THE COMPLETE PREFACES
VOLUME 2: 1914–1929

BERNARD SHAW

THE COMPLETE PREFACES
VOLUME 2: 1914–1929

EDITED BY DAN H. LAURENCE
AND DANIEL J. LEARY

ALLEN LANE
THE PENGUIN PRESS

ALLEN LANE
THE PENGUIN PRESS
Published by the Penguin Group
Penguin Books Ltd, 27 Wrights Lane, London W8 5TZ, England
Penguin Books USA Inc., 375 Hudson Street, New York, New York 10014, USA
Penguin Books Australia Ltd, Ringwood, Victoria, Australia
Penguin Books Canada Ltd, 10 Alcorn Avenue, Toronto, Ontario, Canada M4V 3B2
Penguin Books (NZ) Ltd, 182–190 Wairau Road, Auckland 10, New Zealand

Penguin Books Ltd, Registered Offices: Harmondsworth, Middlesex, England

First published 1995
1 3 5 7 9 10 8 6 4 2

Typset by Datix International Limited, Bungay, Suffolk

Set in 11/13pt Monophoto Bembo
Printed in England by Clays Ltd, St Ives plc

A CIP catalogue record for this book is available from the British Library

ISBN 0–713–990570

Contents

===

Contents

Editors' Note

In the preparation of this edition we have been confronted with a vexing problem in the identification of historic utterances with which Shaw has liberally peppered his prefaces and which he has ascribed to notable personages, many of whom apparently never verbalized their thoughts in the phrasing provided by Shaw. As he himself admitted, he was not only 'a snapper-up of unconsidered trifles' but 'a born improver of occasions', adept at turns of phrase that converted prosaic remarks into highly styled aphorisms and 'Maxims for Revolutionists'.

We have, when possible, suggested a likely origin for an improved 'quotation'. For a typical instance of this, examine the Shavian encapsulation of a passage from Mill's *Autobiography* (see p. 421). In a number of instances, after months of dogged, time-consuming effort, we have had to accept the frustrating possibility that the phrasing we have been seeking was never uttered or written by the individual to whom Shaw has assigned it. Did Napoleon, who was a favourite Shavian phrase-source, actually say that women are 'the occupation of the idle man', as cited by Shaw (see p. 248)? Did Wellington (another favourite source) actually claim that 'martial law is no law at all' (see p. 137)? If so, the documentation is devilishly well secreted.

Few literary artists of our century have shown in their work a degree of familiarity with the Bible comparable to that of Shaw, who read through the entire Old and New Testaments (not to mention the Apocrypha) several times in his life, committing much of them to memory. Biblical allusions and phrases are, consequently, as prevalent in Shaw's prefaces and other writings as are those drawn from Dickens and Shakespeare. Not surprisingly, the book shelves of his London flat and his country home were laden with Bible texts, at least a dozen of them, from the translation of Tyndale (New Testament, 1534) to that of Ronald Knox (1944–8) and *The English Hexapla*. At Ayot one finds Shaw's Bibles in the downstairs study, in the drawing room, in the upstairs Lawrence Room (a guest bedroom frequented by T. E. Lawrence, now a library): the Authorized Version of 1611 in an exact reprint, a 24-volume edition of the *Modern Reader's Bible* edited by Richard G. Moulton, an eight-volume edition (1897–8) with an introduction by J. W. Mackail, a five-volume edition that was used by Charlotte Shaw, Ferrar Fenton's *Complete Bible in Modern English*, a New Testament in Spanish and English and another in Basic English. The text Shaw drew on principally, with occasional variation of his own to make the language more immediate, was the King James Revised Version (New Testament, 1881; Old Testament, 1885).

Readers who have not had occasion to consult the first volume (1889–1913) of this edition of the prefaces are reminded that, except for convenient individual indexes to each volume, the edition is conceived as a running unit, with identifications, annotations and datings provided only at first instance of need and not as a rule repeated in subsequent volumes. In several key instances we have, however, provided cross-references that we believe will be useful. Note too that names misspelled by Shaw (a congenital failing) are retained in that form in the texts, but amended in annotations.

Most regrettably there were inadvertent omissions of prefatory material in Volume 1, including 1933 postscripts to *Widowers' Houses*, *Major Barbara*, *The Doctor's Dilemma*, *Getting Married* and *The Shewing-up of Blanco Posnet*. These will be included in Volume 3 following Shaw's introduction to the 1934 collective edition of *Prefaces*, in which they were first published. A brief foreword to a sixpenny 'Popular Edition' of *Man and Superman* (1911), also overlooked, will be added as an appendix in Volume 3. We blushingly apologize for the oversights.

We are indebted to a number of individuals and institutions for valuable assistance in our researches, to all of whom we extend a benediction: Jacques Barzun, Nicholas Boyle, Revd Father Ronald Creighton-Jobe (Archivist, Brompton Oratory), Rolf Fjelde, Nicholas Grene, Maureen Halligan and all her Dublin relatives, Sir Rupert Hart-Davis, Penelope Hatfield (Archivist, Eton College), Cathy Henderson (Research Librarian) and John Kirkpatrick (Bibliographer, Harry Ransom Humanities Research Center), Father Leo A. Hetzler and Frank A. Petta (the G. K. Chesterton Society), Elizabeth M. Knowles (Senior Editor, New Shorter Oxford English Dictionary), Graham Melville (Cataloguer, British Film Institute), George Newlin and Fred Kameny (*Dickens Studies Annual*), David Parker (Curator, Dickens House Museum), Thomas Postlewait, Nancy Sadek (Archival Collections Librarian, University of Guelph), Becky Simmons (Associate Librarian, George Eastman House), J. Percy Smith, Anne Summers (Curator of Manuscripts) and Tom Pattie (British Library), Kathleen Tillotson, James Tyler (Curator of the Bernard F. Burgunder Collection of Bernard Shaw, Cornell University Libraries) and Michele Whelan, as well as the staffs of Bernard Quaritch Ltd., the Billy Rose Theatre Collection, the New York Public Library for the Performing Arts, and the 42nd Street

Reference Department, New York Public Library, the Ministry of Defence Library, London, the Mitchell Library, Glasgow, and the Trinity University Library, San Antonio.

The proof text of Shaw's *Common Sense about the War: A Word Concerning the 1915 Reprint* and the typescript texts of *What I Said in the Great War: Exordium* (*c*. 1917–18) and *Peace Conference Hints: Preface to the French Edition* (1919) are published by kind permission of the British Library. The extract from Shaw's letter to Beatrice Webb, 21 November 1918, is published by kind permission of the British Library of Political and Economic Science.

D. H. L.
D. J. L.

THE COMPLETE PREFACES

1914–1929

Parents and Children
(Misalliance)

First published in 1914

═══

TRAILING CLOUDS OF GLORY

Childhood is a stage in the process of that continual remanufacture of the Life Stuff by which the human race is perpetuated. The Life Force either will not or cannot achieve immortality except in very low organisms: indeed it is by no means ascertained that even the amœba is immortal. Human beings visibly wear out, though they last longer than their friends the dogs. Turtles, parrots, and elephants are believed to be capable of outliving the memory of the oldest human inhabitant. But the fact that new ones are born conclusively proves that they are not immortal. Do away with death and you do away with the need for birth: in fact if you went on breeding, you would finally have to kill old people to make room for young ones.

Now death is not necessarily a failure of energy on the part of the Life Force. People with no imagination try to make things which will last for ever, and even want to live for ever themselves. But the intelligently imaginative man knows very well that it is waste of labor to make a machine that will last ten years, because it will probably be superseded in half that time by an improved machine answering the same purpose. He also knows that if some devil were to convince us that our dream of personal immortality is no dream but a hard fact, such a shriek of despair would go up from the human race as no other conceivable horror could provoke. With all our perverse nonsense as to John Smith living for a thousand million eons and for ever after, we die voluntarily, knowing that it is time for us to be scrapped, to be remanufactured, to come back, as Wordsworth divined, trailing ever brightening clouds of glory ['Intimations of Immortality', 1807]. We must all be born again, and yet again and again. We should like to live a little longer just as we should like £50: that is, we should take it if we could get it for nothing; but that sort of idle liking is not will. It is amazing—considering the way we talk—how little a man will do to get £50: all the £50 notes I have ever known of have been more easily earned than a laborious sixpence; but the difficulty of inducing a man to make any serious effort to obtain £50 is nothing to the difficulty of inducing him to make a serious effort to keep alive. The moment he sees death approach, he gets into bed and sends for a doctor. He knows very well at the back of his conscience that he is rather a poor job and had better be remanufactured. He knows that his death will make room for a birth; and he hopes that it will be a birth of something that he aspired to be and fell short of. He knows that it is through death and rebirth that this corruptible shall become incorruptible, and this mortal put on immortality. Practise as you will on his ignorance, his fears, and his imagination with bribes of paradises and threats of hells, there is only one belief that can rob death of its sting and the grave of its victory [paraphrase of 1 Corinthians 15: 55]; and that is the belief that we can lay down the burden of our wretched little makeshift individualities for ever at each lift towards the goal of evolution, which can only be a being that cannot be improved upon. After all, what man is capable of the insane self-conceit of believing that an eternity of himself would be tolerable even to himself? Those who try to believe it postulate that they shall be made perfect first. But if you make me perfect I shall no longer be myself, nor will it be possible for me to conceive my present imperfections (and what I cannot conceive I cannot remember); so that you may just as well give me a new name and face the fact that I am a new person and that the old Bernard Shaw is as dead as mutton. Thus, oddly enough, the conventional belief in the matter comes to this: that if you wish to live for ever you must be wicked enough to be irretrievably damned, since the saved are no longer what they were, and in hell alone do people retain their sinful nature: that is to say, their individuality. And this sort of hell, however convenient as a means of intimidating persons who have practically no honor and no conscience, is not a fact. Death is for many of us the gate of hell; but we are inside on the way out, not outside on the way in. Therefore let us give up telling one another idle stories, and rejoice in death as we rejoice in birth; for without death we cannot be born again; and the man who does not wish to be born again and born better is fit only to represent the City of London in Parliament, or perhaps the university of Oxford.

The Child is Father to the Man[1]

Is he? Then in the name of common sense why do we always treat children on the assumption that the man is father to the child? Oh, these fathers! And we are not content with fathers: we must have godfathers, forgetting that the child is godfather to the man. Has it ever struck you as curious that in a country where the first article of belief is that every child is born with a godfather whom we all call "our father which art in heaven," two very limited individual mortals should be allowed to appear at its baptism and explain that they are its godparents, and that they will look after its salvation until it is no longer a child. I had a godmother [Caroline Brabazon] who made herself responsible in this way for me. She presented me with a Bible with a gilt clasp and edges, larger than the Bibles similarly presented to my sisters, because my sex entitled me to a heavier article. I must have seen that lady at least four times in the twenty years following. She never alluded to my salvation in any way. People occasionally ask me to act as godfather to their children with a levity which convinces me that they have not the faintest notion that it involves anything more than calling the helpless child George Bernard without regard to the possibility that it may grow up in the liveliest abhorrence of my notions.

A person with a turn for logic might argue that if God is the Father of all men, and if the child is father to the man, it follows that the true representative of God at the christening is the child itself. But such posers are unpopular, because they imply that our little customs, or, as we often call them, our religion, mean something, or must originally have meant something, and that we understand and believe that something.

However, my business is not to make confusion worse confounded, but to clear it up. Only, it is as well to begin by a sample of current thought and practice which shews that on the subject of children we are very deeply confused. On the whole, whatever our theory or no theory may be, our practice is to treat the child as the property of its immediate physical parents, and to allow them to do what they like with it as far as it will let them. It has no rights and no liberties: in short, its condition is that which adults recognize as the most miserable and dangerous politically possible for themselves: namely, the condition of slavery. For its alleviation we trust

1. The correct reading in Wordsworth's 'My Heart Leaps Up' (1807) is 'The Child is Father of the Man'.

to the natural affection of the parties, and to public opinion. A father cannot for his own credit let his son go in rags. Also, in a very large section of the population, parents finally become dependent on their children. Thus there are checks on child slavery which do not exist, or are less powerful, in the case of manual and industrial slavery. Sensationally bad cases fall into two classes, which are really the same class: namely, the children whose parents are excessively addicted to the sensual luxury of petting children, and the children whose parents are excessively addicted to the sensual luxury of physically torturing them. There is a Society for the Prevention of Cruelty to Children [established in NYC in 1875, and in the UK in 1884] which has effectually made an end of our belief that mothers are any more to be trusted than stepmothers, or fathers than slave-drivers. And there is a growing body of law designed to prevent parents from using their children ruthlessly to make money for the household. Such legislation has always been furiously resisted by the parents, even when the horrors of factory slavery were at their worst; and the extension of such legislation at present would be impossible if it were not that the parents affected by it cannot control a majority of votes in Parliament. In domestic life a great deal of service is done by children, the girls acting as nursemaids and general servants, and the lads as errand boys. In the country both boys and girls do a substantial share of farm labor. This is why it is necessary to coerce poor parents to send their children to school, though in the relatively small class which keeps plenty of servants it is impossible to induce parents to keep their children at home instead of paying schoolmasters to take them off their hands.

It appears then that the bond of affection between parents and children does not save children from the slavery that denial of rights involves in adult political relations. It sometimes intensifies it, sometimes mitigates it; but on the whole children and parents confront oneanother as two classes in which all the political power is on one side; and the results are not at all unlike what they would be if there were no immediate consanguinity between them, and one were white and the other black, or one enfranchised and the other disenfranchised, or one ranked as gentle and the other simple. Not that Nature counts for nothing in the case and political rights for everything. But a denial of political rights, and the resultant delivery of one class into the mastery of another, affects their relations so extensively and profoundly that it is impossible to ascertain what the real natural relations of the two classes are until this political relation is abolished.

WHAT IS A CHILD?

An experiment. A fresh attempt to produce the just man made perfect [Bunyan's *Pilgrim's Progress*]: that is, to make humanity divine. And you will vitiate the experiment if you make the slightest attempt to abort it into some fancy figure of your own: for example, your notion of a good man or a womanly woman. If you treat it as a little wild beast to be tamed, or as a pet to be played with, or even as a means to save you trouble and to make money for you (and these are our commonest ways), it may fight its way through in spite of you and save its soul alive; for all its instincts will resist you, and possibly be strengthened in the resistance; but if you begin with its own holiest aspirations, and suborn them for your own purposes, then there is hardly any limit to the mischief you may do. Swear at a child, throw your boots at it, send it flying from the room with a cuff or a kick; and the experience will be as instructive to the child as a difficulty with a short-tempered dog or a bull. Francis Place[2] tells us that his father always struck his children when he found one within his reach. The effect on the young Places seems to have been simply to make them keep out of their father's way, which was no doubt what he desired, as far as he desired anything at all. Francis records the habit without bitterness, having reason to thank his stars that his father respected the inside of his head whilst cuffing the outside of it; and this made it easy for Francis to do yeoman's service to his country as that rare and admirable thing, a Freethinker: the only sort of thinker, I may remark, whose thoughts, and consequently whose religious convictions, command any respect.

Now Mr Place, senior, would be described by many as a bad father; and I do not contend that he was a conspicuously good one. But as compared with the conventional good father who deliberately imposes himself on his son as a god; who takes advantage of childish credulity and parent worship to persuade his son that what he approves of is right and what he disapproves of is wrong; who imposes a corresponding conduct on the child by a system of prohibitions and penalties, rewards and eulogies, for which he claims divine sanction: compared to this sort of abortionist and monster maker, I say, Place appears almost as a Providence. Not that it is possible to live with children any more than with grown-up people without imposing rules of conduct on them. There is a point at which

2. Shaw's source for the father's behaviour was Graham Wallas, *The Life of Francis Place* (1898).

every person with human nerves has to say to a child "Stop that noise." But suppose the child asks why! There are various answers in use. The simplest: "Because it irritates me," may fail; for it may strike the child as being rather amusing to irritate you; also the child, having comparatively no nerves, may be unable to conceive your meaning vividly enough. In any case it may want to make a noise more than to spare your feelings. You may therefore have to explain that the effect of the irritation will be that you will do something unpleasant if the noise continues. The something unpleasant may be only a look of suffering to rouse the child's affectionate sympathy (if it has any), or it may run to forcible expulsion from the room with plenty of unnecessary violence; but the principle is the same: there are no false pretences involved: the child learns in a straightforward way that it does not pay to be inconsiderate. Also, perhaps, that Mamma, who made the child learn the Sermon on the Mount, is not really a Christian.

The Sin of Nadab and Abihu

But there is another sort of answer in wide use which is neither straightforward, instructive, nor harmless. In its simplest form it substitutes for "Stop that noise," "Dont be naughty," which means that the child, instead of annoying you by a perfectly healthy and natural infantile procedure, is offending God. This is a blasphemous lie; and the fact that it is on the lips of every nurserymaid does not excuse it in the least. Dickens tells us of a nurserymaid who elaborated it into "If you do that, angels wont never love you."[3] I remember a servant who used to tell me that if I were not good, by which she meant if I did not behave with a single eye to her personal convenience, the cock would come down the chimney.[4] Less imaginative but equally dishonest people told me I should go to hell if I did not make myself agreeable to them. Bodily violence, provided it be the hasty expression of normal provoked resentment and not vicious cruelty, cannot harm a child as this sort of pious fraud harms it. There is a legal limit to physical cruelty; and there are also human limits to it. There is an

---

3. 'Nurse's Stories', in Dickens's *The Uncommercial Traveller* (1861): 'The ship was bound for the Indies; and, if you don't know where that is, you ought to it, and angels will never love you.'
4. Recalling the same incident some thirty years later, in *Everybody's Political What's What?* (1944), Shaw added: 'To me the cock was an avenging deity.'

active Society which brings to book a good many parents who starve and torture and overwork their children, and intimidates a good many more. When parents of this type are caught, they are treated as criminals; and not infrequently the police have some trouble to save them from being lynched. The people against whom children are wholly unprotected are those who devote themselves to the very mischievous and cruel sort of abortion which is called bringing up a child in the way it should go. Now nobody knows the way a child should go. All the ways discovered so far lead to the horrors of our existing civilizations, described quite justifiably by Ruskin as heaps of agonizing human maggots, struggling with one another for scraps of food.[5] Pious fraud is an attempt to pervert that divine mystery called the child's conscience into an instrument of our own convenience, and to use that wonderful and terrible power called Shame to grind our own axe. It is the sin of stealing fire from the altar [Leviticus 10 : 1–3]: a sin so impudently practised by popes, parents, and pedagogues, that one can hardly expect the nurserymaids to see any harm in stealing a few cinders when they are worried.

Into the blackest depths of this violation of children's souls one can hardly bear to look; for here we find pious fraud masking the violation of the body by obscene cruelty. Any parent or school teacher who takes a secret and abominable delight in torture is allowed to lay traps into which every child must fall, and then beat it to his or her heart's content. A gentleman once wrote to me and said, with an obvious conviction that he was being most reasonable and highminded, that the only thing he beat his children for was failure in perfect obedience and perfect truthfulness. On these virtues, he said, he must insist. As one of them is not a virtue at all, and the other is the attribute of a god, one can imagine what the lives of this gentleman's children would have been if it had been possible for him

---

5. Ruskin's graphically phrased social and moral criticism is prevalent in the letters and essays collected as *Unto This Last* (1862), *Munera Pulveris* (1872) and *Fors Clavigera* (1871–7). In a report (1881) to the Guild of St George, which he founded in 1871, he summed up the human condition of modern cities in biblical terms:

> The modern cities of all European states have alike in these days become, literally, cities of the plain . . . into which . . . the iniquity of the tribes sinks by instinctive drainage into a slime-pit of central corruption, where sin reacting upon sin, and iniquity festering upon iniquity, curdle and coagulate into forms so monstrous, that the eye hath not seen, nor the ear heard them.
> (*Works of Ruskin*, eds. E. T. Cook and A. Wedderburn, Vol. XXX, 1907.)

to live down to his monstrous and foolish pretensions. And yet he might have written his letter to The Times (he very nearly did, by the way) without incurring any danger of being removed to an asylum, or even losing his reputation for taking a very proper view of his parental duties. And at least it was not a trivial view, nor an ill meant one. It was much more respectable than the general consensus of opinion that if a school teacher can devize a question a child cannot answer, or overhear it calling omega omeega, he or she may beat the child viciously. Only, the cruelty must be whitewashed by a moral excuse, and a pretence of reluctance. It must be for the child's good. The assailant must say "This hurts me more than it hurts you." There must be hypocrisy as well as cruelty. The injury to the child would be far less if the voluptuary said frankly "I beat you because I like beating you; and I shall do it whenever I can contrive an excuse for it." But to represent this detestable lust to the child as Divine wrath, and the cruelty as the beneficent act of God, which is exactly what all our floggers do, is to add to the torture of the body, out of which the flogger at least gets some pleasure, the maiming and blinding of the child's soul, which can bring nothing but horror to anyone.

The Manufacture of Monsters

This industry is by no means peculiar to China. The Chinese (they say) make physical monsters. We revile them for it and proceed to make moral monsters of our own children. The most excusable parents are those who try to correct their own faults in their offspring. The parent who says to his child: "I am one of the successes of the Almighty: therefore imitate me in every particular or I will have the skin off your back" (a quite common attitude) is a much more absurd figure than the man who, with a pipe in his mouth, thrashes his boy for smoking. If you must hold yourself up to your children as an object lesson (which is not at all necessary), hold yourself up as a warning and not as an example. But you had much better let the child's character alone. If you once allow yourself to regard a child as so much material for you to manufacture into any shape that happens to suit your fancy you are defeating the experiment of the Life Force. You are assuming that the child does not know its own business, and that you do. In this you are sure to be wrong: the child feels the drive of the Life Force (often called the Will of God); and you cannot feel it for him. Handel's parents no doubt thought they knew better than their child when they tried to prevent his becoming a musician.[6] They would have been equally wrong and equally unsuccessful if they had tried to prevent the child becoming a great rascal had its genius lain in that direction. Handel would have been Handel, and Napoleon and Peter of Russia *them*selves in spite of all the parents in creation, because, as often happens, they were stronger than their parents. But this does not happen always. Most children can be, and many are, hopelessly warped and wasted by parents who are ignorant and silly enough to suppose that they know what a human being ought to be, and who stick at nothing in their determination to force their children into their moulds. Every child has a right to its own bent. It has a right to be a Plymouth Brother though its parents be convinced atheists. It has a right to dislike its mother or father or sister or brother or uncle or aunt if they are antipathetic to it. It has a right to find its own way and go its own way, whether that way seems wise or foolish to others, exactly as an adult has. It has a right to privacy as to its own doings and its own affairs as much as if it were its own father.

SMALL AND LARGE FAMILIES

These rights have now become more important than they used to be, because the modern practice of limiting families enables them to be more effectually violated. In a family of ten, eight, six, or even four children, the rights of the younger ones to a great extent take care of themselves and of the rights of the elder ones too. Two adult parents, in spite of a house to keep and an income to earn, can still interfere to a disastrous extent with the rights and liberties of one child. But by the time a fourth child has arrived, they are not only outnumbered two to one, but are getting tired of the thankless and mischievous job of bringing up their children in the way they think they should go. The old observation that members of large families get on in the world holds good because in large families it is impossible for each child to receive what schoolmasters call "individual attention." The children may receive a good deal of individual attention from oneanother in the shape of outspoken reproach, ruthless ridicule, and violent resistance to their attempts at aggression; but the parental despots

6. According to Charles Cudworth in the *Encyclopaedia Britannica* (1964): 'At the age of seven the composer already showed signs of musical talent, and it is said that he practised the clavichord secretly at night as his father was opposed to the idea of his son's following music as a profession.'

are compelled by the multitude of their subjects to resort to political rather than personal rule, and to spread their attempts at moral monster-making over so many children, that each child has enough freedom, and enough sport in the prophylactic process of laughing at its elders behind their backs, to escape with much less damage than the single child. In a large school the system may be bad; but the personal influence of the head master has to be exerted, when it is exerted at all, in a public way, because he has little more power of working on the affections of the individual scholar in the intimate way that, for example, the mother of a single child can, than the prime minister has of working on the affections of any individual voter.

CHILDREN AS NUISANCES

Experienced parents, when children's rights are preached to them, very naturally ask whether children are to be allowed to do what they like. The best reply is to ask whether adults are to be allowed to do what they like. The two cases are the same. The adult who is nasty is not allowed to do what he likes: neither can the child who likes to be nasty. There is no difference in principle between the rights of a child and those of an adult: the difference in their cases is one of circumstance. An adult is not supposed to be punished except by process of law; nor, when he is so punished, is the person whom he has injured allowed to act as judge, jury, and executioner. It is true that employers do act in this way every day to their workpeople; but this is not a justified and intended part of the situation: it is an abuse of Capitalism which nobody defends in principle. As between child and parent or nurse it is not argued about because it is inevitable. You cannot hold an impartial judicial inquiry every time a child misbehaves itself. To allow the child to misbehave without instantly making it unpleasantly conscious of the fact would be to spoil it. The adult has therefore to take action of some sort with nothing but his conscience to shield the child from injustice or unkindness. The action may be a torrent of scolding culminating in a furious smack causing terror and pain, or it may be a remonstrance causing remorse, or it may be a sarcasm causing shame and humiliation, or it may be a sermon causing the child to believe that it is a little reprobate on the road to hell. The child has no defence in any case except the kindness and conscience of the adult; and the adult had better not forget this; for it involves a heavy responsibility.

And now comes our difficulty. The responsibility, being so heavy, cannot be discharged by persons of feeble character or intelligence. And yet people of high character and intelligence cannot be plagued with the care of children. A child is a restless, noisy little animal, with an insatiable appetite for knowledge, and consequently a maddening persistence in asking questions. If the child is to remain in the room with a highly intelligent and sensitive adult, it must be told, and if necessary forced, to sit still and not speak, which is injurious to its health, unnatural, unjust, and therefore cruel and selfish beyond toleration. Consequently the highly intelligent and sensitive adult hands the child over to a nurserymaid who has no nerves and can therefore stand more noise, but who has also no scruples, and may therefore be very bad company for the child.

Here we have come to the central fact of the question: a fact nobody avows, which is yet the true explanation of the monstrous system of child imprisonment and torture which we disguise under such hypocrisies as education, training, formation of character and the rest of it. This fact is simply that a child is a nuisance to a grown-up person. What is more, the nuisance becomes more and more intolerable as the grown-up person becomes more cultivated, more sensitive, and more deeply engaged in the highest methods of adult work. The child at play is noisy and ought to be noisy: Sir Isaac Newton at work is quiet and ought to be quiet. And the child should spend most of its time at play, whilst the adult should spend most of his time at work. I am not now writing on behalf of persons who coddle themselves into a ridiculous condition of nervous feebleness, and at last imagine themselves unable to work under conditions of bustle which to healthy people are cheerful and stimulating. I am sure that if people had to choose between living where the noise of children never stopped and where it was never heard, all the goodnatured and sound people would prefer the incessant noise to the incessant silence. But that choice is not thrust upon us by the nature of things. There is no reason why children and adults should not see just as much of oneanother as is good for them, no more and no less. Even at present you are not compelled to choose between sending your child to a boarding school (which means getting rid of it altogether on more or less hypocritical pretences) and keeping it continually at home. Most working folk today either send their children to day schools or turn them out of doors. This solves the problem for the parents. It does not solve it for the children, any more than the tethering of a goat in a field or the chasing of an unlicensed dog into the streets solves it for the goat or the dog; but it shews that in no class are people willing to endure the society of their children, and consequently that it is an error to believe that the family provides children with edifying adult society, or that the family is a social unit. The family is in that, as in so many other respects, a humbug. Old people and young people cannot walk at the same pace without distress and final loss of health to one of the parties. When they are sitting indoors they cannot endure the same degrees of temperature and the same supplies of fresh air. Even if the main factors of noise, restlessness, and inquisitiveness are left out of account, children can stand with indifference sights, sounds, smells, and disorders that would make an adult of fifty utterly miserable; whilst on the other hand such adults find a tranquil happiness in conditions which to children mean unspeakable boredom. And since our system is nevertheless to pack them all into the same house and pretend that they are happy, and that this particular sort of happiness is the foundation of virtue, it is found that in discussing family life we never speak of actual adults or actual children, or of realities of any sort, but always of ideals such as The Home, a Mother's Influence, a Father's Care, Filial Piety, Duty, Affection, Family Life, etc. etc., which are no doubt very comforting phrases, but which beg the question of what a home and a mother's influence and a father's care and so forth really come to in practice. How many hours a week of the time when his children are out of bed does the ordinary bread-winning father spend in the company of his children or even in the same building with them? The home may be a thieves' kitchen, the mother a procuress, the father a violent drunkard; or the mother and father may be fashionable people who see their children three or four times a year during the holidays, and then not oftener than they can help, living meanwhile in daily and intimate contact with their valets and lady's maids, whose influence and care are often dominant in the household. Affection, as distinguished from simple kindliness, may or may not exist: when it does it either depends on qualities in the parties that would produce it equally if they were of no kin to oneanother, or it is a more or less morbid survival of the nursing passion; for affection between adults (if they are really adult in mind and not merely grown-up children) and creatures so relatively selfish and cruel as children necessarily are without knowing it or meaning it, cannot be called natural: in fact the evidence shews that it is easier to love the company of a dog than of a commonplace child between the ages of six and the beginnings of controlled maturity; for women who cannot bear to be separated from their pet dogs send their children to boarding schools cheerfully. They may say and even believe that in allowing their children to leave home they are sacrificing themselves for their children's good; but there are very few pet dogs who would not be the better for a month or two spent elsewhere than in a lady's lap or roasting on a drawingroom hearthrug. Besides, to allege that children are better continually away from home is to give up the whole popular sentimental theory of the family; yet the dogs are kept and the children are banished.

CHILD FANCIERS

There is, however, a good deal of spurious family affection. There is the clannishness that will make a dozen brothers and sisters who quarrel furiously among themselves close up their ranks and make common cause against a brother-in-law or a sister-in-law. And there is a strong sense of property in children, which often makes mothers and fathers bitterly jealous of allowing anyone else to interfere with their children, whom they may none the less treat very badly. And there is an extremely dangerous craze for children which leads certain people to establish orphanages and baby farms and schools, seizing any pretext for filling their houses with children exactly as some eccentric old ladies and gentlemen fill theirs with cats. In such places the children are the victims of all the caprices of doting affection and all the excesses of lascivious cruelty. Yet the people who have this morbid craze seldom have any difficulty in finding victims. Parents and guardians are so worried by children and so anxious to get rid of them that anyone who is willing to take them off their hands is welcomed and whitewashed. The very people who read with indignation of Squeers and Creakle in the novels of Dickens are quite ready to hand over their own children to Squeers [in *Nicholas Nickleby*] and Creakle [in *David Copperfield*], and to pretend that Squeers and Creakle are monsters of the past. But read the autobiography of [Sir Henry] Stanley the traveler,[7] or sit in the company of men talking about their schooldays, and you will soon find that fiction, which must, if it is to be sold and read, stop short of being positively sickening, dare not tell the whole truth about the people to whom children are handed over on educational pretexts. Not very long ago a schoolmaster in Ireland was murdered by his boys; and for reasons which were never made public it was at first decided not to prosecute the murderers.[8] Yet all these flogging schoolmasters and orphanage fiends and

7. Stanley, an illegitimate child, spent his early life with uncaring relatives and in a workhouse. His *Autobiography* was published posthumously in 1909.

8. John Kelly, an assistant headmaster at Trim Industrial School (Co. Meath), was attacked on 12 February 1912 by eight boys of the school, all under seventeen, as he crossed the exercise yard. He died after being beaten about the head with a scrubbing-brush.

baby farmers are "lovers of children." They are really child fanciers (like bird fanciers or dog fanciers) by irresistible natural predilection, never happy unless they are surrounded by their victims, and always certain to make their living by accepting the custody of children, no matter how many alternative occupations may be available. And bear in mind that they are only the extreme instances of what is commonly called natural affection, apparently because it is obviously unnatural.

The really natural feeling of adults for children in the long prosaic intervals between the moments of affectionate impulse is just that feeling that leads them to avoid their care and constant company as a burden beyond bearing, and to pretend that the places they send them to are well conducted, beneficial, and indispensable to the success of the children in after life. The true cry of the kind mother after her little rosary of kisses is "Run away, darling." It is nicer than "Hold your noise, you young devil; or it will be the worse for you;" but fundamentally it means the same thing: that if you compel an adult and a child to live in oneanother's company either the adult or the child will be miserable. There is nothing whatever unnatural or wrong or shocking in this fact; and there is no harm in it if only it be sensibly faced and provided for. The mischief that it does at present is produced by our efforts to ignore it, or to smother it under a heap of sentimental lies and false pretences.

CHILDHOOD AS A STATE OF SIN

Unfortunately all this nonsense tends to accumulate as we become more sympathetic. In many families it is still the custom to treat childhood frankly as a state of sin, and impudently proclaim the monstrous principle that little children should be seen and not heard, and to enforce a set of prison rules designed solely to make cohabitation with children as convenient as possible for adults without the smallest regard for the interests, either remote or immediate, of the children. This system tends to produce a tough, rather brutal, stupid, unscrupulous class, with a fixed idea that all enjoyment consists in undetected sinning; and in certain phases of civilization people of this kind are apt to get the upper hand of more amiable and conscientious races and classes. They have the ferocity of a chained dog, and are proud of it. But the end of it is that they are always in chains, even at the height of their military or political success; they win everything on condition that they are afraid to enjoy it. Their civilizations rest on intimidation, which is so necessary to them that when they cannot find anybody brave enough to intimidate them they intimidate themselves and live in a continual moral and political panic. In the end they get found out and bullied. But that is not the point that concerns us here, which is, that they are in some respects better brought up than the children of sentimental people who are always anxious and miserable about their duty to their children, and who end by neither making their children happy nor having a tolerable life for themselves. A selfish tyrant you know where to have, and he (or she) at least does not confuse your affections; but a conscientious and kindly meddler may literally worry you out of your senses. It is fortunate that only very few parents are capable of doing what they conceive their duty continually or even at all, and that still fewer are tough enough to ride roughshod over their children at home.

School

But please observe the limitation "at home." What private amateur parental enterprize cannot do may be done very effectively by organized professional enterprize in large institutions established for the purpose. And it is to such professional enterprize that parents hand over their children when they can afford it. They send their children to school; and there is, on the whole, nothing on earth intended for innocent people so horrible as a school. To begin with, it is a prison. But it is in some respects more cruel than a prison. In a prison, for instance, you are not forced to read books written by the warders and the governor (who of course would not be warders and governors if they could write readable books), and beaten or otherwise tormented if you cannot remember their utterly unmemorable contents. In the prison you are not forced to sit listening to turnkeys discoursing without charm or interest on subjects that they dont understand and dont care about, and are therefore incapable of making you understand or care about. In a prison they may torture your body; but they do not torture your brains; and they protect you against violence and outrage from your fellow prisoners. In a school you have none of these advantages. With the world's bookshelves loaded with fascinating and inspired books, the very manna sent down from Heaven to feed your souls, you are forced to read a hideous imposture called a schoolbook, written by a man who cannot write: a book from which no human being can learn anything: a book which, though you may decipher it, you cannot in any fruitful sense read, though the enforced attempt will make you loathe the sight of a book all the rest of your life. With millions of acres of woods and valleys and hills and wind and air and birds and streams and fishes and all sorts of instructive and healthy things easily accessible, or with streets and shop windows and crowds and vehicles and all sorts of city delights at the door, you are forced to sit, not in a room with some human grace and comfort of furniture and decoration, but in a stalled pound with a lot of other children, beaten if you talk, beaten if you move, beaten if you cannot prove by answering idiotic questions that even when you escaped from the pound and from the eye of your gaoler, you were still agonizing over his detestable sham books instead of daring to live. And your childish hatred of your gaoler and flogger is nothing to his adult hatred of you; for he is a slave forced to endure your society for his daily bread. You have not even the satisfaction of knowing how you are torturing him and how he loathes you; and you give yourself unnecessary pains to annoy him with furtive tricks and spiteful doing of forbidden things. No wonder he is sometimes provoked to fiendish outbursts of wrath. No wonder men of downright sense, like Dr Johnson, admit that under such circumstances children will not learn anything unless they are so cruelly beaten that they make desperate efforts to memorize words and phrases to escape flagellation.[9] It is a ghastly business, quite beyond words, this schooling.

And now I hear cries of protest arising all round. First my own schoolmasters, or their ghosts, asking whether I was cruelly beaten at school? No; but then I did not learn anything at school. Dr Johnson's schoolmaster presumably did care enough whether Sam learned anything to beat him savagely enough to force him to lame his mind—for Johnson's great mind *was* lamed—by learning his lessons. None of my schoolmasters really cared a rap (or perhaps it would be fairer to them to say that their employers did not care a rap and therefore did not give them the necessary caning powers) whether I learnt my lessons or not, provided my father paid my schooling bill, the collection of which was the real object of the school. Consequently I did not learn my school lessons, having much more important ones in hand, with the result that I have not wasted my life trifling with literary fools in taverns as Johnson did when he should have been shaking England with the thunder of his spirit. My schooling did me a great deal of harm and no good whatever: it was simply dragging a child's soul through the dirt; but I escaped Squeers and Creakle just as I escaped Johnson and Carlyle. And this is what happens to most of us. We are not effectively coerced to learn: we stave off punishment as far as we

9. James Boswell, in *The Life of Samuel Johnson* (1791), reported Johnson as saying, 'A child is afraid of being whipped, and gets his task, and there's an end on't.'

can by lying and trickery and guessing and using our wits; and when this
does not suffice we scribble impositions, or suffer extra imprisonments—
"keeping in" was the phrase in my time—or let a master strike us with a
cane and fall back on our pride at being able to bear it physically (he not
being allowed to hit us too hard) to outface the dishonor we should have
been taught to die rather than endure. And so idleness and worthlessness on
the one hand and a pretence of coercion on the other became a despicable
routine. If my schoolmasters had been really engaged in educating me
instead of painfully earning their bread by keeping me from annoying my
elders they would have turned me out of the school, telling me that I was
thoroughly disloyal to it; that I had no intention of learning; that I was
mocking and distracting the boys who did wish to learn; that I was a liar
and a shirker and a seditious little nuisance; and that nothing could injure
me in character and degrade their occupation more than allowing me
(much less forcing me) to remain in the school under such conditions. But
in order to get expelled, it was necessary to commit a crime of such atrocity
that the parents of the other boys would have threatened to remove their
sons sooner than allow them to be schoolfellows with the delinquent. I can
remember only one case in which such a penalty was threatened; and in
that case the culprit, a boarder, had kissed a housemaid, or possibly, being a
handsome youth, been kissed by her. She did not kiss me; and nobody ever
dreamt of expelling me. The truth was, a boy meant just so much a year to
the institution. That was why he was kept there against his will. That was
why he was kept there when his expulsion would have been an unspeakable
relief and benefit both to his teachers and himself.

It may be argued that if the uncommercial attitude had been taken, and all
the disloyal wasters and idlers shewn sternly to the door, the school would
not have been emptied, but filled. But so honest an attitude was impossible.
The masters must have hated the school much more than the boys did. Just
as you cannot imprison a man without imprisoning a warder to see that he
does not escape, the warder being tied to the prison as effectually by the fear
of unemployment and starvation as the prisoner is by the bolts and bars, so
these poor schoolmasters, with their small salaries and large classes, were as
much prisoners as we were, and much more responsible and anxious ones.
They could not impose the heroic attitude on their employers; nor would
they have been able to obtain places as schoolmasters if their habits had been
heroic. For the best of them their employment was provisional: they looked
forward to escaping from it into the pulpit. The ablest and most impatient of
them were often so irritated by the awkward, slow-witted, slovenly boys:
that is, the ones that required special consideration and patient treatment,

that they vented their irritation on them ruthlessly, nothing being easier than to entrap or bewilder such a boy into giving a pretext for punishing him.

MY SCHOLASTIC ACQUIREMENTS

The results, as far as I was concerned, were what might have been expected. My school made only the thinnest pretence of teaching anything but Latin and Greek. When I went there as a very small boy I knew a good deal of Latin grammar which I had been taught in a few weeks privately by my uncle [Revd William Carroll]. When I had been several years at school this same uncle examined me and discovered that the net result of my schooling was that I had forgotten what he had taught me, and had learnt nothing else. To this day, though I can still decline a Latin noun and repeat some of the old paradigms in the old meaningless way, because their rhythm sticks to me, I have never yet seen a Latin inscription on a tomb that I could translate throughout. Of Greek I can decipher perhaps the greater part of the Greek alphabet. In short, I am, as to classical education, another Shakespear. I can read French as easily as English; and under pressure of necessity I can turn to account some scraps of German and a little operatic Italian; but these I was never taught at school. Instead, I was taught lying, dishonorable submission to tyranny, dirty stories, a blasphemous habit of treating love and maternity as obscene jokes, hopelessness, evasion, derision, cowardice, and all the blackguard's shifts by which the coward intimidates other cowards. And if I had been a boarder at an English public school instead of a day boy at an Irish one, I might have had to add to these, deeper shames still.

SCHOOLMASTERS OF GENIUS

And now, if I have reduced the ghosts of my schoolmasters to melancholy acquiescence in all this (which everybody who has been at an ordinary school will recognize as true), I have still to meet the much more sincere protests of the handful of people who have a natural genius for "bringing up" children. I shall be asked with kindly scorn whether I have heard of [Friedrich] Froebel and [Johann] Pestallozzi,[10] whether I know the work

10. Froebel, a German educator who founded the kindergarten system, was a student of Pestalozzi, a Swiss educational reformer, who sought to emulate the educational theories of Rousseau.

that is being done by Miss [Charlotte] Mason and the Dottoressa [Maria] Montessori[11] or, best of all as I think, the Eurythmics School of Jacques Dalcroze[12] at Hellerau near Dresden. Jacques Dalcroze, like Plato, believes in saturating his pupils with music. They walk to music, play to music, work to music, obey drill commands that would bewilder a guardsman to music, think to music, live to music, get so clearheaded about music that they can move their several limbs each in a different metre until they become complicated living magazines of cross rhythms, and, what is more, make music for others to do all these things to. Stranger still, though Jacques Dalcroze, like all these great teachers, is the completest of tyrants, knowing what is right and that he must and will have the lesson just so or else break his heart (not somebody else's, observe), yet his school is so fascinating that every woman who sees it exclaims "Oh, why was I not taught like this!" and elderly gentlemen excitedly enrol themselves as students and distract classes of infants by their desperate endeavors to beat two in a bar with one hand and three with the other, and start off on earnest walks round the room, taking two steps backward whenever Monsieur Dalcroze calls out "Hop!" Oh yes: I know all about these wonderful schools that you cannot keep children or even adults out of, and these teachers whom their pupils not only obey without coercion, but adore. And if you will tell me roughly how many Masons and Montessoris and Dalcrozes you think you can pick up in Europe for salaries of from thirty shillings to five pounds a week, I will estimate your chances of converting your millions of little scholastic hells into little scholastic heavens. If you are a distressed gentlewoman starting to make a living, you can still open a little school: and you can easily buy a secondhand brass plate inscribed PESTALOZZIAN INSTITUTE and nail it to your door, though you have no more idea of who Pestalozzi was and what he advocated or how he did it than the manager of a hotel which began as a Hydropathic has of the water cure. Or you can buy a cheaper plate inscribed KINDERGARTEN, and imagine, or leave others to imagine, that Froebel is the governing genius of your little *crèche*. No doubt the new brass plates are being inscribed MONTESSORI

---

11. Italian physician and educator, whose method, which stressed freedom of the child, concentrated on the development of a child's imitative sense and on muscle coordination, through the use of specially prepared teaching materials and games.
12. Émile Jaques-Dalcroze was a Swiss composer, who established a school of eurhythmics, visited by Shaw and Granville Barker in early July 1913. Shaw also attended a lecture on the Dalcroze movement in London at the time he drafted his preface.

INSTITUTE, and will be used when the Dottoressa is no longer with us by all the Mrs Pipchins and Mrs Wilfers[13] throughout this unhappy land.

I will go further, and admit that the brass plates may not all be frauds. I will tell you that one of my friends [Pakenham Beatty, poet and amateur pugilist] was led to genuine love and considerable knowledge of classical literature by an Irish schoolmaster whom you would call a hedge school-master[14] (he would not be allowed to teach anything now) and that it took four years of Harrow to obliterate that knowledge and change the love into loathing. Another friend of mine [Edwin Habgood] who keeps a school in the suburbs, and who deeply deplores my "prejudice against schoolmasters," has offered to accept my challenge to tell his pupils that they are as free to get up and go out of the school at any moment as their parents are to get up and go out of a theatre where my plays are being performed. Even among my own schoolmasters I can recollect a few whose classes interested me, and whom I should certainly have pestered for information and instruction if I could have got into any decent human relationship with them, and if they had not been compelled by their position to defend themselves as carefully against such advances as against furtive attempts to hurt them accidentally in the football field or smash their hats with a clod from behind a wall. But these rare cases actually do more harm than good; for they encourage us to pretend that all school-masters are like that. Of what use is it to us that there are always somewhere two or three teachers of children whose specific genius for their occupation triumphs over our tyrannous system and even finds in it its opportunity? For that matter, it is possible, if difficult, to find a solicitor, or even a judge, who has some notion of what law means, a doctor with a glimmer-ing of science, an officer who understands duty and discipline, and a clergyman with an inkling of religion, though there are nothing like enough of them to go round. But even the few who, like Ibsen's Mrs Solness [in *The Master Builder*, 1892], have "a genius for nursing the souls of little children" are like angels forced to work in prisons instead of in

---

13. Mrs Pipchin in Dickens's *Dombey and Son* is a housekeeper who 'had acquired an immense reputation as a great manager of children: and the secret [of her management] was to give them everything they didn't like, and nothing that they did'. Mrs Wilfer in *Our Mutual Friend* is a discontented, foolish, self-pitying woman, who bickers interminably with her daughter Bella. Dickens describes her as always lurking 'like a tragic muse with a face-ache in majestic corners'.
14. A hedge-school was an early Irish school conducted in the open air. The term became an expression of contempt for institutions of inferior quality.

heaven; and even at that they are mostly underpaid and despised. That friend of mine who went from the hedge schoolmaster to Harrow once saw a schoolmaster rush from an elementary school in pursuit of a boy and strike him. My friend, not considering that the unfortunate man was probably goaded beyond endurance, smote the schoolmaster and blackened his eye. The schoolmaster appealed to the law; and my friend found himself waiting nervously in the Hammersmith Police Court to answer for his breach of the peace. In his anxiety he asked a police officer what would happen to him. "What did you do?" said the officer. "I gave a man a black eye" said my friend. "Six pounds if he was a gentleman: two pounds if he wasnt," said the constable. "He was a schoolmaster" said my friend. "Two pounds" said the officer; and two pounds it was. The blood money was paid cheerfully; and I have ever since advised elementary schoolmasters to qualify themselves in the art of self-defence, as the British Constitution expresses our national estimate of them by allowing us to blacken three of their eyes for the same price as one of an ordinary professional man. How many Froebels and Pestalozzis and Miss Masons and Doctoress Montessoris would you be likely to get on these terms even if they occurred much more frequently in nature than they actually do?

No: I cannot be put off by the news that our system would be perfect if it were worked by angels. I do not admit it even at that, just as I do not admit that if the sky fell we should all catch larks. But I do not propose to bother about a supply of specific genius which does not exist, and which, if it did exist, could operate only by at once recognizing and establishing the rights of children.

What We do not Teach, and Why

To my mind, a glance at the subjects now taught in schools ought to convince any reasonable person that the object of the lessons is to keep children out of mischief, and not to qualify them for their part in life as responsible citizens of a free State. It is not possible to maintain freedom in any State, no matter how perfect its original constitution, unless its publicly active citizens know a good deal of constitutional history, law, and political science, with its basis of economics. If as much pains had been taken a century ago to make us all understand [David] Ricardo's[15] law of rent as to

15. English political economist, author of *Principles of Political Economy and Taxation* (1817).

learn our catechisms, the face of the world would have been changed for the better. But for that very reason the greatest care is taken to keep such beneficially subversive knowledge from us, with the result that in public life we are either place-hunters, anarchists, or sheep shepherded by wolves.

But it will be observed that these are highly controversial subjects. Now no controversial subject can be taught dogmatically. He who knows only the official side of a controversy knows less than nothing of its nature. The abler a schoolmaster is, the more dangerous he is to his pupils unless they have the fullest opportunity of hearing another equally able person do his utmost to shake his authority and convict him of error.

At present such teaching is very unpopular. It does not exist in schools; but every adult who derives his knowledge of public affairs from the newspapers can take in, at the cost of an extra halfpenny, two papers of opposite politics. Yet the ordinary man so dislikes having his mind unsettled, as he calls it, that he angrily refuses to allow a paper which dissents from his views to be brought into his house. Even at his club he resents seeing it, and excludes it if it happens to run counter to the opinions of all the members. The result is that his opinions are not worth considering. A churchman who never reads The Freethinker[16] very soon has no more real religion than the atheist who never reads The Church Times. The attitude is the same in both cases: they want to hear nothing good of their enemies; consequently they remain enemies and suffer from bad blood all their lives; whereas men who know their opponents and understand their case, quite commonly respect and like them, and always learn something from them.

Here, again, as at so many points, we come up against the abuse of schools to keep people in ignorance and error, so that they may be incapable of successful revolt against their industrial slavery. The most important simple fundamental economic truth to impress on a child in complicated civilizations like ours is the truth that whoever consumes goods or services without producing by personal effort the equivalent of what he or she consumes, inflicts on the community precisely the same injury that a thief produces, and would, in any honest State, be treated as a thief, however full his or her pockets might be of money made by other people. The nation that first teaches its children that truth, instead of flogging them if they discover it for themselves, may have to fight all the slaves of all the other nations to begin with; but it will beat them as easily

16. A British journal founded in 1881, closely associated with the National Secular Society.

as an unburdened man with his hands free and with all his energies in full play can beat an invalid who has to carry another invalid on his back.

This, however, is not an evil produced by the denial of children's rights, nor is it inherent in the nature of schools. I mention it only because it would be folly to call for a reform of our schools without taking account of the corrupt resistance which awaits the reformer.

A word must also be said about the opposition to reform of the vested interest of the classical and coercive schoolmaster. He, poor wretch, has no other means of livelihood; and reform would leave him as a workman is now left when he is superseded by a machine. He had therefore better do what he can to get the workman compensated, so as to make the public familiar with the idea of compensation before his own turn comes.

TABOO IN SCHOOLS

The suppression of economic knowledge, disastrous as it is, is quite intelligible, its corrupt motive being as clear as the motive of a burglar for concealing his jemmy from a policeman. But the other great suppression in our schools, the suppression of the subject of sex, is a case of taboo. In mankind, the lower the type, and the less cultivated the mind, the less courage there is to face important subjects objectively. The ablest and most highly cultivated people continually discuss religion, politics, and sex: it is hardly an exaggeration to say that they discuss nothing else with fully-awakened interest. Commoner and less cultivated people, even when they form societies for discussion, make a rule that politics and religion are not to be mentioned, and take it for granted that no decent person would attempt to discuss sex. The three subjects are feared because they rouse the crude passions which call for furious gratification in murder and rapine at worst, and, at best, lead to quarrels and undesirable states of consciousness.

Even when this excuse of bad manners, ill temper, and brutishness (for that is what it comes to) compels us to accept it from those adults among whom political and theological discussion does as a matter of fact lead to the drawing of knives and pistols, and sex discussion leads to obscenity, it has no application to children except as an imperative reason for training them to respect other people's opinions, and to insist on respect for their own in these as in other important matters which are equally dangerous: for example, money. And in any case there are decisive reasons, superior, like the reasons for suspending conventional reticences between doctor and patient, to all considerations of mere decorum, for giving proper instruction in the facts of sex. Those who object to it (not counting coarse people who thoughtlessly seize every opportunity of affecting and parading a fictitious delicacy) are, in effect, advocating ignorance as a safeguard against precocity. If ignorance were practicable there would be something to be said for it up to the age at which ignorance is a danger instead of a safeguard. Even as it is, it seems undesirable that any special emphasis should be given to the subject, whether by way of delicacy and poetry or too impressive warning. But the plain fact is that in refusing to allow the child to be taught by qualified unrelated elders (the parents shrink from the lesson, even when they are otherwise qualified, because their own relation to the child makes the subject impossible between them) we are virtually arranging to have our children taught by other children in guilty secrets and unclean jests. And that settles the question for all sensible people.

The dogmatic objection, the sheer instinctive taboo which rules the subject out altogether as indecent, has no age limit. It means that at no matter what age a woman consents to a proposal of marriage, she should do so in ignorance of the relation she is undertaking. When this actually happens (and apparently it does happen oftener than would seem possible) a horrible fraud is being practised on both the man and the woman. He is led to believe that she knows what she is promising, and that he is in no danger of finding himself bound to a woman to whom he is eugenically antipathetic. She contemplates nothing but such affectionate relations as may exist between her and her nearest kinsmen, and has no knowledge of the condition which, if not foreseen, must come as an amazing revelation and a dangerous shock, ending possibly in the discovery that the marriage has been an irreparable mistake. Nothing can justify such a risk. There may be people incapable of understanding that the right to know all there is to know about oneself is a natural human right that sweeps away all the pretences of others to tamper with one's consciousness in order to produce what they choose to consider a good character. But they must here bow to the plain mischievousness of entrapping people into contracts on which the happiness of their whole lives depends without letting them know what they are undertaking.

ALLEGED NOVELTIES IN MODERN SCHOOLS

There is just one more nuisance to be disposed of before I come to the positive side of my case. I mean the person who tells me that my schooldays belong to a bygone order of educational ideas and institutions, and that schools are not now a bit like my old school. I reply, with Sir Walter Raleigh, by calling on my soul to give this statement the lie [actually a paraphrase of Francis Davison's 'The Lie', *Poetical Rhapsody*, 1608]. Some years ago I lectured in Oxford on the subject of Education. A friend to whom I mentioned my intention said, "You know nothing of modern education: schools are not now what they were when you were a boy." I immediately procured the time sheets of half a dozen modern schools, and found, as I expected, that they might all have been my old school: there was no real difference. I may mention, too, that I have visited modern schools, and observed that there is a tendency to hang printed pictures in an untidy and soulless manner on the walls, and occasionally to display on the mantelshelf a deplorable glass case containing certain objects which might possibly, if placed in the hands of the pupils, give them some practical experience of the weight of a pound and the length of an inch. And sometimes a scoundrel who has rifled a bird's nest or killed a harmless snake encourages the children to go and do likewise by putting his victims into an imitation nest and bottling and exhibiting them as aids to "Nature study." A suggestion that Nature is worth study would certainly have staggered my schoolmasters; so perhaps I may admit a gleam of progress here. But as any child who attempted to handle these dusty objects would probably be caned, I do not attach any importance to such modernities in school furniture. The school remains what it was in my boyhood, because its real object remains what it was. And that object, I repeat, is to keep the children out of mischief: mischief meaning for the most part worrying the grownups.

What is to be Done?

The practical question, then, is what to do with the children. Tolerate them at home we will not. Let them run loose in the streets we dare not until our streets become safe places for children, which, to our utter shame, they are not at present, though they can hardly be worse than some homes and some schools.

The grotesque difficulty of making even a beginning was brought home to me by the lady of the manor [Mrs A. C. Ames] in the little village in Hertfordshire [Ayot St Lawrence] where I write these lines. She asked me very properly what I was going to do for the village school. I did not know what to reply. As the school kept the children quiet during my working hours, I did not for the sake of my own personal convenience want to blow it up with dynamite as I should like to blow up most schools. So I asked for guidance. "You ought to give a prize" said the lady. I asked if there was a prize for good conduct. As I expected, there was: one for the best-behaved boy and another for the best-behaved girl. On reflection I offered a handsome prize for the worst-behaved boy and girl on condition that a record should be kept of their subsequent careers and compared with the records of the best-behaved, in order to ascertain whether the school criterion of good conduct was valid out of school. My offer was refused because it would not have had the effect of encouraging the children to give as little trouble as possible, which is of course the real object of all conduct prizes in schools.

I must not pretend, then, that I have a system ready to replace all the other systems. Obstructing the way of the proper organization of childhood, as of everything else, lies our ridiculous misdistribution of the national income, with its accompanying class distinctions and imposition of snobbery on children as a necessary part of their social training. The result of our economic folly is that we are a nation of undesirable acquaintances; and the first object of all our institutions for children is segregation. If, for example, our children were set free to roam and play about as they pleased, they would have to be policed; and the first duty of the police in a State like ours would be to see that every child wore a badge indicating its class in society, and that every child seen speaking to another child with a lower-class badge, or any child wearing a higher badge than that allotted to it by, say, the College of Heralds,[17] should immediately be skinned alive with a birch rod. It might even be insisted that girls with high-class badges should be attended by footmen, grooms, or even military escorts. In short, there is hardly any limit to the follies with which our Commercialism would infect any system that it would tolerate at all. But something like a change of heart is still possible; and since all the evils of snobbery and segregation are rampant in our schools at present we may as well make the best as the worst of them.

CHILDREN'S RIGHTS AND DUTIES

Now let us ask what are a child's rights, and what are the rights of society over the child. Its rights, being clearly those of any other human

17. Heralds' College (originally College of Arms) is a royal corporation, founded in 1484, that records proved pedigrees and grants armorial bearings.

being, are summed up in the right to live: that is, to have all the conclusive arguments that prove that it would be better dead, that it is a child of wrath, that the population is already excessive, that the pains of life are greater than its pleasures, that its sacrifice in a hospital or laboratory experiment might save millions of lives, etc. etc. etc., put out of the question, and its existence accepted as necessary and sacred, all theories to the contrary notwithstanding, whether by Calvin or Schopenhauer or Pasteur or the nearest person with a taste for infanticide. And this right to live includes, and in fact is, the right to be what the child likes and can, to do what it likes and can, to make what it likes and can, to think what it likes and can, to smash what it dislikes and can, and generally to behave in an altogether unaccountable manner within the limits imposed by the similar rights of its neighbors. And the rights of society over it clearly extend to requiring it to qualify itself to live in society without wasting other people's time: that is, it must know the rules of the road, be able to read placards and proclamations, fill voting papers, compose and send letters and telegrams, purchase food and clothing and railway tickets for itself, count money and give and take change, and, generally, know how many beans make five. It must know some law, were it only a simple set of commandments, some political economy, agriculture enough to shut the gates of fields with cattle in them and not to trample on growing crops, sanitation enough not to defile its haunts, and religion enough to have some idea of why it is allowed its rights and why it must respect the rights of others. And the rest of its education must consist of anything else it can pick up; for beyond this society cannot go with any certainty, and indeed can only go this far rather apologetically and provisionally, as doing the best it can on very uncertain ground.

Should Children Earn their Living?

Now comes the question how far children should be asked to contribute to the support of the community. In approaching it we must put aside the considerations that now induce all humane and thoughtful political students to agitate for the uncompromising abolition of child labor under our capitalist system. It is not the least of the curses of that system that it will bequeath to future generations a mass of legislation to prevent capitalists from "using up nine generations of men in one generation," as they began by doing until they were restrained by law[18] at the suggestion of Robert Owen, the founder of English Socialism. Most of this legislation will become an insufferable restraint upon freedom and variety of action when Capitalism goes the way of Druidic human sacrifice (a much less slaughterous institution). There is every reason why a child should not be allowed to work for commercial profit or for the support of its parents at the expense of its own future; but there is no reason whatever why a child should not do some work for its own sake and that of the community if it can be shewn that both it and the community will be the better for it.

CHILDREN'S HAPPINESS

Also it is important to put the happiness of the children rather carefully in its place, which is really not a front place. The unsympathetic, selfish, hard people who regard happiness as a very exceptional indulgence to which children are by no means entitled, though they may be allowed a very little of it on their birthdays or at Christmas, are sometimes better parents in effect than those who imagine that children are as capable of happiness as adults. Adults habitually exaggerate their own capacity in that direction grossly; yet most adults can stand an allowance of happiness that would be quite thrown away on children. The secret of being miserable is to have leisure to bother about whether you are happy or not. The cure for it is occupation, because occupation means preoccupation; and the preoccupied person is neither happy nor unhappy, but simply alive and active, which is pleasanter than any happiness until you are tired of it. That is why it is necessary to happiness that one should be tired. Music after dinner is pleasant: music before breakfast is so unpleasant as to be clearly unnatural. To people who are not overworked holidays are a nuisance. To people who are, and who can afford them, they are a troublesome necessity. A perpetual holiday is a good working definition of hell.

THE HORROR OF THE PERPETUAL HOLIDAY

It will be said here that, on the contrary, heaven is always conceived as a perpetual holiday, and that whoever is not born to an independent income

18. The British Factory Act of 1833 provided enforcing laws to control the apprenticing of pauper children to cotton mill owners, and reduced work hours for children from twelve hours a day to nine in all textile industries.

is striving for one or longing for one because it gives holidays for life. To which I reply, first, that heaven, as conventionally conceived, is a place so inane, so dull, so useless, so miserable, that nobody has ever ventured to describe a whole day in heaven, though plenty of people have described a day at the seaside; and that the genuine popular verdict on it is expressed in the proverb "Heaven for holiness and Hell for company."[19] Second, I point out that the wretched people who have independent incomes and no useful occupation, do the most amazingly disagreeable and dangerous things to make themselves tired and hungry in the evening. When they are not involved in what they call sport, they are doing aimlessly what other people have to be paid to do: driving horses and motor cars; trying on dresses and walking up and down to shew them off; and acting as footmen and housemaids to royal personages. The sole and obvious cause of the notion that idleness is delightful and that Heaven is a place where there is nothing to be done, is our school system and our industrial system. The school is a prison in which work is a punishment and a curse. In avowed prisons, hard labor, the only alleviation of a prisoner's lot, is treated as an aggravation of his punishment; and everything possible is done to intensify the prisoner's inculcated and unnatural notion that work is an evil. In industry we are overworked and underfed prisoners. Under such absurd circumstances our judgment of things becomes as perverted as our habits. If we were habitually underworked and overfed, our notion of heaven would be a place where everybody worked strenuously for twentyfour hours a day and never got anything to eat.

Once realize that a perpetual holiday is beyond human endurance, and that "Satan finds some mischief still for idle hands to do" [Isaac Watts, *Divine Songs*, 1715] and it will be seen that we have no right to impose a perpetual holiday on children. If we did, they would soon outdo the Labor Party in their claim for a Right to Work Bill.

In any case no child should be brought up to suppose that its food and clothes come down from Heaven or are miraculously conjured from empty space by papa. Loathsome as we have made the idea of duty (like the idea of work) we must habituate children to a sense of repayable obligation to the community for what they consume and enjoy, and inculcate the repayment as a point of honor. If we did that today—and nothing but flat dishonesty prevents us from doing it—we should have no idle rich and indeed probably no rich, since there is no distinction in being

19. '[I]f it's heaven for climate, it's hell for company', J. M. Barrie, *The Little Minister* (1891); from a German proverb, '*Himmel für Klima, Hölle für Gesellschaft*'.

rich if you have to pay scot and lot in personal effort like the working folk. Therefore, if for only half an hour a day, a child should do something serviceable to the community.

Productive work for children has the advantage that its discipline is the discipline of impersonal necessity, not that of wanton personal coercion. The eagerness of children in our industrial districts to escape from school to the factory is not caused by lighter tasks or shorter hours in the factory, nor altogether by the temptation of wages, nor even by the desire for novelty, but by the dignity of adult work, the exchange of the humiliating liability to personal assault from the lawless schoolmaster, from which the grownups are free, for the stern but entirely dignified pressure of necessity to which all flesh is subject.

UNIVERSITY SCHOOLBOYISHNESS

Older children might do a good deal before beginning their collegiate education. What is the matter with our universities is that the students are school children, whereas it is of the very essence of university education that they should be adults. The function of a university is not to teach things that can now be taught as well or better by University Extension lectures or by private tutors or modern correspondence classes with gramophones. We go to them to be socialized: to acquire the hallmark of communal training; to become citizens of the world instead of inmates of the enlarged rabbit hutches we call homes; to learn manners and become unchallengeable ladies and gentlemen. The social pressure which effects these changes should be that of persons who have faced the full responsibilities of adults as working members of the general community, not that of a rowdy rabble of half-emancipated school children and unemancipable pedants. It is true that in a reasonable state of society this outside experience would do for us very completely what the university does now so corruptly that we tolerate its bad manners only because they are better than no manners at all. But 'the university will always exist in some form as a community of persons desirous of pushing their culture to the highest pitch they are capable of, not as solitary students reading in seclusion, but as members of a body of individuals all pursuing culture, talking culture, thinking culture, above all, criticizing culture. If such persons are to read and talk and criticize to any purpose, they must know the world outside the university at least as well as the shopkeeper in the High Street does. And this is just what they do not know at present. You may say of them, paraphrasing Mr Kipling, "What do they know of Plato that only Plato know?" ['The English Flag'] If our universities would exclude everybody who had not earned a living by his or her own exertions for at least a couple of years, their effect would be vastly improved.

THE NEW LAZINESS

The child of the future, then, if there is to be any future but one of decay, will work more or less for its living from an early age; and in doing so it will not shock anyone, provided there be no longer any reason to associate the conception of children working for their living with infants toiling in a factory for ten hours a day or boys drudging from nine to six under gas lamps in underground city offices. Lads and lasses in their teens will probably be able to produce as much as the most expensive person now costs in his own person (it is retinue that eats up the big income) without working too hard or too long for quite as much happiness as they can enjoy. The question to be balanced then will be, not how soon people should be put to work, but how soon they should be released from any obligation of the kind. A life's work is like a day's work: it can begin early and leave off early or begin late and leave off late, or, as with us, begin too early and never leave off at all, obviously the worst of all possible plans. In any event we must finally reckon work, not as the curse our schools and prisons and capitalist profit factories make it seem today, but as a prime necessity of a tolerable existence. And if we cannot devize fresh wants as fast as we shorten the process of supplying the old ones, there will come a scarcity of work simultaneously with an excess of leisure. Work may have to be shared out among people who want more of it. Our spurious substitute, exercise, will not serve. A new sort of laziness will become the bugbear of society: the laziness that refuses to face the mental toil and adventure of making work by inventing new ideas or extending the domain of knowledge, and insists on a readymade routine. It may come to forcing people to retire before they are willing to make way for younger ones: that is, to driving all persons of a certain age out of industry, leaving them to find something experimental to occupy them on pain of perpetual holiday. Men will then try to spend twenty thousand a year for the sake of having to earn it. Instead of being what we are now, the cheapest and nastiest of the animals, we shall be the costliest, most fastidious, and best bred. In short, there is no end to the astonishing things that may happen when the curse of Adam becomes first a blessing and then an incurable habit. And in view of that day we must not grudge children their share of it.

THE INFINITE SCHOOL TASK

The question of children's work, however, is only a question of what the child ought to do for the community. How highly it should qualify itself is another matter. But most of the difficulty of inducing children to learn would disappear if our demands became not only definite but finite. When learning is only an excuse for imprisonment, it is an instrument of torture which becomes more painful the more progress is made. Thus when you have forced a child to learn the Church Catechism, a document profound beyond the comprehension of most adults, you are sometimes at a standstill for something else to teach; and you therefore keep the wretched child repeating its catechism again and again until you hit on the plan of making it learn instalments of Bible verses, preferably from the book of Numbers. But as it is less trouble to set a lesson that you know yourself, there is a tendency to keep repeating the already learnt lesson rather than break new ground. At school I began with a fairly complete knowledge of Latin grammar in the childish sense of being able to repeat all the paradigms; and I was kept at this, or rather kept in a class where the master never asked me to do it because he knew I could, and therefore devoted himself to trapping the boys who could not, until I finally forgot most of it. But when progress took place, what did it mean? First it meant Cæsar, with the foreknowledge that to master Cæsar meant only being set at Virgil, with the culminating horror of Greek and Homer in reserve at the end of that. I preferred Cæsar, because his statement that Gaul is divided into three parts, though neither interesting nor true, was the only Latin sentence I could translate at sight: therefore the longer we stuck at Cæsar the better I was pleased. Just so do less classically educated children see nothing in the mastery of addition but the beginning of subtraction, and so on through multiplication and division and fractions, with the black cloud of algebra on the horizon. And if a boy rushes through all that, there is always the calculus to fall back on, unless indeed you insist on his learning music, and proceed to hit him if he cannot tell you the year Beethoven was born.

A child has a right to finality as regards its compulsory lessons. Also as regards physical training. At present it is assumed that the schoolmaster has a right to force every child into an attempt to become [Richard] Porson and [Richard] Bentley, [Gottfried von] Leibniz and [Isaac]

Newton,[20] all rolled into one. This is the tradition of the oldest grammar schools. In our times an even more horrible and cynical claim has been made for the right to drive boys through compulsory games in the playing fields until they are too much exhausted physically to do anything but drop off to sleep. This is supposed to protect them from vice; but as it also protects them from poetry, literature, music, meditation and prayer, it may be dismissed with the obvious remark that if boarding schools are places whose keepers are driven to such monstrous measures lest more abominable things should happen, then the sooner boarding schools are violently abolished the better. It is true that society may make physical claims on the child as well as mental ones: the child must learn to walk, to use a knife and fork, to swim, to ride a bicycle, to acquire sufficient power of self-defence to make an attack on it an arduous and uncertain enterprize, perhaps to fly. What as a matter of common sense it clearly has not a right to do is to make this an excuse for keeping the child slaving for ten hours at physical exercises on the ground that it is not yet as dexterous as [Paul] Cinquevalli and as strong as [Eugene] Sandow.[21]

THE REWARDS AND RISKS OF KNOWLEDGE

In a word, we cannot completely educate a child; for its education can end only with its life and will not even then be complete. Compulsory completion of education is the last folly of a rotten and desperate civilization. All we can fairly do is to prescribe definite acquirements and accomplishments as qualifications for citizenship in general, with further specific qualifications for professional employments; and to secure them, not by the ridiculous method of inflicting artificial injuries on the persons who have not yet mastered them, but by the natural cooperation of self-respect from within with social respect from without.

Most acquirements carry their own privileges with them. Thus a baby has to be pretty closely guarded and imprisoned because it cannot take care

20. Porson and Bentley were English classical scholars; Leibniz was a German philosopher and mathematician. Along with Newton they were classified as child prodigies.
21. Cinquevalli was an internationally celebrated Polish juggler and equilibrist, who frequently performed in British music-halls. Sandow, a German strongman discovered and exploited by the showman Florenz Ziegfeld, was an advocate of physical culture and muscle-building exercises.

of itself. It has even to be carried about (the most complete conceivable infringement of its liberty) until it can walk. But nobody goes on carrying children after they can walk lest they should walk into mischief, though Arab boys make their sisters carry them, as our own spoiled children sometimes make their nurses, out of mere laziness, because sisters in the East and nurses in the West are kept in servitude. But in a society of equals (the only reasonable and permanently possible sort of society) children are in much greater danger of acquiring bandy legs through being left to walk before they are strong enough than of being carried when they are well able to walk. Anyhow, freedom of movement in a nursery is the reward of learning to walk; and in precisely the same way freedom of movement in a city is the reward of learning how to read public notices, and to count and use money. The consequences are of course much larger than the mere ability to read the name of a street or the number of a railway platform and the destination of a train. When you enable a child to read these, you also enable it to read this preface, to the utter destruction, you may quite possibly think, of its morals (its docility). You also expose it to the danger of being run over by taxicabs and trains. The moral and physical risks of education are enormous: every new power a child acquires, from speaking, walking, and coordinating its vision, to conquering continents and founding religions, opens up immense new possibilities of mischief. Teach a child to write and you teach it how to forge: teach it to speak and you teach it how to lie: teach it to walk and you teach it how to kick its mother to death.

The great problem of slavery for those whose aim is to maintain it is the problem of reconciling the efficiency of the slave with the helplessness that keeps him in servitude; and this problem is fortunately not completely soluble; for it is not in fact found possible for a duke to treat his solicitor or his doctor as he treats his laborers, though they are all equally his slaves: the laborer being in fact less dependent on his favor than the professional man. Hence it is that men come to resent, of all things, protection, because it so often means restriction of their liberty lest they should make a bad use of it. If there are dangerous precipices about, it is much easier and cheaper to forbid people to walk near the edge than to put up an effective fence: that is why both legislators and parents and the paid deputies of parents are always inhibiting and prohibiting and punishing and scolding and laming and cramping and delaying progress and growth instead of making the dangerous places as safe as possible and then boldly taking and allowing others to take the irreducible minimum of risk.

English Physical Hardihood and Spiritual Cowardice

It is easier to convert most people to the need for allowing their children to run physical risks than moral ones. I can remember a relative of mine [maternal great-aunt, Ellen Whitcroft] who, when I was a small child, unused to horses and very much afraid of them, insisted on putting me on a rather rumbustious pony with little spurs on my heels (knowing that in my agitation I would use them unconsciously), and being enormously amused at my terrors. Yet when that same lady discovered that I had found a copy of The Arabian Nights and was devouring it with avidity, she was horrified, and hid it away from me lest it should break my soul as the pony might have broken my neck. This way of producing hardy bodies and timid souls is so common in country houses that you may spend hours in them listening to stories of broken collar bones, broken backs, and broken necks without coming upon a single spiritual adventure or daring thought.

But whether the risks to which liberty exposes us are moral or physical, our right to liberty involves the right to run them. A man who is not free to risk his neck as an aviator or his soul as a heretic is not free at all; and the right to liberty begins, not at the age of 21 years but of 21 seconds.

The Risks of Ignorance and Weakness

The difficulty with children is that they need protection from risks they are too young to understand, and attacks they can neither avoid nor resist. You may on academic grounds allow a child to snatch glowing coals from the fire once. You will not do it twice. The risks of liberty we must let everyone take; but the risks of ignorance and self-helplessness are another matter. Not only children but adults need protection from them. At present adults are often exposed to risks outside their knowledge or beyond their comprehension or powers of resistance or foresight: for example, we have to look on every day at marriages or financial speculations that may involve far worse consequences than burnt fingers. And just as it is part of the business of adults to protect children, to feed them, clothe them, shelter them, and shift for them in all sorts of ways until they are able to shift for themselves, it is coming more and more to be seen that this is true not only of the relation between adults and children, but between adults and adults. We shall not always look on indifferently at foolish marriages and financial speculations, nor allow dead men to control live communities by ridiculous wills and living heirs to squander and ruin great estates, nor tolerate a hundred other absurd liberties that we allow today because we are too lazy to find out the proper way to interfere. But the interference must be regulated by some theory of the individual's rights. Though the right to live is absolute, it is not unconditional. If a man is unbearably mischievous, he must be killed. This is a mere matter of necessity, like the killing of a man-eating tiger in a nursery, a venomous snake in the garden, or a fox in the poultry yard. No society could be constructed on the assumption that such extermination is a violation of the creature's right to live, and therefore must not be allowed. And then at once arises the danger into which morality has led us: the danger of persecution. One Christian spreading his doctrines may seem more mischievous than a dozen thieves: throw him therefore to the lions. A lying or disobedient child may corrupt a whole generation and make human Society impossible: therefore thrash the vice out of him. And so on until our whole system of abortion, intimidation, tyranny, cruelty, and the rest is in full swing again.

The Common Sense of Toleration

The real safeguard against this is the dogma of Toleration. I need not here repeat the compact treatise on it which I prepared for the Joint Committee on the Censorship of Stage Plays, and prefixed to The Shewing-up of Blanco Posnet [see Vol. 1, pp. 471–529]. It must suffice now to say that the present must not attempt to schoolmaster the future by pretending to know good from evil in tendency, or protect citizens against shocks to their opinions and convictions, moral, political or religious: in other words it must not persecute doctrines of any kind, or what is called bad taste, and must insist on all persons facing such shocks as they face frosty weather or any of the other disagreeable, dangerous, or bracing incidents of freedom. The expediency of Toleration has been forced on us by the fact that progressive enlightenment depends on a fair hearing for doctrines which at first appear seditious, blasphemous, and immoral, and which deeply shock people who never think originally, thought being with them merely a habit and an echo. The deeper ground for Toleration is the nature of creation, which, as we now know, proceeds by evolution. Evolution finds its way by experiment; and this finding of the way varies according to the stage of development reached, from the blindest groping along the line of least resistance to conscious intellectual speculation, with its routine of hypothesis and verification, induction and deduction; or even into so rapid and intuitive an integration of all these processes in a single brain that we get the inspired guess of the man of genius and the fanatical resolution of the teacher of new truths who is first slain as a blasphemous apostate and then worshipped as a prophet.

Here the law for the child is the same as for the adult. The high priest must not rend his garments and cry "Crucify him" when he is shocked, nor the atheist clamor for the suppression of [William] Law's Serious Call [*to a Devout and Holy Life*, 1729] because it has for two centuries destroyed the natural happiness of innumerable children by persuading pious parents that it is a religious duty to make children miserable. It, and the Sermon on the Mount, and Machiavelli's Prince [1513], and La Rochefoucauld's maxims [*Maximes*], and Hymns Ancient and Modern [1861], and De Glanville's apologue,[22] and Dr Watts's rhymes, and Nietzsche's Gay Science [1882], and [Robert] Ingersoll's [*Some*] Mistakes of Moses [1879], and the speeches and pamphlets of the people who want us to make war on Germany, and the Noodle's Orations[23] and articles of our politicians and journalists, must all be tolerated not only because any of them may for all we know be on the right track but because it is in the conflict of opinion that we win knowledge and wisdom. However terrible the wounds suffered in that conflict, they are better than the barren peace of death that follows when all the combatants are slaughtered or bound hand and foot.

The difficulty at present is that though this necessity for Toleration is a law of political science as well established as the law of gravitation, our rulers are never taught political science: on the contrary, they are taught in school that the master tolerates nothing that is disagreeable to him; that ruling is simply being master; and that the master's method is the method of violent punishment. And our citizens, all school taught, are walking in the same darkness. As I write these lines the Home Secretary [Reginald McKenna] is explaining that he must not release a man who has been imprisoned for blasphemy, as his remarks were painful to the feelings of his pious fellow townsmen.[24] Now it happens that this very Home Secretary

22. Joseph Glanvill was an English philosopher who, in *The Vanity of Dogmatizing, or, Confidence in Opinions . . . and an Apology for Philosophy* (1661), expressed scepticism for scholastic dogmatism as against his own experimental methods, and laid emphasis on the infirmity of human reason.
23. A fool's corruption of formal, elevated discourses. The term is usually applied, as here, to politicians. See also Vol. 1, p. 428.
24. This was McKenna's response in December 1913 to a petition whose signatories included H. G. Wells, Gilbert Murray, Israel Zangwill and the historian G. M.

has driven many thousands of his fellow citizens almost beside themselves by the crudity of his notions of government, and his simple inability to understand why he should not use and make laws to torment and subdue people who do not happen to agree with him. In a word, he is not a politician, but a grown-up schoolboy who has at last got a cane in his hand. And as all the rest of us are in the same condition (except as to command of the cane) the only objection made to his proceedings takes the shape of clamorous demands that *he* should be caned instead of being allowed to cane other people.

THE SIN OF ATHANASIUS[25]

It seems hopeless. Anarchists are tempted to preach a violent and implacable resistance to all law as the only remedy; and the result of that speedily is that people welcome any tyranny that will rescue them from chaos. But there is really no need to choose between anarchy and tyranny. A quite reasonable state of things is practicable if we proceed on human assumptions and not on academic ones. If adults will frankly give up their claim to know better than children what the purposes of the Life Force are, and treat the child as an experiment like themselves, and possibly a more successful one, and at the same time relinquish their monstrous parental claims to personal private property in children, the rest may be left to common sense. It is our attitude, our religion, that is wrong. A good beginning might be made by enacting that any person dictating a piece of conduct to a child or to anyone else as the Will of God, or as absolutely right, should be dealt with as a blasphemer: as, indeed, guilty of the unpardonable sin against the Holy Ghost. If the penalty were death, it would rid us at once of that scourge of humanity, the amateur Pope. As an Irish Protestant, I raise the cry of No Popery with hereditary zest. We are overrun with Popes. From curates and governesses, who may claim a sort of professional standing, to parents and uncles and nurserymaids and school

Trevelyan, calling for remittance of the remainder of a four-month prison sentence imposed on T. W. Stewart on 18 November. The petitioners had urged that 'all punishment which savours of religious persecution should be strenuously avoided'. See also p. 240, fn. 58.

25. Greek bishop and father of the Church, defender of orthodoxy against Arianism. His 'sin' presumably would be his stubborn adherence to his beliefs throughout his life.

teachers and wiseacres generally, there are scores of thousands of human insects groping through our darkness by the feeble phosphorescence of their own tails, yet ready at a moment's notice to reveal the will of God on every possible subject; to explain how and why the universe was made (in my youth they added the exact date[26]) and the circumstances under which it will cease to exist; to lay down precise rules of right and wrong conduct; to discriminate infallibly between virtuous and vicious character; and this with such certainty that they are prepared to visit all the rigors of the law, and all the ruinous penalties of social ostracism on those, however harmless their actions may be, who venture to laugh at their monstrous conceit or to pay their assumptions the extravagant compliment of criticizing them. As to children, who shall say what canings and birchings and terrifyings and threats of hell fire and impositions and humiliations and petty imprisonings and sendings to bed and standing in corners and the like they have suffered because their parents and guardians and teachers knew everything so much better than Socrates or Solon?

It is this ignorant uppishness that does the mischief. A stranger on the planet might expect that its grotesque absurdity would provoke enough ridicule to cure it; but unfortunately quite the contrary happens. Just as our ill health delivers us into the hands of medical quacks and creates a passionate demand for impudent pretences that doctors can cure the diseases they themselves die of daily, so our ignorance and helplessness set us clamoring for spiritual and moral quacks who pretend that they can save our souls from their own damnation. If a doctor were to say to his patients, "I am familiar with your symptoms, because I have seen other people in your condition; and I will bring the very little knowledge we have to your treatment; but except in that very shallow sense I dont know what is the matter with you; and I cant undertake to cure you" he would be a lost man professionally; and if a clergyman, on being called on to award a prize for good conduct in the village school, were to say, "I am afraid I cannot say who is the best-behaved child, because I really do not know what good conduct is; but I will gladly take the teacher's word as to which child has caused least inconvenience" he would probably be unfrocked, if not excommunicated. And yet no honest and intellectually capable doctor or parson can say more. Clearly it would not be wise of the doctor to say it, because optimistic lies have such immense therapeutic value that a doctor who cannot tell them convincingly has mistaken his profession. And a clergyman who is not prepared to lay down the law dogmatically will not be of much

26. 23 October 4004 BC, as found in Archbishop James Ussher's *The Annals of the World*, 1658.

village school, though it behoves him all the more to be very careful what law
he lays down. But unless both the clergyman and the doctor are in the attitude
expressed by these speeches they are not fit for their work. The man who
believes that he has more than a provisional hypothesis to go upon is a
born fool. He may have to act vigorously on it. The world has no use for
the Agnostic who wont believe anything because anything might be false,
and wont deny anything because anything might be true. But there is a
wide difference between saying, "I believe this; and I am going to act on
it," or, "I dont believe it; and I wont act on it," and saying, "it is true; and
it is my duty and yours to act on it," or, "It is false; and it is my duty and
yours to refuse to act on it." The difference is as great as that between the
Apostles' Creed and the Athanasian Creed. When you repeat the Apostles'
Creed you affirm that you believe certain things. There you are clearly
within your rights. When you repeat the Athanasian Creed, you affirm
that certain things are so, and that anybody who doubts that they are so
cannot be saved. And this is simply a piece of impudence on your part, as
you know nothing about it except that as good men as you have never
heard of your creed. The apostolic attitude is a desire to convert others to
our beliefs for the sake of sympathy and light: the Athanasian attitude is a
desire to murder people who dont agree with us. I am sufficient of an
Athanasian to advocate a law for the speedy execution of all Athanasians,
because they violate the fundamental proposition of my creed, which is, I
repeat, that all living creatures are experiments. The precise formula for the
Superman, *ci-devant* [formerly known as] the Just Man Made Perfect, has
not yet been discovered. Until it is, every birth is an experiment in the
Great Research which is being conducted by the Life Force to discover that
formula.

THE EXPERIMENT EXPERIMENTING

And now all the modern schoolmaster abortionists will rise up beaming,
and say, "We quite agree. We regard every child in our school as a subject
for experiment. We are always experimenting with them. We challenge
the experimental test for our system. We are continually guided by our
experience in our great work of moulding the character of our future
citizens, etc. etc. etc." I am sorry to seem irreconcilable; but it is the Life
Force that has to make the experiment and not the schoolmaster; and the
Life Force for the child's purpose is in the child and not in the schoolmaster.
The schoolmaster is another experiment; and a laboratory in which all the

experiments began experimenting on one another would not produce intelligible results. I admit, however, that if my schoolmasters had treated me as an experiment of the Life Force: that is, if they had set me free to do as I liked subject only to my political rights and theirs, they could not have watched the experiment very long, because the first result would have been a rapid movement on my part in the direction of the door, and my disappearance therethrough.

It may be worth inquiring where I should have gone to. I should say that practically every time I should have gone to a much more educational place. I should have gone into the country, or into the sea, or into the National Gallery [of Ireland], or to hear a band if there was one, or to any library where there were no schoolbooks. I should have read very dry and difficult books: for example, though nothing would have induced me to read the budget of stupid party lies that served as a textbook of history in school, I remember reading [William] Robertson's [*History of the Reign of the Emperor*] Charles V [1769] and his [H]istory of Scotland [*during the Reigns of Mary and James VI*, 1759] from end to end most laboriously. Once, stung by the airs of a schoolfellow who alleged that he had read Locke On The Human Understanding [1690], I attempted to read the Bible straight through, and actually got to the Pauline Epistles before I broke down in disgust at what seemed to me their inveterate crookedness of mind. If there had been a school where children were really free, I should have had to be driven out of it for the sake of my health by the teachers; for the children to whom a literary education can be of any use are insatiable: they will read and study far more than is good for them. In fact the real difficulty is to prevent them from wasting their time by reading for the sake of reading and studying for the sake of studying, instead of taking some trouble to find out what they really like and are capable of doing some good at. Some silly person will probably interrupt me here with the remark that many children have no appetite for a literary education at all, and would never open a book if they were not forced to. I have known many such persons who have been forced to the point of obtaining university degrees. And for all the effect their literary exercises have left on them they might just as well have been put on the treadmill. In fact they are actually less literate than the treadmill would have left them; for they might now by chance pick up and dip into a volume of Shakespear or a translation of Homer if they had not been driven to loathe every famous name in literature. I should probably know as much Latin as French, if Latin had not been made the excuse for my school imprisonment and degradation.

Why We Loathe Learning and Love Sport

If we are to discuss the importance of art, learning, and intellectual culture, the first thing we have to recognize is that we have very little of them at present; and that this little has not been produced by compulsory education: nay, that the scarcity is unnatural and has been produced by the violent exclusion of art and artists from schools. On the other hand we have quite a considerable degree of bodily culture: indeed there is a continual outcry against the sacrifice of mental accomplishments to athletics. In other words a sacrifice of the professed object of compulsory education to the real object of voluntary education. It is assumed that this means that people prefer bodily to mental culture; but may it not mean that they prefer liberty and satisfaction to coercion and privation. Why is it that people who have been taught Shakespear as a school subject loathe his plays and cannot by any means be persuaded ever to open his works after they escape from school, whereas there is still, 300 years after his death, a wide and steady sale for his works to people who regard his plays as plays, not as task work? If Shakespear, or for that matter, Newton and Leibniz, are allowed to find their readers and students they will find them. If their works are annotated and paraphrased by dullards, and the annotations and paraphrases forced on all young people by imprisonment and flogging and scolding, there will not be a single man of letters or higher mathematician the more in the country: on the contrary there will be less, as so many potential lovers of literature and mathematics will have been incurably prejudiced against them. Everyone who is conversant with the class in which child imprisonment and compulsory schooling is carried out to the final extremity of the university degree knows that its scholastic culture is a sham; that it knows little about literature or art and a great deal about point-to-point races; and that the village cobbler, who has never read a page of Plato, and is admittedly a dangerously ignorant man politically, is nevertheless a Socrates compared to the classically educated gentlemen who discuss politics in country houses at election time (and at no other time) after their day's earnest and skilful shooting. Think of the years and years of weary torment the women of the piano-possessing class have been forced to spend over the keyboard, fingering scales. How many of them could be bribed to attend a pianoforte recital by a great player, though they will rise from sickbeds rather than miss Ascot or Goodwood [noted English racecourses]?

Another familiar fact that teaches the same lesson is that many women who have voluntarily attained a high degree of culture cannot add up their own housekeeping books, though their education in simple arithmetic was compulsory, whereas their higher education has been wholly voluntary. Everywhere we find the same result. The imprisonment, the beating, the taming and laming, the breaking of young spirits, the arrest of development, the atrophy of all inhibitive power except the power of fear, are real: the education is sham. Those who have been taught most know least.

ANTICHRIST

Among the worst effects of the unnatural segregation of children in schools and the equally unnatural constant association of them with adults in the family is the utter defeat of the vital element in Christianity. Christ stands in the world for that intuition of the highest humanity that we, being members one of another, must not complain, must not scold, must not strike, nor revile nor persecute nor revenge nor punish. Now family life and school life are, as far as the moral training of children is concerned, nothing but the deliberate inculcation of a routine of complaint, scolding, punishment, persecution, and revenge as the natural and only possible way of dealing with evil or inconvenience. "Aint nobody to be whopped for this here?" exclaimed Sam Weller [in *Pickwick Papers*] when he saw his employer's name written up on a stage coach, and conceived the phenomenon as an insult which reflected on himself. This exclamation of Sam Weller is at once the negation of Christianity and the beginning and the end of current morality; and so it will remain as long as the family and the school persist as we know them: that is, as long as the rights of children are so utterly denied that nobody will even take the trouble to ascertain what they are, and coming of age is like the turning of a convict into the streets after twentyone years penal servitude. Indeed it is worse; for the convict, having learnt before his conviction how to live at large, may remember how to set about it, however lamed his power of initiative may have become through disuse; but the child knows no other way of life than the slave's way. Born free, as Rousseau says [in *The Social Contract*, 1762], he has been laid hands on by slaves from the moment of his birth and brought up as a slave. How is he, when he is at last set free, to be anything else than the slave he actually is, clamoring for war, for the lash, for police, prisons, and scaffolds in a wild panic of delusion that without these things he is lost. The grown-up Englishman is to the end of his days a badly brought-up child, beyond belief quarrelsome, petulant, selfish, destructive, and cowardly: afraid that the Germans will come and enslave him; that the burglar will come and rob him; that the bicycle or motor car will run over him; that the smallpox will attack him; and that the devil will run away with him and empty him out like a sack of coals on a blazing fire unless his nurse or his parents or his schoolmaster or his bishop or his judge or his army or his navy will do something to frighten these bad things away. And this Englishman, without the moral courage of a louse, will risk his neck for fun fifty times every winter in the hunting field, and at Badajos[27] sieges and the like will ram his head into a hole bristling with sword blades rather than be beaten in the one department in which he has been brought up to consult his own honor. As a Sportsman (and war is fundamentally the sport of hunting and fighting the most dangerous of the beasts of prey) he feels free. He will tell you himself that the true sportsman is never a snob, a coward, a duffer, a cheat, a thief, or a liar. Curious, is it not, that he has not the same confidence in other sorts of man?

And even sport is losing its freedom. Soon everybody will be schooled, mentally and physically, from the cradle to the end of the term of adult compulsory military service, and finally of compulsory civil service lasting until the age of superannuation. Always more schooling, more compulsion. We are to be cured by an excess of the dose that has poisoned us. Satan is to cast out Satan.

Under the Whip

Clearly this will not do. We must reconcile education with liberty. We must find out some means of making men workers and, if need be, warriors, without making them slaves. We must cultivate the noble virtues that have their root in pride. Now no schoolmaster will teach these any more than a prison governor will teach his prisoners how to mutiny and escape. Self-preservation forces him to break the spirit that revolts against him, and to inculcate submission, even to obscene assault, as a duty. A bishop once had the hardihood to say that he would rather see England free than England sober.[28] Nobody has yet dared to say that he would

27. A city in western Spain. In the Napoleonic Peninsular War it was repeatedly taken by the French. In 1812 it was captured by the British under the Duke of Wellington, with heavy losses.
28. Bishop William Magee, Bishop of Peterborough (later Archbishop of York), in a speech in the House of Lords, 2 May 1872, in opposition to the Intoxicating

rather see an England of ignoramuses than an England of cowards and slaves. And if anyone did, it would be necessary to point out that the antithesis is not a practical one, as we have at present an England of ignoramuses who are also cowards and slaves, and patriotically proud of it at that, because in school they are taught to submit, with what they ridiculously call Oriental fatalism (as if any Oriental has ever submitted more helplessly and sheepishly to robbery and oppression than we Occidentals do), to be driven day after day into compounds and set to the tasks they loathe by the men they hate and fear, as if this were the inevitable destiny of mankind. And naturally, when they grow up, they helplessly exchange the prison of the school for the prison of the mine or the workshop or the office, and drudge along stupidly and miserably, with just enough gregarious instinct to turn furiously on any intelligent person who proposes a change. It would be quite easy to make England a paradise, according to our present ideas, in a few years. There is no mystery about it: the way has been pointed out over and over again. The difficulty is not the way but the will. And we have no will because the first thing done with us in childhood was to break our will. Can anything be more disgusting than the spectacle of a nation reading the biography of Gladstone and gloating over the account [in John Morley's *The Life of William Ewart Gladstone*, Vol. 1, 1903] of how he was flogged at Eton, two of his schoolfellows being compelled to hold him down whilst he was flogged. Not long ago a public body in England had to deal with the case of a schoolmaster who, conceiving himself insulted by the smoking of a cigaret against his orders by a pupil eighteen years old, proposed to flog him publicly as a satisfaction to what he called his honor and authority. I had intended to give the particulars of this case, but find the drudgery of raking over such stuff too sickening, and the effect unjust to a man who was doing only what others all over the country were doing as part of the established routine of what is called education. The astounding part of it was the manner in which the person to whom this outrage on decency seemed quite proper and natural claimed to be a functionary of high character, and had his claim allowed. In Japan he would hardly have been allowed the privilege of committing suicide. What is to be said of a profession in which such obscenities are made points of honor, or of institutions in which they are an accepted part of the daily routine? Wholesome people would not argue about the taste of such nastinesses: they would spit them out; but we are tainted with

Liquor Bill, complained, 'It would be better that England should be free than that England should be compulsorily sober.'

flagellomania from our childhood. When will we realize that the fact that we can become accustomed to anything, however disgusting at first, makes it necessary for us to examine carefully everything we have become accustomed to? Before motor cars became common, necessity had accustomed us to a foulness in our streets which would have horrified us had the street been our drawing-room carpet. Before long we shall be as particular about our streets as we now are about our carpets; and their condition in the XIX century will become as forgotten and incredible as the condition of the corridors of palaces and the courts of castles was as late as the XVIII century. This foulness, we can plead, was imposed on us as a necessity by the use of horses and of huge retinues; but flogging has never been so imposed: it has always been a vice, craved for on any pretext by those depraved by it. Boys were flogged when criminals were hanged, to impress the awful warning on them. Boys were flogged at boundaries, to impress the boundaries on their memory. Other methods and other punishments were always available: the choice of this one betrayed the sensual impulse which makes the practice an abomination. But when its viciousness made it customary, it was practised and tolerated on all hands by people who were innocent of anything worse than stupidity, ill temper, and inability to discover other methods of maintaining order than those they had always seen practised and approved of. From children and animals it extended to slaves and criminals. In the days of Moses it was limited to 39 lashes. In the early XIX century it had become an open madness: soldiers were sentenced to a thousand lashes for trifling offences, with the result (among others less mentionable) that the Iron Duke of Wellington complained that it was impossible to get an order obeyed in the British army except in two or three crack regiments.[29] Such frantic excesses of this disgusting neurosis provoked a reaction against it; but the clamor for it by depraved persons never ceased, and was tolerated by a nation trained to it from childhood in the schools until last year (1913), when, in what must be described as a paroxysm of sexual excitement provoked by the agitation concerning the White Slave Traffic (the purely commercial nature of which I was pre-

---

29. Wellington did not, however, at any time in his military career actively advocate doing away with corporal punishment in the military services. When, in 1829, Prussian reforms led to a re-examination of British military policies, Wellington rejected any reform of punishment in the army. It was not until 1846 that he belatedly took a public stand on reform, announcing in a speech on flogging, in the House of Lords, 'I hope I may live to see it abolished altogether', though warning that 'if you are to have an army, you must have it in a state of discipline.'

vented from exposing on the stage by the Censorship twenty years ago), the Government yielded to an outcry for flagellation led by the Archbishop of Canterbury [Randall T. Davidson], and passed an Act [see preface to *Mrs Warren's Profession*, Vol. 1, p. 139, fn. 22] under which a judge can sentence a man to be flogged to the utmost extremity with any instrument usable for such a purpose that he cares to prescribe. Such an Act is not a legislative phenomenon but a psychopathic one. Its effect on the White Slave Traffic was, of course, to distract public attention from its real cause and from the people who really profit by it to imaginary "foreign scoundrels," and to secure a monopoly of its organization for women.

And all this evil is made possible by the schoolmaster with his cane and birch, by the parents getting rid as best they can of the nuisance of children making noise and mischief in the house, and by the denial to children of the elementary rights of human beings.

The first man who enslaved and "broke in" an animal with a whip would have invented the explosion engine instead could he have foreseen the curse he was laying on his race. For men and women learnt thereby to enslave and break in their children by the same means. These children, grown up, knew no other methods of training. Finally the evil that was done for gain by the greedy was refined on and done for pleasure by the lustful. Flogging has become a pleasure purchasable in our streets, and inhibition a grown-up habit that children play at. "Go and see what baby is doing; and tell him he mustnt" is the last word of the nursery; and the grimmest aspect of it is that it was first formulated by a comic paper as a capital joke.

TECHNICAL INSTRUCTION

Technical instruction tempts to violence (as a short cut) more than liberal education. The sailor in Mr Rudyard Kipling's Captains Courageous [1897], teaching the boy the names of the ship's tackle with a rope's end, does not disgust us as our schoolmasters do, especially as the boy was a spoiled boy. But an unspoiled boy would not have needed that drastic medicine. Technical training may be as tedious as learning to skate or to play the piano or violin; but it is the price one must pay to achieve certain desirable results or necessary ends. It is a monstrous thing to force a child to learn Latin or Greek or mathematics on the ground that they are an indispensable gymnastic for the mental powers. It would be monstrous even if it were true; for there is no labor that might not be imposed on a child or an adult on the same pretext; but as a glance at the average products of our public school and university education shews that it is not true, it need not trouble us. But it is a fact that ignorance of Latin and Greek and mathematics closes certain careers to men (I do not mean artificial, unnecessary, noxious careers like those of the commercial schoolmaster). Languages, even dead ones, have their uses; and, as it seems to many of us, mathematics have their uses. They will always be learned by people who want to learn them; and people will always want to learn them as long as they are of any importance in life: indeed the want will survive their importance: superstition is nowhere stronger than in the field of obsolete acquirements. And they will never be learnt fruitfully by people who do not want to learn them either for their own sake or for use in necessary work. There is no harder schoolmaster than experience; and yet experience fails to teach where there is no desire to learn.

Still, one must not begin to apply this generalization too early. And this brings me to an important factor in the case: the factor of evolution.

DOCILITY AND DEPENDENCE

If anyone, impressed by my view that the rights of a child are precisely those of an adult, proceeds to treat a child as if it were an adult, he (or she) will find that though the plan will work much better at some points than the usual plan, at others it will not work at all; and this discovery may provoke him to turn back from the whole conception of children's rights with a jest at the expense of bachelors' and old maids' children. In dealing with children what is needed is not logic but sense. There is no logical reason why young persons should be allowed greater control of their property the day after they are twentyone than the day before it. There is no logical reason why I, who strongly object to an adult standing over a boy of ten with a Latin grammar, and saying "You must learn this, whether you want to or not," should nevertheless be quite prepared to stand over a boy of five with the multiplication table or a copy book or a code of elementary good manners, and practise on his docility to make him learn them. And there is no logical reason why I should do for a child a great many little offices, some of them troublesome and disagreeable, which I should not do for a boy twice its age, or support a boy or girl when I would unhesitatingly throw an adult on his own resources. But there are practical reasons, and sensible reasons, and affectionate reasons for all these illogicalities. Children do not want to be treated altogether as adults: such treatment terrifies them and overburdens them with responsibility. In truth, very few adults care to be called on for independence and originality: they also are bewildered and terrified in the absence of precedents and precepts and commandments; but modern Democracy allows them a sanctioning and cancelling power if they are capable of using it, which children are not. To treat a child wholly as an adult would be to mock and destroy it. Infantile docility and juvenile dependence are, like death, a product of Natural Selection; and though there is no viler crime than to abuse them, yet there is no greater cruelty than to ignore them. I have complained sufficiently of what I suffered through the process of assault, imprisonment, and compulsory lessons that taught me nothing, which are called my schooling. But I could say a good deal also about the things I was not taught and should have been taught, not to mention the things I was allowed to do which I should not have been allowed to do. I have no recollection of being taught to read or write; so I presume I was born with both faculties; but many people seem to have bitter recollections of being forced reluctantly to acquire them. And though I have the uttermost contempt for a teacher so ill-mannered and incompetent as to be unable to make a child learn to read and write without also making it cry, still I am prepared to admit that I had rather have been compelled to learn to read and write with tears by an incompetent and ill-mannered person than left in ignorance. Reading, writing, and enough arithmetic to use money honestly and accurately, together with the rudiments of law and order, become necessary conditions of a child's liberty before it can appreciate the importance of its liberty, or foresee that these accomplishments are worth acquiring. Nature has provided for this by evolving the instinct of docility. Children are very docile: they have a sound intuition that they must do what they are told or perish. And adults have an intuition, equally sound, that they must take advantage of this docility to teach children how to live properly or the children will not survive. The difficulty is to know where to stop. To illustrate this, let us consider the main danger of childish docility and parental officiousness.

THE ABUSE OF DOCILITY

Docility may survive as a lazy habit long after it has ceased to be a beneficial instinct. If you catch a child when it is young enough to be instinctively docile, and keep it in a condition of unremitted tutelage under the nurserymaid, the governess, the preparatory school, the secondary school, and the university, until it is an adult, you will produce, not a self-reliant, free, fully matured human being, but a grown-up schoolboy or schoolgirl, capable of nothing in the way of original or independent action except outbursts of naughtiness in the women and blackguardism in the men. That is exactly what we get at present in our rich and consequently governing classes; they pass from juvenility to senility without ever touching maturity except in body. The classes which cannot afford this sustained tutelage are notably more self-reliant and grown-up: an office boy of fifteen is often more of a man than a university student of twenty. Unfortunately this precocity is disabled by poverty, ignorance, narrowness, and a hideous power of living without art or love or beauty and being rather proud of it. The poor never escape from servitude: their docility is preserved by their slavery. And so all become the prey of the greedy, the selfish, the domineering, the unscrupulous, the predatory. If here and there an individual refuses to be docile, ten docile persons will beat him or lock him up or shoot him or hang him at the bidding of his oppressors and their own. The crux of the whole difficulty about parents, schoolmasters, priests, absolute monarchs, and despots of every sort, is the tendency to abuse natural docility. A nation should always be healthily rebellious; but rulers have yet to be found who will make trouble for themselves by cultivating that side of the national spirit. A child should begin to assert itself early, and shift for itself more and more not only in washing and dressing itself, but in opinions and conduct; yet as nothing is so exasperating and so unlovable as an uppish child, it is useless to expect parents and schoolmasters to inculcate this uppishness. Such unamiable precepts as Always contradict an authoritative statement, Always return a blow, Never lose a chance of a good fight, When you are scolded for a mistake ask the person who scolds you whether he or she supposes you did it on purpose, and follow the question with a blow or an insult or some other unmistakeable expression of resentment, Remember that the progress of the world depends on your knowing better than your elders, are just as important as those of The Sermon on the Mount; but no one has yet seen them written up in letters of gold in a schoolroom or nursery. The child is taught to be kind, to be respectful, to be quiet, not to answer back, to be truthful when its elders want to find out anything from it, to lie when the truth would shock or hurt its elders, to be above all things obedient, and to be seen and not heard. Here we have two sets of precepts, each of which will spoil an ordinary child if the other be omitted. Unfortunately we do not allow fair play between them. The rebellious, intractable, aggressive, selfish set provoke a corrective resistance, and do not pretend to high moral or religious sanctions; and they are never urged by grown-up people on young people. They are therefore more in danger of neglect or suppression than the other set, which have all the adults, all the laws, all the religions on their side. How is the child to be secured its due share of both bodies of doctrine?

THE SCHOOLBOY AND THE HOMEBOY

In practice what happens is that parents notice that boys brought up at home become mollycoddles, or prigs, or duffers, unable to take care of themselves. They see that boys should learn to rough it a little and to mix with children of their own age. This is natural enough. When you have preached at and punished a boy until he is a moral cripple, you are as much hampered by him as by a physical cripple; and as you do not intend to have him on your hands all your life, and are generally rather impatient for the day when he will earn his own living and leave you to attend to yourself, you sooner or later begin to talk to him about the need for self-reliance, learning to think, and so forth, with the result that your victim, bewildered by your inconsistency, concludes that there is no use trying to please you, and falls into an attitude of sulky resentment. Which is an additional inducement to pack him off to school.

In school, he finds himself in a dual world, under two dispensations. There is the world of the boys, where the point of honor is to be untameable, always ready to fight, ruthless in taking the conceit out of anyone who ventures to give himself airs of superior knowledge or taste, and generally to take Lucifer for one's model. And there is the world of the masters, the world of discipline, submission, diligence, obedience, and continual and shameless assumption of moral and intellectual authority. Thus the schoolboy hears both sides, and is so far better off than the home-bred boy who hears only one. But the two sides are not fairly presented. They are presented as good and evil, as vice and virtue, as villainy and heroism. The boy feels mean and cowardly when he obeys, and selfish and rascally when he disobeys. He loses his moral courage just as he comes to hate books and languages. In the end, John Ruskin, tied so closely to his mother's apron-string that he did not escape even when he went to Oxford, and John Stuart Mill, whose father ought to have been prosecuted for laying his son's childhood waste with lessons, were superior, as products of training, to our schoolboys. They were very conspicuously superior in moral courage; and though they did not distinguish themselves at cricket and football, they had quite as much physical hardihood as any civilized man needs. But it is to be observed that Ruskin's parents were wise people who gave John a full share in their own life, and put up with his presence both at home and abroad when they must sometimes have been very weary of him; and Mill, as it happens, was deliberately educated to challenge all the most sacred institutions of his country. The households they were brought up in were no more average households than a Montessori school is an average school.

THE COMINGS OF AGE OF CHILDREN

All this inculcated adult docility, which wrecks every civilization as it is wrecking ours, is inhuman and unnatural. We must reconsider our institution of the Coming of Age, which is too late for some purposes, and too early for others. There should be a series of Coming of Ages for every individual. The mammals have their first coming of age when they are weaned; and it is noteworthy that this rather cruel and selfish operation on the part of the parent has to be performed resolutely, with claws and teeth; for your little mammal does not want to be weaned, and yields only to a pretty rough assertion of the right of the parent to be relieved of the child as soon as the child is old enough to bear the separation. The same thing occurs with children: they hang on to the mother's apron-string and the father's coat tails as long as they can, often baffling those sensitive parents who know that children should think for themselves and fend for themselves, but are too kind to throw them on their own resources with the ferocity of the domestic cat. The child should have its first coming of age when it is weaned, another when it can talk, another when it can walk, another when it can dress itself without assistance; and when it can read, write, count money, and pass an examination in going a simple errand involving a purchase and a journey by rail or other public method of locomotion, it should have quite a majority. At present the children of laborers are soon mobile and able to shift for themselves, whereas it is possible to find grown-up women in the rich classes who are actually afraid to take a walk in the streets unattended and unprotected. It is true that this is a superstition from the time when a retinue was part of the state of persons of quality, and the unattended person was supposed to be a common person of no quality, earning a living; but this has now become so absurd that children and young women are no longer told why they are forbidden to go about alone, and have to be persuaded that the streets are dangerous places, which of course they are; but people who are not educated to live dangerously have only half a life, and are more likely to die miserably after all than those who have taken all the common risks of freedom from their childhood onward as matters of course.

THE CONFLICT OF WILLS

The world wags in spite of its schools and its families because both schools and families are mostly very largely anarchic: parents and schoolmasters are goodnatured or weak or lazy; and children are docile and affectionate and very shortwinded in their fits of naughtiness; and so most families slummock along and muddle through until the children cease to be children. In the few cases when the parties are energetic and determined, the child is crushed or the parent is reduced to a cipher, as the case may be. When the opposed forces are neither of them strong enough to annihilate the other, there is serious trouble: that is how we get those feuds between parent and child which recur to our memory so ironically when we hear people sentimentalizing about natural affection. We even get tragedies; for there is nothing so tragic to contemplate or so devastating to suffer as the oppression of will without conscience; and the whole tendency of our family and school system is to set the will of the parent and the school despot above conscience as something that must be deferred to abjectly and absolutely for its own sake.

The strongest, fiercest force in nature is human will. It is the highest organization we know of the will that has created the whole universe. Now all honest civilization, religion, law, and convention is an attempt to keep this force within beneficent bounds. What corrupts civilization, religion, law, and convention (and they are at present pretty nearly as corrupt as they dare) is the constant attempts made by the wills of individuals and classes to thwart the wills and enslave the powers of other individuals and classes. The powers of the parent and the schoolmaster, and of their public analogues the lawgiver and the judge, become instruments of tyranny in the hands of those who are too narrowminded to understand law and exercise judgment; and in their hands (with us they mostly fall into such hands) law becomes tyranny. And what is a tyrant? Quite simply a person who says to another person, young or old, "You shall do as I tell you; you shall make what I want; you shall profess my creed; you shall have no will of your own; and your powers shall be at the disposal of my will." It has come to this at last: that the phrase "she has a will of her own," or "he has a will of his own" has come to denote a person of exceptional obstinacy and self-assertion. And even persons of good natural disposition, if brought up to expect such deference, are roused to unreasoning fury, and sometimes to the commission of atrocious crimes, by the slightest challenge to their authority. Thus a laborer may be dirty, drunken, untruthful, slothful, untrustworthy in every way without exhausting the indulgence of the country house. But let him dare to be "disrespectful" and he is a lost man, though he be the cleanest, soberest, most diligent, most veracious, most trustworthy man in the county. Dickens's instinct for detecting social cankers never served him better than when [in *David Copperfield*] he shewed up Mrs Heep teaching her son [Uriah] to "be umble," knowing that if he carried out that precept he might be pretty well anything else he liked. The maintenance of deference to our wills becomes a mania which will carry the best of us to any extremity. We will allow a village of Egyptian fellaheen or Indian tribesmen to live the lowest life they please among themselves without molestation; but let one of them slay an Englishman or even strike him on the strongest provocation, and straightway we go stark mad, burning and destroying, shooting and shelling, flogging and hanging, if only such survivors as we may leave are thoroughly cowed in the presence of a man with a white face. In the committee room of a local council or city corporation, the humblest employees of the committee find defenders if they complain of harsh treatment. Gratuities are voted, indulgences and holidays are pleaded for, delinquencies are excused in the most sentimental manner provided only the employee, however patent a hypocrite or incorrigible a slacker, is hat in hand. But let the most obvious measure of justice be demanded by the secretary of a Trade Union in terms which omit all expressions of subservience, and it is with the greatest difficulty that the cooler-headed can defeat angry motions that the letter be thrown into the wastepaper basket and the committee proceed to the next business.

THE DEMAGOGUE'S OPPORTUNITY

And the employee has in him the same fierce impulse to impose his will without respect for the will of others. Democracy is in practice nothing but a device for cajoling from him the vote he refuses to arbitrary authority. He will not vote for Coriolanus; but when an experienced demagogue comes along and says "Sir: *you* are the dictator: the voice of the people is the voice of God; and I am only your very humble servant" he says at once "All right: tell me what to dictate" and is presently enslaved more effectually with his own silly consent than Coriolanus would ever have enslaved him without asking his leave [in Shakespeare's *Coriolanus*, III: i]. And the trick by which the demagogue defeats Coriolanus is played on him in his turn by *his* inferiors. Everywhere we see the cunning succeeding in the world by seeking a rich or powerful master and practising on his lust for subservience. The political adventurer who gets into parliament by offering himself to the poor voter, not as his representative but as his will-less soulless "delegate," is himself the dupe of a clever wife who repudiates Votes for Women, knowing well that whilst the man is master, the man's mistress will rule. Uriah Heep may be a crawling creature; but his crawling takes him upstairs.

Thus does the selfishness of the will turn on itself, and obtain by flattery what it cannot seize by open force. Democracy becomes the latest trick of tyranny: "womanliness" becomes the latest wile of prostitution.

Between parent and child the same conflict wages and the same destruction of character ensues. Parents set themselves to bend the will of their children to their own—to break their stubborn spirit, as they call it— with the ruthlessness of Grand Inquisitors. Cunning, unscrupulous children learn all the arts of the sneak in circumventing tyranny: children of better character are cruelly distressed and more or less lamed for life by it.

Our Quarrelsomeness

As between adults, we find a general quarrelsomeness which makes political reform as impossible to most Englishmen as to hogs. Certain sections of the nation get cured of this disability. University men, sailors, and politicians are comparatively free from it, because the communal life of the university, the fact that in a ship a man must either learn to consider others or else go overboard or into irons, and the habit of working on committees and ceasing to expect more of one's own way than is included in the greatest common measure of the committee, educate the will socially. But no one who has ever had to guide a committee of ordinary private Englishmen through their first attempts at collective action, in committee or otherwise, can retain any illusions as to the appalling effects on our national manners and character of the organization of the home and the school as petty tyrannies, and the absence of all teaching of self-respect and training in self-assertion. Bullied and ordered about, the Englishman obeys like a sheep, evades like a knave, or tries to murder his oppressor. Merely criticized or opposed in committee, or invited to consider anybody's views but his own, he feels personally insulted and wants to resign or leave the room unless he is apologized to. And his panic and bewilderment when he sees that the older hands at the work have no patience with him and do not intend to treat him as infallible, are pitiable as far as they are anything but ludicrous. That is what comes of not being taught to consider other people's wills, and left to submit to them or to override them as if they were the winds and the weather. Such a state of mind is incompatible not only with the democratic introduction of high civilization, but with the comprehension and maintenance of such civilized institutions as have been introduced by benevolent and intelligent despots and aristocrats.

WE MUST REFORM SOCIETY BEFORE WE CAN REFORM OURSELVES

When we come to the positive problem of what to do with children if we are to give up the established plan, we find the difficulties so great that we begin to understand why so many people who detest the system and look back with loathing on their own schooldays, must helplessly send their children to the very schools they themselves were sent to, because there is no alternative except abandoning the children to undisciplined vagabondism. Man in society must do as everybody else does in his class: only fools and romantic novices imagine that freedom is a mere matter of the readiness of the individual to snap his fingers at convention. It is true that most of us live in a condition of quite unnecessary inhibition, wearing ugly and uncomfortable clothes, making ourselves and other people miserable by the heathen horrors of mourning, staying away from the theatre because we cannot afford the stalls and are ashamed to go to the pit, and in dozens of other ways enslaving ourselves when there are comfortable alternatives open to us without any real drawbacks. The contemplation of these petty slaveries, and of the triumphant ease with which sensible people throw them off, creates an impression that if we only take Johnson's advice to free our minds from cant, we can achieve freedom [Boswell, *The Life of Samuel Johnson*, 15 May 1783]. But if we all freed our minds from cant we should find that for the most part we should have to go on doing the necessary work of the world exactly as we did it before until we organized new and free methods of doing it. Many people believed in secondary co-education (boys and girls taught together) before schools like Bedales[30] were founded: indeed the practice was common enough in elementary schools and in Scotland; but their belief did not help them until Bedales

30. England's first co-educational boarding school, founded in 1893 in Petersfield, Hampshire. Shaw's half-cousin Georgina Gillmore (later his first secretary) was enrolled here in 1897 at the expense of Shaw's future wife Charlotte Payne-Townshend.

and St George's were organized; and there are still not nearly enough co-educational schools in existence to accommodate all the children of the parents who believe in co-education up to university age, even if they could always afford the fees of these exceptional schools. It may be edifying to tell a duke that our public schools are all wrong in their constitution and methods, or a costermonger that children should be treated as in Goethe's Wilhelm Meister[31] instead of as they are treated at the elementary school at the corner of his street; but what are the duke and the coster to do? Neither of them has any effective choice in the matter: their children must either go to the schools that are, or to no school at all. And as the duke thinks with reason that his son will be a lout or a milksop or a prig if he does not go to school, and the coster knows that his son will become an illiterate hooligan if he is left to the streets, there is no real alternative for either of them. Child life must be socially organized: no parent, rich or poor, can choose institutions that do not exist; and the private enterprize of individual schoolmasters appealing to a group of well-to-do parents, though it may shew what can be done by enthusiasts with new methods, cannot touch the mass of our children. For the average parent or child nothing is really available except the established practice; and this is what makes it so important that the established practice should be a sound one, and so useless for clever individuals to disparage it unless they can organize an alternative practice and make it, too, general.

The Pursuit of Manners

If you cross-examine the duke and the coster, you will find that they are not concerned for the scholastic attainments of their children. Ask the duke whether he could pass the standard examination of twelve-year-old children in elementary schools, and he will admit, with an entirely placid smile, that he would almost certainly be ignominiously plucked. And he is so little ashamed of or disadvantaged by his condition that he is not prepared to spend an hour in remedying it. The coster may resent the inquiry instead of being amused by it; but his answer, if true, will be the same. What they both want for their children is the communal training, the apprenticeship to society, the lessons in holding one's own among people of all sorts with whom one is not, as in the home, on privileged terms. These can be

---

31. Meister's son goes to a school that teaches the dignity of labour and the beauty of art. (*Wilhelm Meister's Travels*, 1821–9.)

acquired only by "mixing with the world," no matter how wicked the world is. No parent cares twopence whether his children can write Latin hexameters or repeat the dates of the accession of all the English monarchs since the Conqueror; but all parents are earnestly anxious about the manners of their children. Better Claude Duval than Kaspar Hauser.[32] Laborers who are contemptuously anti-clerical in their opinions will send their daughters to the convent school because the nuns teach them some sort of gentleness of speech and behavior. And peers who tell you that our public schools are rotten through and through, and that our universities ought to be razed to the foundations, send their sons to Eton and Oxford, Harrow and Cambridge, not only because there is nothing else to be done, but because these places, though they turn out blackguards and ignoramuses and boobies galore, turn them out with the habits and manners of the society they belong to. Bad as those manners are in many respects, they are better than no manners at all. And no individual or family can possibly teach them. They can be acquired only by living in an organized community in which they are traditional.

Thus we see that there are reasons for the segregation of children even in families where the great reason: namely, that children are nuisances to adults, does not press very hardly, as, for instance, in the houses of the very poor, who can send their children to play in the streets, or the houses of the very rich, which are so large that the children's quarters can be kept out of the parents' way like the servants' quarters.

NOT TOO MUCH WIND ON THE HEATH, BROTHER

What, then, is to be done? For the present, unfortunately, little except propagating the conception of Children's Rights. Only the achievement of economic equality through Socialism can make it possible to deal thoroughly with the question from the point of view of the total interest of the community, which must always consist of grown-up children. Yet economic equality, like all simple and obvious arrangements, seems impossible to people brought up as children are now. Still, something can be done

---

32. Duval was a French highwayman in England, whose swashbuckling ways were exploited in novels and ballads; he was hanged at Tyburn in 1670. Hauser was a timid German foundling of enigmatic parentage, adopted by aristocrats, who was murdered in 1833 under mysterious circumstances, occasioning a number of literary treatments.

even within class limits. Large communities of children of the same class are possible today; and voluntary organization of outdoor life for children has already begun in Boy Scouting and excursions of one kind or another. The discovery that anything, even school life, is better for the child than home life, will become an overridden hobby; and we shall presently be told by our faddists that anything, even camp life, is better than school life. Some blundering beginnings of this are already perceptible. There is a movement for making our British children into priggish little barefooted vagabonds, all talking like that born fool George Borrow [presumably a reference to his most famous novel, *Lavengro*, 1851], and supposed to be splendidly healthy because they would die if they slept in rooms with the windows shut, or perhaps even with a roof over their heads. Still, this is a fairly healthy folly; and it may do something to establish Mr Harold Cox's[33] claim of a Right to Roam as the basis of a much-needed law compelling proprietors of land to provide plenty of gates in their fences, and to leave them unlocked when there are no growing crops to be damaged nor bulls to be encountered, instead of, as at present, imprisoning the human race in dusty or muddy thoroughfares between walls of barbed wire.

The reaction against vagabondage will come from the children themselves. For them freedom will not mean the expensive kind of savagery now called "the simple life." Their natural disgust with the visions of cockney book fanciers blowing themselves out with "the wind on the heath, brother,"[34] and of anarchists who are either too weak to understand that men are strong and free in proportion to the social pressure they can stand and the complexity of the obligations they are prepared to undertake, or too strong to realize that what is freedom to them may be terror and bewilderment to others, will drive them back to the home and the school if these have meanwhile learned the lesson that children are independent human beings and have rights.

WANTED: A CHILD'S MAGNA CHARTA

Whether we shall presently be discussing a Juvenile Magna Charta or

33. Author of *Land Nationalization* (1892, revised 1906) and editor of the *Edinburgh Review* from 1912 to 1929, a liberal journalist and quondam politician, who endorsed the cause of personal liberty and responsibility.
34. George Borrow, *Lavengro* (1851), Chapter 25: 'There's night and day, brother, both sweet things; sun, moon and stars, brother, all sweet things; there's likewise a wind on the heath. Life is very sweet, brother; who would wish to die?'

Declaration of Rights by way of including children in the Constitution is a question on which I leave others to speculate. But if it could once be established that a child has an adult's Right of Egress from uncomfortable places and unpleasant company, and there were children's lawyers to sue pedagogues and others for assault and imprisonment, there would be an amazing change in the behavior of schoolmasters, the quality of school books, and the amenities of school life. That Consciousness of Consent which, even in its present delusive form, has enabled Democracy to oust tyrannical systems in spite of all its vulgarities and stupidities and rancors and ineptitudes and ignorances, would operate as powerfully among children as it does now among grownups. No doubt the pedagogue would promptly turn demagogue, and woo his scholars by all the arts of demagogy; but none of these arts can easily be so dishonorable or mischievous as the art of caning. And, after all, if larger liberties are attached to the acquisition of knowledge, and the child finds that it can no more go to the seaside without a knowledge of the multiplication and pence tables than it can be an astronomer without mathematics, it will learn the multiplication table, which is more than it always does at present, in spite of all the canings and keepings-in.

THE PURSUIT OF LEARNING

When the Pursuit of Learning comes to mean the pursuit of learning by the child instead of the pursuit of the child by Learning, cane in hand, the danger will be precocity of the intellect, which is just as undesirable as precocity of the emotions. We still have a silly habit of talking and thinking as if intellect were a mechanical process and not a passion; and in spite of the German tutors who confess openly that three out of every five of the young men they coach for examinations are lamed for life thereby; in spite of Dickens and his picture of little Paul Dombey dying of lessons, we persist in heaping on growing children and adolescent youths and maidens tasks Pythagoras would have declined out of common regard for his own health and common modesty as to his own capacity. And this overwork is not all the effect of compulsion; for the average schoolmaster does not compel his scholars to learn: he only scolds and punishes them if they do not, which is quite a different thing, the net effect being that the school prisoners need not learn unless they like. Nay, it is sometimes remarked that the school dunce—meaning the one who does not like—often turns out well afterwards, as if idleness were a sign of ability and character. A much more sensible explanation is that the so-called dunces are not exhausted before they begin the serious business of life. It is said that boys will be boys; and one can only add one wishes they would. Boys really want to be manly, and are unfortunately encouraged thoughtlessly in this very dangerous and overstraining aspiration. All the people who have really worked (Herbert Spencer for instance [as in *A Liberal Education and Where to Find It*, 1868]) warn us against work as earnestly as some people warn us against drink. When learning is placed on the voluntary footing of sport, the teacher will find himself saying every day "Run away and play: you have worked as much as is good for you." Trying to make children leave school will be like trying to make them go to bed; and it will be necessary to surprise them with the idea that teaching is work, and that the teacher is tired and must go play or rest or eat: possibilities always concealed by that infamous humbug the current schoolmaster, who achieves a spurious divinity and a witch doctor's authority by persuading children that he is not human, just as ladies used to persuade them that they have no legs.

CHILDREN AND GAME: A PROPOSAL

Of the many wild absurdities of our existing social order perhaps the most grotesque is the costly and strictly enforced reservation of large tracts of country as deer forests and breeding grounds for pheasants whilst there is so little provision of the kind made for children. I have more than once thought of trying to introduce the shooting of children as a sport, as the children would then be preserved very carefully for ten months in the year, thereby reducing their death rate far more than the fusillades of the sportsmen during the other two would raise it. At present the killing of a fox except by a pack of foxhounds is regarded with horror; but you may and do kill children in a hundred and fifty ways provided you do not shoot them or set a pack of dogs on them. It must be admitted that the foxes have the best of it; and indeed a glance at our pheasants, our deer, and our children will convince the most sceptical that the children have decidedly the worst of it.

This much hope, however, can be extracted from the present state of things. It is so fantastic, so mad, so apparently impossible, that no scheme of reform need ever henceforth be discredited on the ground that it is fantastic or mad or apparently impossible. It is the sensible schemes, unfortunately, that are hopeless in England. Therefore I have great hopes that my own views, though fundamentally sensible, can be made to appear fantastic enough to have a chance.

First, then, I lay it down as a prime condition of sane society, obvious as such to anyone but an idiot, that in any decent community, children should find in every part of their native country, food, clothing, lodging, instruction, and parental kindness for the asking. For the matter of that, so should adults; but the two cases differ in that as these commodities do not grow on the bushes, the adults cannot have them unless they themselves organize and provide the supply, whereas the children must have them as if by magic, with nothing to do but rub the lamp, like Aladdin, and have their needs satisfied.

The Parents' Intolerable Burden

There is nothing new in this: it is how children have always had and must always have their needs satisfied. The parent has to play the part of Aladdin's djinn; and many a parent has sunk beneath the burden of this service. All the novelty we need is to organize it so that instead of the individual child fastening like a parasite on its own particular parents, the whole body of children should be thrown not only upon the whole body of parents, but upon the celibates and childless as well, whose present exemption from a full share in the social burden of children is obviously unjust and unwholesome. Today it is easy to find a widow who has at great cost to herself in pain, danger, and disablement, borne six or eight children. In the same town you will find rich bachelors and old maids, and married couples with no children or with families voluntarily limited to two or three. The eight children do not belong to the woman in any real or legal sense. When she has reared them they pass away from her into the community as independent persons, marrying strangers, working for strangers, spending on the community the life that has been built up at her expense. No more monstrous injustice could be imagined than that the burden of rearing the children should fall on her alone and not on the celibates and the selfish as well.

This is so far recognized that already the child finds, wherever it goes, a school for it, and somebody to force it into the school; and more and more these schools are being driven by the mere logic of facts to provide the children with meals, with boots, with spectacles, with dentists and doctors. In fact, when the child's parents are destitute or not to be found, bread, lodging, and clothing are provided. It is true that they are provided grudgingly and on conditions infamous enough to draw down abundant fire from Heaven upon us every day in the shape of crime and disease and vice; but still the practice of keeping children barely alive at the charge of the community is established; and there is no need for me to argue about it. I propose only two extensions of the practice. One is to provide for all the child's reasonable human wants, on which point, if you differ from me, I shall take leave to say that you are socially a fool and personally an inhuman wretch. The other is that these wants should be supplied in complete freedom from compulsory schooling or compulsory anything except restraint from crime, though, as they can be supplied only by social organization, the child must be conscious of and subject to the conditions of that organization, which may involve such portions of adult responsibility and duty as a child may be able to bear according to its age, and which will in any case prevent it from forming the vagabond and anarchist habit of mind.

One more exception might be necessary: compulsory freedom. I am sure that a child should not be imprisoned in a school. I am not so sure that it should not sometimes be driven out into the open—imprisoned in the woods and on the mountains, as it were. For there are frowsty children, just as there are frowsty adults, who dont want freedom. This morbid result of over-domestication would, let us hope, soon disappear with its cause.

MOBILIZATION

Those who see no prospect held out to them by this except a country in which all the children shall be roaming savages, should consider, first, whether their condition would be any worse than that of the little caged savages of today; and second, whether either children or adults are so apt to run wild that it is necessary to tether them fast to one neighborhood to prevent a general dissolution of society. My own observation leads me to believe that we are not half mobilized enough. True, I cannot deny that we are more mobile than we were. You will still find in the Home Counties old men who have never been to London, and who tell you that they once went to Winchester or St Albans much as if they had been to the South Pole; but they are not so common as the clerk who has been to Paris or to Lovely Lucerne, and who "goes away somewhere" when he has a holiday. His grandfather never had a holiday, and, if he had, would no more have dreamed of crossing the Channel than of taking a box at the opera. But with all allowance for the Polytechnic excursion and the tourist agency, our inertia is still appalling. I confess to having once spent nine years in

London without putting my nose outside it; and though this was better, perhaps, than the restless globetrotting vagabondage of the idle rich, wandering from hotel to hotel and never really living anywhere, yet I should no more have done it if I had been properly mobilized in my childhood than I should have worn the same suit of clothes all that time (which by the way, I very nearly did, my professional income not having as yet begun to sprout). There are masses of people who could afford at least a trip to Margate [seaside resort in Kent], and a good many who could afford a trip round the world, who are more immovable than Aldgate [district in east London] pump. To others, who would move if they knew how, traveling is surrounded with imaginary difficulties and terrors. In short, the difficulty is not to fix people, but to root them up. We keep repeating the silly proverb that a rolling stone gathers no moss, as if moss were a desirable parasite. What we mean is that a vagabond does not prosper. Even this is not true, if prosperity means enjoyment as well as responsibility and money. The real misery of vagabondage is the misery of having nothing to do and nowhere to go, the misery of being derelict of God and Man, the misery of the idle, poor or rich. And this is one of the miseries of unoccupied childhood. The unoccupied adult, thus afflicted, tries many distractions which are, to say the least, unsuited to children. But one of them, the distraction of seeing the world, is innocent and beneficial. Also it is childish, being a continuation of what nurses call "taking notice," by which a child becomes experienced. It is pitiable nowadays to see men and women doing after the age of 45 all the traveling and sightseeing they should have done before they were 15. Mere wondering and staring at things is an important part of a child's education: that is why children can be thoroughly mobilized without making vagabonds of them. A vagabond is at home nowhere because he wanders: a child should wander because it ought to be at home everywhere. And if it has its papers and its passports, and gets what it requires not by begging and pilfering, but from responsible agents of the community as of right, and with some formal acknowledgment of the obligations it is incurring and a knowledge of the fact that these obligations are being recorded: if, further, certain qualifications are exacted before it is promoted from permission to go as far as its legs will carry it to using mechanical aids to locomotion, it can roam without much danger of gypsification.

Under such circumstances the boy or girl could always run away, and never be lost; and on no other conditions can a child be free without being also a homeless outcast. Parents could also run away from disagreeable children or drive them out of doors or even drop their acquaintance, temporarily or permanently, without inhumanity. Thus both parties would be on their good behavior, and not, as at present, on their filial or parental behavior, which, like all unfree behavior, is mostly bad behavior.

As to what other results might follow, we had better wait and see; for nobody now alive can imagine what customs and institutions would grow up in societies of free children. Child laws and child fashions, child manners and child morals are now not tolerated; but among free children there would certainly be surprising developments in this direction. I do not think there would be any danger of free children behaving as badly as grown-up people do now because they have never been free. They could hardly behave worse, anyhow.

CHILDREN'S RIGHTS AND PARENTS' WRONGS

A very distinguished man once assured a mother of my acquaintance that she would never know what it meant to be hurt until she was hurt through her children. Children are extremely cruel without intending it; and in ninetynine cases out of a hundred the reason is that they do not conceive their elders as having any human feelings. Serve the elders right, perhaps, for posing as superhuman! The penalty of the impostor is not that he is found out (he very seldom is) but that he is taken for what he pretends to be, and treated as such. And to be treated as anything but what you really are may seem pleasant to the imagination when the treatment is above your merits; but in actual experience it is often quite the reverse. When I was a very small boy, my romantic imagination, stimulated by early doses of fiction, led me to brag to a still smaller boy so outrageously that he, being a simple soul, really believed me to be an invincible hero. I cannot remember whether this pleased me much; but I do remember very distinctly that one day this admirer of mine, who had a pet goat, found the animal in the hands of a larger boy than either of us, who mocked him and refused to restore the animal to his rightful owner. Whereupon, naturally, he came weeping to me, and demanded that I should rescue the goat and annihilate the aggressor. My terror was beyond description: fortunately for me, it imparted such a ghastliness to my voice and aspect as I, under the eye of my poor little dupe, advanced on the enemy with that hideous extremity of cowardice which is called the courage of despair, and said "You let go that goat," that he abandoned his prey and fled, to my unforgettable, unspeakable relief. I have never since exaggerated my prowess in bodily combat.

Now what happened to me in the adventure of the goat happens very often to parents, and would happen to schoolmasters if the prison door of the school did not shut out the trials of life. I remember once, at school, the resident head master [James de Glanville, of the Dublin English Scientific and Commercial Day School] was brought down to earth by the sudden illness of his wife. In the confusion that ensued it became necessary to leave one of the schoolrooms without a master. I was in the class that occupied that schoolroom. To have sent us home would have been to break the fundamental bargain with our parents by which the school was bound to keep us out of their way for half the day at all hazards. Therefore an appeal had to be made to our better feelings: that is, to our common humanity, not to make a noise. But the head master had never admitted any common humanity with us. We had been carefully broken in to regard him as a being quite aloof from and above us: one not subject to error or suffering or death or illness or mortality. Consequently sympathy was impossible; and if the unfortunate lady did not perish, it was because, as I now comfort myself with guessing, she was too much preoccupied with her own pains, and possibly making too much noise herself, to be conscious of the pandemonium downstairs.

A great deal of the fiendishness of schoolboys and the cruelty of children to their elders is produced just in this way. Elders cannot be superhuman beings and suffering fellow creatures at the same time. If you pose as a little god, you must pose for better for worse.

HOW LITTLE WE KNOW ABOUT OUR PARENTS

The relation between parent and child has cruel moments for the parent even when money is no object, and the material worries are delegated to servants and school teachers. The child and the parent are strangers to oneanother necessarily, because their ages must differ widely. Read Goethe's autobiography [*Poetry and Truth*, 1811–22]; and note that though he was happy in his parents and had exceptional powers of observation, divination, and storytelling, he knew less about his father and mother than about most of the other people he mentions. I myself was never on bad terms with my mother: we lived together until I was fortytwo years old, absolutely without the smallest friction of any kind; yet when her death [several months earlier, on 19 February 1913] set me thinking curiously about our relations, I realized that I knew very little about her. Introduce me to a strange woman who was a child when I was a child, a girl when I was a boy, an adolescent when I was an adolescent; and if we take naturally to

oneanother I will know more of her and she of me at the end of forty days
(I had almost said of forty minutes) than I knew of my mother at the end
of forty years. A contemporary stranger is a novelty and an enigma, also a
possibility; but a mother is like a broomstick or like the sun in the heavens,
it does not matter which as far as one's knowledge of her is concerned: the
broomstick is there and the sun is there; and whether the child is beaten by
it or warmed and enlightened by it, it accepts it as a fact in nature, and does
not conceive it as having had youth, passions, and weaknesses, or as still
growing, yearning, suffering, and learning. If I meet a widow I may ask
her all about her marriage; but what son ever dreams of asking his mother
about her marriage, or could endure to hear of it without violently
breaking off the old sacred relationship between them, and ceasing to be
her child or anything more to her than the first man in the street might be?

Yet though in this sense the child cannot realize its parent's humanity,
the parent can realize the child's; for the parents with their experience of
life have none of the illusions about the child that the child has about the
parents; and the consequence is that the child can hurt its parents' feelings
much more than its parents can hurt the child's, because the child, even
when there has been none of the deliberate hypocrisy by which children
are taken advantage of by their elders, cannot conceive the parent as a
fellow creature, whilst the parents know very well that the children are
only themselves over again. The child cannot conceive that its blame or
contempt or want of interest could possibly hurt its parent, and therefore
expresses them all with an indifference which has given rise to the term
enfant terrible (a tragic term in spite of the jests connected with it); whilst
the parent can suffer from such slights and reproaches more from a child
than from anyone else, even when the child is not beloved, because the
child is so unmistakeably sincere in them.

OUR ABANDONED MOTHERS

Take a very common instance of this agonizing incompatibility. A
widow brings up her son to manhood. He meets a strange woman, and
goes off with and marries her, leaving his mother desolate. It does not
occur to him that this is at all hard on her: he does it as a matter of course,
and actually expects his mother to receive, on terms of special affection, the
woman for whom she has been abandoned. If he shewed any sense of what
he was doing, any remorse; if he mingled his tears with hers and asked her
not to think too hardly of him because he had obeyed the inevitable

destiny of a man to leave his father and mother and cleave to his wife, she could give him her blessing and accept her bereavement with dignity and without reproach. But the man never dreams of such considerations. To him his mother's feeling in the matter, when she betrays it, is unreasonable, ridiculous, and even odious, as shewing a prejudice against his adorable bride.

I have taken the widow as an extreme and obvious case; but there are many husbands and wives who are tired of their consorts, or disappointed in them, or estranged from them by infidelities; and these parents, in losing a son or a daughter through marriage, may be losing everything they care for. No parent's love is as innocent as the love of a child: the exclusion of all conscious sexual feeling from it does not exclude the bitterness, jealousy, and despair at loss which characterize sexual passion: in fact, what is called a pure love may easily be more selfish and jealous than a carnal one. Anyhow, it is plain matter of fact that naïvely selfish people sometimes try with fierce jealousy to prevent their children marrying.

FAMILY AFFECTION

Until the family as we know it ceases to exist, nobody will dare to analyze parental affection as distinguished from that general human sympathy which has secured to many an orphan fonder care in a stranger's house than it would have received from its actual parents. Not even Tolstoy, in The Kreutzer Sonata, has said all that we suspect about it. When it persists beyond the period at which it ceases to be necessary to the child's welfare, it is apt to be morbid; and we are probably wrong to inculcate its deliberate cultivation. The natural course is for the parents and children to cast off the specific parental and filial relation when they are no longer necessary to oneanother. The child does this readily enough to form fresh ties, closer and more fascinating. Parents are not always excluded from such compensations: it happens sometimes that when the children go out at the door the lover comes in at the window. Indeed it happens now oftener than it used to, because people remain much longer in the sexual arena. The cultivated Jewess no longer cuts off her hair at her marriage. The British matron has discarded her cap and her conscientious ugliness; and a bishop's wife at fifty has more of the air of a *femme galante* than an actress had at thirtyfive in her grandmother's time. But as people marry later, the facts of age and time still inexorably condemn most parents to comparative solitude when their children marry. This may be a privation and may be a relief: probably in healthy circumstances it is no worse than a salutary change of habit; but even at that it is, for the moment at least, a wrench. For though parents and children sometimes dislike oneanother, there is an experience of succor and a habit of dependence and expectation formed in infancy which naturally attaches a child to its parent or to its nurse (a foster parent) in a quite peculiar way. A benefit to the child may be a burden to the parent; but people become attached to their burdens sometimes more than the burdens are attached to them; and to "suffer little children" has become an affectionate impulse deep in our nature.

Now there is no such impulse to suffer our sisters and brothers, our aunts and uncles, much less our cousins. If we could choose our relatives, we might, by selecting congenial ones, mitigate the repulsive effect of the obligation to like them and to admit them to our intimacy. But to have a person imposed on us as a brother merely because he happens to have the same parents is unbearable when, as may easily happen, he is the sort of person we should carefully avoid if he were anyone else's brother. All Europe (except Scotland, which has clans instead of families) draws the line at second cousins. Protestantism draws it still closer by making the first cousin a marriageable stranger; and the only reason for not drawing it at sisters and brothers is that the institution of the family compels us to spend our childhood with them, and thus imposes on us a curious relation in which familiarity destroys romantic charm, and is yet expected to create a specially warm affection. Such a relation is dangerously factitious and unnatural; and the practical moral is that the less said at home about specific family affection the better. Children, like grown-up people, get on well enough together if they are not pushed down oneanother's throats; and grown-up relatives will get on together in proportion to their separation and their care not to presume on their blood relationship. We should let children's feelings take their natural course without prompting. I have seen a child scolded and called unfeeling because it did not occur to it to make a theatrical demonstration of affectionate delight when its mother returned after an absence: a typical example of the way in which spurious family sentiment is stoked up. We are, after all, sociable animals; and if we are let alone in the matter of our affections, and well brought up otherwise, we shall not get on any the worse with particular people because they happen to be our brothers and sisters and cousins. The danger lies in assuming that we shall get on any better.

The main point to grasp here is that families are not kept together at present by family feeling but by human feeling. The family cultivates sympathy and mutual help and consolation as any other form of kindly association cultivates them; but the addition of a dictated compulsory affection as an attribute of near kinship is not only unnecessary, but positively detrimental; and the alleged tendency of modern social development to break up the family need alarm nobody. We cannot break up the facts of kinship nor eradicate its natural emotional consequences. What we can do and ought to do is to set people free to behave naturally and to change their behavior as circumstances change. To impose on a citizen of London the family duties of a Highland cateran [a military irregular in Scotland] in the XVIII century is as absurd as to compel him to carry a claymore and target [sword and small shield] instead of an umbrella. The civilized man has no special use for cousins; and he may presently find that he has no special use for brothers and sisters. The parent seems likely to remain indispensable; but there is no reason why that natural tie should be made the excuse for unnatural aggravations of it, as crushing to the parent as they are oppressive to the child. The mother and father will not always have to shoulder the burthen of maintenance which should fall on the Atlas shoulders[35] of the fatherland and motherland. Pending such reforms and emancipations, a shattering break-up of the paternal home must remain one of normal incidents of marriage. The parent is left lonely and the child is not. Woe to the old if they have no impersonal interests, no convictions, no public causes to advance, no tastes or hobbies! It is well to be a mother but not to be a mother-in-law; and if men were cut off artificially from intellectual and public interests as women are, the father-in-law would be as deplorable a figure in popular tradition as the mother-in-law.

It is not to be wondered at that some people hold that blood relationship should be kept a secret from the persons related, and that the happiest condition in this respect is that of the foundling who, if he ever meets his parents or brothers or sisters, passes them by without knowing them. And for such a view there is this to be said: that our family system does unquestionably take the natural bond between members of the same family, which, like all natural bonds, is not too tight to be borne, and superimposes on it a painful burden of forced, inculcated, suggested, and altogether unnecessary affection and responsibility which we should do well to get rid of by making relatives as independent of oneanother as possible.

---

35. Atlas was a Titan in Greek mythology, who supported the pillars 'which hold Heaven and Earth asunder' (Homer, *The Odyssey*).

THE FATE OF THE FAMILY

The difficulty of inducing people to talk sensibly about the family is the same as that which I pointed out in a previous volume as confusing discussions of marriage [see preface to *Getting Married*, Vol. 1, pp. 409–70]. Marriage is not a single invariable institution: it changes from civilization to civilization, from religion to religion, from civil code to civil code, from frontier to frontier. The family is still more variable, because the number of persons constituting a family, unlike the number of persons constituting a marriage, varies from one to twenty: indeed, when a widower with a family marries a widow with a family, and the two produce a third family, even that very high number may be surpassed. And the conditions may vary between opposite extremes: for example, in a London or Paris slum every child adds to the burden of poverty and helps to starve the parents and all the other children, whereas in a settlement of pioneer colonists every child, from the moment it is big enough to lend a hand to the family industry, is an investment in which the only danger is that of temporary over-capitalization. Then there are the variations in family sentiment. Sometimes the family organization is as frankly political as the organization of an army or an industry; fathers being no more expected to be sentimental about their children than colonels about soldiers, or factory owners about their employees, though the mother may be allowed a little tenderness if her character is weak. The Roman father was a despot: the Chinese father is an object of worship: the sentimental modern western father is often a playfellow looked to for toys and pocket-money. The farmer sees his children constantly: the squire sees them only during the holidays, and not then oftener than he can help: the tram conductor, when employed by a joint stock company, sometimes never sees them at all.

Under such circumstances phrases like The Influence of Home Life, The Family, The Domestic Hearth, and so on, are no more specific than The Mammals, or The Man in the Street; and the pious generalizations founded so glibly on them by our sentimental moralists are unworkable. When households average twelve persons with the sexes about equally represented, the results may be fairly good. When they average three the results may be very bad indeed; and to lump the two together under the general term The Family is to confuse the question hopelessly. The modern small family is much too stuffy: children "brought up at home" in it are unfit for society.

But here again circumstances differ. If the parents live in what is called a garden suburb, where there is a good deal of social intercourse, and the family, instead of keeping itself to itself, as the evil old saying is, and glowering at the neighbors over the blinds of the long street in which nobody knows his neighbor and everyone wishes to deceive him as to his income and social importance, is in effect broken up by school life, by out-of-door habits, and by frank neighborly intercourse through dances and concerts and theatricals and excursions and the like, families of four may turn out much less barbarous citizens than families of ten which attain the Boer ideal of being out of sight of oneanother's chimney smoke.

All one can say is, roughly, that the homelier the home, and the more familiar the family, the worse for everybody concerned. The family ideal is a humbug and a nuisance: one might as reasonably talk of the barrack ideal, or the forecastle ideal, or any other substitution of the machinery of social organization for the end of it, which must always be the fullest and most capable life: in short, the most godly life. And this significant word reminds us that though the popular conception of Heaven includes a Holy Family, it does not attach to that family the notion of a separate home, or a private nursery or kitchen or mother-in-law, or anything that constitutes the family as we know it. Even blood relationship is miraculously abstracted from it; and the Father is the father of all children, the Mother the mother of all mothers and babies, and the Son the Son of Man and the Savior of his brothers: one whose chief utterance on the subject of the conventional family was an invitation to all of us to leave our families and follow him, and to leave the dead to bury the dead, and not debauch ourselves at that gloomy festival the family funeral, with its sequel of hideous mourning and grief which is either affected or morbid.

Family Mourning

I do not know how far this detestable custom of mourning is carried in France; but judging from the appearance of the French people I should say that a Frenchwoman goes into mourning for her cousins to the seventeenth degree. The result is that when I cross the Channel I seem to have reached a country devastated by war or pestilence. It is really suffering only from the family. Will anyone pretend that England has not the better of this striking difference? It is such senseless and unnatural conventions as this that make us so impatient of what we call family feeling. Even apart from its insufferable pretensions, the family needs hearty discrediting; for there is hardly any vulnerable part of it that could not be amputated with advantage.

ART TEACHING

By art teaching I hasten to say that I do not mean giving children lessons in freehand drawing and perspective. I am simply calling attention to the fact that fine art is the only teacher except torture. I have already pointed out that nobody, except under threat of torture, can read a schoolbook. The reason is that a schoolbook is not a work of art. Similarly, you cannot listen to a lesson or a sermon unless the teacher or the preacher is an artist. You cannot read the Bible if you have no sense of literary art. The reason why the continental European is, to the Englishman or American, so surprisingly ignorant of the Bible, is that the authorized English version is a great work of literary art, and the continental versions are comparatively artless. To read a dull book; to listen to a tedious play or prosy sermon or lecture; to stare at uninteresting pictures or ugly buildings: nothing, short of disease, is more dreadful than this. The violence done to our souls by it leaves injuries and produces subtle maladies which have never been properly studied by psychopathologists. Yet we are so inured to it in school, where practically all the teachers are bores trying to do the work of artists, and all the books artless, that we acquire a truly frightful power of enduring boredom. We even acquire the notion that fine art is lascivious and destructive to the character. In church, in the House of Commons, at public meetings, we sit solemnly listening to bores and twaddlers because from the time we could walk or speak we have been snubbed, scolded, bullied, beaten and imprisoned whenever we dared to resent being bored or twaddled at, or to express our natural impatience and derision of bores and twaddlers. And when a man arises with a soul of sufficient native strength to break the bonds of this inculcated reverence and to expose and deride and tweak the noses of our humbugs and panjandrums, like Voltaire or Dickens, we are shocked and scandalized, even when we cannot help laughing. Worse, we dread and persecute those who can see and declare the truth, because their sincerity and insight reflects on our delusion and blindness. We are all like Nell Gwynne's footman, who defended Nell's reputation with his fists, not because he believed her to be what he called an honest woman, but because he objected to be scorned as the footman of one who was no better than she should be [as reported by G. K. Chesterton in *Nell Gwyn*, 1912].

This wretched power of allowing ourselves to be bored may seem to give the fine arts a chance sometimes. People will sit through a performance of Beethoven's ninth symphony or of Wagner's Ring just as they will sit through a dull sermon or a front-bench politician saying nothing for two hours whilst his unfortunate country is perishing through the delay of its business in Parliament. But their endurance is very bad for the ninth symphony, because they never hiss when it is murdered. I have heard an Italian conductor [Luigi Arditi] (no longer living) take the *adagio* of that symphony at a lively *allegretto*, slowing down for the warmer major sections into the speed and manner of the heroine's death song in a Verdi opera; and the listeners, far from relieving my excruciation by rising with yells of fury and hurling their programs and opera glasses at the miscreant, behaved just as they do when [Hans] Richter conducts it. The mass of imposture that thrives on this combination of ignorance with despairing endurance is incalculable. Given a public trained from childhood to stand anything tedious, and so saturated with school discipline that even with the doors open and no schoolmasters to stop them they will sit there helplessly until the end of the concert or opera gives them leave to go home; and you will have in great capitals hundreds of thousands of pounds spent every night in the season on professedly artistic entertainments which have no other effect on fine art than to exacerbate the hatred in which it is already secretly held in England.

Fortunately, there are arts that cannot be cut off from the people by bad performances. We can read books for ourselves; and we can play a good deal of fine music for ourselves with the help of a pianola. Nothing stands between us and the actual handwork of the great masters of painting except distance; and modern photographic methods of reproduction are in some cases quite and in many nearly as effective in conveying the artist's message as a modern edition of Shakespear's plays is in conveying the message that first existed in his handwriting. The reproduction of great feats of musical execution is already on the way: the gramophone, for all its wheezing and snarling and braying, is steadily improving in its manners; and what with this improvement on the one hand, and on the other that blessed selective faculty which enables us to ignore a good deal of disagreeable noise if there is a thread of music in the middle of it (few critics of the gramophone seem to be conscious of the very considerable mechanical noise set up by choirs and orchestras) we have at last reached a point at which, for example, a person living in an English village where the church music is the only music, and that music is made by a few well-intentioned ladies with the help of a harmonium, can hear masses by Palestrina very passably executed, and can thereby be led to the discovery that [William]

Jackson[36] in F and Hymns Ancient and Modern are not perhaps the last word of beauty and propriety in the praise of God.

In short, there is a vast body of art now within the reach of everybody. The difficulty is that this art, which alone can educate us in grace of body and soul, and which alone can make the history of the past live for us or the hope of the future shine for us, which alone can give delicacy and nobility to our crude lusts, which is the appointed vehicle of inspiration and the method of the communion of saints, is actually branded as sinful among us because, wherever it arises, there is resistance to tyranny, breaking of fetters, and the breath of freedom. The attempt to suppress art is not wholly successful: we might as well try to suppress oxygen. But it is carried far enough to inflict on huge numbers of people a most injurious art starvation, and to corrupt a great deal of the art that is tolerated. You will find in England plenty of rich families with little more culture than their dogs and horses. And you will find poor families, cut off by poverty and town life from the contemplation of the beauty of the earth, with its dresses of leaves, its scarves of cloud, and its contours of hill and valley, who would positively be happier as hogs, so little have they cultivated their humanity by the only effective instrument of culture: art. The dearth is artificially maintained even when there are the means of satisfying it. Story books are forbidden, picture post cards are forbidden, theatres are forbidden, operas are forbidden, circuses are forbidden, sweetmeats are forbidden, pretty colors are forbidden, all exactly as vice is forbidden. The Creator is explicitly prayed to, and implicitly convicted of indecency every day. An association of vice and sin with everything that is delightful and of goodness with everything that is wretched and detestable is set up. All the most perilous (and glorious) appetites and propensities are at once inflamed by starvation and uneducated by art. All the wholesome conditions which art imposes on appetite are waived: instead of cultivated men and women restrained by a thousand delicacies, repelled by ugliness, chilled by vulgarity, horrified by coarseness, deeply and sweetly moved by the graces that art has revealed to them and nursed in them, we get indiscriminate rapacity in pursuit of pleasure and a parade of the grossest stimulations in catering for it. We have a continual clamor for goodness, beauty, virtue, and sanctity, with such an appalling inability to recognize it or love it when

36. English composer and organist known as Jackson of Exeter, who wrote operas, a musical setting for Milton's 'Lycidas', and much church music, including the Service in F.

it arrives that it is more dangerous to be a great prophet or poet than to promote twenty companies for swindling simple folk out of their savings. Do not for a moment suppose that uncultivated people are merely indifferent to high and noble qualities. They hate them malignantly. At best, such qualities are like rare and beautiful birds: when they appear the whole country takes down its guns; but the birds receive the statuary tribute of having their corpses stuffed.

And it really all comes from the habit of preventing children from being troublesome. You are so careful of your boy's morals, knowing how troublesome they may be, that you keep him away from the Venus of Milo only to find him in the arms of the scullery maid or someone much worse. You decide that the Hermes of Praxiteles and Wagner's Tristan are not suited for young girls; and your daughter marries somebody appallingly unlike either Hermes or Tristan solely to escape from your parental protection. You have not stifled a single passion nor averted a single danger: you have depraved the passions by starving them, and broken down all the defences which so effectively protect children brought up in freedom. You have men who imagine themselves to be ministers of religion openly declaring that when they pass through the streets they have to keep out in the wheeled traffic to avoid the temptations of the pavement. You have them organizing hunts of the women who tempt them—poor creatures whom no artist would touch without a shudder—and wildly clamoring for more clothes to disguise and conceal the body, and for the abolition of pictures, statues, theatres, and pretty colors. And incredible as it seems, these unhappy lunatics are left at large, unrebuked, even admired and revered, whilst artists have to struggle for toleration. To them an undraped human body is the most monstrous, the most blighting, the most obscene, the most unbearable spectacle in the universe. To an artist it is, at its best, the most admirable spectacle in nature, and, at its average, an object of indifference. If every rag of clothing miraculously dropped from the inhabitants of London at noon tomorrow (say as a preliminary to the Great Judgment), the artistic people would not turn a hair; but the artless people would go mad and call on the mountains to hide them. I submit that this indicates a thoroughly healthy state on the part of the artists, and a thoroughly morbid one on the part of the artless. And the healthy state is attainable in a cold country like ours only by familiarity with the undraped figure acquired through pictures, statues, and theatrical representations in which an illusion of natural clotheslessness is produced and made poetic.

In short, we all grow up stupid and mad to just the extent to which we have not been artistically educated; and the fact that this taint of stupidity and madness has to be tolerated because it is general, and is even boasted of as characteristically English, makes the situation all the worse. It is becoming exceedingly grave at present, because the last ray of art is being cut off from our schools by the discontinuance of religious education.

THE IMPOSSIBILITY OF SECULAR EDUCATION

Now children must be taught some sort of religion. Secular education is an impossibility. Secular education comes to this: that the only reason for ceasing to do evil and learning to do well is that if you do not you will be caned. This is worse than being taught in a church school that if you become a dissenter you will go to hell; for hell is presented as the instrument of something eternal, divine, and inevitable: you cannot evade it the moment the schoolmaster's back is turned. What confuses this issue and leads even highly intelligent religious persons to advocate secular education as a means of rescuing children from the strife of rival proselytizers is the failure to distinguish between the child's personal subjective need for a religion and its right to an impartially communicated historical objective knowledge of all the creeds and Churches. Just as a child, no matter what its race and color may be, should know that there are black men and brown men and yellow men, and, no matter what its political convictions may be, that there are Monarchists and Republicans and Positivists, Socialists and Unsocialists, so it should know that there are Christians and Mahometans and Buddhists and Shintoists and so forth, and that they are on the average just as honest and well-behaved as its own father. For example, it should not be told that Allah is a false god set up by the Turks and Arabs, who will all be damned for taking that liberty; but it should be told that many English people think so, and that many Turks and Arabs think the converse about English people. It should be taught that Allah is simply the name by which God is known to Turks and Arabs, who are just as eligible for salvation as any Christian. Further, that the practical reason why a Turkish child should pray in a mosque and an English child in a church is that as worship is organized in Turkey in mosques in the name of Mahomet and in England in churches in the name of Christ, a Turkish child joining the Church of England or an English child following Mahomet will find that it has no place for its worship and no organization of its religion within its reach. Any other teaching of the history and present facts of religion is false teaching, and is politically extremely dangerous in an empire in which a huge majority of the fellow subjects of the governing island do not profess the religion of that island.

But this objectivity, though intellectually honest, tells the child only what other people believe. What it should itself believe is quite another matter. The sort of Rationalism which says to a child "You must suspend your judgment until you are old enough to choose your religion" is Rationalism gone mad. The child must have a conscience and a code of honor (which is the essence of religion) even if it be only a provisional one, to be revised at its confirmation. For confirmation is meant to signalize a spiritual coming of age, and may be a repudiation. Really active souls have many confirmations and repudiations as their life deepens and their knowledge widens. But what is to guide the child before its first confirmation? Not mere orders, because orders must have a sanction of some sort or why should the child obey them? If, as a Secularist, you refuse to teach any sanction, you must say "You will be punished if you disobey." "Yes," says the child to itself, "if I am found out; but wait until your back is turned and I will do as I like, and lie about it." There can be no objective punishment for successful fraud; and as no espionage can cover the whole range of a child's conduct, the upshot is that the child becomes a liar and schemer with an atrophied conscience. And a good many of the orders given to it are not obeyed after all. Thus the Secularist who is not a fool is forced to appeal to the child's vital impulse towards perfection, to the divine spark; and no resolution not to call this impulse an impulse of loyalty to the Fellowship of the Holy Ghost, or obedience to the Will of God, or any other standard theological term, can alter the fact that the Secularist has stepped outside Secularism and is educating the child religiously, even if he insists on repudiating that pious adverb and substituting the word metaphysically.

NATURAL SELECTION AS A RELIGION

We must make up our minds to it therefore that whatever measures we may be forced to take to prevent the recruiting sergeants of the Churches, free or established, from obtaining an exclusive right of entry to schools, we shall not be able to exclude religion from them. The most horrible of all religions: that which teaches us to regard ourselves as the helpless prey of a series of senseless accidents called Natural Selection, is allowed and even welcomed in so-called secular schools because it is, in a sense, the negation of all religion; but for school purposes a religion is a belief which affects conduct: and no belief affects conduct more radically and often so disastrously as the belief that the universe is a product of Natural Selection. What is more, the theory of Natural Selection cannot be kept out of schools, because many of the natural facts that present the most plausible appearance of design can be accounted for by Natural Selection; and it would be as absurd to keep a child in delusive ignorance of so potent a factor in evolution as to keep it in ignorance of radiation or capillary attraction. Even if you make a religion of Natural Selection, and teach the child to regard itself as the irresponsible prey of its circumstances and appetites (or its heredity as you will perhaps call them), you will none the less find that its appetites are stimulated by your encouragement and daunted by your discouragement; that one of its appetites is an appetite for perfection; that if you discourage this appetite and encourage the cruder acquisitive appetites the child will steal and lie and be a nuisance to you; and that if you encourage its appetite for perfection and teach it to attach a peculiar sacredness to it and place it before the other appetites, it will be a much nicer child and you will have a much easier job, at which point you will, in spite of your pseudo-scientific jargon, find yourself back in the old-fashioned religious teaching as deep as Dr Watts and in fact fathoms deeper.

MORAL INSTRUCTION LEAGUES

And now the voices of our Moral Instruction Leagues will be lifted, asking whether there is any reason why the appetite for perfection should not be cultivated in rationally scientific terms instead of being associated with the story of Jonah and the great fish and the thousand other tales that grow up round religions. Yes: there are many reasons; and one of them is that children all like the story of Jonah and the whale (they insist on its being a whale in spite of demonstrations by Bible smashers without any sense of humor that Jonah would not have fitted into a whale's gullet—as if the story would be credible of a whale with an enlarged throat) and that no child on earth can stand moral instruction books or catechisms or any other statement of the case for religion in abstract terms. The object of a moral instruction book is not to be rational, scientific, exact, proof against controversy, nor even credible: its object is to make children good. If it makes them sick instead its place is the wastepaper basket. And if it is to be read it must be readable.

Take for an illustration the story of Elisha and the bears.[37] To the authors of the moral instruction books it is in the last degree reprehensible. It is obviously not true as a record of fact; and the picture it gives us of the temper of God (which is what interests an adult reader) is shocking and blasphemous. But it is a capital story for a child. It interests a child because it is about bears; and it leaves the child with an impression that children who poke fun at old gentlemen and make rude remarks about bald heads are not nice children, which is a highly desirable impression, and just as much as a child is capable of receiving from the story. When a story is about God and a child, children take God for granted and criticize the child. Adults do the opposite, and are thereby often led to talk great nonsense about the bad effect of Bible stories on infants.

But let no one think that a child or anyone else can learn religion from a teacher or a book or by any academic process whatever. It is only by an unfettered access to the whole body of Fine Art: that is, to the whole body of inspired revelation, that we can build up that conception of divinity to which all virtue is an aspiration. And to hope to find this body of art purified from all that is obsolete or dangerous or fierce or lusty, or to pick and choose what will be good for any particular child, much less for all children, is the shallowest of vanities. Such schoolmasterly selection is neither possible nor desirable. Ignorance of evil is not virtue but imbecility: admiring it is like giving a prize for honesty to a man who has not stolen your watch because he did not know you had one. Virtue chooses good from evil; and without knowledge there can be no choice. And even this is a dangerous simplification of what actually occurs. We are not choosing: we are growing. Were you to cut all of what you call the evil out of a child, it would drop dead. If you try to stretch it to full human stature when it is ten years old, you will simply pull it into two pieces and be hanged. And when you try to do this morally, which is what parents and schoolmasters are doing every day, you ought to be hanged; and some day, when we take a sensible view of the matter, you will be; and serve you right. The child does not stand between a good and a bad angel: what it has to deal with is a middling angel who, in normal healthy cases, wants to be a good angel as fast as it can without killing itself in the process, which is a dangerous one.

Therefore there is no question of providing the child with a carefully

---

37. In 2 Kings 2: 23–5, when Elisha is mocked by a street gang of small children he curses them in the name of the Lord. Two she-bears, emerging from the woods at the behest of the Lord, destroy forty-two of the children.

regulated access to good art. There is no good art, any more than there is good anything else in the absolute sense. Art that is too good for the child will either teach it nothing or drive it mad, as the Bible has driven many people mad who might have kept their sanity had they been allowed to read much lower forms of literature. The practical moral is that we must read whatever stories, see whatever pictures, hear whatever songs and symphonies, go to whatever plays we like. We shall not like those which have nothing to say to us; and though everyone has a right to bias our choice, no one has a right to deprive us of it by keeping us from any work of art or any work of art from us.

I may now say without danger of being misunderstood that the popular English compromise called Cowper-Templeism[38] (unsectarian Bible education) is not so silly as it looks. It is true that the Bible inculcates half a dozen religions: some of them barbarous; some cynical and pessimistic; some amoristic and romantic; some sceptical and challenging; some kindly, simple, and intuitional; some sophistical and intellectual; none suited to the character and conditions of western civilization unless it be the Christianity which was finally suppressed by the Crucifixion, and has never been put into practice by any State before or since. But the Bible contains the ancient literature of a very remarkable Oriental race; and the imposition of this literature, on whatever false pretences, on our children left them more literate than if they knew no literature at all, which was the practical alternative. And as our Authorized Version is a great work of art as well, to know it was better than knowing no art, which also was the practical alternative. It is at least not a schoolbook; and it is not a bad story book, horrible as some of the stories are. Therefore as between the Bible and the blank represented by secular education in its most matter-of-fact sense, the choice is with the Bible.

The Bible

But the Bible is not sufficient. The real Bible of modern Europe is the whole body of great literature in which the inspiration and revelation of

38. William Cowper-Temple and his Broad Church League were principally responsible for the inclusion in the 1870 Elementary Education Act of a clause in Section 14 providing that in all public elementary schools 'no catechism or religious formulary which is distinctive of any particular denomination shall be taught'. It was a compromise between absolute secularism and denominationalism.

Hebrew Scripture has been continued to the present day. Nietzsche's Thus Spake Zoroaster [1883–92] is less comforting to the ill and unhappy than the Psalms; but it is much truer, subtler, and more edifying. The pleasure we get from the rhetoric of the book of Job and its tragic picture of a bewildered soul cannot disguise the ignoble irrelevance of the retort of God with which it closes, nor supply the need for such modern revelations as Shelley's Prometheus [*Unbound*, 1820] or The Niblung's Ring [1854–74] of Richard Wagner. There is nothing in the Bible greater in inspiration than Beethoven's ninth symphony; and the power of modern music to convey that inspiration to a modern man is far greater than that of Elizabethan English, which is, except for people steeped in the Bible from childhood like Sir Walter Scott and Ruskin, a dead language.

Besides, many who have no ear for literature or for music are accessible to architecture, to pictures, to statues, to dresses, and to the arts of the stage. Every device of art should be brought to bear on the young; so that they may discover some form of it that delights them naturally; for there will come to all of them that period between dawning adolescence and full maturity when the pleasures and emotions of art will have to satisfy cravings which, if starved or insulted, may become morbid and seek disgraceful satisfactions, and, if prematurely gratified otherwise than poetically, may destroy the stamina of the race. And it must be borne in mind that the most dangerous art for this necessary purpose is the art that presents itself as religious ecstasy. Young people are ripe for love long before they are ripe for religion. Only a very foolish person would substitute the Imitation of Christ for Treasure Island as a present for a boy or girl, or for Byron's Don Juan as a present for a swain or lass. Pickwick is the safest saint for us in our nonage. Flaubert's Temptation of St Anthony [1874] is an excellent book for a man of fifty, perhaps the best within reach as a healthy study of visionary ecstasy; but for the purposes of a boy of fifteen Ivanhoe and the Templar [Sir Brian de Bois-Guilbert] make a much better saint and devil. And the boy of fifteen will find this out for himself if he is allowed to wander in a well-stocked literary garden, and hear bands and see pictures and spend his pennies on cinematograph shows. His choice may often be rather disgusting to his elders when they want him to choose the best before he is ready for it. The greatest Protestant Manifesto ever written, as far as I know, is Houston Chamberlain's[39] Foundations of the

39. Anglo-German writer, remembered chiefly for his racist theories. The thesis of his book is that everything good in the modern world is a contribution of the German 'race', the superior Aryan element in European culture.

Nineteenth Century [1899; tr. 1911]: everybody capable of it should read it. Probably the History of Maria Monk [see Vol. 1, p. 243, fn. 46] is at the opposite extreme of merit (this is a guess: I have never read it); but it is certain that a boy let loose in a library would go for Maria Monk and have no use whatever for Mr Chamberlain. I should probably have read Maria Monk myself if I had not had the Arabian Nights and their like to occupy me better. In art, children, like adults, will find their level if they are left free to find it, and not restricted to what adults think good for them. Just at present our young people are going mad over ragtimes, apparently because syncopated rhythms are new to them. If they had learnt what can be done with syncopation from Beethoven's third Leonora overture, they would enjoy the ragtimes all the more; but they would put them in their proper place as amusing vulgarities.

ARTIST IDOLATRY

But there are more dangerous influences than ragtimes waiting for people brought up in ignorance of fine art. Nothing is more pitiably ridiculous than the wild worship of artists by those who have never been seasoned in youth to the enchantments of art. Tenors and prima donnas, pianists and violinists, actors and actresses enjoy powers of seduction which in the middle ages would have exposed them to the risk of being burnt for sorcery. But as they exercise this power by singing, playing, and acting, no great harm is done except perhaps to themselves. Far graver are the powers enjoyed by brilliant persons who are also connoisseurs in art. The influence they can exercise on young people who have been brought up in the darkness and wretchedness of a home without art, and in whom a natural bent towards art has always been baffled and snubbed, is incredible to those who have not witnessed and understood it. He (or she) who reveals the world of art to them opens heaven to them. They become satellites, disciples, worshippers of the apostle. Now the apostle may be a voluptuary without much conscience. Nature may have given him enough virtue to suffice in a reasonable environment. But this allowance may not be enough to defend him against the temptation and demoralization of finding himself a little god on the strength of what ought to be a quite ordinary culture. He may find adorers in all directions in our uncultivated society among people of stronger character than himself, not one of whom, if they had been artistically educated, would have had anything to learn from him or regarded him as in any way extraordinary apart from his actual achievements as an artist. [Molière's] Tartuffe is not always a priest. Indeed he is not always a rascal: he is often a weak man absurdly credited with omniscience and perfection, and taking unfair advantages only because they are offered to him and he is too weak to refuse. Give everyone his culture, and no one will offer him more than his due.

In thus delivering our children from the idolatry of the artist, we shall not destroy for them the enchantment of art: on the contrary, we shall teach them to demand art everywhere as a condition attainable by cultivating the body, mind, and heart. Art, said Morris, is the expression of pleasure in work [*News from Nowhere*, 1891]. And certainly, when work is made detestable by slavery, there is no art. It is only when learning is made a slavery by tyrannical teachers that art becomes loathsome to the pupil.

"THE MACHINE"

When we set to work at a Constitution to secure freedom for children, we had better bear in mind that the children may not be at all obliged to us for our pains. Rousseau said that men are born free; and this dangerous saying, as Rousseau meant it, was and is a great and true saying; yet let it not lead us into the error of supposing that all men long for freedom and embrace it when it is offered to them. On the contrary, it has to be forced on them; and even then they will give it the slip if it is not religiously inculcated and strongly safeguarded.

Besides, men are born docile, and must in the nature of things remain so with regard to everything they do not understand. Now political science and the art of government are among the things they do not understand, and indeed are not at present allowed to understand. They can be enslaved by a system, as we are at present, because it happens to be there, and nobody understands it. An intelligently worked Capitalist system, as [Auguste] Comte saw, would give us all that most of us are intelligent enough to want [as in *Cours de philosophie positive*, 1830–42]. What makes it produce such unspeakably vile results is that it is an automatic system which is as little understood by those who profit by it in money as by those who are starved and degraded by it: our millionaires and statesmen are manifestly no more "captains of industry" or scientific politicians than our bookmakers are mathematicians. For some time past a significant word has been coming into use as a substitute for Destiny, Fate, and Providence. It is "The Machine": the machine that has no god in it. Why do governments do nothing in spite of reports of Royal Commissions that establish the most frightful urgency? Why do our philanthropic millionaires do nothing, though they are ready to throw bucketfuls of gold into the streets? The Machine will not let them. Always The Machine. In short, they dont know how. They try to reform Society as an old lady might try to restore a broken-down locomotive by prodding it with a knitting needle. And this is not at all because they are born fools, but because they have been educated, not into manhood and freedom, but into blindness and slavery by their parents and schoolmasters, themselves the victims of a similar misdirection, and consequently of The Machine. They do not want liberty. They have not been educated to want it. They choose slavery and inequality; and all the other evils are automatically added to them.

And yet we must have The Machine. It is only in unskilled hands under ignorant direction that machinery is dangerous. We can no more govern modern communities without political machinery than we can feed and clothe them without industrial machinery. Shatter The Machine, and you get Anarchy. And yet The Machine works so detestably at present that we have people who advocate anarchy and call themselves Anarchists.

THE PROVOCATION TO ANARCHISM

The Anarchists are right when they say that governments, like schoolmasters, try to simplify their task by destroying liberty and glorifying authority, especially their own. But the difficulty of combining law and order with free institutions is not a natural one. It is a matter of inculcation. If people are brought up to be slaves, it is useless and dangerous to let them loose at the age of twentyone and say "Now you are free." No one with the tamed soul and broken spirit of a slave can be free. It is like saying to a laborer brought up on a family income of thirteen shillings a week, "Here is one hundred thousand pounds: now you are wealthy." Nothing can make such a man really wealthy. Freedom and wealth are difficult and responsible conditions to which men must be accustomed and socially trained from birth. A nation that is free at twentyone is not free at all; just as a man first enriched at fifty remains poor all his life, even if he does not curtail it by drinking himself to death in the first wild ecstasy of being able to swallow as much as he likes for the first time. You cannot govern men brought up as slaves otherwise than as slaves are governed. You may pile Bills of Right and Habeas Corpus Acts on Great Charters; promulgate American Constitutions; burn the chateaux and guillotine the seigneurs; chop off the heads of kings and queens and set up Democracy on the ruins of feudalism: the end of it all for us is that already in the XX century there has been as much brute coercion and savage intolerance, as much flogging and hanging, as much impudent injustice on the bench and lustful rancor in the pulpit, as much naïve resort to torture, persecution, and suppression of free speech and freedom of the press, as much war, as much of the vilest excess of mutilation, rapine, and delirious indiscriminate slaughter of helpless non-combatants, old and young, as much prostitution of professional talent, literary and political, in defence of manifest wrong, as much cowardly sycophancy giving fine names to all this villainy or pretending that it is "greatly exaggerated," as we can find any record of from the days when the advocacy of liberty was a capital offence and Democracy was hardly thinkable. Democracy exhibits the vanity of Louis XIV, the savagery of Peter of Russia, the nepotism and provinciality of Napoleon, the fickleness of Catherine II: in short, all the childishnesses of all the despots without any of the qualities that enabled the greatest of them to fascinate and dominate their contemporaries.

And the flatterers of Democracy are as impudently servile to the success-ful, and insolent to common honest folk, as the flatterers of the monarchs. Democracy in America has led to the withdrawal of ordinary refined persons from politics; and the same result is coming in England as fast as we make Democracy as democratic as it is in America. This is true also of popular religion: it is so horribly irreligious that nobody with the smallest pretence to culture, or the least inkling of what the great prophets vainly tried to make the world understand, will have anything to do with it except for purely secular reasons.

IMAGINATION

Before we can clearly understand how baleful is this condition of intimidation in which we live, it is necessary to clear up the confusion made by our use of the word imagination to denote two very different powers of mind. One is the power to imagine things as they are not: this I call the romantic imagination. The other is the power to imagine things as they are without actually sensing them; and this I will call the realistic imagination. Take for example marriage and war. One man has a vision of perpetual bliss with a domestic angel at home, and of flashing sabres, thundering guns, victorious cavalry charges, and routed enemies in the field. That is romantic imagination; and the mischief it does is incalculable. It begins in silly and selfish expectations of the impossible, and ends in spiteful disappointment, sour grievance, cynicism, and misanthropic resistance to any attempt to better a hopeless world. The wise man knows that imagination is not only a means of pleasing himself and beguiling tedious hours with romances and fairy tales and fools' paradises (a quite defensible and delightful amusement when you know exactly what you are doing and where fancy ends and facts begin), but also a means of foreseeing and being prepared for realities as yet unexperienced, and of testing the feasibility and desirability of serious Utopias. He does not expect his wife to be an angel; nor does he overlook the facts that war depends on the rousing of all the murderous blackguardism still latent in mankind; that every victory means a defeat; that fatigue, hunger, terror, and disease are the raw material which romancers work up into military glory; and that soldiers for the most part go to war as children go to school, because they are afraid not to. They are afraid even to say they are afraid, as such candor is punishable by death in the military code.

A very little realistic imagination gives an ambitious person enormous power over the multitudinous victims of the romantic imagination. For the romancer not only pleases himself with fictitious glories: he also terrifies himself with imaginary dangers. He does not even picture what these dangers are: he conceives the unknown as always dangerous. When you say to a realist "You must do this" or "You must not do that," he instantly asks what will happen to him if he does (or does not, as the case may be). Failing an unromantic convincing answer, he does just as he pleases unless he can find for himself a real reason for refraining. In short, though you can intimidate him, you cannot bluff him. But you can always bluff the romantic person: indeed his grasp of real considerations is so feeble that you find it necessary to bluff him even when you have solid considerations to offer him instead. The campaigns of Napoleon, with their atmosphere of glory, illustrate this. In the Russian campaign Napoleon's marshals achieved miracles of bluff, especially [Michel] Ney, who, with a handful of men, monstrously outnumbered, repeatedly kept the Russian troops paralyzed with terror by pure bounce. Napoleon himself, much more a realist than Ney (that was why he dominated him), would probably have surrendered; for sometimes the bravest of the brave will achieve successes never attempted by the cleverest of the clever. Wellington was a completer realist than Napoleon. It was impossible to persuade Wellington that he was beaten until he actually was beaten. He was unbluffable; and if Napoleon had understood the nature of Wellington's strength instead of returning Wellington's snobbish contempt for him by an academic contempt for Wellington, he would not have left the attack at Waterloo to Ney and [Jean-Baptiste Drouet, Comte] D'Erlon, who, on that field, did not know when they were beaten, whereas Wellington knew precisely when he was not beaten. The unbluffable would have triumphed anyhow, probably, because Napoleon was an academic soldier, doing the academic thing (the attack in columns and so forth) with superlative ability and energy; whilst Wellington was an original soldier who, instead of outdoing the terrible academic columns with still more terrible and academic columns, outwitted them with the thin red line,[40] not of heroes, but, as this uncompromising realist never hesitated to testify, of the scum of the earth [Philip Henry's *Notes of Conversations with the Duke of Wellington*, 1888].

GOVERNMENT BY BULLIES

These picturesque martial incidents are being reproduced every day in our ordinary life. We are bluffed by hardy simpletons and headstrong bounders as the Russians were bluffed by Ney; and our Wellingtons are threadbound by slave-democracy as Gulliver was threadbound by the Lilliputians. We are a mass of people living in a submissive routine to which we have been drilled from our childhood. When you ask us to take the simplest step outside that routine, we say shyly, "Oh, I really couldnt," or "Oh, I shouldnt like to," without being able to point out the smallest harm that could possibly ensue: victims, not of a rational fear of real dangers, but of pure abstract fear, the quintessence of cowardice, the very negation of "the fear of God." Dotted about among us are a few spirits relatively free from this inculcated paralysis, sometimes because they are half-witted, sometimes because they are unscrupulously selfish, sometimes because they are realists as to money and unimaginative as to other things, sometimes even because they are exceptionally able, but always because they are not afraid of shadows nor oppressed with nightmares. And we see these few rising as if by magic into power and affluence, and forming, with the millionaires who have accidentally gained huge riches by the occasional windfalls of our commerce, the governing class. Now nothing is more disastrous than a governing class that does not know how to govern. And how can this rabble of the casual products of luck, cunning, and folly, be expected to know how to govern? The merely lucky ones and the

40. Rudyard Kipling's inspiration for this line in 'Tommy' (*Barrack Room Ballads*) came from a report of Sir William Russell to *The Times*, 25 October 1854, describing the British infantry at Balaclava: 'The Russians dashed on towards that thin red-line streak tipped with a line of steel'.

hereditary ones do not owe their position to their qualifications at all. As to the rest, the realism which seems their essential qualification often consists not only in a lack of romantic imagination, which lack is a merit, but of the realistic, constructive, Utopian imagination, which lack is a ghastly defect. Freedom from imaginative illusion is therefore no guarantee whatever of nobility of character: that is why inculcated submissiveness makes us slaves to people much worse than ourselves, and why it is so important that submissiveness should no longer be inculcated.

And yet as long as you have the compulsory school as we know it, we shall have submissiveness inculcated. What is more, until the active hours of child life are organized separately from the active hours of adult life, so that adults can enjoy the society of children in reason without being tormented, disturbed, harried, burdened, and hindered in their work by them as they would be now if there were no compulsory schools and no children hypnotized into the belief that they must tamely go to them and be imprisoned and beaten and overtasked in them, we shall have schools under one pretext or another; and we shall have all the evil consequences and all the social hopelessness that result from turning a nation of potential freemen and freewomen into a nation of two-legged spoilt spaniels with everything crushed out of their nature except dread of the whip. Liberty is the breath of life to nations; and liberty is the one thing that parents, schoolmasters, and rulers spend their lives in extirpating for the sake of an immediately quiet and finally disastrous life.

The Dark Lady of the Sonnets

First published in 1914

═══

HOW THE PLAY CAME TO BE WRITTEN

I had better explain why, in this little *pièce d'occasion* [work for a particular occasion], written for a performance in aid of the funds of the project of establishing a National Theatre as a memorial to Shakespear, I have identified the Dark Lady with Mistress Mary Fitton. First, let me say that I do not contend that the Dark Lady was Mary Fitton, because when the case in Mary's favor (or against her, if you please to consider that the Dark Lady was no better than she ought to have been) was complete, a portrait of Mary came to light and turned out to be that of a fair lady, not of a dark one. That settles the question, if the portrait is authentic, which I see no reason to doubt, and the lady's hair undyed, which is perhaps less certain. Shakespear rubbed in the lady's complexion in his sonnets mercilessly; for in his day black hair was as unpopular as red hair was in the early days of Queen Victoria. Any tinge lighter than raven black must be held fatal to the strongest claim to be the Dark Lady. And so, unless it can be shewn that Shakespear's sonnets exasperated Mary Fitton into dyeing her hair and getting painted in false colors, I must give up all pretence that my play is historical. The later suggestion of Mr [Arthur] Acheson [in *Mistress Davenant: The Dark Lady of Shakespeare's Sonnets*, 1913] that the Dark Lady, far from being a maid of honor, kept a tavern in Oxford, and was the mother of [Sir William] Davenant the poet, is the one I should have adopted had I wished to be up to date. Why, then, did I introduce the Dark Lady as Mistress Fitton?

Well, I had two reasons. The play was not to have been written by me at all, but by Dame Edith Lyttelton;[1] and it was she who suggested a scene of jealousy between Queen Elizabeth and the Dark Lady at the expense of

1. English civic-minded socialite and writer, whose novels were published under the pseudonym G. B. Lancaster. Among her plays are *Warp and Woof* (1904) and *Peter's Chance* (1912). Dame Edith was an active member of the Shakespeare Memorial National Theatre Committee.

the unfortunate Bard. Now this, if the Dark Lady was a maid of honor, was quite easy. If she were a tavern landlady, it would have strained all probability. So I stuck to Mary Fitton. But I had another and more personal reason. I was, in a manner, present at the birth of the Fitton theory. Its parent and I had become acquainted; and he used to consult me on obscure passages in the sonnets, on which, as far as I can remember, I never succeeded in throwing the faintest light, at a time when nobody else thought my opinion, on that or any other subject, of the slightest importance. I thought it would be friendly to immortalize him, as the silly literary saying is, much as Shakespear immortalized Mr W. H., as he said he would, simply by writing about him.

Let me tell the story formally.

THOMAS TYLER

Throughout the eighties at least, and probably for some years before, the British Museum reading room was used daily by a gentleman of such astonishing and crushing ugliness that no one who had once seen him could ever thereafter forget him. He was of fair complexion, rather golden red than sandy; aged between fortyfive and sixty; and dressed in frock coat and tall hat of presentable but never new appearance. His figure was rectangular, waistless, neckless, ankleless, of middle height, looking shortish because, though he was not particularly stout, there was nothing slender about him. His ugliness was not unamiable: it was accidental, external, excrescential. Attached to his face from the left ear to the point of his chin was a monstrous goitre, which hung down to his collar bone, and was very inadequately balanced by a smaller one on his right eyelid. Nature's malice was so overdone in his case that it somehow failed to produce the effect of repulsion it seemed to have aimed at. When you first met Thomas Tyler you could think of nothing else but whether surgery could really do nothing for him. But after a very brief acquaintance you never thought of his disfigurements at all, and talked to him as you might to Romeo or Lovelace [the libertine in Samuel Richardson's *Clarissa Harlowe*, 1747–8]; only, so many people, especially women, would not risk the preliminary ordeal, that he remained a man apart and a bachelor all his days. I am not to be frightened or prejudiced by a tumor; and I struck up a cordial acquaintance with him, in the course of which he kept me pretty closely on the track of his work at the Museum, in which I was then, like himself, a daily reader.

He was by profession a man of letters of an uncommercial kind. He was a specialist in pessimism; had made a translation of Ecclesiastes of which eight copies a year were sold; and followed up the pessimism of Shakespear and Swift with keen interest. He delighted in a hideous conception which he called the theory of the cycles, according to which the history of mankind and the universe keeps eternally repeating itself without the slightest variation throughout all eternity; so that he had lived and died and had his goitre before and would live and die and have it again and again and again. He liked to believe that nothing that happened to him was completely novel: he was persuaded that he often had some recollection of its previous occurrence in the last cycle. He hunted out allusions to this favorite theory in his three favorite pessimists. He tried his hand occasionally at deciphering ancient inscriptions, reading them as people seem to read the stars, by discovering bears and bulls and swords and goats where, as it seems to me, no sane human being can see anything but stars higgledy-piggledy. Next to the translation of Ecclesiastes [1874], his *magnum opus* was his work on Shakespear's Sonnets,[2] in which he accepted a previous identification of Mr W. H., the "onlie begetter" of the sonnets, with the Earl of Pembroke (William Herbert), and promulgated his own identification of Mistress Mary Fitton with the Dark Lady. Whether he was right or wrong about the Dark Lady did not matter urgently to me: she might have been Maria Tompkins for all I cared. But Tyler would have it that she was Mary Fitton; and he tracked Mary down from the first of her marriages in her teens to her tomb in Cheshire, whither he made a pilgrimage and whence returned in triumph with a picture of her statue, and the news that he was convinced she was a dark lady by traces of paint still discernible.

In due course he published his edition of the Sonnets, with the evidence he had collected. He lent me a copy of the book, which I never returned. But I reviewed it in the Pall Mall Gazette on the 7th of January 1886, and thereby let loose the Fitton theory in a wider circle of readers than the book could reach. Then Tyler died, sinking unnoted like a stone in the sea. I observe that Mr Acheson, Mrs Davenant's champion, calls him Reverend. It may very well be that he got his knowledge of Hebrew in reading for the Church; and there was always something of the clergyman or the schoolmaster in his dress and air. Possibly he may actually have been ordained. But he never told me that or anything else about his affairs; and his black pessimism would have shot him violently out of any church at

2. Facsimile of the first quarto of the Sonnets, with an introduction by Tyler (1886 [1885]).

present established in the West. We never talked about affairs: we talked about Shakespear, and the Dark Lady, and Swift, and Koheleth, and the cycles, and the mysterious moments when a feeling came over us that this had happened to us before, and about the forgeries of the Pentateuch which were offered for sale to the British Museum,[3] and about literature and things of the spirit generally. He always came to my desk at the Museum and spoke to me about something or other, no doubt finding that people who were keen on this sort of conversation were rather scarce. He remains a vivid spot of memory in the void of my forgetfulness, a quite considerable and dignified soul in a grotesquely disfigured body.

FRANK HARRIS

To the review in the Pall Mall Gazette I attribute, rightly or wrongly, the introduction of Mary Fitton to Mr Frank Harris. My reason for this is that Mr Harris wrote a play about Shakespear and Mary Fitton [*Shakespeare and His Love*, 1910]; and when I, as a pious duty to Tyler's ghost, reminded the world [in ' "The Dark Lady": G. B. S. Replies to Mr Frank Harris', *Daily News*, 24 November 1910] that it was to Tyler we owed the Fitton theory, Frank Harris, who clearly had not a notion of what had first put Mary into his head, believed, I think, that I had invented Tyler expressly for his discomfiture; for the stress I laid on Tyler's claims must have seemed unaccountable and perhaps malicious on the assumption that he was to me a mere name among the thousands of names in the British Museum catalogue. Therefore I make it clear that I had and have personal reasons for remembering Tyler, and for regarding myself as in some sort charged with the duty of reminding the world of his work. I am sorry for

---

3. In 1883 Moses W. Shapira, a Jewish-Christian Jerusalem dealer in antiquities, offered to the Royal Library of Berlin a fragmentary manuscript that followed the order of the Book of Deuteronomy, but with 'singular variations'. When his codex was rejected by theological authorities in Berlin and Leipzig as an 'evident forgery' he offered it to the British Museum. A translation of the manuscript was published in *The Times* on 8, 17 and 22 August 1883. In 1884, after British theologians had concurred with the opinion of their European colleagues, the distraught, dishonoured Shapira committed suicide. Ironically, scholars now believe the Shapira manuscript may have been a genuine fragmented portion of a Dead Sea scroll.

his sake that Mary's portrait is fair, and that [in Acheson's view] Mr W. H. has veered round again from Pembroke to Southampton;[4] but even so his work was not wasted: it is by exhausting all the hypotheses that we reach the verifiable one; and after all, the wrong road always leads somewhere.

Frank Harris's play was written long before mine. I read it in manuscript before the Shakespear Memorial National Theatre was mooted; and if there is anything except the Fitton theory (which is Tyler's property) in my play which is also in Mr Harris's it was I who annexed it from him and not he from me. It does not matter anyhow, because this play of mine is a brief trifle, and full of manifest impossibilities at that; whilst Mr Harris's play is serious both in size, intention, and quality. But there could not in the nature of things be much resemblance, because Frank conceives Shakespear to have been a brokenhearted, melancholy, enormously sentimental person, whereas I am convinced that he was very like myself: in fact, if I had been born in 1556 instead of in 1856, I should have taken to blank verse and given Shakespear a harder run for his money than all the other Elizabethans put together. Yet the success of Frank Harris's book on Shakespear [*The Man Shakespeare*, 1909] gave me great delight.

To those who know the literary world of London there was a sharp stroke of ironic comedy in the irresistible verdict in its favor. In critical literature there is one prize that is always open to competition, one blue ribbon that always carries the highest critical rank with it. To win, you must write the best book of your generation on Shakespear. It is felt on all sides that to do this a certain fastidious refinement, a delicacy of taste, a correctness of manner and tone, and high academic distinction in addition to the indispensable scholarship and literary reputation, are needed; and men who pretend to these qualifications are constantly looked to with a gentle expectation that presently they will achieve the great feat. Now if there is a man on earth who is the utter contrary of everything that this description implies; whose very existence is an insult to the ideal it realizes; whose eye disparages, whose resonant voice denounces, whose cold shoulder jostles every decency, every delicacy, every amenity, every dignity, every sweet usage of that quiet life of mutual admiration in which perfect Shakespearean appreciation is expected to arise, that man is Frank Harris. Here is one who is extraordinarily qualified, by a range of sympathy and understanding that extends from the ribaldry of a buccaneer to the shyest tendernesses of the most sensitive poetry, to be all things to all men, yet whose

4. Henry Wriothesley, Third Earl of Southampton, is best known as the patron of Shakespeare.

proud humor it is to be to every man, provided the man is eminent and pretentious, the champion of his enemies. To the Archbishop he is an atheist, to the atheist a Catholic mystic, to the Bismarckian Imperialist an Anacharsis Klootz,[5] to Anacharsis Klootz a Washington, to Mrs Proudie[6] a Don Juan, to Aspasia[7] a John Knox: in short, to everyone his complement rather than his counterpart, his antagonist rather than his fellow creature. Always provided, however, that the persons thus affronted are respectable persons. Sophie Perovskaia [Russian nihilist revolutionist], who perished on the scaffold for blowing Alexander II to fragments, may perhaps have echoed Hamlet's

> Oh God, Horatio, what a wounded name—
> Things standing thus unknown—I leave behind! [*Hamlet*, V: ii]

but Frank Harris, in his Sonia, has rescued her from that injustice, and enshrined her among the saints. He has lifted the Chicago anarchists out of their infamy, and shewn that, compared with the Capitalism that killed them, they were heroes and martyrs.[8] He has done this with the most unusual power of conviction. The story, as he tells it, inevitably and irresistibly displaces all the vulgar, mean, purblind, spiteful versions. There is a precise realism and an unsmiling, measured, determined sincerity which gives a strange dignity to the work of one whose fixed practice and ungovernable impulse it is to kick conventional dignity whenever he sees it.

Harris "durch Mitleid wissend" ['Through Thoughtful Pity']

Frank Harris is everything except a humorist, not, apparently, from stupidity, but because scorn overcomes humor in him. Nobody ever dreamt of reproaching Milton's Lucifer for not seeing the comic side of his fall; and nobody who has read Mr Harris's stories desires to have them lightened

5. Jean-Baptiste, Baron de Cloots, was a Prussian who migrated to Paris and became a revolutionary. The name he took in Paris – Anacharsis – is that of one of the legendary great sages of ancient times.
6. Character in Trollope's Barsetshire novels, wife of the bishop, always concerned with maintaining appearances.
7. Beautiful, cultured courtesan in Periclean Athens.
8. 'Sonia', in Frank Harris's *Montes the Matador and Other Stories* (1900), is the tale of a woman hanged for her involvement with revolutionaries in the assassination of the Tsar. In *The Bomb: A Story of the Chicago Anarchists of 1886* (1908), Harris related the story of the Haymarket bombings from the point of view of the revolutionists.

by chapters from the hand of Artemus Ward.[9] Yet he knows the taste and the value of humor. He was one of the few men of letters who really appreciated Oscar Wilde, though he did not rally fiercely to Wilde's side until the world deserted Oscar in his ruin. I myself was present at a curious meeting between the two, when Harris, on the eve of the Queensberry trial, prophesied to Wilde with miraculous precision exactly what immediately afterwards happened to him, and warned him to leave the country. It was the first time within my knowledge that such a forecast proved true. Wilde, though under no illusion as to the folly of the quite unselfish suit-at-law he had been persuaded to begin, nevertheless so miscalculated the force of the social vengeance he was unloosing on himself that he fancied it could be stayed by putting up the editor of The Saturday Review (as Mr Harris then was) to declare that he considered Dorian Grey [1891] a highly moral book, which it certainly is. When Harris foretold him the truth, Wilde denounced him as a fainthearted friend who was failing him in his hour of need, and left the room in anger. Harris's idiosyncratic power of pity saved him from feeling or shewing the smallest resentment; and events presently proved to Wilde how insanely he had been advised in taking the action, and how accurately Harris had gauged the situation.

The same capacity for pity governs Harris's study of Shakespear, whom, as I have said, he pities too much; but that he is not insensible to humor is shewn not only by his appreciation of Wilde, but by the fact that the group of contributors who made his editorship of The Saturday Review so remarkable,[10] and of whom I speak none the less highly because I happened to be one of them myself, were all, in their various ways, humorists.

"SIDNEY'S SISTER: PEMBROKE'S MOTHER"[11]

And now to return to Shakespear. Though Mr Harris followed Tyler in identifying Mary Fitton as the Dark Lady, and the Earl of Pembroke as the

9. Pseudonym of Charles Farrar Browne, an American humorous moralist, who was a contributor to *Punch*.
10. Among those Harris hired were J. F. Runciman (music), D. S. MacColl (art), and R. B. Cunninghame-Graham.
11. Sir Philip Sidney was the finest English example of the Renaissance ideal of the perfect gentleman; his sister Mary was of the same tradition. Lady Mary's son, William Herbert, Third Earl of Pembroke, was exiled from court because of his affair with Mary Fitton.

addressee of the other sonnets and the man who made love successfully to Shakespear's mistress, he very characteristically refuses to follow Tyler on one point, though for the life of me I cannot remember whether it was one of the surmises which Tyler published, or only one which he submitted to me to see what I would say about it, just as he used to submit difficult lines from the sonnets.

This surmise was that "Sidney's sister: Pembroke's mother" set Shakespear on to persuade Pembroke to marry, and that this was the explanation of those earlier sonnets which so persistently and unnaturally urged matrimony on Mr W. H. I take this to be one of the brightest of Tyler's ideas, because the persuasions in the sonnets are unaccountable and out of character unless they were offered to please somebody whom Shakespear desired to please, and who took a motherly interest in Pembroke. There is a further temptation in the theory for me. The most charming of all Shakespear's old women, indeed the most charming of all his women, young or old, is the Countess of Rousillon in All's Well That Ends Well. It has a certain individuality among them which suggests a portrait. Mr Harris will have it that all Shakespear's nice old women are drawn from his beloved mother; but I see no evidence whatever that Shakespear's mother was a particularly nice woman or that he was particularly fond of her. That she was a simple incarnation of extravagant maternal pride like the mother of Coriolanus in Plutarch [*Parallel Lives*], as Mr Harris asserts, I cannot believe: she is quite as likely to have borne her son a grudge for becoming "one of these harlotry players" [*Henry IV, Part I*, II: iv] and disgracing the Ardens. Anyhow, as a conjectural model for the Countess of Rousillon, I prefer that one of whom Jonson wrote

> Sidney's sister: Pembroke's mother:
> Death ere thou has slain another,
> Learned and fair and good as she,
> Time shall throw a dart at thee.[12]

But Frank will not have her at any price, because his ideal Shakespear is rather like a sailor in a melodrama; and a sailor in a melodrama must adore his mother. I do not at all belittle such sailors. They are the emblems of human generosity; but Shakespear was not an emblem; he was a man and the author of Hamlet, who had no illusions about his mother. In weak moments one almost wishes he had.

12. Actually by William Browne of Tavistock in 'Epitaph on the Countess of Pembroke' (1621).

SHAKESPEAR'S SOCIAL STANDING

On the vexed question of Shakespear's social standing Mr Harris says that Shakespear "had not had the advantage of a middle-class training." I suggest that Shakespear missed this questionable advantage, not because he was socially too low to have attained to it, but because he conceived himself as belonging to the upper class from which our public school boys are now drawn. Let Mr Harris survey for a moment the field of contemporary journalism. He will see there some men who have the very characteristics from which he infers that Shakespear was at a social disadvantage through his lack of middle-class training. They are rowdy, ill-mannered, abusive, mischievous, fond of quoting obscene schoolboy anecdotes, adepts in that sort of blackmail which consists in mercilessly libelling and insulting every writer whose opinions are sufficiently heterodox to make it almost impossible for him to risk perhaps five years of a slender income by an appeal to a prejudiced orthodox jury; and they see nothing in all this cruel blackguardism but an uproariously jolly rag, although they are by no means without genuine literary ability, a love of letters, and even some artistic conscience. But he will find not one of the models of this type (I say nothing of mere imitators of it) below the rank that looks at the middle class, not humbly and enviously from below, but insolently from above. Mr Harris himself notes Shakespear's contempt for the tradesman and mechanic, and his incorrigible addiction to smutty jokes. He does us the public service of sweeping away the familiar plea of the Bardolatrous ignoramus, that Shakespear's coarseness was part of the manners of his time, putting his pen with precision on the one name, [Edmund] Spenser, that is necessary to expose such a libel on Elizabethan decency. There was nothing whatever to prevent Shakespear from being as decent as [Thomas] More was before him, or Bunyan after him, and as self-respecting as Raleigh or Sidney, except the tradition of his class, in which education or statesmanship may no doubt be acquired by those who have a turn for them, but in which insolence, derision, profligacy, obscene jesting, debt contracting, and rowdy mischievousness, give continual scandal to the pious, serious, industrious, solvent bourgeois. No other class is infatuated enough to believe that gentlemen are born and not made by a very elaborate process of culture. Even kings are taught and coached and drilled from their earliest boyhood to play their part. But the man of family (I am convinced that Shakespear took that view of himself) will plunge into society without a lesson in table manners, into politics without a lesson in history, into the city without a lesson in business, and into the army without a lesson in honor.

It has been said, with the object of proving Shakespear a laborer, that he could hardly write his name. Why? Because he "had not the advantage of a middle-class training." Shakespear himself tells us, through Hamlet, that gentlemen purposely wrote badly lest they should be mistaken for scriveners [*Hamlet*, V: ii]; but most of them, then as now, wrote badly because they could not write any better. In short, the whole range of Shakespear's foibles: the snobbishness, the naughtiness, the contempt for tradesmen and mechanics, the assumption that witty conversation can only mean smutty conversation, the flunkeyism towards social superiors and insolence towards social inferiors, the easy ways with servants which is seen not only between The Two Gentlemen of Verona and their valets, but in the affection and respect inspired by a great servant like Adam [in *As You Like It*]: all these are the characteristics of Eton and Harrow, not of the public elementary or private adventure school. They prove, as everything we know about Shakespear suggests, that he thought of the Shakespears and Ardens as families of consequence, and regarded himself as a gentleman under a cloud through his father's ill luck in business, and never for a moment as a man of the people. This is at once the explanation of and excuse for his snobbery. He was not a *parvenu* trying to cover his humble origin with a purchased coat of arms: he was a gentleman resuming what he conceived to be his natural position as soon as he gained the means to keep it up.

THIS SIDE IDOLATRY

There is another matter which I think Mr Harris should ponder. He says that Shakespear was but "little esteemed by his own generation." He even describes Jonson's description of his "little [a misreading for 'small'] Latin and less Greek" ['To the Memory of Shakespeare'] as a sneer, whereas it occurs in an unmistakeably sincere eulogy of Shakespear, written after his death, and is clearly meant to heighten the impression of Shakespear's prodigious natural endowments by pointing out that they were not due to scholastic acquirements. Now there is a sense in which it is true enough that Shakespear was too little esteemed by his own generation, or, for the matter of that, by any subsequent generation. The bargees on the Regent's Canal do not chant Shakespear's verses as the gondoliers in Venice are said to chant the verses of [Torquato] Tasso (a practice which was suspended for some reason during my stay in Venice: at least no gondolier ever did it in my hearing). Shakespear is no more a popular author than Rodin is a popular sculptor or Richard Strauss a popular composer. But Shakespear was certainly not such a fool as to expect the Toms, Dicks, and Harrys of his time to be any more interested in dramatic poetry than Newton, later on, expected them to be interested in fluxions [mathematical differentials]. And when we come to the question whether Shakespear missed that assurance which all great men have had from the more capable and susceptible members of their generation that they were great men, Ben Jonson's evidence disposes of so improbable a notion at once and for ever. "I loved the man," says Ben, "this side idolatry, as well [a misreading for 'much'] as any" [*Timber*, 1640]. Now why in the name of common sense should he have made that qualification unless there had been, not only idolatry, but idolatry fulsome enough to irritate Jonson into an express disavowal of it? Jonson, the bricklayer, must have felt sore sometimes when Shakespear spoke and wrote of bricklayers as his inferiors. He must have felt it a little hard that being a better scholar, and perhaps a braver and tougher man physically than Shakespear, he was not so successful or so well liked. But in spite of this he praised Shakespear to the utmost stretch of his powers of eulogy: in fact, notwithstanding his disclaimer, he did not stop "this side idolatry." If, therefore, even Jonson felt himself forced to clear himself of extravagance and absurdity in his appreciation of Shakespear, there must have been many people about who idolized Shakespear as American ladies idolize [Ignace] Paderewski,[13] and who carried Bardolatry, even in the Bard's own time, to an extent that threatened to make his reasonable admirers ridiculous.

SHAKESPEAR'S PESSIMISM

I submit to Mr Harris that by ruling out this idolatry, and its possible effect in making Shakespear think that his public would stand anything from him, he has ruled out a far more plausible explanation of the faults of such a play as Timon of Athens than his theory that Shakespear's passion for the Dark Lady "cankered and took on proud flesh in him, and tortured him to nervous breakdown and madness." In Timon the intellectual bankruptcy is obvious enough: Shakespear tried once too often to make a play out of the cheap pessimism which is thrown into despair by a comparison of actual human nature with theoretical morality, actual law and

13. Polish pianist, composer, and Premier (1919) of Poland.

administration with abstract justice, and so forth. But Shakespear's perception
of the fact that all men, judged by the moral standard which they apply to
others and by which they justify their punishment of others, are fools and
scoundrels, does not date from the Dark Lady complication: he seems to
have been born with it. If in The Comedy of Errors and A Midsummer
Night's Dream the persons of the drama are not quite so ready for
treachery and murder as Laertes and even Hamlet himself (not to mention
the procession of ruffians who pass through the latest plays) it is certainly
not because they have any more regard for law or religion. There is only
one place in Shakespear's plays where the sense of shame is used as a human
attribute; and that is where Hamlet is ashamed, not of anything he himself
has done, but of his mother's relations with his uncle. This scene is an
unnatural one: the son's reproaches to his mother, even the fact of his being
able to discuss the subject with her, is more repulsive than her relations
with her deceased husband's brother.

Here, too, Shakespear betrays for once his religious sense by making
Hamlet, in his agony of shame, declare that his mother's conduct makes
"sweet religion a rhapsody of words" [*Hamlet*, III: iv]. But for that passage
we might almost suppose that the feeling of Sunday morning in the
country which Orlando describes so perfectly in As You Like It was the
beginning and end of Shakespear's notion of religion. I say almost, because
Isabella in Measure for Measure has religious charm, in spite of the
conventional theatrical assumption that female religion means an inhumanly
ferocious chastity. But for the most part Shakespear differentiates his heroes
from his villains much more by what they do than by what they are. Don
Juan [Don John] in Much Ado is a true villain: a man with a malicious
will; but he is too dull a duffer to be of any use in a leading part; and when
we come to the great villains like Macbeth, we find, as Mr Harris points
out, that they are precisely identical with the heroes: Macbeth is only
Hamlet incongruously committing murders and engaging in hand-to-hand
combats. And Hamlet, who does not dream of apologizing for the three
murders he commits, is always apologizing because he has not yet committed a fourth, and finds, to his great bewilderment, that he does not want to
commit it. "It cannot be," he says, "but I am pigeon-livered, and lack gall
to make oppression bitter; else, ere this, I should have fatted all the region
kites with this slave's offal" [*Hamlet*, II: ii]. Really one is tempted to suspect
that when Shylock asks "Hates any man the thing he would not kill?" [*The
Merchant of Venice*, IV: i] he is expressing the natural and proper sentiments
of the human race as Shakespear understood them, and not the vindictiveness of a stage Jew.

GAIETY OF GENIUS

In view of these facts, it is dangerous to cite Shakespear's pessimism as evidence of the despair of a heart broken by the Dark Lady. There is an irrepressible gaiety of genius which enables it to bear the whole weight of the world's misery without blenching. There is a laugh always ready to avenge its tears of discouragement. In the lines which Mr Harris quotes only to declare that he can make nothing of them, and to condemn them as out of character, Richard III, immediately after pitying himself because

> There is no creature loves me
> And if I die no soul will pity me,

adds, with a grin,

> Nay, wherefore should they, since that I myself
> Find in myself no pity for myself? [*Richard III*, V: iii]

Let me again remind Mr Harris of Oscar Wilde. We all dreaded to read De Profundis [1905]: our instinct was to stop our ears, or run away from the wail of a broken, though by no means contrite, heart. But we were throwing away our pity. De Profundis was *de profundis* indeed: Wilde was too good a dramatist to throw away so powerful an effect; but none the less it was *de profundis* ['Out of the depths', Psalm 130] *in excelsis*. There was more laughter between the lines of that book than in a thousand farces by men of no genius. Wilde, like Richard and Shakespear, found in himself no pity for himself. There is nothing that marks the born dramatist more unmistakeably than this discovery of comedy in his own misfortunes almost in proportion to the pathos with which the ordinary man announces their tragedy. I cannot for the life of me see the broken heart in Shakespear's latest works. "Hark, hark! the lark at heaven's gate sings" is not the lyric of a broken man; nor is Cloten's comment that if Imogen does not appreciate it, "it is a vice in her ears which horse hairs, and cats' guts, and the voice of unpaved eunuch to boot, can never amend" [both passages are in *Cymbeline*, II: iii], the sally of a saddened one. Is it not clear that to the last there was in Shakespear an incorrigible divine levity, an inexhaustible joy that derided sorrow? Think of the poor Dark Lady having to stand up to this unbearable power of extracting a grim fun from everything. Mr Harris writes as if Shakespear did all the suffering and the Dark Lady all the cruelty. But why does he not put himself in the Dark Lady's place for a moment as he has put himself so successfully in Shakespear's? Imagine her reading the hundred and thirtieth sonnet!

> My mistress' eyes are nothing like the sun;
> Coral is far more red than her lips' red;
> If snow be white, why then her breasts are dun;
> If hairs be wires, black wires grow on her head;
> I have seen roses damasked, red and white,
> But no such roses see I in her cheeks;
> And in some perfumes is there more delight
> Than in the breath that from my mistress reeks.
> I love to hear her speak; yet well I know
> That music hath a far more pleasing sound.
> I grant I never saw a goddess go:
> My mistress, when she walks, treads on the ground.
>   And yet, by Heaven, I think my love as rare
>   As any she belied with false compare.

Take this as a sample of the sort of compliment from which she was never for a moment safe with Shakespear. Bear in mind that she was not a comedian; that the Elizabethan fashion of treating brunettes as ugly women must have made her rather sore on the subject of her complexion; that no human being, male or female, can conceivably enjoy being chaffed on that point in the fourth couplet about the perfumes; that Shakespear's revulsions, as the sonnet immediately preceding shews, were as violent as his ardors, and were expressed with the realistic power and horror that makes Hamlet say that the heavens got sick when they saw the queen's conduct [*Hamlet*, III: iv], and then ask Mr Harris whether any woman could have stood it for long, or have thought the "sugred" compliment ['sug'red words': *Henry VI, Part I*, III: iii] worth the cruel wounds, the cleaving of the heart in twain, that seemed to Shakespear as natural and amusing a reaction as the burlesquing of his heroics by Pistol [in *Henry V*], his sermons by Falstaff [in *Henry IV, Part I*], and his poems by Cloten and Touchstone [in *Cymbeline* and *As You Like It*].

JUPITER AND SEMELE

This does not mean that Shakespear was cruel: evidently he was not; but it was not cruelty that made Jupiter reduce Semele to ashes:[14] it was the fact

14. When Semele, in Greek mythology, was tricked by Hera into asking Zeus to appear to her in his godhead, he materialized in a blaze of lightning and fire. Semele, a mortal who could not bear this divine presence, was consumed.

that he could not help being a god nor she help being a mortal. The one thing Shakespear's passion for the Dark Lady was not, was what Mr Harris in one passage calls it: idolatrous. If it had been, she might have been able to stand it. The man who dotes "yet doubts; suspects, yet strongly loves" [*Othello*, III: iii], is tolerable even by a spoilt and tyrannical mistress; but what woman could possibly endure a man who dotes without doubting; who *knows* and who is hugely amused at the absurdity of his infatuation for a woman of whose mortal imperfections not one escapes him: a man always exchanging grins with Yorick's skull, and inviting "my lady" to laugh at the sepulchral humor of the fact that though she paint an inch thick (which the Dark Lady may have done), to Yorick's favor she must come at last [*Hamlet*, V: i]. To the Dark Lady he must sometimes have seemed cruel beyond description: an intellectual Caliban. True, a Caliban who could say

> Be not afeard: the isle is full of noises,
> Sounds and sweet airs that give delight and hurt not.
> Sometimes a thousand twangling instruments
> Will hum about mine ears; and sometimes voices,
> That, if I then had waked after long sleep,
> Will make me sleep again; and then, in dreaming,
> The clouds, methought, would open and shew riches
> Ready to drop [up]on me: that when I wak'd
> I cried to dream again. [*The Tempest*, III: ii]

which is very lovely; but the Dark Lady may have had that vice in her ears which Cloten dreaded: she may not have seen the beauty of it, whereas there can be no doubt at all that of "My mistress' eyes are nothing like the sun," &c., not a word was lost on her.

And is it to be supposed that Shakespear was too stupid or too modest not to see at last that it was a case of Jupiter and Semele? Shakespear was most certainly not modest in that sense. The timid cough of the minor poet was never heard from him.

> Not marble, nor the gilded monuments
> Of princes, shall outlive this powerful rhyme [Sonnet 55]

is only one out of a dozen passages in which he (possibly with a keen sense of the fun of scandalizing the modest coughers) proclaimed his place and his power in "the wide world dreaming of things to come." The Dark Lady most likely thought this side of him insufferably conceited; for there is no reason to suppose that she liked his plays any better than Minna

Wagner liked Richard's music dramas: as likely as not, she thought The Spanish Tragedy [1594, of Thomas Kyd] worth six Hamlets. He was not stupid either: if his class limitations and a profession that cut him off from actual participation in great affairs of State had not confined his opportunities of intellectual and political training to private conversation and to the Mermaid Tavern, he would probably have become one of the ablest men of his time instead of being merely its ablest playwright. One might surmise that Shakespear found out that the Dark Lady's brains could no more keep pace with his than Anne Hathaway's, if there were any evidence that their friendship ceased when he stopped writing sonnets to her. As a matter of fact the consolidation of a passion into an enduring intimacy generally puts an end to sonnets.

That the Dark Lady broke Shakespear's heart, as Mr Harris will have it she did, is an extremely unShakespearean hypothesis. "Men have died from time to time, and worms have eaten them; but not for love" [*As You Like It*, IV: i], says Rosalind. Richard of Gloster, into whom Shakespear put all his own impish superiority to vulgar sentiment, exclaims

> And this word "love," which greybeards call divine,
> Be resident in men like one another
> And not in me: I am myself alone. [*Henry VI, Part III*, V: vi]

Hamlet has not a tear for Ophelia: her death moves him to fierce disgust for the sentimentality of Laertes by her grave; and when he discusses the scene with Horatio immediately after, he utterly forgets her, though he is sorry he forgot himself, and jumps at the proposal of a fencing match to finish the day with. As against this view Mr Harris pleads Romeo, Orsino [in *Twelfth Night*], and even Antonio [in *The Merchant of Venice*]; and he does it so penetratingly that he convinces you that Shakespear did betray himself again and again in these characters; but self-betrayal is one thing; and self-portrayal, as in Hamlet and Mercutio, is another. Shakespear never "saw himself," as actors say, in Romeo or Orsino or Antonio. In Mr Harris's own play Shakespear is presented with the most pathetic tenderness. He is tragic, bitter, pitiable, wretched and broken among a robust crowd of Jonsons and Elizabeths; but to me he is not Shakespear because I miss the Shakespearean irony and the Shakespearean gaiety. Take these away and Shakespear is no longer Shakespear: all the bite, the impetus, the strength, the grim delight in his own power of looking terrible facts in the face with a chuckle, is gone; and you have nothing left but that most depressing of all things: a victim. Now who can think of Shakespear as a man with a grievance? Even in that most thoroughgoing and inspired of all Shakespear's loves: his love of music (which Mr Harris has been the first to appreciate at anything like its value), there is a dash of mockery. "Spit in the hole, man; and tune again" [*The Taming of the Shrew*, III: i]. "Divine air! Now is his soul ravished. Is it not strange that sheep's guts should hale the souls out of men's bodies?" "An he had been a dog that should have howled thus, they would have hanged him" [both passages in *Much Ado About Nothing*, II: iii]. There is just as much Shakespear here as in the inevitable quotation about the sweet south and the bank of violets.

I lay stress on this irony of Shakespear's, this impish rejoicing in pessimism, this exultation in what breaks the hearts of common men, not only because it is diagnostic of that immense energy of life which we call genius, but because its omission is the one glaring defect in Mr Harris's otherwise extraordinarily penetrating book. Fortunately, it is an omission that does not disable the book as (in my judgment) it disabled the hero of the play, because Mr Harris left himself out of his play, whereas he pervades his book, mordant, deep-voiced, and with an unconquerable style which is the man.

The Idol of the Bardolaters

There is even an advantage in having a book on Shakespear with the Shakespearean irony left out of account. I do not say that the missing chapter should not be added in the next edition: the hiatus is too great: it leaves the reader too uneasy before this touching picture of a writhing worm substituted for the invulnerable giant. But it is none the less probable that in no other way could Mr Harris have got at his man as he has. For, after all, what is the secret of the hopeless failure of the academic Bardolaters to give us a credible or even interesting Shakespear, and the easy triumph of Mr Harris in giving us both? Simply that Mr Harris has assumed that he was dealing with a man, whilst the others have assumed that they were writing about a god, and have therefore rejected every consideration of fact, tradition, or interpretation, that pointed to any human imperfection in their hero. They thus leave themselves with so little material that they are forced to begin by saying that we know very little about Shakespear. As a matter of fact, with the plays and sonnets in our hands, we know much more about Shakespear than we know about Dickens or Thackeray: the only difficulty is that we deliberately suppress it because it proves that

Shakespear was not only very unlike the conception of a god current in Clapham,[15] but was not, according to the same reckoning, even a respectable man. The academic view starts with a Shakespear who was not scurrilous; therefore the verses about "lousy Lucy" cannot have been written by him,[16] and the cognate passages in the plays are either strokes of character-drawing or gags interpolated by the actors. This ideal Shakespear was too well behaved to get drunk; therefore the tradition that his death was hastened by a drinking bout with Jonson and [Michael] Drayton must be rejected, and the remorse of Cassio treated as a thing observed, not experienced: nay, the disgust of Hamlet at the drinking customs of Denmark is taken to establish Shakespear as the superior of Alexander in self-control, and the greatest of teetotalers.

Now this system of inventing your great man to start with, and then rejecting all the materials that do not fit him, with the ridiculous result that you have to declare that there are no materials at all (with your wastepaper basket full of them), ends in leaving Shakespear with a much worse character than he deserves. For though it does not greatly matter whether he wrote the lousy Lucy lines or not, and does not really matter at all whether he got drunk when he made a night of it with Jonson and Drayton, the sonnets raise an unpleasant question which does matter a good deal; and the refusal of the academic Bardolaters to discuss or even mention this question has had the effect of producing a silent verdict against Shakespear. Mr Harris tackles the question openly, and has no difficulty whatever in convincing us that Shakespear was a man of normal constitution sexually, and was not the victim of that most cruel and pitiable of all the freaks of nature: the freak which transposes the normal aim of the affections. Silence on this point means condemnation; and the condemnation has been general throughout the present generation, though it only

15. The Evangelicals had a centre at Clapham in south-west London. The members of this so-called 'Clapham Sect' were convinced of the corruption of human nature and the need for redemption through Christ.
16. Legend has it that the young Shakespeare was accused of deer-stealing in the park of Sir Thomas Lucy of Charlecote, near Stratford. The following lines – and variants – have been attributed to the indignant Shakespeare:

If Lowsie is Lucy as some Volke Miscalle it
Then Lucy is Lowsie whatever befalle it . . .

(Edward Capell, *Commentary, Notes and Various Readings to Shakespeare*, 1783, Vol. II, p. 75.)

needed Mr Harris's fearless handling of the matter to sweep away what is nothing but a morbid and very disagreeable modern fashion. There is always some stock accusation brought against eminent persons. When I was a boy every wellknown man was accused of beating his wife. Later on, for some unexplained reason, he was accused of psychopathic derangement. And this fashion is retrospective. The cases of Shakespear and Michael Angelo are cited as proving that every genius of the first magnitude was a sufferer; and both here and in Germany there are circles in which such derangement is grotesquely reverenced as part of the stigmata of heroic powers. All of which is gross nonsense. Unfortunately, in Shakespear's case, prudery, which cannot prevent the accusation from being whispered, does prevent the refutation from being shouted. Mr Harris, the deep-voiced, refuses to be silenced. He dismisses with proper contempt the stupidity which places an outrageous construction on Shakespear's apologies in the sonnets for neglecting that "perfect ceremony" of love which consists in returning calls and making protestations and giving presents and paying the trumpery attentions which men of genius always refuse to bother about, and to which touchy people who have no genius attach so much importance. No reader who had not been tampered with by the psychopathic monomaniacs could ever put any construction but the obvious and innocent one on these passages. But the general vocabulary of the sonnets to Pembroke (or whoever "Mr W. H." really was) is so over-charged according to modern ideas that a reply on the general case is necessary.

Shakespear's alleged Sycophancy and Perversion

That reply, which Mr Harris does not hesitate to give, is twofold: first, that Shakespear was, in his attitude towards earls, a sycophant; and, second, that the normality of Shakespear's sexual constitution is only too well attested by the excessive susceptibility to the normal impulse shewn in the whole mass of his writings. This latter is the really conclusive reply. In the case of Michael Angelo, for instance, one must admit that if his works are set beside those of Titian or Paul Veronese, it is impossible not to be struck by the absence in the Florentine of that susceptibility to feminine charm which pervades the pictures of the Venetians. But, as Mr Harris points out (though he does not use this particular illustration) Paul Veronese is an anchorite compared to Shakespear. The language of the sonnets addressed to Pembroke, extravagant as it now seems, is the language of compliment and fashion, transfigured no doubt by Shakespear's verbal magic, and hyperbolical, as Shakespear always seems to people who cannot conceive so vividly as he, but still unmistakeable for anything else than the expression of a friendship delicate enough to be wounded, and a manly loyalty deep enough to be outraged. But the language of the sonnets to the Dark Lady is the language of passion: their cruelty shews it. There is no evidence that Shakespear was capable of being unkind in cold blood. But in his revulsions from love, he was bitter, wounding, even ferocious; sparing neither himself nor the unfortunate woman whose only offence was that she had reduced the great man to the common human denominator.

In seizing on these two points Mr Harris has made so sure a stroke, and places his evidence so featly that there is nothing left for me to do but to plead that the second is sounder than the first, which is, I think, marked by the prevalent mistake as to Shakespear's social position, or, if you prefer it, the confusion between his actual social position as a penniless tradesman's son taking to the theatre for a livelihood, and his own conception of himself as a gentleman of good family. I am prepared to contend that though Shakespear was undoubtedly sentimental in his expressions of devotion to Mr W. H. even to a point which nowadays makes both ridiculous, he was not sycophantic if Mr W. H. was really attractive and promising, and Shakespear deeply attached to him. A sycophant does not tell his patron that his fame will survive, not in the renown of his own actions, but in the sonnets of his sycophant. A sycophant, when his patron cuts him out in a love affair, does not tell his patron exactly what he thinks of him. Above all, a sycophant does not write to his patron precisely as he feels on all occasions; and this rare kind of sincerity is all over the sonnets. Shakespear, we are told, was "a very civil gentleman." This must mean that his desire to please people and be liked by them, and his reluctance to hurt their feelings, led him into amiable flattery even when his feelings were not strongly stirred. If this be taken into account along with the fact that Shakespear conceived and expressed all his emotions with a vehemence that sometimes carried him into ludicrous extravagance, making Richard offer his kingdom for a horse and Othello declare of Cassio that

> Had all his hairs been lives, my great revenge
> Had stomach for them all, [*Othello*, V: ii]

we shall see more civility and hyperbole than sycophancy even in the earlier and more coldblooded sonnets.

SHAKESPEAR AND DEMOCRACY

Now take the general case pled against Shakespear as an enemy of democracy by Tolstoy, the late Ernest Crosbie[17] and others, and endorsed by Mr Harris. Will it really stand fire? Mr Harris emphasizes the passages in which Shakespear spoke of mechanics and even of small master tradesmen as base persons whose clothes were greasy, whose breath was rank, and whose political imbecility and caprice moved Coriolanus to say to the Roman Radical who demanded at least "good words" from him

> He that will give good words to thee will flatter
> Beneath abhorring. [*Coriolanus*, I: i]

But let us be honest. As political sentiments these lines are an abomination to every democrat. But suppose they are not political sentiments! Suppose they are merely a record of observed fact. John Stuart Mill told our British workmen [in *Thoughts on Parliamentary Reform*, 1859; repeated in the *Autobiography*, 1873] that they were mostly liars. Carlyle [in *Sartor Resartus*, 1833–4] told us all that we are mostly fools. Matthew Arnold and Ruskin were more circumstantial and more abusive. Everybody, including the workers themselves, knows that they are dirty, drunken, foulmouthed, ignorant, gluttonous, prejudiced: in short, heirs to the peculiar ills of poverty and slavery, as well as co-heirs with the plutocracy to all the failings of human nature. Even Shelley admitted, 200 years after Shakespear wrote Coriolanus, that universal suffrage was out of the question.[18] Surely the real test, not of Democracy, which was not a live political issue in Shakespear's time, but of impartiality in judging classes, which is what one demands from a great human poet, is not that he should flatter the poor and denounce the rich, but that he should weigh them both in the same balance. Now whoever will read Lear and Measure for Measure will find

17. Crosby, an American social reformer, was strongly influenced by Tolstoy, and author of 'Shakespeare's Attitude to the Working Classes' (1902), published in *Tolstoy on Shakespeare* (1906).
18. Although Shelley favoured theoretically the radical drive for universal suffrage, he took a qualified position in his first reform tract, *A Proposal for Putting Reform to the Vote Throughout the Kingdom* (1817, issued pseudonymously as by 'The Hermit of Marion'): 'With respect to Universal Suffrage, I confess I consider its adoption, in the present unprepared state of public knowledge and feeling, a measure fraught with peril.'

stamped on his mind such an appalled sense of the danger of dressing man in a little brief authority [*Measure for Measure*, II: ii], such a merciless stripping of the purple from the "poor, bare, forked animal" [*Lear*, III: iv] that calls itself a king and fancies itself a god, that one wonders what was the real nature of the mysterious restraint that kept "Eliza and our James" [Ben Jonson, 'To the Memory of Shakespeare'] from teaching Shakespear to be civil to crowned heads, just as one wonders why Tolstoy was allowed to go free when so many less terrible levellers went to the galleys or Siberia. From the mature Shakespear we get no such scenes of village snobbery as that between the stage country gentleman Alexander Iden and the stage radical Jack Cade [in *Henry VI, Part II*; IV: x]. We get the shepherd in As You Like It, and many honest, brave, human, and loyal servants, beside the inevitable comic ones. Even in the Jingo play, Henry V, we get Bates and Williams [IV; i] drawn with all respect and honor as normal rank and file men. In Julius Cæsar, Shakespear went to work with a will when he took his cue from Plutarch in glorifying regicide and transfiguring the republicans. Indeed hero–worshippers have never forgiven him for belittling Cæsar and failing to see that side of his assassination which made Goethe denounce it as the most senseless of crimes.[19] Put the play beside the Charles I [1872] of [W. G.] Wills, in which Cromwell is written down to a point at which the Jack Cade of Henry VI becomes a hero in comparison; and then believe, if you can, that Shakespear was one of them that "crook the pregnant hinges of the knee where thrift may follow fawning" [*Hamlet*, III: ii]. Think of Rosencrantz, Guildenstern, Osric, the fop [described in *Henry IV, Part I*, I: iii] who annoyed Hotspur, and a dozen passages concerning such people! If such evidence can prove anything (and Mr Harris relies throughout on such evidence) Shakespear loathed courtiers.

If, on the other hand, Shakespear's characters are mostly members of the leisured classes, the same thing is true of Mr Harris's own plays and mine. Industrial slavery is not compatible with that freedom of adventure, that personal refinement and intellectual culture, that scope of action, which the higher and subtler drama demands. Even Cervantes had finally to drop Don Quixote's troubles with innkeepers demanding to be paid for his food and lodging, and make him as free of economic difficulties as Amadis de

---

19. Statement to J. J. Bodmer, Swiss scholar and critic, in Zürich, early June 1775; reported by Bodmer in a letter to Pastor Schinz of Altstätten, Switzerland, 15 June 1775, as cited in Nicholas Boyle, *Goethe: The Poet and the Age*, I (1991).

Gaul.[20] Hamlet's experiences simply could not have happened to a plumber. A poor man is useful on the stage only as a blind man is: to excite sympathy. The poverty of the apothecary in Romeo and Juliet produces a great effect, and even points the sound moral that a poor man cannot afford to have a conscience; but if all the characters of the play had been as poor as he, it would have been nothing but a melodrama of the sort that the Sicilian players gave us here;[21] and that was not the best that lay in Shakespear's power. When poverty is abolished, and leisure and grace of life become general, the only plays surviving from our epoch which will have any relation to life as it will be lived then will be those in which none of the persons represented are troubled with want of money or wretched drudgery. Our plays of poverty and squalor, now the only ones that are true to the life of the majority of living men, will then be classed with the records of misers and monsters, and read only by historical students of social pathology.

Then consider Shakespear's kings and lords and gentlemen! Would even John Ball or Jeremiah[22] complain that they are flattered? Surely a more mercilessly exposed string of scoundrels never crossed the stage. The very monarch who paralyzes a rebel by appealing to the divinity that hedges a king [Claudius in *Hamlet*, IV: v] is a drunken and sensual assassin, and is presently killed contemptuously before our eyes in spite of his hedge of divinity. I could write as convincing a chapter on Shakespear's Dickensian prejudice against the throne and the nobility and gentry in general as Mr Harris or Ernest Crosbie on the other side. I could even go so far as to contend that one of Shakespear's defects is his lack of an intelligent comprehension of feudalism. He had of course no prevision of democratic Collectivism. He was, except in the commonplaces of war and patriotism, a privateer through and through. Nobody in his plays, whether king or citizen, has any civil public business or conception of such a thing, except in the method of appointing constables, to the abuses in which he called attention quite in the vein of the Fabian Society. He was concerned about

20. Amadís de Gaula, a fictional knight, soul of chivalry, was the central figure in a famous Spanish romance, the earliest known edition of which is dated 1508, though it is probably of much earlier composition.
21. The Sicilian Players performed for a five-week season of variety at the London Hippodrome, opening on 24 April 1911 with an abridged version of Giovanni Verga's *Cavalleria Rusticana*.
22. John Ball, an English priest, was a leader of the Peasants' Revolt of 1381. The prophet Jeremiah's complaints are recorded in the Old Testament as 'The Lamentations of Jeremiah'.

drunkenness and about the idolatry and hypocrisy of our judicial system; but his implied remedy was personal sobriety and freedom from idolatrous illusion in so far as he had any remedy at all, and did not merely despair of human nature. His first and last word on parliament was "Get thee glass eyes, and, like a scurvy politician, seem to see the thing thou dost not" [*Lear*, IV: vi]. He had no notion of the feeling with which the land nationalizers of today regard the fact that he was a party to the enclosure of common lands at Wellcome.[23] The explanation is, not a general deficiency in his mind, but the simple fact that in his day what English land needed was individual appropriation and cultivation, and what the English Constitution needed was the incorporation of Whig principles of individual liberty.

SHAKESPEAR AND THE BRITISH PUBLIC

I have rejected Mr Harris's view that Shakespear died brokenhearted of "the pangs of love despised" [misreading of *Hamlet*, III: i]. I have given my reasons for believing that Shakespear died game, and indeed in a state of levity which would have been considered unbecoming in a bishop. But Mr Harris's evidence does prove that Shakespear had a grievance and a very serious one. He might have been jilted by ten dark ladies and been none the worse for it; but his treatment by the British Public was another matter. The idolatry which exasperated Ben Jonson was by no means a popular movement; and, like all such idolatries, it was excited by the magic of Shakespear's art rather than by his views. He was launched on his career as a successful playwright by the Henry VI trilogy, a work of no originality, depth, or subtlety except the originality, depth, and subtlety of the feelings and fancies of the common people. But Shakespear was not satisfied with this. What is the use of being Shakespear if you are not allowed to express any notions but those of Autolycus [a vagabond in *The Winter's Tale*]? Shakespear did not see the world as Autolycus did: he saw it, if not exactly as Ibsen did (for it was not quite the same world), at least with much of Ibsen's power of penetrating its illusions and idolatries, and with all Swift's horror of its cruelty and uncleanliness.

Now it happens to some men with these powers that they are forced to

23. Welcombe is an area north-east of Stratford where Shakespeare farmed some of his tithes. On 28 October 1614 he was legally assured that he would be recompensed 'for all . . . loss, detriment and hindrance as he . . . shall . . . sustain' by the enclosure of the fields at Welcombe.

impose their fullest exercise on the world because they cannot produce popular work. Take Wagner and Ibsen for instance! Their earlier works are no doubt much cheaper than their later ones; still, they were not popular when they were written. The alternative of doing popular work was never really open to them: had they stooped they would have picked up less than they snatched from above the people's heads. But Handel and Shakespear were not held to their best in this way. They could turn out anything they were asked for, and even heap up the measure. They reviled the British Public, and never forgave it for ignoring their best work and admiring their splendid commonplaces; but they produced the commonplaces all the same, and made them sound magnificent by mere brute faculty for their art. When Shakespear was forced to write popular plays to save his theatre from ruin, he did it mutinously, calling the plays As *You* Like It, and Much Ado About Nothing. All the same, he did it so well that to this day these two genial vulgarities are the main Shakespearean stock-in-trade of our theatres. Later on [Richard] Burbage's power and popularity as an actor enabled Shakespear to free himself from the tyranny of the box office, and to express himself more freely in plays consisting largely of monologue to be spoken by a great actor from whom the public would stand a good deal. The history of Shakespear's tragedies has thus been the history of a long line of famous actors, from Burbage and [Thomas] Betterton to Forbes Robertson; and the man of whom we are told that "when he would have said that Richard died, and cried A horse! A horse! he Burbage cried"[24] was the father of nine generations of Shakespearean playgoers, all speaking of [David] Garrick's Richard, and [Edmund] Kean's Othello, and Irving's Shylock, and Forbes Robertson's Hamlet without knowing or caring how much these had to do with Shakespear's Richard and Othello and so forth. And the plays which were written without great and predominant parts, such as Troilus and Cressida, All's Well That Ends Well, and Measure for Measure, have dropped on our stage as dead as the second part of Goethe's Faust [1832] or Ibsen's Emperor or Galilean [1873].

Here, then, Shakespear had a real grievance; and though it is a sentimental exaggeration to describe him as a brokenhearted man in the face of the passages of reckless jollity and serenely happy poetry in his latest plays, yet the discovery that his most serious work could reach success only when

24. Burbage's impersonation of Richard III was so striking that Richard Corbet, Bishop of Oxford, in his 'Iter Boreale' (first published in *Certaine Elegant Poems*, 1647) tells us of his host in Leicester who, 'when he would have sayd, King Richard dyed,/ And call'd a horse! a horse! – he, Burbidge cry'de.' (Corbet, *Poems*, 1807.)

carried on the back of a very fascinating actor who was enormously overcharging his part, and that the serious plays which did not contain parts big enough to hold the overcharge were left on the shelf, amply accounts for the evident fact that Shakespear did not end his life in a glow of enthusiastic satisfaction with mankind and with the theatre, which is all that Mr Harris can allege in support of his broken-heart theory. But even if Shakespear had had no failures, it was not possible for a man of his powers to observe the political and moral conduct of his contemporaries without perceiving that they were incapable of dealing with the problems raised by their own civilization, and that their attempts to carry out the codes of law and to practise the religions offered to them by great prophets and lawgivers were and still are so foolish that we now call for The Superman, virtually a new species, to rescue the world from mismanagement. This is the real sorrow of great men; and in the face of it the notion that when a great man speaks bitterly or looks melancholy he must be troubled by a disappointment in love seems to me sentimental trifling.

If I have carried the reader with me thus far, he will find that trivial as this little play of mine is, its sketch of Shakespear is more complete than its levity suggests. Alas! its appeal for a National Theatre as a monument to Shakespear failed to touch the very stupid people who cannot see that a National Theatre is worth having for the sake of the National Soul. I had unfortunately represented Shakespear as treasuring and using (as I do myself) the jewels of unconsciously musical speech which common people utter and throw away every day; and this was taken as a disparagement of Shakespear's "originality." Why was I born with such contemporaries? Why is Shakespear made ridiculous by such a posterity?

POSTSCRIPT 1933. The recent death of Frank Harris [26 August 1931] has refreshed the interest of the sketch of him in this preface, especially as he died in the act of finishing a curious biography of me which has attracted a good deal of notice,[25] and which is truthful as to its record of

---

25. The biography consisted, at Harris's death, of a series of disjointed, inaccurate reminiscences and questionable evaluations built round a considerable number of Shaw's letters to Harris, which had been patched together by a journalistic assistant named Frank Scully. When the American publishers submitted galleys to Shaw to protect themselves against suspected libels, he extensively corrected, revised and expanded the book, to strengthen the financial interest of Harris's widow, in the process scrupulously preserving the critical judgements and the critical tone of Harris's work.

bare facts, though its critical side is badly lamed through Frank's having lost touch with me before the end of the XIX century, and never reconsidered his estimates in the light of my later exploits.

The appeal for a national theatre with which the play concludes, and for the sake of which it was written, elicited applause but no subscriptions. Two years ago a great Shakespear Memorial Theatre was completed at Stratford-upon-Avon through the efforts of Sir Archibald Flower, replacing the old Shakespear theatre which owed its existence to his family;[26] but Sir Archibald had wasted no time in appealing to Shakespear's countrymen: he had turned to America and received a noble response. The attempt to establish a National Theatre in London to commemorate Shakespear's exploits in that old city, now expanded into a concentration camp much too big for any civic consciousness, was and still is a complete failure, though there is enough money (not English money, of course) available to carry out the project if the Government would provide a site,[27] and the municipality forgo its rates, as foreign Governments and municipalities do.

26. The Shakespeare Memorial Theatre was first opened on Shakespeare's birthday (23 April) in 1879, on land donated by Charles Flower, a member of a local family of brewers. Destroyed by fire in 1926, it was rebuilt with funds obtained largely from the United States through the efforts of a descendant of the Flowers who was chairman of the theatre's council. The new theatre, which opened in 1932, later became the Royal Shakespeare Theatre.

27. The National Theatre executive committee had purchased a freehold site in Gower Street for £50,000 and laid a foundation in 1913, anticipating the inaugural of the theatre in 1916 for the tercentenary of Shakespeare's death. With the intervention of war the committee shelved its plans and leased the property to the YMCA for construction of a Shakespeare Hut to provide amenities for troops. Eventually the first site was sold to the Rockefeller trustees for construction of a school of hygiene for the University of London. A replacement site was acquired for £75,000 in Cromwell Gardens, South Kensington. On 22 April 1938 Shaw, as representative of the committee, accepted the deeds for the site with the laying of a new foundation stone. After another world war had intruded, the London city planners arranged for a trade-off of the Kensington site for a South Bank site in Southwark adjacent to Waterloo Bridge. After the parliamentary passage of a National Theatre Act in November 1948, guaranteeing up to one million pounds in subvention, and the laying of a third foundation stone, the first of three theatres in the National Theatre scheme at last opened its doors on 16 March 1976. The project was completed a year later, sixty-eight years after Shaw had first helped to launch it.

Fanny's First Play

First published in 1914

═══

Fanny's First Play, being but a potboiler, needs no preface. But its lesson is not, I am sorry to say, unneeded. Mere morality, or the substitution of custom for conscience, was once accounted a shameful and cynical thing: people talked of right and wrong, of honor and dishonor, of sin and grace, of salvation and damnation, not of morality and immorality. The word morality, if we met it in the Bible, would surprise us as much as the word telephone or motor car. Nowadays we do not seem to know that there is any other test of conduct except morality; and the result is that the young had better have their souls awakened by disgrace, capture by the police, and a month's hard labor, than drift along from their cradles to their graves doing what other people do for no other reason than that other people do it, and knowing nothing of good and evil, of courage and cowardice, or indeed anything but how to keep hunger and concupiscence and fashionable dressing within the bounds of good taste except when their excesses can be concealed. Is it any wonder that I am driven to offer to young people in our suburbs the desperate advice: Do something that will get you into trouble? But please do not suppose that I defend a state of things which makes such advice the best that can be given under the circumstances, or that I do not know how difficult it is to find out a way of getting into trouble that will combine loss of respectability with integrity of self-respect and reasonable consideration for other peoples' feelings and interests on every point except their dread of losing their own respectability. But when there's a will there's a way. I hate to see dead people walking about: it is unnatural. And our respectable middle-class people are all as dead as mutton. Out of the mouth of Mrs [Amelia] Knox[1] I have delivered on them the judgment of her God.

---

1. Deeply religious wife and mother in *Fanny's First Play*, who observes in Act III:

    [W]e're ignorant. We dont really know whats right and whats wrong. . . . We bring our children up just as we were brought up; and we go to church or

The critics whom I have lampooned in the induction to this play under the names of Trotter, Vaughan, and Gunn will forgive me:[2] in fact Mr Trotter forgave me beforehand, and assisted the makeup by which Mr Claude King so successfully simulated his personal appearance. The critics whom I did not introduce were somewhat hurt, as I should have been myself under the same circumstances; but I had not room for them all; so I can only apologize and assure them that I meant no disrespect.

The concealment of the authorship,[3] if a *secret de Polichinelle* [secret of Punchinello: an open secret] can be said to involve concealment, was a necessary part of the play. In so far as it was effectual, it operated as a measure of relief to those critics and playgoers who are so obsessed by my strained legendary reputation that they approach my plays in a condition which is really one of derangement, and are quite unable to conceive a play of mine as anything but a trap baited with paradoxes, and designed to compass their ethical perversion and intellectual confusion. If it were possible, I should put forward all my plays anonymously, or hire some less disturbing person, as Bacon is said to have hired Shakespear, to father my plays for me.

chapel just as our parents did; and we say whatever everybody says; and it goes on all right until something out of the way happens . . . And then you know what happens: complaints and quarrels and . . . bad language and bad temper and regular bewilderment . . . We find out then that with all our respectability and piety, weve no real religion and no way of telling right from wrong. Weve nothing but our habits; and when theyre upset, where are we?

2. A. B. Walkley of *The Times* is the model for Trotter, E. A. Baughan of the *Daily News* for Vaughan, and Gilbert Cannan of the *Star* for Gunn.
3. When the play was produced at the Little Theatre in 1911, its authorship was not credited. Shaw did not formally acknowledge authorship until the play's publication in 1914.

Killing for Sport

Preface to Henry S. Salt (ed.), Killing for Sport: Essays by Various Writers *(1914); first published (for American copyright), slightly abridged, as 'Killing for Fun', in* Hearst's Magazine, *New York, July 1914*

======

Sport[1] is a difficult subject to deal with honestly. It is easy for the humanitarian to moralize against it; and any fool on its side can gush about its glorious breezy pleasures and the virtues it nourishes. But neither the moralizings nor the gushings are supported by facts: indeed they are mostly violently contradicted by them. Sportsmen are not crueller than other people. Humanitarians are not more humane than other people. The pleasures of sport are fatigues and hardships: nobody gets out of bed before sunrise on a drizzling wintry morning and rides off into darkness, cold and rain, either for luxury or thirst for the blood of a fox cub. The humanitarian and the sportsman are often the selfsame person drawing altogether unaccountable lines between pheasants and pigeons, between hares and foxes, between tame stags from the cart and wild ones from the heather, between lobsters or *paté de foie gras* and beefsteaks: above all, between man and the lower animals; for people who are sickened by the figures of a *battue* [group of hunters] do not turn a hair over the infantile deathrate in Lisson Grove [north London, west of Regent's Park] or the slums of Dundee.

Clearly the world of sport is a crystal palace in which we had better not throw stones unless we are prepared to have our own faces cut by the falling glass. My own pursuits as a critic and as a castigator of morals by ridicule (otherwise a writer of comedies) are so cruel that in point of giving pain to many worthy people I can hold my own with most dentists, and beat a skilful sportsman hollow. I know many sportsmen; and none of them are ferocious. I know several humanitarians; and they are all ferocious. No book of sport breathes such a wrathful spirit as this book of humanity. No sportsman wants to kill the fox or the pheasant as I want to kill him when I see him doing it. Callousness is not cruel. Stupidity is not cruel. Love of exercise and of feats of skill is not cruel. They may and do produce

---

1. Almost invariably, Shaw confined his use of the term 'sport' to the pastime involving efforts to capture or kill wild animals, notably foxes.

more destruction and suffering than all the neuroses of all the Neros. But they are characteristic of quite amiable and cheerful people, mostly lovers of pet animals. On the other hand, humane sensitiveness is impatient, angry, ruthless, and murderous. [Jean-Paul] Marat was a supersensitive humanitarian, by profession a doctor who had practised successfully in genteel circles in England. What Marat felt towards marquesses most humanitarians feel more or less towards sportsmen. Therefore let no sportsman who reads these pages accuse me of hypocrisy, or of claiming to be a more amiable person than he. And let him excuse me, if he will be so good, for beginning with an attempt to describe how I feel about sport.

To begin with, sport soon bores me when it does not involve killing; and when it does, it affects me much as the murder of a human being would affect me, rather more than less; for just as the murder of a child is more shocking than the murder of an adult (because, I suppose, the child is so helpless and the breach of social faith therefore so unconscionable), the murder of an animal is an abuse of man's advantage over animals: the proof being that when the animal is powerful and dangerous, and the man unarmed, the repulsion vanishes and is replaced by congratulation. But quite humane and cultivated people seem unable to understand why I should bother about the feelings of animals. I have seen the most horrible pictures published in good faith as attractive in illustrated magazines. One of them, which I wish I could forget, was a photograph taken on a polar expedition, shewing a murdered bear with its living cub trying to make it attend to its maternal duties. I have seen a photograph of a criminal being cut into a thousand pieces by a Chinese executioner, which was by comparison amusing. I have also seen thrown on a screen for the entertainment of a large audience a photograph of an Arctic explorer taking away a sledge dog to shoot it for food, the dog jumping about joyously without the least suspicion of its human friend's intentions. If the doomed dog had been a man or a woman, I believe I should have had less sense of treachery. I do not say that this is reasonable: I simply state it as a fact. It was quite evident that the lecturer[2] had no suspicion of the effect the picture was

2. The Irish-born Antarctic explorer Lt. Sir Ernest Shackleton headlined an exhibition of polar cinematograph films, narrated by himself, in a season of matinées at the Alhambra Theatre, 15–25 September 1909. Supplementing these were films taken in the Arctic by the American photographer-explorer Anthony Fiala, commander of the Ziegler polar expedition 1903–5. Among Fiala's films was one of a dog being led to slaughter.

producing on me; and as far as I could see, his audience was just as callous; for if they had all felt as I felt there would have been at least a very perceptible shudder, if not an articulate protest. Now this was not a case of sport. It was necessary to shoot the dog: I should have shot it myself under the same circumstances. But I should have regarded the necessity as a horrible one; and I should have presented it to the audience as a painful episode, like cannibalism in a crew of castaways, and not as a joke. For I must add that a good many people present regarded it as a bit of fun. I absolve the lecturer from this extremity of insensibility. The shooting of a dog was a trifle to what he had endured; and I did not blame him for thinking it by comparison a trivial matter. But to us, who had endured nothing, it might have seemed a little hard on the dog, and calling for some apology from the man.

I am driven to the conclusion that my sense of kinship with animals is greater than most people feel. It amuses me to talk to animals in a sort of jargon I have invented for them; and it seems to me that it amuses them to be talked to, and that they respond to the tone of the conversation, though its intellectual content may to some extent escape them. I am quite sure, having made the experiment several times on dogs left in my care as part of the furniture of hired houses, that an animal who has been treated as a brute, and is consequently undeveloped socially (as human beings remain socially undeveloped under the same circumstances) will, on being talked to as a fellow creature, become friendly and companionable in a very short time. This process has been described by some reproachful dog owners as spoiling the dog, and sincerely deplored by them, because I am glad to say it is easier to do than to undo except by brutalities of which few people are capable. But I find it impossible to associate with animals on any other terms. Further, it gives me extraordinary gratification to find a wild bird treating me with confidence, as robins sometimes do. It pleases me to conciliate an animal who is hostile to me. What is more, an animal who will not be conciliated offends me. There is at the Zoo a morose maned lion who will tear you to pieces if he gets half a chance. There is also a very handsome maneless lion with whom you may play more safely than with most St Bernard dogs,[3] as he seems to need nothing but plenty of attention and admiration to put him into the best of humors. I do not feel towards these two lions as a carpenter does towards two pieces of wood, one hard and knotty, and the other easy to work; nor as I do towards two motor bicycles, one troublesome and dangerous, and the other in perfect order. I

3. Shaw personally petted the lion he speaks of, in Regent's Park Zoo.

feel towards the two lions as I should towards two men similarly diverse. I like one and dislike the other. If they got loose and were shot, I should be distressed in the one case whilst in the other I should say "Serve the brute right!" This is clearly fellow-feeling. And it seems to me that the plea of the humanitarian is a plea for widening the range of fellow-feeling.

The limits of fellow-feeling are puzzling. People who have it in a high degree for animals often seem utterly devoid of it for human beings of a different class. They will literally kill their dogs with kindness whilst behaving to their servants with such utter inconsideration that they have to change their domestic staff once a month or oftener. Or they hate horses and like snakes. One could fill pages with such inconsistencies. The lesson of these apparent contradictions is that fellow-feeling is a matter of dislikes as well as of likes. No man wants to destroy the engine which catches him in its cog-wheels and tears a limb from him. But many a man has tried to kill another man for a very trifling slight. The machine, not being our fellow, cannot be loved or hated. The man, being our fellow, can.

Let us try to get down to the bottom of this matter. There is no use in saying that our fellow creatures must not be killed. That is simply untrue; and the converse proposal that they must be killed is simply true. We see the Buddhist having his path swept before him lest he should tread on an insect and kill it; but we do not see what that Buddhist does when he catches a flea that has kept him awake for an hour; and we know that he has to except certain poisonous snakes from his forbearance. If mice get into your house and you do not kill them, they will end by killing you. If rabbits breed on your farm and you do not exterminate them, you will end by having no farm. If you keep deer in your park and do not thin them, your neighbors or the authorities will finally have to save you the trouble. If you hold the life of a mosquito sacred, malaria and yellow fever will not return the compliment. I have had an interview with an adder, in the course of which it struck repeatedly and furiously at my stick; and I let it go unharmed; but if I were the mother of a family of young children, and I found a cobra in the garden, I would vote for "*La mort sans phrase*" ['Death without a word'] as many humane and honorable persons voted in the case, not of a serpent, but of an anointed king.

I see no logical nor spiritual escape from the theory that evolution (not, please observe, Natural Selection) involves a deliberate intentional destruction by the higher forms of life of the lower. It is a dangerous and difficult business; for in the course of natural selection the lower forms may have become necessary to the existence of the higher; and the gamekeeper shooting everything that could hurt his pheasants or their chicks may be behaving as foolishly as an Arab lunatic shooting horses and camels. But where Man comes, the megatherium must go as surely as where the poultry farmer comes the fox must go unless the hunt will pay for the fox's depredations. To plead for the tiger, the wolf, and the poisonous snake, is as useless as to plead for the spirochete or the tetanus bacillus: we must frankly class these as early and disastrous experiments in creation, and accept it as part of the mission of the later and more successful experiments to recognize them as superseded, and to destroy them purposely. We should, no doubt, be very careful how we jump from the indisputable general law that the higher forms of life must exterminate or limit the lower, to the justification of any particular instance of the slaughter of nonhuman animals by men, or the slaughter of a low type of man by a high type of man. Still, when all due reservations are made, the fact remains that a war of extermination is being waged daily and necessarily by man against his rivals for possession of the earth, and that though an urban humanitarian and vegetarian who never has occasion to kill anything but a microbe may shudder at the callousness with which a farmer kills rats and rabbits and sparrows and moles and caterpillars and ladybirds and many more charming creatures, yet if he were in the farmer's place he would have to do exactly the same, or perish.

In that case why not make a pleasure of necessity, and a virtue of pleasure, as the sportsmen do? I think we must own that there is no objection from the point of view of the animals. On the contrary, it is quite easy to shew that there is a positive advantage to them in the organization of killing as sport. Fox hunting has saved the existing foxes from extermination; and if it were not for the civilization that makes fox hunting possible, the fox would still be hunted and killed by packs of wolves. I am so conscious of this that I have in another place [see preface to *Misalliance*, p. 63] suggested that children should be hunted or shot during certain months of the year, as they would then be fed and preserved by the sportsmen of the counties as generously and carefully as pheasants now are; and the survivors would make a much better nation than our present slum products. And I go further. I maintain that the abolition of public executions was a very bad thing for the murderers. Before that time, we did exactly as our sportsmen now do. We made a pleasure of the necessity for exterminating murderers, and a virtue of the pleasure. Hanging was a popular sport, like racing. Huge crowds assembled to see it and paid large prices for seats. There would have been betting on the result if it had been at all uncertain. The criminal had what all criminals love: a large audience. He had a procession to Tyburn [a former place of public execution, near Hyde

Park]: he had a drink: he was allowed to make a speech if he could; and if he could not, the speech was made for him and published and sold in great numbers. Above all, such fair play as an execution admits of was guaranteed to him by the presence of the public, whereas now he perishes in a horrible secrecy which lends itself to all the abuses of secrecy. Whether the creature slain be man or what we very invidiously call brute, there is no case to be made against sport on its behalf. Even cruelty can justify itself, as far as the victim is concerned, on the ground that it makes sport attractive to cruel people, and that sport is good for the quarry.

The true objection to sport is the one taken by that wise and justly famous Puritan who objected to bear baiting not because it gave pain to the bear but because it gave pleasure to the spectators [in T. B. Macaulay's *History of England*, Vol. 1, Chapter 2]. He rightly saw that it was not important that we should be men of pleasure, and that it was enormously important that we should be men of honor. What the bear would have said if it had had any say in the matter can only be conjectured. Its captors might have argued that if they could not have made money by keeping it alive whilst taking it to England to be baited, they would have killed it at sight in the Pyrenees; so that it owed several months of life, with free board and lodging, to the institution of bear baiting. The bear might have replied that if it had not been for the bear pit in England they would never have come to hunt for it in the Pyrenees, where it could have ended its days in a free and natural manner. Let us admit for the sake of a quiet life that the point is disputable. What is not disputable by any person who has ever seen sport of this character is that the man who enjoys it is degraded by it. We do not bait bears now (I do not quite know why); but we course rabbits in the manner described in one of the essays ['Coursing' by H. S. Salt] in this book. I lived for a time on the south slope of the Hog's Back;[4] and every Sunday morning rabbits were coursed within earshot of me. And I noticed that it was quite impossible to distinguish the cries of the excited terriers from the cries of the sportsmen, although ordinarily the voice of a man is no more like the voice of a dog than like the voice of a nightingale. Sport reduced them all, men and terriers alike, to a common denominator of bestiality. The sound did not make me more humane: on the contrary, I felt that if I were an irresponsible despot with a park of artillery at my disposal, I should (especially after seeing the sportsmen on

4. The North Downs are low chalk hill ranges in Surrey and Kent; Shaw spent much of 1898–1902 in Hindhead, Haslemere and Guildford, Surrey, adjacent to the Downs and the Hog's Back.

their way to and from their sport) have said: "These people have become subhuman, and will be better dead. Be kind enough to mow them down for me."

As a matter of fact there is always a revulsion against these dehumanizing sports in which the killing can be seen, and the actual visible chase shared, by human beings: in short, the sports in which men revert to the excitements of beasts of prey. Several have been abolished by law: among them bear baiting and cock fighting: both of them sports in which the spectators shared at close quarters the excitement of the animals engaged. In the sports firmly established among us there is much less of this abomination. In fox hunting and shooting, predatory excitement is not a necessary part of the sport, and is indeed abhorred by many who practise it. Inveterate fox hunters have been distressed and put off their hunting for days by happening to see a fox in the last despairing stage of its run from the hounds: a sight which can be avoided, and often is, by the hunters, but which they may happen upon some day when they are not hunting. Such people hunt because they delight in meets and in gallops across country as social and healthy incidents of country life. They are proud of their horsemanship and their craftiness in taking a line. They like horses and dogs and exercise and wind and weather, and are unconscious of the fact that their expensive and well-equipped hunting stables and kennels are horse prisons and dog prisons. It is useless to pretend that these ladies and gentlemen are fiends in human form: they clearly are not. By avoiding being in at the death they get all the good out of hunting without incurring the worst of the evil, and so come out with a balance in their favor.

Shooting is subtler: it is a matter of skill with one's weapons. The expert at it is called, not a good chicken butcher, but a good shot. When I want, as I often do, to pick him off, I do so not because I feel that he is cruel or degraded but because he is a nuisance to me with the very disagreeable noise of his explosions, and because there is an unbearable stupidity in converting an interesting, amusing, prettily colored live wonder like a pheasant into a slovenly unhandsome corpse. But at least he does not yap like a terrier, and shake with a detestable excitement, and scream out frantic bets to bookmakers. His expression is that of a man performing a skilled operation with an instrument of precision: an eminently human expression, quite incompatible with the flush of blood to the eyes and the uncovering of the dogtooth that makes a man like a beast of prey. And this is why it is impossible to feel that skilled shooting or fox hunting are as abominable as rabbit coursing, hare hunting with beagles, or otter hunting.

And yet shooting depends for its toleration on custom as much as on the coolness with which it has to be performed. It may be illogical to forgive a man for shooting a pheasant and to loathe him for shooting a seagull; but as a matter of plain fact one feels that a man who shoots seagulls is a cad, and soon makes him feel it if he attempts to do it on board a public ship, whereas the snipe shooter excites no such repulsion. And "fair game" must be skilfully shot if the maximum of toleration is to be enjoyed. Even then it is not easy for some of us to forget that many a bird must have been miserably maimed before the shooter perfected his skill. The late King Edward the Seventh, immediately after his recovery from a serious operation[5] which stirred the whole nation to anxious sympathy with him, shot a stag, which got away to die of just such internal inflammation as its royal murderer had happily escaped. Many people read the account without the least emotion. Others thought it natural that the King should be ashamed, as a marksman, of his failure to kill, but rejected as sentimental nonsense the notion that he should feel any remorse on the stag's behalf. Had he deliberately shot a cow instead, everyone would have been astounded and horrified. Custom will reconcile people to any atrocity; and fashion will drive them to acquire any custom. The English princess [Victoria] who sits on the throne of Spain goes to bullfights because it is the Spanish fashion. At first she averted her face, and probably gave offence by doing so. Now, no doubt, she is a *connoisseuse* of the sport. Yet neither she nor the late King Edward can be classed as cruel monsters. On the contrary, they are conspicuous examples of the power of cruel institutions to compel the support and finally win the tolerance and even the enjoyment of persons of full normal benevolence.

But this is not why I call shooting subtle. It fascinates even humane persons not only because it is a game of skill in the use of the most ingenious instrument in general use, but because killing by craft from a distance is a power that makes a man divine rather than human.

> Oft have I struck
> Those that I never saw, and struck them dead [*Henry VI, Part II*, IV: iv]

said the statesman [Lord Scales] to Jack Cade (who promptly hanged him); and something of the sense of power in that boast stimulates every boy with a catapult and every man with a gun. That is why there is an interest in weapons fathoms deeper than the interest in cricket bats and golf clubs. It is not a question of skill or risk. The men who go to Africa with

5. Two days before his scheduled coronation in June 1902, Edward VII underwent surgery for perityphlitis.

cameras[6] and obtain photographs and even cinematographs of the most dangerous animals at close quarters, shew much more skill and nerve than the gentlemen who disgust us with pictures of themselves sitting on the bodies of the huge creatures they have just killed with explosive bullets. Shooting "big game," like serving as a soldier in the field, is glorified conventionally as a proof of character and courage, though everyone knows that men can be found by the hundred thousand to face such ordeals, including several who would be afraid to walk down Bond Street in an unfashionable hat. The real point of the business is neither character nor courage, but ability to kill. And the greater cowards and the feebler weaklings we are, the more important this power is to us. It is a matter of life and death to us to be able to kill our enemies without coming to handgrips with them; and the consequence is that our chief form of play is to pretend that something is our enemy and kill it. Even to pretend to kill it is some satisfaction: nay, the spectacle of other people pretending to do it is a substitute worth paying for. Nothing more supremely ridiculous as a subject of reasonable contemplation could be imagined than a sham fight in Earls Court between a tribe of North American Indians and a troop of cowboys, both imported by Buffalo Bill as a theatrical speculation.[7] To see these grown-up men behaving like children, galloping about and firing blank cartridges at one another, and pretending to fall down dead, was absurd and incredible enough from any rational point of view; but that thousands of respectable middle-aged and elderly citizens and their wives, all perfectly sober, should pay to be allowed to look on, seems flat madness. Yet the thing not only occurred in London, but occurs now daily in the cinema theatres and yearly at the Military Tournaments. And what honest man dare pretend that he gets no fun out of these spectacles? Certainly not I. They revived enough of my boyish delight in stage fights

6. See Karl Georg Schillings, *With Flashlight and Rifle: Photographing by Flashlight at Night the Wild Animal Life of Equatorial Africa* (1906), tr. Frederic Whyte, and Cherry Kearton, *Wild Life across the World* (1913) and *Through Central Africa from East to West*, with James Barnes (1915). Kearton, with whom Shaw was acquainted, had also created a cinematograph of a native lion hunt in east Africa, and another, 'Lassoing Wild Animals in Africa', shown in the United States in 1911. Both are in the collection of the British Film Institute.
7. Buffalo Bill's Wild West was a leading attraction of the American Exhibition of the Arts, Inventions, Manufactures, Products and Resources of the United States, which ran at Earls Court in West Kensington from 9 May to 31 October 1887. Even Queen Victoria forsook her eternal mourning long enough to attend a performance, on 11 May, in a private visit.

and in the stories of Captain Mayne Reid to induce me to sit them out, conscious as I was of their silliness.[8]

Please do not revile me for telling you what I felt instead of what I ought to have felt. What prevents the sport question and every other question from getting squarely put before us is our habit of saying that the things we think should disgust us and fill us with abhorrence actually do disgust us and fill us with abhorrence, and that the persons who, against all reason and decency, find some sort of delight in them, are vile wretches quite unlike ourselves, though, as everyone can see, we and they are as like as potatoes. You may not agree with Mr Rudyard Kipling about war, or with Colonel Roosevelt about sport; but beware how you pretend that war does not interest and excite you more than printing, or that the thought of bringing down a springing tiger with a well-aimed shot does not interest you more than the thought of cleaning your teeth. Men may be as the poles asunder in their speculative views. In their actual nervous and emotional reactions they are "members one of another" [Ephesians 4: 25] to a much greater extent than they choose to confess. The reason I have no patience with Colonel Roosevelt's tedious string of rhinoceros murders in South Africa is not that I am not interested in weapons, in marksmanship, and in killing, but because my interest in life and creation is still greater than my interest in death and destruction, and because I have sufficient fellow feeling with a rhinoceros to think it a frightful thing that it should be killed for fun.

Consider a moment how one used to feel when an Irish peasant shot his landlord, or when a grand duke was blown to pieces in Russia, or when one read of how Charlotte Corday killed Marat. On the one hand we applauded the courage, the skill, the resolution of the assassin; we exulted in the lesson taught to tyrants and in the overthrow of the strong oppressor by the weak victim; but we were horrified by the breach of law, by the killing of the accused at the decree of an irresponsible Ribbon Lodge [see Vol. 1, p. 273] under no proper public control, by the execution of the grand duke without trial and opportunity of defence, by the suspicion that

8. The Royal Tournament, inaugurated in 1880, is an annual military and naval display held in London, a modern counterpart of a popular medieval pastime, in which the participants not only perform military exercises but exhibit individual skills and daring. Mayne Reid, Irish-born journalist and novelist, drew upon his experiences in America, where he was a US Army captain during the Mexican war, in a series of derring-do fictions, including *The Rifle Rangers* (1850) and *The Scalp Hunters* (1851).

Charlotte Corday was too like Marat in her lust for the blood of oppressors to have the right to kill him. Such cases are extremely complicated, except for those simple victims of political or class prejudice who think Charlotte Corday a saint because she killed a Radical, and the Ribbonmen demons because they were common fellows who dared to kill country gentlemen. But however the cases catch us, there is always that peculiar interest in individual killing, and consequently in the means and weapons by which individuals can kill their enemies, which is at the root of the sport of shooting.

It all comes back to fellow feeling and appetite for fruitful activity and a high quality of life: there is nothing else to appeal to. No commandment can meet the case. It is no use saying "Thou shalt not kill" in one breath, and, in the next "Thou shalt not suffer a witch to live." Men must be killed and animals must be killed: nay, whole species of animals and types of men must be exterminated before the earth can become a tolerable place of habitation for decent folk. But among the men who will have to be wiped out stands the sportsman: the man without fellow feeling, the man so primitive and uncritical in his tastes that the destruction of life is an amusement to him, the man whose outlook is as narrow as that of his dog. He is not even cruel: sport is partly a habit to which he has been brought up, and partly stupidity, which can always be measured by wastefulness and by lack of sense of the importance and glory of life. The horrible murk and grime of the Pottery towns [in Staffordshire] is caused by indifference to a stupid waste of sunlight, natural beauty, cleanliness, and pleasant air, combined with a brutish appetite for money. A *battue* is caused by indifference to the beauty and interest of bird life and song, and callousness to glazed eyes and blood-bedabbled corpses, combined with a boyish love of shooting. All the people who waste beauty and life in this way are characterized by deficiency in fellow feeling: not only have they none of St Francis's feeling that the birds are of our kin, but they would be extremely indignant if a loader or a gamekeeper asserted any claim to belong to their species. Sport is a sign either of limitation or of timid conventionality.

And this disposes of the notion that sport is the training of a conquering race. Even if such things as conquering races existed, or would be tolerable if they did exist, they would not be races of sportsmen. The red scalp-hunting braves of North America were the sportingest race imaginable; and they were conquered as easily as the bisons they hunted. The French can boast more military glory to the square inch of history than any other nation; but until lately they were the standing butt of English humorists for their deficiencies as sportsmen. In the Middle Ages, when they fought as sportsmen and gentlemen, they were annihilated by small bodies of starving

Englishmen who carefully avoided sportsmanlike methods and made a laborious business (learnt at the village target) of killing them. As to becoming accustomed to risks, there are plenty of ways of doing that without killing anything except occasionally yourself. The motorcyclist takes more trying risks than the fox hunter; and motorcycling seems safety itself compared to aviation. A dive from a high springboard will daunt a man as effectually as a stone wall in the hunting field. The notion that if you have no sportsmen you will have no soldiers (as if more than the tiniest fraction of the armies of the world had ever been sportsmen) is as absurd as the notion that burglars and garrotters should be encouraged because they might make hardier and more venturesome soldiers than honest men; but since people foolishly do set up such arguments they may as well be mentioned in passing for what they are worth.

The question then comes to this: which is the superior man? the man whose pastime is slaughter, or the man whose pastime is creative or contemplative? I have no doubt about the matter myself, being on the creative and contemplative side by nature. Slaughter is necessary work, like scavenging; but the man who not only does it unnecessarily for love of it but actually makes as much of it as possible by breeding live things to slaughter, seems to me to be little more respectable than one who befouls the streets for the pleasure of sweeping them. I believe that the line of evolution leads to the prevention of the birth of creatures whose lives are not useful and enjoyable, and that the time will come when a gentleman found amusing himself with a gun will feel as compromised as he does now when found amusing himself with a whip at the expense of a child or an old lame horse covered with sores. Sport, like murder, is a bloody business; and the sportsmen will not always be able to outface that fact as they do at present.

But there is something else. Killing, if it is to give us heroic emotions, must not be done for pleasure. Interesting though the slaying of one man by another may be, it is abhorrent when it is done merely for the fun of doing it (the sportsman's way) or to satisfy the envious spite of the worse man towards the better (Cain's way). When Charlotte Corday stabbed Marat, and when Hamilton of Bothwellhaugh shot the Regent Murray,[9]

9. Lord James Stuart, Earl of Moray (Murray), half-brother of Mary, Queen of Scots, became Regent of Scotland after Mary's abdication, and secured peace in the realm only after urging Elizabeth to imprison Mary. He was assassinated on 20 January 1570 by James Hamilton of Bothwellhaugh at the instigation of adherents of Mary.

they were stung by intolerable social wrongs for which the law offered them no redress. When Brutus and his fellow conspirators killed Cæsar, they had persuaded themselves that they were saving Rome. When Samson slew the lion, he had every reason to feel convinced that if he did not, the lion would slay him. Conceive Charlotte Corday stabbing Marat as an exercise of manual and anatomical skill, or Hamilton bringing down the Regent as a feat of marksmanship! Their deeds at once become, not less, but more horrifying than if they had done them from a love of killing. Jack the Ripper was a madman of the most appalling sort; but the fascination of murder for him must have been compounded of dread, of horror, and of a frightful perversion of an instinct which in its natural condition is a kindly one. He was a ghastly murderer; but he was a hot-blooded one. The perfection of callousness is not reached until a life is sacrificed, and often cruelly sacrificed, solely as a feat of skill. Peter the Great amusing himself by torturing his son to death was a revolting monster;[10] but he was not so utterly inhuman in that crime as he was when, on being interested by a machine for executing criminals which he saw in a museum on his travels, he proposed to execute one of his retinue to see how the machine worked, and could with difficulty be brought to understand that there was a sentimental objection to the proceeding on the part of his hosts which made the experiment impossible. When he tortured his son he knew that he was committing an abomination. When he wanted to try an experiment at the cost of a servant's life he was unconscious of doing anything that was not a matter of course for any nobleman. And in this he was worse than abominable: he was deficient, imbecile, less than human. Just so is the sportsman, shooting quite skilfully and coolly without the faintest sense of any murderous excitement, and with no personal feeling against the birds, really further from salvation than the man who is humane enough to get some sense of wickedness out of his sport. To have one's fellow feeling corrupted and perverted into a lust for cruelty and murder is

10. Peter's son Alexis, a weak, debauched sensualist who dreaded his father, lived abroad to remove himself from Peter's authority. When he imprudently allowed himself to be lured back to Russia and to be interrogated to reveal a 'conspiracy', he was forced by Peter to renounce the succession. Suspected conspirators were tortured in his presence, impaled, broken on the wheel, beheaded. The terrified tsarevich, urged to make a full confession and severely lashed and tortured until he did, confessed to anything he was charged with. He was sentenced to death, his execution occurring on 26 June 1718. A popular rumour circulated that Peter personally beat him to death.

hideous; but to have no fellow feeling at all is to be something less than even a murderer. The man who sees red is more complete than the man who is blind.

The triviality of sport as compared with the risk and trouble of its pursuit and the gravity of its results makes it much sillier than crime. The idler who can find nothing better to do than to kill is past our patience. If a man takes on himself the heavy responsibility of killing, he should not do it for pastime. Pastimes are very necessary; for though a busy man can always find something to do, there comes a point at which his health, his sanity, his very existence may depend on his doing nothing of the smallest importance; and yet he cannot sit still and twiddle his thumbs: besides, he requires bodily exercise. He needs an idle pastime. Now "Satan finds some mischief still for idle hands to do" [Watts, *Divine Songs*] if the idler lets his conscience go to sleep. But he need not let it go to sleep. There are plenty of innocent idle pastimes for him. He can read detective stories. He can play tennis. He can drive a motor car if he can afford one. He can fly. Satan may suggest that it would be a little more interesting to kill something; but surely only an outrageous indifference to the sacredness of life and the horrors of suffering and terror, combined with a monstrously selfish greed for sensation, could drive a man to accept the Satanic suggestion if sport were not organized for him as a social institution. Even as it is, there are now so many other pastimes available that the choice of killing is becoming more and more a disgrace to the chooser. The wantonness of the choice is beyond excuse. To kill as the poacher does, to sell or eat the victim, is at least to act reasonably. To kill from hatred or revenge is at least to behave passionately. To kill in gratification of a lust for death is at least to behave villainously. Reason, passion, and villainy are all human. But to kill, being all the time quite a good sort of fellow, merely to pass away the time when there are a dozen harmless ways of doing it equally available, is to behave like an idiot or a silly imitative sheep.

Surely the broad outlook and deepened consciousness which admits all living things to the commonwealth of fellow feeling, and the appetite for fruitful activity and generous life which come with it, are better than this foolish doing of unamiable deeds by people who are not in the least unamiable.

March, 1914.   G. B. S.

The Prussian Hath Said in His Heart

Preface to a book by Cecil Chesterton, New York, 1915

========

Cecil Chesterton, like his prodigious brother [Gilbert Keith Chesterton], is a man to be reckoned with. He is a journalist in the old and serious sense: that is, a man who combines a mastery of the art of letters with a sympathetic insight into human nature, and a power of seizing on its topical manifestations from day to day, and handling them in such a way as to enlist public passion on his side and supply it with the arguments which make up what is called public opinion. Like most who possess this power in the most effective degree, he has cultivated it *viva voce* as a speaker on various platforms, social, political and religious; and as his utterances are always either audaciously unconventional, or, what is much more danger-ous to an orator, reductions to complete seriousness of the conventional opinions which everyone professes and hardly anyone really means anything by, he continually provokes his audience by inhuman intellectual feats, and as continually conciliates it by the most valuable equipment of the born orator, heartfelt good manners. He has in addition the tremendous advan-tage, from the point of view of the popular orator and journalist, of being absolutely independent of party and indifferent to the rewards which party service bring to men of his gifts who are on sale. He has been pursued legally for his fierce invectives against the influence of finance in politics, and has stood his trial, suffered the inevitable hostile verdict and its sequel of a halfhearted attempt to embarrass him with a fine which was either too much or too little, without losing an inch of ground or allowing his opponents to gain one. Where he will come out in the end I do not know. At present, he has swallowed all the formulas, from the most extreme and sceptical Atheism and Individualism of the mid-Victorian period to the Socialism of the *fin de siècle*, only to land, not in cynicism or eclecticism, but in breaking lances for the most extreme dogmas of medieval Catholi-cism and the grossest prejudices of Henry Fielding, not to say of Squire Western [in Fielding's *Tom Jones*]. He has Latin brains and a very solid XVIII century British stomach; and the combination is so rare that he talks and writes as nobody else in England does. The combination plays him tricks sometimes, for his British shrewdness and humor enable him to use his intellectual ingenuity to play the very exciting game of making the most imposing cases for all sorts of quite desperate causes; but he is saved from this sort of unreality by a genuine and ardent republican conscience and sense of national honor which have drawn him further and further into an attack on the corruption of English public life by dangerous interests which are half trivially private (mostly dinner invitations) and half utterly inhuman, without country or conscience, or any end, except dividend.

G. B. S.

[Cecil E. Chesterton died in active service in 1918.]

Is Britain Blameless?

First published as a review of A. Fenner Brockway's pamphlet, originally titled Is England Blameless?, in the Labour Leader, London, 4 February 1915. Reprinted as a preface to the second edition of the retitled pamphlet, 1915

═══

The time will come when this will seem an extraordinarily silly question. When all is said that possibly can be said for the war, it is a monstrous crime against civilization and humanity; and the notion that any of the parties voluntarily engaged in it can be blameless is absurd. It is impossible to discuss war practically without a suspension of all ordinary morals and all normal religious and humanitarian pretensions. Even that is not enough: it is necessary to set up, alongside of martial law (which, as the Duke of Wellington remarked, is no law at all), an outrageous special morality and religion, in which murder becomes duty and patriotism, and in which our glory lies, not in doing the will of God, but in indulging Lord Roberts's "will to conquer,"[1] which is our more accurate English version of the "will to power" that shocks us so in the pages of Nietzsche. Under such circumstances common sense is turned topsy turvey; "frightfulness" becomes "the truest mercy"; and the world goes mad.

That is a pretty complication to begin with. But here in England our party system has complicated even this insane complication. The war has been declared on our part nominally by a Liberal Government supported by a Liberal majority in the House of Commons, but really by a secret coalition (since revealed) between the Imperialist section of the Cabinet and the Imperialist Opposition,[2] the price paid being the suspension of Liberal

1. In response to advocates of voluntary recruiting, Lord Roberts campaigned strenuously for compulsory military service in the name of the nation's 'will to conquer'. See also p. 267, fn. 4.
2. Sir Edward Grey, Secretary of State for Foreign Affairs, revealed in Parliament on 3 August 1914 that, on 23 August 1911 Herbert Asquith, Liberal Prime Minister (from 1908), convened a secret special meeting of the Imperial Defence Committee to agree on British strategy in the event of war. Those in attendance included Grey, Richard Burdon Haldane (Secretary of State for War), Lloyd George (Chancellor of the Exchequer), Reginald McKenna (First Lord of the

legislation during the war, and consequently the political paralysis of the
nation, with the scandalous result (among others) that the House of
Commons is actually shut up and its members practically disbanded at the
moment when the conduct of an appalling war depends on their vigilance
and criticism. And this situation has been brought about not merely by
pressure of circumstances, but by the deliberate and positive hoodwinking
by the Prime Minister and the Secretary of State for Foreign Affairs of
their own party by assurances which will figure in constitutional history as
the boldest and most successful prevarications to which the official conscience has ever been reconciled by its conception of patriotism.

   Consider now the predicament in which this places the ordinary Liberal
partisan, whose seat in Parliament, and with it all his political and social
ambitions, depends on his sticking to Mr Asquith and Sir Edward Grey, no
matter how contemptuously they may disregard his feelings and his desire
to keep up a pretence of having political principles as well as a side in the
party conflict. He cannot act like the men who really have principles, and
are in politics for the sake of them. The position is quite simple for such
men: when they find that they have been played with, duped, and
betrayed, they simply walk out, like Lord Morley, Mr [John] Burns, and
Mr [Rt. Hon. Charles] Trevelyan, or, if they have no office to walk out of,
denounce their leaders, like Mr [Arthur] Ponsonby.[3] But the poor Partisan,

------

Admiralty) and Winston Churchill (Home Secretary), who met with military
commanders General Henry Wilson and Admiral Sir Arthur Wilson. The secret
understanding committed Britain to a defence of the English Channel and the
North Sea coasts of France against Germany.
3. Lord Morley of Blackburn, Lord President of the Council, resigned as a result
of a fundamental difference of opinion with his colleagues over the national policy
as set forth in Grey's speech to Parliament on 3 August 1914. Burns, President of
the Board of Trade, withdrew for the same reason, as well as for the Government's
decision on 1 August to inform the French it would oppose German naval action
against the French Channel coast, and its further decision to make the decisive issue
the German breach of the 1839 Treaty of London, which guaranteed Belgian
neutrality. Trevelyan, an advocate of pacifism, resigned upon the British declaration
of war. (In an article 'The Peril of Potsdam' in the *Daily News* on 11 August 1914
Shaw commented: 'Mr C. P. Trevelyan's resignation shows how strongly an
Englishman with a cultured historical sense of the Balance of Civilisation in
Europe can regard Germany as so important a bulwark of that civilisation that
even when we are at war with her we must aim finally at the conservation of her
power to defend its eastern frontier.') Ponsonby, Liberal MP, on 3 August denounced

the mere barnacle on the party ship who must sink to the bottom if he is detached from it, has to pocket his betrayal and save his face as best he may.

It is easily done, after all. If a man kicks you, and you cannot knock him down, the best plan is to walk on as if nothing had happened, and speak with enthusiasm of him as your best friend for ever after. When America the other day told us flatly that we had been guilty of repeated breaches of international law,[4] and that she was not going to stand it, we all burst into a chorus of appreciation of her cordial tone and shook her hand warmly until we felt it safe to let go. And the Liberals, having been completely sold by their leaders, have made up their minds not to notice it, and to stand by oneanother in backing up a fairy tale of two noble Liberal apostles of peace suddenly and treacherously surprised by a monstrous and totally unforeseen and unprovoked attack on Belgium by a nation of Odin-worshipping Huns headed by a fiend with upturned moustaches. And they will brazen that out without the least thought of the mischievous effect it may have on neutral opinion or even on the direct fortunes of the war. The French and British Foreign Offices may overwhelm us, as they have done, with White Papers and Orange Books and Blue Books[5] contradicting the Liberal fable in every letter and on every page; and the Germans may flood America with facsimiles of the documents they found in Brussels proving that the violation of Belgium was foreseen and has been provided against (very properly) by us for eight years past: that is, from the moment when the Liberal Party came into power in 1906 [December 1905] and let Sir Edward Grey loose on foreign affairs; but the Liberal papers will still hail

---

in Parliament the speech made by Grey, being reported in *The Times* the next day (in the third person) as saying that 'the speech of the Foreign Secretary showed that what had been rankling all these years was a deep animosity against Germany, in which the balance of power was responsible . . . He regretted, he said, the tone of the Foreign Secretary's speech, believing there was still a ray of hope'.

4. The United States Government, in a publicly issued note on 26 December 1914, criticized His Majesty's Government for a policy constituting 'restrictions . . . on the high seas which are not justified by the rules of international law or required under the principle of self-preservation' (US Department of State, *Papers relating to the Foreign Relations of the United States, Supplement*, 1914, pp. 372–5 (Washington, 1928?).

5. Officially issued documents of the war participants were paper-bound in a wide variety of colours. British Government publications were bound in blue, French in yellow, Russian in orange, German in white, Belgian in grey.

every document (knowing that the public will not read it) with brazen assurances that it proves the precise opposite of what it says, and that the Huns have now indeed been exposed and Peace once more justified in her friend the Foreign Secretary.

And now comes the question: Why should not the Labor Party accept this convenient fiction, and patriotically help to save the face of the Liberal leaders? Why need Mr [Archibald] Fenner Brockway[6] come along with his pamphlet, Is Britain Blameless? to give the Liberal show away and set the Kaiser chuckling? Does not patriotism consist mainly in covering your own country with fictitious whitewash, and the enemy with fictitious soot?

The answer is that it is impossible to hide the proceedings of Mr Asquith and Sir Edward Grey. They are now avowed by themselves and completely published and documented before the whole world; and as the world has not the Liberal partisan reason for shutting its eyes and ears, it is silly to repeat stories that nobody believes. Even at home there is, outside the Liberal Party, no future for the Liberal fable. The Unionists, who are Imperialists almost to a man, glory in the war as an Imperialist war, and will go to the country on the proud plea that it was the support they pledged to Mr Asquith that saved England when he could not trust his Liberals to stand by him when the hour struck for executing the great Imperialist plan to prevent Germany from mastering Europe and reducing us to a third-rate Power.

Among the Labor members the fable is vehemently denounced except by those who are mere Liberal partisans; and the voices of these are practically inaudible because nobody will listen to a man who is neither an official Liberal nor an interesting (because original and independent) Labor champion. In short, the fable is not only incredible but contemptible; for everyone despises the fabulist (to put it politely) who does not tell a good one when he is about it.

Now for the harm the fable does. Unless the neutral nations can be persuaded to believe it, it must seem to them the most paltry hypocrisy; and as the Germans have nothing to do but quote our own official documents and the speeches of the two ministers concerned to knock it into a cocked hat, they will steadily gain on us if we are not as bluntly candid as [Theobald von] Bethmann-Hollweg [German Chancellor, 1909–

---

6. Socialist leader and journalist, who was General Secretary of the Independent Labour Party and author of *Inside the Left* (1942).

17] himself. If it were not that most of the pro-Germans in America have been as childish as the pro-British with their pleas of Injured Innocence, they would have damaged us seriously in American eyes, though the Americans have been so strongly biased against Germany by their horror at the devastation of Belgium that Sir Edward Grey might quite safely have replied to the American note by "My Dear Wilson: You may tell your Copper Kings to go to Jericho, for the American people will never let you turn on us until we have shifted the Huns out of Belgium." But we can wear down even that sympathy if we persist in talking hypocritical nonsense with so clever an advocate as Dr Bernhard Dernburg[7] there to take advantage of every lapse we make from the popular line of the bluffest, frankest, bravest candor. The writers who nag, and snivel, and recriminate, and self-righteously proclaim our moral superiority to our enemies would do us less harm if they put on *pickelhaubes* [spiked helmets] and served in the German trenches against us.

That is why we had better know the worst of ourselves and admit it before we open our own case, which is quite presentable as an Imperialist case, and overwhelming as a democratic case. Every litigant who brings a case to a solicitor is convinced that the strong points in his favor are those which make him out to be a saint and his opponent a mean sneak. And every lawyer has to break gently to his client that these cherished points would only set the judge and jury against him, and that the case as it must go into court is much less flattering to himself. And the litigant thinks his lawyer grossly unjust and inappreciative, and submits with a very bad grace. Just so in this international case, all the belligerent nations kick hard against the impartial unflattering truth as it must be put to the neutral nations, and think it infamously unpatriotic of the Fenner Brockways and other sane spokesmen not to concentrate themselves wholly on their client's blamelessness and their opponents' wickedness. Nevertheless, the counsel who resolutely clears his brief of unsound claims is the one who gets a verdict on the sound ones.

At all events whoever reads this pamphlet will not fall into the mistake of arguing with the pro-Germans like a pettish governess scolding a dirty little boy. He will know that our diplomacy has been no better and no worse than that of our neighbors, though, as we outwitted the Germans on the point of our intentions, we may perhaps claim to have played the game

---

7. German-Jewish economist and politician, a leading member of the German Democratic Party and vigorous defender of the Government's colonial policies.

more cunningly. And he will not force the point about the Scrap of Paper[8] when he understands what very pretty play Dr Dernburg could make with the Act of Algeciras,[9] which we tore up in the face of Germany when she was piously defending the guaranteed independence of Morocco.

It is only too easy to trump up a moral case against all these manœuvres of our aristocratic secret diplomacy; for aristocracy, in England as in Germany, has no middle-class morals, and only gets itself and us into trouble when it pretends to have them for the sake of the middle-class vote. When the vote at stake is not the middle-class vote, but that of the neutral nations, the Foreign Office must take its proper aristocratic, super-moral, Imperialist ground. On that it can shew to considerable advantage to its natural Jingo supporters, especially when it is successful in the field; but to the rest of us it can appeal only by being brave and frank and chivalrous, and not pretending to be better than its own caste abroad, at war or in peace.

8. Britain and Germany were signatories to the 1839 Treaty of London, maintaining the independence of Belgium, which Germany violated by its invasion of Belgium in 1914. When Britain came to the defence of Belgium, declaring war on Germany, the latter's chancellor, Theobald von Bethmann–Hollweg, asserted that Britain had entered the war 'just for a scrap of paper'.
9. The Algeciras Conference (16 January–7 April 1906) was an international meeting held at Germany's insistence to regulate intervention by Spain and France in the internal affairs of Morocco. When in 1911 a French military expedition to Fez prompted Germany to send a gunboat to the port of Agadir, Britain supported France in a speech by Lloyd George. The Germans were forced to withdraw. The crisis strengthened the Anglo-French *entente cordiale*.

Common Sense about the War

Preface to an aborted second edition (1915) of Shaw's polemic, Common Sense about the War, *1914. The preface 'A Word Concerning the 1915 Reprint' is hitherto unpublished*

━━━━

At the risk of having this little volume cast aside contemptuously with the remark, "Why, I saw all this in The Times months ago," I reprint it exactly as it appeared in November 1914 as a supplement to The New Statesman. In that ephemeral form it held the market for six months as a back number. But there is a limit to back number business; and the supply had to be cut off in April. The demand, however, has continued; and it has now become desirable that it should be complied with, for the following reasons.

When Common Sense about the War first appeared, the Germans apparently recognized that in making them a present of the easily answered electioneering official case for the war, and stating the real case for it stripped of every controvertible pretext, I had shewn the weakness of their position as the breakers of the peace of the west of Europe. At all events, I was denounced in the German papers in unmeasured terms, and privately informed that my flourishing career as a popular playwright in Germany was finished for ever by the single word "Potsdamnation."[1] But the Germans found, no doubt to their surprise, that this achievement of mine, far from being appreciated by the British Press, was being frantically denounced here as "Pro-German." To do our enemies justice, they seized their advantage very intelligently. They took the war-demoralized section of the British Press at its word, and claimed me as on their side. And the

---

1. In *Common Sense about the War* Shaw attacked the 'junkers' and Militarists on both sides of the fray, insisting that 'we just simply want to put an end to Potsdamnation, both at home and abroad'. Asquith and Grey, he said, 'want England to out-Potsdam Potsdam and to monopolize the command of the seas: a monstrous aspiration'. Potsdam, centre of Prussian militarism, sixteen miles from Berlin, was the home of the Great Elector, Frederick William I, who was initially responsible, in the seventeenth century, for the development of Germany's strong military machine. See also Shaw's letter to Siegfried Trebitsch, 22 August 1919, in *Collected Letters 1911–1925* (1985).

section aforesaid saw in this a confirmation of its own judgment, and supported the German contention with all its might, evidently believing that it was doing its country an important service. Now this did not greatly matter whilst Common Sense was on sale and in active circulation, as it was speaking for itself. But when it went out of print the misrepresentations began to gain on the truth. The Germans, with a sense of my influence which is very flattering to me, persisted in their claim; and our war-struck journalists, without any sense at all, helped them with heart-broken ravings. In the end they succeeded in persuading a considerable number of people who attach importance to my opinion that I am a declared partisan of Potsdam in this conflict. I do not propose to waste time in arguing with panic; but, as there has been a considerable recovery during the last six months, I put it to the convalescents that if I am an important person, it is hardly wise to advertize me as a Pro-German and thereby discourage recruiting and set up troubles of conscience among those whose belief in me constitutes my importance; and if I am a negligible person it is hardly good sense to waste quarts of ink in giving me a manufactured prominence hardly second to that of the Kaiser himself.

The net result is that I am compelled to launch Common Sense in a more accessible form than before in order that the public may have the opportunity of learning at first hand what I really said. Not, of course, that such a consideration would have moved me if the work of Common Sense had been done. But in some quarters it has hardly been begun. It is true that the horrible paralyzed fear lest a word of common sense should betray us to the Hun, which I broke through with such startling effect, no longer prevails, and has indeed been succeeded by a clamor against the Cabinet, the General Staff, the War Office, the Foreign Office, the Exchequer, and the Trade Unions, so reckless that I sometimes wonder whether I had not better have left undisturbed in full shout the old chorus of British self-congratulation on our possession of the greatest ministers, the ablest generals, the most united and devoted nation, and the most absolute certainty of victory ever combined in human history. When men are terrified, they either assure each other with knocking knees that all is well, or shriek that all is lost. Now I did not write Common Sense merely to change the first cry into the last. All was not well, as the exposure of the shortage of shells soon shewed; but to cry that all was lost was ridiculous. We were in the strongest position in Europe, and have been growing relatively stronger ever since; and yet to this day we have absurd professors talking about "the agony of their country." One friend of mine who is a professional rhetorician gravely told me that England was his mother, and that I had kicked her on her deathbed [Henry Arthur Jones's letter to Shaw, 1 November 1915, in *Collected Letters 1911–1925*].

Now I do not want to trample too brutally on the childish romance that delights in figuring one's country as a persecuted, abandoned, duped, betrayed heroine, or as the little sailor in the melodrama fighting at fearful odds against a treacherous giant. There is a time for such cinematographic indulgences. But it is not war time.

It cannot be affirmed too clearly and sternly that England did not betray her allies by failing to meet her engagements to them, or by blindly and lazily allowing herself to be caught napping by the German army. We had virtually pledged ourselves to France to fight for her; and when the moment came we redeemed our pledge and went far beyond its obligations. We were prepared to the utmost possibility of preparation. The navy was ready, with five years' accumulation of ammunition. The expeditionary force was ready, with a commander [Field Marshal (Sir) John French] virtually appointed five years before, who had been studying the field in Flanders during that time. More than that we had not undertaken; as much as that we carried out without a hitch; and it is monstrous that we should be dishonored, and the seeds of dissension between us and our French ally sown broadcast to please the romantic fancies of our least-instructed patriots, and to save the countenances of Ministers whose replies to questions in the House of Commons before the war fell short of the candor which denotes perfect confidence. Even in peace time playing to the gallery is one of the most dangerous abuses of democracy: in war time it renders direct services to the enemy. For example, Lord Haldane, to whose knowledge of Germany and reorganization of our military system our preparedness was due, and whose capacity for state affairs and disinterestedness of personal character raise him high above the party hacks, the ambitious political adventurers, and inconsecutively minded, jury-humbugging barristers, who act as political solicitors to the Sparklers and Barnacles and Stiltstalkings [all in Dickens's *Little Dorrit*] who still expect complimentary tickets for our Cabinets, is deliberately sacrificed by a Government which has to acknowledge, when it has succeeded in persuading the public that Lord Haldane is all but a German spy, that his services have been "inestimable," and that the Foreign Office would be much the better for his counsel. Blacker national ingratitude, worse faith among political colleagues, a more pitiful truckling to the rabble which sees in war only an excuse for misbehaving itself under pretence of patriotism, can hardly be conceived as possible. Small wonder that Mr Winston Churchill, who also did his share in the preparation for the war, and never condescended to appeal for electoral sympathy as Germany's dupe and England's fool, shook the dust of Parliament off his feet, and went to the trenches, realizing that it was there and not among the politicians, that the war would be won and lost.[2]

My pamphlet has, therefore, still its work to do in getting rid of this silly and dishonorable travesty of the most formidable empire on earth as the feeble and credulous dupe of a stage villain. It has its complement in another legend with which we love to terrify ourselves: that is, the legend of the invincible Prussian army. The Germans have themselves to thank for this popular delusion. For years their officers have taken a childish delight in describing to us the marvelous perfection of their military organization. They have told us across every dinner table how their place was appointed, and even the places of their wives and daughters, so providently and exactly that at a word every wheel and lever of the mighty machine would mobilize into its place, and mow down all Europe as it moved to its objective, whether it were Paris (in a fortnight), or Petrograd, or Constantinople, or London. As I was a student of Ibsen, and familiar with the history of Peer Gynt, "otherwise Human Life's Emperor" [Act 4, Scene 9], I listened with indulgence when this wonderful box of toy soldiers was opened and its millions arrayed on the tablecloth for our entertainment by the German imagination, always so fond of *Märchen*, or fairy stories. Others, unteachable by Ibsen, believed and trembled. Meanwhile, if you asked an English officer what would happen in England if war broke out, he would shrug his shoulders and reply, "The Lord only knows," implying that there would be an appalling mess. Thereby showing that he had a very fair grasp of the realities of the case.

Accordingly, when war actually did break out, the British military and naval forces mobilized without a hitch in very reasonable time; and the human and fallible reality which had been concealed by the idealized Prussian box of toys made a wild rush for Paris, and arrived before the redoubtable Brialmont fortifications of Liège without siege guns, in which amateurish predicament it was held up for a fortnight by the little Belgian army, and, through that delay, probably lost the war.[3] Even when the

---

2. Churchill resigned from the Cabinet in November 1915 (after being demoted from First Lord of the Admiralty, because of the disastrous Dardanelles campaign, to Chancellor of the Duchy of Lancaster), taking a military commission to command a battalion. Openly critical of the Government, he publicly revealed Kitchener's unsatisfactory performance as Secretary of State for War.

3. At the outset of the war, when the German Army invaded Belgium, Liège was the first town to come under attack. It required nearly two weeks of fierce fighting

indispensable guns—known for years beforehand to be indispensable—at last arrived, they were Austrian guns. In short, the Germans were the only belligerents who were unprepared except in their own imaginations, just as we were the only ones who were prepared, with the same ridiculous exception. A little later, the wonderful intelligence department of the box of toys was tested, with the result that the German army was held up before Antwerp for ten days by a handful of devoted horse marines, whom it could have annihilated in ten minutes had it only known. It must not be concluded that the German army is any the less formidable because these lessons have driven it sternly from romance to reality: quite the contrary; but at all events it has left one legend the less for our *gobemouches* [simpletons or boobs] to frighten themselves with.

I may now leave Common Sense to its new readers with the following reminders.

1. As the accident of my being a much-translated playwright has secured me the attention of foreign audiences, Common Sense was written with a constant view to its effect abroad, and especially in Germany, Sweden, and America, without the smallest consideration for the feelings of those readers at home who, when they come upon any writing that does not flatter them and confirm all the outrageous nonsense they are sure to have been talking, repudiate it furiously as unpatriotic.

2. When Common Sense was issued, I knew, though the public as yet did not, that our searching of American and Swedish trading vessels and occasional confiscations of their cargoes, had led to strained relations with those countries, and that it was of great importance that the Americans should have some relief from the irritating anthems in our own praise with which we accompanied our seizures of their copper, and that the Swedes, very nervous about Russia, and with a German queen [Victoria of Baden, consort of Gustav VI] to take advantage of that nervousness, should have some assurance that our military alliance with Russia did not imply the smallest sympathy with the ultra-Prussian methods of the Russian autocracy in Finland and elsewhere. The Germans, remember, had not then been landed in the stupendous blunder of the *Lusitania* disaster [British passenger liner, sunk by a German submarine off the coast of Ireland, 7 May 1915] by their obvious incapacity to control their own navy.

3. Our anti-German propagandists of the last ten years had not then

---

(4–16 August 1914) for the Germans (who had blundered by bringing up field guns instead of siege guns) to defeat the local forces, seriously delaying its advance.

republished all their articles with triumphant cries of "We told you so," and thereby cruelly gravelled the patriots who had madly contradicted any admission of the existence of such a propaganda.

4. Lord Haldane [Lord Chancellor, 1912–15] and Mr Churchill [First Lord of the Admiralty, 1911–15], as the ministers in whose hands England's security had lain, had not then vindicated themselves and our national honor by declaring that we had been vigilant and provident in the face of a well-foreseen danger of war for years past, and that when the war came we were prepared for it as far as such preparation was humanly and politically possible.

5. Mr Bonar Law had not then revealed the secret compact made with him and Lord Lansdowne by Mr Asquith, the terms of which bound the Unionists during the war to support Mr Asquith[4] against his own party, if necessary, Mr Asquith engaging in return to drop the anti-Unionist items in his party's program. This revelation, with the coalition which it made inevitable, and the practical abrogation of the Factory Acts and of our constitutional safeguards of liberty and democracy which followed it, were still in the future.

6. The records of our arrangements for military cooperation with Belgium in the event of a war had not then been published by the Germans; and the Brussels correspondence of the Belgian ministers in London, Paris and Berlin, published later on, were equally unknown. My knowledge of them was like the astronomer [John C.] Adams's knowledge of the planet Neptune:[5] I knew from the forces at work and the situation that there must be something there, as neither we nor the Belgians are imbeciles; but I could not point to any documents. None the less, I felt the extreme unwisdom of forcing the note of virtuous indignation on the neutrality question with the Germans in command of the Brussels pigeon holes, and did what I could to induce our superior persons to dismount from that

---

4. The Unionists Bonar Law and Henry Petty-Fitzmaurice, Fifth Marquess of Lansdowne, were respectively opposition leaders of the House of Commons and the House of Lords. On 2 August 1914, even before the fateful decision to declare war had been made by the Liberals, the Unionists fulfilled their secret-compact commitment when Law wrote to Asquith to tender to him the 'unhesitating support' of the Opposition in any measure necessary. (Shaw, *What I Really Wrote about the War*, 1930.) Asquith confirmed this in his memoirs: 'Bonar Law writes that the Opposition will back us up in any measure we may take for the support of France and Russia' (*Memories and Reflections 1852–1927*, 1928, Vol. II, p. 12).
5. Deduced mathematically the existence and location of the planet Neptune.

high horse, suspecting that he would prove a buckjumper. But I had no evidence. The diplomatic correspondence, by the way, is interesting and rather amusing; and the British and French Governments will be ill-advised if they attempt to suppress it.

7. The overwhelming documentation and elaboration of my statements as to our diplomacy which have since appeared, notably in The Candid Review, and day by day in The Times and other journals during the violent reaction against the Government and the General Staff which followed the discovery of the shortage of ammunition, also in the French Orange Book[6] and other foreign and domestic official publications, did not take place until a great deal of ink had been wasted in attempts to demonstrate that my statements were wild and malicious inventions. I regret to have to add that no one has since apologized to me.

With these points in mind, the reader will not be surprised or irritated by the belated air given to my pages by their paucity in evidence which is now superabundant, and their perhaps overtimid criticism in matters now being angrily discussed in stentorian rhetoric by the ultrawarlike papers. If I be asked why I have not brought my Common Sense up to date, I must reply that I have actually done so,[7] but have decided to keep the results to myself for the present, partly because a good deal has already been done independently by other writers, and partly because so much of the work of the newspaper press is recklessly left to journalists who are much less qualified to handle the European situation than an average Margate tripper to handle the British fleet, that as I do not wish Potsdam to win this war, I deliberately refrain from giving them fresh opportunities of making senseless mischief. Let it suffice to add here a serious warning that as the strain of the war increases, as it must even with the most exhilarating successes, our preoccupations with our own tedious moral attitudes and love of lecturing people on their behavior, will become more and more mischievous, because the effect it produces abroad is one of selfish insular indifference to the point of view and the interests of other nations. Germany, luckily for us, has put herself wrong with America and Sweden, if she has not exactly

---

6. Shaw misrecalled the colour. The *French Yellow Book*, a volume of official documents comprising the diplomatic correspondence preceding the outbreak of war, was published by *The Times*, in translation, in extracts on 1 December 1914 and in full as a Supplement on 19 December.
7. Shaw had completed *More Common Sense about the War*; it was never published. There are shorthand and typescript manuscripts in the British Library: Add. MSS 50699A,B and 63179–80.

put us right with them; but she cannot do us this service with our allies. Our good understanding with France is of supreme importance to both countries. Unfortunately, both Governments are making the mistake of trying to maintain it by using the censorship to prevent the publication of any news that could possibly agitate this understanding. The result, of course, is an atmosphere of suspicion in which the French public, deprived of news, fills up the void by its imagination. For example, our censorship has suppressed all information as to the abuses of the Munitions Act[8] in the interest of the employers, and as to the strikes and disturbances to which the abuses have led. The French would understand these disturbances and sympathize with them as quickly as any people in the world; but they are left to believe that our workers are drunkards and slackers, and that we are prolonging the war at the expense of France, for the sake of capturing German trade, instead of having to fight for our own industrial liberties as well as for the national liberties of Europe. This is only one sample of the mischief that is being done by trying to hide the actual events of the day, and mostly failing because events can seldom be effectively hidden; but unfortunately succeeding in hiding the explanation and discussion of the events, thus leaving them open to the most undesirable interpretations.

I wish I could persuade the two Cabinets that the most awkward human realities do less mischief than the sugariest idealizations and inventions when they proceed from imaginations maddened by war.

November, 1915.   G.B.S.

8. The Munitions of War Act became law five months earlier, at the start of July 1915.

Why a Labor Year Book?
(The Labour Year Book)

First published in 1916

A Labor Year Book will not need any justification to those who have thought the matter out in the light of some experience of the difficulty of finding just the sort of facts they want. They all know the story of the cabinet minister who asked one of his officials to supply him with the statistics of a certain department. To which the young gentleman replied "What is it you want to prove?"

In politics, all facts are selected facts. If you want a book of unselected facts you must buy a Ready Reckoner [a collection of tables supplying results of arithmetical calculations] or the Post Office Directory. They deal with a class of fact that nobody wants to suppress or misrepresent, and that nobody can overlook. The compiler of the Ready Reckoner does not tell you that twice two is four and then forget to tell you that twice three is six. The compiler of the Directory does not give you the name of his friend who lives at number nine and scorn to mention his enemy who lives at number ten. But the moment we come to books in which information is not only given but applied, take care! An election register is very like a directory: it consists of names and addresses only; but it is far from being so trustworthy a document. There are people who ought to be there who are not there: there are people who ought not to be there who are there. Statements of the proportion of taxation borne by the working classes, or of the distribution of income in the country, may be as sound in their simple arithmetic as the Ready Reckoner; but Mr [W. H.] Mallock will bring out a very different result to Mr Sidney Webb every time.

This does not mean that one writer is less truthful than another. It means only that one writer notices things that another overlooks. The human mind is like the human eye. The eye makes a double image of everything except the object the owner of the eye is looking at; but he never notices the double images of all the other objects in sight: he notices only the single one to which he is directing his attention. He never sees a double image in all his life if he is a teetotaler, though he has dozens of them on his retina daily from dawn to dark. It is the same with his mind: he thinks of nothing except the things he focuses his mind on. The idle gentleman understands that the burglar who comes after his spoons is a thief; but he does not understand that he himself bought those spoons out of money stolen from the poor. He sees all the faults of the Labor Party, and none of the faults of the House of Lords. He thinks it splendid and heroic of his son to take a commission and go into the trenches, but takes it quite as a matter of course that his gardener's son should go.

To put it another way, the very honestest man has an unfair mind, and eyes that can see only one side of an object at a time. And that is why Labor must have its own Year Book. There are others, of course. The Statesman's Year Book [a reference book containing historical and statistical information on 'the states of the world'] is as good in its way as the Labor Year Book, and ten times as dear. Whitaker's Almanack [a compendium of general information, akin to the American *World Almanac*] has been the friend of man for many years. But the Statesman's Year Book sees life from the social angle of an Oxford College; and Whitaker has to please everybody and offend nobody. A proper Labor Year Book ought to set all the Oxford Colleges clamoring for its prosecution on a charge of sedition, and to make half the purchasers of Whitaker go blue in the face with indignation. It ought to give all the information that our rich men and their caterers and retainers try to hide from themselves and everybody else, and signpost all the new political roads that democracy has opened to the public, and that used to be closed by boards declaring that Trespassers Will be Prosecuted.

Labor has still a good deal to learn as to facts and ways and means. It does not know the facts. It does not know where to look for them. It could not always get at them even if it did know where to look. Many of its notions of democracy are too crude and general and oldfashioned for practical use; and it often drops the substance in clutching at the shadow. In making Trade Unionism the most jealously democratic institution in the world, it made it in some respects the most autocratic; for it is the simple truth that it used to be easier to turn the whole country against the Prime Minister than to turn a Trade Union against its officials; and the end of that has been a reaction in which officials are hampered in making industrial treaties because they cannot answer for their Unions with sufficient confidence. The Labor world is stuffed with splendid principles; but principles by themselves are very little use. A cockney may wish to take a walk on Wimbledon Common on sound hygienic principles; but if he does not know the way to

Putney[1] he will not get there, and may have to take his constitutional in a slum. It is true that when there is a will there is a way; but the way is through knowledge; and it is surprising how often it lies just in the opposite direction to where we expected to find it. Fortunately it is also sometimes much shorter than we imagined it to be. Very few people know how much has been done already; and we find well-meaning people spending no end of their time and slender means in agitating for laws that already exist; founding schools to teach what is already better taught in the elementary school round the corner; and calling on Parliament to do things that the County Council or City Corporation has had power to do for the last fifty years.

The reason people dont know these things is that nobody tells them. Our governing class mostly does not want them to know. They teach a child the population of China (which they dont know themselves) but take good care to leave him in ignorance of the fact that by sending a postcard to the Home Office or to the local sanitary authority he can strike down tyrants, and dig up drains, and fence in machines, and add years to the lives of women and pounds to the weight of children.

The Labor Year Book is a move in the direction of dispelling this ignorance, and shewing the workers the world from their own point of view instead of from that of their present masters. It is not yet so good as the editors wish and intend it to be. It is not possible to think of everything, and still less possible to do everything that is thought of. You have first to find the right man to do it, and pay him fairly for the job. The war has upset the Year Book as it has upset everything else. Without a good deal of valuable unpaid work it could not have been done at all. No commercial publisher would have ventured on so magnanimous a table of contents. It is not what it will be after a year or two: still, it is a beginning, and not so bad a one, all things considered.

Its improvement will depend largely on those who use it. To them I say, Do not waste time admiring what you find in it: spend a few hours in the year complaining of what you miss in it. The man who writes up to the office to say that it is the rottenest Year Book going because he cannot find the name of his grandmother's third husband in it is the man who will really help us. If he thinks that his grandmother's third husband has nothing to do with the Labor Movement, he may be making a great mistake. What he wants to know, another man may want to know; and if

1. Wimbledon Common and Putney Heath combine to form a residential recreation area in south-west London.

we find by the letters we get that there is a need in the Labor Movement for a table of the third husbands of the grandmothers of the Labor Movement, we shall compile such a table without stopping to ask the use of it, because men neither want nor ask for things that are of no use. "Ask and it shall be given unto you" [Matthew 7: 7] is our editorial principle. We will guess all we can about your wants; but our main standby must be the men who tell us of the bits of information they needed in the Trade Union or Co-operative office and in the Labor candidate's committee room, and which they could not find anywhere. The world is full of books telling us what we do not want to know: the ideal of the editors of the Labor Year Book is a book that will tell its purchasers what they do want to know, and what no other book will tell them.

Androcles and the Lion

I

Prefatory note, in the programme of the St James's Theatre, London, 1 September 1913

=====

The version of the old story of Androcles and the Lion to be played tonight at the St James's Theatre is not hampered by a pedantic retention of the details as given by Aulus Gellius.[1] His Androcles was called Androclus, and Androclus was neither a Greek nor a tailor nor a Christian, but a Roman slave who ran away from the cruelties of his master and was later on captured and condemned to be devoured by wild beasts in the arena. But it happened that during his flight he had taken refuge in a cave; and into this cave came a lion who had a thorn in his paw which Androclus extracted. It was to this very lion that Androclus was afterwards thrown in the arena; and the lion, instead of eating him, caressed him. The story figured in natural histories like those of Aelian and was found to please children, in whose story books it has appeared ever since. Nobody believes it; though everybody believes much more improbable stories. It would be incredible of some lions just as the action of Androclus would be incredible of some men. But there are lions and lions, just as there are men and men. The author of the present version has petted a full-grown lion and had his advances received with much more cordiality than he could expect from most St Bernard dogs. He conceives the lion of Androclus to have been just such a fearless and amiable creature. He conceives Androclus as having that fellow feeling for animals which it becomes the most highly evolved of animals to have (Man is your real king of beasts) and which enables some men to handle bees without being stung and snakes without being bitten. Given such a pair, there is nothing incredible in the story except the theatrical coincidence of the meeting of the two in the arena. Such coincidences are privileged on the stage, and are the special delight of this particular author. And really, when one considers how many men met

1. Second-century AD Roman writer, author of *Noctes Atticae*.

lions in the arena from first to last, it is not too much to ask you to believe that just for once they turned out to be old friends.

If the author is asked why he has made Androcles a Christian, he can only ask why not. St Francis preached to the birds as to his "little brothers"; and St Francis was a Christian. St Anthony preached to the fishes, who probably understood at least as much of his sermon as a modern fashionable congregation would have done; and St Anthony was a Christian. Depend on it, Androcles had that root of the religious matter in him which made all religions free to him except the religion of hunting and killing. That is, the religion of the English country house.

But the XX century Christian need not regard the Christianity of the early Christian martyrs as having much to do with his safe and eminently respectable Sunday profession of faith. Christians in those days were neither safe nor respectable. What is more, some of the most eminent Christians were by no means fond of the average Christians of their time. The author once asked an old Owenite Socialist why he had given up Socialism. He replied that after preaching it for some years he had noticed that it seemed to have a very bad effect on the moral character of those who gave themselves up to its propaganda. The same may be said of all persecuted creeds. A doctrine may be true and important, and its persecutors may be altogether in the wrong; but this makes the position of the man who is persecuted for propagating it all the more morbid. One sane man in a lunatic asylum can no more keep his normal health and temper than one lunatic in a *conseil de prudhommes* [conciliation board]. Add to this consideration the fact that all movements which attack the existing state of society attract both the people who are not good enough for the world and the people for whom the world is not good enough; so that the saint is always embarrassed by finding that the dynamiter and the assassin, the thief and the libertine, make common cause with him; and you will not be surprised to learn, if you do not know it already, that early Christians like Saint Augustine have a good many stories to tell of Christians who thoroughly deserved their evil reputation. The character of Spintho in the present play is by no means a malicious invention of the author's. Indeed had he gone on to exhibit Spintho as having taken the precaution to marry an orthodox Roman in order to shirk the Christian obligation to practise Communism, and as ostentatiously giving the lady black eyes to shew how his conjugal duties revolted his ascetic nature, there would have been warrant for that too, and worse, in the records of the Fathers of the Church.

In representing a Roman centurion and a Roman captain (a pure invention) as corresponding to a British sergeant and a British company officer, some violence may or may not have been done to the petty accuracies of military history. Centurions were much chaffed in Rome as being mostly thick-booted vulgar persons, whacking their men with vine-wood cudgels, and out of place in refined society; and the nearest thing to a modern captain as far as rank was concerned was probably not much more of a patrician. The patrician soldier was not a professional soldier: he commanded armies or adorned Senates or governed provinces as part of the natural pursuits of a patrician. But the relation of patrician officer to plebeian routineer existed as it exists today; and whether my captain should have been called something else, or my Centurion a Decurion, does not trouble me any more than the old controversy as to whether the audience turned their thumbs up or down when they wanted a defeated gladiator slain.

In short, if you demand my authorities for this and that, I must reply that only those who have never hunted up the authorities as I have believe that there is any authority who is not contradicted flatly by some other authority. Marshal [Andoche] Junot, reproached for having no respect for ancestry, said that he was an ancestor himself.[2] In the same spirit I point out that the authorities on the story of Androcles and on the history of the early Christian martyrs are the people who have written about them; and now that I, too, have written about them, I take my place as the latest authority on the subject and ask you to respect me accordingly.

G. B. S.

2. French general who commanded the forces that invaded Portugal in the Peninsular War and who conquered Lisbon (1807), only to be defeated by Wellington the following year. Upon being created Duc d'Abrantes in 1807, he is alleged to have replied to a member of the old aristocracy who caustically asked him to identify his ancestors, 'I am my own ancestor.'

Preface on the Prospects of Christianity

Preface to Androcles and the Lion, *first published in 1916*

======

WHY NOT GIVE CHRISTIANITY A TRIAL?

The question seems a hopeless one after 2000 years of resolute adherence to the old cry of "Not this man, but Barabbas." Yet it is beginning to look as if Barabbas was a failure, in spite of his strong right hand, his victories, his empires, his millions of money, and his moralities and churches and political constitutions. "This man" has not been a failure yet; for nobody has ever been sane enough to try his way. But he has had one quaint triumph. Barabbas has stolen his name and taken his cross as a standard. There is a sort of compliment in that. There is even a sort of loyalty in it, like that of the brigand who breaks every law and yet claims to be a patriotic subject of the king who makes them. We have always had a curious feeling that though we crucified Christ on a stick, he somehow managed to get hold of the right end of it, and that if we were better men we might try his plan. There have been one or two grotesque attempts at it by inadequate people, such as the Kingdom of God in Munster,[1] which was

---

1. In 1534 Anabaptism took a firm hold in Münster, chief city of Westphalia, under the Dutch madman Jan Beuckleson (John of Leiden), self-proclaimed King of the New Zion, who envisioned Münster as destined to be 'the Heavenly Jerusalem'. The revolutionary Anabaptists controlled the city for more than a year until a siege by the army of Prince-Bishop Franz von Waldeck (Shaw's latter-day 'Annas') prevailed in mid 1535. On 22 January 1536 the fanatical leader and two principal cohorts Bernd Knipperdollinck and Bernhardt Krechting were tried as heretics, condemned and publicly tortured, tied to stakes, their flesh burned by hot iron and their tongues torn out, before they were executed by daggers piercing their hearts. Von Waldeck's extinction of the Kingdom of God and its 'Prophet' at Münster put an end to militant Anabaptism. Despite Shaw's dramatic claim that von Waldeck 'went home and died of horror', he appears to have survived for over twenty years, dying in 1557.

ended by a crucifixion so much more atrocious than the one on Calvary that the bishop who took the part of Annas went home and died of horror. But responsible people have never made such attempts. The moneyed, respectable, capable world has been steadily anti-Christian and Barabbasque since the crucifixion; and the specific doctrine of Jesus has not in all that time been put into political or general social practice. I am no more a Christian than Pilate was, or you, gentle reader; and yet, like Pilate, I greatly prefer Jesus to Annas and Caiaphas;[2] and I am ready to admit that after contemplating the world and human nature for nearly sixty years, I see no way out of the world's misery but the way which would have been found by Christ's will if he had undertaken the work of a modern practical statesman.

Pray do not at this early point lose patience with me and shut the book. I assure you I am as sceptical and scientific and modern a thinker as you will find anywhere. I grant you I know a great deal more about economics and politics than Jesus did, and can do things he could not do. I am by all Barabbasque standards a person of much better character and standing, and greater practical sense. I have no sympathy with vagabonds and talkers who try to reform society by taking men away from their regular productive work and making vagabonds and talkers of them too; and if I had been Pilate I should have recognized as plainly as he the necessity for suppressing attacks on the existing social order, however corrupt that order might be, by people with no knowledge of government and no power to construct political machinery to carry out their views, acting on the very dangerous delusion that the end of the world was at hand. I make no defence of such Christians as Savonarola[3] and John of Leyden: they were scuttling the ship before they had learned how to build a raft; and it became necessary to throw them overboard to save the crew. I say this to set myself right with respectable society; but I must still insist that if Jesus could have worked out the practical problems of a Communist constitution, an admitted obligation to deal with crime without revenge or punishment, and a full assumption by humanity of divine responsibilities, he would have conferred an incalculable benefit on mankind, because these distinctive demands of his are now turning out to be good sense and sound economics.

I say distinctive, because his common humanity and his subjection to time and space (that is, to the Syrian life of his period) involved his belief in many things, true and false, that in no way distinguish him from other

2. Both were Hebrew high priests of the Sadducee party at the time of Christ's crucifixion.
3. Italian monk and religious reformer, who was executed for heresy.

Syrians of that time. But such common beliefs do not constitute specific Christianity any more than wearing a beard, working in a carpenter's shop, or believing that the earth is flat and that the stars could drop on it from heaven like hailstones. Christianity interests practical statesmen now because of the doctrines that distinguished Christ from the Jews and the Barabbasques generally, including ourselves.

WHY JESUS MORE THAN ANOTHER?

I do not imply, however, that these doctrines were peculiar to Christ. A doctrine peculiar to one man would be only a craze, unless its comprehension depended on a development of human faculty so rare that only one exceptionally gifted man possessed it. But even in this case it would be useless, because incapable of spreading. Christianity is a step in moral evolution which is independent of any individual preacher. If Jesus had never existed (and that he ever existed in any other sense than that in which Shakespear's Hamlet existed has been vigorously questioned) Tolstoy would have thought and taught and quarreled with the Greek Church all the same.[4] Their creed has been fragmentarily practised to a considerable extent in spite of the fact that the laws of all countries treat it, in effect, as criminal. Many of its advocates have been militant atheists. But for some reason the imagination of white mankind has picked out Jesus of Nazareth as *the* Christ, and attributed all the Christian doctrines to him; and as it is the doctrine and not the man that matters, and, as, besides, one symbol is as good as another provided everyone attaches the same meaning to it, I raise, for the moment, no question as to how far the gospels are original, and how far they consist of Greek and Chinese interpolations. The record that Jesus said certain things is not invalidated by a demonstration that Confucius said them before him. Those who claim a literal divine paternity for him cannot be silenced by the discovery that the same claim was made for Alexander and Augustus. And I am not just now concerned with the credibility of the gospels as records of fact; for I am not acting as a detective, but turning our modern lights on to certain ideas and doctrines in them which disentangle themselves from the rest because they are flatly contrary to common practice,

---

4. During the Russo-Turkish War (1877–8) Tolstoy was filled with disgust on hearing Greek clergy praying for the destruction of the enemy. His attack on the Orthodox Church and defence of the Doukhobors in his novel *Resurrection* (1899) were probably the chief causes of his formal excommunication.

common sense, and common belief, and yet have, in the teeth of dogged incredulity and recalcitrance, produced an irresistible impression that Christ, though rejected by his posterity as an unpractical dreamer, and executed by his contemporaries as a dangerous anarchist and blasphemous madman, was greater than his judges.

WAS JESUS A COWARD?

I know quite well that this impression of superiority is not produced on everyone, even of those who profess extreme susceptibility to it. Setting aside the huge mass of inculcated Christ-worship which has no real significance because it has no intelligence, there is, among people who are really free to think for themselves on the subject, a great deal of hearty dislike of Jesus and of contempt for his failure to save himself and overcome his enemies by personal bravery and cunning as Mahomet did. I have heard this feeling expressed far more impatiently by persons brought up in England as Christians than by Mahometans, who are, like their prophet, very civil to Jesus, and allow him a place in their esteem and veneration at least as high as we accord to John the Baptist. But this British bulldog contempt is founded on a complete misconception of his reasons for submitting voluntarily to an ordeal of torment and death. The modern Secularist is often so determined to regard Jesus as a man like himself and nothing more, that he slips unconsciously into the error of assuming that Jesus shared that view. But it is quite clear from the New Testament writers (the chief authorities for believing that Jesus ever existed) that Jesus at the time of his death believed himself to be the Christ, a divine personage. It is therefore absurd to criticize his conduct before Pilate as if he were Colonel Roosevelt or Admiral [Alfred] von Tirpitz [German naval commander] or even Mahomet. Whether you accept his belief in his divinity as fully as Simon Peter did, or reject it as a delusion which led him to submit to torture and sacrifice his life without resistance in the conviction that he would presently rise again in glory, you are equally bound to admit that, far from behaving like a coward or a sheep, he shewed considerable physical fortitude in going through a cruel ordeal against which he could have defended himself as effectually as he cleared the moneychangers out of the temple. "Gentle Jesus, meek and mild" [by Charles Wesley] is a snivelling modern invention, with no warrant in the gospels. St Matthew would as soon have thought of applying such adjectives to Judas Maccabeus as to Jesus; and even St Luke, who makes Jesus polite and gracious, does not make him meek. The picture of him as an English curate of the farcical comedy type, too meek to fight a policeman, and everybody's butt, may be useful in the nursery to soften children; but that such a figure could ever have become a centre of the world's attention is too absurd for discussion: grown men and women may speak kindly of a harmless creature who utters amiable sentiments and is a helpless nincompoop when he is called on to defend them; but they will not follow him, nor do what he tells them, because they do not wish to share his defeat and disgrace.

WAS JESUS A MARTYR?

It is important therefore that we should clear our minds of the notion that Jesus died, as some of us are in the habit of declaring, for his social and political opinions. There have been many martyrs to those opinions; but he was not one of them, nor, as his words shew, did he see any more sense in martyrdom than Galileo did. He was executed by the Jews for the blasphemy of claiming to be a God; and Pilate, to whom this was a mere piece of superstitious nonsense, let them execute him as the cheapest way of keeping them quiet, on the formal plea that he had committed treason against Rome by saying that he was the King of the Jews. He was not falsely accused, nor denied full opportunities of defending himself. The proceedings were quite straightforward and regular; and Pilate, to whom the appeal lay, favored him and despised his judges, and was evidently willing enough to be conciliated. But instead of denying the charge, Jesus repeated the offence. He knew what he was doing: he had alienated numbers of his own disciples and been stoned in the streets for doing it before. He was not lying: he believed literally what he said. The horror of the High Priest was perfectly natural: he was a Primate confronted with a heterodox street preacher uttering what seemed to him an appalling and impudent blasphemy. The fact that the blasphemy was to Jesus a simple statement of fact, and that it has since been accepted as such by all western nations, does not invalidate the proceedings, nor give us the right to regard Annas and Caiaphas as worse men than the Archbishop of Canterbury and the Head Master of Eton. If Jesus had been indicted in a modern court, he would have been examined by two doctors; found to be obsessed by a delusion; declared incapable of pleading; and sent to an asylum: that is the whole difference. But please note that when a man is charged before a modern tribunal (to take a case that happened the other day) of having asserted and maintained that he was an officer returned from the front to receive the Victoria Cross at the hands of the King, although he was in fact a mechanic,[5] nobody thinks of treating him as afflicted with a delusion. He is punished for false pretences, because his assertion is credible and therefore misleading. Just so, the claim to divinity made by Jesus was to the High Priest, who looked forward to the coming of a Messiah, one that might conceivably have been true, and might therefore have misled the people in a very dangerous way. That was why he treated Jesus as an impostor and a blasphemer where we should have treated him as a madman.

THE GOSPELS WITHOUT PREJUDICE

All this will become clear if we read the gospels without prejudice. When I was young it was impossible to read them without fantastic confusion of thought. The confusion was so utterly confounded that it was called the proper spirit to read the Bible in. Jesus was a baby; and he was older than creation. He was a man who could be persecuted, stoned, scourged, and killed; and he was a god, immortal and all-powerful, able to raise the dead and call millions of angels to his aid. It was a sin to doubt either view of him: that is, it was a sin to reason about him; and the end was that you did not reason about him, and read about him only when you were compelled. When you heard the gospel stories read in church, or learnt them from painters and poets, you came out with an impression of their contents that would have astonished a Chinaman who had read the story without prepossession. Even sceptics who were specially on their guard, put the Bible in the dock, and read the gospels with the object of detecting discrepancies in the four narratives to shew that the writers were as subject to error as the writers of yesterday's newspaper.

All this has changed greatly within two generations. Today the Bible is so little read that the language of the Authorized Version is rapidly becoming obsolete; so that even in the United States, where the old tradition of the verbal infallibility of "the book of books" lingers more strongly than anywhere else except perhaps in Ulster, retranslations into modern English have been introduced perforce to save its bare intelligibility.[6]

5. Shaw alludes to Sam Rutherford, not a mechanic but a pattern maker, arrested in August 1915 for wearing the uniform of a Black Watch captain and military decorations. He informed the arresting officer that he was on his way to Buckingham Palace to receive the VC.

6. For instance, the *Twentieth Century New Testament* (1898–1901). There were also recent translations by R. E. Weymouth (1903) and James Moffatt (1913).

It is quite easy today to find cultivated persons who have never read the New Testament, and on whom therefore it is possible to try the experiment of asking them to read the gospels and state what they have gathered as to the history and views and character of Christ.

THE GOSPELS NOW UNINTELLIGIBLE TO NOVICES

But it will not do to read the gospels with a mind furnished only for the reception of, say, a biography of Goethe. You will not make sense of them, nor even be able without impatient weariness to persevere in the task of going steadily through them, unless you know something of the history of the human imagination as applied to religion. Not long ago I asked a writer of distinguished intellectual competence [William Archer] whether he had made a study of the gospels since his childhood. His reply was that he had lately tried, but "found it all such nonsense that I could not stick it." As I do not want to send anyone to the gospels with this result, I had better here give a brief exposition of how much of the history of religion is needed to make the gospels and the conduct and ultimate fate of Jesus intelligible and interesting.

WORLDLINESS OF THE MAJORITY

The first common mistake to get rid of is that mankind consists of a great mass of religious people and a few eccentric atheists. It consists of a huge mass of worldly people, and a small percentage of persons deeply interested in religion and concerned about their own souls and other people's; and this section consists mostly of those who are passionately affirming the established religion and those who are passionately attacking it, the genuine philosophers being very few. Thus you never have a nation of millions of [John] Wesleys and one Tom Paine. You have a million Mr Worldly Wisemans, one Wesley, with his small congregation, and one Tom Paine, with *his* smaller congregation. The passionately religious are a people apart; and if they were not hopelessly outnumbered by the worldly, they would turn the world upside down, as St Paul was reproached, quite justly, for wanting to do [Acts 17: 6–7]. Few people can number among their personal acquaintances a single atheist or a single Plymouth Brother. Unless a religious turn in ourselves has led us to seek the little Societies to which these rare birds belong, we pass our lives among people who, whatever creeds they may repeat, and in whatever temples they may avouch their respectability and wear their Sunday clothes, have robust consciences, and hunger and thirst, not for righteousness, but for rich feeding and comfort and social position and attractive mates and ease and pleasure and respect and consideration: in short, for love and money. To these people one morality is as good as another provided they are used to it and can put up with its restrictions without unhappiness; and in the maintenance of this morality they will fight and punish and coerce without scruple. They may not be the salt of the earth, these Philistines; but they are the substance of civilization; and they save society from ruin by criminals and conquerors as well as by Savonarolas and Knipperdollings. And as they know, very sensibly, that a little religion is good for children and serves morality, keeping the poor in goodhumor or in awe by promising rewards in heaven or threatening torments in hell, they encourage the religious people up to a certain point: for instance, if Savonarola only tells the ladies of Florence that they ought to tear off their jewels and finery and sacrifice them to God, they offer him a cardinal's hat, and praise him as a saint; but if he induces them to actually do it, they burn him as a public nuisance.

RELIGION OF THE MINORITY. SALVATIONISM

The religion of the tolerated religious minority has always been essentially the same religion: that is why its changes of name and form have made so little difference. That is why, also, a nation so civilized as the English can convert negroes to their faith with great ease, but cannot convert Mahometans or Jews. The negro finds in civilized Salvationism an unspeakably more comforting version of his crude creed; but neither Saracen nor Jew sees any advantage in it over his own version. The Crusader was surprised to find the Saracen quite as religious and moral as himself, and rather more than less civilized. The Latin Christian has nothing to offer the Greek Christian that Greek Christianity has not already provided. They are all, at root, Salvationists.

Let us trace this religion of Salvation from its beginnings. So many things that man does not himself contrive or desire are always happening: death, plagues, tempests, blights, floods, sunrise and sunset, growths and harvests and decay, and Kant's two wonders of the starry heavens above us and the moral law within us [*Fundamental Principles of the Metaphysic of Ethics*, 1785, tr. T. K. Abbott, 1895], that we conclude that somebody must be doing it all, or that somebody is doing the good and somebody else doing the evil, or that armies of invisible persons, beneficent and malevolent, are doing it; hence you postulate gods and devils, angels and demons. You propitiate these powers with presents, called sacrifices, and flatteries, called praises. Then the Kantian moral law within you makes you conceive your god as a judge; and straightway you try to corrupt him, also with presents and flatteries. This seems shocking to us; but our objection to it is quite a recent development: no longer ago than Shakespear's time it was thought quite natural that litigants should give presents to human judges; and the buying off of divine wrath by actual money payments to priests, or, in the reformed churches which discountenance this, by subscriptions to charities and church building and the like, is still in full swing. Its practical disadvantage is that though it makes matters very easy for the rich, it cuts off the poor from all hope of divine favor. And this quickens the moral criticism of the poor to such an extent, that they soon find the moral law within them revolting against the idea of buying off the deity with gold and gifts, though they are still quite ready to buy him off with the paper money of praise and professions of repentance. Accordingly, you will find that though a religion may last unchanged for many centuries in primitive communities where the conditions of life leave no room for poverty and riches, and the process of propitiating the supernatural powers is as well within the means of the least of the members as within those of the headman, yet when commercial civilization arrives, and capitalism divides the people into a few rich and a great many so poor that they can barely live, a movement for religious reform will arise among the poor, and will be essentially a movement for cheap or entirely gratuitous salvation.

To understand what the poor mean by propitiation, we must examine for a moment what they mean by justice.

THE DIFFERENCE BETWEEN ATONEMENT AND PUNISHMENT

The primitive idea of justice is partly legalized revenge and partly expiation by sacrifice. It works out from both sides in the notion that two blacks make a white, and that when a wrong has been done, it should be paid for by an equivalent suffering. It seems to the Philistine majority a matter of course that this compensating suffering should be inflicted on the wrongdoer for the sake of its deterrent effect on other would-be wrongdoers; but a moment's reflection will shew that this utilitarian application corrupts the whole transaction. For example, the shedding of innocent blood cannot be balanced by the shedding of guilty blood. Sacrificing a criminal to propitiate God for the murder of one of his righteous servants is like sacrificing a mangy sheep or an ox with the rinderpest [cattle-plague]: it calls down divine wrath instead of appeasing it. In doing it we offer God as a sacrifice the gratification of our own revenge and the protection of our own lives without cost to ourselves; and cost to ourselves is the essence of sacrifice and expiation. However much the Philistines have succeeded in confusing these things in practice, they are to the Salvationist sense distinct and even contrary. The Baronet's cousin in Dickens's novel, who, perplexed by the failure of the police to discover the murderer of the Baronet's solicitor, said "Far better hang wrong fellow than no fellow,"[7] was not only expressing a very common sentiment, but trembling on the brink of the rarer Salvationist opinion that it is much better to hang the wrong fellow: that, in fact, the wrong fellow is the right fellow to hang.

The point is a cardinal one, because until we grasp it not only does historical Christianity remain unintelligible to us, but those who do not care a rap about historical Christianity may be led into the mistake of supposing that if we discard revenge, and treat murderers exactly as God treated Cain: that is, exempt them from punishment by putting a brand on them as unworthy to be sacrificed, and let them face the world as best they can with that brand on them, we should get rid both of punishment and sacrifice. It would not at all follow: on the contrary, the feeling that there must be an expiation of the murder might quite possibly lead to our putting some innocent person—the more innocent the better—to a cruel death to balance the account with divine justice.

SALVATION AT FIRST A CLASS PRIVILEGE; AND THE REMEDY

Thus, even when the poor decide that the method of purchasing salvation by offering rams and goats or bringing gold to the altar must be wrong because they cannot afford it, we still do not feel "saved" without a sacrifice and a victim. In vain do we try to substitute mystical rites that cost nothing, such as circumcision, or, as a substitute for that, baptism. Our sense of justice still demands an expiation, a sacrifice, a sufferer for our sins. And this leaves the poor man still in his old difficulty; for if it was impossible for him to procure rams and goats and shekels, how much more

7. 'Far better hang wrong fler than no fler': the 'Debilitated Cousin' of the Dedlocks, with affected speech, offers 'the opinion' in *Bleak House*.

impossible is it for him to find a neighbor who will voluntarily suffer for his sins: one who will say cheerfully "You have committed a murder. Well, never mind: I am willing to be hanged for it in your stead"?

Our imagination must come to our rescue. Why not, instead of driving ourselves to despair by insisting on a separate atonement by a separate redeemer for every sin, have one great atonement and one great redeemer to compound for the sins of the world once for all? Nothing easier, nothing cheaper. The yoke is easy, the burden light [Matthew 11: 30]. All you have to do when the redeemer is once found (or invented by the imagination) is to believe in the efficacy of the transaction, and you are saved. The rams and goats cease to bleed; the altars which ask for expensive gifts and continually renewed sacrifices are torn down; and the Church of the single redeemer and the single atonement rises on the ruins of the old temples, and becomes a single Church of the Christ.

RETROSPECTIVE ATONEMENT; AND THE EXPECTATION OF THE REDEEMER

But this does not happen at once. Between the old costly religion of the rich and the new gratuitous religion of the poor there comes an interregnum in which the redeemer, though conceived by the human imagination, is not yet found. He is awaited and expected under the names of the Christ, the Messiah, Baldur the Beautiful [a Teutonic god], or what not; but he has not yet come. Yet the sinners are not therefore in despair. It is true that they cannot say, as we say, "The Christ has come, and has redeemed us" [Luke 1: 68]; but they can say "The Christ will come, and will redeem us," which, as the atonement is conceived as retrospective, is equally consoling. There are periods when nations are seething with this expectation and crying aloud with prophecy of the Redeemer through their poets. To feel that atmosphere we have only to take up the Bible and read Isaiah at one end of such a period and Luke and John at the other.

COMPLETION OF THE SCHEME BY LUTHER AND CALVIN

We now see our religion as a quaint but quite intelligible evolution from crude attempts to propitiate the destructive forces of Nature among savages to a subtle theology with a costly ritual of sacrifice possible only to the rich as a luxury, and finally to the religion of Luther and Calvin. And it must be said for the earlier forms that they involved very real sacrifices. The sacrifice was not always vicarious, and is not yet universally so. In India men pay with their own skins, torturing themselves hideously to attain holiness. In the west, saints amazed the world with their austerities and self-scourgings and confessions and vigils. But Luther delivered us from all that. His reformation was a triumph of imagination and a triumph of cheapness. It brought you complete salvation and asked you for nothing but faith. Luther did not know what he was doing in the scientific sociological way in which we know it; but his instinct served him better than knowledge could have done; for it was instinct rather than theological casuistry that made him hold so resolutely to Justification by Faith as the trump card by which he should beat the Pope, or, as he would have put it, the sign in which he should conquer. He may be said to have abolished the charge for admission to heaven. Paul had advocated this; but Luther and Calvin did it.

JOHN BARLEYCORN[8]

There is yet another page in the history of religion which must be conned and digested before the career of Jesus can be fully understood. People who can read long books will find it in [J. G.] Frazer's Golden Bough [1890; expanded 1907–15]. Simpler folk will find it in the peasant's song of John Barleycorn, now made accessible to our drawing-room amateurs in the admirable collections of Somersetshire Folk Songs [1904–9] by Mr Cecil Sharp. From Frazer's *magnum opus* you will learn how the same primitive logic which makes the Englishman believe today that by eating a beefsteak he can acquire the strength and courage of the bull, and to hold that belief in the face of the most ignominious defeats by vegetarian wrestlers and racers and bicyclists, led the first men who conceived God as capable of incarnation to believe that they could acquire a spark of his divinity by eating his flesh and drinking his blood. And from the song of John Barleycorn you may learn how the miracle of the seed, the growth, and the harvest, still the most wonderful of all the miracles and as inexplicable as ever, taught the primitive husbandman, and, as we must now affirm, taught him quite rightly, that God is in the seed, and that God is immortal. And thus it became the test of Godhead that nothing that you could do to it could kill it, and that when you buried it, it would rise again in renewed life and beauty and give mankind eternal life on condition that

8. Personification of the barley grain from which malt liquor is made.

it was eaten and drunk, and again slain and buried, to rise again for ever and ever. You may, and indeed must, use John Barleycorn "right barbarouslee," cutting him "off at knee" with your scythes, scourging him with your flails, burying him in the earth; and he will not resist you nor reproach you, but will rise again in golden beauty amidst a great burst of sunshine and bird music, and save you and renew your life. And from the interweaving of these two traditions with the craving for the Redeemer, you at last get the conviction that when the Redeemer comes he will be immortal; he will give us his body to eat and his blood to drink; and he will prove his divinity by suffering a barbarous death without resistance or reproach, and rise from the dead and return to the earth in glory as the giver of life eternal.

LOOKING FOR THE END OF THE WORLD

Yet another persistent belief has beset the imagination of the religious ever since religion spread among the poor, or, rather, ever since commercial civilization produced a hopelessly poor class cut off from enjoyment in this world. That belief is that the end of this world is at hand, and that it will presently pass away and be replaced by a kingdom of happiness, justice, and bliss in which the rich and the oppressors and the unjust shall have no share. We are all familiar with this expectation: many of us cherish some pious relative who sees in every great calamity a sign of the approaching end. Warning pamphlets are in constant circulation: advertisements are put in the papers and paid for by those who are convinced, and who are horrified at the indifference of the irreligious to the approaching doom. And revivalist preachers, now as in the days of John the Baptist, seldom fail to warn their flocks to watch and pray, as the great day will steal upon them like a thief in the night [2 Peter 3: 10], and cannot be long deferred in a world so wicked. This belief also associates itself with Barleycorn's second coming; so that the two events become identified at last.

There is the other and more artificial side of this belief, on which it is an inculcated dread. The ruler who appeals to the prospect of heaven to console the poor and keep them from insurrection also curbs the vicious by threatening them with hell. In the Koran we find Mahomet driven more and more to this expedient of government; and experience confirms his evident belief that it is impossible to govern without it in certain phases of civilization. We shall see later on that it gives a powerful attraction to the belief in a Redeemer, since it adds to remorse of conscience, which hardened men bear very lightly, a definite dread of hideous and eternal torture.

THE HONOR OF DIVINE PARENTAGE

One more tradition must be noted. The consummation of praise for a king is to declare that he is the son of no earthly father, but of a god. His mother goes into the temple of Apollo, and Apollo comes to her in the shape of a serpent, or the like. The Roman emperors, following the example of Augustus, claimed the title of God. Illogically, such divine kings insist a good deal on their royal human ancestors. Alexander, claiming to be the son of Apollo, is equally determined to be the son of Philip. As the gospels stand, St Matthew and St Luke give genealogies (the two are different) establishing the descent of Jesus through Joseph from the royal house of David, and yet declare that not Joseph but the Holy Ghost was the father of Jesus. It is therefore now held that the story of the Holy Ghost is a later interpolation borrowed from the Greek and Roman imperial tradition. But experience shews that simultaneous faith in the descent from David and the conception by the Holy Ghost is possible. Such double beliefs are entertained by the human mind without uneasiness or consciousness of the contradiction involved. Many instances might be given: a familiar one to my generation being that of the Tichborne claimant,[9] whose attempt to pass himself off as a baronet was supported by an association of laborers on the ground that the Tichborne family, in resisting it, were trying to do a laborer out of his rights. It is quite possible that Matthew and Luke may have been unconscious of the contradiction: indeed the interpolation theory does not remove the difficulty, as the interpolators themselves must have been unconscious of it. A better ground for suspecting interpolation is that St Paul knew nothing of the divine birth, and taught that Jesus came into the world at his birth as the son of Joseph, but rose from the dead after three days as the son of God. Here again, few notice the discrepancy: the three views are accepted simultaneously without intellectual discomfort. We can provisionally entertain half a dozen contradictory versions of an event if we feel either that it does not

9. A man known as Tom Castro, a butcher in Queensland, claimed to be Roger Charles Tichborne, lost at sea in 1854, and sought to obtain the title and inheritance. After a long trial in 1871 he was declared to be one Arthur Orton, guilty of double perjury.

greatly matter, or that there is a category attainable in which the contradictions are reconciled.

But that is not the present point. All that need be noted here is that the legend of divine birth was sure to be attached sooner or later to very eminent persons in Roman imperial times, and that modern theologians, far from discrediting it, have very logically affirmed the miraculous conception not only of Jesus but of his mother.

With no more scholarly equipment than a knowledge of these habits of the human imagination, anyone may now read the four gospels without bewilderment, and without the contemptuous incredulity which spoils the temper of many modern atheists, or the senseless credulity which sometimes makes pious people force us to shove them aside in emergencies as impracticable lunatics when they ask us to meet violence and injustice with dumb submission in the belief that the strange demeanor of Jesus before Pilate was meant as an example of normal human conduct. Let us admit that without the proper clues the gospels are, to a modern educated person, nonsensical and incredible, whilst the apostles are unreadable. But with the clues, they are fairly plain sailing. Jesus becomes an intelligible and consistent person. His reasons for going "like a lamb to the slaughter" [Isaiah 53: 7] instead of saving himself as Mahomet did, become quite clear. The narrative becomes as credible as any other historical narrative of its period.

MATTHEW

The Annunciation: The Massacre: The Flight

Let us begin with the gospel of Matthew, bearing in mind that it does not profess to be the evidence of an eyewitness. It is a chronicle, founded, like other chronicles, on such evidence and records as the chronicler could get hold of. The only one of the evangelists who professes to give firsthand evidence as an eyewitness naturally takes care to say so; and the fact that Matthew makes no such pretension, and writes throughout as a chronicler, makes it clear that he is telling the story of Jesus as [Raphael] Holinshed told the story of Macbeth [in *Chronicles of England, Scotland and Ireland*, 1577], except that, for a reason to be given later on, he must have collected his material and completed his book within the lifetime of persons contemporary with Jesus. Allowance must also be made for the fact that the gospel is written in the Greek language, whilst the firsthand traditions and the actual utterances of Jesus must have been in Aramaic, the dialect of Palestine. These distinctions are important, as you will find if you read Holinshed or [Jean] Froissart [*Chronicles*, 1523–5] and then read Benvenuto Cellini [*Autobiography*, 1730]. You do not blame Holinshed or Froissart for believing and repeating the things they had read or been told, though you cannot always believe these things yourself. But when Cellini tells you that he saw this or did that, and you find it impossible to believe him, you lose patience with him, and are disposed to doubt everything in his autobiography. Do not forget, then, that Matthew is Holinshed and not Benvenuto. The very first pages of his narrative will put your attitude to the test.

Matthew tells us that the mother of Jesus was betrothed to a man of royal pedigree named Joseph, who was rich enough to live in a house in Bethlehem to which kings could bring gifts of gold without provoking any comment. An angel announces to Joseph that Jesus is the son of the Holy Ghost, and that he must not accuse her of infidelity because of her bearing a son of which he is not the father; but this episode disappears from the subsequent narrative: there is no record of its having been told to Jesus, nor any indication of his having any knowledge of it. The narrative, in fact, proceeds in all respects as if the annunciation formed no part of it.

Herod the Tetrarch, believing that a child has been born who will destroy him, orders all the male children to be slaughtered; and Jesus escapes by the flight of his parents into Egypt, whence they return to Nazareth when the danger is over. Here it is necessary to anticipate a little by saying that none of the other evangelists accepts this story, as none of them except John, who throws over Matthew altogether, shares his craze for treating history and biography as mere records of the fulfilment of ancient Jewish prophecies. This craze no doubt led him to seek for some legend bearing out Hosea's "Out of Egypt have I called my son" [Hosea 11: 1], and Jeremiah's Rachel weeping for her children [Jeremiah 31: 15]: in fact, he says so.[10] Nothing that interests us nowadays turns on the credibility of the massacre of the innocents and the flight into Egypt. We may forget them, and proceed to the important part of the narrative, which skips at once to the manhood of Jesus.

10. The two verses from the Old Testament prophets are echoed in Matthew 2: 15 and 2: 18, each time preceded by the reminder that they 'fulfill what the Lord had spoken by the prophet'.

JOHN THE BAPTIST

At this moment, a Salvationist prophet named John is stirring the people very strongly. John has declared that the rite of circumcision is insufficient as a dedication of the individual to God, and has substituted the rite of baptism. To us, who are accustomed to baptism as a matter of course, and to whom circumcision is a rather ridiculous foreign practice of no consequence, the sensational effect of such a heresy as this on the Jews is not apparent: it seems to us as natural that John should have baptized people as that the rector of our village should do so. But, as St Paul found to his cost later on, the discarding of circumcision for baptism was to the Jews as startling a heresy[11] as the discarding of transubstantiation in the Mass was to the Catholics of the XVI century.

JESUS JOINS THE BAPTISTS

Jesus entered as a man of thirty (Luke says) into the religious life of his time by going to John the Baptist and demanding baptism from him, much as certain well-to-do young gentlemen forty years ago "joined the Socialists." As far as established Jewry was concerned, he burnt his boats by this action, and cut himself off from the routine of wealth, respectability, and orthodoxy. He then began preaching John's gospel, which, apart from the heresy of baptism, the value of which lay in its bringing the Gentiles (that is, the uncircumcized) within the pale of salvation, was a call to the people to repent of their sins, as the kingdom of heaven was at hand. Luke adds that he also preached the communism of charity; told the surveyors of taxes not to over-assess the taxpayers; and advised soldiers to be content with their wages and not to be violent or lay false accusations. There is no record of John going beyond this.

11. Shaw may have had in mind not only the violence of Jewish believers against Paul and his fellow preachers recorded in the second half of Acts, but also the early schism in the Christian Church by the circumcision party of conservative Jewish Christians.

THE SAVAGE JOHN AND THE CIVILIZED JESUS

Jesus went beyond it very rapidly, according to Matthew. Though, like John, he became an itinerant preacher, he departed widely from John's manner of life. John went into the wilderness, not into the synagogues; and his baptismal font was the river Jordan. He was an ascetic, clothed in skins and living on locusts and wild honey, practising a savage austerity. He courted martyrdom, and met it at the hands of Herod. Jesus saw no merit either in asceticism or martyrdom. In contrast to John he was essentially a highly-civilized, cultivated person. According to Luke, he pointed out the contrast himself, chaffing the Jews for complaining that John must be possessed by the devil because he was a teetotaler and vegetarian, whilst, because Jesus was neither one nor the other, they reviled him as a gluttonous man and a winebibber, the friend of the officials and their mistresses. He told straitlaced disciples that they would have trouble enough from other people without making any for themselves, and that they should avoid martyrdom and enjoy themselves whilst they had the chance. "When they persecute you in this city," he says, "flee into the next" [Matthew 10: 23]. He preaches in the synagogues and in the open air indifferently, just as they come. He repeatedly says, "I desire mercy and not sacrifice" [Matthew 9: 13], meaning evidently to clear himself of the inveterate superstition that suffering is gratifying to God. "Be not, as the Pharisees, of a sad countenance" [Matthew 6: 16], he says. He is convivial, feasting with Roman officials and sinners. He is careless of his person, and is remonstrated with for not washing his hands before sitting down to table. The followers of John the Baptist, who fast, and who expect to find the Christians greater ascetics than themselves, are disappointed at finding that Jesus and his twelve friends do not fast; and Jesus tells them that they should rejoice in him instead of being melancholy. He is jocular, and tells them they will all have as much fasting as they want soon enough, whether they like it or not. He is not afraid of disease, and dines with a leper. A woman, apparently to protect him against infection, pours a costly unguent on his head, and is rebuked because what it cost might have been given to the poor. He poohpoohs that lowspirited view, and says, as he said when he was reproached for not fasting, that the poor are always there to be helped, but that he is not there to be anointed always [Matthew 26: 11], implying that you should never lose a chance of being happy when there is so much misery in the world. He breaks the Sabbath; is impatient of conventionality when it is uncomfortable or obstructive; and outrages the feelings of the

Jews by breaches of it. He is apt to accuse people who feel that way of hypocrisy. Like the late Samuel Butler [who died in 1902], he regards disease as a department of sin, and on curing a lame man, says "Thy sins are forgiven" instead of "Arise and walk" [Matthew 9: 5], subsequently maintaining, when the Scribes reproach him for assuming power to forgive sin as well as to cure disease, that the two come to the same thing. He has no modest affectations, and claims to be greater than Solomon or Jonah [Matthew 12: 41–2]. When reproached, as Bunyan was, for resorting to the art of fiction when teaching in parables, he justifies himself on the ground that art is the only way in which the people can be taught. He is, in short, what we should call an artist and a Bohemian in his manner of life.

JESUS NOT A PROSELYTIST

A point of considerable practical importance today is that he expressly repudiates the idea that forms of religion, once rooted, can be weeded out and replanted with the flowers of a foreign faith. "If you try to root up the tares you will root up the wheat as well" [Matthew 13: 29–30]. Our proselytizing missionary enterprizes are thus flatly contrary to his advice; and their results appear to bear him out in his view that if you convert a man brought up in another creed, you inevitably demoralize him. He acts on this view himself, and does not convert his disciples from Judaism to Christianity. To this day a Christian would be in religion a Jew initiated by baptism instead of circumcision, and accepting Jesus as the Messiah, and his teachings as of higher authority than those of Moses, but for the action of the Jewish priests, who, to save Jewry from being submerged in the rising flood of Christianity after the capture of Jerusalem and the destruction of the Temple, set up what was practically a new religious order, with new Scriptures and elaborate new observances, and to their list of the accursed added one Jeschu,[12] a bastard magician, whose comic rogueries brought him to a bad end like Punch or Til Eulenspiegel: an invention which cost them dear when the Christians got the upper hand of them politically. The

12. From the Talmud and from surviving fragments of writings by Celsus (c. AD 178), a Platonist chronicler of pagan reaction against Christianity we learn of Jesus (Jeschu) ben Pandira, procreated by a Roman legionnaire on a Jewish whore, Miriam of Magdala, whose husband was a carpenter. This Jeschu, a sorcerer and false teacher, was known as a najjar (holy man), a worker of miracles, who healed the sick and who foretold the end of the world. Eventually he was stoned and hanged from a tree at Lydda, c. 100 BC, on the eve of Passover.

Jew as Jesus, himself a Jew, knew him, never dreamt of such things, and could follow Jesus without ceasing to be a Jew.

THE TEACHINGS OF JESUS

So much for his personal life and temperament. His public career as a popular preacher carries him equally far beyond John the Baptist. He lays no stress on baptism or vows, and preaches conduct incessantly. He advocates communism, the widening of the private family with its cramping ties into the great family of mankind under the fatherhood of God, the abandonment of revenge and punishment, the counteracting of evil by good instead of by a hostile evil, and an organic conception of society in which you are not an independent individual but a member of society, your neighbor being another member, and each of you members one of another, as two fingers on a hand, the obvious conclusion being that unless you love your neighbor as yourself and he reciprocates you will both be the worse for it. He conveys all this with extraordinary charm, and entertains his hearers with fables (parables) to illustrate them. He has no synagogue or regular congregation, but travels from place to place with twelve men whom he has called from their work as he passed, and who have abandoned it to follow him.

THE MIRACLES

He has certain abnormal powers by which he can perform miracles. He is ashamed of these powers, but, being extremely compassionate, cannot refuse to exercise them when afflicted people beg him to cure them, when multitudes of people are hungry, and when his disciples are terrified by storms on the lakes. He asks for no reward, but begs the people not to mention these powers of his. There are two obvious reasons for his dislike of being known as a worker of miracles. One is the natural objection of all men who possess such powers, but have far more important business in the world than to exhibit them, to be regarded primarily as charlatans, besides being pestered to give exhibitions to satisfy curiosity. The other is that his view of the effect of miracles upon his mission is exactly that taken later on by Rousseau. He perceives that they will discredit him and divert attention from his doctrine by raising an entirely irrelevant issue between his disciples and his opponents.

Possibly my readers may not have studied Rousseau's Letters Written From The Mountain [1764], which may be regarded as the classic work on miracles as credentials of divine mission. Rousseau shews, as Jesus foresaw, that the miracles are the main obstacle to the acceptance of Christianity, because their incredibility (if they were not incredible they would not be miracles) makes people sceptical as to the whole narrative, credible enough in the main, in which they occur, and suspicious of the doctrine with which they are thus associated. "Get rid of the miracles," said Rousseau, "and the whole world will fall at the feet of Jesus Christ." He points out that miracles offered as evidence of divinity, and failing to convince, make divinity ridiculous. He says, in effect, there is nothing in making a lame man walk: thousands of lame men have been cured and have walked without any miracle. Bring me a man with only one leg and make another grow instantaneously on him before my eyes, and I will be really impressed; but mere cures of ailments that have often been cured before are quite useless as evidence of anything else than desire to help and power to cure.

Jesus, according to Matthew, agreed so entirely with Rousseau, and felt the danger so strongly, that when people who were not ill or in trouble came to him and asked him to exercise his powers as a sign of his mission, he was irritated beyond measure, and refused with an indignation which they, not seeing Rousseau's point, must have thought very unreasonable. To be called "an evil and adulterous generation" [Matthew 16 : 4] merely for asking a miracle worker to give an exhibition of his powers, is rather a startling experience. Mahomet, by the way, also lost his temper when people asked him to perform miracles. But Mahomet expressly disclaimed any unusual powers; whereas it is clear from Matthew's story that Jesus (unfortunately for himself, as he thought) had some powers of healing. It is also obvious that the exercise of such powers would give rise to wild tales of magical feats which would expose their hero to condemnation as an impostor among people whose good opinion was of great consequence to the movement started by his mission.

But the deepest annoyance arising from the miracles would be the irrelevance of the issue raised by them. Jesus's teaching has nothing to do with miracles. If his mission had been simply to demonstrate a new method of restoring lost eyesight, the miracle of curing the blind would have been entirely relevant. But to say "You should love your enemies; and to convince you of this I will now proceed to cure this gentleman of cataract" would have been, to a man of Jesus's intelligence, the proposition of an idiot. If it could be proved today that not one of the miracles of Jesus actually occurred, that proof would not invalidate a single one of his didactic utterances; and conversely, if it could be proved that not only did the miracles actually occur, but that he had wrought a thousand other miracles a thousand times more wonderful, not a jot of weight would be added to his doctrine. And yet the intellectual energy of sceptics and divines has been wasted for generations in arguing about the miracles on the assumption that Christianity is at stake in the controversy as to whether the stories of Matthew are false or true. According to Matthew himself, Jesus must have known this only too well; for wherever he went he was assailed with a clamor for miracles, though his doctrine created bewilderment.

So much for the miracles! Matthew tells us further, that Jesus declared that his doctrines would be attacked by Church and State, and that the common multitude were the salt of the earth and the light of the world. His disciples, in their relations with the political and ecclesiastical organizations, would be as sheep among wolves.

MATTHEW IMPUTES BIGOTRY TO JESUS

Matthew, like most biographers, strives to identify the opinions and prejudices of his hero with his own. Although he describes Jesus as tolerant even to carelessness, he draws the line at the Gentile, and represents Jesus as a bigoted Jew who regards his mission as addressed exclusively to "the lost sheep of the house of Israel." When a woman of Canaan begged Jesus to cure her daughter, he first refused to speak to her, and then told her brutally that "It is not meet to take the children's bread and cast it to the dogs." But when the woman said, "Truth, Lord; yet the dogs eat of the crumbs which fall from their master's table," she melted the Jew out of him and made Christ a Christian. To the woman whom he had just called a dog he said, "O woman, great is thy faith: be it unto thee even as thou wilt" [Matthew 15: 24–8]. This is somehow one of the most touching stories in the gospel; perhaps because the woman rebukes the prophet by a touch of his own finest quality. It is certainly out of character; but as the sins of good men are always out of character, it is not safe to reject the story as invented in the interest of Matthew's determination that Jesus shall have nothing to do with the Gentiles. At all events, there the story is; and it is by no means the only instance in which Matthew reports Jesus, in spite of the charm of his preaching, as extremely uncivil in private intercourse.

THE GREAT CHANGE

So far the history is that of a man sane and interesting apart from his special gifts as orator, healer, and prophet. But a startling change occurs. One day, after the disciples have discouraged him for a long time by their misunderstandings of his mission, and their speculations as to whether he is one of the old prophets come again, and if so, which, his disciple Peter suddenly solves the problem by exclaiming, "Thou art the Christ, the son of the living God." At this Jesus is extraordinarily pleased and excited. He declares that Peter has had a revelation straight from God. He makes a pun on Peter's name, and declares him the founder of his Church. And he accepts his destiny as a god by announcing that he will be killed when he goes to Jerusalem; for if he is really the Christ, it is a necessary part of his legendary destiny that he shall be slain. Peter, not understanding this, rebukes him for what seems mere craven melancholy; and Jesus turns fiercely on him and cries, "Get thee behind me, Satan" [Matthew 16: 13–23].

Jesus now becomes obsessed with a conviction of his divinity, and talks about it continually to his disciples, though he forbids them to mention it to others. They begin to dispute among themselves as to the position they shall occupy in heaven when his kingdom is established. He rebukes them strenuously for this, and repeats his teaching that greatness means service and not domination; but he himself, always instinctively somewhat haughty, now becomes arrogant, dictatorial, and even abusive, never replying to his critics without an insulting epithet, and even cursing a fig-tree which disappoints him when he goes to it for fruit. He assumes all the traditions of the folklore gods, and announces that, like John Barleycorn, he will be barbarously slain and buried, but will rise from the earth and return to life. He attaches to himself the immemorial tribal ceremony of eating the god, by blessing bread and wine and handing them to his disciples with the words "This is my body: this is my blood" [Matthew 26: 26–8]. He forgets his own teaching and threatens eternal fire and eternal punishment. He announces, in addition to his Barleycorn resurrection, that he will come to the world a second time in glory and establish his kingdom on earth. He fears that this may lead to the appearance of impostors claiming to be himself, and declares explicitly and repeatedly that no matter what wonders these impostors may perform, his own coming will be unmistakeable, as the stars will fall from heaven, and trumpets be blown by angels. Further he declares that this will take place during the lifetime of persons then present [Matthew 24: 29–35].

JERUSALEM AND THE MYSTICAL SACRIFICE

In this new frame of mind he at last enters Jerusalem amid great popular curiosity; drives the moneychangers and sacrifice sellers out of the temple in a riot; refuses to interest himself in the beauties and wonders of the temple building on the ground that presently not a stone of it shall be left on another; reviles the high priests and elders in intolerable terms; and is arrested by night in a garden to avoid a popular disturbance. He makes no resistance, being persuaded that it is part of his destiny as a god to be murdered and to rise again. One of his followers shews fight, and cuts off the ear of one of his captors. Jesus rebukes him, but does not attempt to heal the wound, though he declares that if he wished to resist he could easily summon twelve million angels to his aid [Matthew 26: 53]. He is taken before the high priest and by him handed over to the Roman governor, who is puzzled by his silent refusal to defend himself in any way, or to contradict his accusers or their witnesses, Pilate having naturally no idea that the prisoner conceives himself as going through an inevitable process of torment, death, and burial as a prelude to resurrection. Before the high priest he has also been silent except that when the priest asks him is he the Christ, the Son of God, he replies that they shall all see the Son of Man sitting at the right hand of power, and coming on the clouds of heaven [Matthew 26: 64]. He maintains this attitude with frightful fortitude whilst they scourge him, mock him, torment him, and finally crucify him between two thieves. His prolonged agony of thirst and pain on the cross at last breaks his spirit, and he dies with a cry of "My God: why hast Thou forsaken me?" [Matthew 27: 46]

NOT THIS MAN BUT BARABBAS

Meanwhile he has been definitely rejected by the people as well as by the priests. Pilate, pitying him, and unable to make out exactly what he has done (the blasphemy that has horrified the high priest does not move the Roman), tries to get him off by reminding the people that they have, by custom, the right to have a prisoner released at that time, and suggests that he should release Jesus. But they insist on his releasing a prisoner named Barabbas instead, and on having Jesus crucified. Matthew gives no clue to the popularity of Barabbas, describing him simply as "a notable prisoner" [Matthew 27: 16]. The later gospels make it clear, very significantly, that his offence was sedition and insurrection; that he was an advocate of physical force; and that he had killed his man. The choice of Barabbas thus appears as a popular choice of the militant advocate of physical force as against the unresisting advocate of mercy.

THE RESURRECTION

Matthew then tells how after three days an angel opened the family vault of one Joseph, a rich man of Arimathea, who had buried Jesus in it, whereupon Jesus rose and returned from Jerusalem to Galilee and resumed his preaching with his disciples, assuring them that he would now be with them to the end of the world.

At that point the narrative abruptly stops. The story has no ending.

DATE OF MATTHEW'S NARRATIVE

One effect of the promise of Jesus to come again in glory during the lifetime of some of his hearers is to date the gospel without the aid of any scholarship. It must have been written during the lifetime of Jesus's contemporaries: that is, whilst it was still possible for the promise of his Second Coming to be fulfilled. The death of the last person who had been alive when Jesus said "There be some of them that stand here that shall in no wise taste death til they see the Son of Man coming in his kingdom" [Matthew 16: 28] destroyed the last possibility of the promised Second Coming, and bore out the incredulity of Pilate and the Jews. And as Matthew writes as one believing in that Second Coming, and in fact left his story unfinished to be ended by it, he must have produced his gospel within a lifetime of the crucifixion. Also, he must have believed that reading books would be one of the pleasures of the kingdom of heaven on earth.

CLASS TYPE OF MATTHEW'S JESUS

One more circumstance must be noted as gathered from Matthew. Though he begins his story in such a way as to suggest that Jesus belonged to the privileged classes, he mentions later on that when Jesus attempted to preach in his own country, and had no success there, the people said, "Is not this the carpenter's son?" [Matthew 13: 55] But Jesus's manner throughout is that of an aristocrat, or at the very least the son of a rich bourgeois, and by no means a lowly-minded one at that. We must be careful therefore to conceive Joseph, not as a modern proletarian carpenter working for weekly wages, but as a master craftsman of royal descent. John the Baptist may have been a Keir Hardie; but the Jesus of Matthew is of the Ruskin-Morris class.

This haughty characterization is so marked that if we had no other documents concerning Jesus than the gospel of Matthew, we should not feel as we do about him. We should have been much less loth to say, "There is a man here who was sane until Peter hailed him as the Christ, and who then became a monomaniac." We should have pointed out that his delusion is a very common delusion among the insane, and that such insanity is quite consistent with the retention of the argumentative cunning and penetration which Jesus displayed in Jerusalem after his delusion had taken complete hold of him. We should feel horrified at the scourging and mocking and crucifixion just as we should if Ruskin had been treated in that way when he also went mad, instead of being cared for as an invalid. And we should have had no clear perception of any special significance in his way of calling the Son of God the Son of Man. We should have noticed that he was a Communist; that he regarded much of what we call law and order as machinery for robbing the poor under legal forms; that he thought domestic ties a snare for the soul; that he agreed with the proverb "The nearer the Church, the farther from God" [C. Tourneur, *The Atheist's Tragedie*, 1611, I: iv]; that he saw very plainly that the masters of the community should be its servants and not its oppressors and parasites; and that though he did not tell us not to fight our enemies, he did tell us to love them, and warned us that they who draw the sword shall perish by the sword. All this shews a great power of seeing through vulgar illusions, and a capacity for a higher morality than has yet been established in any civilized community; but it does not place Jesus above Confucius or Plato, not to mention more modern philosophers and moralists.

MARK

THE WOMEN DISCIPLES AND THE ASCENSION

Let us see whether we can get anything more out of Mark, whose gospel, by the way, is supposed to be older than Matthew's. Mark is brief; and it does not take long to discover that he adds nothing to Matthew except the ending of the story by Christ's ascension into heaven, and the news that many women had come with Jesus to Jerusalem, including Mary Magdalene, out of whom he had cast seven devils. On the other hand Mark says nothing about the birth of Jesus, and does not touch his career until his adult baptism by John. He apparently regards Jesus as a native of Nazareth, as John does, and not of Bethlehem, as Matthew and Luke do, Bethlehem being the city of David, from whom Jesus is said by Matthew and Luke to be descended. He describes John's doctrine as "Baptism of repentance unto remission of sins" [Mark 1: 4]: that is, a form of Salvationism. He tells us that Jesus went into the synagogues and taught, not as the Scribes but as one having authority: that is, we infer, he preaches his own doctrine as an original moralist instead of repeating what the books say. He describes the miracle of Jesus reaching the boat by walking across the sea, but says nothing about Peter trying to do the same. Mark sees what he relates more vividly than Matthew, and gives touches of detail that bring the event more clearly before the reader. He says, for instance, that when Jesus walked on the waves to the boat, he was passing it by when the disciples called out to him. He seems to feel that Jesus's treatment of the woman of Canaan requires some apology, and therefore says that she was a Greek of Syrophenician race [Mark 7: 26], which probably excused any incivility to her in Mark's eyes. He represents the father of the boy whom Jesus cured of epilepsy after the transfiguration as a sceptic who says "Lord, I believe: help thou mine unbelief" [Mark 9: 24]. He tells the story of the widow's mite, omitted by Matthew [Mark 12: 42–4]. He explains that Barabbas was "lying bound with them that made insurrection, men who in the insurrection had committed murder" [Mark 15: 7]. Joseph of Arimathea, who buried Jesus in his own tomb, and who is described by Matthew as a disciple, is described by Mark as "one who also himself was looking for the kingdom of God" [Mark 15: 43], which suggests that he was an independent seeker. Mark earns our gratitude by making no mention of the old prophecies, and thereby not only saves time, but avoids the absurd implication that Christ was merely going through a predetermined ritual, like the works of a clock, instead of living. Finally Mark reports Christ as saying, after his resurrection, that those who believe in him will be saved and those who do not, damned [Mark 16: 16]; but it is impossible to discover whether he means anything by a state of damnation beyond a state of error. The paleographers regard this passage as tacked on by a later scribe.

On the whole Mark leaves the modern reader where Matthew left him.

LUKE

LUKE THE LITERARY ARTIST

When we come to Luke, we come to a later storyteller, and one with a stronger natural gift for his art. Before you have read twenty lines of Luke's gospel you are aware that you have passed from the chronicler writing for the sake of recording important facts, to the artist, telling the story for the sake of telling it. At the very outset he achieves the most charming idyll in the Bible: the story of Mary crowded out of the inn into the stable and laying her newly-born son in the manger, and of the shepherds abiding in the field keeping watch over their flocks by night, and how the angel of the Lord came upon them, and the glory of the Lord shone around them, and suddenly there was with the angel a multitude of the heavenly host. These shepherds go to the stable and take the place of the kings in Matthew's chronicle [Luke 2: 6–16]. So completely has this story conquered and fascinated our imagination that most of us suppose all the gospels to contain it; but it is Luke's story and his alone: none of the others have the smallest hint of it.

THE CHARM OF LUKE'S NARRATIVE

Luke gives the charm of sentimental romance to every incident. The Annunciation, as described by Matthew, is made to Joseph, and is simply a warning to him not to divorce his wife for misconduct. In Luke's gospel it is made to Mary herself, at much greater length, with a sense of the ecstasy of the bride of the Holy Ghost. Jesus is refined and softened almost out of recognition: the stern peremptory disciple of John the Baptist, who never addresses a Pharisee or a Scribe without an insulting epithet, becomes a considerate, gentle, sociable, almost urbane person; and the Chauvinist Jew becomes a pro-Gentile who is thrown out of the synagogue in his own town for reminding the congregation that the prophets had sometimes preferred Gentiles to Jews. In fact they try to throw him down from a sort of Tarpeian rock[13] which they use for executions; but he makes his way through them and escapes [Luke 4: 29–30]: the only suggestion of a feat of

13. A cliff on the Capitoline Hill in Rome, from which traitors to the State were hurled to their death.

arms on his part in the gospels. There is not a word of the Syrophenician woman. At the end he is calmly superior to his sufferings; delivers an address on his way to execution with unruffled composure; does not despair on the cross; and dies with perfect dignity, commending his spirit to God, after praying for the forgiveness of his persecutors on the ground that "They know not what they do" [Luke 23: 34]. According to Matthew, it is part of the bitterness of his death that even the thieves who are crucified with him revile him. According to Luke, only one of them does this; and he is rebuked by the other, who begs Jesus to remember him when he comes into his kingdom. To which Jesus replies, "This day shalt thou be with me in Paradise" [Luke 23: 43], implying that he will spend the three days of his death there. In short, every device is used to get rid of the ruthless horror of the Matthew chronicle, and to relieve the strain of the Passion by touching episodes, and by representing Christ as superior to human suffering. It is Luke's Jesus who has won our hearts.

THE TOUCH OF PARISIAN ROMANCE

Luke's romantic shrinking from unpleasantness, and his sentimentality, are illustrated by his version of the woman with the ointment. Matthew and Mark describe it as taking place in the house of Simon the Leper, where it is objected to as a waste of money. In Luke's version the leper becomes a rich Pharisee; the woman becomes a Dame aux Camellias; and nothing is said about money and the poor. The woman washes the feet of Jesus with her tears and dries them with her hair; and he is reproached for suffering a sinful woman to touch him. It is almost an adaptation of the unromantic Matthew to the Parisian stage. There is a distinct attempt to increase the feminine interest all through. The slight lead given by Mark is taken up and developed. More is said about Jesus's mother and her feelings. Christ's following of women, just mentioned by Mark to account for their presence at his tomb, is introduced earlier; and some of the women are named; so that we are introduced to Joanna the wife of Chuza, Herod's steward, and Susanna. There is the quaint little domestic episode between Mary and Martha [Luke 10: 38–42]. There is the parable of the Prodigal Son [Luke 15: 11–32] appealing to the indulgence romance has always shewn to Charles Surface and Des Grieux.[14] Women follow Jesus to the

14. The first is the good-natured spendthrift in Sheridan's *The School for Scandal* (1777); the second is Chevalier des Grieux, a kind-hearted card cheat in Abbé Prévost's *Manon Lescaut* (1731).

cross; and he makes them a speech beginning "Daughters of Jerusalem" [Luke 23: 28]. Slight as these changes may seem, they make a great change in the atmosphere. The Christ of Matthew could never have become what is vulgarly called a woman's hero (though the truth is that the popular demand for sentiment, as far as it is not simply human, is more manly than womanly); but the Christ of Luke has made possible those pictures which now hang in many ladies' chambers, in which Jesus is represented exactly as he is represented in the Lourdes cinematograph, by a handsome actor. The only touch of realism which Luke does not instinctively suppress for the sake of producing this kind of amenity is the reproach addressed to Jesus for sitting down to table without washing his hands [Luke 11: 37–41]; and that is retained because an interesting discourse hangs on it.

Waiting for the Messiah

Another new feature in Luke's story is that it begins in a world in which everyone is expecting the advent of the Christ. In Matthew and Mark, Jesus comes into a normal Philistine world like our own of today. Not until the Baptist foretells that one greater than himself shall come after him does the old Jewish hope of a Messiah begin to stir again; and as Jesus begins as a disciple of John, and is baptized by him, nobody connects him with that hope until Peter has the sudden inspiration which produces so startling an effect on Jesus. But in Luke's gospel men's minds, and especially women's minds, are full of eager expectation of a Christ not only before the birth of Jesus, but before the birth of John the Baptist, the event with which Luke begins his story. Whilst Jesus and John are still in their mothers' wombs, John leaps at the approach of Jesus when the two mothers visit oneanother. At the circumcision of Jesus pious men and women hail the infant as the Christ.

The Baptist himself is not convinced; for at quite a late period in his former disciple's career he sends two young men to ask Jesus is he really the Christ. This is noteworthy because Jesus immediately gives them a deliberate exhibition of miracles, and bids them tell John what they have seen, and ask him what he thinks *now*. This is in complete contradiction to what I have called the Rousseau view of miracles as inferred from Matthew. Luke shews all a romancer's thoughtlessness about miracles: he regards them as "signs": that is, as proofs of the divinity of the person performing them, and not merely of thaumaturgic powers. He revels in miracles just as he revels in parables: they make such capital stories. He cannot allow the calling of Peter, James, and John from their boats to pass without a comic miraculous overdraft of fishes, with the net sinking the boats and provoking Peter to exclaim, "Depart from me; for I am a sinful man, O Lord" [Luke 5: 8], which should probably be translated, "I want no more of your miracles: natural fishing is good enough for my boats."

There are some other novelties in Luke's version. Pilate sends Jesus to Herod, who happens to be in Jerusalem just then, because Herod had expressed some curiosity about him; but nothing comes of it: the prisoner will not speak to him. When Jesus is ill-received in a Samaritan village James and John propose to call down fire from heaven and destroy it; and Jesus replies that he is come not to destroy lives but to save them. The bias of Jesus against lawyers is emphasized, and also his resolution not to admit that he is more bound to his relatives than to strangers. He snubs a woman who blesses his mother. As this is contrary to the traditions of sentimental romance, Luke would presumably have avoided it had he not become persuaded that the brotherhood of Man and the Fatherhood of God are superior even to sentimental considerations. The story of the lawyer asking what are the two chief commandments is changed by making Jesus put the question to the lawyer instead of answering it.

As to doctrine, Luke is only clear when his feelings are touched. His logic is weak; for some of the sayings of Jesus are pieced together wrongly, as anyone who has read them in the right order and context in Matthew will discover at once. He does not make anything new out of Christ's mission, and, like the other evangelists, thinks that the whole point of it is that Jesus was the long-expected Christ, and that he will presently come back to earth and establish his kingdom, having duly died and risen again after three days. Yet Luke not only records the teaching as to communism and the discarding of hate, which have, of course, nothing to do with the Second Coming, but quotes one very remarkable saying which is not compatible with it, which is, that people must not go about asking where the kingdom of heaven is, and saying "Lo, here!" and "Lo, there!" because the kingdom of heaven is within them [Luke 17: 21]. But Luke has no sense that this belongs to a quite different order of thought to his Christianity, and retains undisturbed his view of the kingdom as a locality as definite as Jerusalem or Madagascar.

JOHN

A NEW STORY AND A NEW CHARACTER

The gospel of John is a surprise after the others. Matthew, Mark and Luke describe the same events in the same order (the variations in Luke are negligible), and their gospels are therefore called the synoptic gospels. They tell substantially the same story of a wandering preacher who at the end of his life came to Jerusalem. John describes a preacher who spent practically his whole adult life in the capital, with occasional visits to the provinces. His circumstantial account of the calling of Peter and the sons of Zebedee is quite different from the others; and he says nothing about their being fishermen [John 1: 35–51]. He says expressly that Jesus, though baptized by John, did not himself practise baptism, and that his disciples did [John 4: 2]. Christ's agonized appeal against his doom in the garden of Gethsemane becomes a coldblooded suggestion made in the temple at a much earlier period [John 12: 27]. Jesus argues much more; complains a good deal of the unreasonableness and dislike with which he is met; is by no means silent before Caiaphas and Pilate; lays much greater stress on his resurrection and on the eating of his body (losing all his disciples except the twelve in consequence); says many apparently contradictory and nonsensical things to which no ordinary reader can now find any clue; and gives the impression of an educated, not to say sophisticated mystic, different both in character and schooling from the simple and downright preacher of Matthew and Mark, and the urbane easy-minded charmer of Luke. Indeed, the Jews say of him "How knoweth this man letters, having never learnt?" [John 7: 15]

JOHN THE IMMORTAL EYE-WITNESS

John, moreover, claims to be not only a chronicler but a witness. He declares that he is "the disciple whom Jesus loved" [John 21: 20], and that he actually leaned on the bosom of Jesus at the last supper and asked in a whisper which of them it was that should betray him. Jesus whispered that he would give a sop to the traitor, and thereupon handed one to Judas, who ate it and immediately became possessed by the devil [John 13: 21–7]. This is more natural than the other accounts, in which Jesus openly indicates Judas without eliciting any protest or exciting any comment. It also implies that Jesus deliberately bewitched Judas in order to bring about his own betrayal. Later on John claims that Jesus said to Peter "If I will that John tarry til I come, what is that to thee?"; and John, with a rather obvious mock modesty, adds that he must not claim to be immortal, as the disciples concluded; for Christ did not use that expression, but merely remarked "If I will that he tarry til I come" [John 21: 22–3]. No other evangelist claims personal intimacy with Christ, or even pretends to be his contemporary (there is no ground for identifying Matthew the publican with Matthew the Evangelist); and John is the only evangelist whose account of Christ's career and character is hopelessly irreconcilable with Matthew's. He is almost as bad as Matthew, by the way, in his repeated explanations of Christ's actions as having no other purpose than to fulfil the old prophecies. The impression is more unpleasant, because, as John, unlike Matthew, is educated, subtle, and obsessed with artificial intellectual mystifications, the discovery that he is stupid or superficial in so simple a matter strikes one with distrust and dislike, in spite of his great literary charm, a good example of which is his transfiguration of the harsh episode of the Syrophenician woman into the pleasant story of the woman of Samaria [John 4: 7–30]. This perhaps is why his claim to be John the disciple, or to be a contemporary of Christ or even of any survivor of Christ's generation, has been disputed, and finally, it seems, disallowed. But I repeat, I take no note here of the disputes of experts as to the date of the gospels, not because I am not acquainted with them, but because, as the earliest codices are Greek manuscripts of the IV century A.D., and the Syrian ones are translations from the Greek, the paleographic expert has no difficulty in arriving at whatever conclusion happens to suit his beliefs or disbeliefs; and he never succeeds in convincing the other experts except when they believe or disbelieve exactly as he does. Hence I conclude that the dates of the original narratives cannot be ascertained, and that we must make the best of the evangelists' own accounts of themselves. There is, as we have seen, a very marked difference between them, leaving no doubt that we are dealing with four authors of well-marked diversity; but they all end in an attitude of expectancy of the Second Coming which they agree in declaring Jesus to have positively and unequivocally promised within the lifetime of his contemporaries. Any believer compiling a gospel after the last of these contemporaries had passed away, would either reject and omit the tradition of that promise on the ground that since it was not fulfilled, and could never now be fulfilled, it could not have been made, or else have had to confess to the Jews, who were the keenest critics of the Christians, that Jesus was either an impostor or the victim of a delusion. Now all the evangelists except Matthew expressly declare themselves to be believers; and Matthew's narrative is obviously not that of a sceptic. I therefore assume as a matter of common sense that, interpolations apart, the gospels are derived from narratives written in the first century A.D. I include John, because though it may be claimed that he hedged his position by claiming that Christ, who specially loved him, endowed him with a miraculous life until the Second Coming, the conclusion being that John is alive at this moment, I cannot believe that a literary forger could hope to save the situation by so outrageous a pretension. Also, John's narrative is in many passages nearer to the realities of public life than the simple chronicle of Matthew or the sentimental romance of Luke. This may be because John was obviously more a man of the world than the others, and knew, as mere chroniclers and romancers never know, what actually happens away from books and desks. But it may also be because he saw and heard what happened instead of collecting traditions about it. The paleographers and daters of first quotations may say what they please: John's claim to give evidence as an eyewitness whilst the others are only compiling history [John 21: 24] is supported by a certain verisimilitude which appeals to me as one who has preached a new doctrine and argued about it, as well as written stories. This verisimilitude may be dramatic art backed by knowledge of public life; but even at that we must not forget that the best dramatic art is the operation of a divinatory instinct for truth. Be that as it may, John was certainly not the man to believe in the Second Coming and yet give a date for it after that date had passed. There is really no escape from the conclusion that the originals of all the gospels date from the period within which there was still a possibility of the Second Coming occurring at the promised time.

THE PECULIAR THEOLOGY OF JESUS

In spite of the suspicions roused by John's idiosyncrasies, his narrative is of enormous importance to those who go to the gospels for a credible modern religion. For it is John who adds to the other records such sayings as that "I and my father are one" [John 10: 30]; that "God is a spirit" [John 4: 24]; that the aim of Jesus is not only that the people should have life, but that they should have it "more abundantly" [John 10: 10] (a distinction much needed by people who think a man is either alive or dead, and never consider the important question how much alive he is); and that men should bear in mind what they were told in the 82nd Psalm: that they are gods, and are responsible for the doing of the mercy and justice of God. The Jews stoned him for saying these things, and, when he remonstrated with them for stupidly stoning one who had done nothing to them but good works, replied "For a good work we stone thee not; but for blasphemy, because that thou, being a man, makest thyself God." He insists (referring to the 82nd Psalm) that if it is part of their own religion that they are gods on the assurance of God himself, it cannot be blasphemy for him, whom the Father sanctified and sent into the world, to say "I am the son of God" [John 10: 33–7]. But they will not have this at any price; and he has to escape from their fury. Here the point is obscured by the distinction made by Jesus between himself and other men. He says, in effect, "If you are gods, then, *a fortiori* [all the more], I am a god." John makes him say this, just as he makes him say "I am the light of the world" [John 9: 5]. But Matthew makes him say to the people "Ye are the light of the world" [Matthew 5: 14]. John has no grip of the significance of these scraps which he has picked up: he is far more interested in a notion of his own that men can escape death and do even more extraordinary things than Christ himself: in fact, he actually represents Jesus as promising this explicitly, and is finally led into the audacious hint that he, John, is himself immortal in the flesh. Still, he does not miss the significant sayings altogether. However inconsistent they may be with the doctrine he is consciously driving at, they appeal to some sub-intellectual instinct in him that makes him stick them in, like a child sticking tinsel stars on the robe of a toy angel.

John does not mention the ascension; and the end of his narrative leaves Christ restored to life, and appearing from time to time among his disciples. It is on one of these occasions that John describes the miraculous draught of fishes which Luke places at the other end of Christ's career, at the call of the sons of Zebedee [the apostles James and John].

John Agreed as to the Trial and Crucifixion

Although John, following his practice of shewing Jesus's skill as a debater, makes him play a less passive part at his trial, he still gives substantially the same account of it as all the rest. And the question that would occur to any modern reader never occurs to him, any more than it occurred to Matthew, Mark, or Luke. That question is, Why on earth did not Jesus defend himself, and make the people rescue him from the High Priest? He was so popular that they were unable to prevent him driving the moneychangers out of the temple, or to arrest him for it. When they did arrest him afterwards, they had to do it at night in a garden. He could have argued with them as he had often done in the temple, and justified himself both to the Jewish law and to Cæsar. And he had physical force at his command to back up his arguments: all that was needed was a speech to rally his followers; and he was not gagged. The reply of the evangelists would have been that all these inquiries are idle, because if Jesus had wished to escape, he could have saved himself all that trouble by doing what John describes him as doing: that is, casting his captors to the earth by an exertion of his miraculous power. If you asked John why he let them get up again and torment and execute him, John would have replied that it was part of the destiny of God to be slain and buried and to rise again, and that to have avoided this destiny would have been to repudiate his Godhead. And that is the only apparent explanation. Whether you believe with the evangelists that Christ could have rescued himself by a miracle, or, as a modern Secularist, point out that he could have defended himself effectually, the fact remains that according to all the narratives he did not do so. He had to die like a god, not to save himself "like one of the princes."* The consensus on this point is important, because it proves the absolute sincerity of Jesus's declaration that he was a god. No impostor would have accepted such dreadful consequences without an effort to save himself. No impostor would have been nerved to endure them by the conviction that he would rise from the grave and live again after three days. If we accept the story at all, we must believe this, and believe also that his promise to return in glory and establish his kingdom on earth within the lifetime of men then living, was one which he believed that he could, and indeed must fulfil. Two evangelists declare that in his last agony he despaired, and reproached God for forsaking him. The other two represent him as dying in unshaken conviction and charity with the simple remark that the ordeal was finished. But all four testify that his faith was not deceived, and that he actually rose again after three days. And I think it unreasonable to doubt that all four wrote their narratives in full faith that the other promise would be fulfilled too, and that they themselves might live to witness the Second Coming.

---

* Jesus himself had referred to that psalm (82) in which men who have judged unjustly and accepted the persons of the wicked (including by anticipation practically all the white inhabitants of the British Isles and the North American continent, to mention no other places) are condemned in the words, "I have said, ye are gods; and all of ye are children of the Most High; but ye shall die like men, and fall like one of the princes." [GBS]

CREDIBILITY OF THE GOSPELS

It will be noted by the older among my readers, who are sure to be obsessed more or less by elderly wrangles as to whether the gospels are credible as matter-of-fact narratives, that I have hardly raised this question, and have accepted the credible and incredible with equal complacency. I have done this because credibility is a subjective condition, as the evolution of religious belief clearly shews. Belief is not dependent on evidence and reason. There is as much evidence that the miracles occurred as that the battle of Waterloo occurred, or that a large body of Russian troops passed through England in 1914 to take part in the war on the western front.[15] The reasons for believing in the murder of Pompey are the same as the reasons for believing in the raising of Lazarus. Both have been believed and doubted by men of equal intelligence. Miracles, in the sense of phenomena we cannot explain, surround us on every hand: life itself is the miracle of miracles. Miracles in the sense of events that violate the normal course of our experience are vouched for every day: the flourishing Church of Christ Scientist is founded on a multitude of such miracles.[16] Nobody believes all the miracles: everybody believes some of them. I cannot tell why men who will not believe that Jesus ever existed yet believe firmly that Shakespear was Bacon. I cannot tell why people who believe that angels appeared and fought on our side at the battle of Mons [Belgium, 1914], and who believe that miracles occur quite frequently at Lourdes, nevertheless boggle at the miracle of the liquefaction of the blood of St Januarius, and reject it as a trick of priestcraft. I cannot tell why people who will not believe Matthew's story of three kings bringing costly gifts to the cradle of Jesus, believe Luke's story of the shepherds and the stable. I cannot tell why people, brought up to believe the Bible in the old literal way as an infallible record and revelation, and rejecting that view later on, begin by rejecting the Old Testament, and give up the belief in a brimstone hell before they give up (if they ever do) the belief in a heaven of harps, crowns, and thrones. I cannot tell why people who will not believe in

15. A rumour that a large contingent of Russian troops had travelled through England was denied by the British Government in the early edition of *The Times* on 12 September 1914.

16. Founded in 1876 by Mary Baker Eddy, the Christian Scientist Association taught that Christ's 'miracles' were natural mental healing, and promised that those who believed could do likewise.

baptism on any terms believe in vaccination with the cruel fanaticism of inquisitors. I am convinced that if a dozen sceptics were to draw up in parallel columns a list of the events narrated in the gospels which they consider credible and incredible respectively, their lists would be different in several particulars. Belief is literally a matter of taste.

FASHIONS IN BELIEF

Now matters of taste are mostly also matters of fashion. We are conscious of a difference between medieval fashions in belief and modern fashions. For instance, though we are more credulous than men were in the Middle Ages, and entertain such crowds of fortunetellers, magicians, miracle workers, agents of communication with the dead, discoverers of the elixir of life, transmuters of metals, and healers of all sorts, as the Middle Ages never dreamed of as possible, yet we will not take our miracles in the form that convinced the Middle Ages. Arithmetical numbers appealed to the Middle Ages just as they do to us, because they are difficult to deal with, and because the greatest masters of numbers, the Newtons and Leibnitzes, rank among the greatest men. But there are fashions in numbers too. The Middle Ages took a fancy to some familiar number like seven; and because it was an odd number, and the world was made in seven days, and there are seven stars in Charles's Wain [the Big Dipper], and for a dozen other reasons, they were ready to believe anything that had a seven or a seven times seven in it. Seven deadly sins, seven swords of sorrow in the heart of the Virgin, seven champions of Christendom,[17] seemed obvious and reasonable things to believe in simply because they were seven. To us, on the contrary, the number seven is the stamp of superstition. We will believe in nothing less than millions. A medieval doctor gained his patient's confidence by telling him that his vitals were being devoured by seven worms. Such a diagnosis would ruin a modern physician. The modern physician tells his patient that he is ill because every drop of his blood is swarming with a million microbes; and the patient believes him abjectly and instantly. Had a bishop told William the Conqueror that the sun was seventyseven miles distant from the earth, William would have believed him not only out of respect for the Church, but because he would have felt that seventyseven

17. In medieval tales these were the seven national saints: George of England, Andrew of Scotland, Patrick of Ireland, David of Wales, Denis of France, James of Spain and Anthony of Italy.

miles was the proper distance. The Kaiser, knowing just as little about it as the Conqueror, would send that bishop to an asylum. Yet he (I presume) unhesitatingly accepts the estimate of ninetytwo and nine-tenths millions of miles, or whatever the latest big figure may be.

CREDIBILITY AND TRUTH

And here I must remind you that our credulity is not to be measured by the truth of the things we believe. When men believed that the earth was flat, they were not credulous: they were using their common sense, and, if asked to prove that the earth was flat, would have said simply, "Look at it." Those who refuse to believe that it is round are exercising a wholesome scepticism. The modern man who believes that the earth is round is grossly credulous. Flat Earth men drive him to fury by confuting him with the greatest ease when he tries to argue about it. Confront him with a theory that the earth is cylindrical, or annular, or hourglass shaped, and he is lost. The thing he believes may be true, but that is not why he believes it: he believes it because in some mysterious way it appeals to his imagination. If you ask him why he believes that the sun is ninety-odd million miles off, either he will have to confess that he doesnt know, or he will say that Newton proved it. But he has not read the treatise in which Newton proved it, and does not even know that it was written in Latin [*Philosophiae naturalis principia mathematica*, 1687]. If you press an Ulster Protestant as to why he regards Newton as an infallible authority, and St Thomas Aquinas or the Pope as superstitious liars whom, after his death, he will have the pleasure of watching from his place in heaven whilst they roast in eternal flame, or if you ask me why I take into serious consideration Colonel Sir Almroth Wright's estimates of the number of streptococci contained in a given volume of serum whilst I can only laugh at the earlier estimates of the number of angels that can be accommodated on the point of a needle, no reasonable reply is possible except that somehow sevens and angels are out of fashion, and billions and streptococci are all the rage. I simply cannot tell you why Bacon, Montaigne, and Cervantes had a quite different fashion of credulity and incredulity from the Venerable Bede and [William Langland's] Piers Plowman and the divine doctors of the Aquinas-Aristotle school, who were certainly no stupider, and had the same facts before them. Still less can I explain why, if we assume that these leaders of thought had all reasoned out their beliefs, their authority seemed conclusive to one generation and blasphemous to another, neither generation having followed the reasoning or gone into the facts of the matter for itself at all.

It is therefore idle to begin disputing with the reader as to what he should believe in the gospels and what he should disbelieve. He will believe what he can, and disbelieve what he must. If he draws any lines at all, they will be quite arbitrary ones. St John tells us that when Jesus explicitly claimed divine honors by the sacrament of his body and blood, so many of his disciples left him that their number was reduced to twelve. Many modern readers will not hold out so long: they will give in at the first miracle. Others will discriminate. They will accept the healing miracles, and reject the feeding of the multitude. To some the walking on the water will be a legendary exaggeration of a swim, ending in an ordinary rescue of Peter; and the raising of Lazarus will be only a similar glorification of a commonplace feat of artificial respiration, whilst others will scoff at it as a planned imposture in which Lazarus acted as a confederate. Between the rejection of the stories as wholly fabulous and the acceptance of them as the evangelists themselves mean them to be accepted, there will be many shades of belief and disbelief, of sympathy and derision. It is not a question of being a Christian or not. A Mahometan Arab will accept literally and without question parts of the narrative which an English Archbishop has to reject or explain away; and many Theosophists and lovers of the wisdom of India, who never enter a Christian Church except as sightseers, will revel in parts of John's gospel which mean nothing to a pious matter-of-fact Bradford manufacturer. Every reader takes from the Bible what he can get. In submitting a précis of the gospel narratives I have not implied any estimate either of their credibility or of their truth. I have simply informed him or reminded him, as the case may be, of what those narratives tell us about their hero.

CHRISTIAN ICONOLATRY AND THE PERIL OF THE ICONOCLAST

I must now abandon this attitude, and make a serious draft on the reader's attention by facing the question whether, if and when the medieval and Methodist will-to-believe the Salvationist and miraculous side of the gospel narratives fails us, as it plainly has failed the leaders of modern thought, there will be anything left of the mission of Jesus: whether, in short, we may not throw the gospels into the wastepaper basket, or put them away on the fiction shelf of our libraries. I venture to reply that we shall be, on the contrary, in the position of the man in Bunyan's riddle who found that "the more he threw away, the more he had" [*Pilgrim's Progress*, Part II]. We get rid, to begin with, of the idolatrous or iconographic worship of Christ. By this I mean literally that worship which is given to pictures and statues of him, and to finished and unalterable stories about him. The test of the prevalence of this is that if you speak or write of Jesus as a real live person, or even as a still active God, such worshippers are more horrified than Don Juan was when the statue stepped from its pedestal and came to supper with him. You may deny the divinity of Jesus; you may doubt whether he ever existed; you may reject Christianity for Judaism, Mahometanism, Shintoism, or Fire Worship; and the iconolaters, placidly contemptuous, will only classify you as a freethinker or a heathen. But if you venture to wonder how Christ would have looked if he had shaved and had his hair cut, or what size in shoes he took, or whether he swore when he stood on a nail in the carpenter's shop, or could not button his robe when he was in a hurry, or whether he laughed over the repartees by which he baffled the priests when they tried to trap him into sedition and blasphemy, or even if you tell any part of his story in the vivid terms of modern colloquial slang, you will produce an extraordinary dismay and horror among the iconolaters. You will have made the picture come out of its frame, the statue descend from its pedestal, the story become real, with all the incalculable consequences that may flow from this terrifying miracle. It is at such moments that you realize that the iconolaters have never for a moment conceived Christ as a real person who meant what he said, as a fact, as a force like electricity, only needing the invention of suitable political machinery to be applied to the affairs of mankind with revolutionary effect.

Thus it is not disbelief that is dangerous in our society: it is belief. The moment it strikes you (as it may any day) that Christ is not the lifeless harmless image he has hitherto been to you, but a rallying centre for revolutionary influences which all established States and Churches fight, you must look to yourselves; for you have brought the image to life; and the mob may not be able to bear that horror.

THE ALTERNATIVE TO BARABBAS

But mobs must be faced if civilization is to be saved. It did not need the present war to shew that neither the iconographic Christ nor the Christ of St Paul has succeeded in effecting the salvation of human society. Whilst I write, the Turks are said to be massacring the Armenian Christians on an unprecedented scale;[18] but Europe is not in a position to remonstrate; for her Christians are slaying oneanother by every device which civilization has put within their reach as busily as they are slaying the Turks. Barabbas is triumphant everywhere; and the final use he makes of his triumph is to lead us all to suicide with heroic gestures and resounding lies. Now those who, like myself, see the Barabbasque social organization as a failure, and are convinced that the Life Force (or whatever you choose to call it) cannot be finally beaten by any failure, and will even supersede humanity by evolving a higher species if we cannot master the problems raised by the multiplication of our own numbers, have always known that Jesus had a real message, and have felt the fascination of his character and doctrine. Not that we should nowadays dream of claiming any supernatural authority for him, much less the technical authority which attaches to an educated modern philosopher and jurist. But when, having entirely got rid of Salvationist Christianity, and even contracted a prejudice against Jesus on the score of his involuntary connection with it, we engage on a purely scientific study of economics, criminology, and biology, and find that our practical conclusions are virtually those of Jesus, we are distinctly pleased and encouraged to find that we were doing him an injustice, and that the nimbus that surrounds his head in the pictures may be interpreted some day as a light of science rather than a declaration of sentiment or a label of idolatry.

The doctrines in which Jesus is thus confirmed are, roughly, the following:

1. The kingdom of heaven is within you. You are the son of God; and God is the son of man. God is a spirit, to be worshipped in spirit and in truth, and not an elderly gentleman to be bribed and begged from. We are members one of another; so that you cannot injure or help your neighbor without injuring or helping yourself. God is your father: you are here to do God's work; and you and your father are one.

2. Get rid of property by throwing it into the common stock. Dissociate your work entirely from money payments. If you let a child starve you are letting God starve. Get rid of all anxiety about tomorrow's dinner and clothes, because you cannot serve two masters: God and Mammon.

3. Get rid of judges and punishment and revenge. Love your neighbor as

18. During 1915–16 an estimated one million Christian Armenians in Turkey died through Turkish Government decrees. See also p. 269, fn. 8.

yourself, he being a part of yourself. And love your enemies: they are your neighbors.

4. Get rid of your family entanglements. Every mother you meet is as much your mother as the woman who bore you. Every man you meet is as much your brother as the man she bore after you. Dont waste your time at family funerals grieving for your relatives: attend to life, not to death: there are as good fish in the sea as ever came out of it, and better. In the kingdom of heaven, which, as aforesaid, is within you, there is no marriage nor giving in marriage, because you cannot devote your life to two divinities: God and the person you are married to.

Now these are very interesting propositions; and they become more interesting every day, as experience and science drive us more and more to consider them favorably. In considering them, we shall waste our time unless we give them a reasonable construction. We must assume that the man who saw his way through such a mass of popular passion and illusion as stands between us and a sense of the value of such teaching was quite aware of all the objections that occur to an average stockbroker in the first five minutes. It is true that the world is governed to a considerable extent by the considerations that occur to stockbrokers in the first five minutes; but as the result is that the world is so badly governed that those who know the truth can hardly bear to live in it, an objection from an average stockbroker constitutes in itself a *prima facie* [obvious] case for any social reform.

THE REDUCTION TO MODERN PRACTICE OF CHRISTIANITY

All the same, we must reduce the ethical counsels and proposals of Jesus to modern practice if they are to be of any use to us. If we ask our stockbroker to act simply as Jesus advised his disciples to act, he will reply, very justly, "You are advising me to become a tramp." If we urge a rich man to sell all that he has and give it to the poor, he will inform us that such an operation is impossible. If he sells his shares and his lands, their purchaser will continue all those activities which oppress the poor. If all the rich men take the advice simultaneously the shares will fall to zero and the lands be unsaleable. If one man sells out and throws the money into the slums, the only result will be to add himself and his dependents to the list of the poor, and to do no good to the poor beyond giving a chance few of them a drunken spree. We must therefore bear in mind that whereas, in the time of Jesus, and in the ages which grew darker and darker after his death until the darkness, after a brief false dawn in the Reformation and the

Renascence, culminated in the commercial night of the XIX century, it was believed that you could not make men good by Act of Parliament, we now know that you cannot make them good in any other way, and that a man who is better than his fellows is a nuisance. The rich man must sell up not only himself but his whole class; and that can be done only through the Chancellor of the Exchequer. The disciple cannot have his bread without money until there is bread for everybody without money; and that requires an elaborate municipal organization of the food supply, rate supported. Being members one of another means One Man One Vote, and One Woman One Vote, and universal suffrage and equal incomes and all sorts of modern political measures. Even in Syria in the time of Jesus his teachings could not possibly have been realized by a series of independent explosions of personal righteousness on the part of the separate units of the population. Jerusalem could not have done what even a village community cannot do, and what Robinson Crusoe himself could not have done if his conscience, and the stern compulsion of Nature, had not imposed a common rule on the half dozen Robinson Crusoes who struggled within him for not wholly compatible satisfactions. And what cannot be done in Jerusalem or Juan Fernandez[19] cannot be done in London, New York, Paris, and Berlin.

In short, Christianity, good or bad, right or wrong, must perforce be left out of the question in human affairs until it is made practically applicable to them by complicated political devices; and to pretend that a field preacher under the governorship of Pontius Pilate, or even Pontius Pilate himself in council with all the wisdom of Rome, could have worked out applications of Christianity or any other system of morals for the XX century, is to shelve the subject much more effectually than Nero and all its other persecutors ever succeeded in doing. Personal righteousness, and the view that you cannot make people moral by Act of Parliament, is, in fact, the favorite defensive resort of the people who, consciously or subconsciously, are quite determined not to have their property meddled with by Jesus or any other reformer.

MODERN COMMUNISM

Now let us see what modern experience and sociology have to say to the suggestion of Jesus that you should get rid of your property by throwing it

19. One of a group of Pacific Islands west of Chile, of which one is Robinson Crusoe Island.

into the common stock. One can hear the Pharisees of Jerusalem and Chorazin and Bethsaida[20] saying, "My good fellow, if you were to divide up the wealth of Judea equally today, before the end of the year you would have rich and poor, poverty and affluence, just as you have today; for there will always be the idle and the industrious, the thrifty and the wasteful, the drunken and the sober; and, as you yourself have very justly observed, the poor we shall have always with us." And we can hear the reply, "Woe unto you, liars and hypocrites; for ye have this very day divided up the wealth of the country yourselves, as must be done every day (for man liveth not otherwise than from hand to mouth, nor can fish and eggs endure for ever); and ye have divided it unjustly; also ye have said that my reproach to you for having the poor always with you was a law unto you that this evil should persist and stink in the nostrils of God to all eternity; wherefore I think that Lazarus will yet see you beside Dives in hell." Modern Capitalism has made short work of the primitive pleas for inequality. The Pharisees themselves have organized communism in capital. Joint stock is the order of the day. An attempt to return to individual properties as the basis of our production would smash civilization more completely than ten revolutions. You cannot get the fields tilled today until the farmer becomes a cooperator. Take the shareholder to his railway, and ask him to point out to you the particular length of rail, the particular seat in the railway carriage, the particular lever in the engine that is his very own and nobody elses; and he will shun you as a madman, very wisely. And if, like Ananias and Sapphira,[21] you try to hold back your little shop or what not from the common stock, represented by the Trust, or Combine, or Kartel, the Trust will presently freeze you out and rope you in and finally strike you dead industrially as thoroughly as St Peter himself. There is no longer any practical question open as to Communism in production: the struggle today is over the distribution of the product: that is, over the daily dividing-up which is the first necessity of organized society.

20. Chorazin and Bethsaida: both towns in Galilee were cursed by Jesus for their unbelief (Matthew 11: 21).
21. When this Jewish-Christian couple withheld some of their profits from the communal pooling, St Peter charged them with falsehood and they were struck dead (Acts 5: 1–10).

REDISTRIBUTION

Now it needs no Christ to convince anybody today that our system of distribution is wildly and monstrously wrong. We have million-dollar babies side by side with paupers worn out by a long life of unremitted drudgery. One person in every five dies in a workhouse, a public hospital, or a madhouse. In cities like London the proportion is very nearly one in two. Naturally so outrageous a distribution has to be effected by violence pure and simple. If you demur, you are sold up. If you resist the selling up you are bludgeoned and imprisoned, the process being euphemistically called the maintenance of law and order. Iniquity can go no further. By this time nobody who knows the figures of the distribution defends them. The most bigoted British Conservative hesitates to say that his king should be much poorer than Mr [John D.] Rockefeller, or to proclaim the moral superiority of prostitution to needlework on the ground that it pays better. The need for a drastic redistribution of income in all civilized countries is now as obvious and as generally admitted as the need for sanitation.

SHALL HE WHO MAKES, OWN?

It is when we come to the question of the proportions in which we are to redistribute that controversy begins. We are bewildered by an absurdly unpractical notion that in some way a man's income should be given to him, not to enable him to live, but as a sort of Sunday School Prize for good behavior. And this folly is complicated by a less ridiculous but quite as unpractical belief that it is possible to assign to each person the exact portion of the national income that he or she has produced. To a child it seems that the blacksmith has made a horseshoe, and that therefore the horseshoe is his. But the blacksmith knows that the horseshoe does not belong solely to him, but to his landlord, to the rate collector and taxgatherer, to the men from whom he bought the iron and anvil and the coals, leaving only a scrap of its value for himself; and this scrap he has to exchange with the butcher and baker and the clothier for the things that he really appropriates as living tissue or its wrappings, paying for all of them more than their cost; for these fellow traders of his have also their landlords and moneylenders to satisfy. If, then, such simple and direct village examples of apparent individual production turn out on a moment's examination to be the products of an elaborate social organization, what is to be said of such products as dreadnoughts, factory-made pins and needles, and steel pens? If God takes the dreadnought in one hand and a steel pen in the other, and asks Job who made them, and to whom they should belong by maker's right, Job must scratch his puzzled head with a potsherd and be dumb, unless indeed it strikes him that God is the ultimate maker, and that all we have a right to do with the product is to feed his lambs.

LABOR TIME

So maker's right as an alternative to taking the advice of Jesus would not work. In practice nothing was possible in that direction but to pay a worker by labor time: so much an hour or day or week or year. But how much? When that question came up, the only answer was "as little as he can be starved into accepting," with the ridiculous results already mentioned, and the additional anomaly that the largest share went to the people who did not work at all, and the least to those who worked hardest. In England nine-tenths of the wealth goes into the pockets of one-tenth of the population.

THE DREAM OF DISTRIBUTION ACCORDING TO MERIT

Against this comes the protest of the Sunday School theorists "Why not distribute according to merit?" Here one imagines Jesus, whose smile has been broadening down the ages as attempt after attempt to escape from his teaching has led to deeper and deeper disaster, laughing outright. Was ever so idiotic a project mooted as the estimation of virtue in money? The London School of Economics is, we must suppose, to set examination papers with such questions as "Taking the money value of the virtues of Jesus as 100, and of Judas Iscariot as zero, give the correct figures for, respectively, Pontius Pilate, the proprietor of the Gadarene swine, the widow who put her mite in the poor-box, Mr Horatio Bottomley,[22] Shakespear, Mr [John] Jack Johnson,[23] Sir Isaac Newton, Palestrina, Offenbach, Sir Thomas Lipton, Mr Paul Cinquevalli, your family doctor,

22. English businessman, politician (of questionable repute) and editor, was a director and, briefly, chairman of the newly founded *Financial Times* in 1888.
23. First Negro world heavyweight boxer, 1908–15.

Florence Nightingale, Mrs [Sarah] Siddons, your charwoman, the Archbishop of Canterbury, and the common hangman." Or "The late Mr
Barney Barnato [Barnett Isaacs][24] received as his lawful income three thousand times as much money as an English agricultural laborer of good
general character. Name the principal virtues in which Mr Barnato exceeded the laborer three thousandfold; and give in figures the loss sustained
by civilization when Mr Barnato was driven to despair and suicide by the
reduction of his multiple to one thousand." The Sunday School idea, with
its principle "to each the income he deserves," is really too silly for
discussion. Hamlet disposed of it three hundred years ago. "Use every man
after his deserts, and who shall scape whipping?" [Hamlet, II: ii] Jesus
remains unshaken as the practical man; and we stand exposed as the fools,
the blunderers, the unpractical visionaries. The moment you try to reduce
the Sunday School idea to figures you find that it brings you back to the
hopeless plan of paying for a man's time; and your examination paper will
read "The time of Jesus was worth nothing (he complained that the foxes
had holes and the birds of the air nests whilst he had not a place to lay his
head [Matthew 8: 20]). Dr [Hawley] Crippen's[25] time was worth, say, three
hundred and fifty pounds a year. Criticize this arrangement; and, if you
dispute its justice, state in pounds, dollars, francs and marks, what their
relative time wages ought to have been." Your answer may be that the
question is in extremely bad taste and that you decline to answer it. But
you cannot object to being asked how many minutes of a bookmaker's
time are worth two hours of an astronomer's?

VITAL DISTRIBUTION

In the end you are forced to ask the question you should have asked at
the beginning. What do you give a man an income for? Obviously to keep
him alive. Since it is evident that the first condition on which he can be
kept alive without enslaving somebody else is that he shall produce an
equivalent for what it costs to keep him alive, we may quite rationally

24. English speculator, who with Cecil Rhodes controlled the Kimberley mines in
South Africa. The failure of his banking company led to his suicide.
25. 'Dr' Crippen studied medicine and dentistry in Michigan. After poisoning his
wife in London he fled to Canada, where he was apprehended in the first
telegraphic arrest on record. Returned to England for trial, he was found guilty of
murder and executed in 1910.

compel him to abstain from idling by whatever means we employ to compel him to abstain from murder, arson, forgery, or any other crime. The one supremely foolish thing to do with him is to do nothing: that is to be as idle, lazy, and heartless in dealing with him as he is in dealing with us. Even if we provided work for him instead of basing, as we do, our whole industrial system on successive competitive waves of overwork with their ensuing troughs of unemployment, we should still sternly deny him the alternative of not doing it; for the result must be that he will become poor and make his children poor if he has any; and poor people are cancers in the commonwealth, costing far more than if they were handsomely pensioned off as incurables. Jesus had more sense than to propose anything of the sort. He said to his disciples, in effect, "Do your work for love; and let the other people lodge and feed and clothe you for love." Or, as we should put it nowadays, "for nothing." All human experience and all natural uncommercialized human aspiration point to this as the right path. The Greeks said, "First secure an independent income; and then practise virtue." We all strive towards an independent income. We all know as well as Jesus did that if we have to take thought for the morrow as to whether there shall be anything to eat or drink it will be impossible for us to think of nobler things, or live a higher life than that of a mole, whose life is from beginning to end a frenzied pursuit of food. Until the community is organized in such a way that the fear of bodily want is forgotten as completely as the fear of wolves already is in civilized capitals, we shall never have a decent social life. Indeed the whole attraction of our present arrangement lies in the fact that it does relieve a handful of us from this fear; but as the relief is effected stupidly and wickedly by making the favored handful parasitic on the rest, they are smitten with the degeneracy which seems to be the inevitable biological penalty of complete parasitism. They corrupt culture and statecraft instead of contributing to them, their excessive leisure being as mischievous as the excessive toil of the laborers. Anyhow, the moral is clear. The two main problems of organized society: how to produce subsistence enough for all its members, and how to prevent the theft of that subsistence by idlers, should be carefully dissociated; for the triumphant solution of the first by our inventors and chemists has been offset by the disastrous failure of our rulers to solve the other. Optimism on this point is only wilful blindness: we all have the hard fact of the failure before us. The only people who cling to the lazy delusion that it is possible to find a just distribution that will work automatically are those who postulate some revolutionary change like land nationalization, which by itself would obviously only force into greater urgency the problem of how to distribute the product of the land among all the individuals in the community.

EQUAL DISTRIBUTION

When that problem is at last faced, the question of the proportion in which the national income shall be distributed can have only one answer. All our shares must be equal. It has always been so: it always will be so. It is true that the incomes of robbers vary considerably from individual to individual; and the variation is reflected in the incomes of their parasites. The commercialization of certain exceptional talents has also produced exceptional incomes, direct and derivative. Persons who live on rent of land and capital are economically, though not legally, in the category of robbers, and have grotesquely different incomes. But in the huge mass of mankind variation of income from individual to individual is unknown, because it is ridiculously impracticable. As a device for persuading a carpenter that a judge is a creature of superior nature to himself, to be deferred and submitted to even to the death, we may give a carpenter a hundred pounds a year and a judge five thousand; but the wage for one carpenter is the wage for all the carpenters: the salary for one judge is the salary for all the judges.

THE CAPTAIN AND THE CABIN BOY

Nothing, therefore, is really in question, or ever has been, but the differences between class incomes. Already there is economic equality between captains, and economic equality between cabin boys. What is at issue still is whether there shall be economic equality between captains and cabin boys. What would Jesus have said? Presumably he would have said that if your only object is to produce a captain and a cabin boy for the purpose of transferring you from Liverpool to New York, or to manœuvre a fleet and carry powder from the magazine to the gun, then you need give no more than a shilling to the cabin boy for every pound you give to the more expensively trained captain. But if in addition to this you desire to allow the two human souls which are inseparable from the captain and the cabin boy, and which alone differentiate them from the donkey-engine, to develop all their possibilities, then you may find the cabin boy costing rather more than the captain, because cabin boy's work does not do so much for the soul as captain's work. Consequently you will have to give him at least as much as the captain unless you definitely wish him to be a lower creature, in which case the sooner you are hanged as an abortionist the better. That is the fundamental argument.

THE POLITICAL AND BIOLOGICAL OBJECTIONS TO INEQUALITY

But there are other reasons for objecting to class stratification of income which have heaped themselves up since the time of Jesus. In politics it defeats every form of government except that of a necessarily corrupt oligarchy. Democracy in the most democratic modern republics: France and the United States for example, is an imposture and a delusion. It reduces justice and law to a farce: law becomes merely an instrument for keeping the poor in subjection; and accused workmen are tried, not by a jury of their peers, but by conspiracies of their exploiters. The press is the press of the rich and the curse of the poor: it becomes dangerous to teach men to read. The priest becomes the mere complement of the policeman in the machinery by which the country house oppresses the village. Worst of all, marriage becomes a class affair: the infinite variety of choice which nature offers to the young in search of a mate is narrowed to a handful of persons of similar income; and beauty and health become the dreams of artists and the advertisements of quacks instead of the normal conditions of life. Society is not only divided but actually destroyed in all directions by inequality of income between classes: such stability as it has is due to the huge blocks of people between whom there is equality of income.

JESUS AS ECONOMIST

It seems therefore that we must begin by holding the right to an income as sacred and equal, just as we now begin by holding the right to life as sacred and equal. Indeed the one right is only a restatement of the other. To hang me for cutting a dock laborer's throat after making much of me for leaving him to starve when I do not happen to have a ship for him to unload is idiotic; for as he does far less mischief with his throat cut than when he is starving, a rational society would esteem the cutthroat more highly than the capitalist. The thing has become so obvious, and the evil so unendurable, that if our attempt at civilization is not to perish like all the previous ones, we shall have to organize our society in such a way as to be able to say to every person in the land, "Take no thought, saying What shall we eat? or What shall we drink? or Wherewithal shall we be clothed?" We shall then no longer have a race of men whose hearts are in their pockets and safes and at their bankers. As Jesus said, where your treasure is, there will your heart be also [Matthew 6: 21]. That was why he recommended that money should cease to be a treasure, and that we should take steps to make ourselves utterly reckless of it, setting our minds free for higher uses [Luke 12: 33–4]. In other words, that we should all be gentlemen and take care of our country because our country takes care of us, instead of the commercialized cads we are, doing everything and anything for money, and selling our souls and bodies by the pound and the inch after wasting half the day haggling over the price. Decidedly, whether you think Jesus was God or not, you must admit that he was a firstrate political economist.

JESUS AS BIOLOGIST

He was also, as we now see, a firstrate biologist. It took a century and a half of evolutionary preachers, from [Georges] Buffon and Goethe to Butler and [Henri] Bergson, to convince us that we and our father are one; that as the kingdom of heaven is within us we need not go about looking for it and crying Lo here! and Lo there!; that God is not a picture of a pompous person in white robes in the family Bible, but a spirit; that it is through this spirit that we evolve towards greater abundance of life; that we are the lamps in which the light of the world burns: that, in short, we are gods though we die like men. All that is today sound biology and psychology; and the efforts of Natural Selectionists like [August] Weismann to reduce evolution to mere automatism have not touched the doctrine of Jesus, though they have made short work of the theologians who conceived God as a magnate keeping men and angels as Lord Rothschild keeps buffaloes and emus at Tring.[26]

26. The Rothschild Museum was erected in 1889 in the market town of Tring, Hertfordshire, by Nathan Meyer, First Baron de Rothschild, to contain an extensive natural history collection, as well as living animals kept in neighbouring cages.

Money the Midwife of Scientific Communism

It may be asked here by some simpleminded reader why we should not resort to crude communism as the disciples were told to do. This would be quite practicable in a village where production was limited to the supply of the primitive wants which nature imposes on all human beings alike. We know that people need bread and boots without waiting for them to come and ask for these things and offer to pay for them. But when civilization advances to the point at which articles are produced that no man absolutely needs and that only some men fancy or can use, it is necessary that individuals should be able to have things made to their order and at their own cost. It is safe to provide bread for everybody because everybody wants and eats bread; but it would be absurd to provide microscopes and trombones, pet snakes and polo mallets, alembics and test tubes for everybody, as nine-tenths of them would be wasted; and the nine-tenths of the population who do not use such things would object to their being provided at all. We have in the invaluable instrument called money a means of enabling every individual to order and pay for the particular things he desires over and above the things he must consume in order to remain alive, plus the things the State insists on his having and using whether he wants to or not: for example, clothes, sanitary arrangements, armies and navies. In large communities, where even the most eccentric demands for manufactured articles average themselves out until they can be foreseen within a negligible margin of error, direct communism (Take what you want without payment, as the people do in Morris's News From Nowhere) will, after a little experience, be found not only practicable but highly economical to an extent that now seems impossible. The sportsmen, the musicians, the physicists, the biologists will get their apparatus for the asking as easily as their bread, or, as at present, their paving, street lighting, and bridges; and the deaf man will not object to contribute to communal flutes when the musician has to contribute to communal ear trumpets. There are cases (for example, radium) in which the demand may be limited to the merest handful of laboratory workers, and in which nevertheless the whole community must pay because the price is beyond the means of any individual worker. But even when the utmost allowance is made for extensions of communism that now seem fabulous, there will still remain for a long time to come regions of supply and demand in which men will need and use money or individual credit, and for which, therefore, they must have individual incomes. Foreign travel is an obvious instance. We are so far from even national communism still, that we shall probably have considerable developments of local communism before it becomes possible for a Manchester man to go up to London for a day without taking any money with him. The modern practical form of the communism of Jesus is therefore, for the present, equal distribution of the surplus of the national income that is not absorbed by simple communism.

JUDGE NOT

In dealing with crime and the family, modern thought and experience have thrown no fresh light on the views of Jesus. When Swift had occasion to illustrate the corruption of our civilization by making a catalogue of the types of scoundrels it produces, he always gave judges a conspicuous place alongside of them they judged.[27] And he seems to have done this not as a restatement of the doctrine of Jesus, but as the outcome of his own observation and judgment. One of Mr Gilbert Chesterton's stories[28] has for its hero a judge who, whilst trying a criminal case, is so overwhelmed by the absurdity of his position and the wickedness of the things it forces him to do, that he throws off the ermine there and then, and goes out into the world to live the life of an honest man instead of that of a cruel idol. There has also been a propaganda of a soulless stupidity called Determinism, representing man as a dead object driven hither and thither by his environment, antecedents, circumstances, and so forth, which nevertheless does remind us that there are limits to the number of cubits an individual can add to his stature morally or physically, and that it is silly as well as cruel to torment a man five feet high for not being able to pluck fruit that is within the reach of men of average height. I have known a case of an unfortunate child being beaten for not being able to tell the time after receiving an

27. For Swift's satiric treatment of judges, see Section II of the *Sermon on False Witness* (1762), the preface to *A Tale of a Tub* (1704) and *Gulliver's Travels*, Part IV, Chapter 5.
28. 'The Tremendous Adventures of Major Brown', the opening tale in Chesterton's *The Club of Queer Trades* (1905), deals with a judge named Basil Grant, who, disillusioned with his calling, suddenly interrupts the case over which he is presiding and, shocking the court, bursts out in a coarse song. Concluding nonsensically 'Rowty owty, Tiddledy owty, Tiddledy owty ow', he bows to the court and vanishes. Turning amateur detective he solves the mysteries in the half-dozen tales that comprise the book.

elaborate explanation of the figures on a clock dial, the fact being that she was shortsighted and could not see them. This is a typical illustration of the absurdities and cruelties into which we are led by the counter-stupidity to Determinism: the doctrine of Free Will. The notion that people can be good if they like, and that you should give them a powerful additional motive for goodness by tormenting them when they do evil, would soon reduce itself to absurdity if its application were not kept within the limits which nature sets to the self-control of most of us. Nobody supposes that a man with no ear for music or no mathematical faculty could be compelled on pain of death, however cruelly inflicted, to hum all the themes of Beethoven's symphonies or to complete Newton's work on fluxions.[29]

LIMITS TO FREE WILL

Consequently such of our laws as are not merely the intimidations by which tyrannies are maintained under pretext of law, can be obeyed through the exercise of a quite common degree of reasoning power and self-control. Most men and women can endure the ordinary annoyances and disappointments of life without committing murderous assaults. They conclude therefore that any person can refrain from such assaults if he or she chooses to, and proceed to reinforce self-control by threats of severe punishment. But in this they are mistaken. There are people, some of them possessing considerable powers of mind and body, who can no more restrain the fury into which a trifling mishap throws them than a dog can restrain himself from snapping if he is suddenly and painfully pinched. People fling knives and lighted paraffin lamps at oneanother in a dispute over a dinner table. Men who have suffered several long sentences of penal servitude for murderous assaults will, the very day after they are released, seize their wives and cast them under drays at an irritating word. We have not only people who cannot resist an opportunity of stealing for the sake of satisfying their wants, but even people who have a specific mania for stealing, and do it when they are in no need of the things they steal. Burglary fascinates some men as sailoring fascinates some boys. Among respectable people how many are there who can be restrained by the warnings of their doctors and the lessons of experience from eating and drinking more than is good for them? It is true that between self-controlled

29. Newton's work on fluxions was begun in *Methodus Fluxionum* (1671), but never completed.

people and ungovernable people there is a narrow margin of moral malingerers who can be made to behave themselves by the fear of consequences; but it is not worth while maintaining an abominable system of malicious, deliberate, costly and degrading ill-treatment of criminals for the sake of these marginal cases. For practical dealing with crime, Determinism or Predestination is quite a good working rule. People without self-control enough for social purposes may be killed, or may be kept in asylums with a view to studying their condition and ascertaining whether it is curable. To torture them and give ourselves virtuous airs at their expense is ridiculous and barbarous; and the desire to do it is vindictive and cruel. And though vindictiveness and cruelty are at least human qualities when they are frankly proclaimed and indulged, they are loathsome when they assume the robes of Justice. Which, I take it, is why Shakespear's Isabella gave such a dressing-down to Judge Angelo [in *Measure for Measure*], and why Swift reserved the hottest corner of his hell for judges.[30] Also, of course, why Jesus said "Judge not that ye be not judged" [Matthew 7: 1] and "If any man hear my words and believe not, I judge him not" because "he hath one that judgeth him" [John 12: 47–8]: namely, the Father who is one with him.

When we are robbed we generally appeal to the criminal law, not considering that if the criminal law were effective we should not have been robbed. That convicts us of vengeance.

I need not elaborate the argument further. I have dealt with it sufficiently elsewhere. I have only to point out that we have been judging and punishing ever since Jesus told us not to; and I defy anyone to make out a convincing case for believing that the world has been any better than it would have been if there had never been a judge, a prison, or a gallows in it all that time. We have simply added the misery of punishment to the misery of crime, and the cruelty of the judge to the cruelty of the criminal. We have taken the bad man, and made him worse by torture and degradation, incidentally making ourselves worse in the process. It does not seem very sensible, does it? It would have been far easier to kill him as kindly as possible, or to label him and leave him to his conscience, or to treat him as an invalid or a lunatic is now treated (it is only of late years, by the way, that madmen have been delivered from the whip, the chain, and the cage); and this, I presume, is the form in which the teaching of Jesus could have been put into practice.

30. No statement to this effect has been discovered in Swift's writings. Possibly Shaw was recalling Swift's sardonic reference to the 'three upright Judges' provided 'for Hell' by the Ancients, in *Intelligencer Papers*, No. XIX (1728).

JESUS ON MARRIAGE AND THE FAMILY

When we come to marriage and the family, we find Jesus making the same objection to that individual appropriation of human beings which is the essence of matrimony as to the individual appropriation of wealth. A married man, he said, will try to please his wife, and a married woman to please her husband, instead of doing the work of God. This is another version of "Where your treasure is, there will your heart be also." Eighteen hundred years later we find a very different person from Jesus, [Charles-Maurice de Talleyrand-Perigord] Talleyrand to wit, saying the same thing. A married man with a family, said Talleyrand, will do anything for money. Now this, though not a scientifically precise statement, is true enough to be a moral objection to marriage. As long as a man has a right to risk his life or his livelihood for his ideas he needs only courage and conviction to make his integrity unassailable. But he forfeits that right when he marries. It took a revolution to rescue Wagner from his Court appointment at Dresden [see Vol. 1, p. 109, fn. 1]; and his wife never forgave him for being glad and feeling free when he lost it and threw her back into poverty. [Jean François] Millet might have gone on painting potboiling nudes to the end of his life if his wife had not been of a heroic turn herself.[31] Women, for the sake of their children and parents, submit to slaveries and prostitutions that no unattached woman would endure.

This was the beginning and the end of the objection of Jesus to marriage and family ties, and the explanation of his conception of heaven as a place where there should be neither marrying nor giving in marriage. Now there is no reason to suppose that when he said this he did not mean it. He did not, as St Paul did afterwards in his name, propose celibacy as a rule of life; for he was not a fool, nor, when he denounced marriage, had he yet come to believe, as St Paul did, that the end of the world was at hand and there was therefore no more need to replenish the earth. He must have meant that the race should be continued without dividing with women and men the allegiance the individual owes to God within him. This raises the practical problem of how we are to secure the spiritual freedom and integrity of the priest and the nun without their barrenness and uncompleted experience. Luther the priest did not solve

31. Millet's second wife Catherine Lemaire shared with him in the poverty he depicted in such works as *The Gleaners* (1857).

the problem by marrying a nun: he only testified in the most convincing and practical way to the fact that celibacy was a worse failure than marriage.

WHY JESUS DID NOT MARRY

To all appearance the problem oppresses only a few exceptional people. Thoroughly conventional women married to thoroughly conventional men should not be conscious of any restriction: the chain not only leaves them free to do whatever they want to do, but greatly facilitates their doing it. To them an attack on marriage is not a blow struck in defence of their freedom but at their rights and privileges. One would expect that they would not only demur vehemently to the teachings of Jesus in this matter, but object strongly to his not having been a married man himself. Even those who regard him as a god descended from his throne in heaven to take on humanity for a time might reasonably declare that the assumption of humanity must have been incomplete at its most vital point if he were a celibate. But the facts are flatly contrary. The mere thought of Jesus as a married man is felt to be blasphemous by the most conventional believers; and even those of us to whom Jesus is no supernatural personage, but a prophet only as Mahomet was a prophet, feel that there was something more dignified in the bachelordom of Jesus than in the spectacle of Mahomet lying distracted on the floor of his harem whilst his wives stormed and squabbled and henpecked round him. We are not surprised that when Jesus called the sons of Zebedee to follow him, he did not call their father, and that the disciples, like Jesus himself, were all men without family entanglements. It is evident from his impatience when people excused themselves from following him because of their family funerals, or when they assumed that his first duty was to his mother, that he had found family ties and domestic affections in his way at every turn, and had become persuaded at last that no man could follow his inner light until he was free from their compulsion. The absence of any protest against this tempts us to declare that on this question of marriage there are no conventional people; and that everyone of us is at heart a good Christian sexually.

INCONSISTENCY OF THE SEX INSTINCT

But the question is not so simple as that. Sex is an exceedingly subtle and complicated instinct; and the mass of mankind neither know nor care much about freedom of conscience, which is what Jesus was thinking about, and are concerned almost to obsession with sex, as to which Jesus said nothing. In our sexual natures we are torn by an irresistible attraction and an overwhelming repugnance and disgust. We have two tyrannous physical passions: concupiscence and chastity. We become mad in pursuit of sex: we become equally mad in the persecution of that pursuit. Unless we gratify our desire the race is lost: unless we restrain it we destroy ourselves. We are thus led to devize marriage institutions which will at the same time secure opportunities for the gratification of sex and raise up innumerable obstacles to it; which will sanctify it and brand it as infamous; which will identify it with virtue and with sin simultaneously. Obviously it is useless to look for any consistency in such institutions; and it is only by continual reform and readjustment, and by a considerable elasticity in their enforcement, that a tolerable result can be arrived at. I need not repeat here the long and elaborate examination of them that I prefixed to my play entitled Getting Married [Vol. 1, pp. 409–70]. Here I am concerned only with the views of Jesus on the question; and it is necessary, in order to understand the attitude of the world towards them, that we should not attribute the general approval of the decision of Jesus to remain unmarried as an endorsement of his views. We are simply in a state of confusion on the subject; but it is part of the confusion that we should conclude that Jesus was a celibate, and shrink even from the idea that his birth was a natural one, yet cling with ferocity to the sacredness of the institution which provides a refuge from celibacy.

FOR BETTER FOR WORSE

Jesus, however, did not express a complicated view of marriage. His objection to it was quite simple, as we have seen. He perceived that nobody could live the higher life unless money and sexual love were obtainable without sacrificing it; and he saw that the effect of marriage as it existed among the Jews (and as it still exists among ourselves) was to make the couples sacrifice every higher consideration until they had fed and pleased oneanother. The worst of it is that this dangerous preposterousness in marriage, instead of improving as the general conduct of married couples improves, becomes much worse. The selfish man to whom his wife is nothing but a slave, the selfish woman to whom her husband is nothing but a scapegoat and a breadwinner, are not held back from spiritual or any other adventures by fear of their effect on the welfare of their mates. Their wives do not make recreants and cowards of them: their husbands do not chain them to the cradle and the cooking range when their feet should be beautiful on the mountains [Isaiah 52: 7]. It is precisely as people become more kindly, more conscientious, more ready to shoulder the heavier part of the burden (which means that the strong shall give way to the weak and the slow hold back the swift), that marriage becomes an intolerable obstacle to individual evolution. And that is why the revolt against marriage of which Jesus was an exponent always recurs when civilization raises the standard of marital duty and affection, and at the same time produces a greater need for individual freedom in pursuit of a higher evolution.

THE REMEDY

This, fortunately, is only one side of marriage; and the question arises, can it not be eliminated? The reply is reassuring: of course it can. There is no mortal reason in the nature of things why a married couple should be economically dependent on oneanother. The communism advocated by Jesus, which we have seen to be entirely practicable, and indeed inevitable if our civilization is to be saved from collapse, gets rid of that difficulty completely. And with the economic dependence will go the force of the outrageous claims that derive their real sanction from the economic pressure behind them. When a man allows his wife to turn him from the best work he is capable of doing, and to sell his soul at the highest commercial prices obtainable; when he allows her to entangle him in a social routine that is wearisome and debilitating to him, or tie him to her apron strings when he needs that occasional solitude which is one of the most sacred of human rights, he does so because he has no right to impose eccentric standards of expenditure and unsocial habits on her, and because these conditions have produced by their pressure so general a custom of chaining wedded couples to oneanother that married people are coarsely derided when their partners break the chain. And when a woman is condemned by her parents to wait in genteel idleness and uselessness for a husband when all her healthy social instincts call her to acquire a profession and work, it is again her economic dependence on them that makes their tyranny effective.

The Case for Marriage

Thus, though it would be too much to say that everything that is obnoxious in marriage and family life will be cured by Communism, yet it can be said that it will cure what Jesus objected to in these institutions. He made no comprehensive study of them: he only expressed his own grievance with an overwhelming sense that it is a grievance so deep that all the considerations on the other side are as dust in the balance. Obviously there are such considerations, and very weighty ones too. When Talleyrand said that a married man with a family is capable of anything, he meant anything evil; but an optimist may declare, with equal half truth, that a married man is capable of anything good; that marriage turns vagabonds into steady citizens; and that men and women will, for love of their mates and children, practise virtues that unattached individuals are incapable of. It is true that too much of this domestic virtue is self-denial, which is not a virtue at all; but then the following of the inner light at all costs is largely self-indulgence, which is just as suicidal, just as weak, just as cowardly as self-denial. Ibsen, who takes us into the matter far more resolutely than Jesus, is unable to find any golden rule: both Brand and Peer Gynt come to a bad end; and though Brand does not do as much mischief as Peer, the mischief he does do is of extraordinary intensity.

Celibacy no Remedy

We must, I think, regard the protest of Jesus against marriage and family ties as the claim of a particular kind of individual to be free from them because they hamper his own work intolerably. When he said that if we are to follow him in the sense of taking up his work we must give up our family ties, he was simply stating a fact; and to this day the Roman Catholic priest, the Buddhist lama, and the fakirs of all the eastern denominations accept the saying. It is also accepted by the physically enterprizing, the explorers, the restlessly energetic of all kinds: in short, by the adventurous. The greatest sacrifice in marriage is the sacrifice of the adventurous attitude towards life: the being settled. Those who are born tired may crave for settlement; but to fresher and stronger spirits it is a form of suicide.

Now to say of any institution that it is incompatible with both the contemplative and adventurous life is to disgrace it so vitally that all the moralizings of all the Deans and Chapters cannot reconcile our souls to its slavery. The unmarried Jesus and the unmarried Beethoven, the unmarried

Joan of Arc, Clare, Teresa, Florence Nightingale seem as they should be; and the saying that there is always something ridiculous about a married philosopher [Nietzsche, *The Genealogy of Morals*, 1887: 'A married philosopher belongs to comedy'] becomes inevitable. And yet the celibate is still more ridiculous than the married man: the priest, in accepting the alternative of celibacy, disables himself; and the best priests are those who have been men of this world before they became men of the world to come. But as the taking of vows does not annul an existing marriage, and a married man cannot become a priest, we are again confronted with the absurdity that the best priest is a reformed rake. Thus does marriage, itself intolerable, thrust us upon intolerable alternatives. The practical solution is to make the individual economically independent of marriage and the family, and to make marriage as easily dissoluble as any other partnership: in other words, to accept the conclusions to which experience is slowly driving both our sociologists and our legislators. This will not instantly cure all the evils of marriage, nor root up at one stroke its detestable tradition of property in human bodies. But it will leave Nature free to effect a cure; and in free soil the root may wither and perish.

This disposes of all the opinions and teachings of Jesus which are still matters of controversy. They are all in line with the best modern thought. He told us what we have to do; and we have had to find the way to do it. Most of us are still, as most were in his own time, extremely recalcitrant, and are being forced along that way by painful pressure of circumstances, protesting at every step that nothing will induce us to go; that is a ridiculous way, a disgraceful way, a socialistic way, an atheistic way, an immoral way, and that the vanguard ought to be ashamed of themselves and must be made to turn back at once. But they find that they have to follow the vanguard all the same if their lives are to be worth living.

AFTER THE CRUCIFIXION

Let us now return to the New Testament narrative; for what happened after the disappearance of Jesus is instructive. Unfortunately, the crucifixion was a complete political success. I remember that when I described it in these terms once before,[32] I greatly shocked a most respectable newspaper in my native town, the Dublin Daily Express, because my journalistic phrase

32. In an address 'Christian Economics', delivered to the City Temple Literary Society, London, 30 October 1913.

shewed that I was treating it as an ordinary event like Home Rule or the
Insurance Act:[33] that is (though this did not occur to the editor), as a real
event which had really happened, instead of a portion of the Church
service. I can only repeat, assuming as I am that it *was* a real event and did
actually happen, that it was as complete a success as any in history.
Christianity as a specific doctrine was slain with Jesus, suddenly and utterly.
He was hardly cold in his grave, or high in his heaven (as you please),
before the apostles dragged the tradition of him down to the level of the
thing it has remained ever since. And that thing the intelligent heathen may
study, if they would be instructed in it by modern books, in Samuel
Butler's novel, The Way of All Flesh.

THE VINDICTIVE MIRACLES AND THE STONING OF STEPHEN

Take, for example, the miracles. Of Jesus alone of all the Christian
miracle workers there is no record, except in certain gospels that all men
reject, of a malicious or destructive miracle. A barren fig-tree was the only
victim of his anger [Mark 11: 12–14]. Every one of his miracles on sentient
subjects was an act of kindness. John declares that he healed the wound of
the man whose ear was cut off (by Peter, John says[34]) at the arrest in the
garden. One of the first things the apostles did with their miraculous power
was to strike dead a wretched man and his wife who had defrauded them
by holding back some money from the common stock. They struck people
blind or dead without remorse, judging because they had been judged.
They healed the sick and raised the dead apparently in a spirit of pure
display and advertisement. Their doctrine did not contain a ray of that
light which reveals Jesus as one of the redeemers of men from folly and
error. They cancelled him, and went back straight to John the Baptist and
his formula of securing remission of sins by repentance and the rite of
baptism (being born again of water and the spirit). Peter's first harangue
softens us by the human touch of its exordium, which was a quaint
assurance to his hearers that they must believe him to be sober because it
was too early in the day to get drunk [Acts 2: 15]; but of Jesus he had
nothing to say except that he was the Christ foretold by the prophets as

33. England's National Insurance Act (1911) established compulsory sickness and
unemployment insurance for those earning less than £160 a year.
34. John's reference to this scene (18: 10) does not include the incident of Jesus
healing the wound. It is related in Luke 22: 50–51.

coming from the seed of David, and that they must believe this and be baptized. To this the other apostles added incessant denunciations of the Jews for having crucified him, and threats of the destruction that would overtake them if they did not repent: that is, if they did not join the sect which the apostles were now forming. A quite intolerable young speaker named Stephen delivered an oration to the council, in which he first inflicted on them a tedious sketch of the history of Israel, with which they were presumably as well acquainted as he, and then reviled them in the most insulting terms as "stiffnecked and uncircumcized" [Acts 7: 51]. Finally, after boring and annoying them to the utmost bearable extremity, he looked up and declared that he saw the heavens open, and Christ standing on the right hand of God. This was too much: they threw him out of the city and stoned him to death. It was a severe way of suppressing a tactless and conceited bore; but it was pardonable and human in comparison to the slaughter of poor Ananias and Sapphira.

PAUL

Suddenly a man of genius, Paul, violently anti–Christian, enters on the scene, holding the clothes of the men who are stoning Stephen. He persecutes the Christians with great vigor, a sport which he combines with the business of a tentmaker. This temperamental hatred of Jesus, whom he has never seen, is a pathological symptom of that particular sort of conscience and nervous constitution which brings its victims under the tyranny of two delirious terrors: the terror of sin and the terror of death, which may be called also the terror of sex and the terror of life. Now Jesus, with his healthy conscience on his higher plane, was free from these terrors. He consorted freely with sinners, and was never concerned for a moment, as far as we know, about whether his conduct was sinful or not; so that he has forced us to accept him as the man without sin. Even if we reckon his last days as the days of his delusion, he none the less gave a fairly convincing exhibition of superiority to the fear of death. This must have both fascinated and horrified Paul, or Saul, as he was first called. The horror accounts for his fierce persecution of the Christians. The fascination accounts for the strangest of his fancies: the fancy for attaching the name of Jesus Christ to the great idea which flashed upon him on the road to Damascus, the idea that he could not only make a religion of his two terrors, but that the movement started by Jesus offered him the nucleus for his new Church. It was a monstrous idea; and the shock of it, as he afterwards declared, struck him blind for days. He heard Jesus calling to him from the clouds, "Why persecute me?" [Acts 9: 4] His natural hatred of the teacher for whom Sin and Death had no terrors turned into a wild personal worship of him which has the ghastliness of a beautiful thing seen in a false light.

The chronicler of the Acts of the Apostles sees nothing of the significance of this. The great danger of conversion in all ages has been that when the religion of the high mind is offered to the lower mind, the lower mind, feeling its fascination without understanding it, and being incapable of rising to it, drags it down to its level by degrading it. Years ago I said that the conversion of a savage to Christianity is the conversion of Christianity to savagery ['The Revolutionist's Handbook' in *Man and Superman*]. The conversion of Paul was no conversion at all: it was Paul who converted the religion that has raised one man above sin and death into a religion that delivered millions of men so completely into their dominion that their own common nature became a horror to them, and the religious life became a denial of life. Paul had no intention of surrendering either his Judaism or his Roman citizenship to the new moral world [name of a journal published by the Owenites, 1834–41] (as Robert Owen called it) of Communism and Jesuism. Just as in our own time Karl Marx, not content to take political economy as he found it, insisted on rebuilding it from the bottom upwards in his own way, and thereby gave a new lease of life to the errors it was just outgrowing, so Paul reconstructed the old Salvationism from which Jesus had vainly tried to redeem him, and produced a fantastic theology which is still the most amazing thing of the kind known to us. Being intellectually an inveterate Roman Rationalist, always discarding the irrational real thing for the unreal but ratiocinable postulate, he began by discarding Man as he is, and substituted a postulate which he called Adam. And when he was asked, as he surely must have been in a world not wholly mad, what had become of the natural man, he replied "Adam *is* the natural man." This was confusing to simpletons, because according to tradition Adam was certainly the name of the natural man as created in the garden of Eden. It was as if a preacher of our own time had described as typically British Frankenstein's monster, and called him Smith, and somebody, on demanding what about the man in the street, had been told "Smith *is* the man in the street." The thing happens often enough; for indeed the world is full of these Adams and Smiths and men in the street and average sensual men and economic men and womanly women and what not, all of them imaginary Atlases carrying imaginary worlds on their unsubstantial shoulders.

The Eden story provided Adam with a sin: the "original sin" for which we are all damned. Baldly stated, this seems ridiculous; nevertheless it corresponds to something actually existent not only in Paul's consciousness but in our own. The original sin was not the eating of the forbidden fruit, but the consciousness of sin which the fruit produced. The moment Adam and Eve tasted the apple they found themselves ashamed of their sexual relation, which until then had seemed quite innocent to them; and there is no getting over the hard fact that this shame, or state of sin, has persisted to this day, and is one of the strongest of our instincts. Thus Paul's postulate of Adam as the natural man was pragmatically true: it worked. But the weakness of Pragmatism is that most theories will work if you put your back into making them work, provided they have some point of contact with human nature. Hedonism will pass the pragmatic test as well as Stoicism. Up to a certain point every social principle that is not absolutely idiotic works: Autocracy works in Russia and Democracy in America; Atheism works in France, Polytheism in India, Monotheism throughout Islam, and Pragmatism, or No-ism, in England. Paul's fantastic conception of the damned Adam, represented by Bunyan as a pilgrim with a great burden of sins on his back, corresponded to the fundamental condition of evolution, which is, that life, including human life, is continually evolving, and must therefore be continually ashamed of itself and its present and past. Bunyan's pilgrim wants to get rid of his bundle of sins; but he also wants to reach "yonder shining light"; and when at last his bundle falls off him into the sepulchre of Christ, his pilgrimage is still unfinished and his hardest trials still ahead of him. His conscience remains uneasy; "original sin" still torments him; and his adventure with Giant Despair, who throws him into the dungeon of Doubting Castle, from which he escapes by the use of a skeleton key, is more terrible than any he met whilst the bundle was still on his back. Thus Bunyan's allegory of human nature breaks through the Pauline theology at a hundred points. His theological allegory, The Holy War [1682], with its troops of Election Doubters, and its cavalry of "those that rode Reformadoes," is, as a whole, absurd, impossible, and, except in passages where the artistic old Adam momentarily got the better of the Salvationist theologian, hardly readable.

Paul's theory of original sin was to some extent idiosyncratic. He tells us definitely that he finds himself quite well able to avoid the sinfulness of sex by practising celibacy; but he recognizes, rather contemptuously, that in this respect he is not as other men are, and says that they had better marry than burn, thus admitting that though marriage may lead to placing the desire to please wife or husband before the desire to please God, yet preoccupation with unsatisfied desire may be even more ungodly than preoccupation with domestic affection. This view of the case inevitably led him to insist that a wife should be rather a slave than a partner, her real function being, not to engage a man's love and loyalty, but on the contrary to release them for God by relieving the man of all preoccupation with sex just as in her capacity of housekeeper and cook she relieves his preoccupation with hunger by the simple expedient of satisfying his appetite. This slavery also justifies itself pragmatically by working effectively; but it has made Paul the eternal enemy of Woman. Incidentally it has led to many foolish surmises about Paul's personal character and circumstances, by people so enslaved by sex that a celibate appears to them a sort of monster. They forget that not only whole priesthoods, official and unofficial, from Paul to Carlyle and Ruskin, have defied the tyranny of sex, but immense numbers of ordinary citizens of both sexes have, either voluntarily or under pressure of circumstances easily surmountable, saved their energies for less primitive activities.

Howbeit, Paul succeeded in stealing the image of Christ crucified for the figurehead of his Salvationist vessel, with its Adam posing as the natural man, its doctrine of original sin, and its damnation avoidable only by faith in the sacrifice of the cross. In fact, no sooner had Jesus knocked over the dragon of superstition than Paul boldly set it on its legs again in the name of Jesus.

THE CONFUSION OF CHRISTENDOM

Now it is evident that two religions having such contrary effects on mankind should not be confused as they are under a common name. There is not one word of Pauline Christianity in the characteristic utterances of Jesus. When Saul watched the clothes of the men who stoned Stephen, he was not acting upon beliefs which Paul renounced. There is no record of Christ's having ever said to any man: "Go and sin as much as you like: you can put it all on me." He said "Sin no more," and insisted that he was putting up the standard of conduct, not debasing it, and that the righteousness of the Christian must exceed that of the Scribe and Pharisee. The notion that he was shedding his blood in order that every petty cheat and adulterator and libertine might wallow in it and come out whiter than snow, cannot be imputed to him on his own authority. "I come as an infallible patent medicine for bad consciences" is not one of the sayings in the gospels. If Jesus could have been consulted on Bunyan's allegory as to that business of the burden of sin dropping from the pilgrim's back when he caught sight of the cross, we must infer from his teaching that he would have told Bunyan in forcible terms that he had never made a greater mistake in his life, and that the business of a Christ was to make self-satisfied sinners feel the burden of their sins and stop committing them instead of assuring them that they could not help it, as it was all Adam's fault, but that it did not matter as long as they were credulous and friendly about himself. Even when he believed himself to be a god, he did not regard himself as a scapegoat. He was to take away the sins of the world by good government, by justice and mercy, by setting the welfare of little children above the pride of princes, by casting all the quackeries and idolatries which now usurp and malversate the power of God into what our local authorities quaintly call the dust destructor [incinerator], and by riding on the clouds of heaven in glory instead of in a thousand-guinea motor car. That was delirious, if you like; but it was the delirium of a free soul, not of a shamebound one like Paul's. There has really never been a more monstrous imposition perpetrated than the imposition of the limitations of Paul's soul upon the soul of Jesus.

THE SECRET OF PAUL'S SUCCESS

Paul must soon have found that his followers had gained peace of mind and victory over death and sin at the cost of all moral responsibility; for he did his best to reintroduce it by making good conduct the test of sincere belief, and insisting that sincere belief was necessary to salvation. But as his system was rooted in the plain fact that as what he called sin includes sex and is therefore an ineradicable part of human nature (why else should Christ have had to atone for the sin of all future generations?) it was impossible for him to declare that sin, even in its wickedest extremity, could forfeit the sinner's salvation if he repented and believed. And to this day Pauline Christianity is, and owes its enormous vogue to being, a premium on sin. Its consequences have had to be held in check by the worldlywise majority through a violently anti-Christian system of criminal law and stern morality. But of course the main restraint is human nature, which has good impulses as well as bad ones, and refrains from theft and murder and cruelty, even when it is taught that it can commit them all at the expense of Christ and go happily to heaven afterwards, simply because it does not always want to murder or rob or torture.

It is now easy to understand why the Christianity of Jesus failed completely to establish itself politically and socially, and was easily suppressed by the police and the Church, whilst Paulinism overran the whole western civilized world, which was at that time the Roman Empire, and was adopted by it as its official faith, the old avenging gods falling helplessly before the new Redeemer. It still retains, as we may see in Africa, its power of bringing to simple people a message of hope and consolation that no other religion offers. But this enchantment is produced by its spurious association with the personal charm of Jesus, and exists only for untrained minds. In the hands of a logical Frenchman like Calvin,[35] pushing it to its utmost conclusions, and devizing "institutes" for hard-headed adult Scots and literal Swiss, it becomes the most infernal of fatalisms; and the lives of civilized children are blighted by its logic whilst negro piccaninnies are rejoicing in its legends.

PAUL'S QUALITIES

Paul, however, did not get his great reputation by mere imposition and reaction. It is only in comparison with Jesus (to whom many prefer him) that he appears common and conceited. Though in The Acts he is only a vulgar revivalist, he comes out in his own epistles as a genuine poet, though by flashes only. He is no more a Christian than Jesus was a Baptist: he is a disciple of Jesus only as Jesus was a disciple of John. He does nothing that Jesus would have done, and says nothing that Jesus would have said, though much, like the famous ode to charity [1 Corinthians 13: 1–13], that he would have admired. He is more Jewish than the Jews, more Roman than the Romans, proud both ways, full of startling confessions and self-revelations that would not surprise us if they were slipped into the pages of Nietzsche, tormented by an intellectual conscience that demanded an argued case even at the cost of sophistry, with all sorts of fine qualities and occasional illuminations, but always hopelessly in the toils of Sin, Death, and Logic, which had no power over Jesus. As we have seen, it was by introducing this bondage and terror of his into the Christian doctrine that he adapted it to the Church and State systems which Jesus transcended, and made it practicable by destroying the specifically Jesuist side of it. He would have been quite in his place in any modern Protestant State; and he, not Jesus, is the true head and founder of our Reformed Church, as Peter is of the Roman Church. The followers of Paul and Peter made Christendom, whilst the Nazarenes were wiped out.

35. John Calvin (Jean Chauvin) was born in Picardy, France. He published his *Institutes of the Christian Religion* at Basel in 1536.

THE ACTS OF THE APOSTLES

Here we may return to the narrative called The Acts of the Apostles, which we left at the point where the stoning of Stephen was followed by the introduction of Paul. The author of The Acts, though a good storyteller, like Luke, was (herein also like Luke) much weaker in power of thought than in imaginative literary art. Hence we find Luke credited with the authorship of The Acts by people who like stories and have no aptitude for theology, whilst the book itself is denounced as spurious by Pauline theologians because Paul, and indeed all the apostles, are represented in it as very commonplace revivalists, interesting us by their adventures more than by any qualities of mind or character. Indeed, but for the epistles, we should have a very poor opinion of the apostles. Paul in particular is described as setting a fashion which has remained in continual use to this day. Whenever he addresses an audience, he dwells with great zest on his misdeeds before his pseudo conversion, with the effect of throwing into stronger relief his present state of blessedness; and he tells the story of that conversion over and over again, ending with exhortations to the hearers to come and be saved, and threats of the wrath that will overtake them if they refuse. At any revival meeting today the same thing may be heard, followed by the same conversions. This is natural enough; but it is totally unlike the preaching of Jesus, who never talked about his personal history, and never "worked up" an audience to hysteria. It aims at a purely nervous effect; it brings no enlightenment; the most ignorant man has only to become intoxicated with his own vanity, and mistake his self-satisfaction for the Holy Ghost, to become qualified as an apostle; and it has absolutely nothing to do with the characteristic doctrines of Jesus. The Holy Ghost may be at work all round producing wonders of art and science, and strengthening men to endure all sorts of martyrdoms for the enlargement of knowledge, and the enrichment and intensification of life ("that ye may have life more abundantly" [John 10: 10]); but the apostles, as described in The Acts, take no part in the struggle except as persecutors and revilers. To this day, when their successors get the upper hand, as in Geneva (Knox's "perfect city of Christ") and in Scotland and Ulster, every spiritual activity but moneymaking and churchgoing is stamped out; heretics are ruthlessly persecuted; and such pleasures as money can purchase are suppressed so that its possessors are compelled to go on making money because there is nothing else to do. And the compensation for all this privation is partly an insane conceit of being the elect of God, with a reserved seat in heaven, and partly, since even the most infatuated idiot cannot spend his life admiring himself, the less innocent excitement of punishing other people for not admiring him, and the nosing out of the sins of the people who, being intelligent enough to be incapable of mere dull self-righteousness, and highly susceptible to the beauty and interest of the real workings of the Holy Ghost, try to live more rational and abundant lives. The abominable amusement of terrifying children with threats of hell is another of these diversions, and perhaps the vilest and most mischievous of them. The net result is that the imitators of the apostles, whether they are called Holy Willies or Stigginses in derision,[36] or, in admiration, Puritans or saints, are, outside their own congregations, and to a considerable extent inside them, heartily detested. Now nobody detests Jesus, though many who have been tormented in their childhood in his name include him in their general loathing of everything connected with the word religion; whilst others, who know him only by misrepresentation as a sentimental pacifist and an ascetic, include him in their general dislike of that type of character. In the same way a student who has had to "get up" Shakespear as a college subject may hate Shakespear; and people who dislike the theatre may include Molière in that dislike without ever having read a line of his or witnessed one of his plays; but nobody with any knowledge of Shakespear or Molière could possibly detest them, or read without pity and horror a description of their being insulted, tortured, and killed. And the same is true of Jesus. But it requires the most strenuous effort of conscience to refrain from crying "Serve him right" when we read of the stoning of Stephen; and nobody has ever cared twopence about the martyrdom of Peter: many better men have died worse deaths: for example, honest Hugh Latimer,[37] who was burned by us, was worth fifty Stephens and a dozen Peters. One feels at last that when Jesus called Peter from his boat, he spoiled an honest fisherman, and made nothing better out of the wreck than a salvation monger.

THE CONTROVERSIES ON BAPTISM AND TRANSUBSTANTIATION

Meanwhile the inevitable effect of dropping the peculiar doctrines of Jesus and going back to John the Baptist, was to make it much easier to

36. Robert Burns's 'Holy Willie's Prayer' satirizes a self-righteous elder of the Church; Dickens's the Revd Mr Stiggins is a hypocritical preacher in *Pickwick Papers*.
37. English prelate and religious reformer, who on the accession of Mary Tudor was excommunicated and burned at the stake in 1555.

convert Gentiles than Jews; and it was by following the line of least resistance that Paul became the apostle to the Gentiles. The Jews had their own rite of initiation: the rite of circumcision; and they were fiercely jealous for it, because it marked them as the chosen people of God, and set them apart from the Gentiles, who were simply the uncircumcized. When Paul, finding that baptism made way faster among the Gentiles than among the Jews, as it enabled them to plead that they too were sanctified by a rite of later and higher authority than the Mosaic rite, he was compelled to admit that circumcision did not matter; and this, to the Jews, was an intolerable blasphemy. To Gentiles like ourselves, a good deal of the Epistle to the Romans is now tedious to unreadableness because it consists of a hopeless attempt by Paul to evade the conclusion that if a man were baptized it did not matter a rap whether he was circumcized or not. Paul claims circumcision as an excellent thing in its way for a Jew; but if it has no efficacy towards salvation, and if salvation is the one thing needful—and Paul was committed to both propositions—his pleas in mitigation only made the Jews more determined to stone him.

Thus from the very beginning of apostolic Christianity, it was hampered by a dispute as to whether salvation was to be attained by a surgical operation or by a sprinkling of water: mere rites on which Jesus would not have wasted twenty words. Later on, when the new sect conquered the Gentile west, where the dispute had no practical application, the other ceremony—that of eating the god—produced a still more disastrous dispute, in which a difference of belief, not as to the obligation to perform the ceremony, but as to whether it was a symbolic or a real ingestion of divine substance, produced persecution, slaughter, hatred, and everything that Jesus loathed, on a monstrous scale.[38]

But long before that, the superstitions which had fastened on the new faith made trouble. The parthenogenetic birth of Christ, simple enough at first as a popular miracle, was not left so simple by the theologians. They began to ask of what substance Christ was made in the womb of the virgin. When the Trinity was added to the faith the question arose, was the virgin the mother of God or only the mother of Jesus? Arian schisms and Nestorian schisms[39] arose on these questions; and the leaders of the resultant

38. Early in the fifteenth century, for example, punishment of death by burning and other depredations were imposed on the Lollards, followers of John Wycliffe, who anticipated the Reformation by questioning the doctrine of transubstantiation.
39. Both were early breaches of unity in Christianity: Arianism, condemned in the fourth century, holds that Christ is neither truly God nor truly man; Nestorianism

agitations rancorously deposed oneanother and excommunicated oneanother according to their luck in enlisting the emperors on their side. In the IV century they began to burn oneanother for differences of opinion in such matters. In the VIII century Charlemagne made Christianity compulsory by killing those who refused to embrace it; and though this made an end of the voluntary character of conversion, Charlemagne may claim to be the first Christian who put men to death for any point of doctrine that really mattered. From his time onward the history of Christian controversy reeks with blood and fire, torture and warfare. The Crusades, the persecutions in Albi [against the Albigenisian heretics in the thirteenth century] and elsewhere, the Inquisition, the "wars of religion" which followed the Reformation, all presented themselves as Christian phenomena; but who can doubt that they would have been repudiated with horror by Jesus? Our own notion that the massacre of St Bartholomew's[40] was an outrage on Christianity, whilst the campaigns of Gustavus Adolphus, and even of Frederick the Great, were a defence of it,[41] is as absurd as the opposite notion that Frederick was Antichrist, and Torquemada and Ignatius Loyola[42] men after the very heart of Jesus. Neither they nor their exploits had anything to do with him. It is probable that Archbishop Laud and John Wesley[43] died equally persuaded that he in whose name they had made themselves famous on earth would receive them in Heaven with

---

taught that Christ is both a divine person and a human person, but not in the unity of a single individual.

40. The mass killing of French Huguenots by Catholics (1572) initiated by Catherine de Medici.

41. In his war against Germany, King Gustavus Adolphus of Sweden regarded himself as a liberator of his fellow Protestants. Frederick the Great was an enlightened monarch who nevertheless waged the Seven Years War (1756–63) to force recognition of Prussia as a major power.

42. Tomás de Torquemada was a Spanish Dominican monk, whose name is identified with the excesses of the Inquisition. Saint Ignatius Loyola, originally an officer in the Spanish Army, founded the Jesuit order as a spiritual counter-Reformation army.

43. Archbishop William Laud, who enforced uniformity in the Church of England, was beheaded by Cromwell's Puritans. John Wesley, of Puritan ancestry, was one of the founders of Methodism in the early eighteenth century, a movement of reaction against the apathy of the Church of England.

open arms. George Fox the Quaker would have had ten times their chance; and yet Fox made rather a miserable business of life.[44]

Nevertheless all these perversions of the doctrine of Jesus derived their moral force from his credit, and so had to keep his gospel alive. When the Protestants translated the Bible into the vernacular and let it loose among the people, they did an extremely dangerous thing, as the mischief which followed proves; but they incidentally let loose the sayings of Jesus in open competition with the sayings of Paul and Koheleth and David and Solomon and the authors of Job and the Pentateuch; and, as we have seen, Jesus seems to be the winning name. The glaring contradiction between his teaching and the practice of all the States and all the Churches is no longer hidden. And it may be that though nineteen centuries have passed since Jesus was born (the date of his birth is now quaintly given as 7 BC, though some contend for 100 BC),[45] and though his Church has not yet been founded nor his political system tried, the bankruptcy of all the other systems when audited by our vital statistics, which give us a final test for all political systems, is driving us hard into accepting him, not as a scapegoat, but as one who was much less of a fool in practical matters than we have hitherto all thought him.

THE ALTERNATIVE CHRISTS

Let us now clear up the situation a little. The New Testament tells two stories for two different sorts of readers. One is the old story of the achievement of our salvation by the sacrifice and atonement of a divine personage who was barbarously slain and rose again on the third day: the story as it was accepted by the apostles. And in this story the political, economic and moral views of the Christ have no importance: the atonement is everything; and we are saved by our faith in it, and not by works or opinions (other than that particular opinion) bearing on practical affairs.

The other is the story of a prophet who, after expressing several very interesting opinions as to practical conduct, both personal and political,

44. Fox was frequently imprisoned (eight times between 1649 and 1673) by those who did not agree with his teachings on non-violence and the need for a personal 'divine light'.
45. According to the New Testament account (Matthew 2: 1–16) Christ must have been born before the death of Herod in 4 BC. The probable date is currently estimated to be 6 BC.

which are now of pressing importance, and instructing his disciples to carry them out in their daily life, lost his head; believed himself to be a crude legendary form of god; and under that delusion courted and suffered a cruel execution in the belief that he would rise from the dead and come in glory to reign over a regenerated world. In this form, the political, economic, and moral opinions of Jesus, as guides to conduct, are interesting and important: the rest is mere psychopathy and superstition. The accounts of the resurrection, the parthenogenetic birth, and the more incredible miracles are rejected as inventions; and such episodes as the conversation with the devil are classed with similar conversations recorded of St Dunstan, Luther, Bunyan, Swedenborg, and Blake.[46]

CREDULITY NO CRITERION

This arbitrary acceptance and rejection of parts of the gospel is not peculiar to the Secularist view. We have seen Luke and John reject Matthew's story of the massacre of the innocents and the flight into Egypt without ceremony. The notion that Matthew's manuscript is a literal and infallible record of facts, not subject to the errors that beset all earthly chroniclers, would have made John stare, being as it is a comparatively modern fancy of intellectually untrained people who keep the Bible on the same shelf with Napoleon's Book of Fate,[47] Old Moore's Almanack,[48] and

46. St Dunstan, Archbishop of Canterbury, tempted by the devil, seized his nose with a pair of blacksmith's pincers. Luther, in his struggles with the devil, threw an inkwell at him. John Bunyan recorded in *Grace Abounding* (1666) the devil's temptations he experienced, which led to doubt and despair. Blake encountered a series of devils in 'The Marriage of Heaven and Hell' (1790), one of whom, he reported, became 'my particular friend; we often read the Bible together'. Emanuel Swedenborg confided in *Heaven and Hell* (1758) that 'I once spoke with a spirit, who ... desired to be the devil himself, that he might continually infest heaven with his self-love'.
47. *The Book of Fate Formerly in the Possession of Napoleon*, tr. Herman Kirchenhoffer, was published in 1823, later editions being issued under the title *Napoleon's Oraculum*. Advertised as 'A New and Complete System of Fortune Telling', it was described as a translation from 'an ancient Egyptian manuscript' found in 1901 'in one of the royal tombs ... in upper Egypt'.
48. Since its founding by Francis Moore in 1699 *Old Moore's Almanack* has provided weather predictions and astrological observations, its range of forecasts growing considerably larger with the passing years.

handbooks of therapeutic herbalism. You may be a fanatical Salvationist and reject more miracle stories than [Thomas] Huxley did; and you may utterly repudiate Jesus as the Savior and yet cite him as a historical witness to the possession by men of the most marvelous thaumaturgical powers. "Christ Scientist" and Jesus the Mahatma are preached by people whom Peter would have struck dead as worse infidels than Simon Magus;[49] and the Atonement is preached by Baptist and Congregationalist ministers whose views of the miracles are those of [Robert] Ingersoll[50] and Bradlaugh. Luther, who made a clean sweep of all the saints with their million miracles, and reduced the Blessed Virgin herself to the status of an idol, concentrated Salvationism to a point at which the most execrable murderer who believes in it when the rope is round his neck, flies straight to the arms of Jesus, whilst Tom Paine and Shelley fall into the bottomless pit to burn there to all eternity. And sceptical physicists like Sir William Crookes[51] demonstrate by laboratory experiments that "mediums" like Dunglas Home can make the pointer of a spring-balance go round without touching the weight suspended from it.

BELIEF IN PERSONAL IMMORTALITY NO CRITERION

Nor is belief in individual immortality any criterion. Theosophists, rejecting vicarious atonement so sternly that they insist that the smallest of our sins brings its Karma, also insist on individual immortality and metempsychosis in order to provide an unlimited field for Karma to be worked out by the unredeemed sinner. The belief in the prolongation of individual life beyond the grave is far more real and vivid among table-rapping Spiritualists than among conventional Christians. The notion that those who reject the Christian (or any other) scheme of salvation by atonement must reject also belief in personal immortality and in miracles is as baseless as the notion that if a man is an atheist he will steal your watch.

I could multiply these instances to weariness. The main difference that

49. The sorcerer of Samaria, whose attempt to purchase miraculous powers from the apostles (Acts 8: 18–19) is alluded to in the word 'Simony'.
50. American lawyer and secular propagandist, widely known for his public lectures attacking the Bible and its reported miracles.
51. English chemist and physicist, published positive accounts in 1871 of his observations of the psychic feats of the Scots-American spiritualist medium D. D. Home.

set Gladstone and Huxley by the ears[52] is not one between belief in super-natural persons or miraculous events and the sternest view of such belief as a breach of intellectual integrity: it is the difference between belief in the efficacy of the crucifixion as an infallible cure for guilt, and a congenital incapacity for believing this, or (the same thing) desiring to believe it.

THE SECULAR VIEW NATURAL, NOT RATIONAL, THEREFORE INEVITABLE

It must therefore be taken as a flat fundamental modern fact, whether we like it or not, that whilst many of us cannot believe that Jesus got his curious grip of our souls by mere sentimentality, neither can we believe that he was John Barleycorn. The more our reason and study lead us to believe that Jesus was talking the most penetrating good sense when he preached Communism; when he declared that the reality behind the popular belief in God was a creative spirit in ourselves called by him the Heavenly Father and by us Evolution, Élan Vital, Life Force and other names; when he protested against the claims of marriage and the family to appropriate that high part of our energy that was meant for the service of his Father, the more impossible it becomes for us to believe that he was talking equally good sense when he so suddenly announced that he was himself a visible concrete God; that his flesh and blood were miraculous food for us; that he must be tortured and slain in the traditional manner and would rise from the dead after three days; and that at his Second Coming the stars would fall from heaven and he become king of an earthly paradise. But it is easy and reasonable to believe that an overwrought preacher at last went mad as Swift and Ruskin and Nietzsche went mad. Every asylum has in it a patient suffering from the delusion that he is a god, yet otherwise sane enough. These patients do not nowadays declare that they will be barbarously slain and will rise from the dead, because they have lost that tradition of the destiny of godhead; but they claim everything appertaining to divinity that is within their knowledge.

Thus the gospels as memoirs and suggestive statements of sociological and biological doctrine, highly relevant to modern civilization, though

---

52. A battle between them, which occurred in the pages of the journal *Nineteenth Century* (November–December 1885; January–February 1886), related to the reliability of the account of Creation in Genesis and the credibility of miracles, focusing on that of the Gadarene swine (Matthew 8: 28–34).

ending in the history of a psychopathic delusion, are quite credible, intelligible, and interesting to modern thinkers. In any other light they are neither credible, intelligible, nor interesting except to people upon whom the delusion imposes.

"The Higher Criticism"

Historical research and paleographic criticism will no doubt continue their demonstrations that the New Testament, like the Old, seldom tells a single story or expounds a single doctrine, and gives us often an accretion and conglomeration of widely discrete and even unrelated traditions and doctrines. But these disintegrations, though technically interesting to scholars, and gratifying or exasperating, as the case may be, to people who are merely defending or attacking the paper fortifications of the infallibility of the Bible, have hardly anything to do with the purpose of these pages. I have mentioned the fact that most of the authorities are now agreed (for the moment) that the date of the birth of Jesus may be placed at about 7 B.C.; but they do not therefore date their letters 1923, nor, I presume, do they expect me to do so. What I am engaged in is a criticism (in the Kantian sense [that is, impartial study]) of an established body of belief which has become an actual part of the mental fabric of my readers; and I should be the most exasperating of triflers and pedants if I were to digress into a criticism of some other belief or nobelief which my readers might conceivably profess if they were erudite Scriptural paleographers and historians, in which case, by the way, they would have to change their views so frequently that the gospel they received in their childhood would dominate them after all by its superior persistency. The chaos of mere facts in which the Sermon on the Mount and the Ode to Charity suggest nothing but disputes as to whether they are interpolations or not, in which Jesus becomes nothing but a name suspected of belonging to ten different prophets or executed persons, in which Paul is only the man who could not possibly have written the epistles attributed to him, in which Chinese sages, Greek philosophers, Latin authors, and writers of ancient anonymous inscriptions are thrown at our heads as the sources of this or that scrap of the Bible, is neither a religion nor a criticism of religion: one does not offer the fact that a good deal of the medieval building in Peterborough Cathedral was found to be flagrant jerry-building[53] as a criticism of the

53. When the west gables of Peterborough Cathedral (built between 1116 and 1528) were deemed unsafe, the architect J. L. Pearson was engaged to deal with the

Dean's sermons. For good or evil, we have made a synthesis out of the literature we call the Bible; and though the discovery that there is a good deal of jerry-building in the Bible is interesting in its way, because everything about the Bible is interesting, it does not alter the synthesis very materially even for the paleographers, and does not alter it at all for those who know no more about modern paleography than Archbishop Ussher did. I have therefore indicated little more of the discoveries than Archbishop Ussher might have guessed for himself if he had read the Bible without prepossessions.

For the rest, I have taken the synthesis as it really lives and works in men. After all, a synthesis is what you want: it is the case you have to judge brought to an apprehensible issue for you. Even if you have little more respect for synthetic biography than for synthetic rubber, synthetic milk, and the still unachieved synthetic protoplasm which is to enable us to make different sorts of men as a pastrycook makes different sorts of tarts, the practical issue still lies as plainly before you as before the most credulous votaries of what pontificates as the Higher Criticism [a movement calling for scientific study of biblical writings].

THE PERILS OF SALVATIONISM

The secular view of Jesus is powerfully reinforced by the increase in our day of the number of people who have had the means of educating and training themselves to the point at which they are not afraid to look facts in the face, even such terrifying facts as sin and death. The result is greater sternness in modern thought. The conviction is spreading that to encourage a man to believe that though his sins be as scarlet he can be made whiter

---

principal restoration (1883–97). His recommendation in 1896 that the entire west front (three immense arches forming a loggia) be removed and rebuilt aroused much controversy, much of the protest coming from the Society for the Preservation of Ancient Buildings (founded by William Morris and architect Philip Webb in 1877), of which Shaw was a vociferous member. Despite all the agitation, including a scathing polemic by Shaw, 'Must Peterborough Perish?', which he signed 'Architect', in the *Saturday Review*, 2 January 1897, the west front was demolished and rebuilt, using most of the old stones in the restoration. The claim by the SPAB that the problems with the west front and the central tower were the result of medieval 'jerry-building' was not substantiated, despite Shaw's 'flagrant' dogmatism.

than snow by an easy exercise of self-conceit, is to encourage him to be a rascal. It did not work so badly when you could also conscientiously assure him that if he let himself be caught napping in the matter of faith by death, a red-hot hell would roast him alive to all eternity. In those days a sudden death—the most enviable of all deaths—was regarded as the most frightful calamity. It was classed with plague, pestilence, and famine, battle and murder, in our prayers. But belief in that hell is fast vanishing. All the leaders of thought have lost it; and even for the rank and file it has fled to those parts of Ireland and Scotland which are still in the XVII century. Even there, it is tacitly reserved for the other fellow.

THE IMPORTANCE OF HELL IN THE SALVATION SCHEME

The seriousness of throwing over hell whilst still clinging to the Atonement is obvious. If there is no punishment for sin there can be no self-forgiveness for it. If Christ paid our score, and if there is no hell and therefore no chance of our getting into trouble by forgetting the obligation, then we can be as wicked as we like with impunity inside the secular law, even from self-reproach, which becomes mere ingratitude to the Savior. On the other hand, if Christ did not pay our score, it still stands against us; and such debts make us extremely uncomfortable. The drive of evolution, which we call conscience and honor, seizes on such slips, and shames us to the dust for being so low in the scale as to be capable of them. The "saved" thief experiences an ecstatic happiness which can never come to the honest atheist: he is tempted to steal again to repeat the glorious sensation. But if the atheist steals he has no such happiness. He is a thief and knows that he is a thief. Nothing can rub that off him. He may try to soothe his shame by some sort of restitution or equivalent act of benevolence; but that does not alter the fact that he did steal; and his conscience will not be easy until he has conquered his will to steal and changed himself into an honest man by developing that divine spark within him which Jesus insisted on as the everyday reality of what the atheist denies.

Now though the state of the believers in the Atonement may thus be the happier, it is most certainly not more desirable from the point of view of the community. The fact that a believer is happier than a sceptic is no more to the point than the fact that a drunken man is happier than a sober one. The happiness of credulity is a cheap and dangerous quality of happiness, and by no means a necessity of life. Whether Socrates got as much happiness out of life as Wesley is an unanswerable question;

but a nation of Socrateses would be much safer and happier than a nation of Wesleys; and its individuals would be higher in the evolutionary scale. At all events it is in the Socratic man and not in the Wesleyan that our hope lies now.

THE RIGHT TO REFUSE ATONEMENT

Consequently, even if it were mentally possible for all of us to believe in the Atonement, we should have to cry off it, as we evidently have a right to do. Every man to whom salvation is offered has an inalienable natural right to say "No, thank you: I prefer to retain my full moral responsibility: it is not good for me to be able to load a scapegoat with my sins: I should be less careful how I committed them if I knew they would cost me nothing." Then, too, there is the attitude of Ibsen: that iron moralist to whom the whole scheme of salvation was only an ignoble attempt to cheat God; to get into heaven without paying the price. To be let off, to beg for and accept eternal life as a present instead of earning it, would be mean enough even if we accepted the contempt of the Power on whose pity we were trading; but to bargain for a crown of glory as well! that was too much for Ibsen: it provoked him to exclaim, "Your God is an old man whom you cheat,"[54] and to lash the deadened conscience of the XIX century back to life with a whip of scorpions.

THE TEACHING OF CHRISTIANITY

And there I must leave the matter to such choice as your nature allows you. The honest teacher who has to make known to a novice the facts about Christianity cannot in any essential regard, I think, put the facts otherwise than as I have put them. If children are to be delivered from the proselytizing atheist on the one hand, and the proselytizing nun in the convent school on the other, with all the other proselytizers that lie between them, they must not be burdened with idle controversies as to whether there was ever such a person as Jesus or not. When Hume said that

54. The reference is to a scene between the clergyman Brand and Einar in Act I of Ibsen's *Brand* (1866).

Joshua's campaigns were impossible, [Richard] Whately[55] did not wrangle about it: he proved, on the same lines, that the campaigns of Napoleon were impossible. Only fictitious characters will stand Hume's sort of examination: nothing will ever make Edward the Confessor [eleventh-century Anglo-Saxon king in Britain] and St Louis [Louis IX of France] as real to us as Don Quixote and Mr Pickwick. We must cut the controversy short by declaring that there is the same evidence for the existence of Jesus as for that of any other person of his time; and the fact that you may not believe everything Matthew tells you no more disproves the existence of Jesus than the fact that you do not believe everything Macaulay tells you disproves the existence of William III. The gospel narratives in the main give you a biography which is quite credible and accountable on purely secular grounds when you have trimmed off everything that Hume or Grimm[56] or Rousseau or Huxley or any modern bishop could reject as fanciful. Without going further than this, you can become a follower of Jesus just as you can become a follower of Confucius or Lao Tse,[57] and may therefore call yourself a Jesuist, or even a Christian, if you hold, as the strictest Secularist quite legitimately may, that all prophets are inspired, and all men with a mission, Christs.

The teacher of Christianity has then to make known to the child, first the song of John Barleycorn, with the fields and seasons as witness to its eternal truth. Then, as the child's mind matures, it can learn, as historical and psychological phenomena, the tradition of the scapegoat, the Redeemer, the Atonement, the Resurrection, the Second Coming, and how, in a world saturated with this tradition, Jesus has been largely accepted as the long expected and often prophesied Redeemer, the Messiah, *the* Christ. It is open to the child also to accept him. If the child is built like Gladstone, he will accept Jesus as his Savior, and Peter and John the Baptist as the Savior's revealer and forerunner respectively. If he is built like Huxley, he will take the secular view, in spite of all that a pious family can do to

55. English Archbishop, logician and theological writer, author of *Historical Doubts Relative to Napoleon Bonaparte* (1819), a satire directed against excessive scepticism as applied to Gospel history such as found in David Hume's *Enquiry Concerning Human Understanding* (1748).
56. Baron Frederick von Grimm, Franco-German critic and author of *Correspondance littéraire, philosophique et critique* (1812–14), friend of Rousseau and Diderot.
57. Lao-tzu: Chinese teacher and sixth-century BC contemporary of Confucius. Reputed founder of Taoism, which encourages unselfish action and is thought to be in some measure in harmony with Christianity.

prevent him. The important thing now is that the Gladstones and Huxleys should no longer waste their time irrelevantly and ridiculously wrangling about the Gadarene swine, and that they should make up their minds as to the soundness of the secular doctrines of Jesus; for it is about these that they may come to blows in our own time.

CHRISTIANITY AND THE EMPIRE

Finally, let us ask why it is that the old superstitions have so suddenly lost countenance that although, to the utter disgrace of the nation's leaders and rulers, the laws by which persecutors can destroy or gag all freedom of thought and speech in these matters are still unrepealed and ready to the hand of our bigots and fanatics (quite recently a respectable shopkeeper was convicted of "blasphemy"[58] for saying that if a modern girl accounted for an illicit pregnancy by saying she had conceived of the Holy Ghost, we should know what to think: a remark which would never have occurred to him had he been properly taught how the story was grafted on the gospel), yet somehow they are used only against poor men, and that only in a halfhearted way. When we consider that from the time when the first scholar ventured to whisper as a professional secret that the Pentateuch could not possibly have been written by Moses to the time within my own recollection when Bishop [John] Colenso,[59] for saying the same thing openly, was inhibited from preaching and actually excommunicated, eight centuries elapsed (the point at issue, though technically interesting to paleographers and historians, having no more bearing on human welfare than the controversy as to whether uncial or cursive is the older form of

58. Thomas W. Stewart, an analytical chemist who was president of the Free Thought Socialist League, was found guilty of blasphemy in August 1911 and sentenced in December to three months' imprisonment. A petition to the Home Secretary in January 1912 urged remittal of the balance of sentence, arguing that 'in the view of great numbers of His Majesty's subjects punishment for blasphemy is a form of religious persecution and inconsistent with modern ideas of toleration'. One of the signatories was Shaw. In 1913 Stewart was again arrested, for a like offence, and served four months at hard labour, despite a second petition (see p. 39, fn. 24), this time with the signature of H. G. Wells in place of Shaw's.
59. Bishop of Natal, South Africa, whose series of tracts, *The Pentateuch and Book of Joshua Critically Examined* (1862–79) concluded that these books were post-exile forgeries. He was excommunicated but confirmed in the possession of his senses by the law courts (1866).

writing [in paleography, large separated letters in contrast to small joined letters]); yet now, within fifty years of Colenso's heresy, there is not a Churchman of any authority living, or an educated layman, who could without ridicule declare that Moses wrote the Pentateuch as Pascal wrote his Thoughts or D'Aubigny [Jean-Henri Merle d'Aubigné] his History of the Reformation [1835–53], or that St Jerome wrote the passage about the three witnesses in the Vulgate [1872–7],[60] or that there are less than three different accounts of the creation jumbled together in the book of Genesis. Now the maddest Progressive will hardly contend that our growth in wisdom and liberality has been greater in the last half century than in the sixteen half centuries preceding: indeed it would be easier to sustain the thesis that the last fifty years have witnessed a distinct reaction from Victorian Liberalism to Collectivism which has perceptibly strengthened the State Churches. Yet the fact remains that whereas Byron's Cain, published a century ago [1821], is a leading case on the point that there is no copyright in a blasphemous book, the Salvation Army might now include it among its publications without shocking anyone.

I suggest that the causes which have produced this sudden clearing of the air include the transformation of many modern States, notably the old self-contained French Republic and the tight little Island of Britain, into empires which overflow the frontiers of all the Churches. In India, for example, there are less than four million Christians out of a population of three hundred and sixteen and a half millions. The King of England is the defender of the faith; but what faith is now *the* faith? The inhabitants of this island would, within the memory of persons still living, have claimed that their faith is surely *the* faith of God, that all others are heathen. But we islanders are only fortyfive millions; and if we count ourselves all as Christians, there are still seventyseven and a quarter million Mahometans in the Empire. Add to these the Hindoos and Buddhists, Sikhs and Jains, whom I was taught in my childhood, by way of religious instruction, to regard as gross idolaters consigned to eternal perdition, but whose faith I can now be punished for disparaging by a provocative word, and you have

60. The passage to which Shaw alludes, known as the Johannine Comma, or the 'Three Witnesses', is an interpolation in the text of 1 John at 5: 7–8, not part of the original epistle. It occurred in early Latin manuscripts, found its way (possibly from North Africa or Spain) into the Latin Bible and eventually entered the Vulgate. It appears in the New Testament of Erasmus (1516) and in the Authorized (King James) Version (1611); but is omitted from the Revised Version of the New Testament (1881) and other scholarly modern translations.

a total of over three hundred and fortytwo and a quarter million heretics to swamp our fortyfive million Britons, of whom, by the way, only six thousand call themselves distinctively "disciples of Christ," the rest being members of the Church of England and other denominations whose discipleship is less emphatically affirmed. In short, the Englishman of today, instead of being, like the forefathers whose ideas he clings to, a subject of a State practically wholly Christian, is now crowded, and indeed considerably overcrowded, into a corner of an Empire in which the Christians are a mere eleven per cent of the population; so that the Nonconformist who allows his umbrella stand to be sold up rather than pay rates towards the support of a Church of England school, finds himself paying taxes not only to endow the Church of Rome in Malta, but to send Christians to prison for the blasphemy of offering Bibles for sale in the streets of Khartoum.

Turn to France, a country ten times more insular in its preoccupation with its own language, its own history, its own character, than we, who have always been explorers and colonizers and grumblers. This once self-centred nation is forty millions strong. The total population of the French Republic is about one hundred and fourteen millions. The French are not in our hopeless Christian minority of eleven per cent; but they are in a minority of thirtyfive per cent, which is fairly conclusive. And, being a more logical people than we, they have officially abandoned Christianity and declared that the French State has no specific religion.

Neither has the British State, though it does not say so. No doubt there are many innocent people in England who take Charlemagne's view, and would, as a matter of course, offer our eightynine per cent of "pagans, I regret to say" the alternative of death or Christianity but for a vague impression that these lost ones are all being converted gradually by the missionaries. But no statesman can entertain such ludicrously parochial delusions. No English king or French president can possibly govern on the assumption that the theology of Peter and Paul, Luther and Calvin, has any objective validity, or that the Christ is more than the Buddha, or Jehovah more than Krishna, or Jesus more or less human than Mahomet or Zoroaster or Confucius. He is actually compelled, in so far as he makes laws against blasphemy at all, to treat all the religions, including Christianity, as blasphemous when paraded before people who are not accustomed to them and do not want them. And even that is a concession to a mischievous intolerance which an empire should use its control of education to eradicate.

On the other hand, governments cannot really divest themselves of religion, or even of dogma. When Jesus said that people should not only live but live more abundantly, he was dogmatizing; and many Pessimist sages, including Shakespear, whose hero begged his friend [Horatio] to refrain from suicide in the words "Absent thee from felicity awhile" [*Hamlet*, V: ii], would say dogmatizing very perniciously. Indeed many preachers and saints declare, some of them in the name of Jesus himself, that this world is a vale of tears, and that our lives had better be passed in sorrow and even in torment, as a preparation for a better life to come. Make these sad people comfortable; and they baffle you by putting on hair shirts.

None the less, governments must proceed on dogmatic assumptions, whether they call them dogmas or not; and they must clearly be assumptions common enough to stamp those who reject them as eccentrics or lunatics. And the greater and more heterogeneous the population the commoner the assumptions must be. A Trappist monastery can be conducted on assumptions which would in twentyfour hours provoke the village at its gates to insurrection. That is because the monastery selects its people; and if a Trappist does not like it he can leave it. But a subject of the British Empire or the French Republic is not selected; and if he does not like it he must lump it; for emigration is practicable only within narrow limits, and seldom provides an effective remedy, all civilizations being now much alike.

To anyone capable of comprehending government at all it must be evident without argument that the set of fundamental assumptions drawn up in the thirtynine articles [doctrinal tenets adopted by the Church of England, 1563] or in the Westminster Confession[61] are wildly impossible as political constitutions for modern empires. A personal profession of them by any person disposed to take such professions seriously would practically disqualify him for high imperial office. A Calvinist Viceroy of India and a Particular Baptist [one who, as in Calvinism, believes redemption is only for the elect] Secretary of State for Foreign Affairs would wreck the empire. The Stuarts wrecked even the tight little island which was the nucleus of the empire by their Scottish logic and theological dogma; and it may be sustained very plausibly that the alleged aptitude of the English for self-government, which is contradicted by every chapter of their history, is really only an incurable inaptitude for theology, and indeed for co-ordinated thought in any direction, which makes them equally impatient of systematic despotism and systematic good government: their history being that of a badly governed and accidentally free people

61. A collective term for the catechism and directories of ritual, polity and discipline framed by the Westminster Assembly of Divines (1643–9). It is accepted as authoritative by nearly all the English-speaking Presbyterian Churches of the world, but did not become accepted doctrine in the Anglican Church.

(comparatively). Thus our success in colonizing, as far as it has not been produced by exterminating the natives, has been due to our indifference to the salvation of our subjects. Ireland is the exception which proves the rule; for Ireland, the standing instance of the inability of the English to colonize without extermination of natives, is also the one country under British rule in which the conquerors and colonizers proceeded on the assumption that their business was to establish Protestantism as well as to make money and thereby secure at least the lives of the unfortunate inhabitants out of whose labor it could be made. At this moment Ulster is refusing to accept fellow-citizenship with the other Irish provinces because the south believes in St Peter and [Jacques-Bénigne] Bossuet,[62] and the north in St Paul and Calvin. Imagine the effect of trying to govern India or Egypt from Belfast or from the Vatican!

The position is perhaps graver for France than for England, because the sixtyfive per cent of French subjects who are neither French nor Christian nor Modernist includes some thirty millions of negroes who are susceptible, and indeed highly susceptible, of conversion to those salvationist forms of pseudo-Christianity which have produced all the persecutions and religious wars of the last fifteen hundred years. When the late explorer Sir Henry Stanley told me of the emotional grip which Christianity had over the Baganda tribes, and read me their letters, which were exactly like medieval letters in their literal faith and ever-present piety, I said "Can these men handle a rifle?" To which Stanley replied with some scorn "Of course they can, as well as any white man."[63] Now at this moment (1915) a vast European war is being waged, in which the French are using Senegalese soldiers. I ask the French Government, which, like our own Government, is deliberately leaving the religious instruction of these negroes in the hands of missions of Petrine Catholics and Pauline Calvinists, whether they have considered the possibility of a new series of crusades, by ardent African Salvationists, to rescue Paris from the grip of the modern scientific "infidel," and to raise the cry of "Back to the Apostles: back to Charlemagne!"

We are more fortunate in that an overwhelming majority of our subjects are Hindoos, Mahometans, and Buddhists: that is, they have, as a

---

62. French prelate, historian, and theologian, among whose works is *Exposition de la doctrine catholique* (1671). His conservative Roman Catholic position is in stark contrast to the Reformist views of Calvin.
63. Shaw's acquaintance with Stanley commenced around 1897. The Shaws, who rented a country house at Woking, near to the Stanleys' retreat in Surrey, visited Sir Henry frequently during his last illness in 1903–4.

prophylactic against salvationist Christianity, highly civilized religions of their own. Mahometanism, which Napoleon at the end of his career classed [in General Gaspard Gourgaud's *Sainte Hélène: Journal inédit*, II, 1889] as perhaps the best popular religion for modern political use, might in some respects have arisen as a reformed Christianity if Mahomet had had to deal with a population of XVII century Christians instead of Arabs who worshipped stones. As it is, men do not reject Mahomet for Calvin; and to offer a Hindoo so crude a theology as ours in exchange for his own, or our Jewish canonical literature as an improvement on Hindoo scripture, is to offer old lamps for older ones in a market where the oldest lamps, like old furniture in England, are the most highly valued.

Yet, I repeat, government is impossible without a religion: that is, without a body of common assumptions. The open mind never acts: when we have done our utmost to arrive at a reasonable conclusion, we still, when we can reason and investigate no more, must close our minds for the moment with a snap, and act dogmatically on our conclusions. The man who waits to make an entirely reasonable will dies intestate. A man so reasonable as to have an open mind about theft and murder, or about the need for food and reproduction, might just as well be a fool and a scoundrel for any use he could be as a legislator or a State official. The modern pseudo-democratic statesman, who says that he is only in power to carry out the will of the people, and moves only as the cat jumps, is clearly a political and intellectual brigand. The rule of the negative man who has no convictions means in practice the rule of the positive mob. Freedom of conscience as Cromwell used the phrase[64] is an excellent thing; nevertheless if any man had proposed to give effect to freedom of conscience as to cannibalism in England, Cromwell would have laid him by the heels almost as promptly as he would have laid a Roman Catholic, though in Fiji at the same moment he would have supported heartily the freedom of conscience of a vegetarian who disparaged the sacred diet of Long Pig [human flesh].

Here then comes in the importance of the repudiation by Jesus of proselytism. His rule "Dont pull up the tares: sow the wheat: if you try to

64. Cromwell wrote to John Sadler in 1650: 'I meddle not with any man's conscience . . . [A]s for the people, what thoughts they have in matters of religion in their own breasts I cannot reach, but shall think it my duty, if they will walk honestly and peaceably, not to cause them in the least to suffer for the same' (*Oliver Cromwell's Letters and Speeches: with Elucidations*, ed. Thomas Carlyle, 1845).

pull up the tares you will pull up the wheat with it" [Matthew 13: 29–30] is the only possible rule for a statesman governing a modern empire, or a voter supporting such a statesman. There is nothing in the teaching of Jesus that cannot be assented to by a Brahman, a Mahometan, a Buddhist or a Jew, without any question of their conversion to Christianity. In some ways it is easier to reconcile a Mahometan to Jesus than a British parson, because the idea of a professional priest is unfamiliar and even monstrous to a Mahometan (the tourist who persists in asking who is the dean of St Sophia puzzles beyond words the sacristan who lends him a huge pair of slippers); and Jesus never suggested that his disciples should separate themselves from the laity: he picked them up by the wayside, where any man or woman might follow him. For priests he had not a civil word; and they shewed their sense of his hostility by getting him killed as soon as possible. He was, in short, a thoroughgoing anti-Clerical. And though, as we have seen, it is only by political means that his doctrine can be put into practice, he not only never suggested a sectarian theocracy as a form of government, and would certainly have prophesied the downfall of the late [Transvaal] President [Paul] Kruger if he had survived to his time, but, when challenged, he refused to teach his disciples not to pay tribute to Cæsar, admitting that Cæsar, who presumably had the kingdom of heaven within him as much as any disciple, had his place in the scheme of things. Indeed the apostles made this an excuse for carrying subservience to the State to a pitch of idolatry that ended in the theory of the divine right of kings, and provoked men to cut kings' heads off to restore some sense of proportion in the matter. Jesus certainly did not consider the overthrow of the Roman empire or the substitution of a new ecclesiastical organization for the Jewish Church or for the priesthood of the Roman gods as part of his program. He said that God was better than Mammon; but he never said that Tweedledum was better than Tweedledee; and that is why it is now possible for British citizens and statesmen to follow Jesus, though they cannot possibly follow either Tweedledum or Tweedledee without bringing the empire down with a crash on their heads. And at that I must leave it.

LONDON.
December, 1915.

Overruled

First published in 1916

======

The Alleviations of Monogamy

This piece is not an argument for or against polygamy. It is a clinical study of how the thing actually occurs among quite ordinary people, innocent of all unconventional views concerning it. The enormous majority of cases in real life are those of people in that position. Those who deliberately and conscientiously profess what are oddly called advanced views by those others who believe them to be retrograde, are often, and indeed mostly, the last people in the world to engage in unconventional adventures of any kind, not only because they have neither time nor disposition for them, but because the friction set up between the individual and the community by the expression of unusual views of any sort is quite enough hindrance to the heretic without being complicated by personal scandals. Thus the theoretic libertine is usually a person of blameless family life, whilst the practical libertine is mercilessly severe on all other libertines, and excessively conventional in professions of social principle.

What is more, these professions are not hypocritical: they are for the most part quite sincere. The common libertine, like the drunkard, succumbs to a temptation which he does not defend, and against which he warns others with an earnestness proportionate to the intensity of his own remorse. He (or she) may be a liar and a humbug, pretending to be better than the detected libertines, and clamoring for their condign punishment; but this is mere self-defence. No reasonable person expects the burglar to confess his pursuits, or to refrain from joining in the cry of Stop Thief when the police get on the track of another burglar. If society chooses to penalize candor, it has itself to thank if its attack is countered by falsehood. The clamorous virtue of the libertine is therefore no more hypocritical than the plea of Not Guilty which is allowed to every criminal. But one result is that the theorists who write most sincerely and favorably about polygamy know least about it; and the practitioners who know most about it keep their knowledge very jealously to themselves. Which is hardly fair to the practice.

Inaccessibility of the Facts

Also, it is impossible to estimate its prevalence. A practice to which nobody confesses may be both universal and unsuspected, just as a virtue which everybody is expected, under heavy penalties, to claim, may have no existence. It is often assumed—indeed it is the official assumption of the Churches and the divorce courts—that a gentleman and a lady cannot be alone together innocently. And that is manifest blazing nonsense, though many women have been stoned to death in the east, and divorced in the west, on the strength of it. On the other hand, the innocent and conventional people who regard gallant adventures as crimes of so horrible a nature that only the most depraved and desperate characters engage in them or would listen to advances in that direction without raising an alarm with the noisiest indignation, are clearly examples of the fact that most sections of society do not know how the other sections live. Industry is the most effective check on gallantry. Women may, as Napoleon said, be the occupation of the idle man just as men are the preoccupation of the idle woman;[1] but the mass of mankind is too busy and too poor for the long and expensive sieges which the professed libertine lays to virtue. Still, wherever there is idleness or even a reasonable supply of elegant leisure there is a good deal of coquetry and philandering. It is so much pleasanter to dance on the edge of a precipice than to go over it that leisured society is full of people who spend a great part of their lives in flirtation, and conceal nothing but the humiliating secret that they have never gone any further. For there is no pleasing people in the matter of reputation in this department: every insult is a flattery: every testimonial is a disparagement: Joseph is despised and promoted, Potiphar's wife admired and condemned [Genesis 39: 7–20]: in short, you are never on solid ground until you get away from the subject altogether. There is a continual and irreconcilable conflict between the natural and conventional sides of the case, between spontaneous human relations between independent men and women on the one hand and the property relation between husband and wife on the other, not to mention the confusion under the common name of love of a generous natural attraction and interest with the murderous jealousy that fastens on and clings to its mate (especially a hated mate) as a tiger fastens on a

1. This aphoristic sentiment is not cited in any principal memoir or biography of Napoleon that we have examined, and appears in none of the standard books of quotations, either in English or French.

carcase. And the confusion is natural; for these extremes are extremes of the same passion; and most cases lie somewhere on the scale between them, and are so complicated by ordinary likes and dislikes, by incidental wounds to vanity or gratifications of it, and by class feeling, that A will be jealous of B and not of C, and will tolerate infidelities on the part of D whilst being furiously angry when they are committed by E.

THE CONVENTION OF JEALOUSY

That jealousy is independent of sex is shewn by its intensity in children, and by the fact that very jealous people are jealous of everybody without regard to relationship or sex, and cannot bear to hear the person they "love" speak favorably of anyone under any circumstances (many women, for instance, are much more jealous of their husbands' mothers and sisters than of unrelated women whom they suspect him of fancying); but it is seldom possible to disentangle the two passions in practice. Besides, jealousy is an inculcated passion, forced by society on people in whom it would not occur spontaneously. In Brieux's Bourgeois aux Champs [*A Bourgeois in His Country Place*, 1914], the benevolent hero finds himself detested by the neighboring peasants and farmers, not because he preserves game, and sets mantraps for poachers, and defends his legal rights over his land to the extremest point of unsocial savagery, but because, being an amiable and public-spirited person, he refuses to do all this, and thereby offends and disparages the sense of property in his neighbors. The same thing is true of matrimonial jealousy: the man who does not at least pretend to feel it, and behave as badly as if he really felt it, is despised and insulted; and many a man has shot or stabbed a friend or been shot or stabbed by him in a duel, or disgraced himself and ruined his own wife in a divorce scandal, against his conscience, against his instinct, and to the destruction of his home, solely because Society conspired to drive him to keep its own lower morality in countenance in this miserable and undignified manner.

Morality is confused in such matters. In an elegant plutocracy, a jealous husband is regarded as a boor. Among the tradesmen who supply that plutocracy with its meals, a husband who is not jealous, and refrains from assailing his rival with his fists, is regarded as a ridiculous, contemptible, and cowardly cuckold. And the laboring class is divided into the respectable section which takes the tradesman's view, and the disreputable section which enjoys the licence of the plutocracy without its money: creeping below the law as its exemplars prance above it; cutting down all expenses of respectability and even decency; and frankly accepting squalor and disrepute as the price of anarchic self-indulgence. The conflict between Malvolio and Sir Toby [in *Twelfth Night*], between the marquis and the bourgeois, the cavalier and the puritan, the ascetic and the voluptuary, goes on continually, and goes on not only between class and class and individual and individual, but in the selfsame breast in a series of reactions and revulsions in which the irresistible becomes the unbearable, and the unbearable the irresistible, until none of us can say what our characters really are in this respect.

THE MISSING DATA OF A SCIENTIFIC NATURAL HISTORY OF MARRIAGE

Of one thing I am persuaded: we shall never attain to a reasonably healthy public opinion on sex questions until we offer, as the data for that opinion, our actual conduct and our real thoughts instead of a moral fiction which we agree to call virtuous conduct, and which we then—and here comes in the mischief—pretend is our conduct and our thoughts. If the result were that we all believed oneanother to be better than we really are, there would be something to be said for it; but the actual result appears to be a monstrous exaggeration of the power and continuity of sexual passion. The whole world shares the fate of Lucrezia Borgia,[2] who, though she seems on investigation to have been quite a suitable wife for a modern British Bishop, has been invested by the popular historical imagination with all the extravagances of a Messalina or a Cenci.[3] Writers of *belles lettres* who are rash enough to admit that their whole life is not one constant preoccupation with adored members of the opposite sex, and who even countenance La Rochefoucauld's remark that very few people would ever imagine themselves in love if they had never read anything about it [*Maximes*], are gravely declared to be abnormal or physically defective by critics of crushing unadventurousness and domestication. French authors of

2. In her earlier marriages Lucrezia Borgia was a victim of the political intrigues of her father and brother. When at the age of twenty-two she married the Duke of Ferrara, her life became peaceful, her court a centre for artists and men of learning.
3. Messalina, wife of the Roman emperor Claudius, was proverbial for her profligacy. Count Francesco Cenci conceived an incestuous passion for his daughter Beatrice; with the help of her brother and stepmother she arranged for his murder. These events provided the subject for Shelley's verse play *The Cenci*.

saintly temperament are forced to include in their retinue countesses of ardent complexion with whom they are supposed to live in sin. Sentimental controversies on the subject are endless; but they are useless, because nobody tells the truth. Rousseau did it [*Les Confessions*, 1782] by an extraordinary effort, aided by a superhuman faculty for human natural history; but the result was curiously disconcerting because, though the facts were so conventionally shocking that people felt that they ought to matter a great deal, they actually mattered very little. And even at that everybody pretends not to believe him.

Artificial Retribution

The worst of this is that busybodies with perhaps rather more than a normal taste for mischief are continually trying to make negligible things matter as much in fact as they do in convention by deliberately inflicting injuries—sometimes atrocious injuries—on the parties concerned. Few people have any knowledge of the savage punishments that are legally inflicted for aberrations and absurdities to which no sanely instructed community would call any attention. We create an artificial morality, and consequently an artificial conscience, by manufacturing disastrous consequences for events which, left to themselves, would do very little harm (sometimes not any) and be forgotten in a few days.

But the artificial morality is not therefore to be condemned offhand. In many cases it may save mischief instead of making it: for example, though the hanging of a murderer is the duplication of a murder, yet it may be less murderous than leaving the matter to be settled by blood feud or vendetta. As long as human nature insists on revenge, the official organization and satisfaction of revenge by the State may be also its minimization. The mischief begins when the official revenge persists after the passion it satisfies has died out of the race. Stoning a woman to death in the east because she has ventured to marry again after being deserted by her husband may be more merciful than allowing her to be mobbed to death; but the official stoning or burning of an adulteress in the west would be an atrocity, because few of us hate an adulteress to the extent of desiring such a penalty, or of being prepared to take the law into our own hands if it were withheld. Now what applies to this extreme case applies also in due degree to the other cases. Offences in which sex is concerned are often needlessly magnified by penalties, ranging from various forms of social ostracism to long sentences of penal servitude, which would be seen to be monstrously disproportionate to the real feeling against them if the removal of both the penalties and the taboo on their discussion made it possible for us to ascertain their real prevalence and estimation. Fortunately there is one outlet for the truth. We are permitted to discuss in jest what we may not discuss in earnest. A serious comedy about sex is taboo: a farcical comedy is privileged.

THE FAVORITE SUBJECT OF FARCICAL COMEDY

The little piece which follows this preface accordingly takes the form of a farcical comedy, because it is a contribution to the very extensive dramatic literature which takes as its special department the gallantries of married people. The stage has been preoccupied by such affairs for centuries, not only in the jesting vein of Restoration Comedy and Palais Royal farce,[4] but in the more tragically turned adulteries of the Parisian school which dominated the stage until Ibsen put them out of countenance and relegated them to their proper place as articles of commerce. Their continued vogue in that department maintains the tradition that adultery is the dramatic subject *par excellence*, and indeed that a play that is not about adultery is not a play at all. I was considered a heresiarch of the most extravagant kind when I expressed my opinion, at the outset of my career as a playwright, that adultery is the dullest of themes on the stage, and that from Francesca and Paolo down to the latest guilty couple of the [social-drama] school of [Alexandre] Dumas *fils*, the romantic adulterers have all been intolerable bores.

THE PSEUDO SEX PLAY

Later on, I had occasion to point out to the defenders of sex as the proper theme of drama, that though they were right in ranking sex as an intensely interesting subject, they were wrong in assuming that sex is an indispensable motive in popular plays. The plays of Molière are, like the novels of the Victorian epoch or Don Quixote, as nearly sexless as anything not absolutely inhuman can be; and some of Shakespear's plays are sexually

4. Paris's Palais-Royal specialized from 1831 in vaudeville and farce. In England in the late nineteenth century the term 'Palais-Royal farce' was employed for broadly suggestive adaptations from the French.

on a par with the census: they contain women as well as men, and that is all. This had to be admitted; but it was still assumed that the plays of the XIX century Paris school are, in contrast with the sexless masterpieces, saturated with sex; and this I strenuously denied. A play about the convention that a man should fight a duel or come to fisticuffs with his wife's lover if she has one, or the convention that he should strangle her like Othello, or turn her out of the house and never see her or allow her to see her children again, or the convention that she should never be spoken to again by any decent person and should finally drown herself, or the convention that persons involved in scenes of recrimination or confession by these conventions should call each other certain abusive names and describe their conduct as guilty and frail and so on: all these may provide material for very effective plays; but such plays are not dramatic studies of sex: one might as well say that Romeo and Juliet is a dramatic study of pharmacy because the catastrophe is brought about through an apothecary. Duels are not sex; divorce cases are not sex; the Trade Unionism of married women is not sex. Only the most insignificant fraction of the gallantries of married people produce any of the conventional results; and plays occupied wholly with the conventional results are therefore utterly unsatisfying as sex plays, however interesting they may be as plays of intrigue and plot puzzles.

The world is finding this out rapidly. The Sunday papers, which in the days when they appealed almost exclusively to the lower middle class were crammed with police intelligence, and more especially with divorce and murder cases, now lay no stress on them; and police papers which confined themselves entirely to such matters, and were once eagerly read, have perished through the essential dulness of their topics. And yet the interest in sex is stronger than ever: in fact, the literature that has driven out the journalism of the divorce courts is a literature occupied with sex to an extent and with an intimacy and frankness that would have seemed utterly impossible to Thackeray or Dickens if they had been told that the change would complete itself within fifty years of their own time.

ART AND MORALITY

It is ridiculous to say, as inconsiderate amateurs of the arts do, that art has nothing to do with morality. What is true is that the artist's business is not that of the policeman; and that such factitious consequences and put-up jobs as divorces and executions and the detective operations that lead up to them are no essential part of life, though, like poisons and buttered slides and red-hot pokers, they provide material for plenty of thrilling or amusing stories suited to people who are incapable of any interest in psychology. But the fine artist must keep the policeman out of his studies of sex and studies of crime. It is by clinging nervously to the policeman that most of the pseudo-sex plays convince me that the writers have either never had any serious personal experience of their ostensible subject, or else have never conceived it possible that the stage dare present the phenomena of sex as they appear in nature.

THE LIMITS OF STAGE PRESENTATION

But the stage presents much more shocking phenomena than those of sex. There is, of course, a sense in which you cannot present sex on the stage, just as you cannot present murder. Macbeth must no more really kill Duncan than he must himself be really slain by Macduff. But the feelings of a murderer can be expressed in a certain artistic convention; and a carefully prearranged sword exercise can be gone through with sufficient pretence of earnestness to be accepted by the willing imaginations of the younger spectators as a desperate combat.

The tragedy of love has been presented on the stage in the same way. In Tristan and Isolde, the curtain does not, as in Romeo and Juliet, rise with the lark: the whole night of love is played before the spectators. The lovers do not discuss marriage in an elegantly sentimental way: they utter the visions and feelings that come to lovers at the supreme moments of their love, totally forgetting that there are such things in the world as husbands and lawyers and duelling codes and theories of sin and notions of propriety and all the other irrelevancies which provide hackneyed and bloodless material for our so-called plays of passion.

PRUDERIES OF THE FRENCH STAGE

To all stage presentations there are limits. If Macduff were to stab Macbeth, the spectacle would be intolerable; and even the pretence which we allow on our stage is ridiculously destructive to the illusion of the scene. Yet pugilists and gladiators will actually fight and kill in public without shame, even as a spectacle for money. But no sober couple of lovers of any delicacy could endure to be watched. We in England, accustomed to consider the French stage much more licentious than the British, are always surprised and puzzled when we learn, as we may do any day if we come within reach of such information, that French actors are often scandalized by what they consider the indecency of the English stage, and that French actresses who desire a greater licence in appealing to the sexual instincts than the French stage allows them, learn English and establish themselves on the English stage.[5] The German and Russian stages are in the same relation to the French and, perhaps more or less, all the Latin stages. The reason is that, partly from a want of respect for the theatre, partly from a sort of respect for art in general which moves them to accord moral privileges to artists, partly from the very objectionable tradition that the realm of art is Alsatia [a sanctuary] and the contemplation of works of art a holiday from the burden of virtue, partly because French prudery does not attach itself to the same points of behavior as British prudery, and has a different code of the mentionable and the unmentionable, and for many other reasons, the French tolerate plays which are never performed in England until they have been spoiled by a process of bowdlerization; yet French taste is more fastidious than ours as to the exhibition and treatment on the stage of the physical incidents of sex. On the French stage a kiss is as obvious a convention as the thrust under the arm by which Macduff runs Macbeth through. It is even a purposely unconvincing convention: the actors rather insisting that it shall be impossible for any spectator to mistake a stage kiss for a real one. In England, on the contrary, realism is carried to the point at which nobody except the two performers can perceive that the caress is not genuine. And here the English stage is certainly in the right; for whatever question there arises as to what incidents are proper for representation on the stage or not, my experience as a playgoer leaves me in no doubt that once it is decided to represent an incident, it will be offensive, no matter whether it be a prayer or a kiss, unless it is presented with a convincing appearance of sincerity.

OUR DISILLUSIVE SCENERY

For example, the main objection to the use of illusive scenery (in most modern plays scenery is not illusive: everything visible is as real as in your

5. French performers on the West End stage in the first half of the century's second decade included Yvonne Arnaud, Alice Delysia and Gaby Deslys. They soon were joined by Odette Myrtil and Jeanne de Casalis.

drawing-room at home) is that it is unconvincing; whilst the imaginary
scenery with which the audience transfigures a platform or tribune like the
Elizabethan stage or the Greek stage used by Sophocles, is quite convincing.
In fact, the more scenery you have the less illusion you produce. The wise
playwright, when he cannot get absolute reality of presentation, goes to the
other extreme, and aims at atmosphere and suggestion of mood rather than
at direct simulative illusion. The theatre, as I first knew it, was a place of
wings and flats which destroyed both atmosphere and illusion. This was
tolerated, and even intensely enjoyed, but not in the least because nothing
better was possible; for all the devices employed in the productions of Mr
Granville Barker [Court Theatre, 1904–7] or Max Reinhardt [Deutsches
Theater, Berlin, 1905] or [K. S. Stanislavsky in] the Moscow Art Theatre
were equally available for Colley Cibber and Garrick, except the intensity
of our artificial light. When Garrick played Richard III in slashed trunk
hose and plumes, it was not because he believed that the Plantagenets
dressed like that, or because the costumiers could not have made him a XV
century dress as easily as a nondescript combination of the state robes of
George III with such scraps of older fashions as seemed to playgoers for
some reason to be romantic. The charm of the theatre in those days was its
makebelieve. It has that charm still, not only for the amateurs, who are
happiest when they are most unnatural and impossible and absurd, but for
audiences as well. I have seen performances of my own plays which were
to me far wilder burlesques than Sheridan's Critic [1779] or [George
Villiers, Second Duke of] Buckingham's Rehearsal [1671]; yet they have
produced sincere laughter and tears such as the most finished metropolitan
productions have failed to elicit. Fielding was entirely right when he
represented Partridge [in *Tom Jones*] as enjoying intensely the performance
of the king in Hamlet because anybody could see that the king was an
actor, and resenting Garrick's Hamlet because it might have been a real
man. Yet we have only to look at the portraits of Garrick to see that his
performances would nowadays seem almost as extravagantly stagey as his
costumes. In our day [Emma] Calvé's intensely real Carmen never pleased
the mob as much as the obvious fancy-ball masquerading of suburban
young ladies in the same character.

HOLDING THE MIRROR UP TO NATURE

Theatrical art begins as the holding up to Nature of a distorting mirror.
In this phase it pleases people who are childish enough to believe that they

can see what they look like and what they are when they look at a true mirror. Naturally they think that a true mirror can teach them nothing. Only by giving them back some monstrous image can the mirror amuse them or terrify them. It is not until they grow up to the point at which they learn that they know very little about themselves, and that they do not see themselves in a true mirror as other people see them, that they become consumed with curiosity as to what they really are like, and begin to demand that the stage shall be a mirror of such accuracy and intensity of illumination that they shall be able to get glimpses of their real selves in it, and also learn a little how they appear to other people.

For audiences of this highly developed class, sex can no longer be ignored or conventionalized or distorted by the playwright who makes the mirror. The old sentimental extravagances and the old grossnesses are of no further use to him. Don Giovanni and Zerlina [whom the Don attempts to ravish] are not gross: Tristan and Isolde are not extravagant or sentimental. They say and do nothing that you cannot bear to hear and see; and yet they give you, the one pair briefly and slightly, and the other fully and deeply, what passes in the minds of lovers. The love depicted may be that of a philosophic adventurer tempting an ignorant country girl, or of a tragically serious poet entangled with a woman of noble capacity in a passion which has become for them the reality of the whole universe. No matter: the thing is dramatized and dramatized directly, not talked about as something that happened before the curtain rose, or that will happen after it falls.

FARCICAL COMEDY SHIRKING ITS SUBJECT

Now if all this can be done in the key of tragedy and philosophic comedy, it can, I have always contended, be done in the key of farcical comedy; and Overruled is a trifling experiment in that manner. Conventional farcical comedies are always finally tedious because the heart of them, the inevitable conjugal infidelity, is always evaded. Even its consequences are evaded. Mr Granville Barker has pointed out rightly that if the third acts of our farcical comedies dared to describe the consequences that would follow from the first and second in real life, they would end as squalid tragedies;[6] and in my opinion they would be greatly improved

6. Shaw presumably is recalling an oral remark, as the statement does not appear in any of Barker's known writings and speeches, or in his correspondence with Shaw.

thereby even as entertainments; for I have never seen a three-act farcical comedy without being bored and tired by the third act, and observing that the rest of the audience were in the same condition, though they were not vigilantly introspective enough to find that out, and were apt to blame oneanother, especially the husbands and wives, for their crossness. But it is happily by no means true that conjugal infidelities always produce tragic consequences, or that they need produce even the unhappiness which they often do produce. Besides, the more momentous the consequences, the more interesting become the impulses and imaginations and reasonings, if any, of the people who disregard them. If I had an opportunity of conversing with the ghost of an executed murderer, I have no doubt he would begin to tell me eagerly about his trial, with the names of the distinguished ladies and gentlemen who honored him with their presence on that occasion, and then about his execution. All of which would bore me exceedingly. I should say, "My dear sir; such manufactured ceremonies do not interest me in the least. I know how a man is tried, and how he is hanged. I should have had you killed in a much less disgusting, hypocritical, and unfriendly manner if the matter had been in my hands. What I want to know about is the murder. How did you feel when you committed it? Why did you do it? What did you say to yourself about it? If, like most murderers, you had not been hanged, would you have committed other murders? Did you really dislike the victim, or did you want his money, or did you murder a person whom you did not dislike, and from whose death you had nothing to gain, merely for the sake of murdering? If so, can you describe the charm to me? Does it come upon you periodically; or is it chronic? Has curiosity anything to do with it?" I would ply him with all manner of questions to find out what murder is really like; and I should not be satisfied until I had realized that I, too, might commit a murder, or else that there is some specific quality present in a murderer and lacking in me. And, if so, what that quality is.

In just the same way, I want the unfaithful husband or the unfaithful wife in a farcical comedy not to bother me with their divorce cases or the stratagems they employ to avoid a divorce case, but to tell me how and why married couples are unfaithful. I dont want to hear the lies they tell oneanother to conceal what they have done, but the truths they tell oneanother when they have to face what they have done without concealment or excuse. No doubt prudent and considerate people conceal such adventures, when they can, from those who are most likely to be wounded by them; but it is not to be presumed that, when found out, they necessarily disgrace themselves by irritating lies and transparent subterfuges.

My playlet, which I offer as a model to all future writers of farcical comedy, may now, I hope, be read without shock. I may just add that Mr Sibthorpe Juno's view [in *Overruled*] that morality demands, not that we should behave morally (an impossibility to our sinful nature) but that we shall not attempt to defend our immoralities, is a standard view in England, and was advanced in all seriousness by an earnest and distinguished British moralist shortly after the first performance of Overruled. My objection to that aspect of the doctrine of original sin is that no necessary and inevitable operation of human nature can reasonably be regarded as sinful at all, and that a morality which assumes the contrary is an absurd morality, and can be kept in countenance only by hypocrisy. When people were ashamed of sanitary problems, and refused to face them, leaving them to solve themselves clandestinely in dirt and secrecy, the solution arrived at was the Black Death. A similar policy as to sex problems has solved itself by an even worse plague than the Black Death; and the remedy for that is not salvarsan,[7] but sound moral hygiene, the first foundation of which is the discontinuance of our habit of telling not only the comparatively harmless lies that we know we ought not to tell, but the ruinous lies that we foolishly think we ought to tell.

7. A trademark for arsphenamine, an arsenical powder used at one time for treating syphilis.

Pygmalion

First published in 1916; revised in 1941

════

A PROFESSOR OF PHONETICS

As will be seen later on, Pygmalion needs, not a preface, but a sequel, which I have supplied in its due place.[1]

The English have no respect for their language, and will not teach their children to speak it. They cannot spell it because they have nothing to spell it with but an old foreign alphabet of which only the consonants—and not all of them—have any agreed speech value. Consequently no man can teach himself what it should sound like from reading it; and it is impossible for an Englishman to open his mouth without making some other Englishman despise him. Most European languages are now accessible in black and white to foreigners: English and French are not thus accessible even to Englishmen and Frenchmen. The reformer we need most today is an energetic phonetic enthusiast: that is why I have made such a one the hero of a popular play.

There have been heroes of that kind crying in the wilderness for many years past. When I became interested in the subject towards the end of the eighteenseventies, the illustrious Alexander Melville Bell,[2] the inventor of Visible Speech, had emigrated to Canada, where his son invented the telephone; but Alexander J. Ellis[3] was still a London patriarch, with an impressive head always covered by a velvet skull cap, for which he would

1. '*Pygmalion* . . . now has a sequel', Shaw informed Mrs Patrick Campbell (19 December 1915), 'not in dialogue, but in prose, which you will never be able to live up to' (*Collected Letters 1911–1925*, 1985, p. 335).
2. Scots-born educationalist, who devoted himself to the education of deaf mutes by the 'visible speech' method, in which the alphabetical characters of his own invention were graphic diagrams of positions and motions of the organs of speech. Among his written works are *A Popular Manual of Vocal Physiology and Visible Speech* (1889) and *The Science of Speech* (1897).
3. Philologist at Cambridge University and officer of the English Spelling Reform Association (1879), author of *The Essentials of Phonetics* (1848). Shaw at ninety-three reminisced (*The Listener*, December 1949), 'I am old enough to have heard

apologize to public meetings in a very courtly manner. He and Tito Pagliardini,[4] another phonetic veteran, were men whom it was impossible to dislike. Henry Sweet,[5] then a young man, lacked their sweetness of character: he was about as conciliatory to conventional mortals as Ibsen or Samuel Butler. His great ability as a phonetician (he was, I think, the best of them all at his job) would have entitled him to high official recognition, and perhaps enabled him to popularize his subject, but for his Satanic contempt for all academic dignitaries and persons in general who thought more of Greek than of phonetics. Once, in the days when the Imperial Institute rose in South Kensington [inaugurated in 1893], and Joseph Chamberlain was booming the Empire, I induced the editor of a leading monthly review to commission an article from Sweet on the imperial importance of his subject. When it arrived, it contained nothing but a savagely derisive attack on a professor of language and literature whose chair Sweet regarded as proper to a phonetic expert only. The article, being libellous, had to be returned as impossible; and I had to renounce my dream of dragging its author into the limelight. When I met him afterwards, for the first time for many years, I found to my astonishment that he, who had been a quite tolerably presentable young man, had actually managed by sheer scorn to alter his personal appearance until he had become a sort of walking repudiation of Oxford and all its traditions. It must have been largely in his own despite that he was squeezed into something called a Readership of phonetics there. The future of phonetics rests probably with his pupils, who all swore by him; but nothing could bring the man himself into any sort of compliance with the university to which he nevertheless clung by divine right in an intensely Oxonian way. I daresay his papers, if he has left any, include some satires that may be published without too destructive results fifty years hence. He was, I believe, not in the least an ill-natured man: very much the opposite, I should say; but he would not suffer fools gladly; and to him all scholars who were not rabid phoneticians were fools.

Those who knew him will recognize in my third act the allusion to the

---

him lecture, in his velvet skull cap . . . After pleading his phonetic brief he read Shakespeare . . .'
4. Former singer, friend of Shaw until his death in 1895, who became a very successful vocal teacher and phoneticist.
5. Principal founder of modern phonetics, for whom a readership was established at Oxford. Among his many publications on language are *A Handbook of Phonetics* (1877) and *A New English Grammar* (1892).

Current Shorthand in which he used to write postcards. It may be acquired from a four-and-sixpenny manual published by the Clarendon Press [*A Manual of Current Shorthand*, 1892]. The postcards which Mrs Higgins describes are such as I have received from Sweet. I would decipher a sound which a cockney would represent by *zerr*, and a Frenchman by *seu*, and then write demanding with some heat what on earth it meant. Sweet, with boundless contempt for my stupidity, would reply that it not only meant but obviously was the word Result, as no other word containing that sound, and capable of making sense with the context, existed in any language spoken on earth. That less expert mortals should require fuller indications was beyond Sweet's patience. Therefore, though the whole point of his Current Shorthand is that it can express every sound in the language perfectly, vowels as well as consonants, and that your hand has to make no stroke except the easy and current ones with which you write m, n, and u, l, p, and q, scribbling them at whatever angle comes easiest to you, his unfortunate determination to make this remarkable and quite legible script serve also as a shorthand reduced it in his own practice to the most inscrutable of cryptograms. His true objective was the provision of a full, accurate, legible script for our language; but he was led past that by his contempt for the popular Pitman system of shorthand, which he called the Pitfall system. The triumph of Pitman was a triumph of business organization: there was a weekly paper to persuade you to learn Pitman: there were cheap textbooks and exercise books and transcripts of speeches for you to copy, and schools where experienced teachers coached you up to the necessary proficiency. Sweet could not organize his market in that fashion. He might as well have been the Sybil who tore up the leaves of prophecy that nobody would attend to.[6] The four-and-sixpenny manual, mostly in his lithographed handwriting, that was never vulgarly advertized, may perhaps some day be taken up by a syndicate and pushed upon the public as The Times pushed the Encyclopedia Britannica; but until then it will certainly not prevail against Pitman. I have bought three copies of it during my lifetime; and I am informed by the publishers that its cloistered existence is still a steady and healthy one. I actually learned the system two several times; and yet the shorthand in which I am writing these lines is Pitman's. And the reason is, that my secretary [Ann Elder] cannot transcribe Sweet, having been perforce taught in the schools of Pitman. In America I

6. Originally the Sibylline Books from Cumae were said to be nine, but the Sibyl destroyed six of them when the Romans, failing to realize their value, attempted to barter for them.

could use the commercially organized Gregg shorthand, which has taken a hint from Sweet by making its letters writable (current, Sweet would have called them) instead of having to be geometrically drawn like Pitman's; but all these systems, including Sweet's, are spoilt by making them available for verbatim reporting, in which complete and exact spelling and word division are impossible. A complete and exact phonetic script is neither practicable nor necessary for ordinary use; but if we enlarge our alphabet to the Russian size, and make our spelling as phonetic as Spanish, the advance will be prodigious.

Pygmalion Higgins is not a portrait of Sweet, to whom the adventure of Eliza Doolittle would have been impossible; still, as will be seen, there are touches of Sweet in the play. With Higgins's physique and temperament Sweet might have set the Thames on fire. As it was, he impressed himself professionally on Europe to an extent that made his comparative personal obscurity, and the failure of Oxford to do justice to his eminence, a puzzle to foreign specialists in his subject. I do not blame Oxford, because I think Oxford is quite right in demanding a certain social amenity from its nurslings (heaven knows it is not exorbitant in its requirements!); for although I well know how hard it is for a man of genius with a seriously underrated subject to maintain serene and kindly relations with the men who underrate it, and who keep all the best places for less important subjects which they profess without originality and sometimes without much capacity for them, still, if he overwhelms them with wrath and disdain, he cannot expect them to heap honors on him.

Of the later generations of phoneticians I know little. Among them towered Robert Bridges,[7] to whom perhaps Higgins may owe his Miltonic sympathies, though here again I must disclaim all portraiture. But if the play makes the public aware that there are such people as phoneticians, and that they are among the most important people in England at present, it will serve its turn.

I wish to boast that Pygmalion has been an extremely successful play, both on stage and screen, all over Europe and North America as well as at home. It is so intensely and deliberately didactic, and its subject is esteemed so dry, that I delight in throwing it at the heads of the wiseacres who repeat the parrot cry that art should never be didactic. It goes to prove my contention that great art can never be anything else.

Finally, and for the encouragement of people troubled with accents that

---

7. English poet and essayist, appointed poet laureate in 1913, and one of the founders of the Society for Pure English.

cut them off from all high employment, I may add that the change wrought by Professor Higgins in the flower-girl is neither impossible nor uncommon. The modern concierge's daughter who fulfils her ambition by playing the Queen of Spain in [Victor Hugo's] Ruy Blas [1838] at the Théâtre Français is only one of many thousands of men and women who have sloughed off their native dialects and acquired a new tongue. Our West End shop assistants and domestic servants are bilingual. But the thing has to be done scientifically, or the last state of the aspirant may be worse than the first. An honest slum dialect is more tolerable than the attempts of phonetically untaught persons to imitate the plutocracy. Ambitious flower-girls who read this play must not imagine that they can pass themselves off as fine ladies by untutored imitation. They must learn their alphabet over again, and different, from a phonetic expert. Imitation will only make them ridiculous.

International Government

Introduction to two reports by Leonard S. Woolf prepared for the Fabian Research Department; first published in New York, 1916, the introduction having been earlier printed separately for copyright deposit

═══

The present war has produced many catchwords, among them, A War to End War, An Inconclusive Peace, The Destruction of Militarism, The Establishment of the Rights of Nationalities on an Unassailable Basis, Free Negotiation by Free Peoples, and This Must Never Occur Again. Most of these shibboleths proclaim their own thoughtlessness. War can do many things, but it cannot end war. No peace can be a conclusive peace: it is beyond the wit of man to draw a treaty of peace which will make it impossible for war to recur between Britain and either her present enemies or her present allies. The destruction of militarism cannot be attained by a military triumph: war is the creator, the sustainer, and the reason-for-existence of militarism. The rights of Nationalities, far from being placed on an unassailable basis by war, are at present wiped out by it: the Englishman is forced to fight as a pressed man for Russia, though his father was slain by the Russians at Inkerman,[1] and for France, though his grandfather fell at Waterloo charging shoulder to shoulder with Blücher's Prussians.[2] The German is compelled by the Prussian, whom he loathes, to die for Turkey and for the Crescent as against Anglo-Saxon Christendom.[3] Every one of the belligerents is holding down some conquered race or nation. The establishment of the rights of nationalities on an unassailable basis would cause the instant dissolution, first of the British Empire, then of the Austrian, with political earthquakes in the French Republic, the Italian Kingdom, and the Russian Empire, leaving Germany, on the whole, the

1. The battle of Inkerman (1854), near Sevastopol, occurred during the Crimean War between the Russians and the allied English and French.
2. At the village of Waterloo in Belgium on 18 June 1815, Wellington's Anglo-Dutch forces and Gebhard von Blücher's German army defeated Napoleon.
3. In August 1916 the Turks, declaring a Holy War, crossed the Sinai peninsula in an effort to seize the Suez Canal. They were led by Colonel Kress von Kressenstein, supported by German artillery and machine-gun companies.

strongest of the survivors. This is so obvious that the phrase can mean nothing but the rescue of Belgium from dependence on the Central Empires, and its restoration to a state of complete political dependence on France and Britain. Free negotiation by free peoples is impossible because there are no free peoples engaged in the present war: nobody pretends that the German people or the Russian people are free; and if we take the belligerent Republics and limited monarchies of the west as comparatively free, yet we find that the one department in which they do not even make a pretense of democracy is diplomacy, which is as autocratic in London as in St Petersburg or Berlin.

Thus we see that none of the catchwords except the last can possibly mean what they say; and when they are cheered each time they reappear in the Prime Minister's [David Lloyd George] stock peroration, it is evident that he himself offers them as no more than oratorical orchestration to the patriotic sentiment of the assembly. They can be taken literally only by ignorant and simple persons to whom a European war is simply a football match conducted with cannons.

The only catchword, then, that has anything in it is, This Must Never Occur Again. But it quite certainly will occur again if nothing is done to prevent it. Crude people recommend the destruction of Germany as a preventive. In Germany the same sort of people recommend the destruction of England. Among the neutrals they say, "By all means let these two quarrelsome and arrogant Powers destroy oneanother like the Kilkenny cats [that fought until only their tails were left] and leave the world in peace." But even if such a solution were physically or morally possible, which everyone who is not a cretinous Yahoo [in Swift's *Gulliver's Travels*, Book IV] knows perfectly well it is not, in what way would the recurrence of war, or even the continuance of the present war in a fight over the spoils, be prevented by it? [Marcus Porcius] Cato's formula for the ending of the Punic wars was, Annihilate Carthage [as was done in 146 BC]. Carthage was annihilated; but its annihilation brought no peace to Rome. The Irish are a contentious and troublesome people; and the proverbial receipt for peace in Ireland is to sink the island for ten minutes into the Atlantic. Let us suppose that Ireland is duly sunk, with England and Prussia moored to it, not for ten minutes, but for ever. The white and yellow races will still confront one another across the Pacific. Italy, France and Spain will still have to divide the heritage of the Moors. Sweden will still watch Russia with her hand on her sword-hilt; and Russia will still burn to protect the Balkans, to wrest Constantinople from the followers of "the accursed Mahound" [Mohammed], to cling to Poland like a big brother, and to pick up more of [what Kipling called] the White Man's Burden [1899] in Asia than the other Powers may think healthy for her, or than India, for instance, may be disposed to cast on any shoulders but her own. Of South America I say nothing except that it does not look convincing as a Temple of Perpetual Peace. At all events, the notion that the most completely decisive victory either by the Allies or the Central Empires, pushed to the most ruthless extremities by the victors with a view to the eternal disablement of the vanquished, would guarantee the peace of the world for five years, or even for five minutes, is on the face of it mere moonshine. The world would remain full of explosive material, and be so heavily demoralized into the bargain that it would be less than ever capable of keeping lighted matches away from the powder magazine.

Besides, the reduction to absurdity of military wars by stalemate, or by increasing the cost of victory beyond any possible advantage, direct or contingent, to be hoped from it, would still leave tariff wars possible, and even encourage them by guaranteeing them against military reprisals. At present a clamorous section of the British public is demanding a perpetual tariff war against Germany, peace or no peace. They openly and recklessly class tariffs with hostilities and insist on their destructive and malicious character. They are naïvely unaware of the fact that if protective duties really bear this construction we are at war with our ally France at this moment; for France has locked the door of her vast dominion in the north of Africa against our manufactures, and it has never been suggested that our alliance should unlock it, either during the war or after it. The modern empire state is not an Arnold von Winkelried,[4] opening the way for all the world to rush in at his heels: on the contrary, the modern Arnold, the moment he is through, turns swiftly and bars the entry against all competitors. The wise man looks for the cause of war not in Nietzsche's gospel of the Will to Power [1901] or Lord Roberts's[5] far blunter gospel of the

4. According to fourteenth-century legend this Swiss patriot, battling the Austrians, rushed into the ranks of the enemy, allowing his body to become pincushioned with their thrown spears, thus opening a way into the enemy lines for his fellow Swiss.
5. In a controversial speech in Manchester, 25 October 1912, General Lord Roberts proclaimed that 'war will take place the instant the German forces by land and sea are, by their superiority at every point, as certain of victory as anything in human calculation can be made certain ... And, gentlemen, it is an excellent policy. It is, or should be, the policy of every nation prepared to play a great part in history' (*Manchester Guardian*, 26 October 1912). See also p. 137.

British Will to Conquer, but in the custom house. The formal conquest of a territory may loom large as a sentimental grievance; but, as the case of Alsace-Lorraine shews,[6] it does not produce war. But the appropriation of a market is another matter: a very small economic grievance will rapidly become the nucleus of an enormous mass of martial and patriotic emotion. There is no prospect of the end of this war being the end of international market-cornering and tariff blockades; and as long as war remains physically possible, such operations will produce it as fatally in the future as in the past.

Again, take the Balance of Power aimed at by our diplomatists. As long as each State works for its own hand, as at present, every diplomatist is necessarily engaged in a constant struggle to upset the balance of power in his own favor. He pretends to aim at nothing beyond preserving it; but he exposes all the rest as aiming at hegemony, at command of the sea, and so forth. Each nation feels that supremacy is absolutely necessary to its security, and that it, and it alone, can be trusted not to abuse it. War intensifies this feeling, and the present war is no exception: it began as a pure Balance of Power war; and it will not only stimulate to the highest degree those passions of fear and jealousy which are the motive force of the equilibrist diplomacy, but will throw political power into the hands of those who are entirely governed by them. The Napoleonic wars threw Europe into the hands of Metternich and Castlereagh, who had no other desire than to stereotype the conditions which had produced the war and to stifle the new moral world in its cradle.[7] In the Franco–Prussian war of 1870–71, even so thoroughpaced a Junker [a German autocratic military officer] as Bismarck went under because he was not reactionary enough for the victorious military party, and Alsace-Lorraine was annexed in spite of him. And if the present war should end in a decisive victory for either side, that victory will be used and abused to the uttermost in spite of the Bismarcks, to say nothing of the moderate men and Pacifists, so vainly urging a

6. In accordance with the Treaty of Frankfurt, which ended the Franco–German War (1870–71), French-speaking Alsace and the greater part of German-speaking Lorraine, seized two centuries earlier by Louis XIV from the Holy Roman Empire, were ceded to Germany.
7. In their efforts to maintain a balance of power in Europe after Napoleon's defeat, they negotiated to restore the Bourbons to the French throne and to reduce France to her former frontiers. Neither was prepared to accept the visionary schemes of Alexander I of Russia for founding an effective confederation of Europe.

friendly settlement whilst the combatants go steadily on fighting for the strongest position at the finish, and most certainly not fighting for it with any intention of foregoing an inch of it when it is gained.

Let us therefore not deceive ourselves with goodnatured dreams. Unless and until Europe is provided with a new organ for supernational action, provided with an effective police, all talk of making an end of war is mere waste of breath. There is only one alternative to government by police, and that is government by massacre. We, like the Ottoman Turks, have found that to be true in our own affairs. The Turks, in the Balkans and in Armenia,[8] and we, in the Indian hills and in Africa and Australia, have found that where our police stops, its place must be taken by raids of soldiers, killing, burning and destroying indiscriminately until enough is judged to have been done to keep the district in awe for some years to come. The fact that we call such expeditions massacres when the Turks resort to them, and punitive expeditions or brigandage commissions when we resort to them, does not change their essential character; and the protests of the few humanitarians who know what the official formulas which occasionally leak out in the press really mean, are quite unavailing; for though the reign of terror is necessarily cruel, anarchy is apt to be crueller still, and the reign of terror is thus forced on us as the best practicable alternative to the reign of law. Our habit of looking the other way and talking busily about the weather on such occasions is not, as we imagine, civilization; it is only our attempt to hide from ourselves the fact that civilization means law, and that where law stops, the most civilized people in the world have to act like Timour the Tartar [Turkish conqueror, known to the West as Tamerlane] and Ivan [IV of Russia] the Terrible, or like the highly respectable and civilized French ladies and gentlemen who, during the French Revolutionary wars, had to connive at the September massacres by pretending that nothing particular was happening when the regular tribunals could not cope with the public danger. In the territories of the United States, pioneered by men quite as civilized by teaching and tradition as their cousins in London and Brighton, the revolver and the bowie knife reigned where the sheriff and the vigilance committee fell short. And the sixteen-inch gun and the submarine torpedo reign in

8. The Ottoman Empire (1909–18) was practically under a military dictatorship of 'the Young Turks', a revolutionary party that used the army to enforce its will to 'Turkify' the Balkans. In 1915 this Turkish Government began a general deportation of Armenians, who resisted being nationalized, in the course of which it committed large-scale atrocities.

Europe at present solely because there is no supernational sheriff or vigilance committee to adjust the disputes of nations.

As this well-established conclusion of political science is not very recondite, there is no lack at present of schemes and proposals for the establishment of some sort of supernational court. American projectors have been specially active, and one of them [Woodrow Wilson] has actually applied to influential persons throughout the world for powers of attorney to enable him to represent them at what may be described roughly as a Hague Conference of the Human Race [the League of Nations]. Besides these more definite schemes, there is a vast mass of opinion which can be compared only to that of the elder [Tony] Weller in Pickwick [Chapter 34]. It will be remembered by good Dickensians that when the case of Bardell *v.* Pickwick was entered, Mr Weller recommended Mr Pickwick to plead an *alibi*; and when Mr Pickwick lost his case, his humble counsellor uttered the famous lamentation, "Why wornt there an alleybi?" Substitute the word Arbitration for Alibi, and you have the state of mind of ninetynine Pacifists out of every hundred now living. They know that a war between England and the United States over the *Alabama*[9] was averted by arbitration, and they have ever since regarded arbitration as a simple and sufficient alternative to war. Since 1899 they have attached a peculiar sanctity to the soil of The Hague, owing to the establishment there of the Hague Conference as a permanent arbitrating body.[10] But it is just this limitation of the Hague Conference to arbitration, and to quite unauthoritative attempts to codify and establish such rules of the ring as war admits of, that makes it practically negligible as a pacific agency.

The present volume will, it is hoped, help to clear away this benevolent vagueness and to explain what is needed as an alternative to war. From it our preachers of arbitration will learn what arbitration really is; and they must set off their disappointment in finding how little it can do against their surprise and satisfaction in learning how much it has already done; for there have been many more arbitrations than the public have heard of, and several of them may fairly claim to have averted war. But no arbitration court can supply the need for a Supernational Legislature, a Supernational

9. One of a number of Confederate warships built in England during the American Civil War. The United States alleged this was a breach of neutrality and demanded, among other things, an apology and reparations for damages inflicted by these ships. The matter was settled by an international tribunal, 1871–2.
10. Assembled in 1898 on the initiative of Nicholas II of Russia, the conference sought ways of limiting international armed forces.

Tribunal, and a Supernational Board of Conciliation; and the members of these bodies must not be private philanthropists on a holiday, qualified in the first instance by their ability to pay the expenses of a trip to Holland, but responsible representatives of the actual Governments of the constituent States. No question can be entertained of any further representative character on their part: the essential and indispensable qualification must be ability to, as the phrase goes, "deliver the goods." Sages and saints, plebiscitary or volunteer representatives of the heart of the people, will not serve the purpose: only the plenipotentiary who has the effective Government of his State behind him, and whose Aye or No may be depended on as the Aye and No of that Government, will be of any use.

How it may all be done if there is the will to do it is suggested in the following pages. It is the peculiar business of the Fabian Society to supply progressive aspirations with practical methods. The process adopted in the present case has been, first, to refer the question to the Fabian Research Department.[11] As practically nobody knew more than bits and scraps of what had actually been done in the way of International Organization, the Department had to begin by finding an investigator and skilled writer with the necessary qualifications and devotion for the task of preparing a report and suggesting conclusions. A certain endowment was also needed, not to remunerate the investigator on the usual professional basis, but to prevent its bare expenses from falling too heavily on a single worker. The endowment was provided by a timely donation from Mr Joseph Rowntree,[12] who, as often happens, is not a member of the Society, but appreciates its manner of doing useful jobs in the building up of social tissue; and the man was found in Mr L. S. Woolf,[13] who turned cheerfully from *belles lettres* to the production of the present volume on terms which would certainly have been rejected with emphasis by a dock laborer.

The report, both in instalments as it was produced, and when it was completely drafted, was subjected to keen discussion in the Research Department, where experts in this kind of work are six a penny. It was

11. Organized by Beatrice Webb in 1912, with Shaw as chairman of the Executive Committee. It developed by 1918 into the Labour Research Department, independent of the Fabian Society.

12. Cocoa manufacturer and industrial and social reformer, who founded a village trust, a social service trust, and a charitable trust, promoted adult education and strongly supported the League of Nations.

13. English publicist and husband of Virginia Woolf, with whom he founded the Hogarth Press. He was editor of the *International Review* and the *Political Quarterly*.

then published as a supplement to The New Statesman, and thus offered for general public discussion. Later on, at a summer meeting on the shore of Lake Derwentwater [in Cumberland], it was submitted to a conference at which the members of a group [that included J. A. Hobson, Graham Wallas and G. Lowes Dickinson] which had been working independently on the subject under the presidency of Lord [James] Bryce[14] were present, with such other non-Fabian experts as could be secured; and a point was there reached at which it was apparent that the sounding of the report by skilled discussion and criticism had been carried to exhaustion. It is now published as being as good as the Fabian Society can at present make it. Nothing but actual experience can determine the limits of its practicability; but it at least plans the experiment as carefully as possible.

The main difficulty will be to make our party politicians aware that any such piece of work has been done in England. It has occurred repeatedly within the experience of the Fabian Society that Ministers, finding themselves under electoral pressure to introduce some reform which is only known to them as a platform phrase, have proceeded in complete ignorance of the work that has been put into the proposal by English thinkers and political scientists, and, after a carefully advertized trip to some country where something of the kind is supposed to be in operation (usually Germany), have come back and introduced a Bill containing every possible blunder that sciolism [shallow learning] can make after five minutes' contemplation of a half-understood subject, and have actually passed it into law, only to be forced to pass an amending Act after a year of easily avoidable wreckage. It is a striking illustration of the want of touch between the intellectual life of the country and the House of Commons, that Cabinet Ministers always assume that political science, as distinguished from the arts of electioneering and managing the House, does not exist in England. German bureaucrats and Swiss and Italian professors are readily credited with political scholarship; but their works are not read; and it is consequently not noticed that they quote English sociologists with respect, and often build on their foundations. The British statesman sails along quite convinced that, except for an occasional university professor's textbook, which is assumed to be unpractical and useless, England has produced nothing but a few agnostic essays, [William] Ruff's Guide to the Turf, The Hundred Best Investments [*The 100 Best Investments* was a London annual, 1911–31], and special articles in the newspapers on Tariff Reform to serve

14. British jurist, historian and ardent Liberal, author of *The American Commonwealth* (1888).

as party kites to test how the electoral wind is blowing, or to set it blowing in a desired direction.

It is a pity; for much excellent work is done; and it is not cheerful for the Fabian Society, which has organized a considerable share of it, to be obliged in common honesty to warn workers that not only will they get no pence for their labors, but that nobody with any executive authority will take the smallest notice of it.

Still, the vocation of the Fabian Society is to chart all the channels into which the ship of State is being irresistibly driven by social evolution. The certainty that the ship will be piloted by a person calling himself a Practical Statesman, fanatically devoted to the method of Trial and Error, and finding all the rocks, both the hidden and the obvious ones, by the simple method of steering the ship crash on to them, and then getting her off as best he can, would not justify the Fabians in leaving the channel uncharted. They are, after all, no worse treated than those English chemists and metallurgists who have seen their discoveries appreciated and exploited in Germany and elsewhere whilst receiving nothing at home but a good-natured contempt as faddists. They do not complain of their own particular share of the general neglect; but they take the opportunity to point out that a supernational political constitution can no more be built without science than an airship or an ironclad, and that a governing class which is still repeating that "The Republic has no need of chemists," and exempting hunt servants from military duty whilst driving scientific workers contemptuously into the trenches by way of "giving them something real to do," must not be surprised if it finds itself outwitted by States which take skilled advice instead of relying on the theory that country gentlemen are, as a class, inspired.

More than this it is not prudent to say, for a total neglect of science may be better than the sudden conversion to it of gentlemen who conceive it as a means of discovering miraculous cures for diseases, especially distemper in foxhounds. Fortunately there is little opportunity in political science for the elixir of life and the philosopher's stone. There will be neither quackery nor science about the Congress which will patch up the present war when it has reached the end of its tether. It will be a repetition of the Congress of Vienna [after the Napoleonic Wars, 1814–15]: that is, a crowd of diplomatists will gather round the booty, and try to secure as much as they can as best they can for their respective States. Few if any of them will have ulterior views; and most of them will regard those who look for an end of war as an institution as vulgar ideologues. Nevertheless, the reaction against the monstrous slaughter and destruction of the war, and the heavy financial burden it will leave, may be too much for diplomatic routine; and it may also happen that the only acceptable terms of peace may be impracticable without new supernational machinery of a much more definite and permanent kind than the old Concert of Europe which it was so hard to keep in tune, and which was so dismal a failure as regards the prevention of war. In such an event the following pages may prove useful, embodying as they do many months of research and discussion of at least as trustworthy a quality as the British Foreign Office, on a comparison of its publications with those of the Fabian Society, can reasonably be expected to achieve.

G. B. S.

How to Settle the Irish Question

First appeared as a series of articles in the Daily Express, London, *on 27–9 November 1917. Separately published as a pamphlet in December 1917*

═══

This book is a reprint of a series of articles written by me at the suggestion of the London Daily Express. They were published simultaneously in London and Dublin, Cork and Belfast, on the 27th, 28th, and 29th November last: a moment chosen in view of the critical stage the deliberations of the Irish Convention[1] were then believed to have reached.

My qualification for dealing with the subject is that though I am an Irishman, of the Protestant landlord variety, I have not lived in Ireland since I left it in 1876, and that though I have since then been occupied almost continually with the problems of modern political science, I have studied them from the point of view of white civilization as a whole, having no constituency to conciliate and no social ambition to further; for it has been my fortune to secure by my artistic activities a public position infinitely preferable to any that political life or office has to offer. I can, without compromising that position, say things that no party politician dares say, and that even those politicians whose public spirit is above party can hardly say without too much offence to the factions they are striving to reconcile.

Thus I am not only disinterested, but disengaged. This is not altogether my own fault. Believing that I might be of some service on the Convention, I conceived it to be my public duty to take steps to have it suggested to the Government and to the Convention itself that I should be nominated or co-opted as a member. By doing so I brought the British Government and the Irish Convention nearer to unanimity than was supposed possible at the time. Fortunately for me, as it turned out when secrecy was imposed on the Convention, I was left free when the officially accredited representatives of Irish opinion were muzzled. That was not the intention; but it has been

---

1. First convened on 25 July 1917 by Prime Minister David Lloyd George, under pressure from the United States, to frame an Irish constitution acceptable to the north and south factions in Ireland and to England. Shaw sought appointment as a delegate, unsuccessfully.

the effect. I mention this circumstance because I want to make it clear that I do not enjoy the confidence of the Government or of any party in the Convention. My articles were not concerted with any individual or group, nor read before they were in print by anyone except in the course of newspaper business. I had discussed the question carefully, in my capacity as chairman of a committee of the Fabian Society called the Empire Reconstruction Committee [January 1917], with English and Australian students of the Empire problem. Without such critical discussion I should have nothing but my personal notions to put forward; and this book would be an impertinence. But my Fabian colleagues are as completely out of Irish party politics as I am myself. I represent nobody on the Convention, though I have valued friends[2] on it. I represent nobody in Parliament or in the Government (this is nowadays not always the same thing). I am only the spokesman of Common Sense, and of the experience already gained in the integration of distinct nations with distinct creeds into a single Power.

In the course of my occasional visits to Ireland and conversations with Irishmen interested in the national question, I had noticed that two considerations which were quite familiar to me were new to them. The first, bearing on the fiscal problem, was the enormous part which socialization of the rents of land, capital, and personal ability, as part of the now irresistible European movement for Redistribution of Income, must play in all but the most provisional and perfunctory schemes of public finance. The other was the final demonstration by the present war of the hollowness of the national independences and neutralities which are set up, not by the internal strength of a nation's position, but by the interested guarantes of foreign Powers. For obvious reasons, it is almost impossible for popular statesmen to be frank on this subject; but diplomatists know perfectly well that a great Power guarantees the independence of a small nation only to acquire control of its foreign policy without responsibility. Many English people are furiously angry with me for giving away this open secret because of its bearing on the case of Belgium. But, as it is the sole really convincing reply to Casement's plan of a German-Irish alliance,[3] I am not prepared to allow numbers of patriotic young Irishmen to involve

2. Shaw's close friend Sir Horace Plunkett was chairman of the Convention. Other friends delegated to the Convention were George Russell (AE), John Redmond MP and Captain Stephen Gwynn MP.
3. Sir Roger Casement, misguided Irish Nationalist rebel, who sought German assistance in 1914–15 in the fight against the British for Irish independence, was captured on his return to Ireland from Berlin in a German submarine. On 3

themselves in treasonable intrigues merely to gratify the taste of patriotic old Englishmen for virtuous indignation.

For the rest I have no novelty to offer except the presentation of the Irish problem in something like reasonable proportion to the rest of the world's business.

AYOT ST LAWRENCE.   G. B. S.
1 December 1917.

August 1916 he was executed as a traitor. Shaw, in June 1917, observed that the 'practical alternative' to union with England

> would be independence under the guarantee of one of the Great Powers. This was Casement's plan. . . . This perfectly legitimate political speculation was in my opinion reduced to absurdity by the fate of Belgium and Greece [as] so-called independent guaranteed States. All it did for them in their foreign relations was to impose on them the burden of an independent and futile armament, and to make them the cockpit of the war between the great Powers. (*Collected Letters 1911–1925*, p. 479.)

What I Said in the Great War

Discarded 'Exordium' (British Library Add. MSS 50670, fos. 3–5), drafted, c. 1917–18, for an abandoned volume (fragment, Add. MSS 50670, fos. 6–47), subsequently rewritten as What I Really Wrote about the War *(Collected Edition, 1930).*

In the Great War it has been my singular destiny to have to choose between making myself intensely unpopular at home, and making England seem ridiculous, hypocritical, and treacherous in the eyes of the neutrals whose respect and friendship was of vital importance to her, and of enemies eagerly seeking for testimony against her. An Englishman in my position would not have hesitated. For the sake of the cheers of his countrymen and the satisfaction of the passions stirred up in him by the war, he would have let himself go without the smallest consideration for the effect of his utterances on foreign opinion or even of the success of his armies in the field. All the public men of England did as a matter of fact let themselves go in that manner. But they were in a much less responsible position than I. Their indignant ravings were not audible beyond the shores of these islands. Their articles were unreadable except by their own countrymen, and were mostly hard reading even at that. As far as the mainland of Europe and the American continent were concerned, it did not matter tuppence what they said. Even in Germany, where their more outrageous sallies would occasionally be quoted in the "Sidelights upon England" columns, it was so obvious that they might have been transferred to the leader columns with a few changes of proper names: Bethmann Hollweg to Asquith, Berlin to London and so forth, that they can hardly have done much harm; and in any case they were so utterly unmemorable that those who read them with the greatest indignation could not possibly have remembered them for half an hour.

I was not in this easy position. Through the accident of my having attained some international fame in the profession of Eschylus, Shakespear, Goethe and Ibsen, not only in Germany and Austria, but in those very countries whose neutrality hung most precariously in the balance (Sweden and the United States of America) I had the ear of these countries, and could say nothing about the war that was not likely to be quoted there. I had to consider the effect of every word I wrote on these countries; and this involved my not considering their effect in England at all, except, at first, on one vital English activity: that of voluntary recruiting. I had plenty [of] reminders of the reach of my pen. Passages from my writings were translated into Arabic and circulated in Morocco as the utterances of a prophet; and I actually had to add another surah to the Koran in that character to counteract the application made of them by the Germans with the object of stirring up an insurrection among the sheikhs and drawing off French troops from the west front.[1] When the Daily Telegraph, always anxiously timid and keeping its eyes glued on a clock forty years slow, first begged me for a contribution to King Albert's Birthday Book, and was afraid to put it in when it got it, the appearance of the book without the promised item was immediately followed by a request from the Belgian Government for an appeal from me to the neutral powers for funds to help them in their desperate need.[2] When Herr Bethmann Hollweg quoted me (a success I had hardly hoped for) it was freely asked, by lunatics who could not conceive that I was not only quoted in Germany but had written expressly that I should be so quoted[3] and that the Germans might

1. Shaw was requested, in October 1915, by a representative of the Naval Intelligence Division, to provide a statement for publication in Arabic in the French zone of Morocco, as a counter-offensive to his anti-British sentiments then being circulated by the Germans to stir the fanatically Muslim Moors to revolt. It is not known whether Shaw's 'surah', which he subsequently alluded to as 'my Moslem Koran chapter', was ever published and circulated. No draft copy survives in his archive. See also p. 553, fn. 1.
2. *King Albert's Book*, edited by Hall Caine, was a collection of contributions by prominent writers and composers, published by the *Daily Telegraph* for the relief of Belgian refugees in England. Shaw's contribution, which he described in a letter to the *New Statesman* editor Clifford Sharp on 21 October 1914 as 'a fierce piece of rhetoric about Belgium', was rejected after publication of his controversial *Common Sense about the War* in November. Urgently solicited by the Belgian relief commission, Shaw produced an article, 'Face the Truth of War', syndicated in the press in January 1915 and issued as a pamphlet *The Case of Belgium*.
3. Despite the war Shaw was able to maintain a correspondence with his German translator Siegfried Trebitsch, through the offices of his literary agent in neutral Holland, which ceased at the end of 1915 after Shaw had been privately warned that the British Government was contemplating action against him, under the Defence of the Realm Act, for 'consorting with the enemy'. For nearly a year, however, Trebitsch had dutifully submitted to the press the criticism of the war that Shaw intended German readers to receive, knowing that at the same time it would be reported in re-translation by British newspapers whose columns otherwise were barred to him.

understand that they had something stronger to meet than the transparent and contemptible official case which was designed to conciliate the non-interventionists of the Liberal party with a reckless disregard of their wider effect.[4] In short I had to weigh every word I wrote whilst all around me were passionately refusing to weigh anything at all.

I said to myself sometimes then that perhaps if I had been an Englishman I should have raved as wildly as the others. But the time was coming when my own patriotism was being tried by the English Government [Easter Uprising, 1916] as ferociously as that of Serbia was tried by Austria. The fact that I kept my head then gives me the right to tell Englishmen that they too can keep their heads if they choose, and that wounded patriotism does not excuse any conduct that would be condemned in a neutral. A great deal of the patriotism elicited by this war has not been distinguishable by a neutral, or indeed by a civilized gentleman, from simple blackguardism; and I do not propose to treat it with more indulgence than it deserves.

4. This long, meandering and convoluted draft sentence is incomplete.

The W. E. A. Education Year Book

Preface to Part I, 1918

Some years ago, in an essay entitled Parents and Children, published, according to my custom, as a preface to a play [*Misalliance*, see p. 3], I gave a fairly exhaustive account of my view of the process commonly called education. Returning to the subject in 1918 by way of a careful perusal of the Education Year Book of The Workers' Educational Association, to which I had been invited to contribute a preface, I found in that very remarkable volume all the relevant essays by other hands which make up this book. I can assure that the facts are fit for publication, all the hopes, all the failures, all the finance, set forth at worst readably, and at best with rare knowledge, penetration, and literary skill. There was nothing left for me to say except the very simple things that stand as mountains in the path of the writer on education, yet that he must usually ignore if he is to get to his subject at all. And I have said most of them before.

First, there is the fact that education is mostly a pretext under cover of which parents get rid of their duties and escape from the noise, the dirt, the unconscious chaperonage, the perpetual questioning of children. By conniving at this evasion our Churchmen and sectarians are enabled to proselytize the rising generations, our plutocrats to segregate and corrupt them, and our schoolmasters to make money. The tense silence in which my exposure of this radical imposture has been received, in contrast with the garrulous discussions of minor points, shews how deeply guilty our society is on this score. Yet the guilt, as I have insisted, does not lie in the parents' quite natural and socially wholesome desire to escape from the intolerable inroads made by the continual presence of children on their privacy, their quiet, their pursuits, and their pleasures, but in our callous indifference to the methods by which the schoolmaster relieves us for so much a year cash.

What does the schoolmaster do with the child when the parent delivers it over with a sigh of relief, having nothing more to dread until the holidays come round? He imprisons it, and hires a body of minor masters to act as warders and turnkeys. An admirable essay by Mr Edmond Holmes in the Year Book deals with the essential slavery of school life, and concludes that we must "defeudalize" education. But strong and deeply felt as Mr Holmes's condemnation is, he flatters our school system in comparing its child victims to feudal serfs. Serfs had rights and a status. School children have neither one nor the other: they are treated as outlaws pure and simple. And their condition is not improving in this respect. One of the contributors to this book [Arthur Clutton-Brock], a man not yet past middle age, tells me that during his last two years at Eton he did what he liked. Recent biographies of Etonians (for example, [Edmund] Gosse's Life of Swinburne [1917]) shew that the public schoolboy was once left to himself sufficiently to enable him to cultivate tastes of his own and approach and commune with Nature in his own way. Compare this picture of Eton life with the recent ones written by young men, especially those who are so proud of having been at a public school that they delight in describing how they were thrashed because they tried to botanize, or naturalize, or take country walks, or read instead of drudging at compulsory games. In our socially pretentious preparatory schools the boys who are too young to play games are actually forced to stand and watch their seniors playing. Is anyone imposed on by the pretence of liking this and believing that it was good for them with which our eager climbers of the social ladder present their credentials as "public school men"? Yet this modern invasion and enslavement of every moment of a child's waking life is represented as a development of education. The most impressive documentary novel of recent years is Mr Alec Waugh's Loom of Youth [1917], which is almost a diary of life at Sherborne [Foster's Grammar School]. Compared with the medieval public school curriculum, in which the wretched scholar rose at six and learned Latin for nearly twelve hours without any play at all, it exhibits the complete capture of the school by the athletic schoolboy and the athletic schoolmaster, the medieval system being restored with the substitution of football and cricket for Latin and Greek. Soon a schoolboy caught reading or looking at pictures or listening to music will be thrashed as he once was when caught playing games.

Meanwhile the schoolmaster must not confess himself a mere boy farmer: he has to make his prisoners learn certain things, whether games or murdered languages. Now there are, unfortunately, two ways of doing this. One way is teaching: a process which requires some natural vocation, a good deal of skill and experience, and an honorable character. The other way is open to any fool or blackguard. You do not teach: you set the pupil a task, and beat him, bully him, ridicule him, or torture him in any other way that may be convenient to you unless he is able to perform it. To naturally cruel men, the Creakles and Murdstones [in *David Copperfield*] and Squeerses [in *Nicholas Nickleby*], this makes schoolkeeping a delightful occupation. The old cries of "See, Udal, see," and "The schoolmaster's delight is to flog"[1] are still stifled in the breasts of many inarticulate victims of much worse men than Creakle or Squeers; for Dickens never told the worst of the orgiast-pseudo-pedagogue, though he need have gone no further than the boasted records of [Andrew] Bell and [Joseph] Lancaster for evidence of them.[2]

This fact has to be faced if the profession of teaching is to be lifted from the abyss of popular dislike and contempt into which it has fallen. Of all men the most naturally reverenced are teachers. Of all men the most naturally despised are executioners. And as long as the schoolmaster is paid, not for teaching, but for saying to the growing child "Learn this, you little devil, or I will cane you until you will not be able to sleep for terror of me," the schoolmaster will be classed with the executioner in popular esteem. That, and that alone, is the secret of the shameful poverty and low social status of the schoolmaster.

If this were merely an abuse in practice such as must arise in all professions when the practitioner is a scoundrel, there would be no disgrace in it. Most unfortunately, it is the accepted and legalized theory of schoolmastering; and, although the practice is seldom as vile as the theory, it is by the theory that the status of the practitioner is determined. The reader of this book may ask me how I can maintain such a proposition in spite of the spirit informing the essays of Mr C. H. C. Osborne on The George Junior Republic and The Little Commonwealth,[3] of Miss M. L. V. Hughes with her admirable Two Decalogues, of Mr Edmond Holmes already quoted, and of Lord Haldane [Richard Burdon Haldane, First

1. Nicholas Udall, a dramatic author, became headmaster at Eton in 1534. Thomas Tusser, writer and poet, in an autobiography in verse (1573) reports that on one occasion Udall gave him fifty-three stripes for 'fault but small or none at all'. 'See Udall, see', exclaims Tusser, 'mercy of thee to mee, poor lad!' (*Dictionary of National Biography*: Udall.) The second cry (with 'joy' for 'delight') is from John Gay's ballad 'Molly Mog' (1726).
2. English educationalists who independently invented a method of teaching that employed older children as monitors and an elaborate system of mechanical drill, by means of which these half-taught youngsters were made to impart the rudiments of reading, writing and arithmetic to large numbers at the same time. Lancaster's *Improvements in Education* (1803) details a number of devices he adopted for punishing offenders.
3. Both were institutions that offered enlightened alternatives to reformatories or industrial schools, part of a movement for founding self-governing communities for delinquent boys and girls. The Republic was founded in 1895 by W. R. George

Viscount of Cloan] with his claim that even the technical formula for calculating the strain on a girder should not be taught without relating it, not to the fear of a caning, but to the Cartesian mathematic which is part of a philosophy. I shall be asked if I have ever read Goethe's Wilhelm Meister; heard of Dr Montessori; or met a pupil from President [Padraic] Pearse's Sgoil Eanna.[4]

I will, therefore, mention something that I have read quite recently and that everyone who takes in a newspaper has read. A schoolboy, with an unusually manly mind, summoned his schoolmaster for assaulting him. The schoolmaster's defence was that he was "teaching" the boy geography. The process, as described by himself, was asking the boy questions in geography and hitting him with a cane when the boy was unable to answer them. The magistrate at once accepted this as the normal and proper business of a schoolmaster; reproved the boy for being (of all things) unmanly; and dismissed the summons.[5] There was no protest either in editorial or correspondence columns. The Press agreed with the magistrate. The parental public agreed with him. That is what education means at present, both in law and public opinion, in spite of the few genuine teachers, who are regarded simply as cranks.

I recommend this case to Dr F. B. Jevons and the other writers who are very justly concerned about the inferior status and wretched pay of schoolmasters as a class. I am a professional man, paid, when I am in luck, two hundred times as much for my work as the poorest schoolmaster is for

---

at Freeville, New York; the Commonwealth in 1913 in Dorset Heights, England, its first superintendent Harold Lane being the American founder of Ford Republic in Detroit.

4. Irish poet and educator, interested in bilingual methods of education, who in 1908 founded Saint Enda's School (Sgoil Eanna) in Rathmines, Dublin (removed to Rathfarnham in 1910), at which Irish was spoken exclusively, both in classroom and playground. The school was closed in 1916 after Pearse, president of a provisional government of Irish insurgents, led an ineffectual rebellion in Dublin against the English at Easter, for which he was executed by the British.

5. The case, brought before the Willesden Police Court on 27 May 1914, was reported (principals unidentified) in the *Daily News* the following day, including the statement of the magistrate, who after denying the boy's request for a summons told him that 'if [he] had taken his punishment [a caning on his hand] like a man, he would not have been caned on the back'. The boy, Shaw argued in a letter to the *Daily News* published on 29 May, 'did exactly what a man would have done.' The whole point of the case, he insisted, 'was that a boy claimed an adult's right to freedom from assault and demanded the legal remedy of an adult.'

his, and perhaps thirty times as much as many an envied headmaster. I am invited to feel indignation because this police-court hero, with his cane and his geography lesson, is not placed on my level as to social esteem and income. I admit the claim as to income because I am a Socialist, and because I am perfectly well aware that my income has no reference whatever to my merit. But as to social esteem I must really ask whether I, who am, for good or evil, a genuine teacher by a highly skilled method, am to admit as my equal a person whose "profession" it is to hit a boy half his size hard enough to make him wince with pain. The schoolmaster's gardener, who could probably hit harder than the schoolmaster, and can at least plead that he produces vegetables without assaulting people, makes no such claim. My feeling is that 30s. a week, and the status of a trainer of performing dogs, is as much as a schoolmaster can reasonably expect until he learns to teach. He would probably think this quite good enough for me if my success as a playwright were obtained by imprisoning my audiences in the theatre and caning them when they omitted to applaud, or whispered, or coughed, or shuffled their feet.

I am not for the moment dealing with the question whether it is possible to make all our children learn in any other way, having regard to the multitudes of them and the dearth of teachers of genuine vocation. And I am certainly not proposing that children, any more than adults, should be artificially exempted from physical coercion, or even from summary natural personal vengeance, to the extent of making them imagine that they are living in a moral vacuum and can do as they like without regard to the feelings and convenience of others. I am simply insisting that the forcing children to learn by beating them is unskilled labor of an unedifying and repulsive character. I call it unskilled advisedly. I am aware that it would break down in practice if the curriculum were not planned with some skilled knowledge of the cane's possibilities, and that you cannot teach the infinitesimal calculus to a child of three by any amount of flogging. But the ordinary schoolmaster does not devize the curriculum: he simply carries out a prearranged routine like the school charwoman; and if some practical joker were to slip the calculus into the junior timetable most of the masters would try to whack it into their youngest pupils as solemnly as they used to try to whack the very difficult subject of grammar. While this state of things lasts they will rebel in vain against the tendency of public common sense to class them with menagerie keepers rather than with men of learning.

The remedy is not to give professional pay and status to unskilled men who cannot even pronounce the alphabet presentably, but to exact genuine professional qualifications from the schoolmaster and pay him their market value. His status will then take care of itself. I have not noticed that genuine teachers who now undertake the care of children are at any disadvantage pecuniarily or socially in ordinary professional society. They have, comparatively, a good time of it; for, I repeat, the true teacher can leave the doctor, the lawyer, and even the parson nowhere in the rapidity with which he can gain respect and liking both in his school and out of it, and that, too, without being by any means an angel in point of temper. Most real teachers have occasionally to pretend to be rather shorter tempered than they really are lest they should mollycoddle their charges. But they do not appear in police courts to explain that in their schools the pupils have to learn without being taught on pain of being beaten, the schoolmaster's department being confined to the beating. They try to make the teaching half of the transaction interesting enough to induce the pupil to do the learning half either for its own sake or for theirs.

The modern tendency is to relieve the caning system for the masters in two ways. One is to confine the use of the cane to the headmaster. That is to say, the head, who ought to be the moral centre of the school, is made a sort of Lord High Executioner, and spends his time between doing the dirty work of his assistants and the making out of the school bills. The other plan, started by [Thomas] Arnold [headmaster of Rugby], is to get the boys to do their own caning by the prefect system. This was a natural move enough; for whereas under the old system the masters, if they did not teach, at least had to cane, under the prefect system they neither teach nor cane; and it becomes possible for a comparatively easygoing, lazy, unauthoritative, donnish sort of person to hang on to a mastership. Also the boy who is caned can look forward to the time when he will cane other boys, and can form a taste in that direction, just as he forms a habit of treating servants as fags [menials]. But these alleviations of the school-master's lot do not entitle him to call himself a teacher, nor to claim the respect and emolument considered proper to a professional man. He still has to depend for any credit he enjoys on such incidentals as holy orders or a University degree. The common schoolmaster who has neither of these qualifications is still in the most embarrassing of all social positions. The gentry inexorably refuse to accept him as a gentleman; and the common people refuse to accept him as a fellow creature. And they will both be entirely justified in their attitude as long as his profession of teaching is only a cloak for the practice of a turnkey and an executioner carrying out a law which is purely lynch law.

Under such circumstances it is not surprising to find that when an educationist is also a statesman, he will not support the schoolmaster's claim to be organized and recognized as the medical profession is organized and recognized: that is, as a monstrous tyranny with legal powers of coercion over the rest of the community, and with unlimited power to dictate its own qualifications; to prevent anyone practising as a teacher without its authority; and to set all lay power at defiance. The schoolmasters are not even aware of the fact that the inevitable operation of these powers has brought the medical profession into such disrepute and open conflict with the public interest that nothing but the gross ignorance and superstition of Parliament in regard to political and hygienic science stands between the General Medical Council and the deprivation of its worst privileges, accompanied by a resolute exercise of the powers already possessed by the Government and the Universities to secure a majority of laymen on it. One of the very first things a true teacher should teach is that such bodies as the General Medical Council, and the ideal at which the National Union of Teachers [founded in 1830] brazenly aims, should be resisted as Star Chambers and Bastilles should be resisted. To Sir Robert Morant's refusal to allow the teachers themselves to be the judges of their own success and the prescribers of their own qualifications, so that they can ruin any teacher who dares to criticize their methods, the Registration Council opposes a simple assumption that a body of men whose notion of teaching is to beat the children for not learning, is omniscient, infallible, and infinitely virtuous, and should, therefore, at once be entrusted with powers which this country made two revolutions sooner than entrust to the Throne and the Church. Those who advance such a demand are not only incapable of teaching, but incapable of learning. By all means let us have a register of teachers; but let the learners keep the key of it.[6]

It must never be forgotten that education is such a dangerous thing that it is very doubtful whether the invention of printing would have been tolerated if more than a very few people had been able to read. The Roman Catholic Church has not to this day consented to place the Scriptures in the hands of the laity. We must either go through with education or let it alone. A state of things like the present, in which

6. Sir Robert Morant, considered to be one of the greatest administrators of modern Britain, was instrumental in the passage of the Education Act of 1902 and served as governor of the Board of Education until 1911. The Teachers' Registration Council, established by Parliament in 1907, granted registration to applicants who fulfilled prescribed conditions of attainment, training and experience.

everybody knows how to read and nobody knows what to read, and in which the crudest, darkest, poorest minds are allowed to propagate their crudity, darkness, and poverty through the Press for a pittance which leaves them no chance of culture, is disastrous: the war is only one of its disasters, and not the worst of them. For it must be added that the richer classes which have gone through the entire routine of schooling, as established at our public schools and Universities, are, except as experts in athletics, sport, and drawing-room accomplishments, as crude and ignorant as the journalists from the elementary school, who have become journalists because they are so incorrigibly inaccurate that they could not keep situations as clerks for a fortnight. The newspapers which cater specially for public schoolmen and University graduates, for the country house and the rectory: that is, for the classes which represent our education untempered by the teaching which men of business or professional men get from their daily pursuits, are frankly organs of savagery and snobbery. The war has revealed an astounding ignorance in the classes that actually govern us: one wonders sometimes how any human beings with so much interest in their own ambitions and amusements could possibly be so void of intellectual interests and curiosities as not to have learnt something by merely walking about with their eyes open, nor have reasoned enough about what they see to become capable of a few simple syllogisms.

Take a topical wartime specimen of their powers of reasoning upon what is one of the main interests of their lives: pheasant shooting. They want pheasants to shoot; therefore nobody must be allowed to kill pheasants except gentlemen with guns. Nevertheless, as we shall lose the war by starvation unless we economize food, we must not feed the pheasants. And there the matter was left. The pheasants were strictly preserved; and their food was cut off. The country houses of England apparently did not contain a single representative person with intelligence enough to infer the result that followed, which was, that the pheasants, not being fed as usual by the gamekeeper, ate the farmer's crops; and the farmer, being forbidden to shoot them, quarreled fiercely with his landlord, their proprietor. In the same way, when the war imposed a need for economy, we had, instead of the educated man's conception of economy as a facilitation of production, the miser's conception of it as mere abstinence. The first thing we were to abstain from was education, which was sacrificed not merely with indifference to its economic value, but positive malice against its superiorities. The next thing was locomotion, the very circulation of the productive organism. Even communication was restricted to such a degree that the penny post is now a thing of the past. A gentleman who was appointed to control the

Air Service because his brother was a rich newspaper proprietor,[7] began by making a speech, in which he described his own official business as murder, like any poor woman in a slum who has seen her child killed by a bomb, and following this up by demanding that the British Museum be cleared out to make room for him and his staff. He did not ask for Westminster Abbey to store petrol in; but it can hardly have been any cultural consideration that hindered him. And the working classes can hardly reproach him after handing over Ruskin College for war purposes[8] with an alacrity which suggested that they were glad of an excuse to get rid of it.

All this means not only that the people we send to school at great expense are ignorant, but that their minds are of very limited use to themselves, and worse than no use to the nation: nay, positively injurious to it. The stupendous blunders made by the Germans, most fortunately for us, shew that their school methods are no better than ours; but they respect education, having an intellectual conception of it, whereas we, having no such conception, dislike and despise it. We actually prefer the ignorant and insolent young barbarians who keep up the reputation of certain Oxford and Cambridge Colleges for rowdiness to those whose civilized instincts and naturally refined tastes lead them to behave like grown-up people with some sense of their duty to their neighbors.

I might say a good deal more about this fundamental vice and error of imposing as education a system of imprisonment and "breaking in" which has no reference to education at all, and is intended only to secure a livelihood for schoolmasters by saving parents trouble and making children quiet and submissive: that is, unfit to be free citizens in a democracy. Suffice it to say here, that the curse of a prison is that by its very nature it reverses every law and aspiration of Christian conduct, being violent,

7. Harold Harmsworth, First Viscount Rothermere, ruthless newspaper proprietor and financial manager, was the brother of Alfred Harmsworth, Viscount North-cliffe, publisher of *The Times*. In November 1917 Harold was appointed head of the Royal Naval Air Service, which he instantly combined with the Royal Flying Corps to create the Royal Air Force. On 3 January 1918 he became Secretary of State for Air and president of the newly established Air Council, but resigned in April on grounds of ill health after losing two sons in the war.

8. Ruskin College announced in September 1914, 'The Executive Committee of Ruskin College, Oxford, have resolved that, owing to the war, the college shall not be open for resident students during the sessions 1914–15, and that the college shall be offered to the government for hospital purposes. The work of the Correspondence Department will be carried on as usual' (*The Times*, 15 September 1914).

revengeful, coercive, and deliberately planned to destroy happiness. In these pages the essays of Mr Osborne, of Miss [Margaret] McMillan, of Mr J. L. Paton, of Miss M. L. V. Hughes, of Dr [Maurice W.] Keatinge, and of Mr Holmes are penetrated with a sense of struggle against the prison morality of our schools; but they do not seem to me to grasp the fact that what they are in revolt against is not fundamentally a bad method of education, but a selfish and mischievous purpose of which neither the parents nor the masters are in the least ashamed. That is why I have felt bound to harp on it.

I need hardly add that the fact that at this moment the majority of schoolmasters are schoolmistresses does not affect my argument. They are quite as handy with the cane as the men. What is more important is that as it is possible to make a case for the statement that "corporal punishment is disappearing," we should bear jealously in mind that corporal punishment is only one of many available methods of intimidation and coercion, and by no means the most cruel and injurious. There are worse tortures, both physical and moral, in actual use (I shall not propagate them by giving particulars) in schools where "corporal punishment is not permitted."

I pass on to the controversy as to technical and liberal education which occupies the contributions of Mr S. G. Hobson and Lord Haldane. I do not think that liberal education, which is really recreation, can ever be attained through compulsory schooling. Until English literature was made a school subject the Shakespear nausea which is now common among the second-arily educated did not exist, though already schoolgirls had learned from their music lessons to loathe Beethoven. Now no adult loathes that indispen-sable subject of compulsory technical education, the multiplication table; nor indeed would any have loathed it in childhood had it been made clear then that a child who knows it can enjoy money and liberty to an extent impossible to one who cannot change a sixpence to buy a tram ticket or visit a picture palace. Technical education is a qualification for living in society. Being necessary to life, it justifies itself by its results even to those who acquire it with difficulty and repugnance, and exercise its accomplish-ments without pleasure for ulterior objects. But a liberal education cannot be acquired without interest and pleasure. Compulsory Shakespear only provides a public for books written to prove that Shakespear was Bacon by people who lack the literary and dramatic sense to know that the fact that Shakespear was not Bacon is not a matter of evidence or argument, but of the direct evidence of the literary and dramatic sense, just as the fact that Bacon's statue at St Albans [Hertfordshire] does not represent the same man as the Stratford bust is a simple matter of eyesight, and the fact that

Wagner was not Brahms is a simple matter of listening to their music. It does not provide audiences for Shakespear's plays: on the contrary, it keeps them away. A liberal education, in short, cannot be imposed: all that can be usefully given is access: water should be provided for the horse; but it must not be forced down with a stomach pump submitted to under threat of the whip.

The distinction between technical and liberal education seems obvious when we contrast a knowledge of the multiplication and pence table with a taste for Shakespear. The obviousness vanishes when democracy forces us to recognize that citizenship is a technical subject and the universal profession of democrat a highly skilled one. Calvin, I take it, though he would perhaps have admitted that the children of Geneva could not be taught to appreciate and enjoy the music of Orlandus Lassus and Josquin Deprès and [J. P.] Van Sweelinck[9] as they could be taught to navigate a ship or build a house, would have maintained that his Institutes should be taught in order to qualify the children technically to become citizens of "the perfect city of God." And I think he would have been right. To live in Geneva in Calvin's time, or in Scotland in the XVI and XVII centuries, as in Ulster today, without intolerable social friction, a knowledge of the Calvinistic scheme of salvation and damnation was as necessary to the man who abhorred it as to the man who accepted it. Dante's scheme of Catholicism was equally a technical subject for the diplomatists of the Holy Roman Empire and their opponents. What is the matter with civilization at present is that Calvin's Institutes and the divine rights of the Holy Roman Empire having become incredible, and the Church Catechism and the Thirtynine Articles in great part unthinkable, chiefly through the discovery of Evolution, there is a void left in our technical education. As Nature abhors a vacuum, this void is being filled by demoralizing pseudo-scientific stupidities like [August] Weismannism and Mechanism[10] on one side, and a mess of crude pseudo-political sentimentalities on the other; whilst the creed of Creative Evolution, obviously the coming religion, has not been formulated and popularized. But it will have to be. The symphonies of Beethoven will

9. Sixteenth-century musicians: Lassus was an eminent Dutch composer of masses, madrigals and motets; Deprès was a French composer, chief contrapuntalist of his day, known as 'the father of modern harmony'; van Sweelinck was a Dutch organ virtuoso, originator of the organ fugue.
10. German biologist, whose *Essays upon Heredity and Kindred Biological Problems* (1889) tended towards 'mechanism' in its view of life solely in terms of the laws of chemistry and physics.

never be possible as textbooks; but the treatises of [Henri] Bergson[11] certainly will if we are to have a society as genuinely organized as the Protestant and Catholic societies of pre-evolutionary times. There must be a common technical theory of the goal of Evolution to replace the old common technical theory of the will of God. Not only those who accept it but those who challenge it will at least know where society stands, which no man knows at present.

Science, admittedly a technical subject, must include political science, not only in its elementary branch of police regulation, but in its modern constitutional developments as industrial democracy and Socialism, which subjects, in a modern democratic State, should be as compulsory, up to the limit of the scholar's capacity for them, as the multiplication table. At least a conception of them should be inculcated: such a conception, for instance, as I have of mathematics, though I cannot do the simplest sum in algebra. Even the uneducated should know what education means. Such an epithet as "half educated" should vanish from the language; for nobody who knows what he is talking about imagines that any individual can confidently claim to be even one per cent educated, much less fifty per cent. The old formula "Know something of everything and everything of something" belongs to an age when so little was known that "one small head could carry all we [he] knew" [Oliver Goldsmith, *The Deserted Village*, 1770]. Three hundred years ago Newton, who came as near to universal knowledge as any merely human animal is ever likely to, could not find a figure infinitesimal enough to express how little he knew, and compared himself to a child on the seashore picking up a few grains of sand. Still, Newton knew what knowledge means and what ignorance means; and though we cannot make every boy and girl a Sidney and Beatrice Webb we can at least save them from the democratic delusion that political capacity is not a scientific acquirement but an intuition which descends on every freeborn Briton at the age of twentyone. It needs no abnormal acumen to see how odd it is that though we will not allow a barrister to practise, or a doctor to call himself a doctor and sign death certificates, or a clergyman to hold a living, unless they undergo a test of technical qualification, anybody may practise political science as voter, or even as Cabinet Minister, without knowing how to read and write. What is worse, anyone may practise abortion and poisoning on the nation's mind and spirit as a journalist or

11. French philosopher, whose *Matière et mémoire* (1896) held that spirit influences matter through the mind and memory. His *L'Évolution créatrice* (1907) also attacked mechanism by supporting the theory of inherited characteristics.

newspaper proprietor with complete impunity and even huge profit, though if he did the same with a mechanical instrument on an unborn baby he would go unpitied to penal servitude. It is even proposed that legislation shall be initiated and imposed, or defeated and cancelled, without discussion or information, by the man in the street acting through a referendum: indeed, this can already be done in some States. The consequences under modern democratic conditions are so appalling that we are in imminent danger of that revulsion against democracy which, instead of saving ancient Athens, hastened its ruin. The people will either throw over democracy altogether in disgust at its disastrous ignorance, and fall back on the hopeless expedient of thrusting dictatorial powers on the nearest adventurer whom they may romantically imagine, at his own suggestion, to be an Earthly Providence, or else they will demand some sort of scientific evidence of political capacity as a qualification for election or office. Already the public services are protected from absolute imbecility and illiteracy by examinations; and sooner or later we shall see the absurdity of demanding educational qualifications from the clerk and none from the Secretary of State, with the result that we have Secretaries of State for Foreign Affairs who cannot speak French at the head of an office in which a knowledge of French is obligatory on everyone else.

The difficulty is that the examination test is useless and even mischievous except for routine workers. Though a knowledge of French and drawing-room dancing may qualify a man to be an attaché, it does not qualify him to be a Foreign Minister. The late President Kruger, who would not have been accepted by the Foreign Office as a hall porter, outwitted all the diplomatists of Britain and Germany until he was in his dotage. People who have a positive genius for passing examinations, and who learn languages with extraordinary facility, are often quite impossible as chiefs of staff, to say nothing of Ministers; and for this reason it has never been possible to apply the examination system throughout the whole public service, the necessary exceptions becoming excuses for a good deal of jobbery. Also, examinations can be manipulated so as to favor or exclude classes; and the shameless resort of our own ruling classes to this device has cooled the enthusiasm with which the examination system was formerly hailed as a democratic reform.

In short, we still lack a trustworthy anthropometric method for high purposes of State. Poets, like other observant people, notice "the straitened forehead of a fool" [Tennyson, 'Locksley Hall', 1842], often in the highest offices or in feudal command of a county; but we have not yet invented the callipers, ascertained the measurements, or discovered the reagents which should test the Prime Minister and the Commander-in-Chief as the tape round the chest and the height measurer test the rank and file of the police and the Army. I remember once being much flattered by a speaker in a discussion following a political harangue of mine, who said, "I did not understand the lecturer's arguments, because, as you will see if you observe the shape of my head, I have not the requisite faculty; but as a professional phrenologist I can assure you that you may trust to his judgment." I followed up this clue far enough to convince myself that the analysis of human faculty made by the phrenologists had not yet carried them beyond classifications so crude and ambiguous as to verge on positive illiteracy here and there, the results being far too imprecise to be of any practical value for political purposes.[12] Nevertheless, the need for some method of measuring personal capacity which shall be as completely beyond the control of the operator or the subject as the measurement of a yard of cloth is beyond the control of the cloth or of the yardstick, is becoming more conscious. I have myself been tested with contrivances designed to ascertain how quickly I can respond to a sensory stimulus, or how long I can distinguish between two colors when they are being substituted for oneanother with increasing rapidity. The inferences from these tests vary from the simplest statement of the result to a certificate classing you with a Fuegian [an indigene of Tierra del Fuego] or with Plato or Shakespear: that is to say, from cautious fact to extravagant romance; but if these contrivances be taken with the various tests used in the Army and other public services, they will appear as part of a growing body of anthropometric devices ranging from the shoemaker's rule to attempts at psychometric machines. These things should not be passed over lightly because some of them are obviously cranky and none have superseded the experienced college tutor who tells an undergraduate what honors it is worth his while to read for in view of his natural capacity. But tutorial measurement is founded on a degree of intimacy and familiarity which is not practicable for general public purposes. We seem far from the day when persons classed by natural capacity (as distinguished from acquirements) will be disqualified or conscribed for public work according to their degree; when Class A1 will be compelled on incorruptible evidence to elect representative peers from their own register to undertake the highest duties of the State, and Class Z17, however self-assertive and noisily popular, will be absolutely debarred from voting at elections, contesting Parliamentary or municipal seats,

12. For Shaw's views on phrenology, see 'Bumps and Brains', *Daily Graphic*, London, 7 January 1907; reprinted in Frederic Whyte, *A Bachelor's London* (1931).

running newspapers, or possibly even procreating their species.

In making this rough suggestion I am not forgetting that one of the uses of democracy is to save people from being intolerably well governed, and, in fact, discouraged out of existence as savages are by civilized men. I would give Class A1 rights of counsel and criticism, but no vote. The mass of men coming between J and K should neither be dragged in the mud by Z nor dragged up to the clouds by A to share the fate of Phaeton;[13] and my old proposal that Parliament should contain fifty aldermen elected by proportional representation under the original [Thomas] Hare[14] scheme, the whole nation voting as one constituency, should be safeguarded by the proviso that their rights of speech in the Assembly should not include access to the voting lobbies. But even with such safeguards, which would not exclude the popular actor of the day and the popular general, however incapable they might be politically, a wise electorate would still ask for some incorruptible scientific test of capacity, taking capacity in its widest sense to include intellectual integrity and social instinct, and giving no more than its due value to that power of working for sixteen hours a day every day for thirty years which at present enables the stupidest routineers to oust from important posts men of much higher faculty, whose real work cannot be sustained except in emergencies for more than two or three hours, and even at that imposes extensive periods of total recreation.

Now secondary education, as we have it today, wholly fails to supply such a test.

Mr J. L. Paton [highly reputed classics teacher] points out how very little secondary education we actually give. People who have attended a secondary school are in an absurd minority. These two propositions are not, however, the same. There is, fortunately, a great deal of secondary self-education: indeed civilization would not hold together if its culture depended on its schools instead of on its bookshops and lectures and summer schools and general currency of intellectual intercourse. Many of our most cultivated people owe absolutely nothing to their schooling; and some of

13. A Greek myth, related in Ovid's *Metamorphoses*, of Phaëthon, whose father Helios the sun-god allowed him to drive the chariot of the sun across the sky. When he lost control of the horses and scorched the earth in driving too near, Zeus destroyed him with a thunderbolt to save the earth from total destruction.
14. Political reformer and lawyer, noted for his plan for securing proportional representation by classes in electoral assemblies of the United Kingdom. He first proposed his plan in *Machinery of Representation* (1857), followed by *A Treatise on the Election of Representatives, Parliamentary and Municipal* (1859).

them, especially among the women, have never been to school at all. Though Ruskin took an Oxford degree, he was never a schoolboy; and he differed from his Etonian and Harrovian fellow graduates only in being, not worse educated (conspicuously the contrary, in fact), but much less of a blackguard. I can lay my hand on my heart and say that nothing that I know was taught me at school except a collection of foul jests on the very subjects that ought to be kept cleanest in a boy's mind; and even these were not in the curriculum. The place where I was imprisoned for half the day, and which was called a school,[15] kept me from the books, the great public picture gallery, the music, and the intercourse with Nature which really educated me; and admirable as the spirit and insight of Mr Paton's plea for more secondary education seem to me, I am not sure that the extension of what is now called secondary education to the age of eighteen or twenty for all classes would not abolish the little culture we have, and produce a generation of young Goths and Vandals which would reduce all Europe to the intellectual level of an officers' mess. The experiment has actually been tried through Eton and Harrow, Oxford and Cambridge; and the result is that the young gentlemen trained in this way are conspicuously absent from the learned societies, political societies, artistic societies, and other cultural organizations, whilst the hunts, shoots, dances, and dinners which enable men to endure the crushing dulness of the drawing room and the tedium of church on Sunday are recognized as their special provinces.

Even in the enlightened pages of the Education Year Book it is remarkable (though I doubt whether anyone will remark it) that with the single exception of a passing reference by Mr Sidney Webb to "subjects requiring exceptional provision," and a paper on Eurythmics by Miss Beryl de Zoete which is too special to save the situation, there is not a word about music, painting, sculpture, literature, or to any other department of that education of the senses and refinement of the imagination without which the inevitable

15. Shaw's education, spread over seven years, was sporadic. He attended the Wesleyan Connexional School in Dublin for the summer term 1865, but was withdrawn at the urgence of his uncle the Revd William Carroll, who privately tutored him. In 1866 (and possibly again briefly in 1867 or 1868) he attended Halpin's Academy at 24 Sandycove Road, Glasthule (near Dalkey). He returned to the Wesleyan Connexional in April 1867 for a term, and again in February 1868 for about nine months. From 1 February to 11 September 1869 he was enrolled in the Central Model Boys' School, Dublin; then transferred to the Dublin English Scientific and Commercial Day School, where he remained until March 1871.

division of a life's activity into work and play, or business and pleasure, means nothing but its division between compulsory necessary money-making and voluntary intemperance in eating, drinking, and sexual sensuality. The appalling fact that nobody in this country seems to know that intellect is a passion for solving problems, and that its exercise produces happiness, satisfaction, and a desirable quality of life, shews that we do not yet know even our crude bodily appetites in their higher aspects as passions: a passion being, I take it, an overwhelming impulse towards a more abundant life. We all have to admit that the greatest poets and dramatists, though great because of their philosophic power and biologic instinct, have been artists. But we talk of professional philosophers as if they were only half men, having brains without eyes or ears or souls. Yet the philosophers who have most deeply moved the world, whether for good or evil, are those who have been artist–philosophers.

I have already insisted on the fact that the fine arts cannot be taught by school methods: the attempts at it end only in trying to make a boy appreciate Venetian painting by asking him the date of Tintoretto's birth, and hitting him if he cannot give the correct answer. What is needed is plenty of books, plenty of picture postcards of masterpieces of design, plenty of good performances of the best plays and the best music obtainable (not necessarily always in the heaviest *genres*, remember), and plenty of rambles in the country. But of what use will these be if the growing boy or girl is always reading that unreadable imposture, a schoolbook, or imprisoned in a school or in a cricket or football field when the music is going on, or the galleries are open, or the view from the mountain is at its best. Ask any schoolmaster to provide for this method of culture; and he will first demand that the manifestations of fine art shall be changed into school lessons; and when they are thus turned into a deadly seed of hatred of all art, and even of Nature, he will sulk furiously over having to find a place for them in his timetable, first declaring it to be utterly impossible, and then grudgingly squeezing them into half an hour a week, perhaps by sacrificing that *bête noire* of his, the drawing lesson. The moment we come down from pompous phrases about education and fine art to the actual facts of the school and the schoolmaster, we are in danger of being driven beyond all patience into a simple declaration that the first step must be the utter annihilation of both, as of Sodom and Gomorrah.

We have, however, admitted that civic education is a technical subject and one of such infinite scope that it overflows the old boundary between technical and liberal education and confines the latter to knowledge as distinguished from practice. Now no real civic education is possible without discussion and controversy. The dogmatic schoolmaster, with his authoritative textbook and his "sanction" of the cane, or the imposition, or the keeping in, will not do here. Mr J. M. Mactavish speaks in these pages of the difficulty of asking for grants of public money for instruction in controversial subjects. But no difficulty is ever made provided only one side is taken in the controversy: provided, that is, that the controversial subject is falsely taught as a closed subject. It is quite true that there is a certain difficulty in obtaining grants of public money to teach that baptism and the Supper of Our Lord are necessary to salvation; but you can get any amount of public money to teach that vaccination is necessary to escape a horrible death from smallpox. No human being could believe these statements if he had all the arguments for and against presented to him fairly: that is, by hearing them, not from one humbug pretending to be an omniscient and impartial judge, but from two well-informed but strongly partial advocates. Both methods have been amply tried; and over and over again the dogmatically schooled professions, on the very questions which concern their own work, have been proved wrong where the laity, especially the unschooled laity, has been proved right. The doctors, the lawyers, the clergy, have had to yield again and again, after the most uppish resistance, to movements conducted by self-educated men. At last a superstition has arisen that popular ignorance has some mystic sanction which makes it more trustworthy than science and knowledge. This is pestilent nonsense: the truth is that the popular movements are educated by open discussion and vehement controversy, and know all the facts and have balanced all the considerations more thoroughly than the professionals. It is not ignorance shaming education: it is controversial education shaming dogmatic cramming. In every street you may find a doctor who is ignorant of a wide range of fact and discovery concerning his own art that is familiar to every member of the debating class in the nearest Young Men's Christian Association, just as any frequenter of Secularist meetings can knock an average curate into a cocked hat in a religious discussion, though he may drop next day to the gun of a Jesuit who has had to defend his intellectual position against continual challenge in Protestant England.

This point is the more vital because we have developed our civilization, and with it the conditions of social intercourse, without revising our philosophic basis, with the result that, though our social structure has reached a degree of communistic complexity at which it is far more important that every adult should be a good citizen than a confirmed member of the Church of England or a successful trader, we are still teaching a code of personal righteousness and riches, and denouncing

Socialism and loyalty to the Common Good, which are now primary necessities of civilized life, as Marxist atrocities. And when any man takes us at our word and, on the authority of his personal righteousness, denies all obligations to accept any State decision of which his individual conscience does not approve, we first admit this anarchic right in the Act of Parliament which imposes the State decision on him, and then, in defiance of that Act, persecute him with murderous ferocity for exercising it. At this moment (1918 war time) the most opprobrious epithet that can be levelled at an Englishman is "conscientious." The controversy is really the old one between the Holy Roman Empire of Dante and Calvin's Perfect City of God, of which our modern Nonconformity and Anglicanism are only muddled, corrupt, and very Laodicean [lukewarm] versions. Now both these formulas of the whole duty of man have, I repeat, been made as incredible and unthinkable by the discovery of Evolution as they have been made impracticable by the industrial revolution. Yet the moment anyone proposes to teach children anything else in public schools he is told that public money cannot be spent on controversial subjects. This ends in the children not being seriously taught anything at all on the plane of philosophy, religion, and political science: they are taught scraps of Dante and Calvin with the tongue in the cheek, and learn from their parents that such doctrines are "rot." In consequence we have such a generation of atheists and anarchists as never existed before. In the XVIII century Frederick the Great, Catherine the Great, and a handful of financiers and philosophers were atheists, with Voltaire defending God and Rousseau defending Jesus Christ against them on modern Free Church Deistic lines; but the common people were Catholic or Lutheran, and men could be and were broken on the wheel for not kneeling down when the Host was carried past them in the street. But today Fred Smith and Kitty Jones are too utterly godless to be even conscious that they are atheists; and the Voltaireans and Rousseauites are classed as ultra-pious chapel folk. Ignorant parsons who used to excite the indignation of Carlyle by absurdly describing Voltaire and Rousseau as atheists are succeeded by the far more dangerously ignorant laymen who imagine that Charles Darwin discovered Evolution and that Natural Selection is an explanation of the universe.

Consider the dilemma we are thus landed in. Nobody who knows what contemporary Governments are would dream for a moment of trusting even the best of them to impose a creed on the children of the nation through the schools. Yet nobody who understands how vitally necessary a common faith is to a common civilization dares persist in the attempt to muddle through as we are. Well, suppose a Minister of Education proposed to adopt Natural Selection or "neo-Darwinism" as the creed of the Empire, with Weismann for its prophet! Instantly he would provoke a raging opposition that would bring any Government to the ground. Calvinist and Catholic alike would declare that they would fight to the last drop of their blood to save their children from the lake of fire and brimstone. The Creative Evolutionists, with Butler and Bergson for their prophets, would offer to swallow the Bible ten times over sooner than the doctrine with which Darwin "banished mind from the universe"[16] and hope from the soul of man. In vain would the Minister of Education exclaim "My good people: what are you making all this fuss about? Dont you know that the scientific sides of our schools and Universities have been teaching nothing else but Natural Selection and purely mechanistic physics for the last half century, and that it would be harder for a teacher who taught anything else to hold a professorship than for Mr Edward Clodd[17] to hold the pulpit of the City Temple [a centre of nonconformist teaching in London] or the Deanery of Westminster?" The reply would be that the people had not known it and would not have stood it if they had, and that all the professors on the scientific side must immediately sign either the Thirtynine Articles or the Westminster Confession, or else be thrown out of their chairs.

The Australian way out of this difficulty is secular education, meaning total exclusion of religious and philosophic teaching. But it does not mean the exclusion of scientific teaching. Now to teach science without any reference to philosophy and religion is to present the world to the child as an automatic machine worked by soulless mechanical forces and energies without purpose or scruple: the organism called Man going through a course of action as an avalanche does when it rolls down a hill or a hydrogen balloon when it rises through the air. The children may not be interested enough or intelligent enough to question this view spontaneously;

16. Shaw reports Butler making this comment to him in the British Museum courtyard (*Observer*, 26 March 1950). (J. L. Wisenthal cites the exchange in *Shaw and Ibsen*, 1979, p. 140.) The aphorism apparently is a variation and Shavian improvement of a less memorable phrasing in Butler's *Luck, or Cunning*, which Shaw reviewed in the *Pall Mall Gazette* (31 May 1887): 'Professor Huxley was trying to expel consciousness and sentience from any causative action in the working of the universe' (p. 141).
17. English author and banker, active in literary and scientific circles, wrote a number of popular scientific works, including *Story of Creation* (1888), *Primitive Man* (1895) and *A Primer of Evolution* (1895).

but as there will be plenty of theologians at hand to prompt them the teacher will soon be asked whether Will and Conscience are not powers as real as gravitation or magnetism, and where they come in under his scheme of things. He must reply, "Oh, that is the science of psychology; we shall come to that presently." But the moment he comes to it he must overleap his noncontroversial limit and plunge into metaphysics; for he cannot enter the domain of Aristotle without poaching on St Thomas Aquinas, nor combine the science of mind and motive with Weismann's dismissal of a butterfly's flight from the sweep of the entomologist's net (and presumably also the movement by which I dodge a motorbus in the Strand) as mere reflex action responding to a purely sensory stimulus of the retina, without presently having to discuss the pre-Weismannic version of Predestination put forward by Calvin, which at least had the mind of God behind it. Once the question of free will is thus raised you are in the controversy about Determinism, to which there is no answer but Bergson's answer. When purpose is once admitted in the course of a psychology lesson the question whether the existence of evil does not prove an evil purpose behind evolution cannot be staved off; and there is no answer to that except, if I may say so, *my* answer.

Now if secular education thus leads inevitably to the discussion of St Thomas Aquinas, Calvin, Darwin, Bergson, and Shaw, what is the use of pretending that it is noncontroversial or that it can steer clear of religion? You can no more draw a line and put a barrier between the temporal and spiritual in education than you can in the soul of man. You may forbid a teacher to mention the Bible or the Koran, or to refer to the Pope or the Archbishop of Canterbury as an authority. But what sense is there in that when you are thrusting on the scholar little textbooks reeking with the crudest theories of creation, destination, and predestination, and claiming an authority for the inoculatory rites of Jenner and Pasteur that St John the Baptist himself would have regarded as blasphemous?

The only solution of the difficulty is controversial education. That is what all the real education we have at present is. The student must be warned that religion, science, and philosophy are all fiercely controversial subjects, and that if he feels interested he must hear champions of the opposed views fighting it out in debate and be permitted to question them afterwards.

The result in many cases will be to leave the student in the very common case of a jury unable to agree on its verdict. But juries learn more from such cases than from the plain sailing ones. Controversy is educational in itself: a controversially educated person with an open mind is better educated than a dogmatically educated one with a closed mind. The student should hear the case, but should never be asked for a verdict. It may take him forty years to arrive at one.

At the same time it must be carefully explained to the young that there is a vast field of human action in which something must be done immediately and they must all agree to do the same thing without stopping to argue about it; for a confident expectation of how other people will behave, though irritating to reformers and improvers and victims of the Tolstoyan *Weltverbesserungswahn* [mania for world improvement] generally is, nevertheless, a first condition of civilization. The child must be taught, in direct contradiction to the current cult of salvation by personal righteousness, that in all public respects men in society must reform society before they can reform themselves. The individual may see a better line for the main road; but he should be educated to understand that his business is to persuade the authorities to make the new road and plough up the old, and not immediately to trample and trespass along his pet line as if the business concerned himself alone.

Yet who will dare to say that this first lesson in civic education is also the last? "Do as everybody else does; and never disappoint expectation" is as necessary a rule in business and general conduct as at a dinner party or when driving a motor car down a crowded street; but it is none the less a law of stagnation and not of evolution. There are departments of the greatest importance in which, far from setting up a rule of perfect expectedness, we must be trained to expect and tolerate and even demand the unexpected. Not only are individuality, originality, initiative, moral courage, and a bold preference of the inner light to the neighboring example vital in society, but mere novelty, change for the sake of change, is needed to make human activity endurable. The schoolmaster or parent who teaches a child the occasionally very necessary lesson that it must not do what it likes, presently finds that a child who is not engaged largely in doing what it likes is the worst sort of spoilt child. All kinds of conflicting rules arise. "Act according to your conscience" is a rule no sooner applied than we find that its validity depends altogether on what sort of conscience you have. Do what you like except when there are good reasons to the contrary is a rule which only leads to the discovery that none of the "natural rights" on the recognition of which all stable society must be built are reasonable; and, if they were, nine people out of ten would be unable to state the reasons for them. President Pearse, of the imaginary Irish Republic of Easter 1916, founded a school of romantic heroism, teaching boys to throw away their lives for their ideals, and sealed his teaching with his blood by throwing away his own life. But is it not clear that these boys of Pearse's, stuffed as they were with legends of the Fianna[18] and of Cuchullain,[19] should have heard the other side from Professors Falstaff, Sganarelle [a servant in Molière's *Le Festin de Pierre*, 1665], and Sancho Panza, and been encouraged to perform The Wild Duck and [William Brough's] A Phenomenon In A Smock Frock [1852] as well as The Coming of Finn and the like? Is a man who does not know the uses of unreason, of perversity, of paradox, of derision, an educated man? Can nothing be done to relieve our unfortunate pioneers from the unwholesome strain of being heroes at the excessive risk of becoming martyrs?

Toleration, Liberty of Conscience, Freedom of Speech and of the Press are all dogmas; consequently no person ignorant of history will accept them; for they are against all reason. It is for want of historical knowledge that they are not accepted at present. No doubt we all profess the deepest regard for liberty; but no sooner does anyone claim to exercise it than we declare with horror that we are in favor of liberty but not of licence, and demand indignantly whether true freedom can ever mean freedom to do wrong, to preach sedition and immorality, to utter blasphemy. Yet this is exactly what liberty does mean. He who remarks that it is a fine morning is not taking a liberty. Galileo took a XVII century liberty when he said that snipe shot would fall as fast as cannon balls, and that the earth moves round the sun; but the most abject slave may say both in the XX century. It is from history alone that we learn that the obvious and immediate evils of allowing individuals and newspapers to utter and publish revolting propositions and to deny sacred beliefs are not so dangerous as the stagnation and retrogression which follow the enforcement of conformity, and that even in the crises of a war the consequences of deceiving the enemy, involving as they do the consequences of deceiving the nation, may easily be more disastrous than fighting strictly on the facts and discarding bluff. Now there is no sign that this lesson has been effectively taught to our educated classes, or even taught at all. It is the received opinion and practice among us that heresy should be persecuted and "bad taste"

---

18. The legendary followers of Finn mac Cumaill, the principal hero of the southern or later cycle of Irish legends. Some of these Fenian or Ossianic tales are chronicled in 'The Coming of Finn' in Lady Gregory's *Gods and Fighting Men* (1904).

19. The principal hero of the northern or Ulster cycle of Irish mythology. Lady Gregory translated much of this material in *Cuchulain of Muirthemne* (1902), and W. B. Yeats dramatized episodes from Cuchulain's life in a series of one-act plays.

punished. There is, it is true, a benefit of clergy and of class and of income allowed in time of peace; and party invective and vulgar abuse are always privileged; but this is not Toleration: we do not tolerate suttee [self-immolation by a Hindu widow on her husband's funeral pyre] in India, nor did the United States tolerate the cult of nakedness introduced by the Doukhobors.

These two examples bring home to us at once that Toleration is no golden rule: in fact, all laws act in restraint of toleration, even when they are laws to enforce toleration. In decently conducted churches a Quaker is allowed to walk to a pew before taking off his hat; but if he were to put his heels up on the back of the pew in front of him, and light a cigar, he would assuredly be thrown out and charged with brawling; and no plea of an imperative inner light would secure his acquittal. Toleration is a matter of degree: we all draw the line somewhere; and nothing will shift that line except education. In a rude village a stranger may be stoned for wearing his hair two inches longer than usual, though on the great bridge across the Golden Horn [inlet of Bosporus, forming Istanbul's harbour] men and women of every race, class, color, fashion, costume or no costume, on earth pass oneanother without even looking round, the reason being that the Turks have been educated by experience to believe that a longhaired man may be as honest a neighbor as a shorthaired one, improbable as that may seem to a British islander. Yet in matters which depend on historical education, the Turk is as intolerant as any other equally ignorant person. One of the main objects of education is to prevent people from defeating their own civilization by refusing to tolerate novelties and heresies which history proves that they had better tolerate. Therefore it is of extraordinary importance that all citizens should be educated in liberty, toleration, and the theory of natural rights. At present they are taught nothing but an idiotic demonstration that natural rights are a fiction of the vulgar imagination, because, forsooth, natural rights *are* natural, and not derived or acquired: in short, not logical.

When we turn from the toleration of acts to the toleration of doctrine, we have to admit that we are not prepared to allow any doctrine which we believe pernicious to be taught to young persons dogmatically. For example, I am not prepared to allow Calvinism to be taught to any infant under any circumstances, nor to older children otherwise than controversially. I have never suffered from the fear of ghosts, because when I was a child, and the servants tried to frighten me with ghost stories, my father assured me that there are no such things as ghosts, and I believed him; but I know people who to this day are afraid to be alone in the dark because their parents were not as careful as my father. Now the dread of ghosts is a trifle compared to the dread of hell; and though there are stages of civilization, like that of the Arabs in Mahomet's time, in which men can be kept under moral restraint only by threatening them with a horribly tortured immortality, yet Mahomet never defeated his own expedient by complicating it and indeed demoralizing it by a doctrine of election and predestination as the Calvinists do. I have enjoyed the friendship and conversation of a gentleman who holds that the two greatest scoundrels who ever lived were Calvin and Robespierre; and though I am not prepared without further consideration to subscribe to this refreshingly vigorous estimate, I should insist that no Calvinist be allowed to proselytize in a school except through controversies with other zealots of the complexion of my friend, and with a sound Nazarene Christian or two as well. This involves, of course, my conceding to the Calvinist in the nominally Christian countries that he should have his say in the schools against Creative Evolution. Calvinism and Paulinism cannot be ignored. The Atonement religions are all much older than Christianity, and have captured it to such a degree that no one can possibly understand human nature or history, even to the very limited extent to which they can be understood at all, without a knowledge of these religions, especially the modern forms of them established by the Reformation.

We are driven to conclude then that civic education must be as compulsory as technical elementary education, but that the former must be controversial, whilst liberal education must be voluntary, though the community must provide the material and conditions for it. But compulsion can only take the form of political or social disability involved by failure to qualify for benefit of clergy. If people have no civic interest or capacity, and therefore cannot be civically educated, it is as absurd to give them political power or admit them to responsible public offices as it would be to give money to a child incapable of counting it. However we may be tempted to say that the only qualification the voter needs is the power of suffering from misgovernment, a moment's reflection will convince us that a baby might claim a vote on this ground. The one thing that is certainly worse than the suffering of a political imbecile is his notion of a remedy for it. Yet if our political imbeciles are disfranchised they will be exploited by their rulers; and the rulers will be corrupted by that power to exploit them. The democratic safeguard against this danger is to give them a choice of rulers. Only, it must be a guided and limited choice. Left to themselves with the whole human race to choose from they will prefer Titus Oates to John Stuart Mill. Elect a world president by universal suffrage, and who would have a chance against Mr Charles Chaplin? The choice must be limited to persons who have passed certain tests and perhaps taken certain vows. Such a limited choice may seem sufficient. Even if it be limited to Cæsar or Pompey (it may be argued) that will keep both of them in order. It will, provided they are both ambitious of rulership. But suppose they are both very reluctant to shoulder the heavy burden of governing! In that case the competition becomes a donkey race in which the candidates vie with oneanother in unpopularity and the loser wins. It is conceivable that when we at last learn how to limit the choice of our electorates to qualified persons we may have to compel those persons to accept the mandate as a public duty just as we now compel jurymen to serve. In any case our rulers must be held to good behavior by forfeiture of rulership if they oppress; and as only new brooms sweep clean, old brooms should not be eligible for re-election too often, however popular they may be.

I am fully aware of the difficulties which my suggestions raise, and how impossible it is to carry them out save as part of a social synthesis which involves the reconstruction of many other institutions besides our schools. Reforming our educational system may end like what is called "restoring" a medieval cathedral: we talk of numbering each stone, and replacing carefully and reverently those which are not too far gone to be saved; but in practice the edifice crumbles to pieces at the first touch of the pick and leaves us contemplating a heap of fragments which have miraculously lost all the shape they had a moment before, and now have neither head nor tail, top nor bottom. The schoolmaster as we know him may, like the cathedral stones, be numbered and registered ever so carefully; but when child slavery is abolished, and a new constitutional edifice of children's rights is set up, he will not fit into it. Genuine born teachers will hold their own, and indeed come to their own; but there will not be enough of them to go round; and the teachers who are not born but made by training will have to be a new generation. Still, the change has to come, for democracy without democrats: that is, without civically educated voters and representatives and officials, means, as we now see, red ruin. And civic education does not mean education in blind obedience to authority, but education in controversy and in liberty, in manners and in courage, in scepticism, in discontent and betterment, tempered by the fear, not of artificially manufactured punishments, but of genuine natural consequences, to be faced or funked, as the case may be, in the light of kindness, humor, and common sense.

The human result will probably be much more like the so-called self-educated man of today than the public school man and the university graduate whose cloistered ignorance and inculcated error have made such a mess of things as they are. Yet what self-educated man, if he can afford to send his son to the public school and university, dares let him run wild? He knows too well that even in the matter of schooling it is a questionable kindness to take a child too far out of the common groove. If, like Romulus or Mowgli, it has to live the life of a wolf,[20] it had better be brought up as a wolf. The good school is now, unfortunately, the crank school: the problem is to make the common school a good school. And good schools are not easily tolerated by bad civilizations. The parent may wish in his soul that his son could be taught that honesty is the best policy; but he has to consider that if he is led to take that precept seriously as a practical rule of life in competitive commerce he may starve for it. All our conventional schools at present teach false ethics, false science, false history, and even false hygiene. And if there were sufficient vested interests in false geography and false arithmetic they would teach these too. Truth is a guilty secret, heavily punishable on discovery; and the parent who allows his child to be taught truth without also leaving him an independent income must be prepared to hear his child curse him. This, I think, is the real reason why we dare not embark on controversial education. It would tear away the camouflage from commercial civilization.

For the rest, I can only repeat that if the advance of education is to mean nothing more than the widening of the net of the child prison and boy farm until not one of us can escape it we had better abolish it altogether. Our main disqualifications for citizenship now are ignorance, unsociability, and terror. And the government of the world by people who have been longest at school has been so far an organization of ignorance, unsociability, and terror, exploding from time to time in such monstrous smashes as the so-called Great War, which the belligerents could bear only by persuading themselves that it was a crusade, though it had really no more ethical character than a railway collision. The root of the evil is that though our national life, which is always assumed to be adult life, is and must always remain at least one-third child life, we have never given children a political constitution with appropriate laws, rights, and safeguards. But this I must reserve for another utterance.

20. Romulus, the legendary founder of Rome, when thrown into the Tiber was saved and suckled by a she-wolf. Mowgli, in Kipling's *The Jungle Books* (1894; 1895) was mothered by the she-wolf Raksha.

A Foreword to the Clerks
(Trade Unionism for Clerks)

Preface to a pamphlet by J. H. Lloyd and R. E. Scouller, first published in 1919

In the XIX century, when I was a clerk, there were two sorts of people whom it was almost impossible to organize. First, the women. Second, the clerks.

They were unorganizable for the same reason. They did not intend to stick to their jobs. Neither of them expected to remain in the position of employee. The woman intended to get married and have a house of her own and be her own mistress, no matter how poor she was. The clerk either hated business and meant to get out of it and become a great man: poet, novelist, polar explorer, field marshal, actor, world's champion pugilist, prime minister, or anything else in the general line of Shakespear and Napoleon (I was myself in this category, which is more numerous than people think), or else, if he was keen on business, he meant to set up for himself unless the boss took him into partnership.

This outlook made all the difference in the world between the clerk and the artisan. Not that the clerk was better paid: quite the contrary. A very common wage was fifteen shillings a week: it was indeed the standard clerk's salary in East London. Although all my main clerking experience was over before I was twenty, I had, through an accident, been put into a position of trust and activity always previously given to a man of mature years and my employer [C. Uniacke Townshend] afterwards testified that I was a treasure (for which I was so ungrateful as to damn his impertinence in the secrecy of my soul); yet the highest salary I touched was either £72 or £84 a year: I forget which. And I began at £18. What is more, I was considered very well placed, and not at all without good reason; for the office was crushingly genteel; and if I had had any serious business intentions I could have made it the jumping-off plank for a lucrative and socially respected career in the business I was supposed to be learning, and would have learnt if it had interested me in the smallest degree.

Now suppose I had been interested in it, and had intended to go through with it all my life! Would I have joined a National Union of Clerks, had there been such a thing in existence? Certainly not. Not only would it have been considered a most ungentlemanly thing to do—almost as outrageous as coming to the office in corduroy trousers with a belcher handkerchief [after Jim Belcher, pugilist: a gaudy neckerchief] round my neck—but, snobbery apart, it would have been stupid, because I should not have intended to remain a clerk, but to employ clerks. I should have taken the employer's point of view from the first, as became a man who was going to be either an employer or a failure in life.

Forty years after I had shaken the dust of that office from my feet I found myself one morning standing in the street outside it, having in the meantime pulled off the Great Man Stunt, and been recently held up to an admiring Europe as "the Molière of the Twentieth Century" [title of a study of Shaw by his French translator, Augustin Hamon]. I was looking for a Commissioner of Oaths [an English notary] to witness some legal profanity or other; and it suddenly struck me that there was one on the first floor of the building [15 Molesworth Street, Dublin] where I had slaved as a clerk. It was a good excuse for going in and peeping through the glass door of my old prison as I passed. I was disgusted to find that they had built a partition which shut off the view of my part of the formerly spacious room, and, as we would have said in my time, "made the place look like a pawnbroker's."

I went upstairs. The Commissioner of Oaths was out. His clerk was no common clerk: he was every inch a churchwarden, frockcoated, large, dignified, prosperous, and, I could swear, a Master Mason in the Lodge next door. Still, only a clerk, legally unable to make anyone swear but his employer. I am by profession a communicative person; and as it was a fine morning, and we were not yet pressed for time, we chatted for a moment. I mentioned that I had been a clerk myself in that building forty years before. Instantly the distinguished consideration he had been beguiled into treating me with by my air of being somebody in particular changed into undisguised contempt, barbed by incredulity. He expressed the contempt in his tone, and the incredulity in these staggering words:

"*I dont remember you.*"

He had been there when I was there. He had been there for forty years. All that time, whilst I was making six or seven reputations, touching nothing that I did not adorn, being abused by all the papers as only the famous are abused, and surveying mankind, if not from China to Peru, at least from Stamboul to Jamaica, he had kept on coming at ten every morning and going home at five every evening, and was good for another ten years of it. And that is what would have happened to me but for the pure accident of my turning out to be the one man in every million or so who happens to have the knack of telling lies so attractively that people go to the theatre to see actors pretending they are true. Granted that he was nothing like so worn out as I, and was obviously on better terms with himself. Granted that he was none of your English Newman Noggses [a down-and-out clerk in Dickens's *Nicholas Nickleby*], but an Irish metropolitan solicitor's right-hand man. Granted that he had never entered a third-class carriage in his life; that he despised shorthand as the craft of a common reporter; that he did not know at sight a typewriter from a cash register. Still, I cannot believe that when he and I were youths together in the eighteenseventies he intended to be a clerk all his life any more than I did.

I fled from his majestic presence recalling many memories. I remembered the old bookkeeper [Frederick Walter], whom I had asked whether his son was a clerk, and who had said, with a ferocity that amazed me, that he would rather see him dead, and told me how he had struggled to save him from that fate by apprenticing him to a pharmaceutical chemist. I remembered how I had been offered his post, and had flatly refused it, to the astonishment of my employer. I remembered how my father [George Carr Shaw], who had managed to obtain a sinecure in the law courts, and had on its abolition received some hundreds of pounds compensation, had thereupon set up in a business he knew nothing about in partnership with a gentleman [George Clibborn] who had been apprenticed to another and quite different business; so that the two had become employers with clerks of their own; and I reflected on how utterly impossible such an absurdity would be now, although then it happened every day. I remembered how my father had been horrified at finding me playing one day with the son of a shopkeeper, and had explained to me that there was a great social gulf fixed between me and the children of men who sold anything retail, he himself being a wholesaler. And I remembered what was odder still: that this claim was allowed by the retailers; so that men twenty times as rich as he, and at least a hundred times as able in business, treated him with deference.

A day or two later I found myself taking tea at the country house of a very great lady [Sybil Viscountess Powerscourt] who in the old days would as soon have thought of entertaining her sweep as my father. Her daughter was going to a ball that night; and I gathered from the conversation that the giver of the ball was one of the rich shopkeepers [Sir John Arnot] (titled, too) with whose sons my father would not allow me to play.

Now I am not treating you to all this autobiography for nothing. I want you, friend and fellow clerk, to reflect on the staggering change in the social world of the peeress, and how sensibly she has adapted herself to it instead of stagnating the prejudices of her grandmother, and on the equally staggering want of change that left that clerk on the first floor exactly what he was and where he had been forty years before. If you take it that the chances against his ever becoming an employer were only ten to one in 1870, you may take the chances against yourself today as a thousand to one. In my father's day it was still gravely contended by economists that there were only three businesses that could be carried on by joint stock companies: banking, insurance, and railways. In my day it was computed that one-third of the entire business of the country was carried on by limited liability companies. Nowadays the companies themselves are superseded by huge trusts, carrying on not only great banking amalgamations and the like, but oilshops and tobacco shops in back streets.

What does that mean for you? It means that not only the clerks, but the managers, representing the oldtime employers, are now employees, and that if one of them wanted to start on his own in the old fashion he would need a hundred thousand pounds for every hundred my father possessed; and even then he would not have a dog's chance if he attempted to compete with the big combinations instead of making it worth their while to annex him.

There is another change. The oldtime clerk whom my father employed could not typewrite nor take down a letter in shorthand. But he could read and write and cipher; and as not one of the mechanics and carmen and laborers employed along with him knew the alphabet or could write his own name, the clerk's "clergy" was a middle-class monopoly: there was no competition outside that class; and he who could read and write presentably was a gentleman. At present every mechanic's son is better educated for the commercial desk than King Edward the Seventh was. Practically every lad in the kingdom is qualified more or less for the job when he leaves school; and the reason why the competition is actually less ruinous than it used to be instead of more is that the skilled trades now absorb thousands of lads whom Victorian snobbery would have condemned to the desk.

Nevertheless the competition is heavy enough to force the clerks to follow the example of their employers in bettering themselves. Fifty years ago the employers began to stop competing and took to combining. A hundred years ago the mechanics and laborers did the same. The professions never competed: the doctors and lawyers were the original trade unionists; and the army, the navy, and the Church were never commercial enough to be even trade unionists. But many clerks are still clinging to the old policy of playing for promotion to the employing class, not realizing that nowadays an average clerk's chance of getting there is about as great as his chance of becoming Emperor of China.

Is clerking, then, a hopeless business? Not at all: it is a better business than ever it was before. When the oldtime clerk achieved his ambition and became an employer, he was for the most part poor, worried, cramped by want of means and the competition of men as poor as himself. He could not afford to pay his clerks well, or to provide decent offices and furniture and sanitation for them. They had long hours, no holidays, and above all, no security; for he was only mortal, and might at any moment fail, retire, die, or lose his temper and give his slaves the boot, being himself the slave of all the vicissitudes that beset poor men. Now a big company, or better still a big combine, can afford to pay its managing clerks far more than they could have made in business for themselves in the old style, and its ordinary clerks more than any small individual employer could ever have afforded to pay them. It has to consider the health and efficiency of its clerks: a thing that never entered the head of an oldtime employer. It has, it is true, "neither a body to be kicked nor a soul to be damned";[1] but one effect of that is that it has no petty social jealousy of its clerks, and never interferes with them outside office hours, when they may give themselves the airs of dukes if they like. It does not die; it does not retire; the risk of its failure is negligible; it does not encourage managers to gratify their tempers at the expense of smooth working; and though it has its evils, they are very much less intense than the same evils in the old small businesses. In short, I should say that there is hardly a managing clerk in a modern big business who is not much better off than my father was as a partner.

But if my father's clerk had a grievance, he could have it out face to face with my father if he dared; and my father, being a goodnatured and reasonable sort of man (though he objected to that startling innovation, bank holiday, as calculated to lead to excessive smoking and idleness), could ease the harness where it galled. Now a modern clerk cannot have it out with a Trust. He is up against a huge impersonal aggregation of capital, where his immediate superior is an employee like himself, and cannot do anything for him without doing it automatically and simultaneously for a hundred and perhaps a thousand other clerks as well. If my father gave a clerk a rise of a pound a month, it cost him only twelve pounds a year.

1. Edward, First Baron Thurlow, eighteenth-century English jurist and Lord Chancellor, is reported in John Poynder's *Literary Extracts* (1844) to have written, 'Corporations have neither bodies to be punished, nor souls to be condemned, they therefore do as they like.'

There are establishments in the world at present, and their number is increasing, in which a rise of a pound a month would cost the firm twelve thousand a year. Thus the individual modern clerk is as helpless as the individual carpenter and mason has always been. At first sight, then, it would seem that my father's clerk was safer; but this is an illusion. There were so few clerks in each office that the employer could take Admiral Fisher's advice, and "sack the lot" just as his temper led him.[2] He could get new ones next day, or, at a pinch, carry on himself for a week without their help. But a Trust cannot sack the lot nor carry on for half a day without them. Therefore it cannot sack even one if all the clerks stand together as the Railwaymen and the Coalminers and Transport Workers do.

And now you see the moral of my tale. First make up your mind that nowadays once an employee always an employee. Even if you are an employer in a small way (comparatively) you will most likely be overtaken by the Trust movement presently and made an employee. Second, realize that as an individual you are now utterly helpless. If you want a rise, if you want shorter hours, if you want any amelioration whatsoever in the conditions of your employment, you must ask it not only for yourself but for all the other clerks as well; and you have no authority to ask in their name (most of them would be terrified at your audacity and would repudiate you in their dread of sharing your inevitable fate of being "fired") even if you could get at any supreme individual from whom you could ask it. In short, unless your demand be made officially through the secretary of a union of clerks it cannot be made at all.

Now go and join the National Union of Clerks before you have time to cool down about it. You will find its credentials in the pages which follow. I can say nothing more to you except that if I were a clerk now I should join it without a moment's hesitation, just as I have joined my own Trade Union, the Society of Authors, Playwrights, and Composers.

G. B. S.

2. John Fisher, First Baron Fisher of Kilverstone, Admiral of the Fleet, was noted for his verbal explosions, often enhanced by biblical allusions and free use of slogans and expletives. In a letter to *The Times* (2 September 1919) his fury was directed at 'the spendthrift crew' in the British Government responsible for daily deficit-spending of two million pounds over income: 'You must be ruthless, relentless, and remorseless! SACK THE LOT!'

Family Life in Germany under the Blockade

Preface to a book edited by Lina Richter, 1919

═══

We are at present at a climax of national exultation over the most magnificent military triumph in our long record of victory. We are the happiest and proudest of empires. Such pageantry of peace, such panoply of war, has never before been seen by living men. The defeat of the Armada, the overthrow of Louis XIV, the conquest of India and Canada, the chaining of Napoleon, were child's play to this last and most tremendous of our exploits. We have stretched out a mighty hand upon the most dreaded power in the world (except ourselves) and choked it until it lies half dead at our feet, buying its bare life from us by concessions so abject that the more generous souls among us are ashamed of having exacted so much. We have been taken into the high mountain as of old; and we have not turned our backs on the power and the glory offered to us.

But the splendor of the end, which is the work of our imagination, had better not blind us to the grimness of the means, which were the work of our hands. Triumphs of this kind cannot be had for nothing. It is now too late to ask whether this one was worth what it cost: the question is not merely could we afford another (our military authorities are already urging us to prepare for it), but whether we can afford to push this one any further, or even to refrain from undoing, as far as possible, a good deal of what we have done, and saving as many lives as we can from the wreck we have made. When Napoleon caught the Russians on a frozen lake, he turned his guns on the ice and broke it. He then took extraordinary pains to rescue the drowning soldiers.[1] Once they were defeated he had no quarrel with them. To win this war, we did a far more horrible thing than the icebreaking. We starved the children of Germany, and of many other lands as well. Having defeated our enemies by that means, are we going to feed the starving children as Napoleon rescued the drowning soldiers, or are we out, not merely for defeat, but for extermination?

1. This statement is unconfirmed in any major study of the Russian campaign or in contemporary memoirs of leading participants, from generals on both sides to Napoleon's valet.

Superficially, extermination seems a logical procedure both during the war and after the victory. But it never works smoothly. When soldiers are asked to do it they refuse, because the fortune of the vanquished may be that of the victor tomorrow; and just as prizefighting would be impossible if pugilists were not protected by a very strict limitation of the extent to which the winner may abuse his victory, so war would be impossible if there were not precisely analogous limits to the abuse of military victories in the field. Everyone must have noticed during the war the contrast between the ferocity of our civilians and the reasonableness and compunction of our soldiers from the front, even of the wounded soldiers who had suffered personally and acutely from the operations of the enemy. The civilian called the German the Hun, and, in the comparative safety of home, clamored for his extermination with a full mouth. The soldier called him Jerry, meaning "companion in misfortune," and spoke no evil of him except when he was specifically ordered to. When the civilian mercilessly went on starving the German children after the armistice, the British soldier fed them out of his rations; and it was from the army that the first protest came against the infernal cruelty of the continued blockade.

This does not mean that the British civilian is one sort of person and the British soldier another. It means that the civilian neither sees nor knows what he is doing, and that the soldier sees it and has to do it. In Coventry it is easy to forget all about the German children, and work yourself up into a drunken frenzy of determination that the Kaiser shall be hanged to avenge the victims of the submarine campaign. In Cologne, with famine-wasted children begging for the refuse of your meals, or mutely watching every morsel you eat with a hungry eye, it is impossible. In the early days of voluntary recruiting, we were exhorted from every hoarding to remember that some day our children would ask us what we did in the great war. That question was dropped when compulsory military service was instituted. It might very well be revived in the form, "Daddy: what did you do when the war was over?" The man who can say "I shared my ration with the poor starving children in Germany" will have a considerable moral advantage over the ardent patriot who has nothing better to say than "I voted for hanging the Kaiser; and he was not hanged after all."[2]

But even men who are naturally cruel, or so desperately afraid of the Germans that no victory can reassure them, are sooner or later forced to

2. Kaiser Wilhelm II, Emperor of Germany, formally abdicated on 28 November 1918 after fleeing to Holland, where he resided at Doorn from 1920 until his death in 1941.

behave themselves by economic considerations. If we and the Germans were two Red Indian tribes, each sufficient to itself for all its needs, then one could exterminate the other and feel all the safer for it without being a penny the worse, except for the incidental casualties. Many of our journalists, like the citizens who accept them as their political instructors, have such primitive notions of society that they are unable to conceive European relations as anything more complicated. But if this were so, we could never have starved Germany, and the war would still be going on with a prospect of lasting until human nature could no longer bear it. Germany was beaten because she was dependent for her very existence on trade with her enemies. But trade means exchange of goods. If Germany lived by selling her products to us, we lived equally by selling our products to Germany. Our blockade cut Germany off from all alternative sources, and so starved her out; but there were moments during the war when Germany, by her submarine campaign, came so near to cutting us off that for some months we read the lists of sunken ships with our hearts in our mouths. It was a frightful starving match, and for nearly a year we were racing neck and neck, or at least seemed to be; for we did not then know how impossible it was for Germany to keep up her submarine fleet.

However, from our point of view all's well that ends well. We won the race. But how is our trade with Germany to be restored? Our primitives say that they do not want it to be restored. They will never shake hands with a Hun as long as they live. They will never buy from him or sell to him. In other words, they have not sense enough to understand modern civilization. In the very same breath with which they gasp out these follies, they declare that Germany must be made to pay for the war; and the Peace Treaty has already imposed on the vanquished a colossal tribute. How is that tribute to be paid if German industry is ruined and German labor is starving? Granted that the Germans are to be our slaves for the next fifty years, must not slaves be fed as well as beaten? There is nothing to be got out of beating them except labor; and how can they labor if they are not fed? Stick is not a very productive diet, is it?

The tribute can be paid only if Germany buys things from us at more than cost price, and sells things to us at less than cost price until her ransom is paid. There is no other way in which it can be done under existing European conditions. That means that German production must continue side-by-side with British production. If we are to have the spoils of victory, German industry must be restored. And if German industry is to be restored, German labor must be fed. That is why, in starving the Germans, we are biting our noses to spite our faces. If our vengeance-mongers cannot divine by spiritual intuition that we are members one of another, they will have it rubbed into them most unsympathetically and uncomfortably by the hard fact that there will be no business doing in many of their own trades until German demand revives: that is, until Germany is producing enough to pay *more than enough* for British goods.

The pages which follow do not go into this economic consideration. They appeal, not to an elementary knowledge of international trade and finance, which most of their readers unfortunately do not possess, but simply, like Athenian tragedy, to pity and horror. There is no literary art about them: they just say crudely to the British conqueror, "Thus didst thou." If he replies that he could not help it, he must be told that he can help it now. The military necessity for starvation has passed: it is now not only a vile revenge on the innocent, but a suicidal blunder.

Also, it is a dangerous precedent. We were able to form an irresistible combination against the late German Empire solely because it had made itself feared throughout the world, and because its military traditions had boasted overmuch of their pseudo-realism and real ruthlessness. Now that we have cast it down from that perilous eminence, we have left ourselves in the position of the most dreaded nation militarily. If we, too, now set up a tradition of the same spurious realism and genuine ruthlessness, the Germany we have emancipated will find it quite easy to form a combination against us which may one day leave us at the mercy of those who are now at our mercy. The old rule, "Treat your friend as one who may some day be your enemy, and your enemy as one who may some day be your friend",[3] is hardly the golden rule; but it is a sound one for those who scorn golden rules.

Let us look to it accordingly.

July, 1919.   G. BERNARD SHAW.

---

3. '[W]e should ever conduct ourselves towards our enemy as if he were one day to be our friend': John Henry Cardinal Newman, *The Idea of a University* (1873), Discourse VIII.

Heartbreak House and Horseback Hall
(Heartbreak House)

First published in 1919

═══

WHERE HEARTBREAK HOUSE STANDS

Heartbreak House is not merely the name of the play which follows this preface. It is cultured, leisured Europe before the war. When the play was begun not a shot had been fired; and only the professional diplomatists and the very few amateurs whose hobby is foreign policy even knew that the guns were loaded. A Russian playwright, Tchekov, had produced four fascinating dramatic studies of Heartbreak House, of which three, The Cherry Orchard, Uncle Vanya, and The Seagull, had been performed in England.[1] Tolstoy, in his Fruits of Enlightenment [1891], had shewn us through it in his most ferociously contemptuous manner. Tolstoy did not waste any sympathy on it: it was to him the house in which Europe was stifling its soul; and he knew that our utter enervation and futilization in that overheated drawing-room atmosphere was delivering the world over to the control of ignorant and soulless cunning and energy, with the frightful consequences which have now overtaken it. Tolstoy was no pessimist: he was not disposed to leave the house standing if he could bring it down about the ears of its pretty and amiable voluptuaries; and he wielded the pickaxe with a will. He treated the case of the inmates as one of opium poisoning, to be dealt with by seizing the patients roughly and exercising them violently until they were broad awake. Tchekov, more of a fatalist, had no faith in these charming people extricating themselves. They would, he thought, be sold up and sent adrift by the bailiffs; therefore he had no scruple in exploiting and even flattering their charm.

1. The first Chekov play to be performed in England was *The Seagull*, by the Glasgow Repertory Theatre, 2 November 1909. The Stage Society mounted the first Chekov play in London, *The Cherry Orchard*, on 28 May 1911; and followed with *Uncle Vanya* on 10 May 1914.

THE INHABITANTS

Tchekov's plays, being less lucrative than swings and roundabouts, got no further in England, where theatres are only ordinary commercial affairs, than a couple of performances by the Stage Society. We stared and said, "How Russian!" They did not strike me in that way. Just as Ibsen's intensely Norwegian plays exactly fitted every middle and professional class suburb in Europe, these intensely Russian plays fitted all the country houses in Europe in which the pleasures of music, art, literature, and the theatre had supplanted hunting, shooting, fishing, flirting, eating, and drinking. The same nice people, the same utter futility. The nice people could read; some of them could write; and they were the only repositories of culture who had social opportunities of contact with our politicians, administrators, and newspaper proprietors, or any chance of sharing or influencing their activities. But they shrank from that contact. They hated politics. They did not wish to realize Utopia for the common people: they wished to realize their favorite fictions and poems in their own lives; and, when they could, they lived without scruple on incomes which they did nothing to earn. The women in their girlhood made themselves look like variety theatre stars, and settled down later into the types of beauty imagined by the previous generation of painters. They took the only part of our society in which there was leisure for high culture, and made it an economic, political, and, as far as practicable, a moral vacuum; and as Nature, abhorring the vacuum, immediately filled it up with sex and with all sorts of refined pleasures, it was a very delightful place at its best for moments of relaxation. In other moments it was disastrous. For prime ministers and their like, it was a veritable Capua.[2]

HORSEBACK HALL

But where were our front benchers to nest if not here? The alternative to Heartbreak House was Horseback Hall, consisting of a prison for horses with an annex for the ladies and gentlemen who rode them, hunted them, talked about them, bought them and sold them, and gave nine-tenths of

---

2. Capua, now a small, dusty Italian town north of Naples, was once a rich city. It is said that Hannibal's soldiers in winter quarters were enervated by its wealth and luxury. See also p. 370, fn. 3.

their lives to them, dividing the other tenth between charity, church-going (as a substitute for religion), and conservative electioneering (as a substitute for politics). It is true that the two establishments got mixed at the edges. Exiles from the library, the music room, and the picture gallery would be found languishing among the stables, miserably discontented; and hardy horsewomen who slept at the first chord of Schumann were born, horribly misplaced, into the [deceptive] garden of Klingsor [in Wagner's *Parsifal*, 1882]; but sometimes one came upon horsebreakers and heartbreakers who could make the best of both worlds. As a rule, however, the two were apart and knew little of oneanother; so the prime-minister folk had to choose between barbarism and Capua. And of the two atmospheres it is hard to say which was the more fatal to statesmanship.

REVOLUTION ON THE SHELF

Heartbreak House was quite familiar with revolutionary ideas on paper. It aimed at being advanced and freethinking, and hardly ever went to church or kept the Sabbath except by a little extra fun at weekends. When you spent a Friday to Tuesday in it you found on the shelf in your bedroom not only the books of poets and novelists, but of revolutionary biologists and even economists. Without at least a few plays by myself and Mr Granville Barker, and a few stories by Mr H. G. Wells, Mr Arnold Bennett, and Mr John Galsworthy, the house would have been out of the movement. You would find Blake among the poets, and beside him Bergson, Butler, Scott Haldane,[3] the poems of Meredith and Thomas Hardy, and, generally speaking, all the literary implements for forming the mind of the perfect modern Socialist and Creative Evolutionist. It was a curious experience to spend Sunday in dipping into these books, and on Monday morning to read in the daily paper that the country had just been brought to the verge of anarchy because a new Home Secretary[4] or chief of police, without an idea in his head that his great-grandmother might not have had to apologize for, had refused to "recognize" some powerful

3. English scientist, among whose works are *Organism and Environment* (1917) and *The New Physiology* (1919).
4. The stress on 'new' reflects the fact that there were no less than five Home Secretaries between 1910 and 1916: Winston Churchill, Reginald McKenna, Rt. Hon. Sir John Simon, Herbert Samuel and Sir George Cave.

Trade Union, just as a gondola might refuse to recognize a 20,000-ton liner.

In short, power and culture were in separate compartments. The barbarians were not only literally in the saddle, but on the front bench in the House of Commons, with nobody to correct their incredible ignorance of modern thought and political science but upstarts from the countinghouse, who had spent their lives furnishing their pockets instead of their minds. Both, however, were practised in dealing with money and with men, as far as acquiring the one and exploiting the other went; and although this is as undesirable an expertness as that of the medieval robber baron, it qualifies men to keep an estate or a business going in its old routine without necessarily understanding it, just as Bond Street tradesmen and domestic servants keep fashionable society going without any instruction in sociology.

THE CHERRY ORCHARD

The Heartbreak people neither could nor would do anything of the sort. With their heads as full of the Anticipations [*of the Reaction of Mechanical and Scientific Progress upon Human Life and Thought*, 1901] of Mr H. G. Wells as the heads of our actual rulers were empty even of the anticipations of Erasmus or Sir Thomas More, they refused the drudgery of politics, and would have made a very poor job of it if they had changed their minds. Not that they would have been allowed to meddle anyhow, as only through the accident of being a hereditary peer can anyone in these days of Votes for Everybody get into parliament if handicapped by a serious modern cultural equipment; but if they had, their habit of living in a vacuum would have left them helpless and ineffective in public affairs. Even in private life they were often helpless wasters of their inheritance, like the people in Tchekov's Cherry Orchard. Even those who lived within their incomes were really kept going by their solicitors and agents, being unable to manage an estate or run a business without continual prompting from those who have to learn how to do such things or starve.

From what is called Democracy no corrective to this state of things could be hoped. It is said that every people has the Government it deserves. It is more to the point that every Government has the electorate it deserves; for the orators of the front bench can edify or debauch an ignorant electorate at will. Thus our democracy moves in a vicious circle of reciprocal worthiness and unworthiness.

NATURE'S LONG CREDITS

Nature's way of dealing with unhealthy conditions is unfortunately not one that compels us to conduct a solvent hygiene on a cash basis. She demoralizes us with long credits and reckless overdrafts, and then pulls us up cruelly with catastrophic bankruptcies. Take, for example, common domestic sanitation. A whole city generation may neglect it utterly and scandalously, if not with absolute impunity, yet without any evil consequences that anyone thinks of tracing to it. In a hospital two generations of medical students may tolerate dirt and carelessness, and then go out into general practice to spread the doctrine that fresh air is a fad, and sanitation an imposture set up to make profits for plumbers. Then suddenly Nature takes her revenge. She strikes at the city with a pestilence and at the hospital with an epidemic of hospital gangrene, slaughtering right and left until the innocent young have paid for the guilty old, and the account is balanced. And then she goes to sleep again and gives another period of credit, with the same result.

This is what has just happened in our political hygiene. Political science has been as recklessly neglected by Governments and electorates during my lifetime as sanitary science was in the days of Charles the Second. In international relations diplomacy has been a boyishly lawless affair of family intrigues, commercial and territorial brigandage, torpors of pseudo-goodnature produced by laziness, and spasms of ferocious activity produced by terror. But in these islands we muddled through. Nature gave us a longer credit than she gave to France or Germany or Russia. To British centenarians who died in their beds in 1914, any dread of having to hide underground in London from the shells of an enemy seemed more remote and fantastic than a dread of the appearance of a colony of cobras and rattlesnakes in Kensington Gardens. In the prophetic works of Charles Dickens we were warned against many evils which have since come to pass; but of the evil of being slaughtered by a foreign foe on our own doorsteps there was no shadow. Nature gave us a very long credit; and we abused it to the utmost. But when she struck at last she struck with a vengeance. For four years she smote our firstborn and heaped on us plagues of which Egypt never dreamed. They were all as preventible as the great Plague of London [1664–5] and came solely because they had not been prevented. They were not undone by winning the war. The earth is still bursting with the dead bodies of the victors.

THE WICKED HALF CENTURY

It is difficult to say whether indifference and neglect are worse than false doctrine; but Heartbreak House and Horseback Hall unfortunately suffered from both. For half a century before the war civilization had been going to the devil very precipitately under the influence of a pseudo-science as disastrous as the blackest Calvinism. Calvinism taught that as we are predestinately saved or damned, nothing that we do can alter our destiny. Still, as Calvinism gave the individual no clue as to whether he had drawn a lucky number or an unlucky one, it left him a fairly strong interest in encouraging his hopes of salvation and allaying his fear of damnation by behaving as one of the elect might be expected to behave rather than as one of the reprobate. But in the middle of the XIX century naturalists and physicists assured the world, in the name of Science, that salvation and damnation are all nonsense, and that predestination is the central truth of religion, inasmuch as human beings are produced by their environment, their sins and good deeds being only a series of chemical and mechanical reactions over which they have no control. Such figments as mind, choice, purpose, conscience, will, and so forth, are, they taught, mere illusions, produced because they are useful in the continual struggle of the human machine to maintain its environment in a favorable condition, a process incidentally involving the ruthless destruction or subjection of its competitors for the supply (assumed to be limited) of subsistence available. We taught Prussia this religion; and Prussia bettered our instruction so effectively that we presently found ourselves confronted with the necessity of destroying Prussia to prevent Prussia destroying us. And that has just ended in each destroying the other to an extent doubtfully reparable in our time.

It may be asked how so imbecile and dangerous a creed ever came to be accepted by intelligent beings. I will answer that question more fully in my next volume of plays [*Back to Methuselah*, 1921], which will be entirely devoted to the subject. For the present I will only say that there were better reasons than the obvious one that such sham science as this opened a scientific career to very stupid men, and all the other careers to shameless rascals, provided they were industrious enough. It is true that this motive operated very powerfully; but when the new departure in scientific doctrine which is associated with the name of the great naturalist Charles Darwin began, it was not only a reaction against a barbarous pseudo-evangelical teleology intolerably obstructive to all scientific progress, but was accompanied, as it happened, by discoveries of extraordinary interest in physics, chemistry, and that lifeless method of evolution which its investigators called Natural Selection. Howbeit, there was only one result possible in the ethical sphere, and that was the banishment of conscience from human affairs, or, as Samuel Butler vehemently put it, "of mind from the universe."

HYPOCHONDRIA

Now Heartbreak House, with Butler and Bergson and Scott Haldane alongside Blake and the other major poets on its shelves (to say nothing of Wagner and the tone poets), was not so completely blinded by the doltish materialism of the laboratories as the uncultured world outside. But being an idle house it was a hypochondriacal house, always running after cures. It would stop eating meat, not on valid Shelleyan grounds, but in order to get rid of a bogey called Uric Acid; and it would actually let you pull all its teeth out to exorcize another demon named Pyorrhea. It was superstitious, and addicted to table-rapping, materialization séances, clairvoyance, palmistry, crystal-gazing and the like to such an extent that it may be doubted whether ever before in the history of the world did soothsayers, astrologers, and unregistered therapeutic specialists of all sorts flourish as they did during this half century of the drift to the abyss. The registered doctors and surgeons were hard put to it to compete with the unregistered. They were not clever enough to appeal to the imagination and sociability of the Heartbreakers by the arts of the actor, the orator, the poet, the winning conversationalist. They had to fall back coarsely on the terror of infection and death. They prescribed inoculations and operations. Whatever part of a human being could be cut out without necessarily killing him they cut out; and he often died (unnecessarily of course) in consequence. From such trifles as uvulas and tonsils they went on to ovaries and appendices until at last no one's inside was safe. They explained that the human intestine was too long, and that nothing could make a child of Adam healthy except short circuiting the pylorus [the opening between the stomach and the small intestine] by cutting a length out of the lower intestine and fastening it directly to the stomach. As their mechanist theory taught them that medicine was the business of the chemist's laboratory, and surgery of the carpenter's shop, and also that Science (by which they meant their practices) was so important that no consideration for the interests of any individual creature, whether frog or philosopher, much less the vulgar commonplaces of sentimental ethics, could weigh for a moment against the remotest off-chance of an addition to the body of scientific knowledge, they operated and vivisected and inoculated and lied on a stupendous scale, clamoring for and actually acquiring such legal powers over the bodies of their fellow citizens as neither king, pope, nor parliament dare ever have claimed. The Inquisition itself was a Liberal institution compared to the General Medical Council.

THOSE WHO DO NOT KNOW HOW TO LIVE MUST MAKE A MERIT OF DYING

Heartbreak House was far too lazy and shallow to extricate itself from this palace of evil enchantment. It rhapsodized about love; but it believed in cruelty. It was afraid of the cruel people; and it saw that cruelty was at least effective. Cruelty did things that made money, whereas Love did nothing but prove the soundness of Larochefoucauld's saying [in *Maximes*] that very few people would fall in love if they had never read about it. Heartbreak House, in short, did not know how to live, at which point all that was left to it was the boast that at least it knew how to die: a melancholy accomplishment which the outbreak of war presently gave it practically unlimited opportunities of displaying. Thus were the firstborn of Heartbreak House smitten; and the young, the innocent, the hopeful expiated the folly and worthlessness of their elders.

WAR DELIRIUM

Only those who have lived through a firstrate war, not in the field, but at home, and kept their heads, can possibly understand the bitterness of Shakespear and Swift, who both went through this experience. The horror of Peer Gynt in the madhouse, when the lunatics, exalted by illusions of splendid talent and visions of a dawning millennium, crowned him as their emperor, was tame in comparison. I do not know whether anyone really kept his head completely except those who had to keep it because they had to conduct the war at first hand. I should not have kept my own (as far as I did keep it) if I had not at once understood that as a scribe and speaker I too was under the most serious public obligation to keep my grip on realities; but this did not save me from a considerable degree of hyperæsthesia. There were of course some happy people to whom the war meant nothing: all political and general matters lying outside their little circle of interest. But the ordinary war-conscious civilian went mad, the main symptom being a conviction that the whole order of nature had been reversed. All foods, he felt, must now be adulterated. All schools must be closed. No advertisements must be sent to the newspapers, of which new editions must appear and be bought up every ten minutes. Traveling must be stopped, or, that being impossible, greatly hindered. All pretences about fine art and culture and the like must be flung off as an intolerable affectation; and the picture galleries and museums and schools at once occupied by war workers. The British Museum itself was saved only by a hairsbreadth. The sincerity of all this, and of much more which would not be believed if I chronicled it, may be established by one conclusive instance of the general craziness. Men were seized with the illusion that they could win the war by giving away money. And they not only subscribed millions to Funds of all sorts with no discoverable object, and to ridiculous voluntary organizations for doing what was plainly the business of the civil and military authorities, but actually handed out money to any thief in the street who had the presence of mind to pretend that he (or she) was "collecting" it for the annihilation of the enemy. Swindlers were emboldened to take offices; label themselves Anti-Enemy Leagues; and simply pocket the money that was heaped on them. Attractively dressed young women found that they had nothing to do but parade the streets, collecting-box in hand, and live gloriously on the profits. Many months elapsed before, as a first sign of returning sanity, the police swept an Anti-Enemy secretary into prison *pour encourager les autres* [as a warning to others], and the passionate penny collecting of the Flag Days was brought under some sort of regulation.[5]

MADNESS IN COURT

The demoralization did not spare the Law Courts. Soldiers were acquitted, even on fully proved indictments for wilful murder, until at last the judges and magistrates had to announce that what was called the Unwritten

---

5. The Commissioner of Police, in 1915, with the approval of the Home Secretary, promulgated regulations under the Streets Act of 1903 that gave him the power to issue or withhold permits for street solicitations, thus curbing unlawful collection of money for bogus charities. The regulations were effected on 12 August. The 'Anti-Enemy secretary' was Edward Chatterton, founder of the Anti-German League, charged in April 1916 with fraudulently converting trust money to his own use.

Law, which meant simply that a soldier could do what he liked with impunity in civil life, was not the law of the land, and that a Victoria Cross did not carry with it a perpetual plenary indulgence. Unfortunately the insanity of the juries and magistrates did not always manifest itself in indulgence. No person unlucky enough to be charged with any sort of conduct, however reasonable and salutary, that did not smack of war delirium had the slightest chance of acquittal. There were in the country, too, a certain number of people who had conscientious objections to war as criminal or unchristian. The Act of Parliament introducing Compulsory Military Service thoughtlessly exempted these persons, merely requiring them to prove the genuineness of their convictions. Those who did so were very ill-advised from the point of view of their own personal interest; for they were persecuted with savage logicality in spite of the law; whilst those who made no pretence of having any objection to war at all, and had not only had military training in Officers' Training Corps, but had proclaimed on public occasions that they were perfectly ready to engage in civil war on behalf of their political opinions, were allowed the benefit of the Act on the ground that they did not approve of this particular war. For the Christians there was no mercy. In cases where the evidence as to their being killed by ill treatment was so unequivocal that the verdict would certainly have been one of wilful murder had the prejudice of the coroner's jury been on the other side, their tormentors were gratuitously declared to be blameless. There was only one virtue, pugnacity: only one vice, pacifism. That is an essential condition of war; but the Government had not the courage to legislate accordingly; and its law was set aside for Lynch law.

The climax of legal lawlessness was reached in France. The greatest Socialist statesman in Europe, [Jean-Léon] Jaurès, was shot and killed by a gentleman who resented his efforts to avert the war. M. [Georges] Clemenceau[6] was shot by another gentleman of less popular opinions, and happily came off no worse than having to spend a precautionary couple of days in bed. The slayer of Jaurès was recklessly acquitted: the would-be

---

6. Jaurès: French political leader and journalist, leader of the French Socialist Party before the Great War. Editor of *La petite république*, in which he defended Dreyfus. Clemenceau: French leader of radical Republicans and newspaper publisher, who became Premier in 1906–9 and again in 1917–20, assuming as well the Cabinet position of Minister of War. He was shot by a young anarchist, Louis Cottin, on 19 February 1919, *en route* to a session of the Peace Conference. The bullet lodged between his ribs, not affecting any vital organs; his physicians decided not to operate. After ten days of rest he returned to his duties.

slayer of M. Clemenceau was carefully found guilty. There is no reason to doubt that the same thing would have happened in England if the war had begun with a successful attempt to assassinate Keir Hardie, and ended with an unsuccessful one to assassinate Mr Lloyd George.

THE LONG ARM OF WAR

The pestilence which is the usual accompaniment of war was called influenza. Whether it was really a war pestilence or not was made doubtful by the fact that it did its worst in places remote from the battlefields, notably on the west coast of North America and in India. But the moral pestilence, which was unquestionably a war pestilence, reproduced this phenomenon. One would have supposed that the war fever would have raged most furiously in the countries actually under fire, and that the others would be more reasonable. Belgium and Flanders, where over large districts literally not one stone was left upon another as the opposed armies drove each other back and forward over it after terrific preliminary bombardments, might have been pardoned for relieving their feelings more emphatically than by shrugging their shoulders and saying "*C'est la guerre.*" England, inviolate for so many centuries that the swoop of war on her homesteads had long ceased to be more credible than a return of the Flood, could hardly be expected to keep her temper sweet when she knew at last what it was to hide in cellars and underground railway stations, or lie quaking in bed, whilst bombs crashed, houses crumbled, and aircraft guns distributed shrapnel on friend and foe alike until certain shop windows in London, formerly full of fashionable hats, were filled with steel helmets. Slain and mutilated women and children, and burnt and wrecked dwellings, excuse a good deal of violent language, and produce a wrath on which many suns go down before it is appeased. Yet it was in the United States of America, where nobody slept the worse for the war, that the war fever went beyond all sense and reason. In European Courts there was vindictive illegality: in American Courts there was raving lunacy. It is not for me to chronicle the extravagances of an Ally: let some candid American do that. I can only say that to us sitting in our gardens in England, with the guns in France making themselves felt by a throb in the air as unmistakeable as an audible sound, or with tightening hearts studying the phases of the moon in London in their bearing on the chances whether our houses would be standing or ourselves alive next morning, the newspaper accounts of the sentences American Courts were passing on young girls and old men alike for the expression of opinions which were being uttered amid thundering applause before huge audiences in England, and the more private records of the methods by which the American War Loans were raised, were so amazing that they would put the guns and the possibilities of a raid clean out of our heads for the moment.

THE RABID WATCHDOGS OF LIBERTY

Not content with these rancorous abuses of the existing law, the war maniacs made a frantic rush to abolish all constitutional guarantees of liberty and well-being. The ordinary law was superseded by Acts under which newspapers were seized and their printing machinery destroyed by simple police raids *à la Russe*, and persons arrested and shot without any pretence of trial by jury or publicity of procedure or evidence. Though it was urgently necessary that production should be increased by the most scientific organization and economy of labor, and though no fact was better established than that excessive duration and intensity of toil reduces production heavily instead of increasing it, the factory laws were suspended, and men and women recklessly overworked until the loss of their efficiency became too glaring to be ignored. Remonstrances and warnings were met either with an accusation of pro-Germanism or the formula, "Remember that we are at war now." I have said that men assumed that war had reversed the order of nature, and that all was lost unless we did the exact opposite of everything we had found necessary and beneficial in peace. But the truth was worse than that. The war did not change men's minds in any such impossible way. What really happened was that the impact of physical death and destruction, the one reality that every fool can understand, tore off the masks of education, art, science, and religion from our ignorance and barbarism, and left us glorying grotesquely in the licence suddenly accorded to our vilest passions and most abject terrors. Ever since Thucydides wrote his history [*History of the Peloponnesian War*], it has been on record that when the angel of death sounds his trumpet the pretences of civilization are blown from men's heads into the mud like hats in a gust of wind. But when this scripture was fulfilled among us, the shock was not the less appalling because a few students of Greek history were not surprised by it. Indeed these students threw themselves into the orgy as shamelessly as the illiterate. The Christian priest joining in the war dance without even throwing off his cassock first, and the respectable school governor expelling the German professor with insult and bodily violence, and declaring that no English child should ever again be taught the language of Luther and Goethe, were kept in countenance by the most impudent repudiations of every decency of civilization and every lesson of political experience on the part of the very persons who, as university professors, historians, philosophers, and men of science, were the accredited custodians of culture. It was crudely natural, and perhaps necessary for recruiting purposes, that German militarism and German dynastic ambition should be painted by journalists and recruiters in black and red as European dangers (as in fact they are), leaving it to be inferred that our own militarism and our own political constitution are millennially democratic (which they certainly are not); but when it came to frantic denunciations of German chemistry, German biology, German poetry, German music, German literature, German philosophy, and even German engineering, as malignant abominations standing towards British and French chemistry and so forth in the relation of heaven to hell, it was clear that the utterers of such barbarous ravings had never really understood or cared for the arts and sciences they professed and were profaning, and were only the appallingly degenerate descendants of the men of the XVII and XVIII centuries who, recognizing no national frontiers in the great realm of the human mind, kept the European comity of that realm loftily and even ostentatiously above the rancors of the battlefield. Tearing the [Order of the] Garter from the Kaiser's leg, striking the German dukes from the roll of our peerage, changing the King's illustrious and historically appropriate surname[7] for that of a traditionless locality [from Saxe-Coburg-Gotha to Windsor, 1917], was not a very dignified business; but the erasure of German names from the British rolls of science and learning was a confession that in England the little respect paid to science and learning is only an affectation which hides a savage contempt for both. One felt that the figure of St George and the Dragon on our coinage should be replaced by that of the soldier driving his spear through Archimedes. But by that time there was no coinage: only paper money in which ten shillings called itself a pound as confidently as the people who were disgracing their country called themselves patriots.

---

7. For the American edition Shaw inserted after 'surname' a parenthetical explanation: 'for the war was the old war of Guelph against Ghibelline' and ended with 'locality', deleting the rest of the sentence.

THE SUFFERINGS OF THE SANE

The mental distress of living amid the obscene din of all these carmagnoles [French Revolutionary dances] and corobberies [warlike dances of Australian aborigines] was not the only burden that lay on sane people during the war. There was also the emotional strain, complicated by the offended economic sense, produced by the casualty lists. The stupid, the selfish, the narrowminded, the callous and unimaginative were spared a great deal. "Blood and destruction shall be so in use that mothers shall but smile when they behold their infants quartered by the hands of war" [*Julius Caesar*, III: i], was a Shakespearean prophecy that very nearly came true; for when nearly every house had a slaughtered son to mourn, we should all have gone quite out of our senses if we had taken our own and our friends' bereavements at their peace value. It became necessary to give them a false value; to proclaim the young life worthily and gloriously sacrificed to redeem the liberty of mankind, instead of to expiate the heedlessness and folly of their fathers, and expiate it in vain. We had even to assume that the parents and not the children had made the sacrifice, until at last the comic papers were driven to satirize fat old men, sitting comfortably in club chairs, and boasting of the sons they had "given" to their country.

No one grudged these anodynes to acute personal grief; but they only embittered those who knew that the young men were having their teeth set on edge because their parents had eaten sour political grapes. Then think of the young men themselves! Many of them had no illusions about the policy that led to the war: they went clearsighted to a horribly repugnant duty. Men essentially gentle and essentially wise, with really valuable work in hand, laid it down voluntarily and spent months forming fours in the barrack yard, and stabbing sacks of straw in the public eye, so that they might go out to kill and maim men as gentle as themselves. These men, who were perhaps, as a class, our most efficient soldiers (Frederick Keeling,[8] for example), were not duped for a moment by the hypocritical melodrama that consoled and stimulated the others. They left their creative work to

---

8. Young Fabian Socialist killed in action in 1916. After reading his posthumously published *Letters and Recollections* (1918) Shaw informed Beatrice Webb: 'I have been reading Keeling with great interest. His intellectual temperament was remarkably like my own in many ways. . . . Pity he was shot: he was the only real Shavio-Webbite we produced [in the Fabian Society].' (TLS, 21 November 1918: British Library of Political and Economic Science.)

drudge at destruction, exactly as they would have left it to take their turn at the pumps in a sinking ship. They did not, like some of the conscientious objectors, hold back because the ship had been neglected by its officers and scuttled by its wreckers. The ship had to be saved, even if Newton had to leave his fluxions and Michael Angelo his marbles to save it; so they threw away the tools of their beneficent and ennobling trades, and took up the bloodstained bayonet and the murderous bomb, forcing themselves to pervert their divine instinct for perfect artistic execution to the effective handling of these diabolical things, and their economic faculty for organization to the contriving of ruin and slaughter. For it gave an ironic edge to their tragedy that the very talents they were forced to prostitute made the prostitution not only effective, but even interesting; so that some of them were rapidly promoted, and found themselves actually becoming artists in war, with a growing relish for it, like Napoleon and all the other scourges of mankind, in spite of themselves. For many of them there was not even this consolation. They "stuck it," and hated it, to the end.

EVIL IN THE THRONE OF GOOD

This distress of the gentle was so acute that those who shared it in civil life, without having to shed blood with their own hands, or witness destruction with their own eyes, hardly care to obtrude their own woes. Nevertheless, even when sitting at home in safety, it was not easy for those who had to write and speak about the war to throw away their highest conscience, and deliberately work to a standard of inevitable evil instead of to the ideal of life more abundant. I can answer for at least one person who found the change from the wisdom of Jesus and St Francis to the morals of Richard III and the madness of Don Quixote extremely irksome. But that change had to be made; and we are all the worse for it, except those for whom it was not really a change at all, but only a relief from hypocrisy.

Think, too, of those who, though they had neither to write nor to fight, and had no children of their own to lose, yet knew the inestimable loss to the world of four years of the life of a generation wasted on destruction. Hardly one of the epoch-making works of the human mind might not have been aborted or destroyed by taking their authors away from their natural work for four critical years. Not only were Shakespears and Platos being killed outright; but many of the best harvests of the survivors had to be sown in the barren soil of the trenches. And this was no mere British consideration. To the truly civilized man, to the good European, the slaughter of the German youth was as disastrous as the slaughter of the English. Fools exulted in "German losses." They were our losses as well. Imagine exulting in the death of Beethoven because Bill Sikes [a murderer and bully in Dickens's *Oliver Twist*] dealt him his death blow!

STRAINING AT THE GNAT AND SWALLOWING THE CAMEL

But most people could not comprehend these sorrows. There was a frivolous exultation in death for its own sake, which was at bottom an inability to realize that the deaths were real deaths and not stage ones. Again and again, when an air raider dropped a bomb which tore a child and its mother limb from limb, the people who saw it, though they had been reading with great cheerfulness of thousands of such happenings day after day in their newspapers, suddenly burst into furious imprecations on "the Huns" as murderers, and shrieked for savage and satisfying vengeance. At such moments it became clear that the deaths they had not seen meant no more to them than the mimic deaths of the cinema screen. Sometimes it was not necessary that death should be actually witnessed: it had only to take place under circumstances of sufficient novelty and proximity to bring it home almost as sensationally and effectively as if it had been actually visible.

For example, in the spring of 1915 there was an appalling slaughter of our young soldiers at Neuve Chapelle [Pas-de-Calais, France] and at the Gallipoli[9] landing. I will not go so far as to say that our civilians were delighted to have such exciting news to read at breakfast. But I cannot pretend that I noticed either in the papers, or in general intercourse, any feeling beyond the usual one that the cinema show at the front was going splendidly, and that our boys were the bravest of the brave. Suddenly there came the news that an Atlantic liner, the *Lusitania*, had been torpedoed [on 7 May 1915], and that several well-known first-class passengers, including a famous theatrical manager and the author of a popular farce,[10] had been

9. Winston Churchill conceived a plan to dislodge the Turks from their position on the Gallipoli Peninsula in European Turkey. Extending from February 1915 to January 1916, the campaign became one of the most calamitous Allied efforts of the war, with some 55,000 Allied men lost and the main objectives not attained.
10. Charles Frohman, American-born theatrical manager, presented plays by Wilde, Barrie, Pinero and Maugham with equal success in England and America. Charles Klein, British-born American playwright, was the author of that season's

drowned, among others. The others included Sir Hugh Lane;[11] but as he had only laid the country under great obligations in the sphere of the fine arts, no great stress was laid on that loss.

Immediately an amazing frenzy swept through the country. Men who up to that time had kept their heads now lost them utterly. "Killing saloon passengers! What next?" was the essence of the whole agitation; but it is far too trivial a phrase to convey the faintest notion of the rage which possessed us. To me, with my mind full of the hideous cost of Neuve Chapelle, Ypres,[12] and the Gallipoli landing, the fuss about the *Lusitania* seemed almost a heartless impertinence, though I was well acquainted personally with the three best-known victims [including the American writer and editor Elbert Hubbard], and understood, better perhaps than most people, the misfortune of the death of Lane. I even found a grim satisfaction, very intelligible to all soldiers, in the fact that the civilians who found the war such splendid British sport should get a sharp taste of what it was to the actual combatants. I expressed my impatience very freely, and found that my very straightforward and natural feeling in the matter was received as a monstrous and heartless paradox. When I asked those who gaped at me whether they had anything to say about the holocaust of Festubert,[13] they gaped wider than before, having totally forgotten it, or rather, having never realized it. They were not heartless any more than I was; but the big catastrophe was too big for them to grasp, and the little one had been just the right size for them. I was not surprised. Have I not seen a public body for just the same reason pass a vote for £30,000 without a word, and then spend three special meetings, prolonged into the

---

London success *Potash and Perlmutter*, previously produced in New York for 457 performances (1913).

11. Nephew of Lady Gregory, he was director of the National Gallery of Ireland and honorary director of the Dublin Municipal Art Gallery. He had recently presented a modern art collection to the City of Dublin.

12. Ypres, a town in north-west Belgium, was the scene of three particularly fierce battles, in October–November 1914, in April–May 1915 and in the autumn of 1917. It remained in English hands, but was completely destroyed. Neuve Chapelle was involved in the second battle: from that village General Sir Douglas Haig launched his offensive.

13. This battle in Normandy began four days after the sinking of the *Lusitania*. In sixteen days the British and French advanced three quarters of a mile at the price of 250,000 lives. The Germans lost 213,000 men. In the sinking of the *Lusitania* well over half of the 2,000 passengers and crew were lost.

night, over an item of seven shillings for refreshments?

LITTLE MINDS AND BIG BATTLES

Nobody will be able to understand the vagaries of public feeling during the war unless they bear constantly in mind that the war in its entire magnitude did not exist for the average civilian. He could not conceive even a battle, much less a campaign. To the suburbs the war was nothing but a suburban squabble. To the miner and navvy it was only a series of bayonet fights between German champions and English ones. The enormity of it was quite beyond most of us. Its episodes had to be reduced to the dimensions of a railway accident or a shipwreck before it could produce any effect on our minds at all. To us the ridiculous bombardments of Scarborough [Yorkshire] and Ramsgate [Kent] were colossal tragedies, and the battle of Jutland[14] a mere ballad. The words "after thorough artillery preparation" in the news from the front meant nothing to us; but when our seaside trippers learned that an elderly gentleman at breakfast in a weekend marine hotel had been interrupted by a bomb dropping into his eggcup, their wrath and horror knew no bounds. They declared that this would put a new spirit into the army, and had no suspicion that the soldiers in the trenches roared with laughter over it for days, and told each other that it would do the blighters at home good to have a taste of what the army was up against. Sometimes the smallness of view was pathetic. A man would work at home regardless of the call "to make the world safe for democracy."[15] His brother would be killed at the front. Immediately he would throw up his work and take up the war as a family blood feud against the Germans. Sometimes it was comic. A wounded man, entitled to his discharge, would return to the trenches with a grim determination to find the Hun who had wounded him and pay him out for it.

It is impossible to estimate what proportion of us, in khaki or out of it, grasped the war and its political antecedents as a whole in the light of any philosophy of history or knowledge of what war is. I doubt whether it was as high as our proportion of higher mathematicians. But there can be no doubt that it was prodigiously outnumbered by the comparatively ignorant

14. Greatest naval battle of the war, in the North Sea, from 31 May to 1 June 1916.
15. From Woodrow Wilson's address to Congress requesting a declaration of war, 2 April 1917.

and childish. Remember that these people had to be stimulated to make the sacrifices demanded by the war, and that this could not be done by appeals to a knowledge which they did not possess, and a comprehension of which they were incapable. When the armistice at last set me free to tell the truth about the war at the following general election, a soldier said to a candidate whom I was supporting "If I had known all that in 1914, they would never have got me into khaki." And that, of course, was precisely why it had been necessary to stuff him with a romance that any diplomatist would have laughed at. Thus the natural confusion of ignorance was increased by a deliberately propagated confusion of nursery bogey stories and melodramatic nonsense, which at last overreached itself and made it impossible to stop the war before we had not only achieved the triumph of vanquishing the German army and thereby overthrowing its militarist monarchy, but made the very serious mistake of ruining the centre of Europe, a thing that no sane European State could afford to do.

The Dumb Capables and the Noisy Incapables

Confronted with this picture of insensate delusion and folly, the critical reader will immediately counterplead that England all this time was conducting a war which involved the organization of several millions of fighting men and of the workers who were supplying them with provisions, munitions, and transport, and that this could not have been done by a mob of hysterical ranters. This is fortunately true. To pass from the newspaper offices and political platforms and club fenders and suburban drawing rooms to the Army and the munition factories was to pass from Bedlam to the busiest and sanest of workaday worlds. It was to rediscover England, and find solid ground for the faith of those who still believed in her. But a necessary condition of this efficiency was that those who were efficient should give all their time to their business and leave the rabble raving to its hearts' content. Indeed the raving was useful to the efficient, because, as it was always wide of the mark, it often distracted attention very conveniently from operations that would have been defeated or hindered by publicity. A precept which I endeavored vainly to popularize early in the war, "If you have anything to do go and do it: if not, for heaven's sake get out of the way," was only half carried out. Certainly the capable people went and did it; but the incapables would by no means get out of the way: they fussed and bawled and were only prevented from getting very seriously into the way by the blessed fact that they never knew where the way was. Thus whilst all the efficiency of England was silent and invisible, all its imbecility was deafening the heavens with its clamor and blotting out the sun with its dust. It was also unfortunately intimidating the Government by its blusterings into using the irresistible powers of the State to intimidate the sensible people, thus enabling a despicable minority of would-be lynchers to set up a reign of terror which could at any time have been broken by a single stern word from a responsible minister. But our ministers had not that sort of courage: neither Heartbreak House nor Horseback Hall had bred it, much less the suburbs. When matters at last came to the looting of shops by criminals under patriotic pretexts, it was the police force and not the Government that put its foot down. There was even one deplorable moment, during the submarine scare, in which the Government yielded to a childish cry for the maltreatment of naval prisoners of war, and, to our great disgrace, was forced by the enemy to behave itself.[16] And yet behind all this public blundering and misconduct and futile mischief, the effective England was carrying on with the most formidable capacity and activity. The ostensible England was making the empire sick with its incontinences, its ignorances, its ferocities, its panics, and its endless and intolerable blarings of Allied national anthems in season and out. The esoteric England

16. On 4 February 1915 the German Government declared the waters surrounding the British islands a war zone, warning that all belligerent ships encountered within that zone, as well as neutral ships, would be subject to submarine attack. The scare resulted in pressure being put upon the British Government to 'punish' German submarine prisoners of war. *The Times*, on 3 April, reported that the German Government, communicating through the United States, had protested against the British Admiralty's decision 'not to accord to officers and crews of German submarines who have become prisoners the treatment due to them as prisoners of war.' It added the threat that 'for each member of the crew of a submarine made prisoner a British army officer held prisoner of war in Germany will receive corresponding harsher treatment.' In his reply Lord Grey took a strong defensive posture, insisting that, as 'they were engaged before capture in sinking innocent British and neutral merchant ships and in "wantonly killing non-combatants"', they 'cannot therefore be regarded as honourable opponents, but as persons who, at the orders of their Government, have offended against the law of nations and common humanity.' The German people, much agitated, called for reprisals, and a number of British officer prisoners of war were imprisoned in solitary confinement. After an announcement by A. J. Balfour, First Lord of the Admiralty, on 9 June, that British policy had been revised so that enemy submarine crews would not receive differential treatment, the officers in Germany were released from special treatment and removed to concentration camps.

was proceeding irresistibly to the conquest of Europe.

THE PRACTICAL BUSINESS MEN

From the beginning the useless people set up a shriek for "practical business men." By this they meant men who had become rich by placing their personal interests before those of the country, and measuring the success of every activity by the pecuniary profit it brought to them and to those on whom they depended for their supplies of capital. The pitiable failure of some conspicuous samples from the first batch we tried of these poor devils helped to give the whole public side of the war an air of monstrous and hopeless farce. They proved not only that they were useless for public work, but that in a well-ordered nation they would never have been allowed to control private enterprize.

HOW THE FOOLS SHOUTED THE WISE MEN DOWN

Thus, like a fertile country flooded with mud, England shewed no sign of her greatness in the days when she was putting forth all her strength to save herself from the worst consequences of her littleness. Most of the men of action, occupied to the last hour of their time with urgent practical work, had to leave to idler people, or to professional rhetoricians, the presentation of the war to the reason and imagination of the country and the world in speeches, poems, manifestos, picture posters, and newspaper articles. I have had the privilege of hearing some of our ablest commanders talking about their work; and I have shared the common lot of reading the accounts of that work given to the world by the newspapers. No two experiences could be more different. But in the end the talkers obtained a dangerous ascendancy over the rank and file of the men of action; for though the great men of action are always inveterate talkers and often very clever writers, and therefore cannot have their minds formed for them by others, the average man of action, like the average fighter with the bayonet, can give no account of himself in words even to himself, and is apt to pick up and accept what he reads about himself and other people in the papers, except when the writer is rash enough to commit himself on technical points. It was not uncommon during the war to hear a soldier, or a civilian engaged on war work, describing events within his own experience that reduced to utter absurdity the ravings and maunderings of his daily paper, and yet echo the opinions of that paper like a parrot. Thus, to escape from the prevailing confusion and folly, it was not enough to seek the company of the ordinary man of action: one had to get into contact with the master spirits. This was a privilege which only a handful of people could enjoy. For the unprivileged citizen there was no escape. To him the whole country seemed mad, futile, silly, incompetent, with no hope of victory except the hope that the enemy might be just as mad. Only by very resolute reflection and reasoning could he reassure himself that if there was nothing more solid beneath these appalling appearances the war could not possibly have gone on for a single day without a total breakdown of its organization.

THE MAD ELECTION

Happy were the fools and the thoughtless men of action in those days. The worst of it was that the fools were very strongly represented in parliament, as fools not only elect fools, but can persuade men of action to elect them too. The election [14 December 1918] that immediately followed the armistice was perhaps the maddest that has ever taken place. Soldiers who had done voluntary and heroic service in the field were defeated by persons who had apparently never run a risk or spent a farthing that they could avoid, and who even had in the course of the election to apologize publicly for bawling Pacifist or Pro-German at their opponent. Party leaders seek such followers, who can always be depended on to walk tamely into the lobby at the party whip's orders, provided the leader will make their seats safe for them by the process which was called, in derisive reference to the war rationing system, "giving them the coupon." Other incidents were so grotesque that I cannot mention them without enabling the reader to identify the parties, which would not be fair, as they were no more to blame than thousands of others who must necessarily be nameless. The general result was patently absurd; and the electorate, disgusted at its own work, instantly recoiled to the opposite extreme, and cast out all the coupon candidates at the earliest bye-elections by equally silly majorities. But the mischief of the general election could not be undone; and the Government had not only to pretend to abuse its European victory as it had promised, but actually to do it by starving the enemies who had thrown down their arms. It had, in short, won the election by pledging itself to be thriftlessly wicked, cruel, and vindictive; and it did not find it as easy to escape from this pledge as it had from nobler ones. The end, as I write, is not yet; but it is clear that this thoughtless savagery will recoil on the heads of the Allies so severely that we shall be forced by the sternest necessity to take up our share of healing the Europe we have wounded almost to death instead of attempting to complete her destruction.

THE YAHOO AND THE ANGRY APE

Contemplating this picture of a state of mankind so recent that no denial of its truth is possible, one understands Shakespear comparing Man to an angry ape, Swift describing him as a Yahoo rebuked by the superior virtue of the horse, and Wellington declaring that the British can behave themselves neither in victory nor defeat.[17] Yet none of the three had seen war as we have seen it. Shakespear blamed great men, saying that "Could great men thunder as Jove himself does Jove would ne'er be quiet; for every pelting petty officer would use his heaven for thunder: nothing but thunder!" [*Measure for Measure*, II: ii] What would Shakespear have said if he had seen something far more destructive than thunder in the hand of every village laborer, and found on the Messines Ridge the craters of the nineteen volcanoes that were let loose there at the touch of a finger that might have been a child's finger without the result being a whit less ruinous?[18] Shakespear may have seen a Stratford cottage struck by one of Jove's thunderbolts, and have helped to extinguish the lighted thatch and clear away the bits of the broken chimney. What would he have said if he had seen Ypres as it is now, or returned to Stratford, as French peasants are returning to their homes today, to find the old familiar signpost inscribed "To Stratford, 1 mile," and at the end of the mile nothing but some holes in the ground and a fragment of a broken churn here and there? Would not the spectacle of the angry ape endowed with powers of destruction that Jove never pretended to, have beggared even his command of words?

17. General Lord Roberts in *The Rise of Wellington* (1895) quotes the Duke as writing (probably to Lord Castlereagh, the War Secretary) after the capture of Oporto (1809) in the Peninsular War: 'I have long been of opinion that a British army could bear neither success nor failure.' To Castlereagh he wrote on 17 June 1809: 'Take my word for it, that either defeat or success would dissolve us' (*Dispatches of Field Marshal the Duke of Wellington*, 12 vols., 1834–8).
18. The ridge dominated the plain east of Ypres. British tunnelling companies drove nineteen shafts into it, packing the chambers at the ends with gigantic charges, which they detonated on 7 June 1917.

And yet, what is there to say except that war puts a strain on human nature that breaks down the better half of it, and makes the worse half a diabolical virtue? Better for us if it broke it down altogether; for then the warlike way out of our difficulties would be barred to us, and we should take greater care not to get into them. In truth, it is, as Byron said, "not difficult to die" [*Manfred*, III: iv], and enormously difficult to live: that explains why, at bottom, peace is not only better than war, but infinitely more arduous. Did any hero of the war face the glorious risk of death more bravely than the traitor Bolo[19] faced the ignominious certainty of it? Bolo taught us all how to die: can we say that he taught us all how to live? Hardly a week passes now without some soldier who braved death in the field so recklessly that he was decorated or specially commended for it, being haled before our magistrates for having failed to resist the paltriest temptations of peace, with no better excuse than the old one that "a man must live." Strange that one who, sooner than do honest work, will sell his honor for a bottle of wine, a visit to the theatre, and an hour with a strange woman, all obtained by passing a worthless cheque, could yet stake his life on the most desperate chances of the battlefield! Does it not seem as if, after all, the glory of death were cheaper than the glory of life? If it is not easier to attain, why do so many more men attain it? At all events it is clear that the kingdom of the Prince of Peace has not yet become the kingdom of this world. His attempts at invasion have been resisted far more fiercely than the Kaiser's. Successful as that resistance has been, it has piled up a sort of National Debt that is not the less oppressive because we have no figures for it and do not intend to pay it. A blockade that cuts off "the grace of our Lord" is in the long run less bearable than the blockades which merely cut off raw materials; and against that blockade our Armada is impotent. In the blockader's house, he has assured us, there are many mansions; but I am afraid they do not include either Heartbreak House or Horseback Hall.

19. Paul Bolo, a financial manipulator and confidence trickster, was charged in France with dealing with the enemy in wartime, after receiving hundreds of thousands of pounds sterling in England from the Germans in 1916. With this he created a movement of opinion in the French press favourable to the enemy, in an effort by Germany to obtain a separate peace with France, thus to conquer Britain with greater ease. Bolo went nonchalantly to his death by firing squad on 17 April 1918.

PLAGUE ON BOTH YOUR HOUSES!

Meanwhile the Bolshevist picks and petards are at work on the foundations of both buildings; and though the Bolshevists may be buried in the ruins, their deaths will not save the edifices. Unfortunately they can be built again. Like Doubting Castle, they have been demolished many times by successive Greathearts, and rebuilt by Simple, Sloth, and Presumption, by Feeble Mind and Much Afraid, and by all the jurymen of Vanity Fair. Another generation of "secondary education" at our ancient public schools and the cheaper institutions that ape them will be quite sufficient to keep the two going until the next war.

For the instruction of that generation I leave these pages as a record of what civilian life was during the war: a matter on which history is usually silent. Fortunately it was a very short war. It is true that the people who thought it could not last more than six months were very signally refuted by the event. As Sir Douglas Haig has pointed out, its Waterloos lasted months instead of hours.[20] But there would have been nothing surprising in its lasting thirty years. If it had not been for the fact that the blockade achieved the amazing feat of starving out Europe, which it could not possibly have done had Europe been properly organized for war, or even for peace, the war would have lasted until the belligerents were so tired of it that they could no longer be compelled to compel themselves to go on with it. Considering its magnitude, the war of 1914–18 will certainly be classed as the shortest in history. The end came so suddenly that the combatants literally stumbled over it; and yet it came a full year later than it should have come if the belligerents had not been far too afraid of oneanother to face the situation sensibly. Germany, having failed to provide for the war she began, failed again to surrender before she was dangerously exhausted. Her opponents, equally improvident, went as much too close to bankruptcy as Germany to starvation. It was a bluff at which both were bluffed. And, with the usual irony of war, it remains doubtful whether Germany and Russia, the defeated, will not be the gainers; for the victors

---

20. In his final despatch, 21 March 1919, Haig wrote: 'The launching and destruction of Napoleon's last reserves at Waterloo was a matter of minutes. In this World War the great sortie of the beleaguered German Armies, commenced on the 21st March, 1918, lasted for four months, yet it represents a corresponding stage in a single colossal battle' (*Sir Douglas Haig's Despatches*, 1919, p. 320).

are already busy fastening on themselves the chains they have struck from the limbs of the vanquished.

How the Theatre Fared

Let us now contract our view rather violently from the European theatre of war to the theatre in which the fights are sham fights, and the slain, rising the moment the curtain has fallen, go comfortably home to supper after washing off their rosepink wounds. It is nearly twenty years since I was last obliged to introduce a play in the form of a book [*Three Plays for Puritans*, 1901] for lack of an opportunity of presenting it in its proper mode by a performance in a theatre. The war has thrown me back on this expedient. Heartbreak House has not yet reached the stage [it was first presented in New York on 10 November 1920 and in England on 18 November 1921]. I have withheld it because the war has completely upset the economic conditions which formerly enabled serious drama to pay its way in London. The change is not in the theatres nor in the management of them, nor in the authors and actors, but in the audiences. For four years the London theatres were crowded every night with thousands of soldiers on leave from the front. These soldiers were not seasoned London playgoers. A childish experience of my own gave me a clue to their condition. When I was a small boy I was taken to the opera. I did not then know what an opera was, though I could whistle a good deal of opera music. I had seen in my mother's album photographs of all the great opera singers, mostly in evening dress. In the theatre I found myself before a gilded balcony filled with persons in evening dress whom I took to be the opera singers. I picked out one massive dark lady as [the contralto Marietta] Alboni, and wondered how soon she would stand up and sing. I was puzzled by the fact that I was made to sit with my back to the singers instead of facing them. When the curtain went up, my astonishment and delight were unbounded.

The Soldier at the Theatre Front

In 1915 I saw in the theatres men in khaki in just the same predicament. To everyone who had my clue to their state of mind it was evident that they had never been in a theatre before and did not know what it was. At one of our great variety theatres I sat beside a young officer, not at all a rough specimen, who, even when the curtain rose and enlightened him as to the place where he had to look for his entertainment, found the dramatic part of it utterly incomprehensible. He did not know how to play his part of the game. He could understand the people on the stage singing and dancing and performing gymnastic feats. He not only understood but intensely enjoyed an artist who imitated cocks crowing and pigs squeaking. But the people who pretended that they were somebody else, and that the painted picture behind them was real, bewildered him. In his presence I realized how very sophisticated the natural man has to become before the conventions of the theatre can be easily acceptable, or the purpose of the drama obvious to him.

Well, from the moment when the routine of leave for our soldiers was established, such novices, accompanied by damsels (called flappers) often as innocent as themselves, crowded the theatres to the doors. It was hardly possible at first to find stuff crude enough to nurse them on. The best music-hall comedians ransacked their memories for the oldest quips and the most childish antics to avoid carrying the military spectators out of their depth. I believe that this was a mistake as far as the novices were concerned. Shakespear, or the dramatized histories of George Barnwell, Maria Marten, or the Demon Barber of Fleet Street,[21] would probably have been quite popular with them. But the novices were only a minority after all. The cultivated soldier, who in time of peace would look at nothing theatrical except the most advanced post-Ibsen plays in the most artistic settings, found himself, to his own astonishment, thirsting for silly jokes, dances, and brainlessly sensuous exhibitions of pretty girls. The author of some of the most grimly serious plays of our time [St John Ervine] told me that after enduring the trenches for months without a glimpse of the female of his species, it gave him an entirely innocent but delightful pleasure merely to see a flapper. The reaction from the battlefield produced a condition of hyperæsthesia in which all the theatrical values were altered. Trivial things gained intensity and stale things novelty. The actor, instead of having to coax his audiences out of the boredom which had driven them to the theatre in an ill humor to seek some sort of distraction, had only to exploit the bliss of smiling men who were no longer under fire and under military discipline, but actually clean and comfortable and in a mood to be pleased with anything and everything that a bevy of pretty girls and a funny man,

---

21. All of these plays are popular melodramas: *The London Merchant; or, the History of George Barnwell* (1731) by George Lillo; *Maria Marten; or, the Murder in the Red Barn* (c. 1830), author unknown; *Sweeney Todd; or, the Fiend of Fleet Street* (1847) by Dibdin Pitt.

or even a bevy of girls pretending to be pretty and a man pretending to be funny, could do for them.

Then could be seen every night in the theatres old-fashioned farcical comedies, in which a bedroom, with four doors on each side and a practicable window in the middle, was understood to resemble exactly the bedroom in the flats beneath and above, all three inhabited by couples consumed with jealousy. When these people came home drunk at night; mistook their neighbor's flats for their own; and in due course got into the wrong beds, it was not only the novices who found the resulting complications and scandals exquisitely ingenious and amusing, nor their equally verdant flappers who could not help squealing in a manner that astonished the oldest performers when the gentleman who had just come in drunk through the window pretended to undress, and allowed glimpses of his naked person to be descried from time to time. Men who had just read the news that [Sir] Charles Wyndham[22] was dying, and were thereby sadly reminded of [James Albery's] Pink Dominos [1877] and the torrent of farcical comedies that followed it in his heyday until every trick of that trade had become so stale that the laughter they provoked turned to loathing: these veterans also, when they returned from the field, were as much pleased by what they knew to be stale and foolish as the novices by what they thought fresh and clever.

COMMERCE IN THE THEATRE

Wellington said that an army moves on its belly [in Philip Henry's *Notes of Conversations with the Duke of Wellington*]. So does a London theatre. Before a man acts he must eat. Before he performs plays he must pay rent. In London we have no theatres for the welfare of the people: they are all for the sole purpose of producing the utmost obtainable rent for the proprietor. If the twin flats and twin beds produce a guinea more than Shakespear, out goes Shakespear, and in come the twin flats and the twin beds.[23] If the brainless bevy of pretty girls and the funny man outbid Mozart, out goes Mozart.

22. Popular actor-manager, a singularly fine light comedian, installed for years in London's Criterion Theatre.
23. The popular American farce *Twin Beds* (1914), by Salisbury Field and Margaret Mayo, was produced in London (1918) as *Be Careful, Baby*.

Unser [Our] Shakespear

Before the war an effort was made to remedy this by establishing a national theatre in celebration of the tercentenary of the death of Shakespear. A committee was formed; and all sorts of illustrious and influential persons lent their names to a grand appeal to our national culture. My play, The Dark Lady of the Sonnets, was one of the incidents of that appeal. After some years of effort the result was a single handsome subscription [£70,000] from a German gentleman [Sir Carl Meyer]. Like the celebrated swearer in the anecdote when the cart containing all his household goods lost its tailboard at the top of the hill and let its contents roll in ruin to the bottom, I can only say, "I cannot do justice to this situation," and let it pass without another word.

The Higher Drama put out of Action

The effect of the war on the London theatres may now be imagined. The beds and the bevies drove every higher form of art out of it. Rents went up to an unprecedented figure. At the same time prices doubled everywhere except at the theatre payboxes, and raised the expenses of management to such a degree that unless the houses were quite full every night, profit was impossible. Even bare solvency could not be attained without a very wide popularity. Now what had made serious drama possible to a limited extent before the war was that a play could pay its way even if the theatre were only half full until Saturday and three-quarters full then. A manager who was an enthusiast and a desperately hard worker, with an occasional grant-in-aid from an artistically disposed millionaire, and a due proportion of those rare and happy accidents by which plays of the higher sort turn out to be potboilers as well, could hold out for some years, by which time a relay might arrive in the person of another enthusiast. Thus and not otherwise occurred that remarkable revival of the British drama at the beginning of the century which made my own career as a playwright possible in England. In America I had already established myself, not as part of the ordinary theatre system, but in association with the exceptional genius of Richard Mansfield. In Germany and Austria I had no difficulty: the system of publicly aided theatres there, Court and Municipal, kept drama of the kind I dealt in alive; so that I was indebted to the Emperor of Austria for magnificent productions of my works at a time when the sole official attention paid me by the British Court was the announcement to the English-speaking world that certain plays of mine [*Mrs Warren's Profession, The Shewing-up of Blanco Posnet, Press Cuttings*] were unfit for public performance, a substantial set-off against this being that the British Court, in the course of its private playgoing,[24] paid no regard to the bad character given me by the chief officer [Lord Chamberlain] of its household.

Howbeit, the fact that my plays effected a lodgment on the London stage, and were presently followed by the plays of Granville Barker, Gilbert Murray, John Masefield, St John Hankin, Laurence Housman, Arnold Bennett, John Galsworthy, John Drinkwater,[25] and others which would in the XIX century have stood rather less chance of production at a London theatre than the Dialogues of Plato, not to mention revivals of the ancient Athenian drama, and a restoration to the stage of Shakespear's plays as he wrote them, was made economically possible solely by a supply of theatres which could hold nearly twice as much money as it cost to rent and maintain them. In such theatres work appealing to a relatively small class of cultivated persons, and therefore attracting only from half to three-quarters as many spectators as the more popular pastimes, could nevertheless keep going in the hands of young adventurers who were doing it for its own sake, and had not yet been forced by advancing age and responsibilities to consider the commercial value of their time and energy too closely. The war struck this foundation away in the manner I have just described. The expenses of running the cheapest west-end theatres rose to a sum which exceeded by twentyfive per cent the utmost that the higher drama can, as an ascertained matter of fact, be depended on to draw. Thus the higher drama, which has never really been a commercially sound speculation, now

24. Edward VII, when Prince of Wales, saw *Arms and the Man* at the Avenue Theatre in 1894. A decade later, as King, he attended a special matinée (Shaw having barred a Command Performance) of *John Bull's Other Island*. Shortly afterwards his son, the Prince of Wales (who became George V in 1910), slipped into the Court Theatre for a private view of the same production. Queen Alexandra attended *You Never Can Tell* at the Court Theatre in 1906, as did the Prince of Wales on 14 July 1906. Alexandra accompanied Edward VII to a performance of *The Devil's Disciple* in the autumn of 1907.
25. Shaw has in mind such plays as Granville Barker's *The Madras House* (1910), Murray's adaptation of Euripides' *The Trojan Women* (1905), Masefield's *The Tragedy of Nan* (1909), Hankin's *The Return of the Prodigal* (1907), Housman's and Granville Barker's *Prunella* (1904), Bennett's *Milestones* (with Edward Knoblock) (1912), Galsworthy's *Justice* (1910) and Drinkwater's *Abraham Lincoln* (1918).

became an impossible one. Accordingly, attempts are being made to provide a refuge for it in suburban theatres in London and repertory theatres in the provinces. But at the moment when the army has at last disgorged the survivors of the gallant band of dramatic pioneers whom it swallowed, they find that the economic conditions which formerly made their work no worse than precarious now put it out of the question altogether, as far as the west end of London is concerned.

CHURCH AND THEATRE

I do not suppose many people care particularly. We are not brought up to care; and a sense of the national importance of the theatre is not born in mankind: the natural man, like so many of the soldiers at the beginning of the war, does not know what a theatre is. But please note that all these soldiers who did not know what a theatre was, knew what a church was. And they had been taught to respect churches. Nobody had ever warned them against a church as a place where frivolous women paraded in their best clothes; where stories of improper females like Potiphar's wife, and erotic poetry like the Song of Songs, were read aloud; where the sensuous and sentimental music of Schubert, Mendelssohn, Gounod, and Brahms was more popular than severe music by greater composers; where the prettiest sort of pretty pictures of pretty saints assailed the imagination and senses through stained-glass windows; and where sculpture and architecture came to the help of painting. Nobody ever reminded them that these things had sometimes produced such developments of erotic idolatry that men who were not only enthusiastic amateurs of literature, painting, and music, but famous practitioners of them, had actually exulted when mobs and even regular troops under express command had mutilated church statues, smashed church windows, wrecked church organs, and torn up the sheets from which the church music was read and sung. When they saw broken statues in churches, they were told that this was the work of wicked godless rioters, instead of, as it was, the work partly of zealots bent on driving the world, the flesh, and the devil out of the temple, and partly of insurgent men who had become intolerably poor because the temple had become a den of thieves. But all the sins and perversions that were so carefully hidden from them in the history of the Church were laid on the shoulders of the Theatre: that stuffy, uncomfortable place of penance in which we suffer so much inconvenience on the slenderest chance of gaining a scrap of food for our starving souls. When the Germans bombed the

Cathedral of Rheims[26] the world rang with the horror of the sacrilege. When they bombed the Little Theatre in the Adelphi [4 September 1917], and narrowly missed bombing two writers of plays [Shaw and J. M. Barrie] who lived within a few yards of it, the fact was not even mentioned in the papers. In point of appeal to the senses no theatre ever built could touch the fane at Rheims: no actress could rival its Virgin in beauty, nor any operatic tenor look otherwise than a fool beside its David. Its picture glass was glorious even to those who had seen the glass of Chartres. It was wonderful in its very grotesques: who would look at the Blondin Donkey[27] after seeing its leviathans? In spite of the [Robert] Adam-Adelphian decoration on which Miss [Gertrude] Kingston [the manager] had lavished so much taste and care, the Little Theatre [seating 250] was in comparison with Rheims the gloomiest of little conventicles: indeed the cathedral must, from the Puritan point of view, have debauched a million voluptuaries for every one whom the Little Theatre had sent home thoughtful to a chaste bed after Mr [G. K.] Chesterton's Magic [:*A Fantastic Comedy*, 1913] or Brieux's Les Avariés [adapted by John Pollock as *Damaged Goods*, 1914]. Perhaps that is the real reason why the Church is lauded and the Theatre reviled. Whether or no, the fact remains that the lady [A. E. F. Horniman] to whose public spirit and sense of the national value of the theatre I owed the first regular public performance of a play of mine [*Arms and the Man*] had to conceal her action as if it had been a crime, whereas if she had given the money to the Church she would have worn a halo for it. And I admit, as I have always done, that this state of things may have been a very sensible one. I have asked Londoners again and again why they pay half a guinea to go to a theatre when they can go to St Paul's or Westminster Abbey for nothing. Their only possible reply is that they want to see something new and possibly something wicked; but the

26. The city of Reims underwent a ceaseless, vicious bombardment assault by the Germans for almost four years, from 3 September 1914, resulting in a heavy loss of civilian lives and wanton destruction of works of art. The thirteenth-century cathedral was left half ruined, most of its stained glass and statuary destroyed.
27. Fred and Joe Delaney created in 1877 a music-hall act known as the Brothers Griffiths, which specialized in comic animal impersonations. Their most successful routine was the 'Blondin Donkey', performed in emulation of the celebrated French aerialist Blondin on a 'tightrope' consisting of a plank whose edge was painted to create the semblance of a rope. The routine, introduced at the Royal Holborn in 1885, reached the height of popularity when the brothers were commanded to perform it before Edward, Prince of Wales, and his family at Marlborough House in 1886.

theatres mostly disappoint both hopes. If ever a revolution makes me Dictator, I shall establish a heavy charge for admission to our churches. But everyone who pays at the church door shall receive a ticket entitling him or her to free admission to one performance at any theatre he or she prefers. Thus shall the sensuous charms of the church service be made to subsidize the sterner virtue of the drama.

THE NEXT PHASE

The present situation will not last. Although the newspaper I read at breakfast this morning before writing these words contains a calculation that no less than twentythree wars are at present being waged to confirm the peace, England is no longer in khaki; and a violent reaction is setting in against the crude theatrical fare of the four terrible years. Soon the rents of theatres will once more be fixed on the assumption that they cannot always be full, nor even on the average half-full week in and week out. Prices will change. The higher drama will be at no greater disadvantage than it was before the war; and it may benefit, first, by the fact that many of us have been torn from the fools' paradise in which the theatre formerly traded, and thrust upon the sternest realities and necessities until we have lost both faith in and patience with the theatrical pretences that had no root either in reality or necessity; second, by the startling change made by the war in the distribution of income. It seems only the other day that a millionaire was a man with £50,000 a year. Today, when he has paid his income tax and super tax, and insured his life for the amount of his death duties, he is lucky if his net income is £10,000, though his nominal property remains the same. And this is the result of a Budget which is called "a respite for the rich." At the other end of the scale millions of persons have had regular incomes for the first time in their lives; and their men have been regularly clothed, fed, lodged, and taught to make up their minds that certain things have to be done, also for the first time in their lives. Hundreds of thousands of women have been taken out of their domestic cages and tasted both discipline and independence. The thoughtless and snobbish middle classes have been pulled up short by the very unpleasant experience of being ruined to an unprecedented extent. We have all had a tremendous jolt; and although the widespread notion that the shock of the war would automatically make a new heaven and a new earth, and that the dog would never go back to his vomit nor the sow to her wallowing in the mire, is already seen to be a delusion, yet we are far more conscious of our condition than we were, and far less disposed to submit to it. Revolution, lately only a sensational chapter in history or a demagogic claptrap, is now a possibility so imminent that hardly by trying to suppress it in other countries by arms and defamation, and calling the process anti-Bolshevism, can our Government stave it off at home.

Perhaps the most tragic figure of the day is the American President [Woodrow Wilson] who was once a historian. In those days it became his task to tell us how, after that great war in America which was more clearly than any other war of our time a war for an idea, the conquerors, confronted with a heroic task of reconstruction, turned recreant, and spent fifteen years in abusing their victory under cover of pretending to accomplish the task they were doing what they could to make impossible [in 'Reconstruction and After', *A History of the American People,* 1902]. Alas! Hegel was right when he said that we learn from history that men never learn anything from history ['Introduction', *Philosophy of History,* 1832]. With what anguish of mind the President sees that we, the new conquerors, forgetting everything we professed to fight for, are sitting down with watering mouths to a good square meal of ten years revenge upon and humiliation of our prostrate foe, can only be guessed by those who know, as he does, how hopeless is remonstrance, and how happy Lincoln was in perishing from the earth before his inspired messages became scraps of paper. He knows well that from the Peace Conference will come, in spite of his utmost, no edict on which he will be able, like Lincoln, to invoke "the considerate judgment of mankind, and the gracious favor of Almighty God" [Emancipation Proclamation, 1 January 1863]. He led his people to destroy the militarism of Zabern;[28] and the army they rescued is busy in Cologne imprisoning every German who does not salute a British officer; whilst the Government at home, asked whether it approves, replies that it does not propose even to discontinue this Zabernism when the Peace is concluded, but in effect looks forward to making Germans salute British officers until the end of the world. That is what war makes of men and women. It will wear off; and the worst it threatens is already proving impracticable; but before the humble and contrite heart ceases to be despised, the President and I, being of the same age, will be dotards. In the

28. Saverne, in Alsace-Lorraine, was annexed by the Germans in 1913. As Zabern, 1913–18, it became a symbol of German militarism at its worst, particularly when in November–December 1913 a German lieutenant provoked a riot by insulting Alsatian recruits. Shaw utilized this as a parallel to unconscionable behaviour by the British in Cologne during the occupation following the 1918 Armistice.

meantime there is, for him, another history to write; for me, another comedy to stage. Perhaps, after all, that is what wars are for, and what historians and playwrights are for. If men will not learn until their lessons are written in blood, why, blood they must have, their own for preference.

THE EPHEMERAL THRONES AND THE ETERNAL THEATRE

To the theatre it will not matter. Whatever Bastilles fall, the theatre will stand. Apostolic Hapsburg [the imperial family of Austria] has collapsed; All Highest Hohenzollern [Kaiser Wilhelm II of Prussia] languishes in Holland, threatened with trial on a capital charge of fighting for his country against England; Imperial Romanoff [Tsar Nicholas II of Russia], said to have perished miserably by a more summary method of murder, is perhaps alive or perhaps dead: nobody cares more than if he had been a peasant; the lord of Hellas [Constantine I] is level with his lackeys in republican Switzerland; Prime Ministers and Commanders-in-Chief have passed from a brief glory as Solons and Cæsars into failure and obscurity as closely on oneanother's heels as the descendants of Banquo; but Euripides and Aristophanes, Shakespear and Molière, Goethe and Ibsen remain fixed in their everlasting seats.

HOW WAR MUZZLES THE DRAMATIC POET

As for myself, why, it may be asked, did I not write two plays about the war instead of two pamphlets on it? The answer is significant. You cannot make war on war and on your neighbor at the same time. War cannot bear the terrible castigation of comedy, the ruthless light of laughter that glares on the stage. When men are heroically dying for their country, it is not the time to shew their lovers and wives and fathers and mothers how they are being sacrificed to the blunders of boobies, the cupidity of capitalists, the ambition of conquerors, the electioneering of demagogues, the Pharisaism of patriots, the lusts and lies and rancors and bloodthirsts that love war because it opens their prison doors, and sets them in the thrones of power and popularity. For unless these things are mercilessly exposed they will hide under the mantle of the ideals on the stage just as they do in real life.

And though there may be better things to reveal, it may not, and indeed cannot, be militarily expedient to reveal them whilst the issue is still in the balance. Truth telling is not compatible with the defence of the realm. We are just now reading the revelations of our generals and admirals,[29] unmuzzled at last by the armistice. During the war, General A, in his moving despatches from the field, told how General B had covered himself with deathless glory in such and such a battle. He now tells us that General B came within an ace of losing us the war by disobeying his orders on that occasion, and fighting instead of running away as he ought to have done. An excellent subject for comedy now that the war is over, no doubt; but if General A had let this out at the time, what would have been the effect on General B's soldiers? And had the stage made known what the Prime Minister and the Secretary of State for War who overruled General A thought of him, and what he thought of them, as now revealed in raging controversy, what would have been the effect on the nation? That is why comedy, though sorely tempted, had to be loyally silent; for the art of the dramatic poet knows no patriotism; recognizes no obligation but truth to natural history; cares not whether Germany or England perish; is ready to cry with Brynhild, "*Lass' uns verderben, lachend zu grunde geh'n*" ['Glide to destruction, gladly go down to death', in Wagner's *Siegfried*] sooner than deceive or be deceived; and thus becomes in time of war a greater military danger than poison, steel, or trinitrotoluene. That is why I had to withhold Heartbreak House from the footlights during the war; for the Germans might on any night have turned the last act from play into earnest, and even then might not have waited for their cues.

June, 1919.

---

29. Recent military 'revelations' included Lord French's *1914*, Admiral Fisher's *Memories and Records*, Naval Commander Alfred von Tirpitz's *My Memoirs*, Sir Douglas Haig's *Despatches* and General Erich Ludendorff's *My War Memories*.

The Author's Apology for Great Catherine

First published in 1919

Exception has been taken to the title of this seeming tomfoolery on the ground that the Catherine it represents is not Great Catherine [II, Empress of Russia], but the Catherine whose gallantries provide some of the lightest pages of modern history. Great Catherine, it is said, was the Catherine whose diplomacy, whose campaigns and conquests, whose plans of Liberal reform, whose correspondence with Grimm and Voltaire enabled her to cut such a magnificent figure in the XVIII century. In reply, I can only confess that Catherine's diplomacy and her conquests do not interest me. It is clear to me that neither she nor the statesmen with whom she played this mischievous kind of political chess had any notion of the real history of their own times, or of the real forces that were moulding Europe. The French Revolution, which made such short work of Catherine's Voltairean principles, surprised and scandalized her as much as it surprised and scandalized any provincial governess in the French chateaux.

The main difference between her and our modern Liberal Governments was that whereas she talked and wrote quite intelligently about Liberal principles before she was frightened into making such talking and writing a flogging matter, our Liberal ministers take the name of Liberalism in vain without knowing or caring enough about its meaning even to talk and scribble about it, and pass their flogging Bills, and institute their prosecutions for sedition and blasphemy and so forth, without the faintest suspicion that such proceedings need any apology from the Liberal point of view.

It was quite easy for Patiomkin [Prince G. A. Potemkin] to humbug Catherine as to the condition of Russia by conducting her through sham cities run up for the occasion by scenic artists; but in the little world of European court intrigue and dynastic diplomacy which was the only world she knew she was more than a match for him and for all the rest of her contemporaries. In such intrigue and diplomacy, however, there was no romance, no scientific political interest, nothing that a sane mind can now retain even if it can be persuaded to waste time in reading it up. But Catherine as a woman, with plenty of character and (as we should say) no morals, still fascinates and amuses us as she fascinated and amused her contemporaries. They were great sentimental comedians, these Peters, Elizabeths, and Catherines who played their Tsarships as eccentric character parts, and produced scene after scene of furious harlequinade with the monarch as clown, and of tragic relief in the torture chamber with the monarch as pantomime demon committing real atrocities, not forgetting the indispensable love interest on an enormous and utterly indecorous scale. Catherine kept this vast Guignol Theatre[1] open for nearly half a century, not as a Russian, but as a highly domesticated German lady whose household routine was not at all so unlike that of Queen Victoria as might be expected from the difference in their notions of propriety in sexual relations.

In short, if Byron leaves you with an impression that he said very little about Catherine [in *Don Juan*], and that little not what was best worth saying, I beg to correct your impression by assuring you that what Byron said was all there really is to say that is worth saying. His Catherine is my Catherine and everybody's Catherine. The young man who gains her favor is a Spanish nobleman in his version. I have made him an English country gentleman [Charles Edstaston], who gets out of his rather dangerous scrape by simplicity, sincerity, and the courage of these qualities. By this I have given some offence to the many Britons who see themselves as heroes: what they mean by heroes being theatrical snobs of superhuman pretensions which, though quite groundless, are admitted with awe by the rest of the human race. They say I think an Englishman a fool. When I do, they have themselves to thank.

I must not, however, pretend that historical portraiture was the motive of a play that will leave the reader as ignorant of Russian history as he may be now before he has turned the page. Nor is the sketch of Catherine complete even idiosyncratically, leaving her politics out of the question. For example, she wrote bushels of plays. I confess I have not yet read any of them. The truth is, this play grew out of the relations which inevitably exist in the theatre between authors and actors. If the actors have sometimes to use their skill as the author's puppets rather than in full self-expression, the author has sometimes to use his skill as the actors' tailor, fitting them with parts written to display the virtuosity of the performer rather than to solve problems of life, character, or history. Feats of this kind may tickle an author's technical vanity; but he is bound on such occasions to admit that

1. A type of entertainment in Paris consisting of short plays crammed with gruesome forms of violence, bloodletting and suicide or murder at the climax, in the Senecan tradition, performed principally at the Théâtre du Grand Guignol.

the performer for whom he writes is "the onlie begetter" ['Mr W. H.' in Shakespeare's dedication of his *Sonnets*, 1609] of his work, which must be regarded critically as an addition to the debt dramatic literature owes to the art of acting and its exponents. Those who have seen Miss Gertrude Kingston play the part of Catherine [18 November 1913] will have no difficulty in believing that it was her talent rather than mine that brought the play into existence. I once recommended Miss Kingston professionally to play queens. Now in the modern drama there were no queens for her to play; and as to the older literature of our stage, did it not provoke the veteran actress [Mrs Telfer, a character] in Sir Arthur Pinero's Trelawny of the Wells [1898] to declare that, as parts, queens are not worth a tinker's oath? Miss Kingston's comment on my suggestion, though more elegantly worded, was to the same effect; and it ended in my having to make good my advice by writing Great Catherine. History provided no other queen capable of standing up to our joint talents.

In composing such bravura pieces, the author limits himself only by the range of the virtuoso, which by definition far transcends the modesty of nature. If my Russians seem more Muscovite than any Russian, and my English people more insular than any Briton, I will not plead, as I honestly might, that the fiction has yet to be written that can exaggerate the reality of such subjects; that the apparently outrageous Patiomkin is but a timidly bowdlerized ghost of the original; and that Captain Edstaston is no more than a miniature that might hang appropriately on the walls of nineteen out of twenty English country houses to this day. An artistic presentment must not condescend to justify itself by a comparison with crude nature; and I prefer to admit that in this kind my *dramatis personae* are, as they should be, of the stage stagey, challenging the actor to act up to them or beyond them, if he can. The more heroic the overcharging, the better for the performance.

In dragging the reader thus for a moment behind the scenes, I am departing from a rule which I have hitherto imposed on myself so rigidly that I never permit myself, even in a stage direction, to let slip a word that could bludgeon the imagination of the reader by reminding him of the boards and the footlights and the sky borders and the rest of the theatrical scaffolding, for which nevertheless I have to plan as carefully as if I were the head carpenter as well as the author. But even at the risk of talking shop, an honest playwright should take at least one opportunity of acknowledging that his art is not only limited by the art of the actor, but often stimulated and developed by it. No sane and skilled author writes plays that present impossibilities to the actor or to the stage engineer. If, as occasionally happens, he asks them to do things that they have never done before and cannot conceive as presentable or possible (as Wagner [in *The Ring*] and Thomas Hardy [in *The Dynasts*, 1904–8] have done, for example), it is always found that the difficulties are not really insuperable, the author having foreseen unsuspected possibilities both in the actor and in the audience, whose will-to-make-believe can perform the quaintest miracles. Thus may authors advance the arts of acting and of staging plays. But the actor also may enlarge the scope of the drama by displaying powers not previously discovered by the author. If the best available actors are only Horatios, the authors will have to leave Hamlet out, and be content with Horatios for heroes. Some of the difference between Shakespear's Orlandos [in *As You Like It*] and Bassanios [in *The Merchant of Venice*] and Bertrams [in *All's Well that Ends Well*] and his Hamlets and Macbeths must have been due not only to his development as a dramatic poet, but to the development of Burbage as an actor. Playwrights do not write for ideal actors when their livelihood is at stake: if they did, they would write parts for heroes with twenty arms like an Indian god. Indeed the actor often influences the author too much; for I can remember a time (I am not implying that it is yet wholly past) when the art of writing a fashionable play had become very largely the art of writing it "round" the personalities of a group of fashionable performers of whom Burbage would certainly have said that their parts needed no acting. Everything has its abuse as well as its use.

It is also to be considered that great plays live longer than great actors, though little plays do not live nearly so long as the worst of their exponents. The consequence is that the great actor, instead of putting pressure on contemporary authors to supply him with heroic parts, falls back on the Shakespearean repertory, and takes what he needs from a dead hand. In the XIX century, the careers of Kean, Macready, Barry Sullivan, and Irving, ought to have produced a group of heroic plays comparable in intensity to those of Eschylus, Sophocles, and Euripides; but nothing of the kind happened: these actors played the works of dead authors, or, very occasionally, of live poets who were hardly regular professional playwrights. Sheridan Knowles, Bulwer Lytton, Wills, and Tennyson produced a few glaringly artificial high horses for the great actors of their time;[2] but

2. Sheridan Knowles, Irish-born actor and playwright, author of the very successful *The Hunchback* (1832), wrote several plays for William Macready and one for Edmund Kean. Edward Bulwer-Lytton was a popular novelist and dramatist, whose plays *The Lady of Lyons* (1838) and *Money* (1840) held the British stage for

the playwrights proper, who really kept the theatre going, and were kept going by the theatre, did not cater for the great actors: they could not afford to compete with a bard who was not of an age but for all time, and who had, moreover, the overwhelming attraction for the actor-managers of not charging author's fees. The result was that the playwrights and the great actors ceased to think of themselves as having any concern with oneanother: Tom Robertson, Ibsen, Pinero, and Barrie might as well have belonged to a different solar system as far as Irving was concerned; and the same was true of their respective predecessors.

Thus was established an evil tradition; but I at least can plead that it does not always hold good. If Forbes-Robertson had not been there to play Cæsar, I should not have written Cæsar and Cleopatra. If Ellen Terry had never been born, Captain Brassbound's conversion would never have been effected. The Devil's Disciple, with which I won my *cordon bleu* in America as a potboiler, would have had a different sort of hero if Richard Mansfield had been a different sort of actor, though the actual commission to write it came from an English actor, William Terriss,[3] who was assassinated before he recovered from the dismay into which the result of his rash proposal threw him. For it must be said that the actor or actress who inspires or commissions a play as often as not regards it as a Frankenstein's monster, and will none of it. That does not make him or her any the less parental in the fecundity of the playwright.

To an author who has any feeling of his business there is a keen and whimsical joy in divining and revealing a side of an actor's genius over-looked before, and unsuspected even by the actor himself. When I snatched Mr Louis Calvert from Shakespear, and made him wear a frock coat and silk hat on the stage for perhaps the first time in his life, I do not think he expected in the least that his performance would enable me to boast of his Tom Broadbent [in *John Bull's Other Island*] as a genuine stage classic. Mrs Patrick Campbell was famous before I wrote for her, but not for playing illiterate cockney flowermaidens [Eliza, in *Pygmalion*]. And in the case which is provoking me to all these impertinences, I am quite sure that Miss

---

decades, the latter proving an ideal vehicle for Barry Sullivan. W. G. Wills, a theatre hack, tailored his plays, including *Charles I* (1872) and *Faust* (1885), to the talents of Henry Irving. Tennyson's *Becket* (1884) also afforded Irving heroic moments, arranged by him for the stage in 1893.

3. Actor-manager who produced first-class melodrama at the Adelphi Theatre, near the stage door of which he was murdered by a knife-wielding assailant in 1897.

Gertrude Kingston, who first made her reputation as an impersonator of the most delightfully featherheaded and inconsequent ingenues, thought me more than usually mad when I persuaded her to play the Helen of Euripides [in the Gilbert Murray translation of *The Trojan Women*], and then launched her on a queenly career as Catherine of Russia.

It is not the whole truth that if we take care of the actors the plays will take care of themselves; nor is it any truer that if we take care of the plays the actors will take care of themselves. There is both give and take in the business. I have seen plays written for actors that made me exclaim, "How oft the sight of means to do ill deeds makes deeds ill done!" But Burbage may have flourished the prompt copy of Hamlet under Shakespear's nose at the tenth rehearsal and cried, "How oft the sight of means to do great deeds makes playwrights great!" [*King John*, IV: ii] I say the tenth because I am convinced that at the first he denounced his part as a rotten one; thought the ghost's speech ridiculously long; and wanted to play the king. Anyhow, whether he had the wit to utter it or not, the boast would have been a valid one. The best conclusion is that every actor should say, "If I create the hero in myself, God will send an author to write his part." For in the long run the actors will get the authors, and the authors the actors, they deserve.

O'Flaherty V. C.

First published in 1919

===

It may surprise some people to learn that in 1915 this little play was a recruiting poster in disguise. The British officer seldom likes Irish soldiers; but he always tries to have a certain proportion of them in his battalion, because, partly from a want of common sense which leads them to value their lives less than Englishmen do (lives are really less worth living in a poor country), and partly because even the most cowardly Irishman feels obliged to outdo an Englishman in bravery if possible, and at least to set a perilous pace for him, Irish soldiers give impetus to those military operations which require for their spirited execution more devilment than prudence.

Unfortunately, Irish recruiting was badly bungled in 1915. The Irish were for the most part Roman Catholics and loyal Irishmen, which means that from the English point of view they were heretics and rebels. But they were willing enough to go soldiering on the side of France and see the world outside Ireland, which is a dull place to live in. It was quite easy to enlist them by approaching them from their own point of view. But the War Office insisted on approaching them from the point of view of Dublin Castle. They were discouraged and repulsed by refusals to give commissions to Roman Catholic officers, or to allow distinct Irish units to be formed. To attract them, the walls were covered with placards headed REMEMBER BELGIUM. The folly of asking an Irishman to remember anything when you want him to fight for England was apparent to everyone outside the Castle: FORGET AND FORGIVE would have been more to the point. Remembering Belgium and its broken treaty[1] led Irishmen to remember Limerick and its broken treaty [see p. 367]; and the recruiting ended in a rebellion, in suppressing which the British artillery quite unnecessarily reduced the centre of Dublin to ruins, and the British

---

1. In spite of its solemn engagement with Britain, France, Austria and Russia in the Treaty of 1839 to maintain Belgian neutrality, Germany invaded Belgium on 4 August 1914 and bombed Louvain, 'the Oxford of Belgium', on 25 August 1914, thus precipitating the Great War.

commanders killed their leading prisoners of war in cold blood morning after morning with an effect of long drawn out ferocity. Really it was only the usual childish petulance in which John Bull does things in a week that disgrace him for a century, though he soon recovers his good humor, and cannot understand why the survivors of his wrath do not feel as jolly with him as he does with them. On the smouldering ruins of Dublin the appeals to remember Louvain were presently supplemented by a fresh appeal. IRISHMEN: DO YOU WISH TO HAVE THE HORRORS OF WAR BROUGHT TO YOUR OWN HEARTHS AND HOMES? Dublin laughed sourly.

As for me, I addressed myself quite simply to the business of obtaining recruits. I knew by personal experience and observation what anyone might have inferred from the records of Irish emigration, that all an Irishman's hopes and ambitions turn on his opportunities of getting out of Ireland. Stimulate his loyalty, and he will stay in Ireland and die for her; for, incomprehensible as it seems to an Englishman, Irish patriotism does not take the form of devotion to England and England's king. Appeal to his discontent, his deadly boredom, his thwarted curiosity and desire for change and adventure, and, to escape from Ireland, he will go abroad to risk his life for France, for the Papal States, for secession in America, and even, if no better may be, for England. Knowing that the ignorance and insularity of the Irishman is a danger to himself and to his neighbors, I had no scruple in making that appeal when there was something for him to fight which the whole world had to fight unless it meant to come under the jackboot of the German version of Dublin Castle.

There was another consideration, unmentionable by the recruiting sergeants and war orators, which must nevertheless have helped them powerfully in procuring soldiers by voluntary enlistment. The happy home of the idealist may become common under millennial conditions. It is not common at present. No one will ever know how many men joined the army in 1914 and 1915 to escape from tyrants and taskmasters, termagants and shrews, none of whom are any the less irksome when they happen by ill-luck to be also our fathers, our mothers, our wives and our children. Even at their amiablest, a holiday from them may be a tempting change for all parties. That is why I did not endow O'Flaherty V. C. with an ideal Irish colleen for his sweetheart, and gave him for his mother a Volumnia [the dominating mother in Shakespeare's *Coriolanus*] of the potato patch rather than an affectionate parent from whom he could not so easily have torn himself away.

I need hardly say that a play thus carefully adapted to its purpose was voted utterly inadmissible;[2] and in due course the British Government, frightened out of its wits for the moment by the rout of the Fifth Army, ordained Irish Conscription, and then did not dare to go through with it. I still think my own line was the more businesslike. But during the war everyone except the soldiers at the front imagined that nothing but an extreme assertion of our most passionate prejudices, without the smallest regard to their effect on others, could win the war. Finally the British blockade won the war; but the wonder is that the British blockhead did not lose it. I suppose the enemy was no wiser. War is not a sharpener of wits; and I am afraid I gave great offence by keeping my head in this matter of Irish recruiting. What can I do but apologize, and publish the play now that it can no longer do any good?

2. Under gentle but firm pressure from British officials in Dublin Castle and from Irish friends whose opinion he respected and who believed it might provoke a riot in Dublin's Abbey Theatre, Shaw in 1916 tactfully withdrew the play, the theatre publicly announcing only that performance had been temporarily postponed.

The Inca of Perusalem

First published in 1919

═══

I must remind the reader that this playlet was written when its principal character [Kaiser Wilhelm II], far from being a fallen foe and virtually a prisoner in our victorious hands, was still the Cæsar whose legions we were resisting with our hearts in our mouths. Many were so horribly afraid of him that they could not forgive me for not being afraid of him: I seemed to be trifling heartlessly with a deadly peril. I knew better; and I have represented Cæsar as knowing better himself. But it was one of the quaintnesses of popular feeling during the war that anyone who breathed the slightest doubt of the absolute perfection of German organization, the Machiavellian depth of German diplomacy, the omniscience of German science, the equipment of every German with a complete philosophy of history, and the consequent hopelessness of overcoming so magnificently accomplished an enemy except by the sacrifice of every recreative activity to incessant and vehement war work, including a heartbreaking mass of fussing and cadging and bluffing that did nothing but waste our energies and tire our resolution, was called a pro-German.

Now that this is all over, and the upshot of the fighting has shewn that we could quite well have afforded to laugh at the doomed Inca, I am in another difficulty. I may be supposed to be hitting Cæsar when he is down. That is why I preface the play with this reminder that when it was written he was not down. To make quite sure, I have gone through the proof sheets very carefully, and deleted everything that could possibly be mistaken for a foul blow. I have of course maintained the ancient privilege of comedy to chasten Cæsar's foibles by laughing at them, whilst introducing enough obvious and outrageous fiction to relieve both myself and my model from the obligations and responsibilities of sober history and biography. But I should certainly put the play in the fire instead of publishing it if it contained a word against our defeated enemy that I would not have written in 1913.

Augustus Does His Bit

First published in 1919

═══

I wish to express my gratitude for certain good offices which Augustus[1] secured for me in January 1917. I had been invited to visit the theatre of war in Flanders by the Commander-in-Chief:[2] an invitation which was, under the circumstances, a summons to duty. Thus I had occasion to spend some days in procuring the necessary passports and other official facilities for my journey. It happened just then that the Stage Society gave a performance of this little play. It opened the heart of every official to me. I have always been treated with distinguished consideration in my contacts with bureaucracy during the war; but on this occasion I found myself *persona grata* in the highest degree. There was only one word when the formalities were disposed of; and that was "We are up against Augustus all day." The shewing-up of Augustus scandalized one or two innocent and patriotic critics who regarded the prowess of the British army as inextricably bound up with Highcastle prestige. But our Government departments knew better: their problem was how to win the war with Augustus on their backs, well-meaning, brave, patriotic, but obstructively fussy, self-important, imbecile, and disastrous.

Save for the satisfaction of being able to laugh at Augustus in the theatre, nothing, as far as I know, came of my dramatic reduction of him to absurdity. Generals, Admirals, Prime Ministers and Controllers, not to mention Emperors, Kaisers and Tsars, were scrapped remorselessly at home and abroad, for their sins or services, as the case might be. But Augustus stood like the Eddystone [lighthouse off Plymouth Sound] in a storm, and

---

1. Lord Augustus Highcastle, chief character in the play, personifies the British governing class as Shaw perceives it, displaying its stupid, selfish behaviour during the war.
2. At the behest of Field Marshal Sir Douglas Haig, Shaw visited the front in France and Belgium from 28 January to 5 February 1917, ranging from Ypres to the Somme and Boulogne. His report of the visit was published as 'Joy Riding at the Front' in the *Daily Chronicle*, 5–8 March 1917; collected in *What I Really Wrote about the War* (1930).

stands so to this day. He gave us his word that he was indispensable; and we took it.

Annajanska the Bolshevik Empress

First published in 1919

═══

Annajanska is frankly a bravura piece. The modern variety theatre demands for its "turns" little plays called sketches, to last twenty minutes or so, and to enable some favorite performer to make a brief but dazzling appearance on some barely passable dramatic pretext. Miss Lillah McCarthy[1] and I, as author and actress, have helped to make oneanother famous on many serious occasions, from Man and Superman to Androcles; and Mr Charles Ricketts[2] has not disdained to snatch moments from his painting and sculpture to design some wonderful dresses for us. We three unbent as Mrs [Sarah] Siddons, Sir Joshua Reynolds, and Dr Johnson might have unbent, to devize a "turn" for the Coliseum variety theatre. Not that we would set down the art of the variety theatre as something to be condescended to, or our own art as elephantine. We should rather crave indulgence as three novices fresh from the awful legitimacy of the highbrow theatre.

Well, Miss McCarthy and Mr Ricketts justified themselves easily in the glamor of the footlights, to the strains of Tchaikovsky's 1812. I fear I did not. I have received only one compliment on my share; and that was from a friend who said "it is the only one of your works that is not too long." So I have made it a page or two longer, according to my own precept: EMBRACE YOUR REPROACHES: THEY ARE OFTEN GLORIES IN DISGUISE.

1. Lillah McCarthy was the eponymous heroine in *Annajanska*'s first production, in a variety bill at the London Coliseum, 21 January 1918.
2. An artist associated with the neo-Pre-Raphaelites, influenced by Rossetti and Millais as well as by the French symbolists. He designed costumes for several of Shaw's productions, most notably *Saint Joan* (1924).

Peace Conference Hints

Shaw's French translator Augustin Hamon, having arranged in September 1919 with a Paris publisher, Librairie de l'Humanité, to publish a translation of Peace Conference Hints *(issued in London in March 1919), urgently requested that Shaw provide a special preface. Shaw complied immediately; but publication was abandoned. Brief portions appear in* Shaw: An Autobiography 1898–1950, *edited by Stanley Weintraub (1970), erroneously identified as from a [non-existent] French edition of* Common Sense about the War. *The manuscript is in the British Library (Add. MSS 50671A)*

In introducing this little book to the French public, it is not necessary to explain that I am not a Frenchman. It is, however, necessary to explain that I am not an Englishman. The secret of my detachment from British chauvinism is that I am an Irishman. When I tried to persuade my countrymen to enlist in the British army (as in fact they did in surprisingly large numbers at first), I did not ask them to rally to the defence of the British crown, but to that of the French nation, which had sent troops to help them in their struggle against England a hundred years ago, and of the French Republic which stood in Europe for their political opinions as against the Hohenzollern regime which stood for the opinions of Dublin Castle, the Bastille of Ireland. When I asked them to subscribe to the War Loans, I explained to them that the interest on their contributions would be money drawn by Ireland from England. I said nothing about the devastation of the three streets of Louvain, because the British cannon had just devastated fifty streets in the Irish capital [during the Easter Rising, April 1916], and left fewer buildings standing in the heart of the city than the German cannon had at that time left standing in Ypres. I said nothing about the sacred national rights of gallant little Serbia and heroic Poland: the irony of the contrast between England's treatment of Irish nationality and her passionate cries for help for all the nationalities she was not herself suppressing was too ghastly. I carefully avoided all reference to the Broken Treaty of 1839, because in Ireland the Broken Treaty means the Treaty of Limerick.[1] Recruiting in Dublin is as different from recruiting in London

---

1. Under a treaty signed on 3 October 1691, following England's defeat of Catholic Ireland as a nation under arms, Irish Catholics were guaranteed religious

as recruiting in Alger[ia] or in Tunis is from recruiting in Paris.

None the less I wanted the Allies to win, even at the risk of their being demoralized by victory, as they actually have been. I wanted Republican rule to supersede Junker rule in Germany. Not, please observe, that I had any illusions about Republican rule: I knew too much about the French and American Republics to overrate the advantage of exchanging Junkers for successful commercial adventurers and barristers and journalists. Such an exchange is not the threshold of the millennium; but it is an inevitable incident of modern development; and the sooner it is accomplished the better.

Of course I was called a pro-German because I advocated the cause of the Allies without hypocrisy, without acclaiming the slaughter of a German by an Englishman as a deed of deathless heroism and in the same breath denouncing the slaughter of an Englishman by a German as a dastardly murder. I could and did distinguish between war on the cinema film and war in the trenches. I knew the diplomatic history of the war as I am about to tell it in this book, and knew it, as it proved, accurately and essentially. All this, added to my Irish detachment from the sentimentalities of British patriotism, was so revolting to Englishmen in the delirium of the war fever, and so contradictory to the current legends of melodramatic patriotism, that my Common Sense about the War, launched in November 1914, when the war fever was at its height, produced furious demands for my immediate execution as a pro-German, a Pacifist, a traitor, a Bolo and what not. It now seems a needlessly discreet document: indeed within six months of its publication the most blatant of the ultra-patriotic papers were shouting what I had whispered; but by that time the sensation made by my Common Sense was remembered and the contents of it forgotten (indeed many of those who execrated it had never read it, and would have been incapable of understanding it if they had read it); so that my unpatriotic reputation remained in spite of all my statements having been confirmed and all my conclusions accepted. Some echoes of the scandal I had caused reached France; and though I am so little known there that no great interest was aroused, yet I found it impossible to have my pamphlet

---

liberty, with those officers and men of the five western counties who had risen against the English being guaranteed retention of their estates or professions in return for a simple oath of allegiance. The parliaments of England and Ireland ratified the Articles of Limerick only after tampering with the letter of the agreement. In Ireland it became known, in consequence, as 'the violated treaty'.

translated and circulated. Thus the present work, which completes the story begun in my Common Sense, is the first to reach the French public.

It may possibly amuse French readers to know what my personal bias was in respect of France and Germany. I had wandered about both countries a good deal, crossing and recrossing the frontiers and marking the change from French to German civilization. In one country I found remarkably efficient and well educated artisans, formidable soldiers, hard materialistic common sense, a jealous and minute legality ruthlessly and pedantically enforced, a certain roughness of life that led to a contemptuous neglect of the niceties of sanitation and cleanliness, curiosity about art without any real sense of it, women always carefully but never well dressed, taking refuge in mourning on every possible pretext (were it only the death of a seventeenth cousin) to escape from the irksome responsibility of choosing colors, children either anarchical or overdisciplined, and an entire absence of sentimental charm. In short, a people to be admired for some things and feared for others, but by no means likely to inspire indulgence and affection, though they lived in a country so beautiful, with such magnificent relics of medieval civilization and with such heart-moving traditions (of which they had for the most part no sense) that it was impossible to travel in their country without acquiring an ineradicable nostalgia for it.

Once across the frontier all was changed. Women dressed carelessly and often tastelessly, but delighting in all the colors of the rainbow and the chemist's laboratory, sentimental men pretending to be soldiers and marching with a swaying willowy motion to songs that made them cry, easygoing beerdrinking men posting up millions of regulations to persuade themselves that they were iron disciplinarians, and yet breaking every one of them twenty times a day, jolly petted children, an enormous romantic sentimentality expressing itself over rivers and old castles and innumerable duly-labelled *schönen aussichten* (*belles vues*) in the country, and in the towns over music, Shakespear, poetry and philosophy, not regarded as antique curiosities but as burning needs of everyday life. Even the sensuality, the beer and sausages, the cleanliness and sanitation of the streets, the fitting up of the houses with automatic telephones and all sorts of domestic inventions, the shops full of rucksacks and alpenstocks and neat sateen bags to pack boots in for pedestrian journeys, all shewed that here you had a people sentimentally wallowing in life and living in the present. No wonder, you said, they cannot get on with the hard, joyless, iron, dangerous French. It was impossible to compare Lille and Bordeaux and Toulouse with Dresden and Munich: they were not in the same epoch. When you sought in France for a Bayreuth or a Hellerau,[2] you were confronted with an antique theatre in Orange or Nîmes, in which Parisian actors declaimed Corneille, or affected an enthusiasm for a fabulous regionalism in postiches by local bards of the uttermost provincialism. If you were saturated with modern drama, modern music, modern religion, and modern social speculation, you felt at home in the German cities. The French cities were still in the XVIII century, except when they were in the XVII.

Let me relate two experiences of mine which have their significance. In Munich once, when I was complimenting a German on the artistic activity of the place (whither I had come to see an enthusiastic but execrable performance of one of my own plays [*Candida*, at the Residenz Theatre, 6 August 1908]), he replied "Do not be deceived: this city is a Capua.[3] When an artist settles down here he produces no more art. Our art will be our ruin."

Some time before this, I had written to the greatest artist France or the world has produced for several centuries. I addressed the letter Monsieur Auguste Rodin, Meudon. If, during one of his visits to London, I addressed it to Rodin, England, the British Post Office, Philistine as it is, would have delivered it to him within twentyfour hours. It was returned to me by the French Post Office marked *Inconnu* [Unknown]. I naturally exclaimed "God has forgotten this people [Psalms 10: 11]: they are hopeless." Rodin explained to me afterwards that as he was not a pupil of the Beaux Arts [École Nationale des Beaux-Arts, Paris, founded in 1671] he was not counted as an artist in France, but only as a common mason. I then understood why Germany was the first country to recognize me as a considerable dramatic author, and why France will be the last. Not that I complain; for it [is] delightful to have one country left in which I can travel as "un monsieur" without being importuned to sign autograph books at every hotel by the whole staff; but I am so deplorably lacking in good taste as the French understand it as to know my own value (and perhaps a little more); and I affirm that Europe can be divided into barbarous countries and civilized countries by the simple test of the presence or absence of a Shaw vogue in the theatres.

2. Shaw attended three of Bayreuth's annual Wagner Festivals, in 1889, 1894 and 1908. Hellerau (founded in 1906), a small village on the outskirts of Dresden, was noted for arts and crafts and was the original home (until the outbreak of war forced a move to Switzerland) of Jaques-Dalcroze's school of eurhythmics, visited by Shaw in 1913.
3. The demise of Capua's artistic capabilities appears to have coincided with the fall of the Roman Empire. See also p. 319, fn. 2.

Now in all this the point I am driving at is that in Europe as I saw it before the war the ideal Prussian was a Frenchman and the ideal Frenchman a German. In France Louis Quatorze was still alive and powerful: in Germany Frederick the Great was as dead as a doornail. The Hohenzollern in his shining armor, with his General Staff and his soldier son full of the Napoleonic legend, [was] only a stage pageant: the big battalions in which their hopes lay were composed of the least military people in the world. The French and the British, imposed on by the pageant, were very much afraid of them. We are still ridiculously afraid of them, even though we have beaten them to the dust. It is true that they might have won in 1914 if their military organization had not been a sham, just as Napoleon III might have won in 1870 if his military organization had not been a sham. But the first brush before Liège[4] exposed their unpreparedness. After that I was not frightened. And that is almost the whole explanation of the disconcerting difference between my attitude and tone and that which was *de rigueur* [fashionable] during the war, and still remains the expected attitude and tone. I am well aware that when we are frightened there is nothing so hateful and terrifying as the intrusion of someone who is not frightened. But even in war some people must keep their heads to save the rest from rushing frantically to their ruin.

I was very well treated during the war by the people who were not frightened and who knew all about the war. At the height of the outcry against me I was able to face large popular audiences and speak my mind to them without opposition and with abundant applause. To many French readers what follows in these pages will require no apology, and may well provoke an enquiry as to whether it was necessary to translate a foreign book to say what most Frenchmen now know, and what many of them could have said, and indeed have said, better in their own language. Nevertheless I do not refuse the opportunity offered me of translation and publication. A book on the war by M. Anatole France would instantly be read with avidity by thousands of English people who would die sooner than read another word on that outworn subject by one of their own compatriots. I am far from having "peacefully penetrated" France as thoroughly as Anatole France has penetrated England; but it may be that here and there a Frenchman or Frenchwoman will take up my booklet with a curiosity that no native writer can now excite. That is why I have consented to its publication, and why I have taken the

4. Shaw uses 'before' in the sense of 'confronting'. For an earlier allusion to the battle for Liège, see p. 146, fn. 3.

pains in this preface to explain what may seem singular in my point of view.

LONDON.   G. B. S.
September, 1919.

Back to Methuselah

First published in 1921. Revised extensively for the World's Classics Edition, 1944

═══

THE INFIDEL HALF CENTURY

The Dawn of Darwinism

One day early in the eighteen hundred and sixties, I, being then a small boy, was with my nurse, buying something in the shop of a petty newsagent, bookseller, and stationer in Camden Street, Dublin, when there entered an elderly man, weighty and solemn, who advanced to the counter, and said pompously, "Have you the works of the celebrated Buffoon?"

My own works were at that time unwritten, or it is possible that the shop assistant might have misunderstood him so far as to produce a copy of Man and Superman. As it was, she knew quite well what he wanted; for this was before the Education Act of 1870 had produced shop assistants who know how to read and know nothing else. The celebrated Buffoon was not a humorist, but the famous naturalist [Georges-Louis de] Buffon.[1] Every literate child at that time knew Buffon's Natural History as well as Esop's Fables. And no living child had heard the name that has since obliterated Buffon's in the popular consciousness: the name of Darwin.

Ten years elapsed. The celebrated Buffoon was forgotten; I had doubled my years and my length; and I had discarded the religion of my forefathers. One day the richest and consequently most dogmatic of my uncles [Richard Frederick Shaw] came into a restaurant where I was dining, and found himself, much against his will, in conversation with the most questionable of his nephews. By way of making myself agreeable, I spoke of modern thought and Darwin. He said, "Oh, thats the fellow who wants to make out that we all have tails like monkeys." I tried to explain that what Darwin had insisted on in this connection was that some monkeys have no tails. But my uncle was as impervious to what Darwin really said as any Neo-Darwinian nowadays. He died impenitent, and did not mention me in his will.

1. French naturalist, director of the Paris Jardin du Roi (Botanical Gardens), and author (with others) of the 44-volume *Histoire Naturelle* (1749–1804).

Twenty years elapsed. If my uncle had been alive, he would have known all about Darwin, and known it all wrong. In spite of the efforts of Grant Allen to set him right [*Charles Darwin*, 1885], he would have accepted Darwin as the discoverer of Evolution, of Heredity, and of modification of species by Selection. For the pre-Darwinian age had come to be regarded as a Dark Age in which men still believed that the book of Genesis was a standard scientific treatise, and that the only additions to it were Galileo's demonstration of Leonardo da Vinci's simple remark that the earth is a moon of the sun, Newton's theory of gravitation, Sir Humphry Davy's invention of the [miner's] safety-lamp [1815], the discovery of electricity, the application of steam to industrial purposes, and the penny post. It was just the same in other subjects. Thus Nietzsche, by the two or three who had come across his writings, was supposed to have been the first man to whom it occurred that mere morality and legality and urbanity lead nowhere, as if Bunyan had never written Badman [*The Life and Death of Mr Badman*, 1680]. Schopenhauer was credited with inventing the distinction between the Covenant of Grace and the Covenant of Works which troubled Cromwell on his deathbed. People talked as if there had been no dramatic or descriptive music before Wagner; no impressionist painting before Whistler; whilst as to myself, I was finding that the surest way to produce an effect of daring innovation and originality was to revive the ancient attraction of long rhetorical speeches; to stick closely to the methods of Molière; and to lift characters bodily out of the pages of Charles Dickens.

THE ADVENT OF THE NEO-DARWINIANS

This particular sort of ignorance does not always or often matter. But in Darwin's case it did matter. If Darwin had really led the world at one bound from the book of Genesis to Heredity, to Modification of Species by Selection, and to Evolution, he would have been a philosopher and a prophet as well as an eminent professional naturalist, with geology as a hobby. The delusion that he had actually achieved this feat did no harm at first, because if people's views are sound, about evolution or anything else, it does not make two straws difference whether they call the revealer of their views Tom or Dick. But later on such apparently negligible errors have awkward consequences. Darwin was given an imposing reputation as discoverer and founder of Evolution when he had really only sidetracked it by shewing that many of its developments can be accounted for by what he called Natural Selection, meaning that instead of being evolved to fulfil some vital purpose they were the aimless and promiscuous results of external material pressures and accidents leading to the survival of the fittest to survive under such circumstances. With, of course, the extinction of the unfit. Of this he gave many examples.

As the vogue of Evolution, begun by Goethe [in *Metamorphose der Pflanzen*, 1790] and maintained by Darwin's grandfather [Erasmus Darwin, in *Zoonomia*, 1794–6], faded out in 1830, neither Darwin nor his contemporaries seem to have been aware of it. The next generation accepted Natural Selection as the only method of biological development, and thereby came into conflict with the old Creative Evolutionists and with Darwin himself: a schism which obliged them to distinguish themselves as Neo-Darwinians.

Before ten more years had elapsed, the Neo-Darwinians were dominating biological Science. It was 1906; I was fifty; I had published my own view of evolution in a play called Man and Superman; and I found that most people were unable to understand how I could be an Evolutionist and not a Neo-Darwinian, or why I derided Neo-Darwinism as a mischievous heresy, and would fall on its professors slaughterously in public discussions. It was in the hope of making me clear the matter up that the Fabian Society, which was then organizing a series of lectures on Prophets of the Nineteenth Century, asked me to deliver a lecture on the prophet Darwin. I did so [on 23 March 1906]; and scraps of that lecture, which was never published, variegate these pages.

POLITICAL INADEQUACY OF THE HUMAN ANIMAL

Ten more years elapsed. Neo-Darwinism in politics had produced a European catastrophe of a magnitude so appalling, and a scope so unpredictable, that as I write these lines in 1920, it is still far from certain whether our civilization will survive it. The circumstances of this catastrophe, the boyish cinema-fed romanticism which made it possible to impose it on the people as a crusade, and especially the ignorance and errors of the victors of Western Europe when its violent phase had passed and the time for reconstruction arrived, confirmed a doubt which had grown steadily in my mind during my forty years public work as a Socialist: namely, whether the human animal, as he exists at present, is capable of solving the social problems raised by his own aggregation, or, as he calls it, his civilization.

COWARDICE OF THE IRRELIGIOUS

Another observation I had made was that goodnatured unambitious men are cowards when they have no religion. They are dominated and exploited not only by greedy and often half-witted and half-alive weaklings who will do anything for cigars, champagne, motor cars, and the more childish and selfish uses of money, but by able and sound administrators who can do nothing else with them than dominate and exploit them. Government and exploitation become synonymous under such circumstances; and the world is finally ruled by the childish, the brigands, and the blackguards. Those who refuse to stand in with them are persecuted and occasionally executed when they give any trouble to the exploiters. They fall into poverty when they lack lucrative specific talents. At the present moment one half of Europe, having knocked the other half down, is trying to kick it to death, and may succeed: a procedure which is, logically, sound Neo-Darwinism. And the goodnatured majority are looking on in helpless horror, or allowing themselves to be persuaded by the newspapers of their exploiters that the kicking is not only a sound commercial investment, but an act of divine justice of which they are the ardent instruments.

But if Man is really incapable of organizing a big civilization, and cannot organize even a village or a tribe any too well, what is the use of giving him a religion? A religion may make him hunger and thirst for righteousness; but will it endow him with the practical capacity to satisfy that appetite? Good intentions do not carry with them a grain of political science, which is a very complicated one, quite beyond the normal parliament man to whom political science is as remote and distasteful as the differential calculus, and to whom such an elementary but vital point as the law of economic rent is a *pons asinorum* [asses' bridge] never to be approached, much less crossed. As to the common voter, he is mostly so hard at work all day earning a living that he cannot keep awake for five minutes over a book.

IS THERE ANY HOPE IN EDUCATION?

The usual answer is that we must educate our masters: that is, ourselves. We must teach citizenship and political science at school. But must we? There is no must about it, the hard fact being that we must *not* teach political science or citizenship at school. The schoolmaster who attempted it would soon find himself penniless in the streets without pupils, if not in the dock pleading to a pompously worded indictment for sedition against the exploiters. Our schools teach the morality of feudalism corrupted by commercialism, and hold up the military conqueror, the robber baron, and the profiteer, as models of the illustrious and the successful. In vain do the prophets who see through this imposture preach and teach a better gospel: the individuals whom they convert are doomed to pass away in a few years; and the new generations are dragged back in the schools to the morality of the XV century, and think themselves Liberal when they are defending the ideas of Henry VII, and gentlemanly when they are opposing to them the ideas of Richard III. Thus the educated man is a greater nuisance than the uneducated one: indeed it is the inefficiency and sham of the educational side of our schools (to which, except under compulsion, children would not be sent by their parents at all if they did not act as prisons in which the immature are kept from worrying the mature) that save us from being dashed on the rocks of false doctrine instead of drifting down the midstream of mere ignorance. There is no way out through our present public schools.

HOMEOPATHIC EDUCATION

Our education, however, is not all false. It must teach mathematics and grammar honestly; and this involves a training in logic. Why does not such training provoke our scholars to detect falsehood? The answer is that it sometimes does. Voltaire was a pupil of the Jesuits; Samuel Butler was a public schoolboy who had had his Latin grammar beaten into him by his father, a hopelessly conventional and erroneous country parson. But then Voltaire was Voltaire, and Butler was Butler: that is, their minds were so abnormally strong that they could throw off the doses of poison that paralyze ordinary minds. When the doctors inoculate you and the homeopathists drug you, they give you an infinitesimally attenuated dose. If they gave you the virus at full strength it would overcome your resistance and produce its direct effect. The doses of false doctrine given at public schools and universities are so big that they overwhelm the resistance that a tiny dose would provoke. The normal student is corrupted beyond redemption, and will drive the genius who resists out of the country if he can. Byron and Shelley had to fly to Italy, whilst [Robert Stewart, Viscount] Castlereagh [Foreign Secretary] and [John Scott, First Earl of] Eldon [Lord Chancellor] ruled the roost at home. Rousseau was hunted from frontier to frontier; Karl Marx starved in exile in a Soho lodging; Ruskin's articles were refused by the magazines (he was too rich to be otherwise persecuted);

whilst mindless forgotten nonentities governed the land; sent men to the prison or the gallows for blasphemy and sedition (meaning the truth about Church and State); and sedulously stored up the social disease and corruption which explode from time to time in mechanized world wars that have neither the romance of chivalry nor the solid gains of conquest.

Homeopathic education has not yet been officially tried, and would obviously be a delicate matter if it were. A body of schoolmasters inciting their pupils to infinitesimal peccadilloes with the object of provoking them to exclaim "Get thee behind me, Satan," or telling them white lies about history for the sake of being contradicted, insulted, and refuted, would certainly do less harm than our present educational allopaths do; but then nobody will advocate homeopathic education. Allopathy has produced the poisonous illusion that it enlightens instead of darkening. The suggestion may, however, explain why, whilst most people's minds succumb to inculcation and environment, a few react vigorously: honest and decent people coming from thievish slums, and sceptics and realists from country parsonages.

THE DIABOLICAL EFFICIENCY OF TECHNICAL EDUCATION

But meanwhile—and here comes the horror of it—our technical instruction is honest and efficient. The public schoolboy who is carefully blinded, duped, and corrupted as to the nature of a society based on profiteering, and is taught to honor parasitic idleness and luxury, learns to shoot and ride and keep fit with all the assistance and guidance that can be procured for him by the most anxiously sincere desire that he may do these things well, and if possible superlatively well. In the army he learns to fly; to drop bombs; to use machine-guns to the utmost of his capacity. The discovery of high explosives is rewarded and dignified: instruction in the manufacture of the weapons, battleships, submarines, and land batteries by which they are applied destructively, is quite genuine: the instructors know their business, and really mean the learners to succeed. The result is that powers of destruction that could hardly without uneasiness be entrusted to infinite wisdom and infinite benevolence are placed in the hands of romantic schoolboy patriots who, however generous by nature, are by education ignoramuses, dupes, snobs, and sportsmen to whom fighting is a religion and killing an accomplishment; whilst political power is left to militarist imperialists in chronic terror of invasion and subjugation, pompous tufthunting fools, commercial adventurers to whom the organization by the nation of its own industrial services would mean checkmate, financial parasites on the money market, stupid people who cling to the *status quo* merely because they are used to it, rich party Yesmen to whom the House of Commons is only a fashionable club, and Anarchist Bohemians and freebooters who want liberties without duties. Place and power are obtainable by heredity, by simple purchase, by keeping newspapers and pretending that they are organs of public opinion, by the wiles of seductive women, and by prostituting ambitious talent to the service of the profiteers, who call the tune because, having secured all the spare plunder, they alone can afford to pay the piper.

Under such circumstances neither the rulers nor the ruled can understand high politics. They do not even know that there is such a branch of knowledge as political science; but between them they can coerce and enslave with the deadliest efficiency, even to the wiping out of civilization, because their education as slayers has been honestly and thoroughly carried out. The commonplace sound people submit, and compel the rest to submit, because they have been taught to do so as an article of religion and a point of honor. Those in whom natural enlightenment has reacted against artificial education submit because they are compelled; but they would resist, and finally resist effectively, if they were not cowards. And they are cowards because they have neither an officially accredited and established religion nor a generally recognized point of honor, and are all at sixes and sevens with their various private speculations, sending their children perforce to the schools where they will be corrupted for want of any other schools. The rulers are equally intimidated by the immense extension and cheapening of the means of slaughter and destruction. The old British caution which maintained a balance of Power through command of the sea is intensified into a terror that sees security in nothing short of absolute military mastery of the entire globe: that is, in an impossibility that will yet seem possible in detail to soldiers and to parochial and insular patriotic civilians.

FLIMSINESS OF CIVILIZATION

This situation has occurred so often before, always with the same result of a collapse of civilization (Professor Flinders Petrie[2] has let out the secret

2. Sir Flinders Petrie, British archaeologist and Professor of Egyptology at University College, London, was the author of *Ten Years' Digging in Egypt* (1892) and *Methods and Aims in Archaeology* (1904).

of previous collapses), that the rich are instinctively crying "Let us eat and drink; for tomorrow we die" [Isaiah 22: 13], and the poor, "How long, O Lord, how long?" [echoes Psalm 13]. But the pitiless reply still is that God helps those who help themselves. This does not mean that if Man cannot find the remedy no remedy will be found. The power that produced Man when the monkey was not up to the mark, can produce a higher creature than Man if Man does not come up to the mark. We must beware; for Man is not yet an ideal creature. At his present best many of his ways are so unpleasant that they are unmentionable in polite society, and so painful that he is compelled to pretend that pain is often a good. Nature, also called Providence, holds no brief for the human experiment: it must stand or fall by its results. If Man will not serve, Nature will try another experiment.

What hope is there then of human improvement? According to the Neo-Darwinists, to the Mechanists, no hope whatever, because improvement can come only through some senseless accident which must, on the statistical average of accidents, be presently wiped out by some other equally senseless accident.

CREATIVE EVOLUTION

But this dismal creed does not discourage those who believe that the impulse that produces evolution is creative. They have observed the simple fact that the will to do anything can and does, at a certain pitch of intensity set up by conviction of its necessity, create and organize new tissue to do it with. To them therefore mankind is by no means played out yet. If the weight lifter, under the trivial stimulus of an athletic competition, can "put up a muscle," it seems reasonable to believe that an equally earnest and convinced philosopher could "put up a brain." Both are directions of vitality to a certain end. Evolution shews us this direction of vitality doing all sorts of things: providing the centipede with a hundred legs, and ridding the fish of any legs at all; building lungs and arms for the land and gills and fins for the sea; enabling the mammal to gestate its young inside its body, and the fowl to incubate hers outside it; offering us, we may say, our choice of any sort of bodily contrivance to maintain our activity and increase our resources.

VOLUNTARY LONGEVITY

Among other matters apparently changeable at will is the duration of individual life. Weismann, a very clever and suggestive biologist who was unhappily stultified by Neo-Darwinism, pointed out [in *Essays upon Heredity*] that as certain living organisms, though they multiply by splitting into living halves, never die, death is neither natural nor inevitable.

Besides, life varies widely in duration. Nobody can explain why a parrot should live ten times as long as a dog, and a turtle centuries longer than a wasp. Even within the same species we find Man's average lifetime varying from generation to generation and from individual to individual. Luigi Cornaro[3] lived sixty years longer than Raphael or Mozart. Even our oldest men do not live long enough: they are, for all the purposes of high civilization, mere children when they die; and our Prime Ministers, though rated as mature, divide their time between the golf course and the Treasury Bench in parliament.

Conceivably, however, the same power that has taken us thus far can take us further. If Man now fixes the term of his life at three score and ten years he can fix it at three hundred or three thousand, or even until a sooner-or-later-inevitable accident makes an end. Surely our ruinous world-wars should convince him of the necessity for at least outliving his taste for golf and cigars if the race is to be saved.

This is not fantastic speculation: it is deductive biology, if there is such a science as biology.

Here, then, is an alternative to the scrapping of our species as a political failure, and its replacement by a new experiment in creative evolution. And so, to make the suggestion more entertaining than it would be to most people in the form of a biological treatise, I have written Back to Methuselah as a contribution to the modern Bible.

Many people, however, can read treatises and cannot read Bibles. Darwin could not read Shakespear.[4] Some who can read both, like to learn the history of their ideas. Some are so entangled in the current confusion of

3. Venetian nobleman who wrote a treatise, at the age of eighty-three, on *The Sure Certain Method of Attaining a Long and Healthful Life* (1558).
4. Darwin confided that as a boy 'I read ... Thomson's "Seasons", and the recently published poems of Byron and Scott. I mention this because later in life I wholly lost, to my great regret, all pleasure from poetry of any kind, including Shakespeare's' (*Life and Letters*, Vol. I, 1887).

Creative Evolution with Circumstantial Selection by their historical ignorance that they are puzzled by any distinction between the two. For all their sakes I must give here a little history of the conflict between the view of Evolution taken by the Darwinians (though not altogether by Darwin himself) and called Natural Selection, and that which is emerging, under the title of Creative Evolution, as the genuinely scientific religion for which all wise men are now anxiously looking.

THE EARLY EVOLUTIONISTS

Empedocles, in the V century B.C., was an Evolutionist; and there is no reason to assume that he was the first. Our contemporary Joseph Needham[5] will certainly not be the last. Erasmus Darwin, the grandfather of Charles, wrote, as his declaration of faith, "The world has been evolved, not created: it has arisen little by little from a small beginning, and has increased through the activity of the elemental forces embodied in itself, and so has rather grown than come into being at an almighty word. What a sublime idea of the infinite might of the great Architect, the Cause of all causes, the Father of all fathers, the Ens Entium [the being of being]! For if we would compare the Infinite, it would surely require a greater Infinite to cause the causes of effects than to produce the effects themselves." In this [*Zoonomia*], published in the year 1794, you have XIX century Evolution precisely defined. And Erasmus Darwin was by no means its only apostle. It was in the air then. A German biologist named [Gottfried] Treviranus, whose book [*Biologie, oder Philosophie der Lebenden Natur*, 1802–22] was published in 1802, wrote, "In every living being there exists a capacity for endless diversity of form. Each possesses the power of adapting its organization to the variations of the external world; and it is this power, called into activity by cosmic changes, which has enabled the simple zoophytes of the primitive world to climb to higher and higher stages of organization, and has brought endless variety into nature." There you have your evolution of Man from the amœba all complete whilst Nelson was still alive on the seas. And in 1809 [in *Philosophie zoologique*], before the battle of Waterloo, a French soldier named [Jean-Baptiste de] Lamarck, who had beaten his musket into a microscope and turned zoologist, declared that species were an illusion produced by the shortness of our individual lives, and that they

5. Evolutionist, surgeon and professor of anatomy at the University of Aberdeen, author of *Man a Machine* (1927).

were constantly changing and melting into oneanother and into new forms as surely as the hand of a clock is continually moving, though it moves so slowly that it looks stationary to us. We have since come to think that its industry is less continuous: that the clock stops for a long time, and then is suddenly "put on" by a mysterious finger. But never mind that just at present.

THE ADVENT OF THE NEO-LAMARCKIANS

I call special attention to Lamarck, who, whilst making many ingenious suggestions as to the reaction of external causes on life and habit, such as changes of climate, food supply, geological upheavals and so forth, really held as his fundamental proposition that living organisms change because they want to. If you have no eyes, and want to see, and keep trying to see, you will finally get eyes. If, like a mole or a subterranean fish, you have eyes and dont want to see, you will lose your eyes. If you like eating the tender tops of trees enough to make you concentrate all your energies on the stretching of your neck, you will finally get a long neck, like the giraffe. This seems absurd to inconsiderate people at the first blush; but it is within the personal experience of all of us that it is just by this process that a child tumbling about on the floor becomes an adult walking erect; and that a man sprawling on the road with a bruised chin, or supine on the ice with a bashed occiput, becomes a bicyclist and a skater. The process is not continuous, as it would be if mere practice had anything to do with it; for though you may improve at each bicycling lesson *during* the lesson, when you begin your next lesson you do not begin at the point at which you left off: you relapse apparently to the beginning. Finally, you succeed quite suddenly, and never relapse again. More miraculous still, you at once exercise the new power unconsciously. Although you are adapting your front wheel to your balance so elaborately and actively that the accidental locking of your handle bars for a second will throw you off; though five minutes before you could not do it at all, yet now you do it as unconsciously as you grow your finger nails. You have a new faculty, and must have created some new bodily tissue as its organ. And you have done it solely by willing. For here there can be no question of Circumstantial Selection, or of the survival of the fittest. The man who is learning how to ride a bicycle has no advantage over the non-cyclist in the struggle for existence: quite the contrary. He has acquired a new habit, an automatic unconscious habit, solely because he wanted to, and kept trying until it was added unto him.

How Acquirements are Inherited

But when your son tries to skate or bicycle in his turn, he does not pick up the accomplishment where you left it, any more than he is born six feet high with a beard and a tall hat. The setback that occurred between your lessons occurs again. The race learns exactly as the individual learns. Your son relapses, not to the very beginning, but to a point which no mortal method of measurement can distinguish from the beginning. Now this is odd; for certain other habits of yours, equally acquired (to the Evolutionist, of course, all habits are acquired), equally unconscious, equally automatic, are transmitted without any perceptible relapse. For instance, the very first act of your son when he enters the world as a separate individual is to yell with indignation: that yell which Shakespear thought the most tragic and piteous of all sounds.[6] In the act of yelling he begins to breathe: another habit, and not even a necessary one, as the object of breathing can be achieved in other ways, as by deep-sea fishes. He circulates his blood by pumping it with his heart. He demands a meal, and proceeds at once to perform the most elaborate chemical operations on the food he swallows. He manufactures teeth; discards them; and replaces them with fresh ones. Compared to these habitual feats, walking, standing upright, and bicycling are the merest trifles; yet it is only by going through the wanting, trying process that he can stand, walk, or cycle, whereas in the other and far more difficult and complex habits he not only does not consciously want nor consciously try, but actually consciously objects very strongly. Take that early habit of cutting the teeth: would he do that if he could help it? Take that later habit of decaying and eliminating himself by death—equally an acquired habit, remember—how his consciousness abhors it! Yet it has become so automatic that he does it in spite of himself, even to his own destruction.

We have here a routine which, given time enough for it to operate, will finally produce the most elaborate forms of organized life on Lamarckian lines without the intervention of Circumstantial Selection at all. If you can turn a pedestrian into a cyclist, and a cyclist into a pianist or violinist,

6. The 'most tragic and piteous of all sounds' is Shaw's conclusion, apparently, in reference to Shakespeare's:

> Thou know'st the first time that we smell the air,
> We wawl and cry . . .
> When we are born, we cry that we are come
> To this great stage of fools. (*Lear*, IV: vi)

without the intervention of Circumstantial Selection, you can turn an amœba into a man, or a man into a superman, without it. All of which is rank heresy to the Neo-Darwinian, who imagines that if you stop Circumstantial Selection, you not only stop development but inaugurate a rapid and disastrous degeneration.

Let us fix the Lamarckian evolutionary process well in our minds. You are alive; and you want to be more alive. You want an extension of consciousness and of power. You want, consequently, additional organs, or additional uses of your existing organs: that is, additional habits. You get them because you want them badly enough to keep trying for them until they come. Nobody knows how: nobody knows why: all we know is that the thing actually takes place. We relapse miserably from effort to effort until the old organ is modified or the new one created, when suddenly the impossible becomes possible and the habit is formed. The moment we form it we want to get rid of the consciousness of it so as to economize our consciousness for fresh conquests of life; for all consciousness means preoccupation and obstruction. If we had to think about breathing or digesting or circulating our blood we should have no attention to spare for anything else, as we find to our cost when anything goes wrong with these operations. We want to be unconscious of them just as we wanted to acquire them; and we finally win what we want. But we win unconsciousness of our habits at the cost of losing our control of them; and we also build one habit and its corresponding functional modification of our organs on another, and so become dependent on our old habits. Consequently we have to persist in them even when they hurt us. We cannot stop breathing to avoid an attack of asthma, nor to escape drowning. We can lose a habit and discard an organ when we no longer need them, just as we acquired them; but this process is slow and broken by relapses; and relics of the organ and the habit long survive their utility. And if other and still indispensable habits and modifications have been built on the ones we wish to discard, we must provide a new foundation for them before we demolish the old ones. This is also a slow process and a very curious one.

THE MIRACLE OF CONDENSED RECAPITULATION

The relapses between the efforts to acquire a habit are important because, as we have seen, they recur not only from effort to effort in the case of the individual, but from generation to generation in the case of the race. This relapsing from generation to generation is an invariable characteristic of the

evolutionary process. For instance, Raphael, though descended from eight
uninterrupted generations of painters, had to learn to paint apparently as if
no Sanzio had ever handled a brush before. But he had also to learn to
breathe, and digest, and circulate his blood. Although his father and
mother were fully grown adults when he was conceived, he was not
conceived or even born fully grown: he had to go back and begin as a
speck of protoplasm, and to struggle through an embryonic lifetime,
during part of which he was indistinguishable from an embryonic dog, and
had neither a skull nor a backbone. When he at last acquired these articles,
he was for some time doubtful whether he was a bird or a fish. He had to
compress untold centuries of development into nine months before he was
human enough to break loose as an independent being. And even then he
was still so incomplete that his parents might well have exclaimed "Good
Heavens! have you learnt nothing from our experience that you come into
the world in this ridiculously elementary state? Why cant you talk and
walk and paint and behave decently?" To that question Baby Raphael had
no answer. All he could have said was that this is how evolution or
transformation happens. The time may come when the same force that
compressed the development of millions of years into nine months may
pack many more millions into even a shorter space; so that Raphaels may
be born painters as they are now born breathers and blood circulators. But
they will still begin as specks of protoplasm, and acquire the faculty of
painting in their mother's womb at quite a late stage of their embryonic
life. They must recapitulate the history of mankind in their own persons,
however briefly they may condense it.

Nothing was so astonishing and significant in the discoveries of the
embryologists, nor anything so absurdly little appreciated, as this recapitula-
tion, as it is now called: this power of hurrying up into months a process
which was once so long and tedious that the mere contemplation of it is
unendurable by men whose span of life is three-score-and-ten. It widened
human possibilities to the extent of enabling us to hope that the most
prolonged and difficult operations of our minds may yet become instantane-
ous, or, as we call it, instinctive. It also directed our attention to examples
of this packing up of centuries into seconds which were staring us in the
face in all directions. As I write these lines the newspapers are occupied by
the exploits of a child of eight,[7] who has just defeated twenty adult chess

7. Samuel Rzeschewski, a Polish chess prodigy of eight, played simultaneous
games against twenty strong amateur players at the Gambit (Club) chess rooms on
10 August 1920, winning eighteen games and drawing two.

players in twenty games played simultaneously, and has been able after-wards to reconstruct all the twenty games without any apparent effort of memory. Most people, including myself, play chess (when they play it at all) from hand to mouth, and can hardly recall the last move but one, or foresee the next but two. Also, when I have to make an arithmetical calculation, I have to do it step by step with pencil and paper, slowly, reluctantly, and with so little confidence in the result that I dare not act on it without "proving" the sum by a further calculation involving more ciphering. But there are men who can neither read, write, nor cipher, to whom the answer to such sums as I can do is instantly obvious without any conscious calculation at all; and the result is infallible. Yet some of these natural arithmeticians have but a small vocabulary; are at a loss when they have to find words for any but the simplest everyday occasions; and cannot for the life of them describe mechanical operations which they perform daily in the course of their trade; whereas to me the whole vocabulary of English literature, from Shakespear to the latest edition of the Encyclopedia Britannica, is so completely and instantaneously at my call that I have never had to consult even a thesaurus except once or twice when for some reason I wanted a third or fourth synonym. Again, though I have tried and failed to draw recognizable portraits of persons I have seen every day for years, Sir Bernard Partridge [*Punch* cartoonist], having seen a man once, will, without more strain than is involved in eating a sandwich, draw him to the life. The keyboard of a piano is a device I have never been able to master; yet Mr Cyril Scott [English pianist and composer] uses it as easily as I use a knife and fork; and to Sir Edward Elgar an orchestral score was as instantaneously intelligible at sight as a page of Shakespear is to me. One man cannot, after trying for years, finger the flute fluently. Another will take up a flute with a newly invented arrangement of keys on it, and play it at once with hardly a mistake. We find people to whom writing is so difficult that they prefer to sign their name with a mark, and beside them men who master systems of shorthand and improvize new systems of their own as easily as they learnt the alphabet. These contrasts are to be seen on all hands, and have nothing to do with variations in general intelligence, nor even in the specialized intelligence proper to the faculty in question: for example, no composer or dramatic poet has ever pretended to be able to perform all the parts he writes for the singers, actors, and players who are his executants. One might as well expect Napoleon to be a fencer, or the Astronomer Royal to know how many beans make five any better than his bookkeeper. Even exceptional command of language does not imply the possession of ideas to express: [Giuseppe, Cardinal] Mezzofanti [chief keeper of the Vatican Library, 1833–8], the master of fiftyeight languages, had less to say in them than Shakespear with his little Latin and less Greek; and public life is the paradise of voluble windbags.

All these are cases in which a long, laborious, conscious, detailed process of acquirement has been condensed into an instinctive and unconscious inborn one. Factors which formerly had to be considered one by one in succession are integrated into what seems a single simple factor. Chains of hardly soluble problems have coalesced in one problem which solves itself the moment it is raised. What is more, they have been pushed back (or forward, if you like) from post-natal to pre-natal ones. The child in the womb may take some time over them; but it is a miraculously shortened time.

The time phenomena involved are curious, and suggest that we are either wrong about our history or else that we enormously exaggerate the periods required for the pre-natal acquirement of habits. In the XIX century we talked very glibly about geological periods, and flung millions of eons about in the most lordly manner in our reaction against Archbishop Ussher's chronology. We had a craze for big figures, and positively liked to believe that the progress made by the child in the womb in a month was represented in prehistoric time by ages and ages. We insisted that Evolution advanced more slowly than any snail ever crawled, and that Nature does not proceed by leaps and bounds. This was all very well as long as we were dealing with such acquired habits as breathing or digestion. It was possible to believe that dozens of epochs had gone to the slow building up of these habits. But when we have to consider the case of a man born not only as an accomplished metabolist, but with such aptitudes that he is a stenographer or pianist at least five-sixths ready-made as soon as he can control his hands intelligently, or a playwright, painter, sculptor, poet or philosopher while still adolescent, we are forced to suspect that acquirements can be assimilated and stored as congenital qualifications in a shorter time than we think; so that, as between [Sir Charles] Lyell[8] and Archbishop Ussher, the laugh may not be with Lyell quite so uproariously as it seemed fifty years ago.

---

8. Scottish geologist, who held that the greatest geological changes have been produced over millennia by forces still at work; author of *Geological Evidences of the Antiquity of Man* (1863).

Heredity an Old Story

It is evident that the evolutionary process is a hereditary one, or, to put it less drily, that human life is continuous and immortal. The Evolutionists took heredity for granted. So did everybody. The human mind has been soaked in heredity as long back as we can trace its thought. Hereditary peers, hereditary monarchs, hereditary castes and trades and classes were the best known of social institutions, and in some cases of public nuisances. Pedigree men counted pedigree dogs and pedigree horses among their most cherished possessions. Far from being unconscious of heredity, or sceptical, men were insanely credulous about it: they not only believed in the transmission of qualities and habits from generation to generation, but expected the son to begin mentally where the father left off.

This belief in heredity led naturally to the practice of Intentional Selection. Good blood and breeding were eagerly sought after in human marriage. In dealing with plants and animals, selection with a view to the production of new varieties and the improvement and modification of species has been practised ever since men began to cultivate them. My pre-Darwinian uncle knew as well as Darwin that the racehorse and the drayhorse are not separate creations from the Garden of Eden, but adaptations by deliberate human selection of the medieval warhorse to modern racing and industrial haulage. He knew that there are nearly two hundred different sorts of dogs, all capable of breeding with oneanother and of producing cross varieties unknown to Adam. He knew that the same thing is true of pigeons. He knew that gardeners had spent their lives trying to breed black tulips and green carnations and unheard-of orchids, and had actually produced flowers just as strange to Eve. His quarrel with the Evolutionists was not a quarrel with the evidence for Evolution: he had accepted enough of it to prove Evolution ten times over before he ever heard of it. What he repudiated was cousinship with the ape, and the implied suspicion of a rudimentary tail, because it was offensive to his sense of his own dignity, and because he thought that apes were ridiculous, and tails diabolical when associated with the erect posture. Also he believed that Evolution was a heresy which involved the destruction of Christianity, of which, as a member of the Protestant Episcopal Irish Church, he conceived himself a pillar. But this was only his ignorance; for a man may deny his descent from an ape and be eligible as a churchwarden without being any the less a convinced Evolutionist.

DISCOVERY ANTICIPATED BY DIVINATION

What is more, the religious folk can claim to be among the pioneers of Evolutionism. Weismann, Neo-Darwinist though he was, devoted a long passage in his History of Evolution [*Studien zur Descendenz-Theorie*, 1875–6] to the Nature Philosophy of Lorenz Oken, published in 1809 [*Lehrbuch der Naturphilosophie*, 1808–11]. Oken defined natural science as "the science of the everlasting transmutations of the Holy Ghost in the world." His religion had started him on the right track, and not only led him to think out a whole scheme of Evolution in abstract terms, but guided his aim in a significantly good scientific shot which brought him within the scope of Weismann. He not only defined the original substance from which all forms of life have developed as protoplasm, or, as he called it, primitive slime (*Urschleim*), but actually declared that this slime took the form of vesicles out of which the universe was built. Here was the modern cell morphology guessed by a religious thinker long before the microscope and the scalpel forced it on the vision of mere laboratory workers who could not think and had no religion. Lorenz Oken *thought* very hard to find out what was happening to the Holy Ghost, and thereby made a contribution of extraordinary biological importance. The man who was scientific enough to see that the Holy Ghost is a scientific fact got easily in front of the laboratory researchers who sinned against it.

The metaphysical side of Evolution was thus no novelty when Darwin arrived. Had Oken never lived, there would still have been millions of persons trained from their childhood to believe that we are continually urged upwards by a force called the Will of God. In 1819 Schopenhauer published his treatise on The World as Will, which is the metaphysical complement to Lamarck's natural history, as it demonstrates that the driving force behind Evolution is a will-to-live, and to live, as Christ said long before, more abundantly [John 10 : 10]. And the earlier philosophers, from Plato to Leibniz, had kept the human mind open for the thought of the universe as one idea behind all its physically apprehensible transformations.

CORRECTED DATES FOR THE DISCOVERY OF EVOLUTION

All this, remember, is the state of things in the pre-Darwin period, which so many of us still think of as a pre-evolutionary period. Evolutionism was the rage before Queen Victoria came to the throne. To fix this chronology, let me repeat the story told by Weismann[9] of the July revolution in Paris in 1830, when the French got rid of Charles the Tenth. Goethe was then still living; and a French friend of his called on him and found him wildly excited. "What do you think of the great event?" said Goethe. "The volcano is in eruption; and all is in flames. There can no longer be discussion with closed doors." The Frenchman replied that no doubt it was a terrible business; but what could they expect with such a ministry and such a king? "Stuff!" said Goethe: "I am not thinking of these people at all, but of the open rupture in the French Academy between [Georges] Cuvier [naturalist and anatomist] and [Geoffroy] St Hilaire [zoologist]. It is of the utmost importance to science." The rupture Goethe meant was about Evolution, Cuvier contending that there were four species, and St Hilaire that there was only one.

From 1830 to 1859, when Darwin published his Origin of Species, there was a slump in Evolutionism. Nobody who knew the theory was adding anything to it. This slump not only heightened the general impression of entire novelty when Darwin brought the subject to the front again but prevented him from realizing how much had been done before, even by his own grandfather, to whom he was accused of being unjust. His insistence on the godless part played in organic development by circumstances delighted the sceptical intelligentsia. Nowadays, when we are turning in weary disgust and disillusion from Neo-Darwinism and Mechanism to Vitalism and Creative Evolution, it is difficult to credit this. Let me therefore try to bring back something of the atmosphere of that time by describing a scene, very characteristic of its superstitions, in which I took what was then considered an unspeakably shocking part.

DEFYING THE LIGHTNING: A FRUSTRATED EXPERIMENT

One evening in 1878 or thereabouts, I, being then in my earliest twenties, was at a bachelor party of young men of the professional class in the house of a rising young London physician [J. Kingston Barton]. We fell to talking about religious revivals; and an anecdote was related of an

9. Shaw's source in Weismann is undetermined. Weismann's source, however, was Frédéric Soret's *Conversations avec Goethe*, ed. A. Robinet de Cléry (Paris, 1832), in the conversation dated 2 August 1830.

"infidel" who, having incautiously scoffed at the mission of Messrs [Dwight L.] Moody and [Ira D.] Sankey, a then famous firm of American evangelists, was subsequently carried home on a shutter, slain by divine vengeance as a blasphemer. A timid minority, without quite venturing to question the truth of the incident—for they naturally did not care to run the risk of going home on shutters themselves—nevertheless shewed a certain disposition to cavil at those who exulted in it; and something approaching to an argument began. At last it was alleged by the most evangelical of the disputants that Charles Bradlaugh, the most formidable atheist on the Secularist platform, had taken out his watch publicly and challenged the Almighty to strike him dead in five minutes if he really existed and disapproved of atheism. The leader of the cavillers, with great heat, repudiated this as a gross calumny, declaring that Bradlaugh had repeatedly and indignantly contradicted it, and implying that the atheist champion was far too pious a man to commit such a blasphemy. This exquisite confusion of ideas roused my sense of comedy. It was clear to me that the challenge attributed to Charles Bradlaugh was a scientific experiment of a quite simple, straightforward, and proper kind to ascertain whether the expression of atheistic opinions really did involve any personal risk. It was certainly the method taught in the Bible, Elijah having confuted the prophets of Baal in precisely that way, with every circumstance of bitter mockery of their god when he failed to send down fire from heaven [I Kings 18: 20–40]. Accordingly I said that if the question at issue were whether the penalty of questioning the theology of Messrs Moody and Sankey was to be struck dead on the spot by an incensed deity, nothing could effect a more convincing settlement of it than the very obvious experiment attributed to Mr Bradlaugh, and that consequently if he had not tried it, he ought to have tried it. The omission, I added, was one which could easily be remedied there and then, as I happened to share Mr Bradlaugh's views as to the absurdity of the belief in these violent interferences with the order of nature by a short-tempered and thin-skinned supernatural deity. Therefore—and at that point I took out my watch.

The effect was electrical. Neither sceptics nor devotees were prepared to abide the result of the experiment. In vain did I urge the pious to trust in the accuracy of their deity's aim with a thunderbolt, and the justice of his discrimination between the innocent and the guilty. In vain did I appeal to the sceptics to accept the logical outcome of their scepticism: it soon appeared that when thunderbolts were in question there were no sceptics. Our host, seeing that his guests would vanish precipitately if the impious challenge were uttered, leaving him alone with a solitary infidel under sentence of extermination in five minutes, interposed and forbade the experiment, pleading at the same time for a change of subject. I of course complied, but could not refrain from remarking that though the dreadful words had not been uttered, yet, as the thought had been formulated in my mind, it was very doubtful whether the consequences could be averted by sealing my lips. However, the rest appeared to feel that the game would be played according to the rules, and that it mattered very little what I thought so long as I said nothing. Only the leader of the evangelical party, I thought, was a little preoccupied until five minutes had elapsed and the weather was still calm.

In Quest of the First Cause

Another reminiscence. In those days we thought in terms of time and space, of cause and effect, as we still do; but we do not now demand from a religion that it shall explain the universe completely in terms of cause and effect, and present the world to us as a manufactured article and as the private property of its Manufacturer. We did then. We were invited to pity the delusion of certain heathens who held that the world is supported by an elephant who is supported by a tortoise.[10] Mahomet decided that the mountains are great weights to keep the world from being blown away into space. But we refuted these orientals by asking triumphantly what the tortoise stands on? Freethinkers asked which came first: the owl or the egg. Nobody thought of saying that the ultimate problem of existence, being clearly insoluble and even unthinkable on causation lines, could not be a causation problem. To pious people this would have been flat atheism, because they assumed that God must be a Cause, and sometimes called him The Great First Cause. To the Rationalists it would have been a renunciation of reason. Here and there a man would confess that he stood as with a dim lantern in a dense fog, and could see but a little way in any direction into infinity. But he did not really believe that infinity was infinite or that the eternal was also sempiternal: he assumed that all things, known and unknown, were caused.

Hence it was that I found myself one day towards the end of the eighteenseventies in a cell in the old Brompton Oratory arguing with

10. In Hindu myth Chukwa (the tortoise) supports Maha-Pudma (the elephant), who in turn supports the world.

Father [William E.] Addis,[11] who had been called by one of his flock to attempt my conversion to Roman Catholicism. The universe exists, said the father: somebody must have made it. If that somebody exists, said I, somebody must have made him. I grant that for the sake of argument, said the Oratorian. I grant you a maker of God. I grant you a maker of the maker of God. I grant you as long a line of makers as you please; but an infinity of makers is unthinkable and extravagant: it is no harder to believe in number one than in number fifty thousand or fifty million; so why not accept number one and stop there, since no attempt to get behind him will remove your logical difficulty? By your leave, said I, it is as easy for me to believe that the universe made itself as that a maker of the universe made himself: in fact much easier; for the universe visibly exists and makes itself as it goes along, whereas a maker for it is a hypothesis.

Of course we two could get no further on these lines. He rose, very sensible and friendly, and said that we were like two men working a saw, he pushing it forward and I pushing it back, and cutting nothing. But when we had dropped the subject and were walking through the refectory, he returned to it for a moment to say that he should go mad if he lost his belief. I, glorying in the robust callousness of youth and the comedic spirit, felt quite comfortable and said so; though I was touched, too, by his evident sincerity.

These two anecdotes are superficially trivial and even comic; but there is an abyss of horror beneath them. They reveal a condition so utterly irreligious that religion means nothing but belief in a nursery bogey, and its inadequacy is demonstrated by a toy logical dilemma, neither the bogey nor the dilemma having anything to do with religion, or being serious enough to impose on or confuse any properly educated child over the age of six. One hardly knows which is the more appalling: the abjectness of the

11. Revd Addis of the Oratory of St Philip Neri (a Roman Catholic church in the Brompton Road, South Kensington) was more likely to have been influenced by the young Shaw than the other way round, being unsettled and insecure in his ecclesiastical commitments through most of his life. The Scottish son of a Free Church minister in Edinburgh, he joined the Church of England while an Oxford scholar, but upon receipt of his degree entered the Roman Catholic Church. He was, from 1868 to 1878, a member of the community at the Oratory, being admitted to the priesthood by Henry Cardinal Manning in 1872. Later he withdrew from active participation in any religious order. In 1899 he was appointed lecturer in Old Testament criticism at Mansfield College; two years later he returned to the Church of England. The church Shaw visited was the second on the Brompton Road site; the third was consecrated in 1882.

credulity or the flippancy of the scepticism. The result was inevitable. All who were strongminded enough not to be terrified by the bogey were left stranded in empty contemptuous negation, and argued, when they argued at all, as I argued with Father Addis. But their position was not intellectually comfortable. A member of parliament expressed their discomfort when, objecting to the admission of Charles Bradlaugh into parliament, he said "Hang it all, a man should believe in something or somebody." It was easy to throw the bogey into the dustbin; but none the less the world, our corner of the universe, did not look like a pure accident: it presented evidences of design in every direction. There was mind and purpose behind it. As the anti-Bradlaugh member would have put it, there must be somebody behind the something: no atheist could get over that.

PALEY'S WATCH

[William] Paley[12] had put the argument in an apparently unanswerable form. If you found a watch, full of mechanism exquisitely adapted to produce a series of operations all leading to the fulfilment of one central purpose of measuring for mankind the march of the day and night, could you believe that it was not the work of a cunning artificer who had designed and contrived it all to that end? And here was a far more wonderful thing than a watch, a man with all his organs ingeniously contrived, cords and levers, girders and kingposts, circulating systems of pipes and valves, dialyzing membranes, retorts, carburettors, pumps, glands, ventilators, inlets and outlets, telephone transmitters in his ears, light recorders and lenses in his eyes: was it conceivable that this was the work of chance? that no artificer had wrought here? that there was no purpose in this, no design, no guiding intelligence? The thing was incredible. In vain did [Hermann] Helmholtz[13] declare that "the eye has every possible defect that can be found in an optical instrument, and even some peculiar to itself," and that "if an optician tried to sell me an instrument which had all these defects I should think myself quite justified in blaming his carelessness in the strongest terms, and sending him back his instrument" [in *Handbook*

12. English theologian and utilitarian philosopher, who published his lectures as *Principles of Moral and Political Philosophy* (1785), adopted as the textbook at Cambridge.
13. German physicist and physiologist, inventor of the ophthalmoscope and founder of the principle of the conservation of energy.

of Physiological Optics, 1856; 1867]. To discredit the optician's skill was not to get rid of the optician. The eye might not be so cleverly made as Paley thought, but it was made somehow, by somebody.

And then my argument with Father Addis began all over again. It was easy enough to say that every man makes his own eyes: indeed the embryologists had actually caught him doing it. But what about the very evident purpose that prompted him to do it? Why did he want to see, if not to extend his consciousness and his knowledge and his power? That purpose was at work everywhere, and must be something bigger than the individual eye-making man. Only the stupidest muckrakers could fail to see this, and even to know it as part of their own consciousness. Yet to admit it seemed to involve letting the bogey come back, so inextricably had we managed to mix up belief in the bogey's existence with belief in the existence of design in the universe.

THE IRRESISTIBLE CRY OF ORDER, ORDER!

Our scornful young scientific and philosophic lions of today must not blame the Church of England for this confusion of thought. In 1562 the Church, in convocation in London "for the avoiding of diversities of opinions and for the establishment of consent touching true religion," proclaimed in their first utterance, and as an Article of Religion, that God is "without body, parts, or passions," or, as we say, an *Élan Vital* or Life Force. Unfortunately neither parents, parsons, nor pedagogues could be induced to adopt that article. St John might say that "God is spirit" [John 4: 24] as pointedly as he pleased; our Sovereign Lady Elizabeth might ratify the Article [one of the thirty-nine articles adopted in 1571] again and again; serious divines might feel as deeply as they could that a God with body, parts, and passions could be nothing but an anthropomorphic idol: no matter: people at large could not conceive a God who was not anthropomorphic: they stood by the Old Testament legends of a God whose parts had been seen by one of the patriarchs, and finally set up as against the Church a God who, far from being without body, parts, or passions, was composed of nothing else, and of very evil passions too. They imposed this idol in practice on the Church itself, in spite of the First Article, and thereby homeopathically produced the atheist, whose denial of God was simply a denial of the idol and a demonstration against an unbearable and most unchristian idolatry. The idol was, as Shelley had been expelled from Oxford for pointing out, an almighty fiend, with a petty character and unlimited power, spiteful, cruel, jealous, vindictive, and physically violent. The most sadistic schoolmasters, the most tyrannical parents, fell far short in their attempts to imitate it. But it was not its social vices that brought it low. What made it scientifically intolerable was that it was ready at a moment's notice to upset the whole order of the universe on the most trumpery provocation, whether by stopping the sun in the valley of Ajalon [Joshua 10: 12–14] or sending an atheist home dead on a shutter (the shutter was indispensable because it marked the utter unpreparedness of the atheist, who, unable to save himself by a deathbed repentance, was subsequently roasted through all eternity in blazing brimstone). It was this disorderliness, this refusal to obey its own laws of nature, that created a scientific need for its destruction. Science could stand a cruel and unjust god; for nature was full of suffering and injustice. But a disorderly god was impossible. In the Middle Ages a compromise had been made by which two different orders of truth, religious and scientific, had been recognized, in order that a schoolman might say that two and two make four without being burnt for heresy. But the XIX century, steeped in a meddling, presumptuous, reading-and-writing, socially and politically powerful ignorance inconceivable by Thomas Aquinas or even Roger Bacon, was incapable of so convenient an arrangement; and science was strangled by bigoted ignoramuses claiming infallibility for their interpretation of the Bible, which was regarded, not as a literature nor even as a book, but partly as an oracle which answered and settled all questions, and partly as a talisman to be carried by soldiers in their breast pockets or placed under the pillows of persons who were afraid of ghosts. The tract shops exhibited in their windows bullet-dinted testaments, mothers' gifts to their soldier sons whose lives had been saved by it; for the muzzle-loaders of those days could not drive a projectile through so many pages.

THE MOMENT AND THE MAN

This superstition of a continual capricious disorder in nature, of a lawgiver who was also a lawbreaker, made atheists in all directions among clever and lightminded people. But atheism did not account for Paley's watch. Atheism accounted for nothing; and it was the business of science to account for everything that was plainly accountable. Science had no use for mere negation: what was desired by it above all things just then was a demonstration that the evidences of design could be explained without resort to the hypothesis of a personal designer. If only some genius, whilst admitting Paley's facts, could knock the brains out of Paley by the discovery of a method whereby watches could happen without watch-makers, that genius was assured of such a welcome from the thought of his day as no natural philosopher had ever enjoyed before.

The time being thus ripe, the genius appeared; and his name was Charles Darwin. And now, what did Darwin really discover?

Here, I am afraid, I shall require once more the assistance of the giraffe, or, as he was called in the days of the celebrated Buffoon, the camelopard (by children, cammyleopard). I do not remember how this animal imposed himself illustratively on the Evolution controversy; but there was no getting away from him then; and I am old-fashioned enough to be unable to get away from him now. How did he come by his long neck? Lamarck would have said, by wanting to get at the tender leaves high up on the tree, and trying until he succeeded in wishing the necessary length of neck into existence. Another answer was also possible: namely, that some prehistoric stockbreeder, wishing to produce a natural curiosity, selected the longest-necked animals he could find, and bred from them until at last an animal with an abnormally long neck was evolved by intentional selection, just as the racehorse or the fantail pigeon has been evolved. Both these explanations, you will observe, involve consciousness, will, design, purpose, either on the part of the animal itself or on the part of a superior intelligence controling its destiny. Darwin pointed out that a third explana-tion, involving neither will nor purpose nor design either in the animal or anyone else, was on the cards. If your neck is too short to reach your food, you die. That may be the simple explanation of the fact that all the surviving animals that feed on foliage have necks or trunks long enough to reach it. So bang goes your belief that the necks must have been designed to reach the food. But Lamarck did not believe that the necks were so designed in the beginning: he believed that the long necks were evolved by wanting and trying. Not necessarily, said Darwin. Consider the effect on the giraffes of the natural multiplication of their numbers, as insisted on by Malthus [in *An Essay on the Principle of Population*, 1798]. Suppose the average height of the foliage-eating animals is four feet, and that they increase in numbers until a time comes when all the trees are eaten away to within four feet of the ground. Then the animals who happen to be an inch or two short of the average will die of starvation. All the animals who happen to be an inch or so above the average will be better fed and stronger than the others. They will secure the strongest and tallest mates; and their progeny will survive whilst the average ones and the sub-average ones will die out. This process, by which the species gains, say, an inch in reach, will repeat itself until the giraffe's neck is so long that he can always find food enough within his reach, at which point, of course, the selective process stops and the length of the giraffe's neck stops with it. Otherwise, he would grow until he could browse off the trees in the moon. And this, mark you, without the intervention of any stock breeder, human or divine, and without will, purpose, design, or even consciousness beyond the blind will to satisfy hunger. It is true that this blind will, being in effect a will to live, gives away the whole case; but still, as compared to the open-eyed intelligent wanting and trying of Lamarck, the Darwinian process may be described as a chapter of accidents. As such, it seems simple, because you do not at first realize all that it involves. But when its whole significance dawns on you, your heart sinks into a heap of sand within you. There is a hideous fatalism about it, a ghastly and damnable reduction of beauty and intelligence, of strength and purpose, of honor and aspiration, to such casually picturesque changes as an avalanche may make in a mountain landscape, or a railway accident in a human figure. To call this Natural Selection is a blasphemy, possible to many for whom Nature is nothing but a casual aggregation of inert and dead matter, but eternally impossible to the spirits and souls of the righteous. If it be no blasphemy, but a truth of science, then the stars of heaven, the showers and dew, the winter and summer, the fire and heat, the mountains and hills, may no longer be called to exalt the Lord with us by praise: their work is to modify all things by blindly starving and murdering everything that is not lucky enough to survive in the universal struggle for hogwash.

THE BRINK OF THE BOTTOMLESS PIT

Thus did the neck of the giraffe reach out across the whole heavens and make men believe that what they saw there was a gloaming of the gods. For if this sort of selection could turn an antelope into a giraffe, it could conceivably turn a pond full of amœbas into the French Academy. Though Lamarck's way, the way of life, will, aspiration, and achievement, remained still possible, this newly shewn way of hunger, death, stupidity, delusion, chance, and bare survival was also possible: was indeed most certainly the way in which many apparently intelligently designed transformations had actually come to pass. Had I not preluded with the apparently idle story of my revival of the controversial methods of Elijah, I should be asked how it was that the explorer who opened up this gulf of despair, far from being stoned or crucified as the destroyer of the honor of the race and the purpose of the world, was hailed as Deliverer, Savior, Prophet, Redeemer, Enlightener, Rescuer, Hope Giver, and Epoch Maker; whilst poor Lamarck was swept aside as a crude and exploded guesser hardly worthy to be named as his erroneous forerunner. In the light of my anecdote, the explanation is obvious. The first thing the gulf did was to swallow up Paley, and the Disorderly Designer, and Shelley's Almighty Fiend [in *Prometheus Unbound*], and all the rest of the pseudo-religious rubbish that had blocked every upward and onward path since the hopes of men had turned to Science as their true Savior. It seemed such a convenient grave that nobody at first noticed that it was nothing less than the bottomless pit, now become a very real terror. For though Darwin left a path round it for his soul, his followers presently dug it right into the crater.

Yet for the moment, there was nothing but wild rejoicing. We had been so oppressed by the notion that everything that happened in the world was the arbitrary personal act of an arbitrary personal god of dangerously jealous and cruel personal character, so that even the relief of the pains of childbed and the operating table by chloroform was objected to as an interference with his arrangements which he would probably resent, that we just jumped at Darwin. When Napoleon was asked what would happen when he died, he said that Europe would express its intense relief with a great "Ouf!" Well, when Darwin killed the god who objected to chloroform, everybody who had ever thought about it said "Ouf!" Paley was buried fathoms deep with his watch, now fully accounted for without any divine artificer at all. We were so glad to be rid of both that we never gave a thought to the consequences. When a prisoner sees the door of his dungeon open, he dashes for it without stopping to think where he shall get his dinner outside. The moment we found that we could do without Shelley's almighty fiend intellectually, he went into the gulf that seemed only a dustbin with a suddenness that made our own lives one of the most astonishing periods in history. If I had told that uncle of mine that within thirty years from the date of our conversation I should be exposing myself to suspicions of the grossest superstition by questioning the sufficiency of Darwin; maintaining the reality of the Holy Ghost; and declaring that the phenomenon of the Thought becoming Flesh was occurring daily, he would have regarded me as the most extravagant madman our family had ever produced. Yet it was so. In 1906 I might have vituperated Jehovah more heartily than ever Shelley did without eliciting a protest in any circle of thinkers, or shocking any public audience accustomed to modern discussion; but when I described Darwin as "an intelligent and industrious pigeon fancier," that blasphemous levity, as it seemed, was received with horror and indignation. The tide has now turned; and every puny whipster may say what he likes about Darwin; but anyone who wants to know what it was to be a Lamarckian during the last quarter of the XIX century has only to read Mr [Henry] Festing Jones's memoir of Samuel Butler [1919] to learn how completely even a man of genius could isolate himself by antagonizing Darwin on the one hand and the Church on the other.

WHY DARWIN CONVERTED THE CROWD

I am well aware that in describing the effect of Darwin's discovery on naturalists and on persons capable of serious reflection on the nature and attributes of God, I am leaving the vast mass of the British public out of account. I have pointed out elsewhere that the British nation does not consist of atheists and Plymouth Brothers; and I am not now going to pretend that it ever consisted of Darwinians and Lamarckians. The average citizen is irreligious and unscientific: you talk to him about cricket and golf, market prices and party politics, not about evolution and relativity, transubstantiation and predestination. Nothing will knock into his head the fateful distinction between Evolution as promulgated by Erasmus Darwin, and Circumstantial (so-called Natural) Selection as revealed by his grandson. Yet the doctrine of Charles reached him, though the doctrine of Erasmus had passed over his head. Why did not Erasmus Darwin popularize the word Evolution as effectively as Charles?

The reason was, I think, that Circumstantial Selection is easier to understand, more visible and concrete, than Lamarckian evolution. Evolution as a philosophy and physiology of the will is a mystical process, which can be apprehended only by a trained, apt, and comprehensive thinker. Though the phenomena of use and disuse, of wanting and trying, of the manufacture of weight lifters and wrestlers from men of ordinary strength, are familiar enough as facts, they are extremely puzzling as subjects of thought, and lead you into metaphysics the moment you try to account for them. But pigeon fanciers, dog fanciers, gardeners, stock breeders, or stud grooms, can understand Circumstantial Selection, because it is their business to produce transformation by imposing on flowers and animals a Selection From Without. All that Darwin had to say to them was that the mere chapter of accidents is always doing on a huge scale what they themselves are doing on a very small scale. There is hardly a laborer attached to an English country house who has not taken a litter of kittens or puppies to the bucket, and drowned all of them except the one he thinks the most promising. Such a man has nothing to learn about the survival of the fittest except that it acts in more ways than he has yet noticed; for he knows quite well, as you will find if you are not too proud to talk to him, that this sort of selection occurs naturally (in Darwin's sense) too: that, for instance, a hard winter will kill off a weakly child as the bucket kills off a weakly puppy. Then there is the farm laborer. Shakespear's Touchstone [in *As You Like It*], a court-bred fool, was shocked to find in the shepherd a natural philosopher, and opined that he would be damned for the part he took in the sexual selection of sheep. As to the production of new species by the selection of variations, that is no news to your gardener. Now if you are familiar with these three processes: the survival of the fittest, sexual selection, and variation leading to new kinds, there is nothing to puzzle you in Darwinism.

That was the secret of Darwin's popularity. He never puzzled anybody. If very few of us have read The Origin of Species from end to end, it is not because it overtaxes our mind, but because we take in the whole case and are prepared to accept it long before we have come to the end of the innumerable instances and illustrations of which the book mainly consists. Darwin becomes tedious in the manner of a man who insists on continuing to prove his innocence after he has been acquitted. You assure him that there is not a stain on his character, and beg him to leave the court; but he will not be content with enough evidence to acquit him: he will have you listen to all the evidence that exists in the world. Darwin's industry was enormous. His patience, his perseverance, his conscientiousness reached the human limit. But he never got deeper beneath or higher above his facts than an ordinary man could follow him. He was not conscious of having raised a stupendous issue, because, though it arose instantly, it was not his business. He was conscious of having discovered a process of transformation and modification which accounted for a great deal of natural history. But he did not put it forward as accounting for the whole of natural history. He included it under the heading of Evolution, though it was only pseudo-evolution at best; but he revealed it as *a* method of evolution, not as *the* method of evolution. He did not pretend that it excluded other methods, or that it was the chief method. Though he demonstrated that many transformations which had been taken as functional adaptations (the current phrase for Lamarckian evoluti∨n) either certainly were or conceivably might be due to Circumstantial Selection, he was careful not to claim that he had superseded Lamarck or disproved Functional Adaptation. In short, he was not a Darwinian, but an honest naturalist working away at his job with so little preoccupation with theological speculation that he never quarreled with the theistic Unitarianism into which he was born, and remained to the end the engagingly simple and socially easygoing soul he had been in his boyhood, when his elders doubted whether he would ever be of much use in the world.

How We Rushed Down a Steep Place

Not so the rest of us intellectuals. We all began going to the devil with the utmost cheerfulness. Everyone who had a mind to change, changed it. Only Samuel Butler, on whom Darwin had acted homeopathically, reacted against him furiously; ran up the Lamarckian flag to the top-gallant peak; declared with penetrating accuracy that Darwin had "banished mind from the universe" [see p. 300, fn. 16]; and even attacked Darwin's personal character, unable to bear the fact that the author of so abhorrent a doctrine was an amiable and upright man. Nobody would listen to him. He was so completely submerged by the flowing tide of Darwinism that when Darwin wanted to clear up the misunderstanding on which Butler was basing his personal attacks, Darwin's friends, very foolishly and snobbishly, persuaded him that Butler was too ill-conditioned and negligible to be answered. That they could not recognize in Butler a man of genius mattered little: what did matter was that they could not understand the provocation under which he was raging. They actually regarded the banishment of mind from the universe as a glorious enlightenment and emancipation for which he was ignorantly ungrateful. Even now, when Butler's eminence is unchallenged, and his biographer, Mr Festing Jones is enjoying a vogue like that of Boswell or [John] Lockhart [biographer of Sir Walter Scott], his memoirs shew him rather as a shocking example of the bad controversial manners of our country parsonages than as a prophet who tried to head us back when we were gaily dancing to our damnation across the rainbow bridge which Darwinism had thrown over the gulf which separates life and hope from death and despair. We were intellectually intoxicated with the idea that the world could make itself without design, purpose, skill, or intelligence: in short, without life. We completely overlooked the difference between the modification of species by adaptation to their environment and the appearance of new species: we just threw in the word "variations" or the word "sports" (fancy a man of science talking of an unknown factor as a sport instead of as x!) and left them to "accumulate" and account for the difference between a cockatoo and a hippopotamus. Such phrases set us free to revel in demonstrating to the Vitalists and Bible worshippers that if we once admit the existence of any kind of force, however unintelligent, and stretch out the past to unlimited time for such force to operate accidentally in, that force may conceivably, by the action of Circumstantial Selection, produce a world in which every function has an organ perfectly adapted to perform it, and therefore presents every appearance of having been designed, like Paley's watch, by a conscious and intelligent artificer for the purpose. We took a perverse pleasure in arguing, without the least suspicion that we were reducing ourselves to absurdity, that all the books in the British Museum library might have been written word for word as they stand on the shelves if no human being had ever been conscious, just as the trees stand in the forest doing wonderful things without consciousness.

And the Darwinians went far beyond denying consciousness to trees. Weismann insisted that the chick breaks out of its eggshell automatically; that the butterfly, springing into the air to avoid the pounce of the lizard, "does not wish to avoid death; knows nothing about death," what has happened being simply that a flight instinct evolved by Circumstantial Selection reacts promptly to a visual impression produced by the lizard's movement. His proof is that the butterfly immediately settles again on the flower, and repeats the performance every time the lizard springs, thus shewing that it learns nothing from experience, and—Weismann concludes—is not conscious of what it does.

It should hardly have escaped so curious an observer that when the cat jumps up on the dinner table, and you put it down, it instantly jumps up again, and finally establishes its right to a place on the cloth by convincing you that if you put it down a hundred times it will jump up a hundred and one times; so that if you desire its company at dinner you can have it only on its own terms. If Weismann really thought that cats act thus without any consciousness or any purpose, immediate or ulterior, he must have known very little about cats. But a thoroughgoing Weismannite, if any such still survive from those mad days, would contend that I am not at present necessarily conscious of what I am doing; that my writing of these lines, and your reading of them, are effects of Circumstantial Selection; that I need know no more about Darwinism than a butterfly knows of a lizard's appetite; and that the proof that I actually am doing it unconsciously is that as I have spent forty years in writing in this fashion without, as far as I can see, producing any visible effect on public opinion, I must be incapable of learning from experience, and am therefore a mere automaton. And the Weismannite demonstration of this would of course be an equally unconscious effect of Circumstantial Selection.

Darwinism not Finally Refutable

Do not too hastily say that this is inconceivable. To Circumstantial Selection all mechanical and chemical reactions are possible, provided you accept the geologists' estimates of the great age of the earth, and therefore allow time enough for the circumstances to operate. It is true that mere survival of the fittest in the struggle for existence plus sexual selection fail as hopelessly to account for Darwin's own life work as for my conquest of the bicycle; but who can prove that there are not other soulless factors, unnoticed or undiscovered, which only require imagination enough to fit them to the evolution of an automatic Jesus or Shakespear? When a man tells you that you are a product of Circumstantial Selection solely, you cannot finally disprove it. You can only tell him out of the depths of your inner conviction that he is a fool and a liar. But as this, though British, is uncivil, it is wiser to offer him the counter-assurance that you are the product of Lamarckian evolution, formerly called Functional Adaptation and now Creative Evolution, and challenge him to disprove *that*, which he can no more do than you can disprove Circumstantial Selection, both forces being conceivably able to produce anything if you only give them rope enough. You may also defy him to act for a single hour on the assumption that he may safely cross Oxford Street in a state of unconsciousness, trusting to his dodging reflexes to react automatically and promptly enough to the visual impression produced by a motorbus, and the audible impression produced by its hooter. But if you allow yourself to defy him to explain any particular action of yours by Circumstantial Selection, he should always be able to find some explanation that will fit the case if only he is ingenious enough and goes far enough to find it. Darwin found several such explanations in his controversies. Anybody who really wants to believe that the universe has been produced by Circumstantial Selection cooperating with a force as inhuman as we conceive magnetism to be can find a logical excuse for his belief if he tries hard enough.

Traumatic Selection

The stultification and damnation which ensued are illustrated by a comparison of the ease and certainty with which Butler's mind moved to humane and inspiring conclusions with the grotesque stupidities and cruelties of the idle and silly controversy which arose among the Darwinians as to whether acquired habits can be transmitted from parents to offspring. Consider, for example, how Weismann set to work on that subject. An Evolutionist with a live mind would first have dropped the popular expression "acquired habits," because to an Evolutionist there are no other habits and can be no others, a man being only an amœba with acquirements. He would then have considered carefully the process by which he himself had acquired his habits. He would have assumed that the habits with which he was born must have been acquired by a similar process. He would have known what a habit is: that is, an action voluntarily attempted until it has become more or less automatic and involuntary; and it would never have occurred to him that injuries or accidents coming from external sources against the will of the victim could possibly establish a habit; that, for instance, a family could acquire a habit of being killed in railway accidents.

And yet Weismann began to investigate the point by behaving like the farmer's wife in the old catch. He got a colony of mice, and cut off their tails. Then he waited to see whether their children would be born without tails. They were not, as Butler could have told him beforehand. He then cut off the children's tails, and waited to see whether the grandchildren would be born with at least rather short tails. They were not, as I could have told him beforehand. So with the patience and industry on which men of science pride themselves, he cut off the grandchildren's tails too, and waited, full of hope, for the birth of curtailed great-grandchildren. But their tails were quite up to the mark, as any fool could have told him beforehand. Weismann then gravely drew the inference that acquired habits cannot be transmitted. And yet Weismann was not a born imbecile. He was an exceptionally clever and studious man, not without roots of imagination and philosophy in him which Darwinism killed as weeds. How was it that he did not see that he was not experimenting with habits or characteristics at all? How had he overlooked the glaring fact that his experiment had been tried for many generations in China on the feet of Chinese women without producing the smallest tendency on their part to be born with abnormally small feet? He must have known about the bound feet even if he knew nothing of the mutilations, the clipped ears and docked tails, practised by dog fanciers and horse breeders on many generations of the unfortunate animals they deal in. Such amazing blindness and stupidity on the part of a man who was naturally neither blind nor stupid is a telling illustration of what Darwin unintentionally did to the minds of his disciples by turning their attention so exclusively towards the part played in Evolution by accident and violence operating with entire callousness to suffering and sentiment.

A vital conception of Evolution would have taught Weismann that biological problems are not to be solved by assaults on mice. The scientific form of his experiment would have been something like this. First, he should have procured a colony of mice highly susceptible to hypnotic suggestion. He should then have hypnotized them into an urgent conviction that the fate of the *musqué* [musky] world depends on the disappearance of its tail, just as some ancient and forgotten experimenter seems to have convinced the cats of the Isle of Man. Having thus made the mice desire to lose their tails with a life-or-death intensity, he would very soon have seen a few mice born with little or no tail. These would be recognized by the other mice as superior beings, and privileged in the division of food and in sexual selection. Ultimately the tailed mice would be put to death as monsters by their fellows, and the miracle of the tailless mouse completely achieved.

The objection to this experiment is not that it seems too funny to be taken seriously, and is not cruel enough to overawe the mob, but simply that it is impossible because the human experimenter cannot get at the mouse's mind. And that is what is wrong with all the barren cruelties of the laboratories. Darwin's followers did not think of this. Their only idea of investigation was to imitate "Nature" by perpetrating violent and senseless cruelties, and watch the effect of them with a paralyzing fatalism which forbade the smallest effort to use their minds instead of their knives and eyes, and established an abominable tradition that the man who hesitates to be as cruel as Circumstantial Selection itself is a traitor to science. For Weismann's experiment upon the mice was a mere joke compared to the atrocities committed by other Darwinians in their attempts to prove that mutilations could not be transmitted. Granted that the worst of these experiments may not have been experiments at all, but cruelties committed by cruel men attracted to the laboratory as a secret refuge left by law and public superstition for the amateur of passionate torture. But there is no reason to suspect Weismann of Sadism. Cutting off the tails of several generations of mice is not voluptuous enough to tempt a scientific Nero. It was a mere piece of one-eyedness; and it was Darwin who put out Weismann's humane and sensible eye. He blinded many another eye and paralyzed many another will also. Ever since he set up Circumstantial Selection as the creator and ruler of the universe, the scientific world has been the very citadel of stupidity and cruelty. Fearful as the tribal god of the Hebrews was, nobody ever shuddered as they passed even his meanest and narrowest little Bethel[14] or his proudest war-consecrating cathedral as we shudder now when we pass a physiological laboratory. If we dreaded and mistrusted the priest, we could at least keep him out of the house; but what of the modern Darwinist surgeon whom we dread and mistrust ten times more, but into whose hands we must all give ourselves from time to time? Miserably as religion had been debased, it did at least still proclaim that our relation to oneanother was that of a fellowship in which we were all equal and members one of another before the judgment seat of our common father. Darwinism proclaimed that our true relation is that of competitors and combatants in a struggle for mere survival, and that every act of pity or loyalty to the old fellowship is a vain and mischievous attempt to lessen the severity of the struggle and preserve inferior varieties from the efforts of Nature to weed them out. Even in Socialist Societies which existed solely to substitute the law of fellowship for the law of competition, and the method of providence and wisdom for the method of rushing violently down a steep place into the sea, I found myself regarded as a blasphemer and an ignorant sentimentalist because whenever the Neo-Darwinian doctrine was preached there I made no attempt to conceal my intellectual contempt for its blind coarseness and shallow logic, or my natural abhorrence of its sickening inhumanity.

THE GREATEST OF THESE IS SELF-CONTROL

As there is no place in Darwinism for free will, or any other sort of will, the Neo-Darwinists held that there is no such thing as self-control. Yet self-control is just the one quality of survival value which Circumstantial Selection must invariably and inevitably develop in the long run. Uncontroled qualities may be selected for survival and development for certain periods and under certain circumstances. For instance, since it is the ungovernable gluttons who strive the hardest to get food and drink, their efforts would develop their strength and cunning in a period of such scarcity that the utmost they could do would not enable them to over-eat themselves. But a change of circumstances involving a plentiful supply of food would destroy them. We see this very thing happening often enough in the case of the healthy and vigorous poor man who becomes a millionaire by one of the accidents of our competitive commerce, and immediately proceeds

14. Any small place where God is worshipped, from Bethel in Palestine, scene of Jacob's vision of a ladder (Genesis 28: 17–19).

to dig his grave with his teeth. But the self-controled man survives all such changes of circumstance, because he adapts himself to them, and eats neither as much as he can hold nor as little as he can scrape along on, but as much as is good for him. What *is* self-control? It is nothing but a highly developed vital sense, dominating and regulating the mere appetites. To overlook the very existence of this supreme sense; to miss the obvious inference that it is the quality that distinguishes the fittest to survive; to omit, in short, the highest moral claim of Evolutionary Selection: all this, which the Neo-Darwinians did in the name of Natural Selection, shewed the most pitiable want of mastery of their own subject, the dullest lack of observation of the forces upon which Natural Selection works.

The Humanitarians and the Problem of Evil

The humanitarians were as delighted as anybody with Darwinism at first. They had been perplexed by the Problem of Evil and the Cruelty of Nature. They were Shelleyists, but not atheists. Those who believed in God were at a terrible disadvantage with the atheist. They could not deny the existence of natural facts so cruel that to attribute them to the will of a god is to make that god a demon. Belief in Jehovah was hard for any thoughtful person without belief in the Devil as well. The painted Devil, with his horns, his barbed tail, and his abode of burning brimstone, was an incredible bogey; but the evil attributed to him was real enough; and the atheists argued that the author of evil, if he exists, must be strong enough to overcome God, else God is morally responsible for everything he permits the Devil to do. Neither conclusion delivered us from the horror of attributing the cruelty of nature to the workings of an evil will, or could reconcile it with our impulses towards justice, mercy, and a higher life.

A complete deliverance was offered by the discovery of Circumstantial Selection: that is to say, of a method by which horrors having every appearance of being elaborately planned by some intelligent contriver are only accidents without any moral significance at all. Suppose a watcher from the stars saw a frightful accident produced by two crowded trains at full speed crashing into oneanother! How could he conceive that a catastrophe brought about by such elaborate machinery, such ingenious preparation, such skilled direction, such vigilant industry, was quite unintentional? Would he not conclude that the signalmen were devils?

Well, Circumstantial Selection is largely a theory of collisions: that is, a theory of the innocence of much apparently designed devilry. In this way

Darwin brought intense relief as well as an enlarged knowledge of facts to the humanitarians. He destroyed the omnipotence of God for them; but he also exonerated God from a hideous charge of cruelty. Granted that the comfort was shallow, and that deeper reflection was bound to shew that worse than all conceivable devil-deities is a blind, deaf, dumb, heartless, senseless mob of forces that strike as a tree does when it is blown down by the wind, or as the tree itself is struck by lightning. This did not occur to the humanitarians at the moment: people do not reflect deeply when they are in the first happiness of escape from an intolerably oppressive situation.

Happily for our uneasy souls the problem of evil yields easily to Creative Evolution. If the driving power behind Evolution is omnipotent only in the sense that there seems no limit to its final achievement; and if it must meanwhile struggle with matter and circumstance by the method of trial and error, then the world must be full of its unsuccessful experiments. Christ may meet a tiger, or a High Priest arm-in-arm with a Roman Governor, and be the unfittest to survive under the circumstances. Mozart may have a genius that prevails against Emperors and Archbishops, and a lung that succumbs to some obscure and noxious property of foul air. If all our calamities are either accidents or sincerely repented mistakes, there is no malice in the Cruelty of Nature and no Problem of Evil in the Victorian sense at all. The theology of the women who told us that they became atheists when they sat by the cradles of their children and saw them strangled by the hand of God is succeeded by the theology of [Shaw's] Blanco Posnet, with his "It was early days when He made the croup, I guess. It was the best He could think of then; but when it turned out wrong on His hands He made you and me to fight the croup for Him."

WHY DARWIN PLEASED THE SOCIALISTS

The Humanitarians were not alone among the agitators in their welcome to Darwin. He had the luck to please everybody who had an axe to grind. The Militarists were as enthusiastic as the Humanitarians, the Socialists as the Capitalists. The Socialists were specially encouraged by Darwin's insistence on the influence of environment. Perhaps the strongest moral bulwark of Capitalism is the belief in the efficacy of individual righteousness. Robert Owen made desperate efforts to convince England that her criminals, her drunkards, her ignorant and stupid masses, were the victims of circumstance: that if we would only establish his new moral world we should find that the masses born into an educated and moralized community would be themselves educated and moralized. The stock reply to this is to be found in [George Henry] Lewes's Life of Goethe [1855]. Lewes[15] scorned the notion that circumstances govern character. He pointed to the variety of character in the governing rich class to prove the contrary [in *Biographical History of Philosophy*, 1845–6]. Similarity of circumstance can hardly be carried to a more desolating dead level than in the case of the individuals who are born and bred in English country houses, and sent first to Eton or Harrow, and then to Oxford or Cambridge, to have their minds and habits formed. Such a routine would destroy individuality if anything could. Yet individuals come out from it as different as Pitt from Fox. There was no more effective retort to the Socialist than to tell him to reform himself before he pretends to reform society. If you were rich, how pleasant it was to feel that you owed your riches to the superiority of your own character! The industrial revolution had turned numbers of greedy dullards into monstrously rich men. Nothing could be more humiliating and threatening to them than the view that the falling of a shower of gold into their pockets was as pure an accident as the falling of a shower of hail on their umbrellas, and happened alike to the just and unjust. Nothing could be more flattering and fortifying to them than the assumption that they were rich because they were virtuous.

Now Darwinism made a clean sweep of all such selfrighteousness. It more than justified Robert Owen by discovering in the environment of an organism an influence on it more potent than Owen had ever claimed. It implied that street arabs are produced by slums and not by original sin: that prostitutes are produced by starvation wages and not by feminine concupiscence. It threw the authority of science on the side of the Socialist who said that he who would reform himself must first reform society. It suggested that if we want healthy and wealthy citizens we must have healthy and wealthy towns; and that these can exist only in healthy and wealthy countries. It led straight to the conclusion that the type of character which remains indifferent to the welfare of its neighbors as long as its own personal appetites are satisfied is the disastrous type, and the type which is deeply concerned about its environment the only possible type for a permanently prosperous community. It shewed that the surprising changes which Robert Owen had produced in factory children by a change in their circumstances which does not seem any too generous to us nowadays were

15. English philosopher and essayist, largely influenced by the philosophy of Auguste Comte. From 1854 he was the companion of George Eliot. His greatest work is *The Problems of Life and Mind* (1874–9).

as nothing to the changes—changes not only of habits but of species, not only of species but of orders—which might conceivably be the work of environment acting on individuals without any character or intellectual consciousness whatever. No wonder the Socialists received Darwin with open arms.

Darwin and Karl Marx

Besides, the Socialists had an evolutionary prophet of their own, Karl Marx, who discredited Manchester as Darwin discredited the Garden of Eden. To him civilization was an organism evolving irresistibly by circumstantial selection; and he published the first volume of his Das Kapital in 1867. The revolt against anthropomorphic idolatry, which was, as we have seen, the secret of Darwin's success, had been accompanied by a revolt against the conventional respectability which covered not only the brigandage and piracy of feudal robber barons, but the hypocrisy, inhumanity, snobbery, and greed of the bourgeoisie, who were deeply corrupted by an essentially diabolical identification of success in life with big profits. The moment Marx shewed that the relation of the bourgeoisie to society was grossly immoral and disastrous, and that the whited wall of starched shirt fronts concealed and defended the most infamous of all tyrannies and the basest of all robberies, he became an inspired prophet in the mind of every generous soul whom his book reached. He had said and proved what they wanted to have proved; and they would hear nothing against him. Now Marx was by no means infallible: his economics, half borrowed, and half homemade by a literary amateur, were not, when strictly followed up, even favorable to Socialism. His theory of civilization had been promulgated already in [Henry] Buckle's History of Civilization [*in England,* 1857–61], a book as epoch-making in the minds of its readers as Das Kapital. There was nothing about Socialism in the widely read first volume of Das Kapital: every reference it made to workers and capitalists shewed that Marx had never breathed industrial air, and had dug his case out of bluebooks in the British Museum. Compared to Darwin, he seemed to have no power of observation: there was not a fact in Das Kapital that had not been taken out of a book, nor a discussion that had not been opened by somebody else's pamphlet. No matter: he exposed the bourgeoisie and made an end of its moral prestige. That was enough: like Darwin he had for the moment the World Will by the ear. Marx had, too, what Darwin had not: implacability and a fine Jewish literary gift, with terrible powers of hatred, invective, irony, and all the bitter qualities bred, first in the oppression of a rather pampered young genius (Marx was the spoilt child of a well-to-do family) by a social system utterly uncongenial to him, and later on by exile and poverty. Thus Marx and Darwin between them toppled over two closely related idols, and became the prophets of two new creeds.

WHY DARWIN PLEASED THE PROFITEERS ALSO

But how, at this rate, did Darwin succeed with the profiteers too? It is not easy to make the best of both worlds when the two are at war, as the proletariat and the proprietors were and are over their shares in the national income. But Darwin kept a foot in each camp easily. He got his main postulate, the pressure of population on the available means of subsistence, from the treatise of Malthus on Population, just as he got his other postulate of a practically unlimited time for that pressure to operate from the geologist Lyell, who made an end of Archbishop Ussher's Biblical estimate of the age of the earth as 4004 B.C. plus A.D. The treatise of Ricardo on the Law of Diminishing Return presented profit and rent as natural perquisites for which no man was responsible nor could avert. Long before Darwin published a line, the disciples of Malthus and Ricardo were preaching the fatalistic Wages Fund doctrine, and assuring the workers that Trade Unionism is a vain defiance of the inexorable laws of political economy. The Neo-Darwinians were presently assuring us that temperance legislation is a vain defiance of Natural Selection, and that the right way to deal with drunkenness is to flood the country with cheap gin and let the fittest survive. Cobdenism is, after all, nothing but the abandonment of trade to Circumstantial Selection.

It is hardly possible to exaggerate the importance of this preparation for Darwinism by a vast political and clerical propaganda of its moral atmosphere. Never in history, as far as we know, had there been such a determined, richly subsidized, politically organized attempt to persuade the human race that all progress, all prosperity, all salvation, individual and social, depend on an unrestrained conflict for food and money, on the suppression and elimination of the weak by the strong, on Free Trade, Free Contract, Free Competition, Natural Liberty, *Laisser-faire*: in short, on "doing the other fellow down" with impunity. Even the proletariat sympathized, though to them Capitalist liberty meant only wage slavery without the legal safeguards of chattel slavery. People were tired of governments and kings and priests and providences, and wanted to find out how Nature would arrange matters if she were let alone. And they found it out to their cost in the days when Lancashire used up nine generations of wage slaves [in the coal mines] in one generation of their masters, who, becoming richer and richer, had their uneasy consciences soothed when [Claude-Frédéric] Bastiat[16] proved convincingly that Nature had arranged Economic Harmonies which would settle social questions far better than theocracies or aristocracies or mobocracies, the real *deus ex machina* being unrestrained plutocracy.

THE POETRY AND PURITY OF MATERIALISM

Thus the stars in their courses fought for Darwin. Every faction drew a moral from him; every catholic hater of faction founded a hope on him; every blackguard felt justified by him; and every saint felt encouraged by him. The notion that any harm could come of so splendid an enlightenment seemed as silly as the notion that the atheists would steal all our spoons. The physicists went further than the Darwinians. Tyndall declared that he saw in Matter the promise and potency of all forms of life, and with his Irish graphic lucidity made a picture of a world of magnetic atoms, each atom with a positive and a negative pole, arranging itself by attraction and repulsion in orderly crystalline structure [in *Researches on Diamagnetism and Magne-crystallic Action*, 1870]. Such a picture is dangerously fascinating to thinkers oppressed by the bloody disorders of the living world. Craving for purer subjects of thought, they find in the contemplation of crystals and magnets a happiness more dramatic and less childish than the happiness found by the mathematicians in abstract numbers, because they see in the crystals beauty and movement without the corrupting appetites of fleshly vitality. In such Materialism as that of Lucretius and Tyndall there is a nobility which produces poetry: the poet [John] Davidson[17] found his highest inspiration in it. Even its pessimism as it faces the cooling of the sun and the return of the ice-caps does not degrade the pessimist: for example,

16. French anti-Socialist economist, author of *Sophismes économiques* (1845) and an important series of pamphlets and essays on property, protectionism, credit and rent.
17. British poet and playwright, author of *The Triumph of Mammon* (1907) and *Mammon and His Message* (1908), Parts 1 and 2 of an uncompleted trilogy *God and Mammon*.

the Quincy Adamses,[18] with their insistence on modern democratic degradation as an inevitable result of solar shrinkage, are not dehumanized as the
vivisectionists are. Perhaps nobody is at heart fool enough to believe that
life is at the mercy of temperature: Dante was not troubled by the
objection that Brunetto could not have lived in the fire nor Ugolino in the
ice [in *The Divine Comedy*].

But the physicists found their intellectual vision of the world incommuni-
cable to those who were not born with it. It came to the public simply as
Materialism; and Materialism lost its peculiar purity and dignity when it
entered into the Darwinian reaction against Bible fetishism. Between the
two of them religion was knocked to pieces; and where there had been
God, a cause, a faith that the universe was ordered, and therefore a sense of
moral responsibility as part of that order, there was now an utter void.
Chaos had come again.

The first effect was exhilarating: we had the runaway child's sense of
freedom before it gets hungry and lonely and frightened. Not that we
desired God back again. We printed the verses in which William Blake, the
most religious of our great poets, called the anthropomorphic idol Old
Nobodaddy [in 'Motto' to the *Songs of Innocence*, 1789], and gibed at him
in terms which the printer had to leave us to guess from dashes and
asterisks. It did not occur to us that Old Nobodaddy, instead of being a
ridiculous fiction, might be a real impostor, and that he could not have
impersonated anybody if there had not been Somebodaddy to impersonate.
We did not see the significance of the fact that on the last occasion on
which God had been "expelled with a pitchfork,"[19] men so different as
Voltaire and Robespierre had said, the one that if God did not exist it

18. Henry Adams, grandson of the American president John Quincy Adams,
outlined a theory of energy in the solar system, paralleling it to and linking it with
a similar decline in the human race: '[Earlier epochs] allowed ample time for
shrinkage before the Miocene first proved by its temperate vegetation that the sun
had approached its present diameter, and could no longer equitably warm the
world' (*The Degradation of the Democratic Dogma*, 1919). In an extended introduction
to the book, Henry's brother Brooks Adams applied Henry's theory to the career
of their grandfather. He recalled John Quincy Adams's enlightened commitment to
service and to science, particularly astronomy. This era in American democracy, he
noted, was succeeded by the 'spoils system' of Andrew Jackson's administration, in
which 'selfishness, greed, and competition in rapidly expanding America were
making science and education the tools of evil'.
19. 'You may drive out nature with a pitchfork, yet she still will hurry back'
(Horace, *Epistles* I; iv: 24).

would be necessary to invent him [Voltaire, *Épître à l'auteur du livre des trois imposteurs*, 1769], and the other that after an honest attempt to dispense with a Supreme Being in practical politics, some such hypothesis had been found quite indispensable, and could not be replaced by a sham Goddess of Reason.[20] If these two opinions were quoted at all, they were quoted as jokes at the expense of Nobodaddy. We were quite sure for the moment that whatever lingering superstition might have daunted these men of the XVIII century, we Darwinians could do without God, and had made a good riddance of Him.

THE VICEROYS OF THE KING OF KINGS

Now in politics it is much easier to do without God than to do without his viceroys and vicars and lieutenants; and we begin to miss the lieutenants long before we begin to miss their principal. Roman Catholics do what their confessors advise without troubling God; and Royalists are content to worship the King and ask the policeman. But God's trustiest lieutenants often lack official credentials. They may be professed atheists who are also men of honor and high public spirit. The old belief that it matters dreadfully to God whether a man thinks himself an atheist or not, and that the extent to which it matters can be stated with exactness as one single damn, was an error; for the divinity is in the honor and public spirit, not in the mouthed *credo* or *non credo*. The consequences of this error became grave when the fitness of a man for public trust was tested, not by his honor and public spirit, but by asking him whether he belonged to the Church of England. Darwin destroyed this test; but when it was dropped, there remained no test at all; and the door to public trust was open to the man who had no sense of God because he had no sense of anything beyond his own business interests and personal appetites and ambitions. As a result, the people who did not feel in the least inconvenienced by being no longer governed by Nobodaddy soon found themselves very acutely inconvenienced by being governed by fools and commercial adventurers. They had

20. On 7 May 1794 Robespierre secured from the National Convention a decree recognizing the existence of a Supreme Being. The worship of this Supreme Being was patterned after views expressed in Rousseau's *The Social Contract*. 'Atheism is aristocratic', Robespierre declared in a speech at the Jacobin Club on 1 November 1793. 'The idea of a Great Being who watches over oppressed innocence and punishes triumphant crime is entirely democratic.'

forgotten not only God but Goldsmith, who had warned them that "honor sinks where commerce long prevails" [*The Traveller*, 1764].

The lieutenants of God are not always persons: some of them are legal and parliamentary fictions. One of them is Public Opinion. The pre-Darwinian statesmen and publicists were not restrained directly by God; but they restrained themselves by setting up an image of a Public Opinion which would not tolerate any attempt to tamper with British liberties. Their favorite way of putting it was that any Government which proposed such and such an infringement of such and such a British liberty would be hurled from office in a week. Compulsory military service was the stock instance of this in England.

All this had no foundation on the facts. There was no limit to what the British people would put up with. It was this very helplessness of the people that forced their rulers to pretend that they were not helpless, and that the certainty of a sturdy and unconquerable popular resistance forbade any trifling with Magna Carta or the Petition of Rights or the authority of parliament. Now the reality behind this fiction was the divine sense that liberty is a need vital to human growth. Accordingly, though it was difficult enough to effect a political reform, yet, once parliament had passed it, its wildest opponent had no hope that the Government would cancel it, or shelve it, or be bought off from executing it. From Walpole to Campbell-Bannerman there was no Prime Minister to whom such re-naguing or trafficking would ever have occurred, though there were plenty who employed corruption unsparingly to procure the votes of members of parliament for their policy.

Political Opportunism in Excelsis

The moment Nobodaddy was slain by Darwin, Public Opinion, as divine deputy, lost its sanctity. Politicians no longer told themselves that the British public would never suffer this or that: they allowed themselves to know that for their own personal purposes, which are limited to their ten or twenty years on the front benches in parliament, the British Public can be humbugged and coerced into believing and suffering everything that it pays their rulers to impose on them, and that any excuse for an unpopular step will serve if it can be kept in countenance for three days: that is, until the terms of the excuse are forgotten. With its last ideal gone, policy died and was succeeded by unprincipled opportunism. All Governments became like the tramp who walks always with the wind and ends as a pauper, or the stone that rolls down the hill and ends as an avalanche: their way was the way to destruction.

THE BETRAYAL OF WESTERN CIVILIZATION

Within sixty years from the publication of Darwin's Origin of Species political opportunism had brought parliaments into contempt; created a popular demand for direct action by the organized industries ("Syndicalism"); and wrecked the centre of Europe in a paroxysm of that chronic terror of oneanother, that cowardice of the irreligious, which, masked in the bravado of militarist patriotism, had ridden the Powers like a nightmare since the Franco-Prussian war of 1870–71. The sturdy old cosmopolitan Liberalism evaporated. Ordinances for the government of our Crown Colonies contain, as a matter of course, prohibitions of all criticism, spoken or written, of their ruling officials, which would have scandalized George III and elicited Liberal pamphlets from Catherine II. Statesmen are afraid of the suburbs, of the newspapers, of the profiteers, of the diplomatists, of the militarists, of the country houses, of the trade unions, of everything ephemeral on earth except the revolutions they are provoking; and they would be afraid of these if they were not too ignorant of society and history to appreciate the risk, and to know that a revolution always seems hopeless and impossible the day before it breaks out, and indeed never does break out until it seems hopeless and impossible; for rulers who think it possible take care to insure the risk by ruling reasonably. This brings about a condition fatal to all political stability: namely, that you never know where to have the politicians. If the fear of God was in them it might be possible to come to some general understanding as to what God disapproves of; and Europe might pull together on that basis. But the present panic, in which Prime Ministers drift from election to election, either fighting or running away from everybody who shakes a fist at them, makes a European civilization impossible; for peace and prosperity depend on the loyalty of States to civilization. Every meaner consideration should have given way to this loyalty. What actually happened was that France and England made an alliance with Russia to defend themselves against Germany; Germany made an alliance with Turkey to defend herself against the three; whilst the United States held aloof as long as they could, and the other States either did the same or joined in the fray through compulsion, bribery, or their judgment as to which side their bread was buttered.

In 1918 the surrender of Germany on terms which the victors never dreamt of observing did not change the situation. If the Western Powers had selected their allies in the Lamarckian manner intelligently, purposely, and vitally, *ad majorem Dei gloriam* [to the greater glory of God], as good Europeans, there would have been a durable League of Nations and no war. But because the selection relied on was purely circumstantial opportunist selection, so that the alliances were mere marriages of convenience, they have turned out, not merely as badly as might have been expected, but far worse than the blackest pessimist had ever imagined possible. How it will all end we do not yet know. When wolves combine to kill a horse, the death of the horse only sets them fighting oneanother for the choicest morsels.

THE HOMEOPATHIC REACTION AGAINST DARWINISM

Throughout all this godless welter of the infidel century, Darwinism has been acting not only directly but homeopathically, its poison rallying our vital forces not only to resist it and cast it out, but to achieve a new Reformation and put a credible and healthy religion in its place. Samuel Butler was the pioneer of the reaction as far as the casting out was concerned; but the issue was confused by the physiologists, who were divided on the question into Mechanists and Vitalists. The Mechanists said that life is nothing but physical and chemical action; that they have demonstrated this in many cases of so-called vital phenomena; and that there is no reason to doubt that with improved methods they will presently be able to demonstrate it in all of them. The Vitalists said that a dead body and a live one are physically and chemically identical, and that the difference can be accounted for only by the existence of a Vital Force. This seems simple; but the Anti-Mechanists objected to be called Vitalists (obviously the right name for them) on two contradictory grounds. First, that vitality is scientifically inadmissible, because it cannot be isolated and experimented with in the laboratory. Second, that force, being by definition anything that can alter the speed or direction of matter in motion (briefly, that can overcome inertia), is essentially a mechanistic conception. Here we had the new Vitalism only half extricated from the upstart Mechanism, objecting to be called either, and unable to give a clear lead to the new direction.

These professional faction fights are ephemeral, and need not trouble us here. The old Vitalist, who was essentially a Materialist, has evolved into the Neo-Vitalist, who is, as every genuine scientist must be, finally a metaphysician. And as the Neo-Vitalist turns from the disputes of his youth to the future of his science, he will cease to boggle at the name Vitalist, or at the inevitable, ancient, popular, and quite correct use of the term Force to denote metaphysical as well as physical overcomers of inertia.

Since the discovery of Evolution as the method of the Life Force, the religion of metaphysical Vitalism has been gaining the definiteness and concreteness needed to make it assimilable by the educated critical man. But it has always been with us. The popular religions, disgraced by their Opportunist cardinals and bishops, have been kept in credit by canonized saints whose secret was their conception of themselves as the instruments and vehicles of divine power and aspiration: a conception which at moments becomes an actual experience of ecstatic possession by that power. And above and below all have been millions of humble and obscure persons, sometimes totally illiterate, sometimes unconscious of having any religion at all, sometimes believing in their simplicity that the gods and temples and priests of their district stood for their instinctive righteousness, who have kept sweet the tradition that good people follow a light that shines within and above and ahead of them, that bad people care only for themselves, and that the good are saved and blessed and the bad damned and miserable. Protestantism was a movement towards the pursuit of a light called an inner light because every man must see it with his own eyes and not take any priest's word for it or any Church's account of it. In short, there is no question of a new religion, but rather of redistilling the eternal spirit of religion and thus extricating it from the sludgy residue of temporalities and legends that are making belief impossible, though they are the stock-in-trade of all the Churches and all the Schools.

RELIGION AND ROMANCE

It is the adulteration of religion by the romance of miracles and paradises and torture chambers that makes it reel at the impact of every advance in science, instead of being clarified by it. If you take an English village lad, and teach him that religion means believing that the stories of Noah's Ark and the Garden of Eden are literally true on the authority of God himself, and if that boy becomes an artisan and goes into the town among the sceptical city proletariat, then, when the jibes of his mates set him thinking, and he sees that these stories cannot be literally true, and learns that no candid prelate now pretends to believe them, he does not make any fine distinctions: he declares at once that religion is a fraud, and parsons and teachers hypocrites and liars. He becomes indifferent to religion if he has little intellectual conscience, and indignantly hostile to it if he has a good deal.

The same revolt against wantonly false teaching is happening daily in the professional classes whose recreation is reading and whose intellectual sport is controversy. They banish the Bible from their houses, and sometimes put into the hands of their unfortunate children Ethical and Rationalist tracts of the deadliest dulness, compelling these wretched infants to sit out the discourses of Secularist lecturers (I have delivered some of them myself), who wearied them at a length now abandoned in the Church of England. Our minds have reacted so violently towards provable logical theorems and demonstrable mechanical or chemical facts that we have become incapable of metaphysical truth, and try to cast out incredible and silly lies by credible and clever ones, calling in Satan to cast out Satan, and getting more into his clutches than ever in the process. Thus the world is kept sane less by the saints than by the vast mass of the indifferent, who neither act nor react in the matter. Butler's preaching of the gospel of Laodicea[21] was a piece of common sense founded on his observation of this.

But indifference will not guide nations through civilization to the establishment of the perfect city of God. An indifferent statesman is a contradiction in terms; and a statesman who is indifferent on principle, a *Laisser-faire* or Muddle-Through doctrinaire, plays the deuce with us in the long run. Our statesmen must get a religion by hook or crook; and while we are ruled by Adult Suffrage it must be a religion capable of vulgarization. The thought first put into words by the Mills when they said "There is no God; but this is a family secret,"[22] and long held unspoken by aristocratic statesmen and diplomatists, will not serve now; for the revival

21. The 'gospel' appears to be 'The Message of Laodicea' (Revelation 3: 15–22), addressed to those who are 'neither hot nor cold', but 'lukewarm' in their faith. Ernest Pontifex in Butler's *The Way of All Flesh* (Chapter 85) maintains 'The Church herself should approach as nearly to that of Laodicea as [is] compatible with her continuing to be a Church at all, as each individual member should only be hot in striving to be as lukewarm as possible.'
22. This phrasing is of Shaw's own creation, summing up Mill's account in the *Autobiography* (Chapter 2) of his father passing on to him the sceptical 'convictions and feelings' he held concerning religion. 'I am thus', Mill stated, 'one of the very few examples, in this country, of one who has, not thrown off religious belief, but never had it'. He added, however, that in giving him 'an opinion contrary to that of the world', his father 'thought it necessary to give it as one which could not prudently be avowed to the world.'

of civilization after the war cannot be effected by artificial breathing: the driving force of an undeluded popular consent is indispensable, and will be impossible until the statesman can appeal to the vital instincts of the people in terms of a common religion.

THE DANGER OF REACTION

And here arises the danger that when we realize this we shall run back in terror to our old superstitions. We jumped out of the frying-pan into the fire; and we are just as likely to jump back again, now that we feel hotter than ever. History records very little in the way of mental activity on the part of the mass of mankind except a series of stampedes from affirmative errors into negative ones and back again. It must therefore be said very precisely and clearly that the bankruptcy of Darwinism does not mean that Nobodaddy was Somebodaddy *with* "body, parts, and passions" after all; that the world was made in the year 4004 B.C.; that damnation means an eternity of blazing brimstone; that the Immaculate Conception means that sex is sinful and that Christ was parthenogenetically brought forth by a virgin descended in like manner from a line of virgins right back to Eve; that the Trinity is an anthropomorphic monster with three heads which are yet only one head; that in Rome the bread and wine on the altar become flesh and blood, and in England, in a still more mystical manner, they do and they do not; that the Bible is an infallible scientific manual, an accurate historical chronicle, and a complete guide to conduct; that we may lie and cheat and murder and then wash ourselves innocent in the blood of the Lamb on Sunday at the cost of a *credo* and a penny in the plate; and so on and so forth. Civilization cannot be saved by people not only crude enough to believe these things, but irreligious enough to believe that such belief constitutes a religion. The education of children cannot safely be left in their hands. If dwindling sects like the Church of England, the Church of Rome, the Greek Church, and the rest, persist in trying to cramp the human mind within the limits of these grotesque perversions of natural truths and poetic metaphors, then they must be ruthlessly banished from the schools to free the soul that is hidden in every dogma. The real Class War will be a war of intellectual classes; and its conquest will be the souls of the children.

A TOUCHSTONE FOR DOGMA

The test of a dogma is its universality. Any doctrine that the British churchgoer, the Brahman, the Jainist, the Buddhist, the Mussulman cannot hold in common, however varied their rituals, is an obstruction to the fellowship of the Holy Ghost. The only frontier to the currency of a sound dogma as such is the frontier of capacity for understanding it.

This does not mean that we should throw away legend and parable and drama: they are the natural vehicles of dogma; but woe to the Churches and rulers who substitute the legend for the dogma, the parable for the history, the drama for the religion! Better by far declare the throne of God empty than set a liar and a fool on it. What are called wars of religion are always wars to destroy religion by affirming the historical truth or material substantiality of some legend, and killing those who refuse to accept it as historical or substantial. But who has ever refused to accept a good legend with delight *as* a legend? The legends, the parables, the dramas, are among the choicest treasures of mankind. No one is ever tired of stories of miracles. In vain did Mahomet repudiate the miracles ascribed to him: in vain did Christ furiously scold those who asked him to give them an exhibition as a conjurer: in vain did the saints declare that God chose them not for their powers but for their weaknesses; that the humble might be exalted, and the proud rebuked. People will have their miracles, their stories, their heroes and heroines and saints and martyrs and divinities to exercise their gifts of affection, admiration, wonder, and worship, and their Judases and devils to enable them to be angry and yet feel that they do well to be angry. Every one of these legends is the common heritage of the human race; and there is only one inexorable condition attached to their healthy enjoyment, which is that no one shall believe them literally. The reading of stories and delighting in them made Don Quixote a gentleman: the believing them literally made him a madman who slew lambs instead of feeding them. In England today good books of Eastern religious legends are read eagerly; and Protestants and Atheists read legends of the saints with pleasure. Sceptical Freethinkers read the Bible: indeed they seem to be its only readers now except the parsons at the Church lecterns. This is because the imposition of the legends as literal truths at once changes them from legends into falsehoods. The feeling against the Bible has become so strong at last that educated people will not tolerate even the chronicles of King David, which may be historical, and are certainly more candid than the official biographies of our contemporary monarchs.

WHAT TO DO WITH THE LEGENDS

What we should do, then, is to pool our legends and make a delightful stock of religious folklore on an honest basis for all children. With our minds freed from pretence and falsehood we could enter into the heritage of all the faiths. China would share her sages with Spain, and Spain her saints with China. The Belfast Orangeman who gives his son a thrashing if the boy is so tactless as to ask how the evening and the morning could be the first day before the sun was created, or to betray an innocent calf-love for the Virgin Mary, would buy him a bookful of legends of the creation and of mothers of God from all parts of the world, and be very glad to find his laddie as interested in such things as in marbles or Police and Robbers. That would be better than beating all good feeling towards religion out of the child, and blackening his mind by teaching him that the worshippers of the holy virgins, whether of the Parthenon or St Peter's, are fire-doomed heathens and idolaters. All the sweetness of religion is conveyed to children by the hands of storytellers and image-makers. Without their fictions the truths of religion would for the multitude be neither intelligible nor even apprehensible; and the prophets would prophesy and the philosophers cerebrate in vain. And nothing stands between the people and the fictions except the silly falsehood that the fictions are literal truths, and that there is nothing in religion but fiction.

A LESSON FROM SCIENCE TO THE CHURCHES

Let the Churches ask themselves why there is no revolt against the dogmas of mathematics though there is one against the dogmas of religion. It is not that the mathematical dogmas are more comprehensible. The law of inverse squares is as incomprehensible to the common man as the Athanasian creed. It is not that science is free from legends, witchcraft, miracles, biographic boostings of quacks as heroes and saints, and of barren scoundrels as explorers and discoverers. On the contrary, the iconography and hagiology of Scientism are as copious as they are mostly squalid. But no student of science has yet been taught that specific gravity consists in the belief that Archimedes[23] jumped out of his bath and ran naked through

---

23. Ancient Greek mathematician who, according to legend, shouted 'Eureka – I have found it!' on discovering a method of determining the weight of gold by comparing the displacements of liquid when metals were immersed.

the streets of Syracuse shouting Eureka, Eureka, or that the law of inverse squares must be discarded if anyone can prove that Newton was never in an orchard in his life. When some unusually conscientious or enterprizing bacteriologist reads the pamphlets of Jenner, and discovers that they might have been written by an ignorant but curious and observant nurserymaid, and could not possibly have been written by any person with a scientifically trained mind, he does not feel that the whole edifice of science has collapsed and crumbled, and that there is no such thing as smallpox. It may come to that yet; for hygiene, as it forces its way into our schools, is being taught as falsely as religion is taught there; but in mathematics and physics the faith is still kept pure, and you may take the law and leave the legends without suspicion of heresy. Accordingly, the tower of the mathematician stands unshaken whilst the temple of the priest rocks to its foundation.

THE RELIGIOUS ART OF THE XX CENTURY

Creative Evolution is already a religion, and is indeed now unmistakeably the religion of the XX century, newly arisen from the ashes of pseudo-Christianity, of mere scepticism, and of the soulless affirmations and blind negations of the Mechanists and Neo-Darwinians. But it cannot become a popular religion until it has its legends, its parables, its miracles. And when I say popular I do not mean apprehensible by villagers only. I mean apprehensible by Cabinet Ministers as well. It is unreasonable to look to the professional politician and administrator for light and leading in religion. He is neither a philosopher nor a prophet: if he were, he would be philosophizing and prophesying, and not neglecting both for the drudgery of practical government. Not being an expert, he must take religion as he finds it; and before he can take it, he must have been told stories about it in his childhood and had before him all his life an elaborate iconography of it produced by writers, painters, sculptors, temple architects, and artists of all the higher sorts. Even if, as sometimes happens, he is a bit of an amateur in metaphysics as well as a professional politician, he must still govern according to the popular iconography, and not according to his own interpretations if these happen to be heterodox.

It will be seen then that the revival of religion on a scientific basis does not mean the death of art, but a glorious rebirth of it. Indeed art has never been great when it was not providing an iconography for a live religion. And it has never been quite contemptible except when imitating the iconography after the religion had become a superstition. Italian painting from Giotto to Carpaccio is all religious painting; and it moves us deeply and has real greatness. Compare with it the attempts of our painters a century ago to achieve the effects of the old masters by imitation when they should have been illustrating a faith of their own. Contemplate, if you can bear it, the dull daubs of [William] Hilton and [Benjamin] Haydon,[24] who knew so much more about drawing and scumbling and glazing and perspective and anatomy and "marvelous foreshortening" than Giotto, the latchet of whose shoe they were nevertheless not worthy to unloose. Compare Mozart's Magic Flute, Beethoven's Ninth Symphony, and Wagner's Ring cycle, all of them reachings-forward to the new Vitalist art, with the dreary pseudo-sacred oratorios and cantatas produced for no better reason than that Handel made splendid thunder in that way. Compare [John] Flaxman and [Bertel] Thorwaldsen and [John] Gibson[25] with Phidias and Praxiteles, [Alfred] Stevens[26] with Michael Angelo, [Adolphe William] Bouguereau's[27] Virgin with Cimabue's, or the best operatic Christs of [Ary] Scheffer[28] and [Charles-Louis] Müller[29] with the worst Christs that the worst painters could paint before the end of the XV century, and you must feel that until we have a great religious movement we cannot hope for a great artistic one. The disillusioned Raphael could paint a mother and child, but not a queen of Heaven as much less skilful men had done in the days of his great-grandfathers; yet he could reach forward to the XX century and paint a Transfiguration of the Son of Man as they could not. Also, please note, he could decorate a house of pleasure for a plutocrat very beautifully with voluptuous pictures of Cupid and Psyche; for this simple sort of Vitalism is always with us, and, like portrait painting, keeps the artist supplied with subject matter in the intervals between the ages of faith; so that your sceptical Rembrandts and Velasquezs are at least not

24. Once-famous historical-religious painters of the early nineteenth century.
25. The three were early nineteenth-century sculptors: the second a Dane, the others English.
26. Mid nineteenth-century English designer and sculptor, who sculpted Wellington's monument in St Paul's.
27. French nineteenth-century painter, known for academic works on religious and allegorical themes.
28. French historical and religious painter of German extraction, who worked in the romantic French style. Among his canvases are *Christus Consolator* (1836) and *Christ Interred* (1845).
29. Parisian painter of religious and historical pictures, one of whose best-known works is *Christ's Entry into Jerusalem*.

compelled to paint shop fronts for want of anything else to paint in which they can really believe.

THE ARTIST-PROPHETS

And there are always great anticipations. Michael Angelo painted the Superman three hundred years before Nietzsche wrote Thus Spake Zoroaster [whose Persian name is Zarathustra]. As a painter of prophets and sibyls he is greatest among the very greatest in his craft, because we aspire to a world of prophets and sibyls. Beethoven never heard of radioactivity nor of electrons dancing in vortices of inconceivable energy; but pray can anyone explain the last movement of his Hammerklavier Sonata, Opus 106, otherwise than as a musical picture of these whirling electrons? His contemporaries said he was mad, partly perhaps because the movement was so hard to play; but we, who can make a pianola play it to us over and over until it is as familiar as Pop Goes the Weazel, know that it is sane and methodical. As such, it must represent something; and as all Beethoven's serious compositions represent some process within himself, some nerve storm or soul storm, and the storm here is clearly one of physical movement, I should much like to know what other storm than the atomic storm could have driven him to this oddest of all those many expressions of cyclonic energy which have given him the same distinction among musicians that Michael Angelo has among draughtsmen.

In Beethoven's day the business of art was held to be "the sublime and beautiful." In our day it has fallen to be the imitative and voluptuous. In both periods the word passionate has been freely employed; but in the XVIII century passion meant irresistible impulse of the loftiest kind: for example, a passion for astronomy or for truth. For us it has come to mean concupiscence and nothing else. One might say to the art of Europe what [Shakespeare's] Antony said to the corpse of Caesar: "Are all thy conquests, glories, triumphs, spoils, shrunk to this little measure?" [*Julius Caesar*, III: i] But in fact it is the mind of Europe that has shrunk, being, as we have seen, wholly preoccupied with a busy springcleaning to get rid of its superstitions before readjusting itself to the creative conception of Evolution.

EVOLUTION IN THE THEATRE

On the stage (and here I come at last to my own particular function in the matter), Comedy, as a destructive, derisory, critical, negative art, kept the theatre open when sublime tragedy perished. From Molière to Oscar Wilde we had a line of comedic playwrights who, if they had nothing fundamentally positive to say, were at least in revolt against falsehood and imposture, and were not only, as they claimed, "chastening morals by ridicule,"[30] but, in Johnson's phrase, clearing our minds of cant,[31] and thereby shewing an uneasiness in the presence of error which is the surest symptom of intellectual vitality. Meanwhile the name of Tragedy was assumed by plays in which everyone was killed in the last act, just as, in spite of Molière, plays in which everyone was married in the last act called themselves comedies. Now neither tragedies nor comedies can be produced according to a prescription which gives only the last moments of the last act.

Ever since Shakespear, playwrights have been struggling with their lack of positive religion. Many of them were forced to become mere pandars and sensation-mongers because, though they had higher ambitions, they could find no better subject matter. From Congreve to Sheridan they were so sterile in spite of their wit that they did not achieve between them the output of Molière's single lifetime; and they were all (not without reason) ashamed of their profession, and preferred to be regarded as mere men of fashion with a rakish hobby. Goldsmith's was the only saved soul in that pandemonium. Consider the great exception of Goethe. He is Olympian: the other giants are infernal in everything but their veracity and their repudiation of the irreligion of their time: that is, they are bitter and hopeless. It is not a question of mere dates. Goethe was an Evolutionist in 1830: many modern playwrights, even young ones, are still untouched by Creative Evolution. Even Ibsen was Darwinized to the extent of exploiting heredity on the stage much as the ancient Athenian playwrights exploited the Eumenides. Evolution as a poetic aspiration is plain enough in his Emperor or Galilean;[32] but it is one of Ibsen's distinctions that nothing was valid for him but science; and he left that vision of the future which his Roman seer calls "the third Empire" behind him when he settled down to his serious grapple with realities in those plays of XIX century life with which he overcame Europe, and broke the dusty windows of every dry-rotten theatre in it from Moscow to Manchester.

30. '*Castigat ridendo mores*' ('He corrects morals by ridicule') was the motto of the seventeenth-century Italian harlequin Joseph Biancolelli.
31. Boswell, *The Life of Samuel Johnson*, 15 May 1783.
32. Ibsen's *Emperor and Galilean* (1873) consists of two full-length plays, *Caesar's Apostasy* and *The Emperor Julian*, forming a 'double drama' of ten acts.

MY OWN PART IN THE MATTER

In my own activities as a playwright I found this state of things intolerable. The fashionable theatre prescribed one serious subject: clandestine adultery: the dullest of all subjects for a serious author, whatever it may be for audiences who read the police intelligence and skip the reviews and leading articles. I tried slum-landlordism, doctrinaire Free Love (pseudo-Ibsenism), prostitution, militarism, marriage, history, current politics, natural Christianity, national and individual character, paradoxes of conventional society, husband hunting, questions of conscience, professional delusions and impostures, all worked into a series of comedies of manners in the classic fashion, which was then very much out of fashion, the mechanical tricks of Parisian "construction" being held obligatory in the theatre. But this, though it occupied me and established me professionally, did not constitute me an iconographer of the religion of my time, fulfilling my natural function as an artist. I knew that civilization needs a religion as a matter of life or death; and as the conception of Creative Evolution developed I saw that we were at last within reach of a faith which complied with the first condition of all the religions that have ever taken hold of humanity: namely, that it must be, first and fundamentally, a science of metabiology. This was a crucial point with me; for I had seen Bible fetichism, after standing up to all the rationalistic batteries of Hume, Voltaire, and the rest, collapse before the onslaught of much less gifted Evolutionists, solely because they discredited it as a biological document; so that from that moment it lost its hold, and left literate Christendom faithless. My own Irish XVIII centuryism made it impossible for me to believe anything until I could conceive it as a scientific hypothesis, even though the abominations, quackeries, impostures, venalities, credulities, and delusions of the camp followers of science, and the brazen lies and priestly pretensions of the pseudo-scientific cure-mongers, all sedulously inculcated by modern "secondary education," were so monstrous that I was sometimes forced to make a verbal distinction between science and knowledge lest I should mislead my readers. But I never forgot that without knowledge even wisdom is more dangerous than mere opportunist ignorance, and that somebody must take the Garden of Eden in hand and weed it properly.

Accordingly, in 1901, I took the legend of Don Juan in its Mozartian form and made it a dramatic parable of Creative Evolution ['Don Juan in Hell', which became the third Act of *Man and Superman*, 1903]. But being then at the height of my invention and comedic talent, I decorated it too brilliantly and lavishly. I surrounded it with a comedy of which it formed only one act, and that act was so completely episodical (it was a dream which did not affect the action of the piece) that the comedy could be detached and played by itself. Also I supplied the published work with an imposing framework consisting of a preface, an appendix called The Revolutionist's Handbook, and a final display of aphoristic fireworks. The effect was so vertiginous, apparently, that nobody noticed the new religion in the centre of the intellectual whirlpool. Now I protest I did not cut these cerebral capers in mere inconsiderate exuberance. I did it because the worst convention of the criticism of the theatre current at that time was that intellectual seriousness is out of place on the stage; that the theatre is a place of shallow amusement; that people go there to be soothed after the enormous intellectual strain of a day in the city: in short, that a playwright is a person whose business it is to make unwholesome confectionery out of cheap emotions. My answer to this was to put all my intellectual goods in the shop window under the sign of Man and Superman. That part of my design succeeded. By good luck and acting, the comedy triumphed on the stage; and the book was a good deal discussed. But as its tale of a husband huntress obscured its evolutionary doctrine I try again with this cycle of plays that keep to the point all through. I abandon the legend of Don Juan with its erotic associations, and go back to the legend of the Garden of Eden. I exploit the eternal interest of the philosopher's stone which enables men to live for ever. I am not, I hope, under more illusion than is humanly inevitable as to my contribution to the scriptures of Creative Evolution. It is my hope that a hundred parables by younger hands will soon leave mine as far behind as the religious pictures of the XV century left behind the first attempts of the early Christians at iconography. In that hope I withdraw and ring up the curtain.

AYOT ST LAWRENCE, 1921.
Revised, 1944.

The World of the Theatre

J. T. Grein wrote to Shaw in 1921 to elicit an introduction to his book The World of the Theatre: Impressions and Memoirs, March 1920–1921 *(1921). Shaw responded with a letter intended to serve as a prefatory note, which Grein sandwiched between opening and closing paragraphs of his own (deleted here), headed 'Introductory'*

My Dear Grein: It is now very close on thirty years since you madly began an apparently hopeless attempt to bring the English theatre into some sort of relation with contemporary culture. Matthew Arnold had suggested that step;[1] but nobody in the theatre took the slightest notice of him, because nobody in the theatre knew of the existence of such a person as Matthew Arnold. That was what was the matter with the theatre then. There was nothing wrong with the acting: I cannot remember any actor or actress then occupying a leading position who could be called an amateur or a duffer: they had all been "through the mill," and could make intruders who had not, look ridiculous. The theatres were better managed than they are now: the front of the house was not always controled by the bar; and at the best theatres all petty cadgings like charges for programs and cloak-room fees were abolished. The public was so seriously interested in the theatre that it booked seats months in advance: in fact, it was by the booking that a manager knew when his run was coming to an end. Photographs of actors and actresses cost a shilling each; and at this price the Stereoscopic Company did a big trade in them. At every point except the one point of culture and contact with the life of the time the theatre was in a more dignified position than it occupies today. If you and I could have set the Bancrofts, the Kendals, the Rorkes, Hare and Wyndham and Irving and Forbes-Robertson and Ada Rehan, to work in live contemporary drama, the London stage would have led Europe triumphantly. Forbes-Robertson's Cæsar proved it.[2]

As it was, these artists were kept up to the mark by the continual effort

1. 'The French Play in London,' collected in *Irish Essays* (1882).
2. Forbes-Robertson toured the United States and Canada in Shaw's *Caesar and Cleopatra* in 1906–7. He then successfully recreated the role in the Vedrenne-Barker season at the Savoy Theatre, London, in November 1907.

to pass off literary scarecrows as heroes and heroines. The generation which succeeded them at the *fin de siècle* acquired this art and acquired nothing else (never having had the chance); so that you got actors and actresses who had an enchanting power of persuading you that they could say and do the most wonderful things when the moment came; but the author had to be particularly careful to get the curtain down before it came; for when you called on them, as Shakespear does for instance, not for suggestion, but for execution, they knew better than to give themselves away by trying. Shakespear then became physically impossible. As the notion of performing his plays as he meant them to be performed never occurred to anyone but Mr William Poel,[3] who was regarded consequently as the absurdest of cranks, the Bard had already become a mere stalking-horse for the scene painter, the costumier, and the spectacular artists generally. His plays were presented in mutilated fragments, divided into acts with long waits between, in which form they were so horribly boresome, being mostly unintelligible, that only the most powerful personal fascination could induce playgoers to endure him. As long as this fascination was associated with great executive power, Shakespear did not always "spell ruin," as the phrase went then. Whilst the actor could not only look as if he could say tremendous things, but could actually say them tremendously when he got the chance, it was possible for Barry Sullivan, who turned his back on London with disdain because he lost £800 in three months and was not used to such treatment, to die worth £100,000. But when the fascination was divorced from executive power, the Shakespearean game was up for the young of the old school. It was the young of the new school who discovered that Poel had really struck the trail. Then you got Granville Barker, [John] Drinkwater, [William] Bridges Adams, and [James Bernard] Fagan establishing genuine Shakespear on the English stage, and extracting from the play the fascination for which their fathers would have looked to the actor alone.[4]

3. Poel singlehandedly revolutionized English production of Shakespeare by return-ing to the unedited texts and restoring long-omitted scenes and speeches; and by reinstituting the Elizabethan style of staging, sans scenery and act and scene breaks, to achieve an unbroken flow in performance.
4. Granville-Barker created now legendary, influential productions of *The Winter's Tale*, *Twelfth Night* and *A Midsummer Night's Dream* at the Savoy Theatre in 1912–14. Drinkwater, a poet and playwright, was for some years general manager of the Birmingham Repertory Theatre, where he directed *Macbeth* (1916) and others of the eleven Shakespeare plays included in the repertory in 1913–18. Bridges-Adams, quondam assistant manager to Poel, became managing director of the Shakespeare Memorial Theatre at Stratford-on-Avon (1919), where he staged twenty-nine plays

Now you may ask what this has to do with you, who never meddled with Shakespear. I assure you you had a great deal to do with it. When you first desperately stuck an advertisement into the papers to say that an unheard-of enterprize called the Independent Theatre would on a certain Sunday night and Monday afternoon perform an unheard-of play, totally unlike any play then current in the theatrical market; when the papers thereupon declared that the manager of the theatre ought to be prosecuted for keeping a disorderly house, and that you and the foreign blackguard named Ibsen who was your accomplice, should be deported as obvious undesirables, you made a hole in the dyke; and the weight of the flood outside did the rest. When you declared that you would bring to light treasures of unacted English drama grossly suppressed by the managers of that day, you found that there was not any unacted English drama except two acts of an unfinished play (begun and laid aside eight years before) by me; but it was the existence of the Independent Theatre that made me finish that play, and by giving me the experience of its rehearsal and performance, revealed the fact (to myself among others) that I possessed the gift of "fingering" the stage. That old play now seems as remote and oldfashioned as Still Waters Run Deep or London Assurance;[5] but the newspapers of 1892 raged over it for a whole fortnight. Everything followed from that: the production of Arms and the Man by Miss Horniman and Florence Farr at the Avenue Theatre, Miss Horniman's establishment of Repertory Theatres in Dublin and Manchester, the Stage Society, H. Granville Barker's tentative matinées of Candida at the Court Theatre, the fullblown management of Vedrenne and Barker, Edie Craig's Pioneers,[6] and the final relegation of the XIX Century London theatre to the dustbin by Barrie. At present the cry in the papers is that the theatre is hopelessly out of date, that it needs fresh air, new ideas, scrapping of

---

in the Shakespeare canon before retirement in 1932. Fagan, an Irish playwright and director, assumed management of the Royal Court Theatre in 1918, helming *Twelfth Night* and a memorable production of *The Merchant of Venice* (1919), starring the eminent Jewish actor Maurice Moskovitch as Shylock, which moved to the West End.

5. Popular Victorian plays, frequently revived. The first, a farce, was written by Tom Taylor; the second, a comedy, by Dion Boucicault.

6. Edith Craig, daughter of Ellen Terry, founded the Pioneer Players in 1911. During the ten years of its existence she directed, and designed most of the scenery and costumes for, more than 150 productions.

traditions and conventions. The most famous apostle of the new theatre [Edward Gordon Craig] has declared publicly that what has been holding the theatre back for twenty years past and making all reform impossible is not Sardou but Shaw.[7] If only we could give the young lions a ride on [H. G.] Wells's Time Machine [1895] and take them back to 1892!

Well, more power to their elbows! I am always delighted to hear a clamor for new ideas, or indeed for ideas of any sort, in the theatre. So, I have no doubt, are you. But the clamorers will hardly see a revolution like the one you began by making the hole in the dyke. It is the second revolution that England owes to a Dutchman.[8]

G. B. S.

---

7. In a debate with Shaw at the Art Workers Guild, 18 June 1920, following a paper read by Craig on stage decoration and costume. See Shaw, *Collected Letters 1898–1910*, p. 682.
8. The first was the Glorious Revolution (1688), led by William of Orange, subsequently Britain's William III.

The Quintessence of Ibsenism

Preface to the third English edition, 1922

Since the last edition of this book was printed [1913], war, pestilence, and famine have wrecked civilization and killed a number of people of whom the first batch is calculated as not less than fifteen millions. Had the gospel of Ibsen been understood and heeded, these fifteen millions might have been alive now; for the war was a war of ideals. Liberal ideals, Feudal ideals, National ideals, Dynastic ideals, Republican ideals, Church ideals, State ideals, and Class ideals, bourgeois and proletarian, all heaped up into a gigantic pile of spiritual high explosive, and then shoveled daily into every house with the morning milk by the newspapers, needed only a bomb thrown at Serajevo by a handful of regicide idealists to blow the centre out of Europe. Men with empty phrases in their mouths and foolish fables in their heads have seen each other, not as fellow creatures, but as dragons and devils, and have slaughtered each other accordingly. Now that our frenzies are forgotten, our commissariats disbanded, and the soldiers they fed demobilized to starve when they cannot get employment in mending what we broke, even the iron-mouthed Ibsen, were he still alive, would perhaps spare us, disillusioned wretches as we are, the well-deserved "I told you so."

Not that there is any sign of the lesson being taken to heart. Our reactions from Militarist idealism into Pacifist idealism will not put an end to war: they are only a practical form of the *reculer pour mieux sauter* [stepping back in order to make a better leap]. We still cannot bring ourselves to criticize our ideals, because that would be a form of self-criticism. The vital force that drives men to throw away their lives and those of others in the pursuit of an imaginative impulse, reckless of its apparent effect on human welfare, is, like all natural forces, given to us in enormous excess to provide against an enormous waste. Therefore men, instead of economizing it by consecrating it to the service of their highest impulses, grasp at a phrase in a newspaper article, or in the speech of a politician on a vote-catching expedition, as an excuse for exercising it violently, just as a horse turned out to grass will gallop and kick merely to let off steam. The shallowness of the ideals of men ignorant of history is their destruction.

But I cannot spend the rest of my life drawing the moral of the war. It must suffice to say here that as war throws back civilization inevitably, leaving everything worse than it was, from razors and scissors to the characters of the men that make and sell and buy them, old abuses revive eagerly in a world that dreamed it had got rid of them for ever; old books on morals become new and topical again; and old prophets stir in their graves and are read with a new sense of the importance of their message. That is perhaps why a new edition of this book is demanded.

In spite of the temptation to illustrate it afresh by the moral collapse of the last ten years, I have left the book untouched. To change a pre-war book into a post-war book would in this case mean interpreting Ibsen in the light of a catastrophe of which he was unaware. Nobody can pretend to say what view he would have taken of it. He might have thought the demolition of three monstrous idealist empires cheap at the cost of fifteen million idealists' lives. Or he might have seen in the bourgeois republics which have superseded them a more deeply entrenched fortification of idealism at its suburban worst. So I have refrained from tampering with what I wrote when I, too, was as pre-war as Ibsen.

1922.   G. B. S.

Imprisonment

First published as a preface to Sidney and Beatrice Webb's English Prisons under Local Government, *1922, with a title and foreword added for a slightly revised separate American edition, 1925. Further amended in 1931 for the Collected Works*

When I was a boy in my teens in Dublin I was asked by an acquaintance of mine who was clerk to a Crown Solicitor, and had business in prisons, whether I would like to go through Mountjoy Prison, much as he might have asked me whether I would like to go through the Mint, or the cellars at the docks. I accepted the invitation with my head full of dungeons and chains and straw pallets and stage gaolers: in short, of the last acts of Il Trovatore and Gounod's Faust, and of the Tower of London in Richard III. I expected the warders to look like murderers, and the murderers like heroes. At least I suppose I did, because what struck me most was that the place was as bright and clean as whitewash and scrubbing and polish could make it, with all the warders looking thoroughly respectable, and all the prisoners ruffianly and degenerate, except one tall delicate figure tramping round in the exercise ring, a Lifer by the color of his cap, who had chopped up his family with a hatchet, and been recommended to mercy on account of his youth. I thought, and still think, imprisonment for life a curious sort of mercy. My main impression of the others, and the one that has stuck longest and hardest, was that as it was evidently impossible to reform such men, it was useless to torture them, and dangerous to release them.

I have never been imprisoned myself; but in my first years as a public speaker I had to volunteer for prison martyrdom in two Free Speech conflicts with the police.[1] As my luck would have it, on the first occasion the police capitulated on the eve of the day on which I had undertaken to address a prohibited meeting and refuse to pay a fine; and on the second a rival political organization put up a rival martyr, and, on a division, carried

---

1. The principal of these occasions was in September 1885 when, after the police had broken up a Socialist League demonstration in the East End's Dod Street, near the docks, and arrested seven participants, Shaw pledged 'to speak next Sunday, to get arrested, to refuse to pay the fine, and to do the month' (letter to Ida Beatty, 22 September 1885, in *Collected Letters 1874–1897*, 1965). To his great relief the

his election over my head, to my great relief. These incidents are not very impressive now; but the fact that my acquaintance with the subject of the following essay began with the sight of an actual prison, and that twice afterwards I was for a week or so firmly convinced that I was about to spend at least a fortnight and possibly a month in the cells, gave me an interest in the subject less perfunctory than that of the ordinary citizen to whom prison is only a reference in the police news, denoting simply a place where dishonest and violent people are very properly locked up.

This comfortable ignorance, by the way, is quite commonly shared by judges. A Lord Chief Justice of England, grieved at hearing from a lady of social importance that her son had been sent to prison as a Conscientious Objector, told her that he hoped she would get to see him often, and keep up his spirits with frequent letters, and send him in nice things to eat. He was amazed to learn from her that he might just as well have suggested a motor ride every afternoon and a visit to the opera in the evening. He had been sentencing people all through his judicial career to terms of imprisonment, some of them for life, without knowing that it meant anything more than being confined to the house and wearing a dress with broad arrows all over it. No doubt he thought, quite rightly, that such confinement was bad enough for anybody, however wicked.

I had no such illusions about prison life. My political activities often brought me into contact with men of high character and ability who had been victims of modern forms of persecution under the very elastic headings of treason, sedition, obstruction, blasphemy, offences against press laws, and so forth. I knew that Karl Marx had declared that British prisons were the cruellest in the world; and I thought it quite probable that he was right. I knew Prince Peter Kropotkin, who, after personal experience of the most villainous convict prisons in Siberia and the best model prison in France, said that they were both so bad that the difference was not worth talking about. What with European "politicals" and amnestied Irish Fenians, those who, like myself, were in the way of meeting such people could hardly feel easy in their consciences about the established methods of handling criminals.

---

police took no action on that day. The second occasion was at World's End, Chelsea, after the police had threatened to arrest agitators. Shaw volunteered to speak, but 'a member of a rival Socialist Society disputed the martyr's palm with me,' he recalled in *Sixteen Self Sketches* (1949), 'and, on a division, defeated me by two votes'.

Also I was in occasional touch with certain efforts made by the now extinct Humanitarian League, and by a little Society called the Police and Public Vigilance Society, to call attention to the grievances of prisoners. The League dealt with punishments: the Society, which was really an agitation conducted by one devoted man with very slender means, the late James Timewell,[2] tried to obtain redress for people who alleged that they had been the victims of petty frame-ups by the police. But the witnesses on whose testimony these two bodies had to proceed were mostly either helpless creatures who could not tell the truth or scoundrels who would not tell it. The helpless creatures told you what they wanted to believe themselves: the scoundrels told you what they wanted you to believe.

Anyone who has tried to find out what war is like from our demobilized soldiers will understand. Their consciousness is limited and utterly uncritical; their memory is inaccurate and confused; their judgment is perverted by personal dislikes and vanities; and as to reflection, reason, self-criticism, and the rest of the intellectual counterchecks, they have no more of them than a mouse has of mathematics. If this is the case with normal men like soldiers, even less is to be expected from subnormal men like criminals. Neither the Humanitarian League nor Mr Timewell could rouse general public compunction with such testimony, or attract special subscriptions enough to enable them to conduct a serious investigation. And John Galsworthy had not then arisen to smite our consciences with such plays as The Silver Box and Justice.

This situation was changed by the agitation for Votes for Women and the subsequent war of 1914–18, both of which threw into prison an unprecedented number of educated, critical, public-spirited, conscientious men and women who under ordinary circumstances would have learnt no more about prisons than larks learn about coal mines. They came out of prison unembittered by their personal sufferings: their grievance was the public grievance of the whole prison system and its intense irreligiousness. In prison they had been capable of observing critically what they saw; and out of prison they were able to describe it. The official whitewash of the Prison Commissioners could not impose on them. They and their friends had money enough to take an office and engage a secretarial staff, besides supplying some voluntary educated labor. They formed a committee[3] with Lord Olivier as chairman, which investigated the condition of English prisons and incidentally read some interesting reports of American ones.

2. A master tailor, much involved in municipal affairs, who served for two decades as Secretary to the Society he had helped to found in 1902.
3. The Prison System Enquiry Committee.

Eventually they issued their report as a volume entitled English Prisons Today [1922], edited by Stephen Hobhouse and Fenner Brockway, who had both been in prison during the war.

I was a member of that committee; and the essay which follows was written as a preface to the report. But I did not find it possible to keep a thorough sifting of the subject within the limits of the sixth commandment ['Thou shalt not kill'] on which Mr Hobhouse took an uncompromising stand [as a Quaker and conscientious objector]. Fortunately my friends Sidney and Beatrice Webb were just then reinforcing the work of the committee by issuing the volume of their monumental history of English Local Government which deals with prisons. By transferring my preface to their book I was able to secure the intended publicity for it, and to please everybody concerned, myself included.

I give this history of the essay lest it should be taken as a fanciful exercise by a literary man making up the subject out of his own head. I have not made a parade of facts and figures because my business is to change the vindictive attitude towards criminals which has made the facts possible; but I know the facts better, apparently, than the Prison Commissioners, and relevant figures quite as well.

However, the matter did not stop with the issue of Mr and Mrs Webb's Prisons Under Local Government. That work, though read throughout the civilized world by serious students of political science, has a specialized circulation. Fortunately, my preface to it attracted the attention of the Department of Christian Social Service of the National Council of the Protestant Episcopal Church in the United States. That body put it into general circulation in America [under the title *Imprisonment*, published by Brentano's, New York].

(It now appears among my own works for the first time in the British Isles, 1931.)

MADEIRA.   G. B. S
January, 1925.

THE SPIRIT IN WHICH TO READ THIS ESSAY

Imprisonment as it exists today is a worse crime than any of those committed by its victims; for no single criminal can be as powerful for evil, or as unrestrained in its exercise, as an organized nation. Therefore, if any person is addressing himself to the perusal of this dreadful subject in the spirit of a philanthropist bent on reforming a necessary and beneficent public institution, I beg him to put it down and go about some other business. It is just such reformers who have in the past made the neglect, oppression, corruption, and physical torture of the old common gaol the pretext for transforming it into that diabolical den of torment, mischief, and damnation, the modern model prison.

If, on the contrary, the reader comes as a repentant sinner, let him read on.

THE OBSTACLE OF VINDICTIVENESS

The difficulty in finding repentant sinners when this crime is in question has two roots. The first is that we are all brought up to believe that we may inflict injuries on anyone against whom we can make out a case of moral inferiority. We have this thrashed into us in our childhood by the infliction on ourselves of such injuries by our parents and teachers, or indeed by any elder who happens to be in charge of us. The second is that we are all now brought up to believe, not that the king can do no wrong, because kings have been unable to keep up that pretence, but that Society can do no wrong. Now not only does Society commit more frightful crimes than any individual, king or commoner: it legalizes its crimes, and forges certificates of righteousness for them, besides torturing anyone who dares expose their true character. A society like ours, which will, without remorse, ruin a boy body and soul for life for trying to sell newspapers in a railway station, is not likely to be very tender to people who venture to tell it that its laws would shock the Prince of Darkness himself if he had not been taught from his earliest childhood to respect as well as fear them.

Consequently we have a desperately sophisticated public, as well as a quite frankly vindictive one. Judges spend their lives consigning their fellow creatures to prison; and when some whisper reaches them that prisons are horribly cruel and destructive places, and that no creature fit to live should be sent there, they only remark calmly that prisons are not meant to be comfortable, which is no doubt the consideration that reconciled Pontius Pilate to the practice of crucifixion.

THE OBSTACLE OF STUPIDITY

Another difficulty is the sort of stupidity that comes from lack of imagination. When I tell people that I have seen with these eyes [in 1877] a man (no less a man than Richard Wagner, by the way) who once met a crowd going to see a soldier broken on the wheel by the crueller of the two legalized methods of carrying out that hideous sentence, they shudder, and are amazed to hear that what they call medieval torture was used in civilized Europe so recently. They forget that the punishment of half-hanging, unmentionably mutilating, beheading, and quartering, was on the British statute book within my own memory. The same people will read of a burglar being sentenced to ten years' penal servitude without turning a hair. They are like Ibsen's Peer Gynt, who was greatly reassured when he was told that the pains of hell are mental: he thought they cannot be so very bad if there is no actual burning brimstone. When such people are terrified by an outburst of robbery with violence, or sadistically excited by reports of the White Slave traffic, they clamor to have sentences of two years' hard labor supplemented by a flogging, which is a joke by comparison. They will try to lynch a criminal who illtreats a child in some sensationally cruel manner; but on the most trifling provocation they will inflict on the child the prison demoralization and the prison stigma which condemn it for the rest of its life to crime as the only employment open to a prison child. The public conscience would be far more active if the punishment of imprisonment were abolished, and we went back to the rack, the stake, the pillory, and the lash at the cart's tail.

BLOOD SPORTS DISGUISED AS PUNISHMENT ARE LESS CRUEL THAN IMPRISONMENT BUT MORE DEMORALIZING TO THE PUBLIC

The objection to retrogression is not that such punishments are more cruel than imprisonment. They are less cruel, and far less permanently injurious. The decisive objection to them is that they are sports in disguise. The pleasure to the spectators, and not the pain to the criminal, condemns them. People will go to see Titus Oates flogged or Joan of Arc burnt with equal zest as an entertainment. They will pay high prices for a good view. They will reluctantly admit that they must not torture oneanother as long as certain rules are observed; but they will hail a breach of the rules with delight as an excuse for a bout of cruelty. Yet they can be shamed at last into recognizing that such exhibitions are degrading and demoralizing; that the executioner is a wretch whose hand no decent person cares to take; and that the enjoyment of the spectators is fiendish. We have then to find some form of torment which can give no sensual satisfaction to the tormentor, and which is hidden from public view. That is how imprisonment, being just such a torment, became the normal penalty. The fact that it may be worse for the criminal is not taken into account. The public is seeking its own salvation, not that of the lawbreaker. For him it would be far better to suffer in the public eye; for among the crowd of sightseers there might be a Victor Hugo or a Dickens, able and willing to make the sightseers think of what they are doing and ashamed of it. The prisoner has no such chance. He envies the unfortunate animals in the zoo, watched daily by thousands of disinterested observers who never try to convert a tiger into a Quaker by solitary confinement, and would set up a resounding agitation in the papers if even the most ferocious maneater were made to suffer what the most docile convict suffers. Not only has the convict no such protection: the secrecy of his prison makes it hard to convince the public that he is suffering at all.

How we all become inured to Imprisonment

There is another reason for this incredulity. The vast majority of our city populations are inured to imprisonment from their childhood. The school is a prison. The office and the factory are prisons. The home is a prison. To the young who have the misfortune to be what is called well brought up it is sometimes a prison of inhuman severity. The children of John Howard,[4] as far as their liberty was concerned, were treated very much as he insisted criminals should be treated, with the result that his children were morally disabled, like criminals. This imprisonment in the home, the school, the office, and the factory is kept up by browbeating, scolding, bullying, punishing, disbelief of the prisoner's statements and acceptance of those of the official, essentially as in a criminal prison. The freedom given by the adult's right to walk out of his prison is only a freedom to go into another or starve: he can choose the prison where he is best treated: that is all. On the other hand, the imprisoned criminal is free from care as to his board, lodging, and clothing: he pays no taxes, and has no responsibilities. Nobody expects him to work as an unconvicted man must work if he is to keep his job: nobody expects him to do his work well, or cares twopence whether it is well done or not.

Under such circumstances it is very hard to convince the ordinary citizen

---

4. English philanthropist, whose active interest in prison reform began in 1773 with his acceptance of the office of High Sheriff at Bedford. Author of *The State of Prisons in England and Wales* (1777).

that the criminal is not better off than he deserves to be, and indeed on the verge of being positively pampered. Judges, magistrates, and Home Secretaries are so commonly under the same delusion that people who have ascertained the truth about prisons have been driven to declare that the most urgent necessity of the situation is that every judge, magistrate, and Home Secretary should serve a six months' sentence incognito; so that when he is dealing out and enforcing sentences he should at least know what he is doing.

COMPETITION IN EVIL BETWEEN PRISON AND SLUM

When we get down to the poorest and most oppressed of our population we find the conditions of their life so wretched that it would be impossible to conduct a prison humanely without making the lot of the criminal more eligible than that of many free citizens. If the prison does not underbid the slum in human misery, the slum will empty and the prison will fill. This does in fact take place to a small extent at present, because slum life at its worst is so atrocious that its victims, when they are intelligent enough to study alternatives instead of taking their lot blindly, conclude that prison is the most comfortable place to spend the winter in, and qualify themselves accordingly by committing an offence for which they will get six months. But this consideration affects only those people whose condition is not defended by any responsible publicist: the remedy is admittedly not to make the prison worse but the slum better. Unfortunately the admitted claims of the poor on life are pitifully modest. The moment the treatment of the criminal is decent and merciful enough to give him a chance of moral recovery, or, in incorrigible cases, to avoid making bad worse, the official descriptions of his lot become so rosy that a clamor arises against thieves and murderers being better off than honest and kindly men; for the official reports tell us only of the care that is taken of the prisoner and the advantages he enjoys, or can earn by good conduct, never of his sufferings; and the public is not imaginative or thoughtful enough to supply the deficiency.

What sane man, I ask the clamorers, would accept an offer of free board, lodging, clothing, waiters in attendance at a touch of the bell, medical treatment, spiritual advice, scientific ventilation and sanitation, technical instruction, liberal education, and the use of a carefully selected library, with regular exercise daily and sacred music at frequent intervals, even at the very best of the Ritz Hotels, if the conditions were that he should never leave the hotel, never speak, never sing, never laugh, never see a newspaper, and write only one sternly censored letter and have one miserable interview at long intervals through the bars of a cage under the eye of a warder? And when the prison is not the Ritz Hotel, when the lodging, the food, the bed, are all deliberately made so uncomfortable as to be instruments of torture, when the clothes are rags promiscuously worn by all your fellow prisoners in turn with yourself, when the exercise is that of a turnspit, when the ventilation and sanitation are noisome, when the instruction is a sham, the education a fraud, when the doctor is a bully to whom your ailments are all malingerings, and the chaplain a moral snob with no time for anything but the distribution of unreadable books, when the waiters are bound by penalties not to speak to you except to give you an order or a rebuke, and then to address you as you would not dream of addressing your dog, when the manager holds over your head a continual threat of starvation and confinement in a punishment cell (as if your own cell were not punishment enough), then what man in his senses would voluntarily exchange even the most harassed freedom for such a life, much less wallow luxuriously in it, as the Punch burglar[5] always does on paper the moment anyone suggests the slightest alleviation of the pains of imprisonment?

GIVING THEM HELL

Yet people cannot be brought to see this. They ask, first, what right the convict has to complain when he has brought it on himself by his own misconduct, and second, what he has to complain of. You reply that his grievances are silence, solitude, idleness, waste of time, and irresponsibility. The retort is, "Why call that torture, as if it were boiling oil or red-hot irons or something like that? Why, I have taken a cottage in the country for the sake of silence and solitude; and I should be only too glad to get rid of my responsibilities and waste my time in idleness like a real gentleman. A jolly sight too well off, the fellows are. I should give them hell."

Thus imprisonment is at once the most cruel of punishments and the one that those who inflict it without having ever experienced it cannot believe to be cruel. A country gentleman with a big hunting stable will indignantly discharge a groom and refuse him a reference for cruelly thrashing a horse.

5. A generic reference to any cartoon in the British humour magazines that treated the jailed criminal's situation with cavalier comicality.

But it never occurs to him that his stables are horse prisons, and the stall a cell in which it is quite unnatural for the horse to be immured. In my youth I saw the great Italian actress [Adelaide] Ristori play Mary Stuart [in Johann Schiller's play of that name, 1801]; and nothing in her performance remains more vividly with me than her representation of the relief of Mary at finding herself in the open air after months of imprisonment. When I first saw a stud of hunters turned out to grass, they reminded me so strongly of Ristori that I at once understood that they had been prisoners in their stables, a fact which, obvious as it was, I had not thought of before. And this sort of thoughtlessness, being continuous and unconscious, inflicts more suffering than all the malice and passion in the world. In prison you get one piled on the other: to the cruelty that is intended and contrived, that grudges you even the inevitable relief of sleep, and makes your nights miserable by plank beds and the like, is added the worse cruelty that is not intended as cruelty, and, when its perpetrators can be made conscious of it at all, deludes them by a ghastly semblance of pampered indulgence.

THE THREE OFFICIAL AIMS OF IMPRISONMENT

And now comes a further complication. When people are at last compelled to think about what they are doing to our unfortunate convicts, they think so unsuccessfully and confusedly that they only make matters worse. Take for example the official list of the results aimed at by the Prison Commissioners. First, imprisonment must be "retributory" (the word vindictive is not in official use). Second, it must be deterrent. Third, it must be reformative.

THE RETRIBUTION MUDDLE

Now, if you are to punish a man retributively, you must injure him. If you are to reform him, you must improve him. And men are not improved by injuries. To propose to punish and reform people by the same operation is exactly as if you were to take a man suffering from pneumonia, and attempt to combine punitive and curative treatment. Arguing that a man with pneumonia is a danger to the community, and that he need not catch it if he takes proper care of his health, you resolve that he shall have a severe lesson, both to punish him for his negligence and pulmonary weakness and to deter others from following his example. You therefore strip him naked, and in that condition stand him all night in the snow. But as you admit the duty of restoring him to health if possible, and discharging him with sound lungs, you engage a doctor to superintend the punishment and administer cough lozenges, made as unpleasant to the taste as possible so as not to pamper the culprit. A Board of Commissioners ordering such treatment would prove thereby that either they were imbeciles or else they were hotly in earnest about punishing the patient and not in the least in earnest about curing him.

When our Prison Commissioners pretend to combine punishment with moral reformation they are in the same dilemma. We are told that the reformation of the criminal is kept constantly in view; yet the destruction of the prisoner's self-respect by systematic humiliation is deliberately ordered and practised; and we learn from a chaplain that he "does not think it is good to give opportunity for the exercise of Christian and social virtues one towards another" among prisoners. The only consolation for such contradictions is their demonstration that, as the tormentors instinctively feel that they must be liars and hypocrites on the subject, their consciences cannot be very easy about the torment. But the contradictions are obvious here only because I put them on the same page. The Prison Commissioners keep them a few pages apart; and the average reader's memory, it seems, is not long enough to span the gap when his personal interests are not at stake.

PLAUSIBILITY OF THE DETERRENCE DELUSION

Deterrence, which is the real object of the courts, has much more to be said for it, because it is neither simply and directly wicked like retribution, nor a false excuse for wickedness like reformation. It is an unquestionable fact that, by making rules and forcing those who break them to suffer so severely that others like them become afraid to break them, discipline can be maintained to a certain extent among creatures without sense enough to understand its necessity, or, if they do understand it, without conscience enough to refrain from violating it. This is the crude basis of all our disciplines: home discipline, school discipline, factory discipline, army and navy discipline, as well as of prison discipline, and of the whole fabric of criminal law. It is imposed not only by cruel rulers, but by unquestionably humane ones: the only difference being that the cruel rulers impose it with alacrity and gloat over its execution, and the humane rulers are driven to it reluctantly by the failure of their appeals to the consciences of people who have no conscience. Thus we find Mahomet, a conspicuously humane and conscientious Arab, keeping his fierce staff in order, not by unusual punishments, but by threats of a hell after death which he invented for the purpose in revolting detail of a kind which suggests that Mahomet had perhaps too much of the woman and the artist in him to know what would frighten a Bedouin most. Wellington, a general so humane that he sacrificed the exercise of a military genius of the first order to his moral horror of war and his freedom from its illusions, nevertheless hanged and flogged his soldiers mercilessly because he had learnt from experience that, as he put it, nothing is worse than impunity. All revolutions have been the work of men who, like Robespierre, were sentimental humanitarians and conscientious objectors to capital punishment and to the severities of military and prison discipline; yet all the revolutions have after a very brief practical experience been driven to Terrorism (the proper name of Deterrence) as ruthless as the Counter-Revolutionary Terror of Sulla, a late example being that of the Russian revolution of 1917. Whether it is Sulla, Robespierre, Trotsky, or the fighting mate of a sailing ship with a crew of loafers and wastrels, the result is the same: there are people to be dealt with who will not obey the law unless they are afraid to disobey it, and whose disobedience would mean disaster.

CRIME CANNOT BE KILLED BY KINDNESS

It is useless for humanitarians to shirk this hard fact, and proclaim their conviction that all lawbreakers can be reformed by kindness. That may be true in many cases, provided you can find a very gifted practitioner to take the worst ones in hand, with unlimited time and means to treat them. But if these conditions are not available, and a policeman and an executioner who will disable the wrongdoer instantaneously are available, the police remedy is the only practicable one, even for rulers filled with the spirit of the Sermon on the Mount. The late G. W. Foote, President of the English National Secular Society [see Vol. 1, p. 273], a strenuous humanitarian, once had to persuade a very intimate friend of his, a much smaller and weaker man, to allow himself to be taken to an asylum for lunatics. It took four hours of humanitarian persuasion to get the patient from the first floor of his house to the cab door. Foote told me that he had not only recognized at once that no asylum attendant, with several patients to attend to, could possibly spend four hours in getting each of them downstairs, but found his temper so intolerably strained by the unnatural tax on his patience that if the breaking point had been reached, as it certainly would have been in the case of a warder or asylum attendant, he would have been far more violent, not to say savage, than if he had resorted to force at once, and finished the job in five minutes.

From resorting to this rational and practically compulsory use of kindly physical coercion to making it so painful that the victim will be afraid to give any trouble next time is a pretty certain step. In prisons the warders have to protect themselves against violence from prisoners, of which there is a constant risk and very well-founded dread, as there are always ungovernably savage criminals who have little more power of refraining from furious assaults than some animals, including quite carefully bred dogs and horses, have of refraining from biting and savaging. The official punishment is flogging and putting in irons for months. But the immediate rescue of the assaulted warder has to be effected by the whole body of warders within reach; and whoever supposes that the prisoner suffers nothing more at their hands than the minimum of force necessary to restrain him knows nothing of prison life and less of human nature.

Any criticism of the deterrent theory of our prison system which ignores the existence of ungovernable savages will be discredited by the citation of actual cases. I should be passed over as a sentimentalist if I lost sight of them for a moment. On any other subject I could dispose of the matter by reminding my critics that hard cases make bad law. On this subject I recognize that the hard cases are of such a nature that provision must be made for them. Indeed hard cases may be said to be the whole subject matter of criminal law; for the normal human case is not that of the criminal, but of the law-abiding person on whose collar the grip of the policeman never closes. Only, it does not follow that the hardest cases should dictate the treatment of the relatively soft ones.

The Seamy Side of Deterrence

Let us now see what are the objections to the Deterrent or Terrorist system.

1. It necessarily leaves the interests of the victim wholly out of account. It injures and degrades him; destroys the reputation without which he cannot get employment; and when the punishment is imprisonment under our system, atrophies his powers of fending for himself in the world. Now this would not materially hurt anyone but himself if, when he had been duly made an example of, he were killed like a vivisected dog. But he is

not killed. He is, at the expiration of his sentence, flung out of the prison into the streets to earn his living in a labor market where nobody will employ an ex-prisoner, betraying himself at every turn by his ignorance of the common news of the months or years he has passed without newspapers, lamed in speech, and terrified at the unaccustomed task of providing food and lodging for himself. There is only one lucrative occupation available for him; and that is crime. He has no compunction as to Society: why should he have any? Society having for its own selfish protection done its worst to him, he has no feeling about it except a desire to get a bit of his own back. He seeks the only company in which he is welcome: the society of criminals; and sooner or later, according to his luck, he finds himself in prison again. The figures of recidivism shew that the exceptions to this routine are so few as to be negligible for the purposes of our argument. The criminal, far from being deterred from crime, is forced into it; and the citizen whom his punishment was meant to protect suffers from his depredations.

OUR PLAGUE OF UNRESTRAINED CRIME

It is, in fact, admitted that the deterrent system does not deter the convicted criminal. Its real efficacy is sought in its deterrent effect on the free citizens who would commit crimes but for their fear of punishment. The Terrorist can point to the wide range of evil-doing which, not being punished by law, is rampant among us; for though a man can get himself hanged for a momentary lapse of self-control under intolerable provocation by a nagging woman, or into prison for putting the precepts of Christ above the orders of a Competent Military Authority, he can be a quite infernal scoundrel without breaking any penal law. If it be true, as it certainly is, that it is conscience and not the fear of punishment that makes civilized life possible, and that Dr Johnson's

> How small, of all that human hearts endure,
> That part that laws or kings can cause or cure! [inserted in Oliver Goldsmith's
> *The Traveller*]

is as applicable to crime as to human activity in general, it is none the less true that commercial civilization presents an appalling spectacle of pillage and parasitism, of corruption in the press and in the pulpit, of lying advertisements which make people buy rank poisons in the belief that they are health restorers, of traps to catch the provision made for the widow and the fatherless and divert it to the pockets of company-promoting rogues, of villainous oppression of the poor and cruelty to the defenceless; and it is arguable that most of this could, like burglary and forgery, be kept within bearable bounds if its perpetrators were dealt with as burglars and forgers are dealt with today. It is, let us not forget, equally arguable that if we can afford to leave so much villainy unpunished we can afford to leave all villainy unpunished. Unfortunately, we cannot afford it: our toleration is threatening our civilization. The prosperity that consists in the wicked flourishing like a green bay tree, and the humble and contrite hearts being thoroughly despised, is a commercial delusion. Facts must be looked in the face, rascals told what they are, and all men called on to justify their ways to God and Man up to the point at which the full discharge of their social duties leaves them free to exercise their individual fancies. Restraint from evil-doing is within the rights as well as within the powers of organized society over its members; and it cannot be denied that the exercise of these powers, as far as it could be made inevitable, would incidentally deter from crime a certain number of people with only marginal consciences or none at all, and that an extension of the penal code would create fresh social conscience by enlarging the list of things which law-abiding people make it a point of honor not to do, besides calling the attention of the community to grave matters in which they have hitherto erred through thoughtlessness.

DETERRENCE A FUNCTION OF CERTAINTY, NOT OF SEVERITY

But there is all the difference in the world between deterrence as an incident of the operation of criminal law, and deterrence as its sole object and justification. In a purely deterrent system, for instance, it matters not a jot who is punished provided somebody is punished and the public persuaded that he is guilty. The effect of hanging or imprisoning the wrong man is as deterrent as hanging or imprisoning the right one. This is the fundamental explanation of the extreme and apparently fiendish reluctance of the Home Office to release a prisoner when, as in the Beck case,[6]

6. The Beck case (also known as the Croydon Poisoning Case) involved the unintentional killing in April 1907 of Richard and Elizabeth Beck by a carpenter, Richard Brinkley, who was attempting to do away with an inconvenient witness to another (non-capital) crime by use of prussic acid. Brinkley was found guilty and hanged on 13 August 1907.

the evidence on which he was convicted has become discredited to a point at which no jury would maintain its verdict of guilty. The reluctance is not to confess that an innocent man is being punished, but to proclaim that a guilty man has escaped. For if escape is possible deterrence shrinks almost to nothing. There is no better established rule of criminology than that it is not the severity of punishment that deters, but its certainty. And the flaw in the case of Terrorism is that it is impossible to obtain enough certainty to deter. The police are compelled to confess every year, when they publish their statistics, that against the list of crimes reported to them they can set only a percentage of detections and convictions. And the list of reported crimes can form only a percentage, how large or small it is impossible to say, but probably small, of the crimes actually committed; for it is the greatest mistake to suppose that everyone who is robbed runs to the police: on the contrary, only foolish and ignorant or very angry people do so without very serious consideration and great reluctance. In most cases it costs nothing to let the thief off, and a good deal to prosecute him. The burglar in Heartbreak House, who makes his living by breaking into people's houses, and then blackmailing them by threatening to give himself up to the police and put them to the expense and discomfort of attending his trial and giving evidence after enduring all the worry of the police enquiries, is not a joke; he is a comic dramatization of a process that is going on every day. As to the black sheep of respectable families who blackmail them by offering them the alternative of making good their thefts and frauds, even to the extent of honoring their forged cheques, or having the family name disgraced, ask any experienced family solicitor.

Besides the chances of not being prosecuted, there are the chances of acquittal; but I doubt whether they count for much except with very attractive women. Still, it is worth mentioning that juries will snatch at the flimsiest pretexts for refusing to send people who engage their sympathy to the gallows or to penal servitude, even on evidence of murder or theft which would make short work of a repulsive person.

SOME PERSONAL EXPERIENCES

Take my own experience as probably common enough. Fifty years ago a friend of mine [Alexander Maclagan, cashier of the Uniacke Townshend land agency, 1873], hearing that a legacy had been left him, lent himself the expected sum out of his employers' cash; concealed the defalcation by falsifying his accounts; and was detected before he could repay. His employers angrily resented the fraud, and had certainly no desire to spare him. But a public exposure of the affair would have involved shock to their clients' sense of security, loss of time and consequently of money, an end to all hope of his ever making good the loss, and the unpleasantness of attendance in court at the trial. All this put any recourse to the police out of the question; and my friend obtained another post after a very brief interval during which he supported himself as a church organist. This, by the way, was a quite desirable conclusion, as he was for all ordinary practical purposes a sufficiently honest man. It would have been pure mischief to make him a criminal; but that is not the present point. He serves here as an illustration of the fact that our criminal law, far from inviting prosecution, attaches serious losses and inconveniences to it.

It may be said that whatever the losses and inconveniences may be, it is a public duty to prosecute. But is it? Is it not a Christian duty not to prosecute? A man stole £500 from me by a trick.[7] He speculated in my character with subtlety and success; and yet he ran risks of detection which no quite sensible man would have ventured on. It was assumed that I would resort to the police. I asked why. The answer was that he should be punished to deter others from similar crimes. I naturally said, "You have been punishing people cruelly for more than a century for this kind of fraud; and the result is that I am robbed of £500. Evidently your deterrence does not deter. What it does do is to torment the swindler for years, and then throw him back upon society, a worse man in every respect, with no other employment open to him except that of fresh swindling. Besides, your elaborate arrangements to deter me from prosecuting are convincing and effective. I could earn £500 by useful work in the time it would take to prosecute this man vindictively and worse than uselessly. So I wish him joy of his booty, and invite him to swindle me again if he can." Now this was not sentimentality. I am not a bit fonder of being swindled than other people; and if society would treat swindlers properly I should denounce them without the slightest remorse, and not grudge a reasonable expenditure of time and energy in the business. But to

7. In May 1913 a confidence man swindled £525 from Shaw by the trick of delivering a letter supposedly from a Fabian colleague F. W. Pethick Lawrence containing a crossed cheque payable to himself and asking Shaw to deliver to bearer an open cheque in the same amount, thus relieving Pethick Lawrence of a financial difficulty. Shaw, naïvely accepting letter and cheque as genuine, complied. Only when the forged cheque was returned by his bank stamped 'Drawer has no account' did Shaw realize he had been duped.

throw good money after bad in setting to work a wicked and mischievous routine of evil would be to stamp myself as a worse man than the swindler, who earned the money more energetically, and appropriated it no more unjustly, if less legally, than I earn and appropriate my dividends.

I must however warn our thieves that I can promise them no immunity from police pursuit if they rob me. Some time after the operation just recorded, an uninvited guest came to a luncheon party in my house. He (or she) got away with an overcoat and a pocketful of my wife's best table silver. But instead of selecting my overcoat, he took the best overcoat, which was that of one of my guests. My guest [T. E. Lawrence] was insured against theft; the insurance company had to buy him a new overcoat; and the matter thus passed out of my hands into those of the police. But the result, as far as the thief was concerned, was the same. He was not captured; and he had the social satisfaction of providing employment for others in converting into a strongly fortified obstacle the flimsy gate through which he had effected an entrance, thereby giving my flat the appearance of a private madhouse.

On another occasion a drunken woman obtained admission by presenting an authentic letter from a softhearted member of the House of Lords. I had no guests at the moment; and as she, too, wanted an overcoat, she took mine, and actually interviewed me with it most perfunctorily concealed under her jacket. When I called her attention to it she handed it back to me effusively; begged me to shake hands with her; and went her way.

Now these things occur by the dozen every day, in spite of the severity with which they are punished when the thief is dealt with by the police. I daresay all my readers, if not too young to have completed a representative experience, could add two or three similar stories. What do they go to prove? Just that detection is so uncertain that its consequences have no really effective deterrence for the potential offender, whilst the unpleasant and expensive consequences of prosecution, being absolutely certain, have a very strong deterrent effect indeed on the prosecutor. In short, all the hideous cruelty practised by us for the sake of deterrence is wasted: we are damning our souls at great expense and trouble for nothing.

JUDICIAL VENGEANCE AS AN ALTERNATIVE TO LYNCH LAW

Thus we see that of the three official objects of our prison system: vengeance, deterrence, and reformation of the criminal, only one is achieved; and that is the one which is nakedly abominable. But there is a plea for it which must be taken into account, and which brings us to the root of the matter in our own characters. It is said, and it is in a certain degree true, that if the Government does not lawfully organize and regulate popular vengeance, the populace will rise up and execute this vengeance lawlessly for itself. The standard defence of the Inquisition is that without it no heretic's life would have been safe. In Texas today the people are not satisfied with the prospect of knowing that a murderer or ravisher will be electrocuted inside a gaol if a jury can resist the defence put up by his lawyer. They tear him from the hands of the sheriff; pour lamp oil over him; and burn him alive. Now the burning of human beings is not only an expression of outraged public morality: it is also a sport for which a taste can be acquired much more easily and rapidly than a taste for coursing hares, just as a taste for drink can be acquired from brandy and cocktails more easily and rapidly than from beer or sauterne. Lynching mobs begin with negro ravishers and murderers; but they presently go on to any sort of delinquent, provided he is black. Later on, as a white man will burn as amusingly as a black one, and a white woman react to tarring and feathering as thrillingly as a negress, the color line is effaced by what professes to be a rising wave of virtuous indignation, but is in fact an epidemic of Sadism. The defenders of our penal systems take advantage of it to assure us that if they did not torment and ruin a boy guilty of sleeping in the open air, an indignant public would rise and tear that boy limb from limb.

Now the reply to such a plea, from the point of view of civilized law, cannot be too sweeping. The government which cannot restrain a mob from taking the law into its own hands is no government at all. If [Henri-Desiré] Landru could go to the guillotine unmolested in France,[8] and his British prototype who drowned all his wives in their baths could be peaceably hanged in England,[9] Texas can protect its criminals by simply bringing its civilization up to the French and British level. But indeed the besetting sin of the mob is a morbid hero worship of great criminals rather

8. French murderer, known as 'the modern Bluebeard', who defrauded middle-aged women and was put to death after allegedly slaying at least ten of them between 1915 and 1919.
9. George Joseph Smith, who had 'married' at least seven women for profit motives, and who was suspected of having drowned three of them in their baths, was convicted of the 1912 murder of the first of the three, Bessie Mundy. He was executed on 13 August 1915. The case became known in the press as the 'Brides in the Bath Murders'.

than a ferocious abhorrence of them. In any case nobody will have the effrontery to pretend that the number of criminals who excite popular feeling enough to provoke lynching is more than a negligible percentage of the whole. The theory that the problem of crime is only one of organizing, regulating, and executing the vengeance of the mob will not bear plain statement, much less discussion. It is only the retributive theory over again in its most impudent form.

THE HARD CASES THAT MAKE BAD LAW

Having now disposed of all the official theories as the trash they are, let us return to the facts, and deal with the hard ones first. Everyone who has any extensive experience of domesticated animals, human or other, knows that there are negatively bad specimens who have no consciences, and positively bad ones who are incurably ferocious. The negative ones are often very agreeable and even charming companions; but they beg, borrow, steal, defraud, and seduce almost by reflex action: they cannot resist the most trifling temptation. They are indulged and spared to the extreme limit of endurance; but in the end they have to be deprived of their liberty in some way. The positive ones enjoy no such tolerance. Unless they are physically restrained they break people's bones, knock out their eyes, rupture their organs, or kill them.

Then there are the cruel people, not necessarily unable to control their tempers, nor fraudulent, nor in any other way disqualified for ordinary social activity or liberty, possibly even with conspicuous virtues. But, by a horrible involution, they lust after the spectacle of suffering, mental and physical, as normal men lust after love. Torture is to them a pleasure except when it is inflicted on themselves. In scores of ways, from the habitual utterance of wounding speeches, and the contriving of sly injuries and humiliations for which they cannot be brought to book legally, to thrashing their wives and children or, as bachelors, paying prostitutes of the hardier sort to submit to floggings, they seek the satisfaction of their desire wherever and however they can.

POSSIBILITIES OF THERAPEUTIC TREATMENT

Now in the present state of our knowledge it is folly to talk of reforming these people. By this I do not mean that even now they are all quite incurable. The cases of no conscience are sometimes, like Parsifal's when he shot the swan, cases of unawakened conscience. Violent and quarrelsome people are often only energetic people who are underworked: I have known a man cured of wife-beating by setting him to beat the drum in a village band; and the quarrels that make country life so very unarcadian are picked mostly because the quarrelers have not enough friction in their lives to keep them goodhumored.

Psychoanalysis, too, which is not all quackery and pornography, might conceivably cure a case of Sadism as it might cure any of the phobias. And psychoanalysis is a mere fancy compared to the knowledge we now pretend to concerning the function of our glands and their effect on our character and conduct. In the XIX century this knowledge was pursued barbarously by crude vivisectors whose notion of finding out what a gland was for was to cut it violently out and see what would happen to the victim, meanwhile trying to bribe the public to tolerate such horrors by promising to make old debauchees young again. This was rightly felt to be a villainous business; besides, who could suppose that the men who did these things would hesitate to lie about the results when there was plenty of money to be made by representing them as cures for dreaded diseases? But today we are not asked to infer that because something has happened to a violently mutilated dog it must happen also to an unmutilated human being. We can now make authentic pictures of internal organs by means of rays to which flesh is transparent. This makes it possible to take a criminal and say authoritatively that he is a case, not of original sin, but of an inefficient, or excessively efficient, thyroid gland, or pituitary gland, or adrenal gland, as the case may be. This of course does not help the police in dealing with a criminal: they must apprehend and bring him to trial all the same. But if the prison doctor were able to say "Put some iodine in this man's skilly [porridge], and his character will change," then the notion of punishing instead of curing him would become ridiculous. Of course the matter is not so simple as that; and all this endocrinism, as it is called, may turn out to be only the latest addition to our already very extensive collection of pseudo-scientific mares' nests; still, we cannot ignore the fact that a considerable case is being made out by eminent physiologists for at least a conjecture that many cases which are now incurable may be disposed of in the not very remote future by inducing the patient to produce more thyroxin or pituitrin or adrenalin or what not, or even administering them to him as thyroxin is at present administered in cases of myxœdema. Yet the reports of the work of our prison medical officers suggest that hardly any of them has ever heard of these discoveries, or regards a convict as anything more interesting scientifically than a malingering rascal.

The Incorrigible Villains

It will be seen that I am prepared to go to lengths which still seem fantastic as to the possibility of changing a criminal into an honest man. And I have more faith than most prison chaplains seem to have in the possibilities of religious conversion. But I cannot add too emphatically that the people who imagine that all criminals can be reformed by setting chaplains to preach at them, by giving them pious books and tracts to read, by separating them from their companions in crime and locking them up in solitude to reflect on their sins and repent, are far worse enemies both to the criminal and to Society than those who face the fact that these are merely additional cruelties which make their victims worse, or even than those who frankly use them as a means of "giving them hell." But when this is recognized, and the bigoted reformers with their sermons, their tracts, their horrors of separation, silence, and solitude to avoid contamination, are bundled out of our prisons as nuisances, the problem remains, how are you to deal with your incorrigibles? Here you have a man who supports himself by gaining the confidence and affection of lonely women; seducing them; spending all their money; and then burning them in a stove or drowning them in a bath. He is quite an attractive fellow, with a genuine taste for women and no taste at all for murder, which is only his way of getting rid of them when their money is spent and they are in the way of the next woman. There is no more malice or Sadism about the final operation than there is about tearing up a letter when it is done with, and throwing it into the wastepaper basket. You electrocute him or hang him or chop his head off. But presently you have to deal with a man who lives in exactly the same way, but has not executive force or courage enough to commit murder. He only abandons his victims and turns up in a fresh place with a fresh name. He generally marries them, as it is easier to seduce them so.

Alongside him you have a married couple united by a passion for cruelty. They amuse themselves by tying their children to the bedstead; thrashing them with straps; and branding them with red-hot pokers. You also have to deal with a man who on the slightest irritation flings his wife under a dray, or smashes a lighted kerosene lamp into her face. He has been in prison again and again for outbursts of this kind; and always, within a week of his release, or within a few hours of it, he has done it again.

Now you cannot get rid of these nuisances and monsters by simply cataloguing them as subthyroidics and superadrenals or the like. At present you torment them for a fixed period, at the end of which they are set free to resume their operations with a savage grudge against the community which has tormented them. That is stupid. Nothing is gained by punishing people who cannot help themselves, and on whom deterrence is thrown away. Releasing them is like releasing the tigers from the Zoo to find their next meal in the nearest children's playing ground.

THE LETHAL CHAMBER

The most obvious course is to kill them. Some of the popular objections to this may be considered for a moment. Death, it is said, is irrevocable; and after all, they may turn out to be innocent. But really you cannot handle criminals on the assumption that they may be innocent. You are not supposed to handle them at all until you have convinced yourself by an elaborate trial that they are guilty. Besides, imprisonment is as irrevocable as hanging. Each is a method of taking a criminal's life; and when he prefers hanging or suicide to imprisonment for life, as he sometimes does, he says, in effect, that he had rather you took his life all at once, painlessly, than minute by minute in long-drawn-out torture. You can give a prisoner a pardon; but you cannot give him back a moment of his imprisonment. He may accept a reprieve willingly in the hope of a pardon or an escape or a revolution or an earthquake or what not; but as you do not mean him to evade his sentence in any way whatever, it is not for you to take such clutchings at straws into account.

Another argument against the death penalty for anything short of murder is the practical one of the policeman and the householder, who plead that if you hang burglars they will shoot to avoid capture on the ground that they may as well be hanged for a sheep as for a lamb. But this can be disposed of by pointing out, first, that even under existing circumstances the burglar occasionally shoots, and, second, that acquittals, recommendations to mercy, verdicts of manslaughter, successful pleas of insanity and so forth, already make the death penalty so uncertain that even red-handed murderers shoot no oftener than burglars—less often, in fact. This uncertainty would be actually increased if the death sentence were, as it should be, made applicable to other criminals than those convicted of wilful murder, and no longer made compulsory in any case.

The Sacredness of Human Life from the Warder's Side

Then comes the plea for the sacredness of human life. The State should not set the example of killing, or of clubbing a rioter with a policeman's *bâton*, or of dropping bombs on a sleeping city, or of doing many things that States nevertheless have to do. But let us take the plea on its own ground, which is, fundamentally, that life is the most precious of all things, and its waste the worst of crimes. We have already seen that imprisonment does not spare the life of the criminal: it takes it and wastes it in the most cruel way. But there are others to be considered beside the criminal and the citizens who fear him so much that they cannot sleep in peace unless he is locked up. There are the people who have to lock him up, and fetch him his food, and watch him. Why are their lives to be wasted? Warders, and especially wardresses, are almost as much tied to the prison by their occupation, and by their pensions, which they dare not forfeit by seeking other employment, as the criminals are. If I had to choose between a spell under preventive detention among hardened criminals in Camp Hill [on the Isle of Wight] and one as a warder in an ordinary prison, I think I should vote for Camp Hill. Warders suffer in body and mind from their employment; and if it be true, as our examination seems to prove, that they are doing no good to society, but very active harm, their lives are wasted more completely than those of the criminals; for most criminals are discharged after a few weeks or months; but the warder never escapes until he is superannuated, by which time he is an older gaolbird than any Lifer in the cells.

The Price of Life in Communities

How then does the case stand with your incurable pathological case of crime? If you treat the life of the criminal as sacred, you find yourself not only taking his life but sacrificing the lives of innocent men and women to keep him locked up. There is no sort of sense or humanity in such a course. The moment we face it frankly we are driven to the conclusion that the community has a right to put a price on the right to live in it. That price must be sufficient self-control to live without wasting and destroying the lives of others, whether by direct attack like a tiger, parasitic exploitation like a leech, or having to be held in a leash with another person at the end of it. Persons lacking such self-control have been thrust out into the sagebrush to wander there until they die of thirst, a cruel and cowardly way of killing them. The dread of clean and wilful killing often leads to evasions of the commandment "Thou shalt not kill" which are far more cruel than its frank violation. It has never been possible to obey it unreservedly, either with men or with animals; and the attempts to keep the letter of it have led to burying vestal virgins and nuns alive, crushing men to death in the press-yard, handing heretics over to the secular arm, and the like, instead of killing them humanely and without any evasion of the heavy responsibility involved. It was a horrible thing to build a vestal virgin into a wall with food and water enough for a day; but to build her into a prison for years as we do, with just enough loathsome food to prevent her from dying, is more than horrible: it is diabolical. If no better alternatives to death can be found than these, then who will not vote for death? If people are fit to live, let them live under decent human conditions. If they are not fit to live, kill them in a decent human way. Is it any wonder that some of us are driven to prescribe the lethal chamber as the solution for the hard cases which are at present made the excuse for dragging all the other cases down to their level, and the only solution that will create a sense of full social responsibility in modern populations?

THE SIXTH COMMANDMENT

The slaughtering of incorrigibly dangerous persons, as distinguished from the punitive execution of murderers who have violated the commandment not to kill, cannot be established summarily by these practical considerations. In spite of their cogency we have not only individuals who are resolutely and uncompromisingly opposed to slaying under any provocation whatever, we have nations who have abolished the death penalty, and regard our grim retention of it as barbarous. Wider than any nation we have the Roman Catholic Church, which insists literally on absolute obedience to the commandment, and condemns as murder even the killing of an unborn child to save the mother's life. In practice this obligation has been evaded so grossly—by the Inquisition, for example, which refused to slay the heretic, but handed him over to the secular arm with a formal recommendation to mercy, knowing that the secular arm would immediately burn him—that the case of the Church might be cited to illustrate the uselessness of barring the death penalty. But it also illustrates the persistence and antiquity of a point of conscience which still defies the argument from expediency. That point of conscience may be called a superstition because it is as old as the story of Cain and Abel, and because it is difficult to find any rational basis for it. But there is something to be said for it all the same.

Killing is a dangerously cheap way out of a difficulty. "Stone dead hath no fellow" [English adage dating to the early seventeenth century] was a handy formula for Cromwell's troops in dealing with the Irish; still, that precedent is not very reassuring. All the social problems of all the countries can be got rid of by extirpating the inhabitants; but to get rid of a problem is not to solve it. Even perfectly rational solutions of our problems must be humane as well if they are to be accepted by good men: otherwise the logic of the inquisitor, the dynamiter, and the vivisectionist would rule the world for ever as it unfortunately does to far too great an extent already. It may also be argued that if society were to forgo its power of slaying, and also its practice of punishment, it would have a stronger incentive to find out how to correct the apparently incorrigible. Although whenever it has renounced its power to slay sane criminals it has substituted a horribly rigorous and indeed virtually lethal imprisonment, this does not apply to homicidal lunatics, the comparatively lenient treatment of whom could obviously be extended to sane murderers. The Oxford Dictionary owes several of its pages to a homicide who was detained at Broadmoor (the English Asylum for Criminal Lunatics) during the pleasure of the Crown.[10] As to the cases which, when not disposed of by the lethal method, involve caging men as tigers are caged, can they not be dealt with by the padded room? Granted that it is questionable whether the public conscience which tolerates such caging is really more sensitive or thoughtful than that which

10. Dr William C. Minor, an American surgeon suffering from chronic delusional insanity, murdered an innocent passer-by in the street shortly after his arrival in London in 1872, and was committed to Broadmoor Criminal Lunatic Asylum. A highly educated man, he volunteered from the asylum to be a reader of selected book texts for the *New English Dictionary* (later the *Oxford English Dictionary*), recording early appearances of words and phrases. He served in this lexicographic capacity for more than twenty years, supplying over 12,000 quotations before his health failed. He was repatriated to his American family in 1910. Shaw's knowledge of Dr Minor was derived from a brace of highly coloured and inaccurate articles by his friend Hayden Church in the *Strand*, September 1915 and January 1916. For a full and accurate treatment see Elizabeth M. Knowles, 'Dr Minor and the *Oxford English Dictionary*', *Dictionaries: Journal of the Dictionary Society of North America*, No. 12 (1990).

demands the lethal solution, and that at the present time executions, and even floggings, do not harden the authorities and lower the standard of humanity all through our penal system as much as continuing penalties do, yet the reluctance to kill persists. The moment it is pointed out that if we kill incurable criminals we may as well also kill incurable troublesome invalids, people realize with a shock that the urge of horror, hatred, and vengeance is needed to nerve them—or unnerve them—to slay. When I force humane people to face their political powers of life and death apart from punishment as I am doing now, I produce a terrified impression that I want to hang everybody. In vain I protest that I am dealing with a very small class of human monsters, and that as far as crime is concerned our indiscriminate hanging of wilful murderers and traitors slays more in one year than dispassionate lethal treatment would be likely to slay in ten. I am asked at once who is to be trusted with the appalling responsibility of deciding whether a man is to live or die, and what government could be trusted not to kill its enemies under the pretence that they are enemies of society.'

GOVERNMENTS MUST PRESUME OR ABDICATE

The reply is obvious. Such responsibilities must be taken, whether we are fit for them or not, if civilized society is to be organized. No unofficial person denies that they are abused: the whole effect of this essay is to shew that they are horribly abused. I can say for my own part as a vehement critic and opponent of all the governments of which I have had any experience that I am the last person to forget that governments use the criminal law to suppress and exterminate their opponents whenever the opposition becomes really acute, and that the more virtuous the revolutionist and the more vicious the government, the more likely it is to kill him, and to do so under pretence of his being one of the dangerous persons for whom the lethal treatment would be reserved. It has been pointed out again and again that it is in the very nature of power to corrupt those to whom it is entrusted, and that to God alone belongs the awful prerogative of dismissing the soul from the body. Tolstoy has exhausted the persuasions of literary art in exhorting us that we resist not evil; and men have suffered abominable persecutions sooner than accept military service with its chief commandment, Thou shalt kill.

All this leaves the problem just where it was. The irresponsible humanitarian citizen may indulge his pity and sympathy to his heart's content, knowing that whenever a criminal passes to his doom there, but for the grace of God, goes he; but those who have to govern find that they must either abdicate, and that promptly, or else take on themselves as best they can many of the attributes of God. They must decide what is good and what evil; they must force men to do certain things and refrain from doing certain other things whether individual consciences approve or not; they must resist evil resolutely and continually, possibly and preferably without malice or revenge, but certainly with the effect of disarming it, preventing it, stamping it out, and creating public opinion against it. In short, they must do all sorts of things which they are manifestly not ideally fit to do, and, let us hope, do with becoming misgiving, but which must be done, all the same, well or ill, somehow and by somebody. If I were to ignore this, everyone who has had any experience of government would throw these pages aside as those of an inexperienced sentimentalist or an Impossibilist Anarchist.

Nevertheless, certain lines have to be drawn limiting the activities of governments, and allowing the individual to be a law unto himself. For instance, we are obliged (if we are wise) to tolerate sedition and blasphemy to a considerable extent because sedition and blasphemy are nothing more than the advocacy of changes in the established forms of government, morals, and religion; and without such changes there can be no social evolution. But as governments are not always wise, it is difficult enough to secure this intellectual anarchy, or as we call it, freedom of speech and conscience; and anyone who proposed to extend it to such actions as are contemplated by the advocates of lethal treatment would be dismissed as insane. No country at peace will tolerate murder, whether it is done on principle or in sin. What is more, no country at war will tolerate a refusal to murder the enemy. Thus, whether the powers of the country are being exercised for good or evil, they never remain in abeyance; and whoever proposes to set to those powers the limit of an absolute obedience to the commandment "Thou shalt not kill," must do so quite arbitrarily. He cannot give any reason that I can discover for saying that it is wickeder to break a man's neck than to cage him for life: he can only say that his instinct places an overwhelming ban on the one and not on the other; and he must depend on the existence of a similar instinct in the community for his success in having legal slaying ruled out.

THE RUTHLESSNESS OF THE PURE HEART

In this he will have little difficulty as long as the slaying is an act of revenge and expiation, as it is at present: that is why capital punishment has been abolished in some countries, and why its abolition is agitated for in the countries which still practise it. But if these sinful elements be discarded, and the slaying is made a matter of pure expediency, the criminal being pitied as sincerely as a mad dog is pitied, the most ardent present advocate of the abolition of capital punishment may not only consent to the slaying as he does in the case of the mad dog, but even demand it to put an end to an unendurable danger and horror. Malice and fear are narrow things, and carry with them a thousand inhibitions and terrors and scruples. A heart and brain purified of them gain an enormous freedom; and this freedom is shewn not only in the many civilized activities that are tabooed in the savage tribe, but also in the ruthlessness with which the civilized man destroys things that the savage prays to and propitiates. The attempt to reform an incurably dangerous criminal may come to be classed with the attempt to propitiate a sacred rattlesnake. The higher civilization does not make still greater sacrifices to the snake: it kills it.

I am driven to conclude, that though, if voluntary custodians can be found for dangerous incorrigibles, as they doubtless can by attaching compensating advantages to their employment, it is quite possible to proceed with slaying absolutely barred, there is not enough likelihood of this renunciation by the State of the powers of life and death to justify me in leaving lethal treatment out of the question. In any case it would be impossible to obtain any clear thinking on the question unless its possibilities were frankly faced and to some extent explored. I have faced them frankly and explored them as far as seems necessary; and at that I must leave it. Nothing that I have to say about the other sorts of criminals will be in the least invalidated if it should be decided that killing is to be ruled out. I think it quite likely that it may be ruled out on sentimental grounds. By the time we have reached solid ground the shock of reintroducing it (though this has been effected and even clamored for in some countries) may be too great to be faced under normal conditions. Also, as far as what we call crime is concerned, the matter is not one of the first importance. I should be surprised if, even in so large a population as ours, it would ever be thought necessary to extirpate one criminal as utterly unmanageable every year; and this means, of course, that if we decide to cage such people, the cage need not be a very large one.

I am not myself writing as an advocate one way or the other. I have to deal with European and American civilization, which, having no longer than a century ago executed people for offences now punished by a few months or even weeks of imprisonment, has advanced to a point at which less than half a dozen crimes are punishable by death: murder, piracy, rape,

arson, and (in Scotland) vitriol throwing. The opponents of capital punishment usually believe, naturally enough, that the effect of abandoning the
notion of punishment altogether as sinful (which it is) will sweep away the
scaffold from these crimes also, and thus make an end of the death penalty.
No doubt it will; but I foresee that it will reintroduce the idea of killing
dangerous people simply because they are dangerous, without the least
desire to punish them, and without specific reference to the actions which
have called attention to their dangerousness. That extremity may be met
with an absolute veto, or it may not. I cannot foresee which side I should
take: a wise man does not ford a stream till he gets to it. But I am so sure
that the situation will arise, that I have to deal with it here as impersonally
as may be, without committing myself or anyone else one way or the
other.

THE SOFT CASES THAT WE TURN INTO HARD ONES

Now let us look at the other end of the scale, where the soft cases are.
Here we are confronted with the staggering fact that many of our prisoners
have not been convicted of any offence at all. They are awaiting their trial,
and are too poor and friendless to find bail; whilst others have been
convicted of mere breaches of bye-laws of which they were ignorant, and
which they could not have guessed by their sense of right and wrong; for
many bye-laws have no ethical character whatever. For example, a boy
sells a newspaper on the premises of a railway company, and thereby
infringes a bye-law the object of which is to protect the commercial
monopoly of the newsagents who have paid the company for the right to
have a bookstall on the platform. The boy's brother jostles a passenger
who is burdened with hand luggage, and says "Carry your bag, sir?" These
perfectly innocent lads are sent to prison, though the warders themselves
admit that a sentence of imprisonment is so ruinous to a boy's morals that
they would rather see their own sons dead than in prison.

But let us take the guilty. The great majority of them have been
convicted of petty frauds compared to which the common practices of the
commercial world are serious crimes. Herbert Spencer's essays [*Essays*,
1858; 1863; 1885] on the laxity of the morals of trade have called no trader
successfully to repentance. It is not too much to say that any contractor in
Europe or America who does not secure business by tenders and estimates
and specifications for work and materials which he has not the smallest
intention of doing or putting in, and who does not resort to bribery to

have the work and materials he actually does do and put in passed by anybody whose duty it is to check them, is an exceptional man. The usage is so much a matter of course, and competition has made it so compulsory, that conscience is awakened only when the fraud is carried to some unusual length. I can remember two cases which illustrate what I mean very well. A builder of high commercial standing contracted to put up a public building. When the work began he found that the clerk of the works, whose business it was to check the work on behalf of the purchaser, lived opposite the building site. The contractor immediately protested that this was not part of the bargain, and that his estimate had been obtained on false pretences. The other is the case of the omnibus conductors of London when the alarum punch was invented and introduced. They immediately struck for higher wages, and got them, frankly on the ground that the punch had cut off the percentage they had been accustomed to add to their wages by peculation, and that it should be made up to them.

Both these cases prove that dishonesty does not pay when it becomes general. The contractor might just as well estimate for the work he really does and the material he actually uses; for, after all, since his object is to tempt the purchaser by keeping prices down, he has to give him the benefit of the fraud. If the purchaser finds him out and says, for example, "You estimated for galvanized pipes; and you have put in plain ones," the contractor can reply, "If I had put in galvanized pipes I should have had to charge you more." In the same way, the bus conductors might just as well have struck for an increase of wage as stolen it: the event proved they could have got it. But they thought they could secure employment more easily by asking for a low wage and making it up to their needs surreptitiously. It is one of the grievances of clerks in many businesses that they have to connive at dishonest practices as part of the regular routine of the office; but neither they nor their employers are any the richer, because business always finally settles down to the facts, and is conducted in terms not of the pretence but of the reality.

MOST PRISONERS NO WORSE THAN OURSELVES

We may take it, then, that the thief who is in prison is not necessarily more dishonest than his fellows at large, but mostly only one who, through ignorance or stupidity, steals in a way that is not customary. He snatches a loaf from the baker's counter and is promptly run into gaol. Another man snatches bread from the tables of hundreds of widows and orphans and simple credulous souls who do not know the ways of company promoters; and, as likely as not, he is run into Parliament. You may say that the remedy for this is not to spare the lesser offender but to punish the greater; but there you miss my present point, which is, that as the great majority of prisoners are not a bit more dishonest naturally than thousands of people who are not only at liberty, but highly pampered, it is no use telling me that society will fall into anarchic dissolution if these unlucky prisoners are treated with common humanity. On the contrary, when we see the outrageous extent to which the most shamelessly selfish rogues and rascals can be granted not only impunity but encouragement and magnificent remuneration, we are tempted to ask ourselves have we any right to restrain anyone at all from doing his worst to us. The first prison I ever saw had inscribed on it CEASE TO DO EVIL: LEARN TO DO WELL; but as the inscription was on the outside, the prisoners could not read it. It should have been addressed to the self-righteous free spectator in the street, and should have run ALL HAVE SINNED, AND FALLEN SHORT OF THE GLORY OF GOD.

We must get out of the habit of painting human character in soot and whitewash. It is not true that men can be divided into absolutely honest persons and absolutely dishonest ones. Our honesty varies with the strain put on it: this is proved by the fact that every additional penny of income tax brings in less than the penny preceding. The purchaser of a horse or motor car has to beware much more carefully than the purchaser of an article worth five shillings. If you take Landru at one extreme, and at the other the prisoner whose crime is sleeping out: that is to say, whose crime is no crime at all, you can place every sane human being, from the monarch to the tramp, somewhere on the scale between them. Not one of them has a blank page in the books of the Recording Angel. From the people who tell white lies about their ages, social positions, and incomes, to those who grind the faces of the poor, or marry whilst suffering from contagious disease, or buy valuable properties from inexperienced owners for a tenth of their value, or sell worthless shares for the whole of a widow's savings, or obtain vast sums on false pretences held forth by lying advertisements, to say nothing of bullying and beating in their homes, and drinking and debauching in their bachelorhood, you could at any moment find dozens of people who have never been imprisoned and never will be, and are yet worse citizens than any but the very worst of our convicts. Much of the difference between the bond and the free is a difference in circumstances only: if a man is not hungry, and his children are ailing only because they are too well fed, nobody can tell whether he would steal a loaf if his children were crying for bread and he himself had not tasted a mouthful for twentyfour hours. Therefore, if you are in an attitude of moral superiority to our convicts: if you are one of the Serve Them Right and Give Them Hell brigade, you may justly be invited, in your own vernacular, either to Come Off It, or else Go Inside and take the measure you are meting out to others no worse than yourself.

GOOD SOLDIERS OFTEN BAD CITIZENS, AND BAD CITIZENS GOOD PRISONERS

The distinction between the people the criminal law need deal with and those it may safely leave at large is not a distinction between depravity and good nature: it is a distinction between people who cannot, as they themselves put it, go straight except in leading strings, and those who can. Incurable criminals make wellbehaved soldiers and prisoners. The war of 1914–18 almost emptied our prisons of able-bodied men; and in the leading strings of military discipline these men ceased to be criminals. Some soldiers who were discharged with not only firstrate certificates of their good conduct as soldiers, but with a Victoria Cross "For Valor," were no sooner cast adrift into ordinary civil life than they were presently found in the dock pleading their military services and good character as soldiers in mitigation of sentences of imprisonment for frauds and thefts of the meanest sort. When we consider how completely a soldier is enslaved by military discipline, and how abhorrent military service consequently is to civically capable people, we cannot doubt, even if there were no firsthand testimony on the subject, that many men enlist voluntarily, not because they want to lead a drunken and dissolute life (the reason given by the Iron Duke [Wellington]), or because they are under any of the romantic illusions on which the recruiting sergeant is supposed to practise, but because they know themselves to be unfit for full moral responsibility, and conclude that they had better have their lives ordered for them than face the effort (intolerably difficult for them) of ordering it themselves.

This effort is not made easier by our civilization. A man who treated his children as every laborer treated them as a matter of course a hundred years ago would now be imprisoned for neglecting them and keeping them away from school. The statute book is crammed with offences unknown to our grandfathers and unintelligible to uneducated men; and the list needs startling extension; for, as Mr H. G. Wells has pointed out [in *The Outline of History*, 1920], its fundamental items date from the Mosaic period, when modern Capitalism, which involves a new morality, was unknown. In more obvious matters we notice how the standard of dress, manners, and lodging which qualifies a man socially for employment as a factory hand or mechanic has risen since the days when no person of any refinement could travel, as everybody now travels, third-class.

REMEDIES IN THE ROUGH

We may now begin to arrange our problem comprehensively. The people who have to be dealt with specially by the Government because for one reason or another they cannot deal satisfactorily with themselves may be roughly divided into three sections. First, the small number of dangerous or incorrigibly mischievous human animals. With them should be associated all hopeless defectives, from the idiot children who lie like stranded jellyfish on asylum floors, and have to be artificially fed, to the worst homicidal maniacs. Second, a body of people who cannot provide for or order their lives for themselves, but who, under discipline and tutelage, with their board and lodging and clothing provided for them, as in the case of soldiers, are normally happy, wellbehaved, useful citizens. (There would be several degrees of tutelage through which they might be promoted if they are fit and willing.) Third, all normal persons who have trespassed in some way during one of those lapses of self-discipline which are as common as colds, and who have been unlucky enough to fall into the hands of the police in consequence. These last should never be imprisoned. They should be required to compensate the State for the injury done to the body politic by their misdeeds, and, when possible, to compensate the victims, as well as pay the costs of bringing them to justice. Until they have done this they cannot complain if they find themselves distrained upon; harassed by frequent compulsory appearances in court to excuse themselves; and threatened with consignment to the second class as defectives. It is quite easy to make carelessness and selfishness or petty violence and dishonesty unremunerative and disagreeable, without resorting to imprisonment. In the cases where the offender has fallen into bad habits and bad company, the stupidest course to take is to force him into the worst of all habits and the worst of all company: that is, prison habits and prison company. The proper remedies are good habits and good company. If these are not available, then the offender must be put into the second class, and kept straight under tutelage until he is fit for freedom.

Difficulty of the Undisciplined

The difficulty lies, it will be seen, in devizing a means of dealing with the second class. The first is easy: too easy, in fact. You kill or you cage: that is all. In the third class, summoning and fining and admonishing are easy and not mischievous: you may worry a man considerably by badgering him about his conduct and dunning him for money in a police court occasionally; but you do not permanently disable him morally and physically thereby. It is the offender of the second class, too good to be killed or caged, and not good enough for normal liberty, whose treatment bothers us.

The Indeterminate Sentence

Any proposal to place men under compulsory tutelage immediately raises the vexed question of what is called "the indeterminate sentence." The British parliament has never been prevailed on to create a possibility of a criminal being "detained preventively" for life: it has set a limit of ten years to that condition. This is inevitable as long as the tutelage is primarily not a tutelage but a punishment. In England there is a law under which a drunkard, politely called an inebriate, can voluntarily sentence himself to a term of detention for the sake of being restrained from yielding to a temptation which he is unable to resist when left to himself. Under existing circumstances nobody is likely to do that twice, or even once if he has any knowledge of how the unfortunate inebriates are treated. The only system of detention available is the prison system; and the only sort of prisoner the officials have any practice in dealing with is the criminal. Every detained person is therefore put through the dismal routine of punishment in the first place, deterrence in the second place, and reform in the very remote third place. The inebriate volunteer prisoner very soon finds that he is being treated as a criminal, and tries in vain to revoke his renunciation of his liberty.

Otherwise, say the authorities very truly, they would be overwhelmed with volunteers. This reminds us of the Westminster Abbey verger who charged a French gentleman with brawling in church. The magistrate, inquiring what, exactly, the foreigner had done, was told that he had knelt in prayer. "But," said the magistrate, "is not that what a church is for?" The verger was scandalized. "If we allowed that," he said, "we should have people praying all over the place." The Prison Commissioners know that if prisons were made reasonably happy places, and thrown open to volunteers like the army, they might speedily be overcrowded. And this, with its implied threat of an enormous increase of taxation, seems a conclusive objection.

THE ECONOMY ASPECT

But if its effect would be to convert a large mass of more or less dishonest, unproductive or half productive, unsatisfactory, feckless, nervous, anxious, wretched people into good citizens, it is absurd to object to it as costly. It would be unbearably costly, of course, if the life and labor of its subjects were as stupidly wasted as they are in our prisons; but any scheme into which the conditions of our present system are read will stand condemned at once. Whether the labor of the subject be organized by the State, as in Government dockyards, post offices, municipal industries and services and so forth, or by private employers obtaining labor service from the authorities, organized and used productively it must be; and anyone who maintains that such organization and production costs the nation more than wasting the labor power of able-bodied men and women either by imprisonment or by throwing criminals on the streets to prey on society and on themselves, is maintaining a monstrous capitalistic paradox. Obviously it will not cost the nation anything at all: it will enrich it and protect it. The real commercial objection to it is that it would reduce the supply of sweatable labor available for unscrupulous private employers. But so much the better if it does. Sweating may make profits for private persons here and there; but their neighbors have to pay through the nose for these profits in poor rates, police rates, public health rates (mostly disease rates), and all the rest of the gigantic expenditure, all pure waste and mischief, which falls on the ratepayer and taxpayer in his constant struggle with the fruits of the poverty which he is nevertheless invited to maintain for the sake of making two or three of his neighbors unwholesomely and unjustly rich.

It is not altogether desirable that State tutelage should be available without limit for all who may volunteer for it. We can imagine a magistrate's court as a place in which men clamoring to be literally "taken in charge" are opposed by Crown lawyers and court officials determined to prove, if possible, that these importunate volunteers are quite well able to take care of themselves if they choose. Evidence of defective character would be sternly demanded; and if these were manufactured (as in the not uncommon case of a poor woman charging her son with theft to get him taken off her hands and sent to a reformatory) the offender would be ruthlessly consigned to my third division, consisting of offenders who are not to be taken in charge at all, but simply harried and bothered and attached and sold up until they pay the damages of their offences.

But as a matter of experience men do not seek the avowed tutelage of conditions which imply deficiency of character. Most of them resent any sort of tutelage unless they are brought up to it and therefore do not feel it as an infringement of their individuality. The army and navy are not overcrowded, though the army has always been the refuge of the sort of imbecile called a ne'er-do-well. Indeed the great obstacle to the realization of the Socialist dream of a perfectly organized and highly prosperous community, without poverty or overwork or idleness, is the intense repugnance of the average man to the degree of public regulation of his life which it would involve. This repugnance is certainly not weaker in England and America than elsewhere. Both Americans and Englishmen are born Anarchists; and, as complete Anarchism is practically impossible, they seek the minimum of public interference with their personal initiative, and overshoot the mark so excessively that it is no exaggeration to say that civilization is perishing of Anarchism. If civilization is to be saved for the first time in history it will have to be by a much greater extension of public regulation and organization than any community has hitherto been willing to submit to. When this extension takes place it will provide the discipline of public service for large masses of the population who now look after themselves very indifferently, and are only nominally free to control their own destinies; and in this way many people of the sort that now finds itself in prison will be kept straight automatically. But in any case there is no danger of a tutelary system being swamped by a rush of volunteers qualifying themselves for it by hurling stones through shop windows or the like.

All this does not mean that we must have indeterminate sentences of tutelage. The mischief of the present system is not that the criminal under preventive detention must be released at the end of ten years, but that if he relapses he is sent to penal servitude instead of being simply and sensibly returned to Camp Hill. What it does mean is that if the tutelage be made humane and profitable, the criminal, far from demanding his discharge, will rather threaten the authorities with a repetition of his crime if they turn him out of doors. The change that is needed is to add to the present power of the detaining authorities to release the prisoner at any time if they consider him fit for self-responsibility, the power of the prisoner to remain if he finds himself more comfortable and safe under tutelage, as voluntary soldiers feel themselves more comfortable in the army, or enclosed nuns in a convent, than cast on the world on his own resources.

WHITHER THE FACTS ARE DRIVING US

So much for the difficulty of the indeterminate sentence, which is quite manageable. Its discussion has led us to the discovery that in spite of the unchristian spirit of our criminal law, and the cruelty of its administration, the mere logic of facts is driving us to humane solutions. Already in England no judge or magistrate is obliged to pass any sentence whatever for a first offence except when dealing with a few extraordinary crimes which have affected our imagination so strongly that we feel bound to mark our abhorrence of them by special rigor not only to those convicted of them, but to those accused of them: for example, persons accused of high treason were formerly not allowed the help of counsel in defending themselves. And when the account of the English system of preventive detention at Camp Hill is studied in connection with the remarkable series of experiments now being made in America,[11] it will be seen that nothing stands between us and humanity and decency but our cruelty, vindictiveness, terror, and thoughtless indifference.

CRIME AS DISEASE

It must not be imagined that any system will reach every anti-social deed that is committed. I have already shewn that most crime goes undetected,

---

11. Among the many American experiments in penal reform at this time were special schools for adolescent female delinquents, as in Geneva, Illinois, and adult reformatories for female offenders whose convictions were on indictments, as at Bedford, New York. The principal American reform effort, however, was the institution judicially of 'the indeterminate sentence' (as addressed by Shaw on p. 471), a movement that sought to eliminate the 'retributory' element in punishment of crime – the judge's 'power to inflict a definite sentence for a definite offence'. The indeterminate sentence concentrated not on guilt but on the criminal's potential for reform and release 'without danger to the community' (Sir Evelyn Ruggles-Brise, *Prison Reform at Home and Abroad*, 1924).

unreported, and even unforbidden; and I have suggested that if our system of dealing with crime were one with which any humane and thoughtful person could conscientiously cooperate, if we compensated injured persons for bringing criminals to justice instead of, as at present, making the process expensive and extremely disagreeable and even terrifying to them, and if we revised our penal laws by striking out of their list of criminal acts a few which ought not to be there and adding a good many which ought to be there, we might have a good many more delinquents to deal with than at present unless we concurrently improved the education and condition of the masses sufficiently to do away with the large part of lawbreaking which is merely one of the symptoms of poverty, and would disappear with it. But in any case we should diligently read Samuel Butler's Erewhon [1872], and accustom ourselves to regard crime as pathological, and the criminal as an invalid, curable or incurable. There is, in fact, hardly an argument that can be advanced for the stern suppression of crime by penal methods that does not apply equally to the suppression of disease; and we have already an elaborate sanitary code under which persons neglecting certain precautions against disease are not only prosecuted but in some instances (sometimes quite mistaken ones, as the history of vaccination has proved) persecuted very cruelly. We actually force parents to subject their children to surgical operations, some of which are both dangerous and highly questionable. But we have so far stopped short of making it a punishable offence to be attacked by smallpox or typhus fever, though no legal assumption is more certain than that both diseases can be extinguished by sanitation more completely than crime by education. Yet there would be no greater injustice in such punishment than there is in the imprisonment of any thief; and the sanctimonious speech in which the judge in Erewhon, sentencing a man for phthisis, recapitulated the career of crime which began with an accident in childhood, and ended with pulmonary tuberculosis, was not a whit more ridiculous than the similar speeches made at every session by our own judges. Why a man who is punished for having an inefficient conscience should be privileged to have an inefficient lung is a debatable question. If one is sent to prison and the other to hospital, why make the prison so different from the hospital?

But I make the parallel here because it brings out the significance of the fact that we admit without protest that we have to put up with a good deal of illness in the world, and to treat the sufferers with special indulgence and consideration, instead of turning on them like a herd of buffaloes and goring them to death, as we do in the case of our moral invalids. We even punish people very severely for neglecting their invalids or treating them in such a way as to make them worse instead of better: that is, for doing to them exactly what we should do ourselves if instead of doing wrong in body and losing health they had gone wrong in mind and stolen a handkerchief. There are people in the world so incredibly foolish that they expect their children to be always perfectly truthful and perfectly obedient; but even these idiots do not expect their children to be perfectly well always, nor thrash them if they catch cold. In short, if crime were not punished at all, the world would not come to an end any more than it does now that disease is not punished at all. The real gist of the distinction we make is that the consequences of crime, if unpunished, are pleasant, whereas the consequences of catching a chill are its own punishment; but this will not bear examination. A bad conscience is quite as uncomfortable as a bad cold; and though there are people so hardily constituted in this respect that they can behave very selfishly without turning a hair, so are there people of such hardy physical constitution that they can abuse their bodies with impunity to an extent that would be fatal to ordinary persons. Anyhow, it is not proposed that abnormal subjects should be unrestrained.

On the other hand avoidable illnesses are just like avoidable crimes in respect of being the result of some form of indulgence, positive or negative. For all practical purposes the parallel between the physical and moral invalid holds good; only, we may have to reconsider the absolute sacredness of the physical invalid's life. I shall not here attempt to prejudge the result of that consideration; but it is clear that if we decide that this sacredness must be maintained at all costs, and that the idiot in Darenth [mental asylum in Kent], who lies there having food poured into it so that its heart may continue to beat and its lungs to breathe automatically (for it can do nothing voluntarily), must be preserved from death much more laboriously than Einstein, then we must hold the criminal equally fetish unless we are to keep the whole subject in its present disastrous confusion.

REFORMING OUR CONSCIENCES

The change in the public conscience which is necessary before these considerations can take effect in abolishing our villainous system of dealing with crime will never be induced by sympathy with the criminal or even disgust at the prison. The proportion of the population directly concerned is so small that to the great majority imprisonment is something so unlikely to occur—indeed, so certain statistically never to occur—that they cannot be persuaded to take any interest in the matter. As long as the question is only one of the comfort of the prisoner, nothing will be done, because as long as the principle of punishment is admitted, and the Sermon on the Mount ridiculed as an unpractical outburst of anarchism and sentimentality, the public will always be reassured by learning from the judges (none of whom, by the way, seems to know what really happens to a prisoner after he leaves the dock) that our prisons are admirable institutions, and by the romances of Prison Commissioners like [Sir Edmund F.] Du Cane and Sir Evelyn Ruggles-Brise, who arrange prisons as children build houses with toy bricks, and finally become so pleased with their arrangements that they describe them in terms which make us wonder that they do not commit serious crimes to qualify themselves for prolonged residence in their pet paradises.[12] I must therefore attack the punitive position at another angle by dealing with its psychological effect on the criminal.

EXPIATION AND MORAL ACCOUNTANCY

No ordinary criminal will agree with me for a moment that punishment is a mistake and a sin. His opinions on that point are precisely those of the policeman who arrests him; and if I were to preach this gospel of mine to the convicts in a prison I should be dismissed as a hopeless crank far more summarily than if I were to interview the Chief Commissioner at Scotland Yard about it.

Punishment is not a simple idea: it is a very complex one. It is not merely some injury that an innocent person inflicts on a guilty one, and that the guilty one evades by every means in his power. It is also a balancing of accounts with the soul. People who feel guilty are apt to inflict it on themselves if nobody will take the job off their hands. Confessions, though less common than they would be if the penalties were not so soul-destroying, are received without surprise. From the criminals' point of view punishment is expiation; and their bitterest complaints of injustice refer, not to their sentences, but to the dishonesty with which society, having exacted the price of the crime, still treats the criminal as a defaulter. Even so sophisticated a man of the world as Oscar Wilde claimed that by his two years' imprisonment he had settled accounts with the world

12. Du Cane's principal work was *The Punishment and Prevention of Crime* (1885). Ruggles-Brise was the author of *The English Prison System* (1921).

and was entitled to begin again with a clean slate.[13] But the world persisted in ostracizing him as if it had not punished him at all.

This was inevitable; but it was dishonest. If we are absurd enough to engage in a retributive trade in crime, we should at least trade fairly and give clean receipts when we are paid. If we did, we should soon find that the trade is impracticable and ridiculous; for neither party can deliver the goods. No discharge that the authorities can give can procure the ex-prisoner an eligible situation; and no atonement that a thief or murderer can make in suffering can make him any the less a thief or murderer. And nobody shirks this demonstration as much as the thief himself. Human self-respect wants so desperately to have its sins washed away, however purgatorially, that we are willing to go through the most fantastic ceremonies, conjurations, and ordeals to have our scarlet souls made whiter than snow. We naturally prefer to lay our sins on scapegoats or on the Cross, if our neighbors will let us off so easily; but when they will not, then we will cleanse ourselves by suffering a penalty sooner than be worried by our consciences. This is the real foundation of the criminal law in human superstition. This is why, when we refuse to employ a discharged prisoner, he invariably pleads that what he did is paid for, and that we have no right to bring it against him after he has suffered the appointed penalty.

As we cannot admit the plea, we should consider whether we should exact the penalty. I am not arguing that the plea should be admitted: I am arguing that the bargain should never have been made. I am more merciless than the criminal law, because I would destroy the evildoer's delusion that there can be any forgiveness of sin. What is done cannot be undone; and the man who steals must remain a thief until he becomes another man, no matter what reparation or expiation he may make or suffer. A

---

13. Nowhere in his 1897 post-prison letters to the *Daily Chronicle* concerning needs of prison reform nor in the long letter written in jail in 1897 to Lord Alfred Douglas, published in a condensed version as *De Profundis* (1905), did Oscar Wilde make the precise statement to which Shaw alludes. What he does say in *De Profundis* is:

> When the man's punishment is over, [society] leaves him to himself: that is to say it abandons him at the very moment when its highest duty towards him begins. It is really ashamed of its own actions and shuns those whom it has punished, as people shun a creditor whose debt they cannot pay, or one on whom they have inflicted an irreparable, an irredeemable wrong. I can claim on my side that if I realise what I have suffered, society should realise what it has inflicted on me; and that there should be no bitterness or hate on either side.

punishment system means a pardon system: the two go together insep-
arably. Once admit that if I do something wicked to you we are quits
when you do something equally wicked to me and you are bound to admit
also that the two blacks make a white. Our criminal system is an organized
attempt to produce white by two blacks. Common sense should doggedly
refuse to believe that evil can be abolished by duplicating it. But common
sense is not so logical; and thus we get the present grotesque spectacle of a
judge committing thousands of horrible crimes in order that thousands of
criminals may feel that they have balanced their moral accounts.

FAMILIAR FRAUDS OF THE TRADE IN SIN

It is a game at which there is plenty of cheating. The prisoner pleads Not
Guilty, and tries his best to get off, or to have as light a sentence as possible.
The commercial brigand, fining himself for his plunderings by subscribing
to charities, never subscribes as much as he stole. But through all the folly
and absurdity of the business, and the dense mental confusion caused by the
fact that it is never frankly faced and clearly stated, there shines the fact that
conscience is part of the equipment of the normal man, and that it never
fails in its work. It is retributive because it makes him uncomfortable; it is
deterrent because detection and retribution are absolutely certain; and it is
reformative because reformation is the only way of escape. That is to say, it
does to perfection by divine methods what the Prison Commissioners are
trying to do by diabolical methods without hope or even possibility of
success.

REVENGE THE DESTROYER OF CONSCIENCE

The effect of revenge, or retribution from without, is to destroy the
conscience of the aggressor instantly. If I stand on the corn of a man in the
street, and he winces or cries out, I am all remorse, and overwhelm him
with heartfelt apologies. But if he sets about me with his fists, the first
blow he lands changes my mind completely; and I bend all my energies on
doing intentionally to his eyes and nose and jaw what I did unintentionally
to his toes. Vengeance is mine, saith the Lord [Deuteronomy 32: 35]; and
that means that it is not the Lord Chief Justice's. A violent punishing, such
as a flogging, carries no sense of expiation with it: whilst its effect lasts,
which is fortunately not very long, its victim is in a savage fury in which

he would burn down the gaol and roast the warders and the governor and the justices alive in it with intense satisfaction if he could.

Imprisonment, on the other hand, gives the conscience a false satisfaction. The criminal feels that he is working off his crime, though he is doing it involuntarily, and would escape at any moment if he could. He preserves his sense of solvency without ceasing to be a thief, as a gambler preserves it by paying his losses without ceasing to be a gambler.

THE SENTIMENTALITY OF REVENGE

There is a mysterious psychological limit to punishment. We somehow dare not kill a hopelessly diseased or dangerous man by way of punishment for any offence short of murder, though we chloroform a hopelessly diseased or dangerous dog by way of kindness without the least misgiving. Until we have purged our souls of malice, which is pure sentiment, we cannot get rid of sentimentality; and the sentimentality which makes us abominably cruel in one direction makes us foolishly and superstitiously afraid to act sternly in others. Homicidal lunatics say in their asylums "They cannot hang *us*." I could give here, but refrain for obvious reasons, simple instructions by carrying out which any person can commit a murder with the certainty, if detected, of being sent to an asylum instead of to the gallows. They ought to have just the contrary effect; for the case of the homicidal lunatic is the clearest case for judicial killing that exists. It is the killing of the sane murderer that requires consideration: it should never be a matter of course, because there are murders which raise no convincing presumption that those who commit them are exceptionally likely to commit another. But about a chronically homicidal lunatic there should be no hesitation whatever as long as we practise judicial killing at all; and there would not be if we simply considered without malice the question of his fitness to live in society. We spare him because the gallows is a punishment, and we feel that we have no right to punish a lunatic. When we realize that we have no right to punish anybody, the problem of disposing of impossible people will put itself on its proper footing. We shall drop our moral airs; but unless we rule killing out absolutely, persons who give more trouble than they are worth will run the risk of being apologetically, sympathetically, painlessly, but effectually returned to the dust from which they sprung.

MAN IN SOCIETY MUST JUSTIFY HIS EXISTENCE

This would at least create a sense of moral responsibility in our citizens. We are all too apt to take our lives as a matter of course. In a civilized community life is not a matter of course: it can be maintained only on complicated artificial conditions; and whoever enlarges his life by violating these conditions enlarges it at the expense of the lives of others. The extent to which we tolerate such vital embezzlement at present is quite outrageous: we have whole classes of persons who waste, squander, and luxuriate in the hard-earned income of the nation without even a pretence of social service or contribution of any kind; and instead of sternly calling on them to justify their existence or go to the scrap heap, we encourage and honor them, and indeed conduct the whole business of the country as if its object were to produce and pamper them. How can a prison chaplain appeal with any effect to the conscience of a professional criminal who knows quite well that his illegal and impecunious modes of preying on society are no worse morally, and enormously less mischievous materially, than the self-legalized plutocratic modes practised by the chaplain's most honored friends with the chaplain's full approval? The moment we cease asking whether men are good or bad, and ascertain simply whether they are pulling their weight in the social boat, our persistent evildoers may have a very unpleasant surprise. Far from having an easy time under a Government of softhearted and softheaded sentimentalists, cooing that "to understand everything is to pardon everything"[14] they may find themselves disciplined to an extent at present undreamed of by the average man-about-town.

CIVILIZED MAN IS NOT BORN FREE

And here it will occur to some of my readers that a book about imprisonment should be also a book about freedom. Rousseau said that Man is born free. Rousseau was wrong. No government of a civilized State can possibly regard its citizens as born free. On the contrary, it must regard them as born in debt, and as necessarily incurring fresh debt every day they live; and its most pressing duty is to hold them to that debt and see that they pay it. Not until it is paid can any freedom begin for the

14. '*Tout comprendre, c'est tout pardonner*': attributed to Madame de Staël, *Corinne* (1807), Book XVIII, Chapter 5.

individual. When he cannot walk a hundred yards without using such a very expensive manufactured article as a street, care must be taken that he produces his share of its cost. When he has paid scot and lot his leisure begins, and with it his liberty. He can then say boldly, "Having given unto Cæsar the things that are Cæsar's I shall now, under no tutelage or compulsion except that of my conscience, give to God the things that are God's" [Matthew 22: 21]. That is the only possible basis for civil liberty; and we are unable to attain it because our governments corruptly shirk the duties of Cæsar; usurp the attributes of God; and make an unholy mess of which this horrible prison system of ours is only one symptom.

Our Nature not so bad as our Prison System

We must, however, be on our guard against ascribing all the villainy of that system to our cruelty and selfish terrors. I have pointed out how the operation of the criminal law is made very uncertain, and therefore loses the deterrence it aims at, by the reluctance of sympathetic people to hand over offenders to the police. Vindictive and frivolous as we are, we are not downright fiends, as we should be if our modern prison system had been deliberately invented and constructed by us all in one piece. It has grown upon us, and grown evilly, having evil roots; but its worst developments have been well meant; for the road to hell is paved with good intentions [Samuel Johnson in Boswell's *Life*, 16 April 1775], not with bad ones. The history of it is too long to be told here in detail; but a word or two of it is needed to save the reader from closing the volume in despair of human nature.

The History of our Prisons

Imprisonment was not originally a punishment any more than chaining up a dog, cruel as that practice is, is a punishment. It was simply a method of detention. The officer responsible for the custody of an offender had to lock or chain him up somewhere to prevent him from running away, and to be able to lay his hand on him on the day of trial or execution. This was regarded as the officer's own affair: the law looked to him for the delivery of the offender, and did not concern itself as to how it was effected. This seems strange nowadays; but I can remember a case of a lunatic on a battleship, who had one man told off to act as his keeper. The lunatic was violent and troublesome, and gave his keeper plenty of severe exercise; but the rest of the crew looked on with the keenest enjoyment of the spectacle, and gave the lunatic the strictest fair play by letting his keeper fight it out with him unaided. And that is what the law did mostly in England until well into the XIX century. To this day there is no prison in some of the Virgin Islands. The prisoner is tied by the leg to a tree, and plays cards with the constable who guards him.

The result was that the provision of lockups became a private commercial speculation, undertaken and conducted for the sake of what could be made out of it by the speculator. There was no need for these places to be lockups: the accused could be chained up or gyved or manacled if no safe prison was available; and when lockups came to be provided as a matter of business, the practice of chaining was continued as a matter of tradition, and formed a very simple method of extorting money from prisoners by torture. No food was provided by the State: what the prisoner ate was charged against him as if he were in a hotel; and it often happened that when he was acquitted he was taken back to prison as security for his bill and kept there until he had paid it.

Under these circumstances the prison was only a building into which all classes and sorts of detained persons were thrown indiscriminately. The rich could buy a private room, like Mr Pickwick in the Fleet [a debtors' prison]; but the general herd of poor criminals, old and young, innocent and hardened, virgin and prostitute, mad and sane, clean and verminous, diseased and whole, pigged together in indescribable promiscuity. I repeat: nobody invented this. Nobody intended it. Nobody defended it except the people who made money by it. Nobody else except the prisoners knew about it: they were as innocent as Mr Pickwick of what went on inside the prison walls. And, as usual in England, nobody bothered about it, because people with money could avoid its grossest discomforts on the negligibly rare occasions when they fell into the hands of the officers of the law. It was by the mere accident of being pricked for sheriff that John Howard learned what the inside of a gaol was like.

HOWARD'S GOOD INTENTIONS

As a result of Howard's agitation prisons are now State prisons: the State accepts full responsibility for the prisoner from the moment of his arrest. So far, so good. But in the meantime imprisonment, instead of being a means of detention, has become not only a punishment, but, for the reasons given at the outset of this essay, *the* punishment. And official shallowness, prevailing against the poet [George] Crabbe's depth [as in *The Borough*, 1810, where he juxtaposes 'Prisons' (XXIII) and 'Schools' (XXIV)], has made it an infernal punishment. Howard saw that the prisoners in the old gaol contaminated oneanother; and his remedy was to give them separate cells in which they could meditate on their crimes and repent. When prisons with separate cells were built accordingly, the prison officials soon found that it saved trouble to keep the prisoners locked up in them; and the philanthropists out-Howarded Howard in their efforts to reform criminals by silence, separation, and the wearing of masks, lest they should contaminate oneanother by the expression of their faces. Until 1920 the convicts in Belgian prisons wore iron masks. Our own convicts wore cloth masks for some time, and would probably be wearing them still had not our solicitude for their salvation killed and driven them mad in such numbers that we were forced to admit that thorough segregation, though no doubt correct in principle (which is just where it is fatally incorrect), does not work. Frightful things in the way of solitude, separation, and silence, not for months, but for many years at a time, were done in American prisons.

The reader will find as much as he can stand in English Prisons Under Local Government, by Sidney and Beatrice Webb, and a good deal more in English Prisons Today, edited by Stephen Hobhouse and Fenner Brockway, in which the system is described from the prison cells, not by common criminals, but by educated and thoughtful men and women who, as agitators for Votes for Women or as Conscientious Objectors to military service, have been condemned to imprisonment of late years. Our horror at their disclosures must not blind us to my immediate point, which is that our prison system is a horrible accidental growth and not a deliberate human invention, and that its worst features have been produced with the intention, not of making it worse, but of making it better. Howard is not responsible: he warned us that "absolute solitude is more than human nature can bear without the hazard of distraction and despair" [in *The State of Prisons in England and Wales*]. Elizabeth Fry[15] saw nothing but mischief in prison silence and prison solitude. Their followers were fools: that is all.

The So-called Criminal Type

Perhaps the most far-reaching service done by the Brockway-Hobhouse report is the light it throws on the alleged phenomenon of a Criminal Type. The belief in this has gone through several vicissitudes. At first a

15. English philanthropist Quaker, after Howard the chief promoter of prison reform in Europe.

criminal was supposed to be a beetle-browed, bulldog-jawed person for whom no treatment could be too bad. This suited the prison authorities, as nothing is so troublesome to them as waves of public sympathy with criminals, founded on imaginative idealizations of them. But the authorities changed their note when a scientific account of the type was put forward by [Cesare] Lombroso and a body of investigators calling themselves psychiatrists. These gentlemen found that criminals had asymmetrical features and other stigmata (an effective word). They contended that the criminals were the victims of these congenital peculiarities, and could not help themselves. As the obvious conclusion was that they were not morally responsible for their actions, and therefore should not be punished for them, the prison authorities saw their occupation threatened, and denied that there was any criminal type, always excepting the beetle-brows and bulldog-jaws which the criminal was assumed to have imposed on his naturally Grecian features by a life of villainy. They were able to point out that everybody has asymmetrical features, and that the alleged stigmata of the Lombrosic criminal are as characteristic of the Church, the Stock Exchange, the Bench, and the Legislature as of Portland and Dartmoor [sites of convict prisons in Dorsetshire and Devonshire respectively]. That settled the matter for the moment. The criminal type was off.

But nobody who has ever visited a prison has any doubt that there is a prison type, and a very marked one at that. And if he is saturated with the teachings of the Natural Selectionists, according to which changes of type are the result of the slow accumulation of minute variations, and therefore cannot be visibly produced in less than, say, a million years, he will conclude, like Lombroso, that the criminal is a natural species, and therefore incorrigible.

How Types are Manufactured

But XX century observation has lately been knocking XIX century science into a cocked hat by shewing that the types that were said to take a million years to produce can be produced in five. I have in my hand number seventyfour of the privately printed *opuscula* [small volumes] issued by the Society which calls itself the Set of Odd Volumes.[16] It is

16. The Sette of Odd Volumes was founded in 1878 as a literary dining club by the bookseller Bernard Quaritch. It continues to meet in various London clubs, though literary interest is no longer predominant. Since its founding it has published over one hundred 'opuscula' for its members.

entitled The Influence Which Our Surroundings Exert On Us [1920], and is the work of Sir William Arbuthnot Lane, one of our most distinguished surgeons. In it he shews that by keeping a man at work as a deal porter, a coal trimmer, a shoemaker or what not, you can, within a period no longer than that spent in prison by typical criminals, produce a typical deal porter, coal trimmer and so on, the changes involved being visible grotesque skeletal changes for which Huxley or Owen would have demanded a whole evolutionary epoch. No Bolshevik has yet written so revolutionary a pamphlet as this little record of a recent after-dinner speech.

What it means is that the criminal type is an artificial type, manufactured in prison by the prison system. It means that the type is not one of the accidents of the system, but must be produced by imprisonment no matter how normal the victim is at the beginning, or how anxious the authorities are to keep him so. The simple truth is that the typical criminal is a normal man when he first enters a prison, and develops the type during his imprisonment.

PSYCHIATRISTS AND ENDOCRINISTS

This does not mean that no other types are to be noted in prison. By all means let the endocrinists go on dividing abnormal people, in prison and out, into hyper and sub pituitaries and thyroidics and adrenals. They need not, as the habit of the scientific world is, quarrel furiously with me for remarking that another type can be externally imposed on their pituitaries and thyroidics and adrenals impartially. The fact that a man has an excessive adrenal secretion may be a reason for trying to check it instead of punishing him. It does not alter the fact that if you keep one adrenal in penal servitude and another in the House of Lords for ten years, the one will shew the stigmata of a typical convict, and the other of a typical peer, in addition to the stigmata of adrenalism.

To realize the importance of this, we must recall the discredit into which Lombroso fell when it was pointed out that by his diagnosis everybody was more or less a criminal. I suggest that this was not quite so complete a *reductio ad absurdum* as it seemed. I have already accounted for the curious insensibility of the public to the misery they are inflicting on their prisoners by the fact that some of the most mischievous and unhappy conditions of prison life are imposed on all respectably brought-up children as a matter of course. It is arguable that what Lombroso took to be criminal stigmata were genuine prison stigmata, and that their prevalence among respectable people who have never been in gaol is due to the prison conditions to which such people are conventionally subjected for the first twenty years of their life.

THE CASE OF QUEEN VICTORIA

I take up another much discussed and most readable modern book: Queen Victoria [1921], by Lytton Strachey. It contains some shocking pages, made bearable by the comedic power of the author, but still ghastly reading. Queen Victoria was very carefully brought up. When she was eighteen they came to her and told her that she was Queen of England. She asked whether she could really do what she liked; and when this was reluctantly admitted by her careful mother, Victoria considered what wonderful and hitherto impossible happiness she could confer on herself by her new powers. And she could think of nothing more delightful than an hour of separate solitary confinement. She had never been alone before, never been unwatched by people whose business it was to see that she behaved herself, and to rebuke her and punish her if she did anything they disapproved of. In short, she had been treated as a dangerous criminal, unfit to be trusted with any initiative or moral responsibility.

It would carry me too far to trace the effects of this monstrous bringing-up on the course of history. The book should be given to every prisoner who finds his solitary confinement every day from half-past four in the afternoon to next morning more than he can bear. He will find that there are worse things than solitude when the only company available is that of the warders and governor. And he will understand why the next thing the queen did was to turn her mother practically out of the house. She was, as he would put it, getting a bit of her own back. Let him then, if he is an intellectually curious prisoner, and has not been long enough in prison to have his intellect atrophied, make a list of the miseries that are common to the lot of our little Queen Victorias out of prison and our thieves and murderers in prison. Confinement, obedience, silence at associated work, continual supervision by hostile guardians reporting every infraction of rule for punishment, regulation of every moment of one's life from outside, compulsory exercise instead of play, systematic extirpation of initiative and responsibility, uncongenial and sometimes impossible tasks, and a normal assumption that every original and undictated action will be a

wrong action. This is the lot of the well-brought-up child, whether heiress
to a throne or heir to a country rector, like Samuel Butler, who was beaten
by his father until he acquired and retained until his death some of the
stigmata of a chained dog. The British statesman Mr Winston Churchill, a
duke's grandson, tells us in his reminiscences that when he was a child of
seven he was sent to an expensive school where the discipline was more
ferocious than would be permitted in a Reformatory for young criminals
of twice that age.[17]

Prevalence of Criminal Characteristics in Polite Society

Butler, a man of exceptionally strong character which reacted violently
against his training, would have been what the Prison Commissioners call a
bad prisoner, and therefore does not illustrate the normal social effect of the
system. Even Queen Victoria, with all her characteristic prison transitions
from tutelage to tyranny, and her inability to understand or tolerate any
other conditions, was too energetic, uneducated, and original, not to react
vigorously against her circumstances. It is when we look at modern
civilization in bulk that we are forced to admit that child training (or
rather taming), as we practise it, produces moral imbecility. About a dozen
millions of persons, on whose education enormous sums had been spent
publicly and privately, went like sheep to the slaughter in 1914–18; and the
survivors are making elaborate arrangements to go again. A glance at
the newspapers which cater specially for the classes which go through the
respectable routine of preparatory school, public school, and university,
will shew that the ideals of those classes, their points of honor, their sense
of humor, their boasts, their anticipations of future exploits, are precisely
those of criminals. They always are ready (Steady, boys, steady)[18] to fight
and to conquer again and again. Ned Kelly, Charles Peace, Dick Turpin
and Claude Duval,[19] the Black Prince, Harry the Fifth, Robin Hood, [John]
Paul Jones, [Robert] Clive, [Horatio] Nelson and Captain Kidd, [Hernando]

17. 'When I was Young', *Strand Magazine* (December 1924), pp. 604–12; incorpor-
ated into *A Roving Commission: My Early Life* (1930), Chapter 1.
18. Line from a song 'Hearts of Oak' by David Garrick, in his Christmas pantomime *Harlequin's Invasion* (1759).
19. Legendary felons: Ned Kelly, Australian bushranger; Charles Peace, Victorian
burglar-murderer; Dick Turpin, eighteenth-century horse-stealer and smuggler;
Claude Duval, French highwayman in Restoration England.

Cortez and Lord Roberts, were not all on the side of the law; but their morality was the same: they all held that pugnacity, the will to conquer, and the sort of courage that makes pugnacity and the will to conquer effective, are virtues so splendid that they sanctify plunder, devastation, and murder in direct proportion to the magnitude of these operations. The relaxations of the operators are love affairs and luxurious banquets. Now pray what else is the romance of the thieves' kitchen and of the surreptitious conversations of the prison exercise ring and associated labor shop? The difference is no more essential than that between whiskey and champagne, between an ounce of shag and a box of Havanas, between a burglary and a bombardment, between a jemmy [a crowbar used by burglars] and a bayonet, between a chloroformed pad and a gas shell, between a Browning pistol bought at a pawnbroker's and a service revolver. Gild the reputable end of it as thickly as we like with the cant of courage, patriotism, national prestige, security, duty, and all the rest of it: smudge the disreputable end with all the vituperation that the utmost transports of virtuous indignation can inspire: such tricks will not induce the divine judgment, by which all mankind must finally stand or fall, to distinguish between the victims of these two bragging predatory insects the criminal and the gentleman.

The gentleman beats the criminal hollow in the magnitude of his operations and the number of people employed in them. For the depredations of the criminal are negligibly small compared to the military holocausts and ravaged areas, the civic slums, the hospitals, the cemeteries crowded with the prematurely dead, and the labor markets in which men and women are exposed for sale for all purposes, honorable and dishonorable. These are the products of criminal ideas imposed on the entire population. The common thief and burglar, miserably sweated by the receiver to whom he has to sell his plunder, steals a few spoons or diamonds at a monstrous risk, and gets less than a tenth of their value from a rascal who runs no risk worth considering; and the poor wretch is content with the trumpery debauch his hard-earned percentage brings him. The gentleman steals a whole country, or a perpetual income for himself and his descendants, and is never satisfied until he has more conquests and more riches to boast of. What is more, the illicit thief does not defend his conduct ethically. He may cry "To hell with the parsons and with honesty and white-livered respectability!" and so forth; but he does so as a defier of God, a public enemy, a Satanic hero. The gentleman really believes that he is a creator of national prestige, a defender of the faith, a pillar of society; and with this conviction to strengthen him he is utterly unscrupulous in his misplaced pride and honor, and plays the wholesaler in evil to the criminal's petty retail enterprizes.

THE ROOT OF THE EVIL

And what is at the bottom of it all? Just the belief that virtue is something to be imposed on us from without, like the tricks taught to a performing animal, by the whip. Such manufactured virtue has no ethical value whatever, as appears promptly enough when the whip is removed. All communities must live finally by their ethical values: that is, by their genuine virtues. Living virtuously is an art that can be learnt only by living in full responsibility for our own actions; and as the process is one of trial and error even when seeking the guidance of others' experience, society must, whether it likes it or not, put up with a certain burden of individual error. The man who has never made a mistake will never make anything; and the man who has never done any harm will never do any good. The disastrous people are the indelicate and conceited busybodies who want to reform criminals and mould children's characters by external pressure and abortion. The cowards who refuse to accept the inevitable risks of human society, and would have everybody handcuffed if they could lest they should have their pockets picked or their heads punched, are bad enough; and the flagellomaniacs who are for ever shrieking the exploded falsehood that garotting was put down by flogging, and that all crimes, especially the sexually exciting ones, can be put down by more flogging, are worse; but such obvious cases of phobia and libido soon make themselves ridiculous if they are given a free platform. It is the busybody, the quack, the pseudo God Almighty, the Dr Moreau of Mr H. G. Wells's ghastliest romance [*The Island of Dr Moreau*, 1896], continually lusting to lay hands on living creatures and by reckless violation of their souls and bodies abort them into some monster representing their ideal of a Good Man, or a Model Citizen, or a Perfect Wife and Mother: he is the irreconcilable enemy, the ubiquitous and iniquitous nuisance, and the most difficult to get rid of because he has imposed his moral pretensions on public opinion, and is accepted as just the sort of philanthropist our prisons and criminals should be left to, whereas he (or she) is really the only sort of person who should never be admitted to any part of a prison except the gallows on which so many less mischievous egotists have expired. No one who has not a profound instinctive respect for the right of all living creatures to moral and religious liberty: that is, to liberty of moral and religious experiment on themselves, limited only by their obligations not to become unduly burdensome to others, should be let come within ten miles of a child, a criminal, or any other person in a condition of tutelage. Indelicacy on this point is the most conclusive of social disqualifications. When it is ignorant and shortsighted it produces criminals. When it is worldly-wise and pompous it produces Prison Commissioners.

RECAPITULATION

For the reader's mental convenience, I recapitulate the contentions presented above.

1. Modern imprisonment: that is, imprisonment practised as a punishment as well as a means of detention, is extremely cruel and mischievous, and therefore extremely wicked. The word extremely is used advisedly because the system has been pushed to a degree at which prison mortality and prison insanity forced it back to the point at which it is barely endurable, which point may therefore be regarded as the practicable extreme.

2. Although public vindictiveness and public dread are largely responsible for this wickedness, some of the most cruel features of the prison system are not understood by the public, and have not been deliberately invented and contrived for the purpose of increasing the prisoner's torment. The worst of these are (a) unsuccessful attempts at reform, (b) successful attempts to make the working of the prison cheaper for the State and easier for the officials, and (c) accidents of the evolution of the old privately owned detention prison into the new punitive State prison.

3. The prison authorities profess three objects: (a) Retribution (a euphemism for vengeance), (b) Deterrence (a euphemism for Terrorism), and (c) Reform of the prisoner. They achieve the first by simple atrocity. They fail in the second through lack of the necessary certainty of detection, prosecution, and conviction; partly because their methods are too cruel and mischievous to secure the cooperation of the public; partly because the prosecutor is put to serious inconvenience and loss of time; partly because most people desire to avoid an unquestionable family disgrace much more than to secure a very questionable justice; and partly because the proportion of avowedly undetected crimes is high enough to hold out reasonable hopes to the criminal that he will never be called to account. The third (Reform) is irreconcilable with the first (Retribution); for the figures of recidivism, and the discovery that the so-called Criminal Type is really a

prison type, prove that the retributive process is one of uncompensated deterioration.

4. The cardinal vice of the system is the anti-Christian vice of vengeance, or the intentional duplication of malicious injuries partly in pure spite, partly in compliance with the expiatory superstition that two blacks make a white. The criminal accepts this, but claims that punishment absolves him if the injuries are equivalent, and still more if he has the worse of the bargain, as he almost always has. Consequently, when absolution on his release is necessarily denied him, and he is forced back into crime by the refusal to employ him, he feels that he is entitled to revenge this injustice by becoming an enemy of society. No beneficial reform of our treatment of criminals is possible unless and until this superstition of expiation and this essentially sentimental vice of vengeance are unconditionally eradicated.

5. Society has a right of self-defence, extending to the destruction or restraint of lawbreakers. This right is separable from the right to revenge or punish: it need have no more to do with punishment or revenge than the caging or shooting of a man-eating tiger. It arises from the existence of (A) intolerably mischievous human beings, and (B) persons defective in the self-control needed for free life in modern society, but well behaved and at their ease under tutelage and discipline. Class A can be painlessly killed or permanently restrained. The requisite tutelage and discipline can be provided for Class B without rancor or insult. The rest can be treated not as criminals but as civil defendants, and made to pay for their depredations in the same manner. At present many persons guilty of conduct much viler than that for which poor men are sent to prison suffer nothing worse than civil actions for damages when they do not (unhappily) enjoy complete impunity.

6. The principle to be kept before the minds of all citizens is that as civilized society is a very costly arrangement necessary to their subsistence and security they must justify their enjoyment of it by contributing their share to its cost, and giving no more than their share of trouble, subject to every possible provision by insurance against innocent disability. This is a condition precedent to freedom, and justifies us in removing cases of incurable noxious disability by simply putting an end to their existence.

7. An unconquerable repugnance to judicial killing having led to the abolition of capital punishment in several countries, and to its reservation for specially dangerous or abhorrent crimes in all the others, it is possible that the right to kill may be renounced by all civilized States. This repugnance may be intensified as we cease to distinguish between sin and

infirmity, or, in prison language, between crime and disease, because of our fear of being led to the extirpation of the incurable invalid who is excessively troublesome as well as to that of the incurable criminal.

On the other hand, the opposite temperament, which is not squeamish about making short work of hard cases, and which is revolted by the daily sacrifice of the lives of prison officials, and of relatives and nurses, to incurable criminals and invalids, may be reinforced by the abandonment of ethical pretentiousness, vengeance, malice, and all uncharitableness in the matter, and may become less scrupulous than at present in advocating euthanasia for all incurables.

Whichever party may prevail, punishment as such is likely to disappear, and with it the earmarking of certain offences as calling for specially deterrent severities. But it does not follow that lethal treatment of extreme cases will be barred. On the contrary, it may be extended from murder to social incompatibility of all sorts. If it be absolutely barred, sufficient restraint must be effected, not as a punishment but as a necessity for public safety. But there will be no excuse for making it more unpleasant than it need be.

8. When detention and restraint are necessary, the criminal's right to contact with all the spiritual influences of his day should be respected, and its exercise encouraged and facilitated. Conversation, access to books and pictures and music, unfettered scientific, philosophic, and religious activity, change of scene and occupation, the free formation of friendships and acquaintances, marriage and parentage: in short, all the normal methods of creation and recreation, must be available for criminals as for other persons, partly because deprivation of these things is severely punitive, and partly because it is destructive to the victim, and produces what we call the criminal type, making a cure impossible. Any specific liberty which the criminal's specific defects lead him to abuse will, no doubt, be taken from him; but if his life is spared his right to live must be accepted in the fullest sense, and not, as at present, merely as a right to breathe and circulate his blood. In short, a criminal should be treated, not as a man who has forfeited all normal rights and liberties by the breaking of a single law, but as one who, through some specific weakness or weaknesses, is incapable of exercising some specific liberty or liberties.

9. The main difficulty in applying this concept of individual freedom to the criminal arises from the fact that the concept itself is as yet unformed. We do not apply it to children, at home or at school, nor to employees, nor to persons of any class or age who are in the power of other persons. Like Queen Victoria, we conceive Man as being either in authority or

subject to authority, each person doing only what he is expressly permitted to do, or what the example of the rest of his class encourages him to consider as tacitly permitted. The concept of the evolving free man in an evolving society, making all sorts of experiments in conduct, and therefore doing everything he likes as far as he can unless there are express prohibitions to which he is politically a consenting party, is still unusual, and consequently terrifying, in spite of all the individualist pamphlets of the XVIII and XIX centuries. It will be found that those who are most scandalized by the liberties I am claiming for the convict would be equally scandalized if I claimed them for their own sons, or even for themselves.

The conclusion is that imprisonment cannot be fully understood by those who do not understand freedom. But it can be understood quite well enough to have it made a much less horrible, wicked, and wasteful thing than it is at present.

AYOT ST LAWRENCE.
December–January, 1921–22 [Revised 1925 and 1931.].

The Perfect Wagnerite

Preface to the fourth English edition, 1923

=====

Much water, some of it deeply stained with blood, has passed under the bridges since this book was first published twentyfour years ago. Musically Wagner is now more old-fashioned than Handel and Bach, Mozart and Beethoven, whose fashions have perished though their music remains; whilst his own fashion has been worn to rags by young composers in their first efforts to draw the bow of Ulysses. Finally, it has been discarded as Homerically impossible; and England, after two centuries of imitative negligibility, has suddenly flung into the field a cohort of composers whose methods have made a technical revolution in musical composition so complete that the conductor does not dare to correct the most cacophonous errors in band parts lest the composer should have intended them, and looks in vain for key signatures because young men no longer write in keys but just mark their notes flat or sharp as they come. One can imagine Wagner trying to conduct the latest British tone poem, and exclaiming in desperation, "Is this music?" just as his own contemporaries did when they were confronted with the "false relations" [chromatic conflict between two notes of the same chord] in the score of Tristan. It is true that most of the modern developments, as far as they are really developments and not merely experimental eccentricities, are implicit in Parsifal. Indeed, for that matter, they are implicit in Bach: still, the first man to be scandalized by a new departure is usually he that found the path for it; and I cannot feel sure that Wagner would have encouraged Messrs [Arnold] Bax, [John] Ireland, Cyril Scott, [Gustav] Holst, [Eugene] Goossens, [Ralph] Vaughan Williams, Frank Bridge, [Rutland] Boughton, [Josef] Holbrooke, [Herbert] Howells[1] and the rest (imagine being able to remember offhand so many names of British composers turning out serious music in native styles of their own!!!) any more than Haydn encouraged Beethoven. Wagner, after his 1855 London season as conductor of the Philharmonic, would not have believed that such a thing could happen in England. Had he been told that within

1. All were living British composers in 1923.

two years a British baby [Edward] Elgar[2] would arrive who would attain classic rank as a European composer, he would hardly have kept his temper. Yet all this has happened very much as it happened before in Shakespear's time; and the English people at large are just as unconcerned about it, and indeed unconscious of it, as they were then.

Also the English have taken, as I said in this book they might, to Wagner singing and acting; and there is now no question of going to Bayreuth or importing German singers when we wish to hear The Ring or Parsifal; for much better performances of both can be heard now from English companies in England than Wagner ever heard at Bayreuth; and even a transpontine theatre like the Old Vic[3] thinks no more of doing Tannhäuser than it would have thought of doing [Douglas Jerrold's] Black-Eyed Susan [1829] half a century ago.

Another change has outmoded my description of the Bayreuth Festival Playhouse as an ultramodern theatre. Bayreuth has a pictorial stage framed by a proscenium, and the framed picture stage is not now in the latest fashion. When the monarchy and the theatre were restored in England simultaneously on the accession of Charles II, the representation of Shakespear's plays as he planned them was made impossible by the introduction of pictorial scenery and of the proscenium with its two curtains, the act drop and the final green baize, to divide the plays into acts and hide the stage for intervals during which elaborate scenes were built up on it. His plays had to be chopped into fragments; divided into acts; rewritten and provided with new endings to make effective "curtains," in which condition they were intolerably tedious except as mere pedestals for irresistibly attractive actors and actresses.

Thus the pictorial stage not only murdered Shakespear, and buried the old Athenian drama, but dictated the form of opera (which grew up with it) and changed the form of the spoken drama. Wagner submitted to it as inevitable; but when he conceived the performances of The Ring, and planned a theatre for them, he made a desperate effort to elaborate its machinery so as to enable complete changes of scene to be made without stopping the performance and keeping the audience staring idly for fifteen

2. Composer of the popular oratorio *The Dream of Gerontius* (1900), two symphonies, the *Enigma Variations* (1899), and *Pomp and Circumstance* marches (1901–7).
3. A transpontine theatre is a playhouse literally 'across the bridge'. The Old Vic (originally the Royal Coburg, then the Royal Victoria), south of the Thames, long specialized in popular entertainment; but in the early twentieth century it became a home for opera and for top-quality Shakespearian production.

minutes at a dropped curtain, or scrambling to and from their seats to fill up the time by smoking cigarets and drinking. One of his devices was to envelop the stage in mists produced by what was called a steam curtain, which looked exactly like what it really was, and made the theatre smell like a laundry. By its aid The Rhine Gold was performed without a break instead of in three acts with long intervals between each.

One had to admit at Bayreuth that here was the utmost perfection of the pictorial stage, and that its machinery could go no further. Nevertheless, having seen it at its best, fresh from Wagner's own influence, I must also admit that my favorite way of enjoying a performance of The Ring is to sit at the back of a box, comfortable on two chairs, feet up, and listen without looking. The truth is, a man whose imagination cannot serve him better than the most costly devices of the imitative scenepainter, should not go to the theatre, and as a matter of fact does not. In planning his Bayreuth theatre, Wagner was elaborating what he had better have scrapped altogether.

But as this did not occur to him, he allowed his technical plan of The Ring to be so governed by pictorial visions that it is as unreasonable to ask Bayreuth to scrap the Wagner tradition as it would be to ask the Théâtre Français [home of the Comédie Française] to scrap the Molière tradition. Only, I must now treat that tradition as old-fashioned, whereas when this book was first published it was the latest development. What has happened since in England is that an Englishman, Mr Harley Granville-Barker, developing certain experiments made from time to time by Mr William Poel, another Englishman, inaugurated XX century Shakespear by a series of performances in which the plays were given with unprecedented artistic splendor without the omission of a single decently presentable line, undivided into acts, without the old pictorial scenery, and with, as a result, a blessed revelation of Shakespear as the Prince of Entertainers instead of the most dreaded of bores, and a degree of illusion which the pictorial theatre had not only failed to attain, but had sedulously destroyed, nowhere more effectively than (save only in certain scenes of pure ritual in Parsifal) at Bayreuth.

Almost simultaneously with Mr Granville-Barker's revolutionary restoration of Shakespear, the pictorial stage triumphantly announced that at the English Bayreuth, which is the Shakespear Memorial Theatre at Stratford-on-Avon, the play of Coriolanus had been, by a climax of Procrustean adaptation, cut down to a performance lasting only one hour, in which state it was humbly hoped that the public would steel itself to bear it just once or twice for the sake of our national playwright. That was too much.

Mr Bridges-Adams, who had started with Mr Granville-Barker, took the new method to Stratford, where the former victims of the pictorial stage now find to their amazement that three hours of unabbreviated Shakespear fly faster than one hour of Procrusty Coriolanus. And at the Old Vic in London, where the reform was adopted by Mr [Robert] Atkins,[4] Shakespear now draws better than would-be popular melodrama.

Thus have Englishmen left Wagner behind as to methods, and made obsolete all that part of this book which presents him as a pioneer. I must add that nobody who knows the snobbish contempt in which most Englishmen hold oneanother will be surprised when I mention that in England the exploits of Poel, Granville-Barker, Bridges-Adams, Atkins, and the English designers and painters who have worked for them, are modestly attributed to Herr [Max] Reinhardt,[5] their eminent German contemporary. The only Englishman who is given any credit by his countrymen is Mr Gordon Craig, a fascinating propagandist who still loves the stage picture better than the stage play, and, living in the glamor of the Continent, seldom meddles with the actual theatre except to wipe his boots on it and on all the art that grows on its boards.

As to the sociological aspect of The Ring, which is unaffected by the rapid ageing of its technical aspect as a musical composition and a theatrical spectacle, it seems to challenge the so-called Great War to invalidate it if it can. Gross as the catastrophe has been, it has not shaken Bayreuth. But postwar contemplation of The Ring must not make us forget that all the progress Wagner saw was from the revolutions of 1848, when he was with the barricaders, to the Imperialist climax of 1871, when he sang:

> Hail, hail, our Cæsar!
> Royal William!
> Rock and ward of German freedom![6]

What would he have said had he lived to see 1917 in Russia and 1918 in Germany, with England singing "Hang, hang that Kaiser!" and Germany sympathizing to such an extent that the grandson of Wagner's William

4. Actor and director at the Old Vic, 1915–25, who specialized in Shakespeare throughout his career.
5. Pre-eminent, innovative German director, equally adept with intimate theatre and large-scale, elaborate staging.
6. William I, King of Prussia, proclaimed German Emperor. The lyric is a contemporary revision of the German 1793 adaptation to its own use of 'God Save the King' ('Heil dir im Siegerkrantz'/'Hail thee in victor's crown').

[William II (Frederick Wilhelm)] had to seek safety in Holland? Rhine maidens walking out with British Tommies, Senegalese negroes in Goethe's house, Marx enthroned in Russia, pistoled Romanoffs, fugitive Hapsburgs, exiled Hohenzollerns marking the ruins of empires with no more chance of restoration than the Stuarts and Bourbons: such a Götterdämmerung [night falls on the gods], in short, as in its craziness can be fitted into no allegory until its upshot becomes plainer than it now is: all this has so changed the political atmosphere in which Wagner lived, and in which this book was written, that it says much for the comprehensiveness of his grasp of things that his allegory should still be valid and important. Indeed the war was more a great tearing off of masks than a change of face: the main difference is that Alberic is richer, and his slaves hungrier and harder worked when they are so lucky as to have any work to do. The Ring ends with everybody dead except three mermaids; and though the war went far enough in that conclusive direction to suggest that the next war may possibly kill even the mermaids with "depth charges," the curtain is not yet down on our drama, and we have to carry on as best we can. If we succeed, this book may have to pass into yet another edition: if not, the world itself will have to be re-edited.

AYOT ST LAWRENCE, 1922.

Saint Joan

First published in 1924

═══

JOAN THE ORIGINAL AND PRESUMPTUOUS

Joan of Arc, a village girl from the Vosges [a district in east France], was born about 1412; burnt for heresy, witchcraft, and sorcery in 1431; rehabilitated after a fashion in 1456; designated Venerable in 1904; declared Blessed in 1908; and finally canonized in 1920. She is the most notable Warrior Saint in the Christian calendar, and the queerest fish among the eccentric worthies of the Middle Ages. Though a professed and most pious Catholic, and the projector of a Crusade against the Husites,[1] she was in fact one of the first Protestant martyrs. She was also one of the first apostles of Nationalism, and the first French practitioner of Napoleonic realism in warfare as distinguished from the sporting ransom-gambling chivalry of her time. She was the pioneer of rational dressing for women, and, like Queen Christina of Sweden two centuries later, to say nothing of Catalina de Erauso[2] and innumerable obscure heroines who have disguised themselves as men to serve as soldiers and sailors, she refused to accept the specific woman's lot, and dressed and fought and lived as men did.

As she contrived to assert herself in all these ways with such force that she was famous throughout western Europe before she was out of her teens (indeed she never got out of them), it is hardly surprising that she was judicially burnt, ostensibly for a number of capital crimes which we no longer punish as such, but essentially for what we call unwomanly and insufferable presumption. At eighteen Joan's pretensions were beyond those

1. Followers of John Hus, a Czech priest and Church reformer. Hus's stand on papal indulgences anticipated Martin Luther's by a hundred years. When he refused to recant on this issue and others, he was burned at the stake as a heretic.
2. Ex-nun, who fled from a convent, disguised herself in male garb and sailed to America, where she served in the army as a second lieutenant. Her story was told in a picaresque 'biography' allegedly by herself but written by Joaquin María de Ferrer, *Historia de la monja alférez Doña Catalina de Erauso, escrita por ella misma* (1829).

of the proudest Pope or the haughtiest emperor. She claimed to be the ambassador and plenipotentiary of God, and to be, in effect, a member of the Church Triumphant [see p. 530] whilst still in the flesh on earth. She patronized her own king, and summoned the English king to repentance and obedience to her commands. She lectured, talked down, and overruled statesmen and prelates. She pooh-poohed the plans of generals, leading their troops to victory on plans of her own. She had an unbounded and quite unconcealed contempt for official opinion, judgment, and authority, and for War Office tactics and strategy. Had she been a sage and monarch in whom the most venerable hierarchy and the most illustrious dynasty converged, her pretensions and proceedings would have been as trying to the official mind as the pretensions of Cæsar were to Cassius.[3] As her actual condition was pure upstart, there were only two opinions about her. One was that she was miraculous: the other that she was unbearable .

JOAN AND SOCRATES

If Joan had been malicious, selfish, cowardly or stupid, she would have been one of the most odious persons known to history instead of one of the most attractive. If she had been old enough to know the effect she was producing on the men whom she humiliated by being right when they were wrong, and had learned to flatter and manage them, she might have lived as long as Queen Elizabeth. But she was too young and rustical and inexperienced to have any such arts. When she was thwarted by men whom she thought fools, she made no secret of her opinion of them or her impatience with their folly; and she was naïve enough to expect them to be obliged to her for setting them right and keeping them out of mischief. Now it is always hard for superior wits to understand the fury roused by their exposures of the stupidities of comparative dullards. Even Socrates, for all his age and experience, did not defend himself at his trial like a man who understood the long accumulated fury that had burst on him, and was clamoring for his death. His accuser [Anytus, an Athenian politician], if born 2300 years later, might have been picked out of any first-class carriage on a suburban railway during the evening or morning rush from or to the City; for he had really nothing to say except that he and his like could not endure being shewn up as idiots every time Socrates opened his mouth.

3. Shaw refers apparently to Caesar's pretentious reply to Cassius, who has pleaded for a pardon for Publius Cimber, in Shakespeare's *Julius Caesar* (III: i).

Socrates, unconscious of this, was paralyzed by his sense that somehow he was missing the point of the attack. He petered out after he had established the fact that he was an old soldier and a man of honorable life, and that his accuser was a silly snob. He had no suspicion of the extent to which his mental superiority had roused fear and hatred against him in the hearts of men towards whom he was conscious of nothing but good will and good service.

CONTRAST WITH NAPOLEON

If Socrates was as innocent as this at the age of seventy, it may be imagined how innocent Joan was at the age of seventeen. Now Socrates was a man of argument, operating slowly and peacefully on men's minds, whereas Joan was a woman of action, operating with impetuous violence on their bodies. That, no doubt, is why the contemporaries of Socrates endured him so long, and why Joan was destroyed before she was fully grown. But both of them combined terrifying ability with a frankness, personal modesty, and benevolence which made the furious dislike to which they fell victims absolutely unreasonable, and therefore inapprehensible by themselves. Napoleon, also possessed of terrifying ability, but neither frank nor disinterested, had no illusions as to the nature of his popularity. When he was asked how the world would take his death, he said it would give a gasp of relief. But it is not so easy for mental giants who neither hate nor intend to injure their fellows to realize that nevertheless their fellows hate mental giants and would like to destroy them, not only enviously because the juxtaposition of a superior wounds their vanity, but quite humbly and honestly because it frightens them. Fear will drive men to any extreme; and the fear inspired by a superior being is a mystery which cannot be reasoned away. Being immeasurable it is unbearable when there is no presumption or guarantee of its benevolence and moral responsibility: in other words, when it has no official status. The legal and conventional superiority of Herod and Pilate, and of Annas and Caiaphas, inspires fear; but the fear, being a reasonable fear of measurable and avoidable consequences which seem salutary and protective, is bearable; whilst the strange superiority of Christ and the fear it inspires elicit a shriek of Crucify Him from all who cannot divine its benevolence. Socrates has to drink the hemlock, Christ to hang on the cross, and Joan to burn at the stake, whilst Napoleon, though he ends in St Helena, at least dies in his bed there; and many terrifying but quite comprehensible official scoundrels die natural deaths in all the glory of the kingdoms of this world, proving that it is far more dangerous to be a saint than to be a conqueror. Those who have been both, like Mahomet and Joan, have found that it is the conqueror who must save the saint, and that defeat and capture mean martyrdom. Joan was burnt without a hand lifted on her own side to save her. The comrades she had led to victory and the enemies she had disgraced and defeated, the French king she had crowned and the English king whose crown she had kicked into the Loire, were equally glad to be rid of her.

WAS JOAN INNOCENT OR GUILTY?

As this result could have been produced by a crapulous inferiority as well as by a sublime superiority, the question which of the two was operative in Joan's case has to be faced. It was decided against her by her contemporaries after a very careful and conscientious trial; and the reversal of the verdict twentyfive years later, in form a rehabilitation of Joan, was really only a confirmation of the validity of the coronation of Charles VII [Dauphin in Shaw's play]. It is the more impressive reversal by a unanimous Posterity, culminating in her canonization, that has quashed the original proceedings, and put her judges on their trial, which, so far, has been much more unfair than their trial of her. Nevertheless the rehabilitation of 1456, corrupt job as it was, really did produce evidence enough to satisfy all reasonable critics that Joan was not a common termagant, not a harlot, not a witch, not a blasphemer, no more an idolater than the Pope himself, and not ill conducted in any sense apart from her soldiering, her wearing of men's clothes, and her audacity, but on the contrary goodhumored, an intact virgin, very pious, very temperate (we should call her meal of bread soaked in the common wine which is the drinking water of France ascetic), very kindly, and, though a brave and hardy soldier, unable to endure loose language or licentious conduct. She went to the stake without a stain on her character except the overweening presumption, the superbity as they called it, that led her thither. It would therefore be waste of time now to prove that the Joan of the first part of the Elizabethan chronicle play of Henry VI (supposed to have been tinkered by Shakespear[4]) grossly libels

4. Shakespearian scholars in Shaw's time tended to conjecture that *Henry VI* was the work predominantly of another author, nominating such candidates as Robert Greene, Christopher Marlowe and Thomas Nashe. Thus, it is possible that, as Shaw suggests, the libelling of Joan in the play was not the work of Shakespeare. One

her in its concluding scenes in deference to Jingo patriotism. The mud that was thrown at her has dropped off by this time so completely that there is no need for any modern writer to wash up after it. What is far more difficult to get rid of is the mud that is being thrown at her judges, and the whitewash which disfigures her beyond recognition. When Jingo scurrility had done its worst to her, sectarian scurrility (in this case Protestant scurrility) used her stake to beat the Roman Catholic Church and the Inquisition. The easiest way to make these institutions the villains of a melodrama was to make The Maid its heroine. That melodrama may be dismissed as rubbish. Joan got a far fairer trial from the Church and the Inquisition than any prisoner of her type and in her situation gets nowadays in any official secular court; and the decision was strictly according to law. And she was not a melodramatic heroine: that is, a physically beautiful lovelorn parasite on an equally beautiful hero, but a genius and a saint, about as completely the opposite of a melodramatic heroine as it is possible for a human being to be.

Let us be clear about the meaning of the terms. A genius is a person who, seeing farther and probing deeper than other people, has a different set of ethical valuations from theirs, and has energy enough to give effect to this extra vision and its valuations in whatever manner best suits his or her specific talents. A saint is one who having practised heroic virtues, and enjoyed revelations or powers of the order which The Church classes technically as supernatural, is eligible for canonization. If a historian is an Anti-Feminist, and does not believe women to be capable of genius in the traditional masculine departments, he will never make anything of Joan, whose genius was turned to practical account mainly in soldiering and politics. If he is Rationalist enough to deny that saints exist, and to hold that new ideas cannot come otherwise than by conscious ratiocination, he will never catch Joan's likeness. Her ideal biographer must be free from XIX century prejudices and biases; must understand the Middle Ages, the Roman Catholic Church, and the Holy Roman Empire much more intimately than our Whig historians have ever understood them; and must be capable of throwing off sex partialities and their romance, and regarding woman as the female of the human species, and not as a different kind of animal with specific charms and specific imbecilities.

---

assumes, however, that the editors of the 1623 First Folio would not have included it as the work of a man with whom they were personally familiar as theatre colleagues unless they believed him to have been the author.

JOAN'S GOOD LOOKS

To put the last point roughly, any book about Joan which begins by describing her as a beauty may be at once classed as a romance. Not one of Joan's comrades, in village, court, or camp, even when they were straining themselves to please the king by praising her, ever claimed that she was pretty. All the men who alluded to the matter declared most emphatically that she was unattractive sexually to a degree that seemed to them miraculous, considering that she was in the bloom of youth, and neither ugly, awkward, deformed, nor unpleasant in her person. The evident truth is that like most women of her hardy managing type she seemed neutral in the conflict of sex because men were too much afraid of her to fall in love with her. She herself was not sexless: in spite of the virginity she had vowed up to a point, and preserved to her death, she never excluded the possibility of marriage for herself. But marriage, with its preliminary of the attraction, pursuit, and capture of a husband, was not her business: she had something else to do. Byron's formula, "Man's love is of man's life a thing apart: 'tis woman's whole existence" [*Don Juan*, I], did not apply to her any more than to George Washington or any other masculine worker on the heroic scale. Had she lived in our time, picture postcards might have been sold of her as a general: they would not have been sold of her as a sultana. Nevertheless there is one reason for crediting her with a very remarkable face. A sculptor of her time in Orleans made a statue of a helmeted young woman with a face that is unique in art in point of being evidently not an ideal face but a portrait, and yet so uncommon as to be unlike any real woman one has ever seen.[5] It is surmised that Joan served unconsciously as the sculptor's model. There is no proof of this; but those extraordinarily spaced eyes raise so powerfully the question "If this woman be not Joan, who is she?" that I dispense with further evidence, and challenge those who disagree with me to prove a negative. It is a wonderful face, but quite neutral from the point of view of the operatic beauty fancier.

Such a fancier may perhaps be finally chilled by the prosaic fact that Joan was the defendant in a suit for breach of promise of marriage, and that she conducted her own case and won it.

5. The helmeted figure was later identified as St Maurice.

JOAN'S SOCIAL POSITION

By class Joan was the daughter of a working farmer who was one of the headmen of his village, and transacted its feudal business for it with the neighboring squires and their lawyers. When the castle in which the villagers were entitled to take refuge from raids became derelict, he organized a combination of half a dozen farmers to obtain possession of it so as to occupy it when there was any danger of invasion. As a child, Joan could please herself at times with being the young lady of this castle. Her mother and brothers were able to follow and share her fortune at court without making themselves notably ridiculous. These facts leave us no excuse for the popular romance that turns every heroine into either a princess or a beggarmaid. In the somewhat similar case of Shakespear a whole inverted pyramid of wasted research has been based on the assumption that he was an illiterate laborer, in the face of the plainest evidence that his father was a man of business, and at one time a very prosperous one, married to a woman of some social pretensions. There is the same tendency to drive Joan into the position of a hired shepherd girl, though a hired shepherd girl in Domrémy [Joan's native village] would have deferred to her as the young lady of the farm.

The difference between Joan's case and Shakespear's is that Shakespear was not illiterate. He had been to school, and knew as much Latin and Greek as most university passmen retain: that is, for practical purposes, none at all. Joan was absolutely illiterate. "I do not know A from B" she said. But many princesses at that time and for long after might have said the same. Marie Antoinette, for instance, at Joan's age could not spell her own name correctly. But this does not mean that Joan was an ignorant person, or that she suffered from the diffidence and sense of social disadvantage now felt by people who cannot read or write. If she could not write letters, she could and did dictate them and attach full and indeed excessive importance to them. When she was called a shepherd lass to her face she very warmly resented it, and challenged any woman to compete with her in the household arts of the mistresses of well-furnished houses. She understood the political and military situation in France much better than most of our newspaper-fed university women-graduates understand the corresponding situation of their own country today. Her first convert was the neighboring commandant at Vaucouleurs; and she converted him by telling him about the defeat of the Dauphin's troops at the Battle of

Herrings[6] so long before he had official news of it that he concluded she must have had a divine revelation. This knowledge of and interest in public affairs was nothing extraordinary among farmers in a war-swept country-side. Politicians came to the door too often sword in hand to be disregarded: Joan's people could not afford to be ignorant of what was going on in the feudal world. They were not rich; and Joan worked on the farm as her father did, driving the sheep to pasture and so forth; but there is no evidence or suggestion of sordid poverty, and no reason to believe that Joan had to work as a hired servant works, or indeed to work at all when she preferred to go to confession, or dawdle about waiting for visions and listening to the church bells to hear voices in them. In short, much more of a young lady, and even of an intellectual, than most of the daughters of our petty bourgeoisie.

JOAN'S VOICES AND VISIONS

Joan's voices and visions have played many tricks with her reputation. They have been held to prove that she was mad, that she was a liar and impostor, that she was a sorceress (she was burned for this), and finally that she was a saint. They do not prove any of these things; but the variety of the conclusions reached shew how little our matter-of-fact historians know about other people's minds, or even about their own. There are people in the world whose imagination is so vivid that when they have an idea it comes to them as an audible voice, sometimes uttered by a visible figure. Criminal lunatic asylums are occupied largely by murderers who have obeyed voices. Thus a woman may hear voices telling her that she must cut her husband's throat and strangle her child as they lie asleep; and she may feel obliged to do what she is told. By a medico-legal superstition it is held in our courts that criminals whose temptations present themselves under these illusions are not responsible for their actions, and must be treated as insane. But the seers of visions and the hearers of revelations are not always criminals. The inspirations and intuitions and unconsciously reasoned conclusions of genius sometimes assume similar illusions. Socrates, Luther,

6. The defeat occurred near Rouvray in February 1429. Sir John Fastolf was transporting barrels of herrings intended for the Lenten fast. When the French attacked, the English successfully used the barrels for shields.

[Emanuel] Swedenborg,[7] Blake saw visions and heard voices just as Saint Francis and Saint Joan did. If Newton's imagination had been of the same vividly dramatic kind he might have seen the ghost of Pythagoras[8] walk into the orchard and explain why the apples were falling. Such an illusion would have invalidated neither the theory of gravitation nor Newton's general sanity. What is more, the visionary method of making the discovery would not be a whit more miraculous than the normal method. The test of sanity is not the normality of the method but the reasonableness of the discovery. If Newton had been informed by Pythagoras that the moon was made of green cheese, then Newton would have been locked up. Gravitation, being a reasoned hypothesis which fitted remarkably well into the Copernican version of the observed physical facts of the universe, established Newton's reputation for extraordinary intelligence, and would have done so no matter how fantastically he had arrived at it. Yet his theory of gravitation is not so impressive a mental feat as his astounding chronology, which establishes him as the king of mental conjurors, but a Bedlamite king whose authority no one now accepts. On the subject of the eleventh horn of the beast seen by the prophet Daniel [*Observations upon the Prophecies of Daniel and the Apocalypse of St John*, 1733] he was more fantastic than Joan, because his imagination was not dramatic but mathematical and therefore extraordinarily susceptible to numbers: indeed if all his works were lost except his chronology we should say that he was as mad as a hatter. As it is, who dares diagnose Newton as a madman?

In the same way Joan must be judged a sane woman in spite of her voices because they never gave her any advice that might not have come to her from her mother wit exactly as gravitation came to Newton. We can all see now, especially since the late war threw so many of our women into military life, that Joan's campaigning could not have been carried on in petticoats. This was not only because she did a man's work, but because it was morally necessary that sex should be left out of the question as between her and her comrades-in-arms. She gave this reason herself when she was pressed on the subject; and the fact that this entirely reasonable necessity came to her imagination first as an order from God delivered through the mouth of Saint Catherine does not prove that she was mad. The soundness of the order proves that she was unusually sane; but its form

7. Swedish scientist and religious philosopher, who engendered a religious sect known as the Church of the New Jerusalem.
8. Sixth-century BC Greek philosopher and mathematician to whom the doctrine of metempsychosis has been ascribed.

proves that her dramatic imagination played tricks with her senses. Her policy was also quite sound: nobody disputes that the relief of Orleans, followed up by the coronation at Rheims of the Dauphin as a counterblow to the suspicions then current of his legitimacy and consequently of his title, were military and political masterstrokes that saved France. They might have been planned by Napoleon or any other illusionproof genius. They came to Joan as an instruction from her Counsel, as she called her visionary saints; but she was none the less an able leader of men for imagining her ideas in this way.

THE EVOLUTIONARY APPETITE

What then is the modern view of Joan's voices and visions and messages from God? The XIX century said that they were delusions, but that as she was a pretty girl, and had been abominably ill-treated and finally done to death by a superstitious rabble of medieval priests hounded on by a corrupt political bishop, it must be assumed that she was the innocent dupe of these delusions. The XX century finds this explanation too vapidly commonplace, and demands something more mystic. I think the XX century is right, because an explanation which amounts to Joan being mentally defective instead of, as she obviously was, mentally excessive, will not wash. I cannot believe, nor, if I could, could I expect all my readers to believe, as Joan did, that three ocularly visible well-dressed persons, named respectively Saint Catherine, Saint Margaret, and Saint Michael [Blessed Michael the Archangel, not a saint], came down from heaven and gave her certain instructions with which they were charged by God for her. Not that such a belief would be more improbable or fantastic than some modern beliefs which we all swallow; but there are fashions and family habits in belief, and it happens that, my fashion being Victorian and my family habit Protestant, I find myself unable to attach any such objective validity to the form of Joan's visions.

But that there are forces at work which use individuals for purposes far transcending the purpose of keeping these individuals alive and prosperous and respectable and safe and happy in the middle station in life, which is all any good bourgeois can reasonably require, is established by the fact that men will, in the pursuit of knowledge and of social readjustments for which they will not be a penny the better, and are indeed often many pence the worse, face poverty, infamy, exile, imprisonment, dreadful hardship, and death. Even the selfish pursuit of personal power does not nerve men to the efforts and sacrifices which are eagerly made in pursuit of extensions of our power over nature, though these extensions may not touch the personal life of the seeker at any point. There is no more mystery about this appetite for knowledge and power than about the appetite for food: both are known as facts and as facts only, the difference between them being that the appetite for food is necessary to the life of the hungry man and is therefore a personal appetite, whereas the other is an appetite for evolution, and therefore a superpersonal need.

The diverse manners in which our imaginations dramatize the approach of the superpersonal forces is a problem for the psychologist, not for the historian. Only, the historian must understand that visionaries are neither impostors nor lunatics. It is one thing to say that the figure Joan recognized as St Catherine was not really St Catherine, but the dramatization by Joan's imagination of that pressure upon her of the driving force that is behind evolution which I have just called the evolutionary appetite. It is quite another to class her visions with the vision of two moons seen by a drunken person, or with Brocken spectres,[9] echoes and the like. Saint Catherine's instructions were far too cogent for that; and the simplest French peasant who believes in apparitions of celestial personages to favored mortals is nearer to the scientific truth about Joan than the Rationalist and Materialist historians and essayists who feel obliged to set down a girl who saw saints and heard them talking to her as either crazy or mendacious. If Joan was mad, all Christendom was mad too; for people who believe devoutly in the existence of celestial personages are every whit as mad in that sense as the people who think they see them. Luther, when he threw his inkhorn at the devil, was no more mad than any other Augustinian monk: he had a more vivid imagination, and had perhaps eaten and slept less: that was all.

THE MERE ICONOGRAPHY DOES NOT MATTER

All the popular religions in the world are made apprehensible by an array of legendary personages, with an Almighty Father, and sometimes a mother and divine child, as the central figures. These are presented to the mind's eye in childhood; and the result is a hallucination which persists strongly throughout life when it has been well impressed. Thus all the

---

9. Brocken, chief summit of the Hartz Mountains in north Germany, is the traditional meeting place of witches on Walpurgis Night, famous for the optical phenomenon called the 'specter of the Brocken'.

thinking of the hallucinated adult about the fountain of inspiration which is continually flowing in the universe, or about the promptings of virtue and the revulsions of shame: in short, about aspiration and conscience, both of which forces are matters of fact more obvious than electro-magnetism, is thinking in terms of the celestial vision. And when in the case of exceptionally imaginative persons, especially those practising certain appropriate austerities, the hallucination extends from the mind's eye to the body's, the visionary sees Krishna or the Buddha or the Blessed Virgin or St Catherine as the case may be.

THE MODERN EDUCATION WHICH JOAN ESCAPED

It is important to everyone nowadays to understand this, because modern science is making short work of the hallucinations without regard to the vital importance of the things they symbolize. If Joan were reborn today she would be sent, first to a convent school in which she would be mildly taught to connect inspiration and conscience with St Catherine and St Michael exactly as she was in the XV century, and then finished up with a very energetic training in the gospel of Saints Louis Pasteur and Paul Bert,[10] who would tell her (possibly in visions but more probably in pamphlets) not to be a superstitious little fool, and to empty out St Catherine and the rest of the Catholic hagiology as an obsolete iconography of exploded myths. It would be rubbed into her that Galileo was a martyr, and his persecutors incorrigible ignoramuses, and that St Teresa's[11] hormones had gone astray and left her incurably hyperpituitary or hyperadrenal or hysteroid or epileptoid or anything but asteroid. She would have been convinced by precept and experiment that baptism and receiving the body of her Lord were contemptible superstitions, and that vaccination and vivisection were enlightened practices. Behind her new Saints Louis and Paul there would be not only Science purifying Religion and being purified by it, but hypochondria, melancholia, cowardice, stupidity, cruelty, muckraking curiosity, knowledge without wisdom, and everything that the eternal soul in Nature loathes, instead of the virtues of which St Catherine was the figure head. As to the new rites, which would be the saner Joan? the one who carried little children to be baptized of water and

10. French physiologist, author of *Notes d'anatomie et de physiologie comparées* (1867) and *Barometric Pressure: Researches in Experimental Physiology* (1878).
11. St Teresa of Avila, canonized in 1622, was noted for her mystical visions.

the spirit, or the one who sent the police to force their parents to have the most villainous racial poison we know thrust into their veins? the one who told them the story of the angel and Mary, or the one who questioned them as to their experiences of the Edipus complex? the one to whom the consecrated wafer was the very body of the virtue that was her salvation, or the one who looked forward to a precise and convenient regulation of her health and her desires by a nicely calculated diet of thyroid extract, adrenalin, thymin, pituitrin, and insulin, with pick-me-ups of hormone stimulants, the blood being first carefully fortified with antibodies against all possible infections by inoculations of infected bacteria and serum from infected animals, and against old age by surgical extirpation of the reproductive ducts or weekly doses of monkey gland?[12]

It is true that behind all these quackeries there is a certain body of genuine scientific physiology. But was there any the less a certain body of genuine psychology behind St Catherine and the Holy Ghost? And which is the healthier mind? the saintly mind or the monkey-gland mind? Does not the present cry of Back to the Middle Ages, which has been incubating ever since the pre-Raphaelite movement began, mean that it is no longer our Academy pictures that are intolerable, but our credulities that have not the excuse of being superstitions, our cruelties that have not the excuse of barbarism, our persecutions that have not the excuse of religious faith, our shameless substitution of successful swindlers and scoundrels and quacks for saints as objects of worship, and our deafness and blindness to the calls and visions of the inexorable power that made us, and will destroy us if we disregard it? To Joan and her contemporaries we should appear as a drove of Gadarene swine, possessed by all the unclean spirits cast out by the faith and civilization of the Middle Ages, running violently down a steep place into a hell of high explosives. For us to set up our condition as a standard of sanity, and declare Joan mad because she never condescended to it, is to prove that we are not only lost but irredeemable. Let us then once for all drop all nonsense about Joan being cracked, and accept her as at least as sane as Florence Nightingale, who also combined a very simple iconography of religious belief with a mind so exceptionally powerful that it kept her in continual trouble with the medical and military panjandrums of her time.

---

12. Medical use of the glands of monkeys for the rejuvenation of aging humans motivated a highly amusing letter by Shaw, published on 29 May 1928, to the editor of the *Daily News*, London, 'Do Apes Make War', which was signed 'Consul Junior', a well-known performing chimpanzee in Regent's Park Zoo. It is reprinted in Shaw's *Agitations* (1985).

FAILURES OF THE VOICES

That the voices and visions were illusory, and their wisdom all Joan's own, is shewn by the occasions on which they failed her, notably during her trial, when they assured her that she would be rescued. Here her hopes flattered her; but they were not unreasonable: her military colleague La Hire was in command of a considerable force not so very far off; and if the Armagnacs, as her party was called, had really wanted to rescue her, and had put anything like her own vigor into the enterprize, they could have attempted it with very fair chances of success. She did not understand that they were glad to be rid of her, nor that the rescue of a prisoner from the hands of the Church was a much more serious business for a medieval captain, or even a medieval king, than its mere physical difficulty as a military exploit suggested. According to her lights her expectation of a rescue was reasonable; therefore she heard Madame Saint Catherine assuring her it would happen, that being her way of finding out and making up her own mind. When it became evident that she had miscalculated: when she was led to the stake, and La Hire was not thundering at the gates of Rouen nor charging Warwick's men at arms, she threw over Saint Catherine at once, and recanted. Nothing could be more sane or practical. It was not until she discovered that she had gained nothing by her recantation but close imprisonment for life that she withdrew it, and deliberately and explicitly chose burning instead: a decision which shewed not only the extraordinary decision of her character, but also a Rationalism carried to its ultimate human test of suicide. Yet even in this the illusion persisted; and she announced her relapse as dictated to her by her voices.

JOAN A GALTONIC VISUALIZER

The most sceptical scientific reader may therefore accept as a flat fact, carrying no implication of unsoundness of mind, that Joan was what Francis Galton[13] and other modern investigators of human faculty call a visualizer. She saw imaginary saints just as some other people see imaginary diagrams and landscapes with numbers dotted about them, and are thereby

13. English anthropologist and eugenicist, known for pioneering studies of human intelligence. His major works include *Heredity and Genius* (1869) and *Inquiries into Human Faculty* (1883).

able to perform feats of memory and arithmetic impossible to non–visualizers. Visualizers will understand this at once. Non-visualizers who have never read Galton will be puzzled and incredulous. But a very little inquiry among their acquaintances will reveal to them that the mind's eye is more or less a magic lantern, and that the street is full of normally sane people who have hallucinations of all sorts which they believe to be part of the normal permanent equipment of all human beings.

JOAN'S MANLINESS AND MILITARISM

Joan's other abnormality, too common among uncommon things to be properly called a peculiarity, was her craze for soldiering and the masculine life. Her father tried to frighten her out of it by threatening to drown her if she ran away with the soldiers, and ordering her brothers to drown her if he were not on the spot. This extravagance was clearly not serious: it must have been addressed to a child young enough to imagine that he was in earnest. Joan must therefore as a child have wanted to run away and be a soldier. The awful prospect of being thrown into the Meuse and drowned by a terrible father and her big brothers kept her quiet until the father had lost his terrors and the brothers yielded to her natural leadership; and by that time she had sense enough to know that the masculine and military life was not a mere matter of running away from home. But the taste for it never left her, and was fundamental in determining her career.

If anyone doubts this, let him ask himself why a maid charged with a special mission from heaven to the Dauphin (this was how Joan saw her very able plan for retrieving the desperate situation of the uncrowned king) should not have simply gone to the court as a maid, in woman's dress, and urged her counsel upon him in a woman's way, as other women with similar missions had come to his mad father and his wise grandfather. Why did she insist on having a soldier's dress and arms and sword and horse and equipment, and on treating her escort of soldiers as comrades, sleeping side by side with them on the floor at night as if there were no difference of sex between them? It may be answered that this was the safest way of traveling through a country infested with hostile troops and bands of marauding deserters from both sides. Such an answer has no weight because it applies to all the women who traveled in France at that time, and who never dreamt of traveling otherwise than as women. But even if we accept it, how does it account for the fact that when the danger was over, and she could present herself at court in feminine attire with perfect safety and obviously with greater propriety, she presented herself in her man's dress, and instead of urging Charles, like Queen Victoria urging the War Office to send Roberts to the Transvaal, to send D'Alençon, De Rais, La Hire and the rest to the relief of [Jean de] Dunois at Orleans,[14] insisted that she must go herself and lead the assault in person? Why did she give exhibitions of her dexterity in handling a lance, and of her seat as a rider? Why did she accept presents of armor and chargers and masculine surcoats, and in every action repudiate the conventional character of a woman? The simple answer to all these questions is that she was the sort of woman that wants to lead a man's life. They are to be found wherever there are armies on foot or navies on the seas, serving in male disguise, eluding detection for astonishingly long periods, and sometimes, no doubt, escaping it entirely. When they are in a position to defy public opinion they throw off all concealment. You have your Rosa Bonheur[15] painting in male blouse and trousers, and George Sand living a man's life and almost compelling her Chopins and De Mussets to live women's lives to amuse her. Had Joan not been one of those "unwomanly women," she might have been canonized much sooner.

But it is not necessary to wear trousers and smoke big cigars to live a man's life any more than it is necessary to wear petticoats to live a woman's. There are plenty of gowned and bodiced women in ordinary civil life who manage their own affairs and other people's, including those of their menfolk, and are entirely masculine in their tastes and pursuits. There always were such women, even in the Victorian days when women had fewer legal rights than men, and our modern women magistrates, mayors, and members of Parliament were unknown. In reactionary Russia in our own century a woman soldier organized an effective regiment of amazons, which disappeared only because it was Aldershottian enough to be against the Revolution.[16] The exemption of women from military service is founded, not on any natural inaptitude that men do not share, but

14. Dunois, soldier and diplomat, known because of his illegitimate birth as 'the Bastard of Orleans', defended that city (1428–9) until the siege was lifted by Joan.
15. French nineteenth-century nonconformist painter of animal life and landscape.
16. Maria Bochkareva, Siberian daughter of a former serf, organized and commanded the Women's Battalion of Death in the Great War; it supported defensively the February revolutionists in 1917. See Bochkareva's *Yashka: My Life as Peasant, Officer, and Exile* (1919). Aldershot, a municipal borough of Hampshire, south-west of London, is the site of the largest of all British military stations – dedicated, presumably, to preservation of the *status quo*.

on the fact that communities cannot reproduce themselves without plenty of women. Men are more largely dispensable, and are sacrificed accordingly.

WAS JOAN SUICIDAL?

These two abnormalities were the only ones that were irresistibly prepotent in Joan; and they brought her to the stake. Neither of them was peculiar to her. There was nothing peculiar about her except the vigor and scope of her mind and character, and the intensity of her vital energy. She was accused of a suicidal tendency; and it is a fact that when she attempted to escape from Beaurevoir Castle by jumping from a tower said to be sixty feet high, she took a risk beyond reason, though she recovered from the crash after a few days fasting. Her death was deliberately chosen as an alternative to life without liberty. In battle she challenged death as Wellington did at Waterloo, and as Nelson habitually did when he walked his quarter deck during his battles with all his decorations in full blaze. As neither Nelson nor Wellington nor any of those who have performed desperate feats, and preferred death to captivity, has been accused of suicidal mania, Joan need not be suspected of it. In the Beaurevoir affair there was more at stake than her freedom. She was distracted by the news that Compiègne was about to fall; and she was convinced that she could save it if only she could get free. Still, the leap was so perilous that her conscience was not quite easy about it; and she expressed this, as usual, by saying that Saint Catherine had forbidden her to do it, but forgave her afterwards for her disobedience.

JOAN SUMMED UP

We may accept and admire Joan, then, as a sane and shrewd country girl of extraordinary strength of mind and hardihood of body. Everything she did was thoroughly calculated; and though the process was so rapid that she was hardly conscious of it, and ascribed it all to her voices, she was a woman of policy and not of blind impulse. In war she was as much a realist as Napoleon: she had his eye for artillery and his knowledge of what it could do. She did not expect besieged cities to fall Jerichowise at the sound of her trumpet, but, like Wellington, adapted her methods of attack to the peculiarities of the defence; and she anticipated the Napoleonic calculation that if you only hold on long enough the other fellow will give in: for example, her final triumph at Orleans was achieved after her commander Dunois had sounded the retreat at the end of a day's fighting without a decision. She was never for a moment what so many romancers and playwrights have pretended: a romantic young lady. She was a thorough daughter of the soil in her peasantlike matter-of-factness and doggedness, and her acceptance of great lords and kings and prelates as such without idolatry or snobbery, seeing at a glance how much they were individually good for. She had the respectable countrywoman's sense of the value of public decency, and would not tolerate foul language and neglect of religious observances, nor allow disreputable women to hang about her soldiers. She had one pious ejaculation "En nom Dé!" ['In God's name!'] and one meaningless oath "Par mon martin" ['By my martin': French name for a donkey]; and this much swearing she allowed to the incorrigibly blasphemous La Hire equally with herself. The value of this prudery was so great in restoring the self-respect of the badly demoralized army that, like most of her policy, it justified itself as soundly calculated. She talked to and dealt with people of all classes, from laborers to kings, without embarrassment or affectation, and got them to do what she wanted when they were not afraid or corrupt. She could coax and she could hustle, her tongue having a soft side and a sharp edge. She was very capable: a born boss.

JOAN'S IMMATURITY AND IGNORANCE

All this, however, must be taken with one heavy qualification. She was only a girl in her teens. If we could think of her as a managing woman of fifty we should seize her type at once; for we have plenty of managing women among us of that age who illustrate perfectly the sort of person she would have become had she lived. But she, being only a lass when all is said, lacked their knowledge of men's vanities and of the weight and proportion of social forces. She knew nothing of iron hands in velvet gloves: she just used her fists. She thought political changes much easier than they are, and, like Mahomet in his innocence of any world but the tribal world, wrote letters to kings calling on them to make millennial rearrangements. Consequently it was only in the enterprizes that were really simple and compassable by swift physical force, like the coronation and the Orleans campaign, that she was successful.

Her want of academic education disabled her when she had to deal with such elaborately artificial structures as the great ecclesiastical and social institutions of the Middle Ages. She had a horror of heretics without suspecting that she was herself a heresiarch, one of the precursors of a schism that rent Europe in two, and cost centuries of bloodshed that is not yet staunched. She objected to foreigners on the sensible ground that they were not in their proper place in France; but she had no notion of how this brought her into conflict with Catholicism and Feudalism, both essentially international. She worked by common sense; and where scholarship was the only clue to institutions she was in the dark, and broke her shins against them, all the more rudely because of her enormous self-confidence, which made her the least cautious of human beings in civil affairs.

This combination of inept youth and academic ignorance with great natural capacity, push, courage, devotion, originality and oddity, fully accounts for all the facts in Joan's career, and makes her a credible historical and human phenomenon; but it clashes most discordantly both with the idolatrous romance that has grown up round her, and the belittling scepticism that reacts against that romance.

The Maid in Literature

English readers would probably like to know how these idolizations and reactions have affected the books they are most familiar with about Joan. There is the first part of the Shakespearean, or pseudo-Shakespearean trilogy of Henry VI, in which Joan is one of the leading characters. This portrait of Joan is not more authentic than the descriptions in the London papers of George Washington in 1780, of Napoleon in 1803, of the German Crown Prince in 1915, or of Lenin in 1917. It ends in mere scurrility. The impression left by it is that the playwright, having begun by an attempt to make Joan a beautiful and romantic figure, was told by his scandalized company that English patriotism would never stand a sympathetic representation of a French conqueror of English troops, and that unless he at once introduced all the old charges against Joan of being a sorceress and a harlot, and assumed her to be guilty of all of them, his play could not be produced. As likely as not, this is what actually happened: indeed there is only one other apparent way of accounting for the sympathetic representation of Joan as a heroine culminating in her eloquent appeal to the Duke of Burgundy [*Henry VI, Part I*, III: iii], followed by the blackguardly scurrility of the concluding scenes. That other way is to assume that the original play was wholly scurrilous, and that Shakespear touched up the earlier scenes. As the work belongs to a period at which he was only beginning his practice as a tinker of old works, before his own style was fully formed and hardened, it is impossible to verify this guess. His finger is not unmistakably evident in the play, which is poor and base in its moral tone; but he may have tried to redeem it from downright infamy by shedding a momentary glamor on the figure of The Maid.

When we jump over two centuries to Schiller, we find Die Jungfrau von Orleans [*The Maid of Orleans*, 1802] drowned in a witch's caldron of raging romance. Schiller's Joan has not a single point of contact with the real Joan, nor indeed with any mortal woman that ever walked this earth. There is really nothing to be said of his play but that it is not about Joan at all, and can hardly be said to pretend to be; for he makes her die on the battlefield, finding her burning unbearable. Before Schiller came Voltaire, who burlesqued Homer in a mock epic called La Pucelle [*The Virgin*, 1755, the name referring to Joan's village]. It is the fashion to dismiss this with virtuous indignation as an obscene libel; and I certainly cannot defend it against the charge of extravagant indecorum. But its purpose was not to depict Joan, but to kill with ridicule everything that Voltaire righteously hated in the institutions and fashions of his own day. He made Joan ridiculous, but not contemptible nor (comparatively) unchaste; and as he also made Homer and St Peter and St Denis and the brave Dunois ridiculous, and the other heroines of the poem very unchaste indeed, he may be said to have let Joan off very easily. But indeed the personal adventures of the characters are so outrageous, and so Homerically free from any pretence at or even possibility of historical veracity, that those who affect to take them seriously only make themselves Pecksniffian. Samuel Butler believed The Iliad to be a burlesque of Greek Jingoism and Greek religion, written by a hostage or a slave [*Humour of Homer*, 1892]; and La Pucelle makes Butler's theory almost convincing. Voltaire represents Agnes Sorel, the Dauphin's mistress, whom Joan never met, as a woman with a consuming passion for the chastest concubinal fidelity, whose fate it was to be continually falling into the hands of licentious foes and suffering the worst extremities of rapine. The combats in which Joan rides a flying donkey, or in which, taken unaware with no clothes on, she defends Agnes with her sword, and inflicts appropriate mutilations on her assailants, can be laughed at as they are intended to be without scruple; for no sane person could mistake them for sober history; and it may be that their ribald irreverence is more wholesome than the beglamored sentimentality of Schiller. Certainly Voltaire should not have asserted that Joan's father was a priest; but when he was out to *écraser l'infâme* [wipe out the disgrace] (the French Church) he stuck at nothing.

So far, the literary representations of The Maid were legendary. But the publication by [Jules] Quicherat in 1841 [*Procès de condamnation et de réhabilitation de Jeanne d'Arc*, 1841–9] of the reports of her trial and rehabilitation placed the subject on a new footing. These entirely realistic documents created a living interest in Joan which Voltaire's mock Homerics and Schiller's romantic nonsense missed. Typical products of that interest in America and England are the histories of Joan by Mark Twain [*Personal Recollections of Joan of Arc*, 1895] and Andrew Lang [*The Maid of France*, 1908]. Mark Twain was converted to downright worship of Joan directly by Quicherat. Later on, another man of genius, Anatole France, reacted against the Quicheratic wave of enthusiasm, and wrote a Life of Joan [*La Vie de Jeanne d'Arc*, 1908] in which he attributed Joan's ideas to clerical prompting and her military success to an adroit use of her by Dunois as a *mascotte*: in short, he denied that she had any serious military or political ability. At this Andrew saw red, and went for Anatole's scalp in a rival Life of her which should be read as a corrective to the other. Lang had no difficulty in shewing that Joan's ability was not an unnatural fiction to be explained away as an illusion manufactured by priests and soldiers, but a straightforward fact.

It has been lightly pleaded in explanation that Anatole France is a Parisian of the art world, into whose scheme of things the able, hardheaded, hardhanded female, though she dominates provincial France and business Paris, does not enter; whereas Lang was a Scot, and every Scot knows that the grey mare is as likely as not to be the better horse.[17] But this explanation does not convince me. I cannot believe that Anatole France does not know what everybody knows. I wish everybody knew all that he knows. One feels antipathies at work in his book. He is not anti-Joan; but he is anti-clerical, anti-mystic, and fundamentally unable to believe that there ever was any such person as the real Joan.

Mark Twain's Joan, skirted to the ground, and with as many petticoats as Noah's wife in a toy ark, is an attempt to combine Bayard with Esther Summerson from Bleak House[18] into an unimpeachable American school teacher in armor. Like Esther Summerson she makes her creator ridiculous,

---

17. Scots adage: 'The old grey mare she ain't what she used to be but she's better than what we'll get.'

18. Pierre du Terrail, Chevalier de Bayard, French military hero of knightly character, known as '*le chevalier sans peur et sans reproche*' ('the knight without fear

and yet, being the work of a man of genius, remains a credible human goodygoody in spite of her creator's infatuation. It is the description rather than the valuation that is wrong. Andrew Lang and Mark Twain are equally determined to make Joan a beautiful and most ladylike Victorian; but both of them recognize and insist on her capacity for leadership, though the Scots scholar is less romantic about it than the Mississippi pilot. But then Lang was, by lifelong professional habit, a critic of biographies rather than a biographer, whereas Mark Twain writes his biography frankly in the form of a romance.

PROTESTANT MISUNDERSTANDINGS OF THE MIDDLE AGES

They had, however, one disability in common. To understand Joan's history it is not enough to understand her character: you must understand her environment as well. Joan in a XIX–XX century environment is as incongruous a figure as she would appear were she to walk down Piccadilly today in her XV century armor. To see her in her proper perspective you must understand Christendom and the Catholic Church, the Holy Roman Empire and the Feudal System, as they existed and were understood in the Middle Ages. If you confuse the Middle Ages with the Dark Ages, and are in the habit of ridiculing your aunt for wearing "medieval clothes," meaning those in vogue in the eighteen-nineties, and are quite convinced that the world has progressed enormously, both morally and mechanically, since Joan's time, then you will never understand why Joan was burnt, much less feel that you might have voted for burning her yourself if you had been a member of the court that tried her; and until you feel that you know nothing essential about her.

That the Mississippi pilot should have broken down on this misunderstanding is natural enough. Mark Twain, the Innocent Abroad, who saw the lovely churches of the Middle Ages without a throb of emotion, author of A Yankee at the Court of King Arthur [British title of *A Connecticut Yankee in King Arthur's Court*, 1889], in which the heroes and heroines of medieval chivalry are guys seen through the eyes of a street arab, was clearly out of court from the beginning. Andrew Lang was better read;

---

and without reproach'), distinguished himself in the Italian campaigns of Charles VIII, Louis XII and Francis I. Esther Summerson, in *Bleak House*, is the supposed orphan whom John Jarndyce takes into his house and later into his heart.

but, like Walter Scott, he enjoyed medieval history as a string of [Scottish] Border romances rather than as the record of a high European civilization based on a catholic faith. Both of them were baptized as Protestants, and impressed by all their schooling and most of their reading with the belief that Catholic bishops who burnt heretics were persecutors capable of any villainy; that all heretics were Albigensians[19] or Husites or Jews or Protestants of the highest character; and that the Inquisition was a Chamber of Horrors invented expressly and exclusively for such burnings. Accordingly we find them representing Peter Cauchon, Bishop of Beauvais, the judge who sent Joan to the stake, as an unconscionable scoundrel, and all the questions put to her as "traps" to ensnare and destroy her. And they assume unhesitatingly that the two or three score of canons and doctors of law and divinity who sat with Cauchon as assessors, were exact reproductions of him on slightly less elevated chairs and with a different headdress.

COMPARATIVE FAIRNESS OF JOAN'S TRIAL

The truth is that Cauchon was threatened and insulted by the English for being too considerate to Joan. A recent French writer denies that Joan was burnt [Émile Grillot de Givry, *La Survivance . . . de Jeanne d'Arc*, 1914] and holds that Cauchon spirited her away and burnt somebody or something else in her place, and that the pretender who subsequently personated her at Orleans and elsewhere was not a pretender but the real authentic Joan. He is able to cite Cauchon's pro-Joan partiality in support of his view. As to the assessors, the objection to them is not that they were a row of uniform rascals, but that they were political partisans of Joan's enemies. This is a valid objection to all such trials; but in the absence of neutral tribunals they are unavoidable. A trial by Joan's French partisans would have been as unfair as the trial by her French opponents; and an equally mixed tribunal would have produced a deadlock. Such recent trials as those of Edith Cavell[20] by a German tribunal and Roger Casement by an English one

19. Anti-sacerdotal sects in the south of France in the twelfth and thirteenth centuries, who revolted against the established Church and held that matter was intrinsically evil.
20. English nurse who was First Matron of a Brussels medical institution but became a Red Cross nurse in 1914. She was arrested by the Germans for assisting some 200 soldiers of various nationalities, from November 1914 to July 1915, to escape across the Dutch border. She admitted her actions and was condemned to death.

were open to the same objection; but they went forward to the death nevertheless, because neutral tribunals were not available. Edith, like Joan, was an arch heretic: in the middle of the war she declared before the world that "Patriotism is not enough." She nursed enemies back to health, and assisted their prisoners to escape, making it abundantly clear that she would help any fugitive or distressed person without asking whose side he was on, and acknowledging no distinction before Christ between Tommy and Jerry and Pitou the *poilu* [the shaggy one].[21] Well might Edith have wished that she could bring the Middle Ages back, and have fifty civilians, learned in the law or vowed to the service of God, to support two skilled judges in trying her case according to the Catholic law of Christendom, and to argue it out with her at sitting after sitting for many weeks. The modern military Inquisition was not so squeamish. It shot her out of hand; and her countrymen, seeing in this a good opportunity for lecturing the enemy on his intolerance, put up a statue to her [in St Martin's Place, London], but took particular care not to inscribe on the pedestal "Patriotism is not enough," for which omission, and the lie it implies, they will need Edith's intercession when they are themselves brought to judgment, if any heavenly power thinks such moral cowards capable of pleading to an intelligible indictment.

The point need be no further labored. Joan was persecuted essentially as she would be persecuted today. The change from burning to hanging or shooting may strike us as a change for the better. The change from careful trial under ordinary law to recklessly summary military terrorism may strike us as a change for the worse. But as far as toleration is concerned the trial and execution in Rouen in 1431 might have been an event of today; and we may charge our consciences accordingly. If Joan had to be dealt with by us in London she would be treated with no more toleration than Miss Sylvia Pankhurst,[22] or the Peculiar People, or the parents who keep their children from the elementary school, or any of the others who cross the line we have to draw, rightly or wrongly, between the tolerable and the intolerable.

21. Names given respectively to British, German or French private soldiers.
22. English feminist and journalist, frequently imprisoned for militant suffrage activities.

Joan not tried as a Political Offender

Besides, Joan's trial was not, like Casement's, a national political trial. Ecclesiastical courts and the courts of the Inquisition (Joan was tried by a combination of the two) were Courts Christian: that is, international courts; and she was tried, not as a traitress, but as a heretic, blasphemer, sorceress and idolater. Her alleged offences were not political offences against England, nor against the Burgundian faction in France, but against God and against the common morality of Christendom. And although the idea we call Nationalism was so foreign to the medieval conception of Christian society that it might almost have been directly charged against Joan as an additional heresy, yet it was not so charged; and it is unreasonable to suppose that the political bias of a body of Frenchmen like the assessors would on this point have run strongly in favor of the English foreigners (even if they had been making themselves particularly agreeable in France instead of just the contrary) against a Frenchwoman who had vanquished them.

The tragic part of the trial was that Joan, like most prisoners tried for anything but the simplest breaches of the ten commandments, did not understand what they were accusing her of. She was much more like Mark Twain than like Peter Cauchon. Her attachment to the Church was very different from the Bishop's, and does not, in fact, bear close examination from his point of view. She delighted in the solaces the Church offers to sensitive souls: to her, confession and communion were luxuries beside which the vulgar pleasures of the senses were trash. Her prayers were wonderful conversations with her three saints. Her piety seemed superhuman to the formally dutiful people whose religion was only a task to them. But when the Church was not offering her her favorite luxuries, but calling on her to accept its interpretation of God's will, and to sacrifice her own, she flatly refused, and made it clear that her notion of a Catholic Church was one in which the Pope was Pope Joan. How could the Church tolerate that, when it had just destroyed Hus, and had watched the career of [John] Wycliffe[23] with a growing anger that would have brought him, too, to the stake, had he not died a natural death before the wrath fell on

---

23. English religious reformer, who opposed the doctrine of transsubstantiation, resulting in a denial to him of priestly powers and a forced retirement from his post at Oxford. He was a forerunner of the Protestant Reformation, and initiator of the first full translation of the Bible.

him in his grave? Neither Hus nor Wycliffe was as bluntly defiant as Joan: both were reformers of the Church like Luther; whilst Joan, like Mrs Eddy, was quite prepared to supersede St Peter as the rock on which the Church was built, and, like Mahomet, was always ready with a private revelation from God to settle every question and fit every occasion.

The enormity of Joan's pretension was proved by her own unconsciousness of it, which we call her innocence, and her friends called her simplicity. Her solutions of the problems presented to her seemed, and indeed mostly were, the plainest common sense, and their revelation to her by her Voices was to her a simple matter of fact. How could plain common sense and simple fact seem to her to be that hideous thing, heresy? When rival prophetesses came into the field, she was down on them at once for liars and humbugs; but she never thought of them as heretics. She was in a state of invincible ignorance as to the Church's view; and the Church could not tolerate her pretensions without either waiving its authority or giving her a place beside the Trinity during her lifetime and in her teens, which was unthinkable. Thus an irresistible force met an immovable obstacle, and developed the heat that consumed poor Joan.

Mark and Andrew would have shared her innocence and her fate had they been dealt with by the Inquisition: that is why their accounts of the trial are as absurd as hers might have been could she have written one. All that can be said for their assumption that Cauchon was a vulgar villain, and that the questions put to Joan were traps, is that it has the support of the inquiry which rehabilitated her twentyfive years later. But this rehabilitation was as corrupt as the contrary proceeding applied to Cromwell by our Restoration reactionaries.[24] Cauchon had been dug up, and his body thrown into the common sewer. Nothing was easier than to accuse him of cozenage, and declare the whole trial void on that account. That was what everybody wanted, from Charles the Victorious, whose credit was bound up with The Maid's, to the patriotic Nationalist populace, who idolized Joan's memory. The English were gone; and a verdict in their favor would have been an outrage on the throne and on the patriotism which Joan had set on foot.

We have none of these overwhelming motives of political convenience and popularity to bias us. For us the first trial stands valid; and the rehabilitation would be negligible but for the mass of sincere testimony it

---

24. After the Restoration of Charles II, Cromwell's embalmed remains were removed from the tomb and hung up at Tyburn. His head was stuck on a pole atop Westminster Hall, where it remained until the end of Charles's reign.

produced as to Joan's engaging personal character. The question then arises: how did The Church get over the verdict at the first trial when it canonized Joan five hundred years later?

THE CHURCH UNCOMPROMISED BY ITS AMENDS

Easily enough. In the Catholic Church, far more than in law, there is no wrong without a remedy. It does not defer to Joanesque private judgment as such, the supremacy of private judgment for the individual being the quintessence of Protestantism; nevertheless it finds a place for private judgment *in excelsis* [in the highest] by admitting that the highest wisdom may come as a divine revelation to an individual. On sufficient evidence it will declare that individual a saint. Thus, as revelation may come by way of an enlightenment of the private judgment no less than by the words of a celestial personage appearing in a vision, a saint may be defined as a person of heroic virtue whose private judgment is privileged. Many innovating saints, notably Francis and Clare,[25] have been in conflict with the Church during their lives, and have thus raised the question whether they were heretics or saints. Francis might have gone to the stake had he lived longer. It is therefore by no means impossible for a person to be excommunicated as a heretic, and on further consideration canonized as a saint. Excommunication by a provincial ecclesiastical court is not one of the acts for which the Church claims infallibility. Perhaps I had better inform my Protestant readers that the famous Dogma of Papal Infallibility[26] is by far the most modest pretension of the kind in existence. Compared with our infallible democracies, our infallible medical councils, our infallible astronomers, our infallible judges, and our infallible parliaments, the Pope is on his knees in the dust confessing his ignorance before the throne of God, asking only that as to certain historical matters on which he has clearly more sources of

25. St Francis of Assisi was the founder of the Order of Franciscans. In the first general chapter meeting of the Order in 1217, many of the friars agitated for more 'practicalness'. St Clare of Assisi founded the Poor Clares or Minoresses, inspired by the preaching of St Francis. Though she insisted that the sisters should possess no property, Popes Gregory IX and Innocent IV published recensions of the rule of poverty permitting the holding of property in common.
26. This dogma that the Pope cannot err in defining doctrines of faith or morals was decreed at the Vatican Council (18 July 1870) in the pontificate of Pope Pius IX.

information open to him than anyone else his decision shall be taken as final. The Church may, and perhaps some day will, canonize Galileo without compromising such infallibility as it claims for the Pope, if not without compromising the infallibility claimed for the Book of Joshua by simple souls whose rational faith in more important things has become bound up with a quite irrational faith in the chronicle of Joshua's campaigns as a treatise on physics.[27] Therefore the Church will probably not canonize Galileo yet awhile, though it might do worse. But it has been able to canonize Joan without any compromise at all. She never doubted that the sun went round the earth: she had seen it do so too often.

Still, there was a great wrong done to Joan and to the conscience of the world by her burning. *Tout comprendre, c'est tout pardonner*, which is the Devil's sentimentality, cannot excuse it. When we have admitted that the tribunal was not only honest and legal, but exceptionally merciful in respect of sparing Joan the torture which was customary when she was obdurate as to taking the oath, and that Cauchon was far more self-disciplined and conscientious both as priest and lawyer than any English judge ever dreams of being in a political case in which his party and class prejudices are involved, the human fact remains that the burning of Joan of Arc was a horror, and that a historian who would defend it would defend anything. The final criticism of its physical side is implied in the refusal of the Marquesas islanders [Polynesian cannibals] to be persuaded that the English did not eat Joan. Why, they ask, should anyone take the trouble to roast a human being except with that object? They cannot conceive its being a pleasure. As we have no answer for them that is not shameful to us, let us blush for our more complicated and pretentious savagery before we proceed to unravel the business further, and see what other lessons it contains for us.

CRUELTY, MODERN AND MEDIEVAL

First, let us get rid of the notion that the mere physical cruelty of the burning has any special significance. Joan was burnt just as dozens of less interesting heretics were burnt in her time. Christ, in being crucified, only shared the fate of thousands of forgotten malefactors. They have no pre-eminence in mere physical pain: much more horrible executions than theirs

27. In the battle of the Israelites against the Amorites, Joshua's prayer was fulfilled that the Sun and Moon would stand still (Joshua 10: 12).

are on record, to say nothing of the agonies of so-called natural death at its worst.

Joan was burnt more than five hundred years ago. More than three hundred years later: that is, only about a hundred years before I was born, a woman was burnt on Stephen's Green in my native city of Dublin for coining,[28] which was held to be treason. In my preface to the recent volume on English Prisons under Local Government, by Sidney and Beatrice Webb, I have mentioned that when I was already a grown man I saw Richard Wagner conduct two concerts, and that when Richard Wagner was a young man he saw and avoided a crowd of people hastening to see a soldier broken on the wheel by the more cruel of the two ways of carrying out that hideous method of execution. Also that the penalty of hanging, drawing, and quartering, unmentionable in its details, was abolished so recently that there are men living who have been sentenced to it. We are still flogging criminals, and clamoring for more flogging. Not even the most sensationally frightful of these atrocities inflicted on its victim the misery, degradation, and conscious waste and loss of life suffered in our modern prisons, especially the model ones, without, as far as I can see, rousing any more compunction than the burning of heretics did in the Middle Ages. We have not even the excuse of getting some fun out of our prisons as the Middle Ages did out of their stakes and wheels and gibbets. Joan herself judged this matter when she had to choose between imprisonment and the stake, and chose the stake. And thereby she deprived The Church of the plea that it was guiltless of her death, which was the work of the secular arm. The Church should have confined itself to excommunicating her. There it was within its rights: she had refused to accept its authority or comply with its conditions; and it could say with truth "You

---

28. Judicial incineration of bodies following death by hanging (apparently rooted in superstitions relating to witchcraft, the sentence being confined to female felons) continued in Ireland until as late as 1784. The Dublin *Hibernian Journal* of 24 March 1783 reported such a sentence carried out in the execution two days earlier at Gallows-green, Kilmainham, of Mary Purfield for the crime of arson. On 23 August 1784 the *Hibernian Journal* noted the execution, on Stephen's-green on 21 August, of Mary Fairfield, a young woman who had conspired with her lover, Constable Funt, in the stabbing to death of his wife. 'After the poor wretch was strangled', the journal reported, 'the body was thrown into the fire, to fulfil the sentence'. One result of the sentence was deprival of the conventional ceremony by families of giving the body a 'wake'. (See Brian Henry, *Crime, Law Enforcement and Punishment in Dublin 1780–95*. Ph.D. dissertation, Trinity College, Dublin, 1992.)

are not one of us: go forth and find the religion that suits you, or found one for yourself." It had no right to say "You may return to us now that you have recanted; but you shall stay in a dungeon all the rest of your life." Unfortunately, The Church did not believe that there was any genuine soul-saving religion outside itself; and it was deeply corrupted, as all the Churches were and still are, by primitive Calibanism (in Browning's sense[29]), or the propitiation of a dreaded deity by suffering and sacrifice. Its method was not cruelty for cruelty's sake, but cruelty for the salvation of Joan's soul. Joan, however, believed that the saving of her soul was her own business, and not that of *les gens d'église* [the clergy]. By using that term as she did, mistrustfully and contemptuously, she announced herself as, in germ, an anti-Clerical as thoroughgoing as Voltaire or Anatole France. Had she said in so many words "To the dustbin with the Church Militant and its blackcoated officials: I recognize only the Church Triumphant in heaven," she would hardly have put her view more plainly.

Catholic Anti-Clericalism

I must not leave it to be inferred here that one cannot be an anti-Clerical and a good Catholic too. All the reforming Popes have been vehement anti-Clericals, veritable scourges of the clergy. All the great Orders arose from dissatisfaction with the priests: that of the Franciscans with priestly snobbery, that of the Dominicans with priestly laziness and Laodiceanism, that of the Jesuits with priestly apathy and ignorance and indiscipline. The most bigoted Ulster Orangeman or Leicester Low Church bourgeois (as described by Mr Henry Nevinson[30]) is a mere [Junius] Gallio[31] compared to Machiavelli, who, though no Protestant, was a fierce anti-Clerical. Any Catholic may, and many Catholics do, denounce any priest or body of priests, as lazy, drunken, idle, dissolute, and unworthy of their great Church and their function as the pastors of their flocks of human souls. But

29. In Browning's 'Caliban upon Setebos; or, Natural Theology in the Island' (1864) Browning uses the slave Caliban of Shakespeare's *The Tempest* to depict a savage meditating on his anthropomorphic god, Setebos, who has all the human vices of jealousy, envy, maliciousness and, above all, vengefulness.
30. Journalist and essayist, who became a celebrated foreign and war correspondent.
31. As proconsul (c. AD 51–5) under Emperor Claudius, he dismissed the charge brought by the Jews against the apostle Paul (Acts 18).

to say that the souls of the people are no business of the Churchmen is to go a step further, a step across the Rubicon.[32] Joan virtually took that step.

CATHOLICISM NOT YET CATHOLIC ENOUGH

And so, if we admit, as we must, that the burning of Joan was a mistake, we must broaden Catholicism sufficiently to include her in its charter. Our Churches must admit that no official organization of mortal men whose vocation does not carry with it extraordinary mental powers (and this is all that any Church Militant can in the face of fact and history pretend to be), can keep pace with the private judgment of persons of genius except when, by a very rare accident, the genius happens to be Pope, and not even then unless he is an exceedingly overbearing Pope. The Churches must learn humility as well as teach it. The Apostolic Succession cannot be secured or confined by the laying on of hands: the tongues of fire have descended on heathens and outcasts too often for that, leaving anointed Churchmen to scandalize History as worldly rascals. When the Church Militant behaves as if it were already the Church Triumphant,[33] it makes these appalling blunders about Joan and [Giordano] Bruno[34] and Galileo and the rest which make it so difficult for a Freethinker to join it; and a Church which has no place for Freethinkers: nay, which does not inculcate and encourage free-thinking with a complete belief that thought, when really free, must by its own law take the path that leads to The Church's bosom, not only has no future in modern culture, but obviously has no faith in the valid science of its own tenets, and is guilty of the heresy that theology and science are two different and opposite impulses, rivals for human allegiance.

I have before me the letter of a Catholic priest [Joseph Leonard]. "In your play," he writes, "I see the dramatic presentation of the conflict of the Regal,

32. A small river in north Italy crossed by Caesar in 49 BC, which began the civil war with Pompey. Thus, to 'cross the Rubicon' means to commit oneself to a final, irrevocable action.
33. The Church Militant consists of the whole community of living believers, 'waging the war of faith' against 'the world, the flesh, and the devil'. The Church Triumphant consists of the dead who, having fought, triumphed and, where needed, atoned in purgatory for sins, have attained their reward in Heaven.
34. Italian philosopher, whose dialogue *Cena de la Ceneri* (*Ash Wednesday Conversation*) (1584) was devoted to an exposition of the Copernican astrological system. He was brought to Rome in 1593, imprisoned, excommunicated and in 1600 burned at the stake.

sacerdotal, and Prophetical powers, in which Joan was crushed. To me it is not the victory of any one of them over the others that will bring peace and the Reign of the Saints in the Kingdom of God, but their fruitful interaction in a costly but noble state of tension." The Pope himself could not put it better; nor can I. We must accept the tension, and maintain it nobly without letting ourselves be tempted to relieve it by burning the thread. This is Joan's lesson to The Church; and its formulation by the hand of a priest emboldens me to claim that her canonization was a magnificently Catholic gesture as the canonization of a Protestant saint by the Church of Rome. But its special value and virtue cannot be apparent until it is known and understood as such. If any simple priest for whom this is too hard a saying tells me that it was not so intended, I shall remind him that the Church is in the hands of God, and not, as simple priests imagine, God in the hands of the Church; so if he answers too confidently for God's intentions he may be asked "Hast thou entered into the springs of the sea? or hast thou walked in the recesses of the deep?" And Joan's own answer is also the answer of old: "Though He slay me, yet will I trust in Him; *but I will maintain my own ways before Him*" [Job 13: 15].

The Law of Change is the Law of God

When Joan maintained her own ways she claimed, like Job, that there was not only God and the Church to be considered, but the Word made Flesh: that is, the unaveraged individual, representing life possibly at its highest actual human evolution and possibly at its lowest, but never at its merely mathematical average. Now there is no deification of the democratic average in the theory of the Church: it is an avowed hierarchy in which the members are sifted until at the end of the process an individual stands supreme as the Vicar of Christ. But when the process is examined it appears that its successive steps of selection and election are of the superior by the inferior (the cardinal vice of democracy), with the result that great popes are as rare and accidental as great kings, and that it has sometimes been safer for an aspirant to the Chair and the Keys to pass as a moribund dotard than as an energetic saint. At best very few popes have been canonized, or could be without letting down the standard of sanctity set by the self-elected saints.

No other result could have been reasonably expected; for it is not possible that an official organization of the spiritual needs of millions of men and women, mostly poor and ignorant, should compete successfully in the selection of its principals with the direct choice of the Holy Ghost as it flashes with unerring aim upon the individual. Nor can any College of Cardinals pray effectively that its choice may be inspired. The conscious prayer of the inferior may be that his choice may light on a greater than himself; but the subconscious intention of his self-preserving individuality must be to find a trustworthy servant for his own purposes. The saints and prophets, though they may be accidentally in this or that official position or rank, are always really self-selected, like Joan. And since neither Church nor State, by the secular necessities of its constitution, can guarantee even the recognition of such self-chosen missions, there is nothing for us but to make it a point of honor to privilege heresy to the last bearable degree on the simple ground that all evolution in thought and conduct must at first appear as heresy and misconduct. In short, though all society is founded on intolerance, all improvement is founded on tolerance, or the recognition of the fact that the law of evolution is Ibsen's law of change.[35] And as the law of God in any sense of the word which can now command a faith proof against science is a law of evolution, it follows that the law of God is a law of change, and that when the Churches set themselves against change as such, they are setting themselves against the law of God.

CREDULITY, MODERN AND MEDIEVAL

When [John] Abernethy, the famous doctor, was asked why he indulged himself with all the habits he warned his patients against as unhealthy, he replied that his business was that of a direction post, which points out the way to a place, but does not go thither itself. He might have added that neither does it compel the traveler to go thither, nor prevent him from seeking some other way. Unfortunately our clerical direction posts always do coerce the traveler when they have the political power to do so. When the Church was a temporal as well as a spiritual power, and for long after to the full extent to which it could control or influence the temporal power, it enforced conformity by persecutions that were all the more ruthless because their intention was so excellent. Today, when the doctor has succeeded to the priest, and can do practically what he likes with parliament and the press through the blind faith in him which has succeeded to the far more critical faith in the parson, legal compulsion to take the

---

35. That is, man is constantly outgrowing his ideals and replacing them with new ones.

doctor's prescription, however poisonous, is carried to an extent that would have horrified the Inquisition and staggered Archbishop Laud. Our credulity is grosser than that of the Middle Ages, because the priest had no such direct pecuniary interest in our sins as the doctor has in our diseases: he did not starve when all was well with his flock, nor prosper when they were perishing, as our private commercial doctors must. Also the medieval cleric believed that something extremely unpleasant would happen to him after death if he was unscrupulous, a belief now practically extinct among persons receiving a dogmatically materialist education. Our professional corporations are Trade Unions without souls to be damned; and they will soon drive us to remind them that they have bodies to be kicked. The Vatican was never soulless: at worst it was a political conspiracy to make the Church supreme temporally as well as spiritually. Therefore the question raised by Joan's burning is a burning question still, though the penalties involved are not so sensational. That is why I am probing it. If it were only an historical curiosity I would not waste my readers' time and my own on it for five minutes.

TOLERATION, MODERN AND MEDIEVAL

The more closely we grapple with it the more difficult it becomes. At first sight we are disposed to repeat that Joan should have been excommunicated and then left to go her own way, though she would have protested vehemently against so cruel a deprivation of her spiritual food; for confession, absolution, and the body of her Lord were first necessaries of life to her. Such a spirit as Joan's might have got over that difficulty as the Church of England got over the Bulls of Pope Leo,[36] making a Church of her own, and affirming it to be the temple of the true and original faith from which her persecutors had strayed. But as such a proceeding was, in the eyes of both Church and State at that time, a spreading of damnation and anarchy, its toleration involved a greater strain on faith in freedom than political and ecclesiastical human nature could bear. It is easy to say that the Church should have waited for the alleged evil results instead of assuming that they would occur, and what they would be. That sounds

36. Leo X's bull of 3 January 1521 excommunicated Luther and directed Charles V, Emperor of Germany, and the Holy Roman Empire, to take action against heresy. Ironically, by bull of 11 October 1521, the title 'Defender of the Faith' was conferred on Henry VIII.

simple enough; but if a modern Public Health Authority were to leave people entirely to their own devices in the matter of sanitation, saying, "We have nothing to do with drainage or your views about drainage; but if you catch smallpox or typhus we will prosecute you and have you punished very severely like the authorities in Butler's Erewhon," it would either be removed to the County Asylum or reminded that A's neglect of sanitation may kill the child of B two miles off, or start an epidemic in which the most conscientious sanitarians may perish.

We must face the fact that society is founded on intolerance. There are glaring cases of the abuse of intolerance; but they are quite as characteristic of our own age as of the Middle Ages. The typical modern example and contrast is compulsory inoculation replacing what was virtually compulsory baptism. But compulsion to inoculate is objected to as a crudely unscientific and mischievous anti-sanitary quackery, not in the least because we think it wrong to compel people to protect their children from disease. Its opponents would make it a crime, and will probably succeed in doing so; and that will be just as intolerant as making it compulsory. Neither the Pasteurians nor their opponents the Sanitarians would leave parents free to bring up their children naked, though that course also has some plausible advocates. We may prate of toleration as we will; but society must always draw a line somewhere between allowable conduct and insanity or crime, in spite of the risk of mistaking sages for lunatics and saviors for blasphemers. We must persecute, even to the death; and all we can do to mitigate the danger of persecution is, first, to be very careful what we persecute, and second, to bear in mind that unless there is a large liberty to shock conventional people, and a well-informed sense of the value of originality, individuality, and eccentricity, the result will be apparent stagnation covering a repression of evolutionary forces which will eventually explode with extravagant and probably destructive violence.

VARIABILITY OF TOLERATION

The degree of tolerance attainable at any moment depends on the strain under which society is maintaining its cohesion. In war, for instance, we suppress the gospels and put Quakers in prison, muzzle the newspapers, and make it a serious offence to shew a light at night. Under the strain of invasion the French Government in 1792 struck off 4000 heads, mostly on grounds that would not in time of settled peace have provoked any Government to chloroform a dog; and in 1920 the British Government slaughtered and burnt in Ireland to persecute the advocates [Irish Republicans] of a constitutional change which it had presently to effect itself.[37] Later on the Fascisti in Italy did everything that the Black and Tans did in Ireland,[38] with some grotesquely ferocious variations, under the strain of an unskilled attempt at industrial revolution by Socialists who understood Socialism even less than Capitalists understand Capitalism. In the United States an incredibly savage persecution of Russians took place during the scare spread by the Russian Bolshevik revolution after 1917. These instances could easily be multiplied; but they are enough to shew that between a maximum of indulgent toleration and a ruthlessly intolerant Terrorism there is a scale through which toleration is continually rising or falling, and that there was not the smallest ground for the self-complacent conviction of the XIX century that it was more tolerant than the XV, or that such an event as the execution of Joan could not possibly occur in what we call our own more enlightened times. Thousands of women, each of them a thousand times less dangerous and terrifying to our Governments than Joan was to the Government of her day, have within the last ten years been slaughtered, starved to death, burnt out of house and home, and what not that Persecution and Terror could do to them, in the course of Crusades far more tyrannically pretentious than the medieval Crusades which proposed nothing more hyperbolical than the rescue of the Holy Sepulchre from the Saracens. The Inquisition, with its English equivalent the Star Chamber,[39] are gone in the sense that their names are now disused; but can any of the modern substitutes for the Inquisition, the Special Tribunals and Commissions, the punitive expeditions, the suspensions of the Habeas Corpus Act, the proclamations of martial law and of minor states of siege, and the rest of them, claim that their victims have as fair a trial, as well-considered a body of law to govern their cases, or as conscientious a judge to insist on strict legality of procedure as Joan had from the Inquisition and from the spirit of the Middle Ages even when her country was under the heaviest

37. Under a treaty of 1921 with the Irish, the British Government was obliged to create an Irish Free State of twenty-six counties, excluding the six counties of Ulster.

38. The Black and Tans were undisciplined, newly demobilized soldiers recruited by Britain's Chief Secretary for Ireland for the Royal Irish Constabulary. The name denoted the mixed colours of the uniforms of the demobbed men. See also Vol. 1, pp. 240–41.

39. An ancient English high court of wide jurisdiction composed largely of the King's Privy Council; abolished in 1641 by the Long Parliament.

strain of civil and foreign war? From us she would have had no trial and no law except a Defence of The Realm Act suspending all law;[40] and for judge she would have had, at best, a bothered major, and at worst a promoted advocate in ermine and scarlet to whom the scruples of a trained ecclesiastic like Cauchon would seem ridiculous and ungentlemanly.

THE CONFLICT BETWEEN GENIUS AND DISCIPLINE

Having thus brought the matter home to ourselves, we may now consider the special feature of Joan's mental constitution which made her so unmanageable. What is to be done on the one hand with rulers who will not give any reason for their orders, and on the other with people who cannot understand the reasons when they are given? The government of the world, political, industrial, and domestic, has to be carried on mostly by the giving and obeying of orders under just these conditions. "Dont argue: do as you are told" has to be said not only to children and soldiers, but practically to everybody. Fortunately most people do not want to argue: they are only too glad to be saved the trouble of thinking for themselves. And the ablest and most independent thinkers are content to understand their own special department. In other departments they will unhesitatingly ask for and accept the instructions of a policeman or the advice of a tailor without demanding or desiring explanations.

Nevertheless, there must be some ground for attaching authority to an order. A child will obey its parents, a soldier his officer, a philosopher a railway porter, and a workman a foreman, all without question, because it is generally accepted that those who give the orders understand what they are about, and are duly authorized and even obliged to give them, and because, in the practical emergencies of daily life, there is no time for lessons and explanations, or for arguments as to their validity. Such obediences are as necessary to the continuous operation of our social system as the revolutions of the earth are to the succession of night and day. But they are not so spontaneous as they seem: they have to be very carefully arranged and maintained. A bishop will defer to and obey a king; but let a curate venture to give him an order, however necessary and sensible, and the bishop will forget his cloth and damn the curate's impudence. The

---

40. An act known by the acronym DORA, instituted in 1914, curbed liberty of speech through various measures granted to the government by Parliament, which allowed for exclusionary jurisdiction by various tribunals.

more obedient a man is to accredited authority the more jealous he is of allowing any unauthorized person to order him about.

With all this in mind, consider the career of Joan. She was a village girl, in authority over sheep and pigs, dogs and chickens, and to some extent over her father's hired laborers when he hired any, but over no one else on earth. Outside the farm she had no authority, no prestige, no claim to the smallest deference. Yet she ordered everybody about, from her uncle to the king, the archbishop, and the military General Staff. Her uncle obeyed her like a sheep, and took her to the castle of the local commander, who, on being ordered about, tried to assert himself, but soon collapsed and obeyed. And so on up to the king, as we have seen. This would have been unbearably irritating even if her orders had been offered as rational solutions of the desperate difficulties in which her social superiors found themselves just then. But they were not so offered. Nor were they offered as the expression of Joan's arbitrary will. It was never "I say so," but always "God says so."

JOAN AS THEOCRAT

Leaders who take that line have no trouble with some people, and no end of trouble with others. They need never fear a lukewarm reception. Either they are messengers of God, or they are blasphemous impostors. In the Middle Ages the general belief in witchcraft greatly intensified this contrast, because when an apparent miracle happened (as in the case of the wind changing at Orleans) it proved the divine mission to the credulous, and proved a contract with the devil to the sceptical. All through, Joan had to depend on those who accepted her as an incarnate angel against those who added to an intense resentment of her presumption a bigoted abhorrence of her as a witch. To this abhorrence we must add the extreme irritation of those who did not believe in the voices, and regarded her as a liar and impostor. It is hard to conceive anything more infuriating to a statesman or a military commander, or to a court favorite, than to be overruled at every turn, or to be robbed of the ear of the reigning sovereign, by an impudent young upstart practising on the credulity of the populace and the vanity and silliness of an immature prince by exploiting a few of those lucky coincidences which pass as miracles with uncritical people. Not only were the envy, snobbery, and competitive ambition of the baser natures exacerbated by Joan's success, but among the friendly ones that were clever enough to be critical a quite reasonable scepticism and mistrust of her ability, founded on a fair observation of her obvious ignorance and temerity, were at work against her. And as she met all remonstrances and all criticisms, not with arguments or persuasion, but with a flat appeal to the authority of God and a claim to be in God's special confidence, she must have seemed, to all who were not infatuated by her, so insufferable that nothing but an unbroken chain of overwhelming successes in the military and political field could have saved her from the wrath that finally destroyed her.

Unbroken Success essential in Theocracy

To forge such a chain she needed to be the King, the Archbishop of Rheims, the Bastard of Orleans, and herself into the bargain; and that was impossible. From the moment when she failed to stimulate Charles to follow up his coronation with a swoop on Paris she was lost. The fact that she insisted on this whilst the king and the rest timidly and foolishly thought they could square the Duke of Burgundy, and effect a combination with him against the English,[41] made her a terrifying nuisance to them; and from that time onward she could do nothing but prowl about the battle-fields waiting for some lucky chance to sweep the captains into a big move. But it was to the enemy that the chance came: she was taken prisoner by the Burgundians fighting before Compiègne, and at once discovered that she had not a friend in the political world. Had she escaped she would probably have fought on until the English were gone, and then had to shake the dust of the court off her feet, and retire to Domrémy as [Giuseppe] Garibaldi[42] had to retire to Caprera.

Modern Distortions of Joan's History

This, I think, is all that we can now pretend to say about the prose of Joan's career. The romance of her rise, the tragedy of her execution, and the comedy of the attempts of posterity to make amends for that execution,

41. Charles and Philip the Good, Duc of Burgundy, who had until this time allied himself with Henry V of England, finally settled their differences in the Treaty of Arras four years after Joan's death.
42. Italian statesman and patriot, who frequently retired to his home on the island of Caprera when faced with reversals.

belong to my play and not to my preface, which must be confined to a sober essay on the facts. That such an essay is badly needed can be ascertained by examining any of our standard works of reference. They give accurately enough the facts about the visit to Vaucouleurs, the annunciation to Charles at Chinon, the raising of the siege of Orleans and the subsequent battles, the coronation at Rheims, the capture at Compiègne, and the trial and execution at Rouen, with their dates and the names of the people concerned; but they all break down on the melodramatic legend of the wicked bishop and the entrapped maiden and the rest of it. It would be far less misleading if they were wrong as to the facts, and right in their view of the facts. As it is, they illustrate the too little considered truth that the fashion in which we think changes like the fashion of our clothes, and that it is difficult, if not impossible, for most people to think otherwise than in the fashion of their own period.

HISTORY ALWAYS OUT OF DATE

This, by the way, is why children are never taught contemporary history. Their history books deal with periods of which the thinking has passed out of fashion, and the circumstances no longer apply to active life. For example, they are taught history about Washington, and told lies about Lenin. In Washington's time they were told lies (the same lies) about Washington, and taught history about Cromwell. In the XV and XVI centuries they were told lies about Joan, and by this time might very well be told the truth about her. Unfortunately the lies did not cease when the political circumstances became obsolete. The Reformation, which Joan had unconsciously anticipated, kept the questions which arose in her case burning up to our own day (you can see plenty of the burnt houses[43] still in Ireland), with the result that Joan has remained the subject of anti-Clerical lies, of specifically Protestant lies, and of Roman Catholic evasions of her unconscious Protestantism. The truth sticks in our throats with all the sauces it is served with: it will never go down until we take it without any sauce at all.

---

43. Many Irish country houses (including the family home of Charlotte Shaw) were burned, first by the Black and Tans in the Anglo-Irish War, and later by the Republicans in the Civil War (1922–3).

The Real Joan not Marvelous Enough for Us

But even in its simplicity, the faith demanded by Joan is one which the anti-metaphysical temper of XIX century civilization, which remains powerful in England and America, and is tyrannical in France, contemptuously refuses her. We do not, like her contemporaries, rush to the opposite extreme in a recoil from her as from a witch self-sold to the devil, because we do not believe in the devil nor in the possibility of commercial contracts with him. Our credulity, though enormous, is not boundless; and our stock of it is quite used up by our mediums, clairvoyants, hand readers, slate writers, Christian Scientists, psychoanalysts, electronic vibration diviners, therapeutists of all schools registered and unregistered, astrologers, astronomers who tell us that the sun is nearly a hundred million miles away and that Betelgeuse [a giant red star in the constellation of the Twins] is ten times as big as the whole universe, physicists who balance Betelgeuse by describing the incredible smallness of the atom, and a host of other marvel mongers whose credulity would have dissolved the Middle Ages in a roar of sceptical merriment. In the Middle Ages people believed that the earth was flat, for which they had at least the evidence of their senses: we believe it to be round, not because as many as one per cent of us could give the physical reasons for so quaint a belief, but because modern science has convinced us that nothing that is obvious is true, and that everything that is magical, improbable, extraordinary, gigantic, microscopic, heartless, or outrageous is scientific.

I must not, by the way, be taken as implying that the earth is flat, or that all or any of our amazing credulities are delusions or impostures. I am only defending my own age against the charge of being less imaginative than the Middle Ages. I affirm that the XIX century, and still more the XX, can knock the XV into a cocked hat in point of susceptibility to marvels and miracles and saints and prophets and magicians and monsters and fairy tales of all kinds. The proportion of marvel to immediately credible statement in the latest edition of the Encyclopedia Britannica is enormously greater than in the Bible. The medieval doctors of divinity who did not pretend to settle how many angels could dance on the point of a needle cut a very poor figure as far as romantic credulity is concerned beside the modern physicists who have settled to the billionth of a millimetre every movement and position in the dance of the electrons. Not for worlds would I question the precise accuracy of these calculations or the existence of electrons (whatever they may be). The fate of Joan is a warning to me against such heresy. But why the men who believe in electrons should regard themselves as less credulous than the men who believed in angels is not apparent to me. If they refuse to believe, with the Rouen assessors of 1431, that Joan was a witch, it is not because that explanation is too marvelous, but because it is not marvelous enough.

THE STAGE LIMITS OF HISTORICAL REPRESENTATION

For the story of Joan I refer the reader to the play which follows. It contains all that need be known about her; but as it is for stage use I have had to condense into three and a half hours a series of events which in their historical happening were spread over four times as many months; for the theatre imposes unities of time and place from which Nature in her boundless wastefulness is free. Therefore the reader must not suppose that Joan really put Robert de Baudricourt in her pocket in fifteen minutes, nor that her excommunication, recantation, relapse, and death at the stake were a matter of half an hour or so. Neither do I claim more for my dramatizations of Joan's contemporaries than that some of them are probably slightly more like the originals than those imaginary portraits of all the Popes from Saint Peter onward through the Dark Ages which are still gravely exhibited in the Uffizi in Florence (or were when I was there last). My Dunois would do equally well for the Duc d'Alençon [a close companion of Joan]. Both left descriptions of Joan so similar that, as a man always describes himself unconsciously whenever he describes anyone else, I have inferred that these goodnatured young men were very like oneanother in mind; so I have lumped the twain into a single figure, thereby saving the theatre manager a salary and a suit of armor. Dunois' face, still on record at Châteaudun [in north-central France], is a suggestive help. But I really know no more about these men and their circle than Shakespear knew about Falconbridge and the Duke of Austria [in *King John*], or about Macbeth and Macduff. In view of the things they did in history, and have to do again in the play, I can only invent appropriate characters for them in Shakespear's manner.

A VOID IN THE ELIZABETHAN DRAMA

I have, however, one advantage over the Elizabethans. I write in full view of the Middle Ages, which may be said to have been rediscovered in the middle of the XIX century after an eclipse of about four hundred and fifty years. The Renascence of antique literature and art in the XVI century, and the lusty growth of Capitalism, between them buried the Middle Ages; and their resurrection is a second Renascence. Now there is not a breath of medieval atmosphere in Shakespear's histories. His John of Gaunt [in *Richard II*] is like a study of the old age of [Sir Francis] Drake.[44] Although he was a Catholic by family tradition, his figures are all intensely Protestant, individualist, sceptical, selfcentred in everything but their love affairs, and completely personal and selfish even in them. His kings are not statesmen: his cardinals have no religion: a novice can read his plays from one end to the other without learning that the world is finally governed by forces expressing themselves in religions and laws which make epochs rather than by vulgarly ambitious individuals who make rows. The divinity which shapes our ends, rough hew them how we will [*Hamlet*, V: ii], is mentioned fatalistically only to be forgotten immediately like a passing vague apprehension. To Shakespear as to Mark Twain, Cauchon would have been a tyrant and a bully instead of a Catholic, and the inquisitor Lemaître would have been a Sadist instead of a lawyer. Warwick would have had no more feudal quality than his successor the King Maker has in the play of Henry VI. We should have seen them all completely satisfied that if they would only to their own selves be true they could not then be false to any man [*Hamlet*, I: iii] (a precept which represents the reaction against medievalism at its intensest) as if they were beings in the air, without public responsibilities of any kind. All Shakespear's characters are so: that is why they seem natural to our middle classes, who are comfortable and irresponsible at other people's expense, and are neither ashamed of that condition nor even conscious of it. Nature abhors this vacuum in Shakespear; and I have taken care to let the medieval atmosphere blow through my play freely. Those who see it performed will not mistake the startling event it records for a mere personal accident. They will have before them not only the visible and human puppets, but the Church, the Inquisition, the Feudal System, with divine inspiration always beating against their too inelastic limits: all more terrible in their dramatic force than any of the little mortal figures clanking about in plate armor or moving silently in the frocks and hoods of the order of St Dominic.

44. Drake's abortive attempts to restore Don Antonio, King of Portugal, and to destroy Spanish settlements in the West Indies were the principal causes of his death.

TRAGEDY, NOT MELODRAMA

There are no villains in the piece. Crime, like disease, is not interesting: it is something to be done away with by general consent, and that is all about it. It is what men do at their best, with good intentions, and what normal men and women find that they must and will do in spite of their intentions, that really concern us. The rascally bishop and the cruel inquisitor of Mark Twain and Andrew Lang are as dull as pickpockets; and they reduce Joan to the level of the even less interesting person whose pocket is picked. I have represented both of them as capable and eloquent exponents of The Church Militant and The Church Litigant, because only by doing so can I maintain my drama on the level of high tragedy and save it from becoming a mere police court sensation. A villain in a play can never be anything more than a *diabolus ex machina*, possibly a more exciting expedient than a *deus ex machina*, but both equally mechanical, and therefore interesting only as mechanism. It is, I repeat, what normally innocent people do that concerns us; and if Joan had not been burnt by normally innocent people in the energy of their righteousness her death at their hands would have no more significance than the Tokyo earthquake,[45] which burnt a great many maidens. The tragedy of such murders is that they are not committed by murderers. They are judicial murders, pious murders; and this contradiction at once brings an element of comedy into the tragedy: the angels may weep at the murder, but the gods laugh at the murderers.

THE INEVITABLE FLATTERIES OF TRAGEDY

Here then we have a reason why my drama of Saint Joan's career, though it may give the essential truth of it, gives an inexact picture of some accidental facts. It goes almost without saying that the old Jeanne d'Arc melodramas, reducing everything to a conflict of villain and hero, or in Joan's case villain and heroine, not only miss the point entirely, but falsify the characters, making Cauchon a scoundrel, Joan a prima donna, and Dunois a lover. But the writer of high tragedy and comedy, aiming at the innermost attainable truth, must needs flatter Cauchon nearly as much as

45. An earthquake of great magnitude (8.3 on the Richter scale) occurred in September 1923 in Yokohama (near Tokyo), in which 200,000 Japanese lost their lives.

the melodramatist vilifies him. Although there is, as far as I have been able to discover, nothing against Cauchon that convicts him of bad faith or exceptional severity in his judicial relations with Joan, or of as much anti-prisoner, pro-police, class and sectarian bias as we now take for granted in our own courts, yet there is hardly more warrant for classing him as a great Catholic churchman, completely proof against the passions roused by the temporal situation. Neither does the inquisitor Lemaître, in such scanty accounts of him as are now recoverable, appear quite so able a master of his duties and of the case before him as I have given him credit for being. But it is the business of the stage to make its figures more intelligible to themselves than they would be in real life; for by no other means can they be made intelligible to the audience. And in this case Cauchon and Lemaître have to make intelligible not only themselves but the Church and the Inquisition, just as Warwick has to make the feudal system intelligible, the three between them having thus to make a XX century audience conscious of an epoch fundamentally different from its own. Obviously the real Cauchon, Lemaître, and Warwick could not have done this: they were part of the Middle Ages themselves, and therefore as unconscious of its peculiarities as of the atomic formula of the air they breathed. But the play would be unintelligible if I had not endowed them with enough of this consciousness to enable them to explain their attitude to the XX century. All I claim is that by this inevitable sacrifice of verisimilitude I have secured in the only possible way sufficient veracity to justify me in claiming that as far as I can gather from the available documentation, and from such powers of divination as I possess, the things I represent these three exponents of the drama as saying are the things they actually would have said if they had known what they were really doing. And beyond this neither drama nor history can go in my hands.

SOME WELL-MEANT PROPOSALS FOR THE IMPROVEMENT OF THE PLAY

I have to thank several critics on both sides of the Atlantic, including some whose admiration for my play is most generously enthusiastic, for their heartfelt instructions as to how it can be improved. They point out that by the excision of the epilog and all the references to such undramatic and tedious matters as the Church, the feudal system, the Inquisition, the theory of heresy and so forth, all of which, they point out, would be ruthlessly blue pencilled by any experienced manager, the play could be considerably shortened. I think they are mistaken. The experienced knights of the blue pencil, having saved an hour and a half by disembowelling the play, would at once proceed to waste two hours in building elaborate scenery, having real water in the river Loire and a real bridge across it, and staging an obviously sham fight for possession of it, with the victorious French led by Joan on a real horse. The coronation would eclipse all previous theatrical displays, shewing, first, the procession through the streets of Rheims, and then the service in the cathedral, with special music written for both. Joan would be burnt on the stage, as Mr Matheson Lang[46] always is in The Wandering Jew, on the principle that it does not matter in the least why a woman is burnt provided she is burnt, and people can pay to see it done. The intervals between the acts whilst these splendors were being built up and then demolished by the stage carpenters would seem eternal, to the great profit of the refreshment bars. And the weary and demoralized audience would lose their last trains and curse me for writing such inordinately long and intolerably dreary and meaningless plays. But the applause of the press would be unanimous. Nobody who knows the stage history of Shakespear will doubt that this is what would happen if I knew my business so little as to listen to these well-intentioned but disastrous counsellors: indeed it probably will happen when I am no longer in control of the performing rights. So perhaps it will be as well for the public to see the play while I am still alive.

THE EPILOG

As to the epilog, I could hardly be expected to stultify myself by implying that Joan's history in the world ended unhappily with her execution, instead of beginning there. It was necessary by hook or crook to shew the canonized Joan as well as the incinerated one; for many a woman has got herself burnt by carelessly whisking a muslin skirt into the drawing-room fireplace, but getting canonized is a different matter, and a more important one. So I am afraid the epilog must stand.

46. Canadian-Scots actor-manager, who had one of his greatest successes in E. Temple Thurston's *The Wandering Jew* (1920), which ran for 391 performances. The production currently was touring the provinces in Lang's repertory before returning to London late in 1924.

To the Critics, lest they should feel Ignored

To a professional critic (I have been one myself) theatregoing is the curse of Adam. The play is the evil he is paid to endure in the sweat of his brow; and the sooner it is over, the better. This would seem to place him in irreconcilable opposition to the paying playgoer, from whose point of view the longer the play, the more entertainment he gets for his money. It does in fact so place him, especially in the provinces, where the playgoer goes to the theatre for the sake of the play solely, and insists so effectively on a certain number of hours' entertainment that touring managers are sometimes seriously embarrassed by the brevity of the London plays they have to deal in.

For in London the critics are reinforced by a considerable body of persons who go to the theatre as many others go to church, to display their best clothes and compare them with other people's; to be in the fashion, and have something to talk about at dinner parties; to adore a pet performer; to pass the evening anywhere rather than at home: in short, for any or every reason except interest in dramatic art as such. In fashionable centres the number of irreligious people who go to church, of unmusical people who go to concerts and operas, and of undramatic people who go to the theatre, is so prodigious that sermons have been cut down to ten minutes and plays to two hours; and, even at that, congregations sit longing for the benediction and audiences for the final curtain, so that they may get away to the lunch or supper they really crave for, after arriving as late as (or later than) the hour of beginning can possibly be made for them.

Thus from the stalls and in the Press an atmosphere of hypocrisy spreads. Nobody says straight out that genuine drama is a tedious nuisance, and that to ask people to endure more than two hours of it (with two long intervals of relief) is an intolerable imposition. Nobody says "I hate classical tragedy and comedy as I hate sermons and symphonies; but I like police news and divorce news and any kind of dancing or decoration that has an aphrodisiac effect on me or on my wife or husband. And whatever superior people may pretend, I cannot associate pleasure with any sort of intellectual activity; and I dont believe anyone else can either." Such things are not said; yet nine-tenths of what is offered as criticism of the drama in the metropolitan Press of Europe and America is nothing but a muddled paraphrase of it. If it does not mean that, it means nothing.

I do not complain of this, though it complains very unreasonably of me. But I can take no more notice of it than Einstein of the people who are incapable of mathematics. I write in the classical manner for those who pay for admission to a theatre because they like classical comedy or tragedy for its own sake, and like it so much when it is good of its kind and well done that they tear themselves away from it with reluctance to catch the very latest train or omnibus that will take them home. Far from arriving late from an eight or half-past eight o'clock dinner so as to escape at least the first half-hour of the performance, they stand in queues outside the theatre doors for hours beforehand in bitingly cold weather to secure a seat. In countries where a play lasts a week, they bring baskets of provisions and sit it out. These are the patrons on whom I depend for my bread. I do not give them performances twelve hours long, because circumstances do not at present make such entertainments feasible; though a performance beginning after breakfast and ending at sunset is as possible physically and artistically in Surrey or Middlesex as in Oberammergau [Bavaria, where the Passion Play is given every tenth year]; and an all-night sitting in a theatre would be at least as enjoyable as an all-night sitting in the House of Commons, and much more useful. But in St Joan I have done my best by going to the well-established classical limit of three and a half hours practically continuous playing, barring the one interval imposed by considerations which have nothing to do with art. I know that this is hard on the pseudo-critics and on the fashionable people whose playgoing is a hypocrisy. I cannot help feeling some compassion for them when they assure me that my play, though a great play, must fail hopelessly, because it does not begin at a quarter to nine and end at eleven. The facts are overwhelmingly against them. They forget that all men are not as they are. Still, I am sorry for them; and though I cannot for their sakes undo my work and help the people who hate the theatre to drive out the people who love it, yet I may point out to them that they have several remedies in their own hands. They can escape the first part of the play by their usual practice of arriving late. They can escape the epilog by not waiting for it. And if the irreducible minimum thus attained is still too painful, they can stay away altogether. But I deprecate this extreme course, because it is good neither for my pocket nor for their own souls. Already a few of them, noticing that what matters is not the absolute length of time occupied by a play, but the speed with which that time passes, are discovering that the theatre, though purgatorial in its Aristotelian moments, is not necessarily always the dull place they have so often found it. What do its discomforts matter when the play makes us forget them?

AYOT ST LAWRENCE.
May, 1924.

Translator's Note
(Jitta's Atonement)

First published as a loosely inserted leaflet in the programme for the first London performance, 26 January 1925. Subsequently published, with revision, as a preface to the play in Translations and Tomfooleries, *1926*

═══

Siegfried Trebitsch, a well-known Austrian novelist and playwright, was born in Vienna on the 21st December 1869 [1868]. The list of his original works includes eight novels and volumes of stories, and six or seven plays, including Frau Gitta's Sühne, of which the present work is a translation. I have to stress the word original, because, with a devotion extraordinary in the case of a writer with a successful career open to him as an original writer, he has undertaken and carried out the heavy additional task of translating and introducing to the German-speaking public and to the German theatre the entire body of my own works, both literary and theatrical.

This enterprize is the more remarkable because it was begun at a time when my position in the English theatre was one not of good repute, but of infamy. I was rated in the theatrical world of London as an absurd pamphleteer, who had been allowed to display his ignorance of the rudiments of stage technique, and his hopeless incapacity for representing human nature dramatically or otherwise, in a few performances at coterie theatres quite outside recognized theatrical commerce. Trebitsch knew better. He also knew English. He was quite unknown to me when he appeared one day at my house[1] and asked to see me with a view to his becoming my interpreter and apostle in Central Europe. I attempted to

---

1. There are two versions to this story by Shaw. In the first, published in German (*Die Zeit*, 22 February 1903), Shaw correctly described two visits, both in mid March 1902, as corroborated by Trebitsch in his autobiography (and elsewhere). In the first visit Trebitsch met Charlotte Shaw, but not GBS. Shaw's 1926 description is dramatically effective, but fictional. Trebitsch was received by Shaw on 18 March 1902, his second visit to Adelphi Terrace, only after he had written for an appointment and received a response from Mrs Shaw inviting him to lunch. In Shaw's later recollection, the two visits are conflated.

dodge his visit by asking my wife to see him and to explain politely that a proposal to translate could be entertained only when made by the responsible manager of a theatre with a view to immediate production. The evasion failed ignominiously. My wife came to me and said that the young gentleman, though he seemed a very nice young gentleman, had swept aside her excuse with explosive contempt, and would take no denial. If I was to get rid of him (which she already regarded as doubtful policy) I must go down and do it myself. I came down; and the result was that the young gentleman carried the citadel by storm as successfully as he had carried the outworks. I did what I could to dissuade him from what seemed a desperate undertaking; but his faith in my destiny was invincible. I surrendered at discretion; and the result was that I presently found myself a successful and respected playwright in the German language whilst the English critics were still explaining laboriously that my plays were not plays, and urging me, in the kindest spirit, to cease my vain efforts to enter a profession for which Nature had utterly unfitted me. In the last decade of the XIX century I was deriving a substantial income as a playwright from America and Central Europe. Not until the middle of the first decade of the XX could I have lived by my theatrical earnings in London. Today I have only to lift up my finger to attract a hundred translators. When Trebitsch volunteered for the job, the hundred would have fled from my invitation as one man.

It is not for me to say how far English drama is indebted to Herr Trebitsch for its present prestige abroad. It *is* for me to say that my personal debt to him is incalculable. When the horrible catastrophe of the war had torn Anglo-German relations to fragments, and only the fools who would not heed Mr Lloyd George's warning to "stop snarling" could doubt the vital European necessity for mending them, I could do no less than take advantage of the fact that Trebitsch has written plays of his own, to translate one of them from German into English for the man who has translated so many plays from English into German.

There were technical difficulties: how great I never realized until I took the job in hand. At first I was preoccupied with a quite minor matter. I can neither claim knowledge of the German language nor plead ignorance of it. I am like most literary persons: I have spent several holidays in Germany (mostly in Bayreuth), and have just managed to ask my way, and get what I wanted in the shops and railway stations, without the aid of an interpreter. The proverbial bits of Goethe and Wagner and Nietzsche are familiar to me; and when a German writes to me I can generally make out what he wants provided he uses the Latin and not the Gothic script. And that is all.

When I opened the pages of Frau Gitta's Sühne, I was driven to the dictionary, only to discover that Trebitsch apparently does not use words that are in the dictionary. It was not by any process known to men of learning, but rather by some telepathic method of absorption, that I managed at last to divine, infer, guess, and co-invent the story of Gitta, or Jitta, as I have had to spell her to avert having her name pronounced with a hard G. Trebitsch is amiable enough to say that I have succeeded wonderfully;[2] but even a very bad translation may be a wonderful feat for a translator who does not know the language.

However, when it comes to translating a play the mere translation is only the tiniest fraction of the business. I soon found that a literal translation would fail completely to convey the play to an Anglo-American audience. It was necessary to translate the audience as well as the play: that is, to translate Vienna into London and New York. And this involved translating one theatrical epoch into another. Vienna is still romantic in the manner of Verdi's operas, and modern in the manner of De Maupassant and Baudelaire. And as the conqueror always acquires some of the qualities of the conquered, even now that he no longer eats him, there is a touch of the east in Vienna, not only brought by the winds along the Danube, but left by the Turks when [John] Sobieski[3] drove them back from the gates. Add to this that Vienna has never weaned itself from the sweet milk of XVIII century art, when even woe was a luxury, and the heroine could not die in gloom too deep to please the audience. When natural history (sometimes ambiguously called realism) is banished from the theatre, cruelty, horror and death become painless there, and even luxurious, because nobody believes in them. The most frightful torments may be heaped on the heroine until she dies of poison or a broken heart: the villain may, like the wicked Count [di Luna] in Il Trovatore, live only to *centuplicar la morte* of the hero in *mille atroci spasimi*,[4] and the hero [Manrico] himself may not

2. 'It is much better than the original', Trebitsch tactfully informed Shaw in 1920. After Shaw's death, however, in his autobiography *Chronicle of a Life* (1951; tr. 1953) he remarked that Shaw 'took liberties that he himself would never have forgiven his translator'; and added, 'The drama as I had written it exist[s] in print as evidence of what I had set out to do.'
3. John III, King of Poland, as Commander-in-Chief of the Polish Army, inflicted several defeats on the invading Turks. In 1683, after concluding a treaty with Leopold II of Hungary, he relieved the siege of Vienna, which led eventually to the ejection of the Turks from Hungary.
4. 'By all the pangs of hell itself/I'd still have him tormented . . .' (Verdi, *Il Trovatore*, Part IV, Scene 2).

know a moment of happiness or security until misfortune dogs him to his death; yet no one will turn a hair: the more dreadful it all is the better it is liked, because romance can never come home to reality. To preserve this delicious anæsthesia there must be no bringing down to earth of the business by the disillusioning touch of comedy.

In England and America nowadays, such romance is privileged only in Italian Opera, and is not tolerated without the music. The Anglo-American audience wants a happy ending because it wants a credible ending, and therefore cannot bear an utterly unhappy one. It is true, as the late St John Hankin pointed out and illustrated by his Plays With Happy Endings,[5] that the conventional happy ending is often as unhappy and disastrous as the marriages which foolish magistrates and police-court missionaries force on young people who have been no better than they ought to be. But the fact remains that in proportion as a play succeeds in producing an illusion of real life, it must dispense with the frantic agonies and despairs and poisonings and butcheries of the romantic theatre. Consequently, if you take a play written under the tyranny of a romantic audience and present it without modification to a comparatively matter-of-fact audience, it will miss its mark, and may even miss fire altogether.

To avert this result in the case of Frau Gitta's Sühne, I have taken advantage of the fortunate circumstance that in real life the consequences of conjugal infidelity are seldom either so serious as they are assumed to be in romantic tragedy or so trivial as in farcical comedy. I may as well confess at once that in the original play Jitta lives miserably ever after, and that her husband bears malice, and presents a character study much subtler and more elusive than you will gather from my frankly comedic British version of him. Also Trebitsch, being a German poet, has a certain melancholic delicacy which escapes my comparatively barbarous and hilarious occidental touch. I could not help suggesting, by a few translator's treacheries here and there, that the ill-assorted pair settle down on reasonable human terms, and find life bearable after all.

Trebitsch goes so far as to say [in a letter of 11 October 1921, which Shaw partially misquotes] "You have made my last act almost a comedy"; but he is too amiable to reproach me, and tolerates my variations, which affect, not the story itself, but only the key in which it ends. Though the assumptions of the audience as to what will happen after the fall of the

---

5. Hankin was a promising Edwardian social satirist, who committed suicide in 1909. *Three Plays with Happy Endings* (New York, 1907) contained *The Return of the Prodigal*, *The Charity That Began at Home* and *The Cassilis Engagement*.

curtain will be more cheerful in England and America than they were in Vienna, the action of the play remains unaltered. Nevertheless those who can should read the original, to the idiosyncratic literary quality of which I have been shamefully unable to do justice.

T. E. Lawrence

Preface to Catalogue of an Exhibition of Paintings, Pastels, Drawings and Woodcuts illustrating Col. T. E. Lawrence's Book 'Seven Pillars of Wisdom', *The Leicester Gallery, London, 1927*

======

The circumstances of the present exhibition are so extraordinary that if most of them were not unquestioned parts of recent history I should certainly be accused of inventing them for the entertainment of the visitors.

In the war of 1914–18, all those of the belligerent Powers which were holding alien peoples in subjection, for their own good or otherwise, had to face the risk of such peoples seeing in the war their opportunity to rise and strike for independence. The Germans banked on a rising in Ireland. What is more to the present point, they considered the possibility of a nationalist rising in Algeria against the French. If they could have brought that about, the consequences might have been serious. But the steps they took to provoke it were futile, ending in a merely literary propaganda which was easily and effectively countered, not from France but from England: I myself being concerned in the affair in a comic opera manner as a reputed Prophet.[1] Nevertheless the thing could have been done had there been a man of genius on the German side to do it.

The proof of this is that England, having a man of genius at her disposal, succeeded in effecting the parallel operation of stirring up a nationalist rebellion against the Turkish Empire in Arabia. The genius in question was a young archæologist with a careless fancy for calling himself by any name that came into his head at the moment. His mission caught him when he was T.E. Lawrence, and immortalized him under that name in spite of all his subsequent efforts to discard it, which included, by the way, an avatar as [T. E.] Shaw. As this caused him to be taken for my son one day by a clergyman at the house of Thomas Hardy, I had better, perhaps, explain

1. The reference is to a now lost 'Epistle to the Moors' written in 1915 in an ornate style 'founded on the New Testament, the Koran, and Captain Burton's translation of the "Arabian Nights"' (Archibald Henderson, *Table-Talk of G. B. S.*, 1925), for distribution in north-west Africa to counter German anti-British war propaganda. See p. 279, fn. 1.

that we are two different people, not related in the way of vulgar consanguinity.

Lawrence, like the Prophet of the Latter Day Saints, had a passion for digging up old civilizations, to gratify which he had to go to the East, where such excavations are not obstructed by precarious and extremely uninteresting new civilizations. He picked up some Arabic, and found out the sort of people the Arabs are. Knowing already only too well the sort of people we are, he saw that if he came to our rescue by making the Arabs revolt during the war he would have more trouble with us than with them; for British public opinion and official routine disapproves intensely of geniuses, even when they have been hallmarked at Oxford. As to the British army, its feelings when, after being compelled in some unaccountable manner to make Lawrence a Colonel rather than be ordered about by a nobody, it found him leading his hosts to battle on camelback in a picturesque Arab costume, can be more easily imagined in messrooms than described by me. Even the camel did not get its regulation meals.

The limelight of history follows the authentic hero as the theatre limelight follows the *prima ballerina assoluta*. It soon concentrated in its whitest radiance on Colonel Lawrence, *alias* Luruns Bey, *alias* Prince of Damascus, the mystery man, the wonder man, the man who might have, if provoked, put on Arabia Felix and Arabia Deserta[2] as a shepherd putteth on his garment, and who did, when all the lies and all the legends are subtracted, authentically and unquestionably in his own way and largely with his own hands explode and smash the Turkish dominion in Arabia and join up with [Field Marshal Edmund Hynman, First Viscount] Allenby[3] in Damascus at the head of Arabia Liberata, Arabia Redenta, Arabia allied to Britannia just when Britannia wanted her.

This might have left Britannia in a difficulty when the war was over. It is said that in 1918 Marshal [Ferdinand] Foch[4] was asked how Napoleon

2. Arabia Felix was the name given by ancient geographers to the entire Arabian peninsula. Ptolemy, in the second century, in his *Geographike Huphegesis* (*Guide to Geography*) divided Arabia into three areas: Arabia Petrae (stony: Hejaz); Arabia Felix (fruitful: Oman, Yemen); and Arabia Deserta (desert: Nejd). To these Shaw appended three modern political distinctions to signal the efforts and accomplishments of Lawrence in the 1914–18 war: Liberata (liberated), Redenta (restored) and 'Arabia allied to Britannia'.
3. Commander-in-Chief of the Egyptian Expeditionary Force, who in 1919 was appointed High Commissioner for Egypt.
4. Commander of the Tenth Army Corps, who was appointed Supreme Commander of all Allied armies in March 1918 and Marshal of France in August 1918.

would have fought the Great War. "Superbly" said the Marshal; "but what the devil should we have done with him afterwards?" The Prince of Damascus solved that problem for Britannia. He simply walked away and became a nobody again under another name. Any country with a Valhalla or a spark of gratitude would have rewarded him with a munificent pension and built him another Blenheim.[5] The British Government left him to pension himself like any ex-minister by writing a book about it all and living on the proceeds.

Now it happened that Lawrence's genius included literary genius; and that his maddeningly intense conscientiousness obliged him to write the book in order that the truth might be disentangled from the legends and lies, and history enjoy another of her rare escapes from romance and partisan scurrility. But he had inexorably determined that he would not coin the blood of the Arabs or his own into drachmas. He wrote the history, and, when it got lost, stolen or strayed, rewrote it as Carlyle rewrote his French Revolution when the housemaid lit the fire with it. It was a prodigious task; and the result was a masterpiece of literature. Commercially it was worth to the author a very large sum, a big advance on which was ready on the nail from eager publishers.

Lawrence made up his mind to lose money by it. He set able painters to work to make portraits of his Arab comrades in arms, and imaginative draughtsmen to let their fancy play on illustrations in black and white. He had the portraits reproduced in color. He had paper specially made, and directed the printing himself in the manner of Morris or [William] Caxton.[6] Finally he produced a private subscription edition of one hundred copies[7] after bringing the cost per copy up to ninety pounds or so, the subscription price being thirty. It was scarcely out when advertisements appeared in The Times offering £5 a week for the loan of a copy.

The pictures in this exhibition are those he had procured for the book. Except a few which belong to the artists, they are the property of a Trust set up by Lawrence to liquidate the bankruptcy which he had so ruthlessly contrived. Perhaps you would like to buy them and pay extravagant sums for them over and above their value to you as works of art with the

5. The castle in England built for John Churchill, First Duke of Marlborough, after his rout of the French (1704) at Blenheim, Bavaria, during the War of the Spanish Succession.
6. The first English printer, who issued his first dated book in 1477.
7. Actually there were 170 complete copies of the private subscription edition, printed in 1926.

intention of benefiting Luruns Bey in his own despite. You would not succeed: the Trust is to devote all residual assets (I shall explain in the next paragraph that there may finally be some) to a fund for the relief of the Belisariuses[8] of the Air Force. Not one farthing of the price of Arabia's independence and her timely aid to England will ever go into the pockets of the Prince of Damascus.

If you ask me, as you well may, how all these extravagances were financed, I can point only to the subscription, and to a mortgage on the popular abridgment of the book which is to be issued [in 1927] by the firm of Jonathan Cape [under the title *Revolt in the Desert*], and which will presently take its place among our treasures of military chronicle, travel, confession, and ethnology. An Oxford grant which Lawrence refused to exploit for his private ends, and some remnants of his own property, were sunk in the enterprize. As to Arabian booty, it seems to have consisted in a presentation camel which he shot under himself in the excitement of battle: an incident illustrated in the exhibition.

How, then, did he live whilst all this expenditure was going on? Well, how does a nobody live when he has made himself totally unintelligible to commercial civilization? The Government was not wholly ungrateful; but it did not understand. It offered him all sorts of jobs that he did not want. Military commands in time of peace did not appeal to a man who had for years played skittles with army routine as masterfully as he had blown up the Turkish army of occupation on its railway trips through the desert. Civilian bureaucracy was even more hopeless. What more could a Government offer? Money enough to follow his star does not seem to have suggested itself to the departmental mind. In the Middle Ages Lawrence would have gone into a monastery as a retired *condottiero* [captain of a band of mercenaries]. Living as he was, and is, in the Dark Ages, he deliberately chose the lot of a common soldier. It was objected that this was not fair, as he would be a most embarrassingly uncommon soldier, and that Private Lawrence would make the army ridiculous. He promptly took another name, and wore down the War Office as he had worn down Headquarters in Egypt. As a private soldier living humbly with his comrades (though I must confess that when they invited me to tea he looked very like Colonel Lawrence with several *aides-de-camp*) he finished the great book, and directed its manufacture even to ordering a different binding for every

---

8. Greatest of Justinian's generals, he was accused of conspiracy, but later restored to favour. A beggar's cry, 'Give an obolus to Belisarius', is based on an unfounded report that Belisarius's eyes had been put out by Justinian's tormentors.

copy, so that there might be no "first edition" in the collector's sense. He then transferred his patronage from the regular army, changing into the Air Force, and becoming Aircraftsman XXXX [John Hume Ross],[9] still refusing any position in which he would have to give an order, and still making me wonder whether he ever did anything else. At all events, having made up his mind to run away to India from the book and its inevitable rekindling of the Lawrence limelight, he ordered his regiment (or whatever they call a regiment in the Air Force) thither, and is now out of reach of this exhibition and this preface, which is perhaps lucky for me, as I am able to say all these things behind his back.

What will happen in India next, Heaven only knows.

G. B. S.

9. Shaw has confused the sequence. Lawrence joined the Royal Air Force as an enlisted man, using the name John Hume Ross, until his discharge in December 1922. He then (1923) joined the Royal Tank Corps, using the name T. E. Shaw. In 1925 he transferred to the Royal Air Force, from which he was discharged in 1935.

How William Archer Impressed Bernard Shaw

Preface to the posthumous publication of William Archer's Three Plays, *1927*

=====

William Archer, though the most lucid and unequivocal of writers, was in person and manner probably the most deceptive man of his time. Nobody could have been less of an impostor in character; yet he took in all his contemporaries, even those who were fairly intimate with him. One of the cleverest of our younger essayists has described him as a dour Scot, without the slightest sense of humor, hard, logical, with an ability that was always in cold storage.[1] This was not a stranger's deduction from his writings. It was a personal impression so strong that no study of his writings could quite dispel it. Not until the last London journalist who has met him has perished will William Archer be judged by his writings; and even in them there is an emotional reticence that will leave an incomplete picture of the man, though they will do him more justice than he ever did to himself. For the present, there is a fabulous Archer who is extremely unlike the real Archer, and much less amiable.

Had the fabulous Archer been the real one, our long friendship would have been impossible: indeed any friendship with him would have been impossible. Fortunately the real Archer was, like myself, the victim of an unsleeping and incorrigible sense of humor: the very quality (or fault) which the fabulous Archer utterly lacked. No doubt when we first met as young men of the same age some fortyfive years ago [1883], I interested him as a person free from certain superstitions that had been oppressive to him; but I interested him still more by being so laughably free, not only from superstitions recognized by him as such, but from many conventions which he had never dreamt of challenging, that I appealed irresistibly to him as an incarnate joke. The Shavianismus tickled him enormously; and he was never tired of quoting not only my jokes, but my heresies and paradoxes, many of which have by this time become platitudes. The way to get on with Archer was to amuse him: to argue with him was dangerous. The invaluable precept of Robert Owen: "Never argue: repeat

---

1. The description is Max Beerbohm's, in substance though not in wording, in an unsigned appreciation in *The Times*, 6 January 1925, ten days after Archer's death.

your assertion," established me with Archer on the footing of a privileged lunatic, and made quarrels impossible.

Archer had the air of a stoic: he was really a humorist to whom a jest was worth more than most of the things common men prize. For instance, he was unlucky enough to have trouble with one of his eyes. He went to an oculist, and returned so radiant that I concluded that the oculist had cured him. On the contrary, the oculist had diagnosed amblyopia. "What is amblyopia?" said Archer. "Well," said the oculist, "the eye is quite perfect. There is no lesion or defect of any sort. A first-class eye. Only, it does not see anything." Archer found this so funny that he thought half his sight well lost for the fun of repeating it to me and everyone else.

Another instance, in which money was at stake. Though a thoroughbred Scot, he was usually so indifferent to it, so untouched by vulgar ambition or by the least taint of snobbery, so sensibly unpretentious in his habits, so content to go to the pit when he paid to enter a theatre or even in the steerage when he made a long voyage, that nothing but a stroke of luck could ever have made him rich; but when he got married he conscientiously set to work to accumulate savings; and by doing too much journalism he succeeded in making some provision for family contingencies. Unfortunately, on the best advice, he invested it all in Australian banks; and Australian banks presently went smash. I have known men reduced to fury and despair by less serious losses. Archer was sustained and even elated by our friend John Mackinnon Robertson.[2] Robertson, not at that time the Right Honorable (he had not yet entered on the distinguished parliamentary career which he managed to combine so oddly with an equally distinguished literary activity), had just written an economic treatise entitled The Fallacy of Saving. He sent a copy to Archer; and it arrived simultaneously with the bad news from Australia. Archer at once sat down and wrote, "My dear Robertson: I am already completely convinced of the fallacy of saving, thank you." He came to me to tell me the story, chuckling with the enjoyment of a man who had just heard that his uncle had died in Australia and left him a million. Had he been a giggling fribble, incapable of his own distress, I should have had no patience with him. But, as I shall presently shew, never was there a man less a trifler than William Archer. He laughed at his misfortunes because things of the mind were important to him (humor is purely mental), and things of the body and of the pocket, as long as they stopped short of disablement and painful privation, relatively

2. Journalist, literary scholar and politician, author of a book critical of Shaw's play, *Mr Shaw and 'The Maid'* (1926).

trivial. The sight of one eye did not matter provided he could see with the other; and he, who set very little store by what people call good living, could hardly be expected to feel much concern about savings whilst he could pay his way with earnings: a comic speech consoled him for both losses.

Why was it, then, that he produced so strong an impression of dourness, unbending Puritan rigidity, and total lack of humor?

The explanation is that in spite of his lifelong preoccupation with the theatre, he was not a dramatic, self-expressive person. Physically he was a tall upstanding wellbuilt goodlooking Scot, keeping his figure and bearing to the last. He had an agreeable voice and unaffected manners, and no touch of malice in him. But nobody could tell from any external sign what he was thinking about, or how he felt. The amblyopic eye may have contributed to this air of powerful reserve; but the reserve was real: it was a habit that had become first nature to him. In modern psycho-pathological terms it was a repression that had become a complex. Accustomed as I was to this, he amazed even me once. He had just completed his translation of Ibsen's Little Eyolf; and he read it to two or three friends of whom I was one [on 3 December 1894]. His reading was clear, intelligent, cold, without a trace of emotion, and rather wooden in the more moving passages. When he came to the last pages he suddenly handed me the book, and said, formally and with a marked access of woodenness, "Shaw: I must ask you to finish the reading for me. My feelings will not allow me to proceed." The contrast between the matter and the manner of this speech would have been irresistibly comic had any doubt of the sincerity of his distress been possible. I took the proofsheets in silence, and finished the reading as desired. We were face to face with a man in whom dissimulation had become so instinctive that it had become his natural form of emotional expression. No wonder he seemed a monster of insensibility to those who did not know him very intimately.

To explain this, I must cast back to the year 1730 as a date in religious history. In that year, just before Wesley began Methodism in England, a Scots minister named John Glas was cast out by the General Assembly of the Kirk in Scotland as a Congregationalist heretic. Glas thought this was so much the worse for the Kirk in Scotland. Bible in hand, and strong in the Protestant right to private judgment, he founded one of the innumerable Separatist sects [of independent Presbyterians] that arose in the XVIII century. Shakespear would have called him a Brownist.[3] He maintained

3. Robert Browne, a sixteenth-century English clergyman, was the founder of a sect called Brownist, a predecessor of the Congregationalist movement, which

that any group of persons organized according to the instructions of St Paul to Timothy, and qualified as godly according to the prescription of Matthew, was independent of any Kirk or General Assembly or ecclesiastical authority whatsoever, and was answerable to God alone. The aim of his own group was the realization of Christ's kingdom as defined in the famous reply to Pilate, "My kingdom is not of this world" [John 18: 36]. Glas's son-in-law, [Robert] Sandeman, carried this doctrine to England, where the groups became known as Sandemanians.

Now of Separation there is no end until every human being is a Separate Church, for which there is much to be said. The Separatists continue to separate. In 1804 John Walker, Bachelor of Divinity (for so I construe the letters B.D.) and Fellow of Trinity College, Dublin, separated himself from the Episcopal Church of Ireland, and founded a sect called by him The Church of God, and by the profane The Walkerites. Its tenets resembled those of the Glasites so closely that there was talk of an amalgamation; but the Glasites were Sabbatarians; the Walkerites held that Christ had discarded the Sabbath; and so they could not agree. Anyhow Walkerism was superfluous in Scotland, where its numbers were often so small that worship among them was a family affair conducted by the head of the household, assisted by such male members of the sect as happened to be present. As the Glasites had flourishing congregations in many centres, Walkerite children would be sent to a Glasite Meeting when there was no Walkerite Meeting to send them to.

In the second generation of Walkerites, a Miss Walker married a Mr Archer. And one of their sons complicated the faith by marrying a daughter of James Morison, one of the shining lights of Glasism. From that exogamous alliance William Archer sprang. If ever there was a doubly predestined heir of grace, William, one would think, was he. And, on the whole, he lived up to his antecedents. But God fulfils Himself in many ways, and often in extremely unexpected ones. As William grew up, he felt obliged to pursue his hereditary Separatism to the point of separating himself not only from the Separatists, but from the curious fetish worship of the Bible, and the idolization of Christ, with which all the sects and Churches were still saturated.

This looks like a complete explanation of the reserve that was a second nature with him. But, if you are an English reader, do not infer too much from your ignorance of Scoto-Norwegian Separatism. Long before Archer's views had formed themselves sufficiently to threaten a schism in

---

holds each Church as independent in ecclesiastical matters but united in fellowship.

the family if he gave voice to them, he had profited, without the smallest friction, by the fact that both Walkerites and Glasites regarded religion as too sacred to be made a subject of private conversation. They actually barred private prayer, and not only neither asked their children controversial questions nor permitted them to put any, but would not allow even a catechism to come between them and their God. In their view, you were either damned or saved by your own nature and the act of God; and any attempt to force God's hand in the transaction was sedition in His kingdom. Thus William was never driven to lie about his beliefs or about the family beliefs. He was simply not allowed to talk about either. He was, however, expected to go to Meeting when there was a meeting (Walkerite or Glasite) within reach, and not to laugh when his sense of humor got the better of the solemnity of the occasion. In the latter observance the Archer children were by no means uniformly successful. In William as in Mark Twain, the meetings had a marked homeopathic effect.

Another feature of Separatism which favored his freedom of thought was its anti-clericalism. The common English association of clericalism with piety is often misleading. The revolt against institutional religion which moved George Fox to regard a priest of any denomination as Mr Winston Churchill regards a Bolshevist, and to revile a church as a steeple house, has produced all the Separatist sects, and has in our day invaded even the Church of England in the person of the most intellectually eminent of its dignitaries. William Archer's father [Thomas] would have been surprised if anyone had called him an anti-clerical; but he had the Separatist habit of assuming that parsons are inadmissible acquaintances. The family atmosphere, if not explicitly anti-clerical, was, to say the least, not prelatical.

Archer's brother [Charles] and collaborator in their translation of Peer Gynt tells me that he never heard his father say a word of any kind on any religious subject. This gives in a single sentence a vision of the extraordinary reserve imposed by the Separatism of Glas and Walker, surviving as a habit long after the original impulse had lost its fervor, and had even provoked a reaction. The reaction in William Archer carried him to a Modernism which would have been taken by Glas and Walker as unmistakeable evidence of his predestined damnation; but the habit of reserve remained.

It was reinforced as he grew older by the clash of his political opinions with those of the Glasites, who interpreted Christ's declaration that His kingdom was not of this world as implying a duty of unquestioning submission to all duly constituted secular authority. This view had settled down into simple political Conservatism; and when Archer's inner light led him to a vigorous Radicalism, it became necessary for him to extend his reserve from religion to politics, or else grieve his people very sorely, a cruelty of which he was quite incapable. He was hereditarily affectionate, and even suffered from a family inability to control his diaphragm (I borrow this quaint diagnosis from an expert) which made it impossible for him to command his voice when he was deeply moved, which explains both why he could not finish reading Little Eyolf and why up to the moment of relinquishing the attempt he had had to constrain himself so rigidly as to seem a wooden image rather than a very emotional man.

He was not himself conscious of the extent to which the Glasite diathesis influenced him. I do not believe that he knew or cared anything about the constitution or origin of Glasism: all he could tell me to satisfy my curiosity as a connoisseur in religious beliefs was that the performance, as he called it, consisted mainly in his grandfather reading the Bible phrase by phrase, and extracting from every phrase some not immediately obvious significance, the more farfetched and fantastic the better. The grandson was interested neither in Kirk nor Conventicle, but in the theatre. He was prepared to attend to Shakespear, but not to Glasite hermeneutics. He had a certain admiration for his grandfather's ingenuity as an exegete, and was rather proud of him; but he soon learnt to defend himself from his expositions by an acquirement that often stood him in good stead in the theatre later on. He could slip his finger under the next page of his open Bible; go fast asleep; and turn the page without waking up when the rustling of all the other Bibles as their readers turned over struck on his sleeping ear and started a reflex action.

If I had known this when I attempted to read my first play to him I might not have abandoned it for years as an unfinished failure. He was utterly contemptuous of its construction; but this I did not mind, as I classed constructed plays with artificial flowers, clockwork mice, and the like. Unfortunately, when I came to the second act, something—possibly something exegetic in my tone—revived the old protective habit. He fell into a deep slumber; and I softly put the manuscript away and let him have his sleep out. When I mentioned this to our friend Henry Arthur Jones he reminded me of a member of the *Comédie Française*, who, on being remonstrated with for sleeping whilst an author was reading a play, said "Sleep is a criticism." This was my own view of the case; and I might never have meddled with the stage again had not Archer unconsciously discounted the incident one day by telling me the tale of his famous grandfather.

Thus he never came to know what his grandfather's religion was. He dismissed it, and most of Scriptural theology with it, as flat nonsense. And from this estimate he never to the end of his days retreated. It may seem strange that a man whose literary bent was so strong that he made literature his profession, whose ear was so musical that he could write excellent verse, and whose judgment was so respected that he was accepted as the most serious critic of his day, should be able to read the dregs of Elizabethan drama and not to read the Bible; but the fact remains that when I was writing my preface on Christianity (to Androcles and the Lion) and, having just read the New Testament through, asked him whether he had read the Gospels lately, and what he made of them, he replied that he had tried, but "could not stick it." The doctrine was nonsense to him; and he had no patience with it because he took no interest in it. I pleaded that though Matthew had muddled his gospel by stringing sayings together in the wrong order, a more intelligible arrangement of them could be discovered by reading the other evangelists; but this produced no impression on him: the subject simply bored him; and he rather resented any attempt on my part to give the slightest importance to it. This was a very natural consequence of dosing a clever child prematurely with mental food that Ecumenical Councils have before now failed to digest; and parents and school committees will do well to make a careful note of it; but in Archer's case the intolerance it produced became a quality, as his book on India proves. There was no morbid nonsense about understanding everything and pardoning everything in the Archer family. The glimpses I had of them were quite convincing as to their being healthy-minded sensible open-air colonially rejuvenated people who, having to keep an inherited form of worship from making social life impossible, instinctively avoided sophistry and speculation, and took their intellectual course simply and downrightly. When, in what was then called The Conflict Between Religion and Science, William Archer took the side of Science, he broke away as cleanly and confidently as Glas had broken away from the Assembly or Walker from the Church of Ireland. He expressly denied having ever had any internal struggle or qualm. His only difficulty was to maintain his convictions without making his parents unhappy; and the Separatist reserve made it quite easy to do this whilst he lived with them.

When he came to London and began to write for the Secularist press, thus breaking the Separatist silence, he resorted to a *nom de plume*, for which, in those days, there were other reasons than family ones. A then future president of the National Secular Society had been actually imprisoned for a year for publishing in The Freethinker, his weekly journal, a picture of Samuel anointing Saul, in which the costumes and accessories were those of a modern hairdresser's shop; and until the expiration of the sentence Archer had to help with a monthly review which the victim of persecution edited for his more scholarly and fastidious followers.[4] The leaders of the Secularist movement, including at that time Mrs Besant, were delighted to welcome Archer as a brilliant young recruit, and were somewhat taken aback when he would not enter into intimate social relations with them lest they should meet his parents, and quite simply told them so in his most expressionless manner. But for the strained relations which ensued, and for his preoccupation with the theatre, he might, like Robertson, have become a familiar figure in the pulpit of South Place Chapel, and been as definitely associated with Rationalism as Mr Edward Clodd. As it was, his position was sufficiently affirmed to make me ask him one day what his parents had to say about it. His reply was that the subject was never mentioned between them, but that he supposed they must have noticed that he did not attend any place of worship. Clearly there was no bitterness nor bigotry in the matter; and the fact that there was no resistance to break down made it impossible for a man of Archer's affectionate sensitiveness not to shield his father and mother from every contact with his heresy and its associations that could possibly be avoided without a sacrifice of his convictions.

Presently another interest came into his life. One showery day [1884] I was in New Oxford Street, probably going to or from the British Museum reading room, when I saw Archer coming towards me past Mudie's, looking much more momentous than usual. He seemed eight feet high; and his aspect was stern and even threatening, as if he were defying all Oxford Street, buses and all, to take the smallest liberty with him. His air of formidable height was partly due, perhaps, to his having draped himself in a buff-colored mackintosh which descended to his calves. But it was quaintly aided by the contrast of his inches with those of a lady who clung to his arm to keep pace with his unmerciful strides. She had a small head and a proportionately small comely face, winsome and ready to smile when not actually smiling. I had never seen Archer with a woman on his arm before, nor indeed concerning himself with one in any way; and, as the future author of Man and Superman, I feared the worst. And, sure

4. G. W. Foote, editor of the secularist weekly *The Freethinker*, was imprisoned for twelve months for a 'blasphemous libel' in that journal (see also Vol. 1, p. 273). Archer, writing under the pseudonym Norman Britton, held the fort for him on *Progress*, which was Foote's monthly journal.

enough, I was immediately introduced to the lady as his selection for the destiny of being Mrs Archer [the former Frances Trickett].

The marriage seemed a great success. Mrs Archer fitted herself into the simple and frugal life of her husband quite naturally, caring no more for fashion or manufactured pleasures and luxuries than he did. There came a wonderful son: he who figures in the correspondence of Robert Louis Stevenson as Tomarcher. Mrs Archer found the world paradise enough first with her Willie, and then with her man and her boy. She tolerated me and indulged me as an incarnate joke because he did; and I saw rather more of him after his marriage than before it, instead of less: a rare privilege for a bachelor friend.

But the more Archer's slender means obliged him to put Mrs Archer and the boy first, and literature comparatively nowhere, the more I, having among my budget of novels that nobody would publish a book called The Irrational Knot (meaning the marriage tie), began to doubt whether domesticity was good for his career. At last I read an anonymous article on one of Archer's subjects which seemed to me a poor one. I was on the point of abusing it roundly to him one day when, to my consternation, he said, just in time, that he had written it. My concern was not because I thought the article unsatisfactory: every writer produces unsatisfactory articles occasionally. But that, good or bad, I had not recognized it as his: a failure unprecedented so far, proved to me that he had lost some of the brilliancy and unmistakeable individuality of style which had attracted me in his articles in The London Figaro long before I made his acquaintance. I knew that the way to make money in journalism is to turn out rapidly great quantities of undistinguished stuff; and I knew also that when a man marries he gives up his right to put quality of work first, and income second. I did not conceive it possible at that time that I should ever become a married man myself. With an artistic recklessness which shocks me in retrospect I told Archer that Mrs Archer was spoiling him, and that he would be a lost man unless he broke loose. He said, with that wooden formality which was the surest sign that he was deeply moved, that he must ask me not to visit his house whilst I held opinions so disparaging to Mrs Archer.

I was not in the least offended. Indeed I never was offended by anything Archer ever said to me or wrote about me, though he sometimes expressed a quite unnecessary remorse for speeches or articles which he supposed must have been painful to me. For some time I remained under his interdict, and saw nothing of Mrs Archer. Then the unexpected happened. Archer did not break loose; but Mrs Archer did. Let me not be misunderstood. There was no gentleman in the case. It was much more interesting than that.

I forget how long Mrs Archer remained a dropped subject between us; but it was Archer himself who resumed it. I found him in a state of frank anxiety which in him indicated considerable distress of mind; and he told me that Mrs Archer fancied that there was something the matter with her, though she was, as he believed, in perfect health. Now Mrs Archer, like her husband, was not at all the sort of person her appearance suggested. She seemed dainty, unassuming, clinging. Really, she was a woman of independent character, great decision and pertinacity, and considerable physical hardihood. This I had half guessed that day in Oxford Street, but I kept the guess to myself, as it might have been taken as a wanton paradox until the sequel bore it out. When Archer told me of his perplexity I shared it, and could think of nothing to suggest.

To the rescue of this male helplessness came a remarkable lady from America, Miss Annie Payson Call, authoress of a book entitled Power through Repose, and of a system, partly manipulative, partly sympathetic, of straightening out tangled nerves. Miss Call had the same sort of amiability as Mrs Archer, and the same overflow of energy for which selfishness was not enough. She tackled Mrs Archer; she tackled me; she tackled everybody; and as she was a charming person, nobody objected. But she found in Mrs Archer something more than the passive subject of a cure. She found a pupil, a disciple, and finally an apostle in England. Mrs Archer's vocation also was for healing sore minds and wandering wits. With what seems to me in retrospect a staggering suddenness, though in fact she had to see Tom through to his independent manhood first, she created the nerve training institution at King's Langley which survives her. Literary people in the eighteen-nineties used to write futile sequels to Ibsen's Doll's House: Mrs Archer found a real and perfectly satisfactory sequel. She became an independent professional woman most affectionately married to an independent professional man, the two complementing instead of hampering each other; for in practical matters he was full of inhibitions and diffidences from which she was vigorously free. Incidentally I ceased to be one of Willie's bachelor encumbrances. Mrs Archer, having developed considerably more practical initiative and ability than ever I possessed, took me in hand fearlessly on her new footing, and admitted me, I think, to as much of her friendship as I deserved.

Thus Archer's domesticity ceased to be a problem; and you may set him down for good and all as fortunate in his marriage. But to suggest all that his marriage meant for him I must return to the child Tom Archer. The extraordinary companionship which Archer found in his little son could not have existed but for a double bond between them. First, Archer had retained much more of his own childhood than even his most intimate friends suspected. He must have been a very imaginative child; and he had retained so much of a child's imagination and fun that it was for some time a puzzle to me that he could be so completely fascinated as he was by Ibsen's imagination, and that yet, when I produced my Quintessence of Ibsenism, he dismissed much of the specifically adult and worldly part of it precisely as he had dismissed the Scriptural exegetics of his grandfather. This devoted Ibsenite, who translated the Master's works so forcibly and vividly, was never in the least an Ibsenist: he delighted in Ibsen's plays just as a child delights in The Arabian Nights without taking in anything of the passages which Captain Burton left unexpurgated. It was this innocence that limited his own excursions into dramatic literature; he could not see that the life around him, including his own, was teeming with dramatic material, and persisted in looking for his subjects either in literature or in fairyland.

Now it happened that Tom Archer, though so entirely his mother's son in most respects that, save for an occasional fleeting revelation in his expression, he was not a bit like Archer, had a prodigious imagination. Having no derisive brothers and sisters to make him sensitive and secretive about it, but, on the contrary, a father who took it with the tenderest seriousness, and in fact became an accomplice in all its extravagances, Tom was able to let himself go gloriously. He invented a *pays de Cocagne* [land of plenty] which he called Peona [error for Piona], which went far beyond the garret-forest in The Wild Duck, as it had no contact with limited mechanical realities. I heard much of Peona and its inhabitants at second hand, and even a little at first hand, on which occasions I swallowed every adventure with a gravity not surpassed by Archer's own. I am sure that Archer, whose youth as one of a large and robust family enjoyed no such protection, could never have felt this delicacy had he not remembered his own youth, and recognized his own imagination in his son's.

There was another experience from which he was determined to protect Tom; and that was the British boarding school, or boy farm, as William Morris called it. It was useless to romance to him about the character-forming virtues and historic glories of Eton and Harrow, Winchester and Rugby and Marlborough: he anticipated the opinions of [Frederick W.] Sanderson[5]

5. Sanderson was headmaster of the Oundle School, whose roots go back to the fifteenth century, and which stressed modern educational techniques favouring engineering.

of Oundle, who heartily agreed with me when I expressed my opinion that these places should be razed to the ground, and their foundations sown with salt. Archer had taken his own schooling as a dayboy, and was convinced, with good reason, that this arrangement, however inconvenient for the parents, was much more wholesome for the child. Accordingly, Tom spent his childish schooldays with his people in a Surrey cottage on the façade of which Mr Edward Rimbault Dibdin[6] inscribed the name Walden (a compliment to Thoreau) in highly artistic lettering. When he outgrew the educational resources of that primitive neighborhood the family moved to Dulwich and sent him to the college there.

Meanwhile my comment on Tom was that he was a second Rudyard Kipling; for, as I happened to know from William Morris, Mr Kipling had been a great Peoneer in his nonage. The years in which Archer and Tom explored Peona together passed as fast as real years in a real country until at last the once inexhaustible subject of Tom dropped so completely that I actually had to ask Archer about him. To my amazement he conveyed to me, with a manner that would have done credit to a piece of mahogany, that the firm of Archer & Son of Peona had dissolved partnership. Tom, he explained, had been ill; and Archer opined that the illness had affected his character, which, he said, was totally changed. This theory of the alleged change was too summary and too surgical to convince me. But I forbore to probe; and the truth came out gradually. The child Tom, developing into the incipient man, emerged from Peona a most unnatural son. He was as keen about the glories of public schools as if he were indeed the author [Rudyard Kipling] of Stalky and Co. He distinguished himself at Dulwich by the facility with which he turned out Latin verses, becoming Captain of the Classical Side. He joined the Officers' Training Corps, and actually made his father enlist in the Inns of Court Volunteers, a trial which Archer supported because, being a private, and having to salute Tom, who was an officer, the situation appealed to his sense of humor as well as to his conscientious public spirit. In short, he dragged Archer out of Peona with him, and imposed public schools ideals on him. Military romance alone survived from fairyland; and even that took the fashionable imperialist shape.

Up to this time Archer had, without knowing it, been a true Glasite in the essential sense. His kingdom had not been of this world. But now, what with the son grasping with all his imaginative power at conventional

6. A close friend of Archer, he was curator of the Walker Art Gallery, Liverpool, and a former art critic.

military ideals, and this world beginning to treat the father with more and more of the distinguished consideration which his work earned and his unworldly character commanded, Archer had to adapt himself as far as he could to the responsibilities of his celebrity, and to set himself to make the best of convention instead of criticizing it with the independence of a young and comparatively unknown man. Every freelance who makes a reputation has to go through this phase; but Archer was under the special emotional pressure of having to adapt himself to Tom's Kiplingesque war mentality in and out of season. He became as conventional as it was in his nature to be, and indeed, for Tom's sake, perhaps a little more, though the public school had taken away his playmate.

Presently Tom's boyhood passed like his childhood, and left him a young man, still his mother's son in respect of being under average military size and considerably over average military vigor of mind and practical initiative. Oxford, where he had expected to distinguish himself because he had done so at Dulwich, did not suit him. True, his aptitude for classical exercises did not desert him. He took honors in law, and was in no sense a failure. But Oxford was something of a failure for him. The struggle for life was not real enough there for a youth who had a passion for the military realism of soldiering. When he left Oxford to begin adult life, he worked as a solicitor for a couple of years in London. Then an opening in America, with a promise of a speedy return to rejoin his family at home, took him across the Atlantic.

Two months later the gulf of war opened at the feet of our young men. Tom rushed back to hurl himself into it. Amid the volcanoes of Messines he was serving as a lance-corporal in "the dear old G Company" of the London Scottish. Invalided home, he accepted a commission, and for a year was able to do no more than sit on the brink of the gulf in the Ordnance until his strength returned, when he volunteered afresh for the firing line as lieutenant in the King's Own Scottish Borderers. In February 1918 he married Alys Morty, cousin to a comrade-at-arms fallen at Messines, and had a deliriously happy honeymoon in Ireland. Then, the war still dragging on, he hurled himself into the gulf again; and this time, at Mount Kemmel, it closed on him, and his father saw him no more. He left his young widow to take his place in his parents' affections, the newly found beloved daughter succeeding to the newly lost beloved son. Yet Archer was loth to let the son go. He renewed an old interest in super-rational research; investigated dreams and the new psychoanalysis; and even experimented unsuccessfully in those posthumous conversations in which so many of the bereaved found comfort. And so, between daughter and son, the adventure of parentage never ended for Archer.

When the war broke out he was past military age, and had to confine his part in it to countering the German propaganda service and doing some of our own, an employment in which his knowledge of languages stood him in good stead. When the Armistice made an end of that, his own bent reasserted itself and took him back to the theatre, and (save where his memories of Tom were concerned) to militant Rationalism.

His great work of translating Ibsen had by this time been brought to an end by Ibsen's death. I am myself a much-translated author; and I know how hard the lot of a translator is if he is sensitive to frantic abuse both by rival or would-be rival translators, and by literary men inflamed by an enthusiasm for the author (gained from the translations they abuse) which convinces them that his opinions are their own, and that the translator, not seeing this, has missed the whole point of the work. I use the word frantic advisedly: the lengths to which these attacks go are incredible. At one time it was the fashion in the literary cliques to dismiss Archer's translations as impossible. I told them it was no use: that Archer-Ibsen had seized the public imagination as it had seized theirs, and would beat any other brand of Ibsen in English. And it was so. Whenever a translation was produced without the peculiar character that Archer gave to his, it had no character at all, no challenge, at best only a drawing-room elegance that was a drawback rather than an advantage. When Mr [F.] Anstey [pseudonym of Thomas Anstey Guthrie] burlesqued Ibsen in Punch, he did it by burlesquing Archer: without Archer the plays would not have bitten deep enough to be burlesqued. Even in the case of Peer Gynt, which moved several enthusiasts to attempt translations following the rhymes and metres of the original (I began one myself, with our friend Braekstad translating for me literally, line by line, and got as far as a couple of pages or so [see Vol. 1, p. 184, fn. 14]), the unrhymed translation by Archer and his brother Colonel Charles Archer held its own against the most ingenious and elaborate rival versions. Whenever Peer Gynt was quoted it was always in the Archer version. I have already given the explanation. Archer understood and cared for Ibsen's imagination. For his sociological views he cared so little that he regarded them mostly as aberrations when he was conscious of them. Thus, undistracted by Ibsen's discussions, he went straight for his poetry, and reproduced every stroke of imagination in a phraseology that invented itself *ad hoc* in his hands. As nothing else really mattered, the critics who could not see this, and would have it that everything else mattered, neither made nor deserved to make any permanent impression. Besides, the air of Norway breathed through his versions. He had breathed it himself from his childhood during his frequent visits, beginning at the age of three, to the

Norwegian home of his grandparents, where he had two unmarried aunts who exercised his tenderness and powers of admiration very beneficently. As to the few lyrics which occur in Ibsen's plays, and which would have baffled a prosaic translator, they gave Archer no trouble at all: he was at his best in them. If it had been possible for the father of a family to live by writing verse in the XIX century, Archer would probably have done more in that manner on his own account.

How far he sacrificed a career as an original playwright to putting the English-speaking peoples in possession of Ibsen is an open question. In my opinion he instinctively chose the better part, because the theatre was not to him a workshop but part of his fairyland. He never really got behind the scenes, and never wanted to. The illusion that had charmed his youth was so strong and lasting that not even fifty years of professional theatregoing in London could dispel it. Inevitably then he liked the theatre as he found it at first: the theatre of the French "well-made play." But the attraction of this school of theatrical art for him did not lie in its ingenuities and neatnesses of construction, though he sometimes wrote as if it did. He liked it because it also lived in fairyland. Sophisticated as it was, yet was its kingdom not of this world. Archer, though he approached it as a reformer, did not want to reform it out of existence: he wanted to strengthen it by giving some sort of subsistence to its make-believe, which had worn thin and stale, ignorant and incredible. He did not want to drag the heroine from her fairyland; but how could he believe in her if she had an obviously impossible solicitor and butler and lady's maid? If she lived in a world totally exhausted of ideas, created by authors who, outside their little theatrical clique, knew nothing of their country, and conceived it as a complete vacuum in respect of the things it had most at heart: business, sport, politics, and religion, how could a man of any strength of mind or sense of verisimilitude take her seriously? That was why Archer cried out in one breath for naturalness in the theatre and for artifice in dramatic authorship. In the novel, which raises no question of technique, he welcomed the most uncompromising naturalness, making me read De Maupassant's Une Vie [1883], applauding Zola, and coming into my rooms one day full of his discovery of a new novelist of our own, who had burst on the world with a naturalistic novel entitled A Mummer's Wife [1885]. I was so impressed with his account of it that I eagerly asked the name of the author; but when he told me it was George Moore I burst into irreverent laughter, knowing the said George personally as an inveterate romancer, whose crimson inventions, so far delivered orally for private circulation only, suggested that he had been brought into the world by a union of

Victor Hugo with Ouida.[7] But Archer insisted on my reading the book, as he had insisted on my reading Une Vie; and I stood rebuked for my incredulity.

I never read Archer's one novel, a youthful exploit called The Doom of the Destroyed, which had been published serially in a Scottish newspaper [*North Briton*, in 1875–6], and was one of his favorite jokes. I gathered that in point of romance it left George Moore's unpublished *quasi* autobiographical tales of adventure nowhere; but it is certain that Archer's adult taste in novels was for merciless realism. Therefore when one day he proposed that we two should collaborate in writing a play, he to supply the constructional scaffolding or scenario, and I to fill in the dialogue, I assumed that I might be as realistic as Zola or De Maupassant with his entire sympathy. But he was always upsetting my assumptions as to his sympathies; and he did so signally on this occasion.

It happened in this way. Archer had planned for two heroines, a rich one and a poor one. The hero was to prefer the poor one to the rich one; and in the end his disinterestedness was to be rewarded by the lucrative discovery that the poor one was really the rich one. When I came to fill in this scheme I compressed the two heroines into one; but I made up the one out of two models, whom I will now describe.

Once, when I was walking homewards at midnight through Wigmore Street, taking advantage of its stillness and loneliness at that hour to contemplate, like Kant, the starry heaven above me, the solitude was harshly broken by the voices of two young women who came out of Mandeville Place on the other side of the street a couple of hundred yards behind me. The dominant one of the pair was in a black rage: the other was feebly trying to quiet her. The strained strong voice and the whimpering remonstrant one went on for some time. Then came the explosion. The angry one fell on the other, buffeting her, tearing at her hair, grasping at her neck. The victim, evidently used to it, cowered against the railings, covering herself as best she could, and imploring and remonstrating in a carefully subdued tone, dreading a police rescue more than the other's violence. Presently the fit passed, and the two came on their way, the lioness silent, and the lamb reproachful and rather emboldened by her sense of injury. The scene stuck in my memory, to be used in due time.

Also I had about this time a friendship with a young independent professional woman, who enjoyed, as such, an exceptional freedom of

7. Pseudonym of novelist Marie Louise de la Ramée, whose forty-five novels deal chiefly with fashionable life.

social intercourse in artistic circles in London. As she was clever, good-natured, and very goodlooking, all her men friends fell in love with her. This had occurred so often that she had lost all patience with the hesitating preliminaries of her less practised adorers. Accordingly, when they clearly longed to kiss her, and she did not dislike them sufficiently to make their gratification too great a strain on her excessive goodnature, she would seize the stammering suitor firmly by the wrists, bring him into her arms by a smart pull, and saying "Let's get it over," allow the startled gentleman to have his kiss, and then proceed to converse with him at her ease on subjects of more general interest.

I provided Archer with a heroine by inventing a young woman who developed from my obliging but impatient friend in the first act to the fury of Wigmore Street in the second: such a heroine as had not been seen on the London stage since Shakespear's Taming of the Shrew. And my shrew was never tamed.

Now Archer was not such a simpleton as to be unaware that some women are vulgar, violent, and immodest according to Victorian conceptions of modesty. He would probably have assented to the proposition that as vulgarity, violence, and immodesty are elements in human nature, it is absurd to think of them as unwomanly, unmanly, or unnatural. But he also knew that a character practically free from these three vices could be put on the stage without any departure from nature, for the excellent reason that his own character was most unusually free from them, even his strong Scottish sense of humor being, like his conversation, entirely clean. Why, then, impose them wantonly on his charming and refined heroine? He repudiated all complicity in such an outrage. He reproached me for my apparent obsession with abominably ill-tempered characters, oversexed to saturation. My way in the theatre was evidently not his way; and it was not until, at my third attempt as a playwright, I achieved a play (Mrs Warren's Profession) which appealed to his sense of Zolaistic naturalism, that he ceased to dissuade me from pursuing the occupation into which he had innocently tempted me.

I must mention that his decisive and indignant retirement from the collaboration occurred whilst the play was still in shorthand, and therefore quite illegible by him, and not legible enough by myself to admit of my reading it aloud to him tolerably. But I had made demands on him which betrayed my deliberate and unconscionable disregard of his rules of the art of play construction. His scenario had been communicated to me *viva voce*; and when I told him I had finished the first act, and had not yet come to his plot, asking him to refresh my memory about it, he felt as the architect of a cathedral might if the builder had remarked one day that he had finished the nave and transepts according to his own fancy, and, having lost the architect's plans, would like to have another copy of them before he tackled the tower, the choir, and the lady chapel. I managed to appease my architect by arguing that it was not until the second act that a well-made play came to business seriously, and that meanwhile I had fulfilled his design by making the river Rhine the scene of the meeting of the lovers in the first act. But when, having written some pages of the second act, I said I had used up all his plot and wanted some more to go on with, he retired peremptorily from the firm. He was of course quite right: I was transmogrifying not only his design but the whole British drama of that day so recklessly that my privilege as a paradoxical lunatic broke down under the strain; and he could no longer with any self-respect allow me to play the fool with his scenario. For it was not a question of this particular scenario only. He did not agree with me that the form of drama which had been perfected in the middle of the XIX century in the French theatre was essentially mechanistic and therefore incapable of producing vital drama. That it was exhausted and, for the moment, sterile, was too obvious to escape an observer of his intelligence; but he saw nothing fundamentally wrong with it, and to the end of his life maintained that it was indispensable as a form for sound theatrical work, needing only to be brought into contact with life by having new ideas poured into it. I held, on the contrary, that a play is a vital growth and not a mechanical construction; that a plot is the ruin of a story and therefore of a play, which is essentially a story; that Shakespear's plays and Dickens's novels, though redeemed by their authors' genius, were as ridiculous in their plots as Goldsmith's hopelessly spoilt Good-Natured Man [1768]: in short, that a play should never have a plot, because, if it has any natural life in it, it will construct itself, like a flowering plant, far more wonderfully than its author can consciously construct it.

On such terms collaboration between us was impossible: indeed my view practically excludes collaboration. His view does not; and we shall presently see him returning to it after an interval of many years, during which I had become an established playwright, possibly wrong in my theory, but beyond all question successful in my practice.

He had already written plays singlehanded. I remember a one-act play called Clive, dealing with the failure of that hero's attempt at suicide, and his conclusion that Heaven had other views for him. As this has disappeared, he may have destroyed it as puerile; but I thought it promising, and more alive than a play about a prima donna who lost her voice, a theme frankly taken from George Eliot's Armgart.[8] George Eliot's reputation was then enormous, in spite of the protests of Ruskin, and of the alliterative vituperations of Swinburne; and it was very far from being undeserved. When I read Middlemarch in my teens I was impressed by it as by a masterpiece of a new order; and I have no doubt that Archer was equally impressed, though I do not remember discussing George Eliot with him. But the impression she made was not encouraging. The effect of the fatalistic determinism into which the scientific thought of that day had driven her was distinctly depressing and laming. Her characters seemed the helpless victims of their environment and inherited dispositions, contributing nothing except a few follies and weaknesses to the evolutionary struggle, if the word struggle can be used where there is no real resistance to what Darwin called natural selection. Now a fatalist, as George Eliot proved, can write so well that a capable man of letters like the late Lord Bryce, in a public eulogy of Tolstoy,[9] could think of nothing more complimentary to say of him than that as a novelist he was second only to George Eliot. But, for all that, she discouraged many noble spirits; and I think she disabled Archer to some extent, directly or indirectly. The last drop of dramatic vitality in her school was drained by Ibsen; and when Archer had translated Ibsen there was nothing left for the translator.

Archer had various theories as to this disablement: as, for instance, that he could not write dialogue, which was nonsense; but the fact was that a George Eliotish philosophy of life, and a mechanistic limitation of the possibilities of the theatre, combined with his natural and very amiable diffidence and his unconsciously Glasite unworldliness, kept him back from the newly broken and rather unsightly ground in which alone a new drama could germinate.

At last, quite late in life, he had a dream; and the dream was a good story about an Asiatic Rajah made cynical by a Western education, and a Green Goddess who had to be propitiated by blood sacrifices, some English captives becoming available for that purpose. The result proved that the complexes which inhibited him from writing effective plays when he was awake, did not operate when he was asleep. When he turned his dream into a play it was prodigiously successful, first in America and then in

---

8. The poem 'Armgart' (1871) is included in Eliot's *The Legend of Jubal, and Other Poems* (1874).
9. James Viscount Bryce, scholar, jurist, diplomat and Chief Secretary for Ireland under Campbell-Bannerman, was one of the speakers (Shaw was another) at the Tolstoy Commemoration in Kingsway Hall on 30 November 1920.

England;[10] and Archer ceased at last to be a much underpaid man. I had urged at every opportunity that the great national services he had done by his Englishing of Ibsen should be acknowledged by a pension (a title without one is only a source of expense); but I was always met with the difficulty that in this Philistine country parliamentary grants are made only to generals, pro-consuls, and Polar explorers. Literature and art have nothing to look for but an occasional knighthood or a civil list pension; and to obtain the pension it is necessary to assert that the postulant is in straitened circumstances. For Ashton Ellis, the translator of Richard Wagner's voluminous prose works, it had been possible, when he was almost destitute, to obtain a wretched pittance of £80 a year; but Archer was at no time at a loss for his livelihood. After the success of The Green Goddess a pension was more than ever out of the question; and Archer never had any official recognition of his public service, out of which, by the way, he steadfastly refused to make money through translator's performing fees, lest he should compromise his disinterestedness as a critic.

Here let me say, parenthetically, that Archer was incorruptible as a critic. In his day there were various methods of amiable corruption in vogue. One was called simply Chicken & Champagne, which explains itself. It includes various degrees of blandishment; and some of them were tried on Archer; but they were hopelessly thrown away on him, because he never had the least suspicion of their nature, and either accepted them in unconquerable innocence at their face value, or declined them because they bored him. Another way was available if the critic was known to have written a play. The manager asked for it; put it on the shelf; promised production at some future unspecified time; and offered an advance on account of author's fees. A third method was almost a routine. An actor-manager would write to a critic to say that he wanted to consult him as an expert. An interview would follow. The manager would explain that he had acquired the performing right of some foreign play, and was thinking of attempting a part in it. Would the critic advise him about the translation? Would he care to undertake the translation? If so, would he sell a six months option on the translation for, say, £50? If the critic was amenable, the £50 changed hands; and nothing more was heard of the play or the translation. If not, he recommended another translator; the manager shrugged his shoulders; and the two parted smiling. The managers did this, I believe, rather because it was the fashion, and almost the due of a leading

10. *The Green Goddess* (1921), which starred George Arliss, achieved a run of 440 performances in New York, followed by 416 in London.

critic, than with any sense that the proposal was in any way improper. Certainly the actor-managers who made it to me when I was a critic thought no worse of it than of tipping a waiter, and probably considered it rather unsocial on my part to evade the transaction.

Notwithstanding Archer's reputation as a translator, no such proposals were made, as far as I know, to him. His integrity was unassailed because it was so obviously impregnable. I doubt if he even knew the game as a usage, though he must have been aware of instances in which dealings in options had been followed by marked accesses of eulogy. After all, the instances were exceptional; besides, he went his own way so completely as a matter of course that he passed through the theatrical world without noticing all its aberrations, as indeed he passed through the kingdom of this world in general. He was much too scrupulous in the matter of the Ibsen translations; but the position of a critic who is also a proprietor of performing rights of any kind is certainly a very delicate one; and it was characteristic of Archer to carry his delicacy too far rather than accept a commercial interest in the plays of an author whom his critical conscience obliged him to recommend with all his might.

Diffident to the last, Archer had no sooner constructed The Green Goddess according to rule, and finished the two main acts, than he lost self-confidence, and perhaps patience, over the *dénouement* in the third act, and asked me to finish the play for him on the old ground that he could not write dialogue. I overwhelmed him with denunciations of his laziness; told him he could finish it perfectly well for himself if he chose to; and threatened that if I did the work I would make the lady get the better of the wicked Rajah in the vein of Captain Brassbound's Conversion. This threat was effectual; and he turned to Arthur Pinero to finish the play for him. Pinero, with great tact, made an alternative suggestion which opened Archer's eyes to the fact that if it was not worth his while to write the last act because it was to be hack work, he should offer it to a hack writer. Archer thereupon finished the play himself, and was, I hope, delivered by the result from all further misgivings as to his own competence. But it was too late in the day to begin life anew as a fashionable playwright; and The Green Goddess stands, by no means as the crown of his career, but rather as a proof that the inhibitions which prevented him from achieving this sort of worldly success earlier were not due, as he himself feared, to lack of faculty, but to Providence, which had other fish for him to fry.

In his predestined work I do not include the whole of his huge output of notices of theatrical performances, nor even the plans for a national theatre, which he prepared in collaboration with Harley Granville-Barker [A

National Theatre: Scheme and Estimates, 1907], then the most wonderful of the younger generation knocking at our doors. Journalistic criticism, after the first years, becomes necessarily for the most part repetitive breadwinning; and the theatre planning was rather like building sand castles in the face of a flood tide, a pastime to which Granville-Barker was much addicted as a refuge from his proper business of writing plays. Archer's essays on the censorship, on Diderot's Paradox (Masks or Faces?), and on Macready, with his reprints of the theatrical criticisms of [George Henry] Lewes and [John] Forster, are all valuable and readable;[11] but they lay in his path as a professional critic of the theatre, and are therefore not so significant as the excursions to which his spirit drove him.

In 1906 a Spanish educationalist and philanthropist who was also strongly anti-clerical (meaning really anti-obscurantist), and was therefore supposed by the officers of the Spanish army to be in his nature essentially diabolical, and in his habits an assassin of all royal persons, had the misfortune to fall into the hands of a court-martial in Barcelona, where he was shamefully ill-used whilst in custody, and finally shot. It was a monstrous case of class ignorance and vindictive bigotry; and Archer willingly accepted a journalistic commission to visit Spain and investigate it. He exposed it so effectually that the biographical dictionaries and encyclopedias now refer to him as their authority for their accounts of the martyrdom—for that is what it came to—of Ferrer.[12]

His subsequent visit to India, though it had no such sensational provocation, produced his remarkable book on the subject [India and the Future, 1917]. At that time it was the fashion for literary European travelers returning from Asia to display their susceptibilities to the call of the East by

---

11. Archer's *Masks and Faces: A Study of the Psychology of Acting* (1888) contains his essay on Diderot's *Paradox of Acting* (1830), published in the *Theatre*, March 1884. His work on W. C. Macready (Vol. 1 in the Eminent Actors series) was published in 1890. The criticisms of Forster and Lewes were collected by Archer and Robert Lowe in *Dramatic Essays*, Vol. III (1896). Forster, an English biographer and literary and dramatic critic of the *True Sun* and the *Examiner*, is remembered particularly for his *Life of Dickens* (1872–4).

12. Archer was commissioned by *McClure's Magazine* to investigate the case of Francisco Ferrer, a secularist editor and theoretical anarchist, executed in Spain in 1909 after a military trial on the charge of having been the instigator and leader of the Barcelona riots in July 1909. Archer's finding that the charges against Ferrer were unfounded and probably trumped up appeared in *McClure's* in November–December 1910, and issued as a book *The Life, Trial, and Death of Francisco Ferrer* in 1911.

depicting an India of boundless and magical fascination, lit up with Bengal lights, saturated with the charm of Pierre Loti's[13] romances, adorned with the temples of a living religion more profound than our own, and inhabited by Rabindranath Tagores[14] and darkeyed enchantresses, with Mahatmas in the mountain background. These enthusiasts were more Indian than any Indian; and their readers, who had never been in India, began where they left off, and went much further into an imaginary East. Archer went to see for himself, and instantly and uncompromisingly denounced the temples as the shambles of a barbarous ritual of blood sacrifice, and the people as idolaters with repulsive rings through their noses. He refused to accept the interest of Indian art and the fictions of Indian romance as excuses. He remained invincibly faithful to Western civilization, and told the Indians flatly what a civilized Western gentleman must think of them and feel about some of their customs. Had he been able to get behind the scenes of Indian domestic life as Katherine Mayo [in *Mother India*, 1927] did some years later, his book might have made as great a sensation as hers.

In writing thus he did India the only service in his power. If Western civilization is not more enlightened than Eastern we have clearly no right to be in India. When once the British conqueror and master of India comes to think that suttee is a touching and beautiful act of wifely sacrifice, he had better abdicate, come home, and introduce suttee in England. When he ceases to treat the car of Juggernaut precisely as he would treat a motorbus driven to the public danger, his mission in India is over. What we owe to the Roman occupation of Britain we do not know: in fact there is too much ground for Mr George Trevelyan's conclusion that we relapsed the moment the Romans left us to ourselves; but we should certainly owe nothing at all if the Romans had had the slightest doubt that the augur represented a less grossly superstitious religion than the Druid, and that Roman law and Roman civilization were higher than British. They may have been as hasty and superficial as Sir John Woodroffe[15] declares Archer to have been; but they did not think so; and anyhow the sole justification of their conquest and occupation was that they were right. We shall have to clear out of India some day as the Romans had to clear out of Britain:

13. Pen-name of Louis-Marie Viaud, French naval officer who became an accomplished writer of popular romances, such as *Fantôme d'Orient* (1892).
14. Bengali poet and philosopher, awarded the Nobel Prize for Literature in 1913.
15. Professor of the University of Calcutta (1919) and Puisne Judge of the High Court of Calcutta 1904–22, who published *Is India Civilized?* in 1919.

perhaps the sooner the better for both parties. But it is certain that if, after that happens, the Indians are ever to say "It was a good thing for us that the westerners came and taught us something," it will be because the English criticism of India was Archer's criticism, and not that of the occidental renegades who swell the heads of our Indian students by assuring them that we are crude barbarians compared to them. Archer would have been the last man to deny that we are shocking barbarians according to our own standards; that white women with small earrings cannot logically despise brown women with large noserings; and that the Fundamentalist who prosecutes a school teacher for refusing to bow the knee to the god to whom Jephthah sacrificed his daughter [Judges 11: 29–40] can hardly hope to impose himself on an educated Hindu as a pioneer of thought. All the same, the Fundamentalist does not sacrifice his daughter or even his calf, and would send anyone who did to the electric chair or the lunatic asylum; and the Eastern toleration of noserings is not justified by the Western toleration of earrings. People who make the one an excuse for the other will never do anything to lighten the load of human superstition; and as this was really Archer's appointed task in life he wrote one of the most useful because one of the most resolutely unsympathetic books on India produced in his generation. It is not all unsympathetic or anti-Indian: very far from it. But it was the unsympathetic part that was needed and effective. If you like, he wrote about the Indians as John Glas would have written about the heathen. But why not rather put it that he wrote about the Indians as Dickens wrote about the Americans [*American Notes*, 1842]? And does anyone now doubt that Dickens told the Americans what they needed to be told, and that his honesty did not prevent his becoming more popular with them than any of their romantic flatterers?

I have no more to say about William Archer that matters enough to be printed. Looking back as far as the days when, finding me full of literary ability but ridiculously incapable of obtaining literary employment and desperately in need of it, he set me on my feet as a critical journalist by simply handing me over a share of his own work, and making excuses for having deputed it until the Pall Mall Gazette and The World, then in the van of fashionable journalism, accepted the deputy as a principal, I am conscious that many of our contemporaries must have seen him much oftener than I, and that this sketch of him must be incomplete and perhaps in some points misleading. And there is the other possibility: that I may have been too close to him, and known him too early, to realize his full stature. But I am sure that I never could get him to think as well of himself as I thought of him. I leave it to others to compose a proper full-dress literary portrait of him: all I have tried to do here is to give some sort of life to a sketch of a friend of whom, after more than forty years, I have not a single unpleasant recollection, and whom I was never sorry to see or unready to talk to.

One day I received from him the following letter:

27, FITZROY SQUARE, W.I
17th December 1924

MY DEAR G. B. S.

Since I wrote you, I have learnt that I shall have to undergo an operation one of these days—go into a nursing home tomorrow. I don't know that the operation is a very serious one, and as a matter of fact I feel as fit as a fiddle, so I suppose my chances are pretty good. Still, accidents will happen; and this episode gives me an excuse for saying, what I hope you don't doubt—namely, that though I may sometimes have played the part of all-too candid mentor, I have never wavered in my admiration and affection for you, or ceased to feel that the Fates had treated me kindly in making me your contemporary and friend. I thank you from my heart for forty years of good comradeship.

Whatever happens, let it never be said that I did not move in good society—I lunched today with the King of Norway and Prince Olaf.

Very kind regards to Mrs Shaw, and all good wishes for 1925.
—Ever yours,

W. A.

I was not seriously alarmed, and presently sailed for Madeira. On landing there, the first words that caught my eye on the news bulletin in the hall of Reid's Hotel were "Death of Mr William Archer." They threw me into a transport of fury. The operation had killed him. I am unfashionable enough to hold that an operation which does not justify itself by its promised results should always be the subject of a stringent inquest; for I have never been able to regard a death caused by an operation as a natural death. My rage may have been unjust to the surgeons; but it carried me over my first sense of bereavement. When I returned to an Archerless London it seemed to me that the place had entered on a new age in which I was lagging superfluous.

I still feel that when he went he took a piece of me with him.

Author's Note

Preface to a series of reprints of prefaces to Shaw's plays, in John O'London's Weekly, *28 January 1928*

The articles which follow were written from time to time as prefaces to the published volumes of my plays and have therefore never reached the very considerable body of people who do not read plays. Some of them do not even read books, having no leisure and no money to spare for anything but the papers and magazines. The purpose of John O'London's Weekly is to see that this limitation of their resources shall not cut them off from the literary culture which is so important to them, and which they are quite as capable of appreciating as richer and idler folk. That is why I very gladly accept the hospitality of its columns for a republication which will make these essays accessible to many whom they have hitherto, to my great regret, failed to reach.

Those who are unacquainted with the oddities of literary tradition may ask how it is possible to separate the prefaces from the plays. Nothing is easier. The only connection between the prefaces and the plays is that they have hitherto kept company within the same book covers. Most of the prefaces were written long after the plays had been performed. The practice of attaching polemical pamphlets to plays as prefaces has persisted from the days of Dryden and Molière to those of Victor Hugo, Dumas *fils*, and myself. A playwright who deals with human nature instead of artificial "plots" is like a shipwright who finds, when he has built his ship, that he has a store of material left, rejected as unsuitable or superfluous for the ship, but sound and useful for, say, housebuilding. If he is master of the two trades, he builds a house after building the ship. I happen to have the two trades at my fingers' ends; and I hate to waste good material. These prefaces are the houses; and you can inhabit them without having ever seen the ships, just as you can travel in the ship without knowing anything about the house.

G. B. S.

The Intelligent Woman's Guide to Socialism and Capitalism

I

A Foreword for American Readers, 1928

═══

I have never been in America;[1] therefore I am free from the delusion, commonly entertained by the people who happen to have been born there, that they know all about it, and that America is their country in the same sense that Ireland is my country by birth, and England my country by adoption and conquest. You, dear madam, are an American in the sense that I am a European, except that the American States have a language in common and are federated, and the European states are still on the tower of Babel and are separated by tariff fortifications. When I hear people asking why America does not join the League of Nations I have to point out to them that America *is* a League of Nations, and sealed the covenant of her solidity as such by her blood more than sixty years ago, whereas the affair at Geneva is not a League of Nations at all, but only a so far unsuccessful attempt to coax Europe to form one at the suggestion of a late American President, with the result that the British Secretary of State for Foreign Affairs makes occasional trips to Geneva, and, on returning, reassures the British House of Commons by declaring that in spite of all Woodrow-Wilsonic temptations to combine with other nations he remains an Englishman [Shavian parody of W. S. Gilbert lyric in *H.M.S. Pinafore*, 1878] first, last, and all the time; that the British Empire comes before everything with him; and that it is on this understanding and this alone that he consents to discuss with foreigners any little matters in which he can oblige them without detriment to the said reserved interests. And this attitude seems to us in England so natural, so obvious, so completely a matter of

---

1. Shaw first visited the United States in 1933 and again in 1936, both times very briefly.

course, that the newspapers discuss the details of Mr [Austen] Chamberlain's[2] report of his trip without a word about the patriotic exordium which reduces England's membership of the League to absurdity.

Now your disadvantage in belonging to a league of nations instead of to a nation is that if you belong to New York or Massachusetts, and know anything beyond the two mile radius of which you are the centre, you probably know much more of England, France, and Italy than you do of Texas or Arizona, though you are expected, as an American, to know all about America. Yet I never met an American who knew anything about America except the bits she had actually set eyes on or felt with her boots; and even of that she could hardly see the wood for the trees. By comparison I may be said to know almost all about America. I am far enough off to get a good general view, and, never having assumed, as the natives do, that a knowledge of America is my intuitional birthright, I have made enquiries, read books, availed myself of the fact that I seem to be personally an irresistible magnet for every wandering American, and even gathered something from the recklessly confidential letters which every American lady who has done anything unconventional feels obliged to write me as a testimony to the ruinous efficacy of my books and plays. I could and should have drawn all the instances in this book from American life were it not that America is such a fool's paradise that no American would have believed a word of them, and I should have been held up, in exact proportion to my accuracy and actuality, as a grossly ignorant and prejudiced Britisher, defaming the happy West as ludicrously as the capitalist West defames Russia. What I tell you of England you will believe. What I could tell you of America might provoke you to call on me with a gun. Also it would lead you to class me as a bitter enemy to America, whereas I assure you that though I do not adore your country with the passion professed by English visitors at public banquets when you have overwhelmed them with your reckless hospitality, I give it a good deal of my best attention as a very interesting if still very doubtful experiment in civilization.

But this much I will permit myself to say. Do not imagine that because at this moment certain classes of American workmen are buying bathtubs and Ford cars, and investing in building societies and the like the money that they formerly spent in the saloons, that America is doing as well as can be expected. If you were at this moment a miner's wife in South Wales

2. British politician, who as Foreign Secretary (1924–9) attended all meetings of the League of Nations Council and Assembly.

you would be half starving; but the wife of a Colorado miner might think you very lucky in having nothing more violent than half starving to endure. The sweated women workers in the tenements of your big cities are told that in America anyone can make a fortune who wants to. Here we spare them that mockery, at least. You must take it from me, without driving me to comparisons that between nations wound as personalities do between individuals, that Capitalism is the same everywhere, and that if you look for its evils at home you will miss nothing of them except perhaps some of the socialistic defences which European States have been forced to set up against their worst extremities.

In truth it is odd that this book should not have been written by an American. Its thesis is the hopelessness of our attempts to build up a stable civilization with units of unequal income; and it was in America that this inequality first became monstrous not only in money but in its complete and avowed dissociation from character, rank, and the public responsibility traditionally attached to rank. On the eastern shores of the Atlantic the money makers formed a middle class between the proletariat, or manual working class, and the aristocracy, or governing class. Thus labor was provided for; business was provided for; and government was provided for; and it was possible to allow and even encourage the middle class to make money without regard to public interests, as these were the business of the aristocracy.

In America, however, the aristocracy was abolished; and the only controling and directing force left was business, with nothing to restrain it in its pursuit of money except the business necessity for maintaining property in land and capital and enforcing contracts, the business prudence which perceives that it would be ruinous to kill outright the proletarian goose that lays the golden eggs, and the fear of insurrection. There was no longer a king and an aristocratic governing class to say to the tradesman "Never mind the public interest: that is our business: yours is to get as rich as you can, incidentally giving employment to the proletariat and increasing our rent rolls." All that remained was the tradition of unscrupulous irresponsibility in business; and when the American millionaires first began to astonish Europe with their wealth it was possible for the most notorious of them [William Vanderbilt], in the course of an enquiry into the proceedings of a Trust with which he was connected, to reply to a criticism as to the effect of his business policy on the public with a simple "Damn the public!".[3] Had

3. Vanderbilt's exact words, to a Chicago reporter on 8 October 1882, were 'The public be damned.'

he been a middle-class man in a country where there was a governing class outside and above business, or a monarch with a council in the same position, or even a State Church, his answer would have been entirely in order apart from its verbal profanity. Duly bowdlerized it would have run "I am a man of business, not a ruler and a lawgiver. The public interest is not my job: I do not presume to meddle with it. My sole function is to make as much money as I can." Queen Elizabeth would have applauded such an attitude as socially sound and highly becoming: nothing angered her more than presumptuous attempts on the part of common persons to concern themselves with *her* business of high politics.

When America got rid of monarchs and prelates and popes and British cabinets and the like, and plunged into the grand republican experiment which has become the rule instead of the exception in Europe since the war swept all the emperors into the dustbin of history, she raised the middle classes to the top of the social structure and thus delivered its civilization into their hands without ennobling their traditions. Naturally they raced for money, for more money, and still more money, and damned the public when they were not doping it with advertisements which were by tacit agreement exempted from the law against obtaining money by false pretences or practising medicine without qualifications. It is true that they were forced to govern as well by the impossibility of maintaining civilization without government; but their government was limited and corrupted by their principle of letting nothing stand in the way of their getting rich quickly. And the ablest of them at that game (which has no attraction for the ability that plays the higher games by which finally civilization must live) soon became rich at a rate that made the European middle classes envious. In my youth I heard little of great men arising in America—not that America did not produce them, but that her money masters were more apt to persecute than to advertize them—but I heard much of the great fortunes that were being made there. Vanderbilt, Jay Gould,[4] Carnegie, Rockefeller became famous by bringing our civilization to the point to which Crassus and the other millionaire contemporaries of Sulla and Julius Cæsar brought the civilization of ancient republican Rome just before it set up Emperor idolatry as a resting place on the road to ruin. Nowadays we have multimillionaires everywhere; but they began in America; and that is why I wonder this book of mine was not written in America by an American fifty years ago. Henry George had a shot at it: indeed it was his oratory (to which I was exposed for fortyfive minutes

4. American financier and railway baron, owner of the New York *World*.

fortyfive years ago by pure chance) that called my attention to it; but though George impressed his generation with the outrageous misdistribution of income resulting from the apparently innocent institution of private property in land, he left untouched the positive problem of how else income was to be distributed, and what the nation was to do with the rent of its land when it was nationalized, thus leaving the question very much where it had been left a century earlier by the controversy between Voltaire and the elder Mirabeau,[5] except for the stupendous series of new illustrations furnished by the growth of the great cities of the United States. Still, America can claim that in this book I am doing no more than finishing Henry George's job.

Finally, I have been asked whether there are any intelligent women in America. There must be; for politically the men there are such futile gossips that the United States could not possibly carry on unless there were some sort of practical intelligence back of them. But I will let you into a secret which bears on this point. By this book I shall get at the American men through the American women. In America as in England every male citizen is supposed to understand politics and economics and finance and diplomacy and all the rest of a democratic voter's business on the strength of a Fundamentalist education that excites the public scorn of the Sioux chiefs who have seen their country taken from them by palefaced lunatics. He is ashamed to expose the depths of his ignorance by asking elementary questions; and I dare not insult him by volunteering the missing information. But he has no objection to my talking to his wife as to one who knows nothing of these matters: quite the contrary. And if he should chance to overhear——!!!

CONWAY, NORTH WALES.
17th April 1928.　　　　　　　　　　　　　　　　　　　　　　　G. B. S.

---

5. Victor Riqueti, Marquis de Mirabeau, author of *L'Ami des hommes, ou Traité de la population* (1756–8), was a member of the Physiocrat school of economists, single-taxers who regarded land as the sole resource of the nation's wealth and therefore as bound to pay for all State expenses. Voltaire took exception to this in a well-reasoned but savage satire on Physiocracy, *L'Homme aux quarante écus* (1768).

II

Author's Note for Popular Edition, 1929

======

The demand for an edition of this book at a price within the means of the severely equalized incomes of the vast majority of women in this country has been continuous and sometimes vigorously reproachful. In knocking two thirds off the price[1] I am only too conscious of the fact that I am not meeting the case of the lady who asked me how I could have the face to ask her to pay three weeks wages for one book. Evidently that lady is subsidized by somebody, husband or father, or she could not live on five shillings a week, and spare three ha'pence to stamp a letter of remonstrance to the author. However, I welcome the proof that there are still subsidized women working for five shillings a week, and thereby dragging unsubsidized women down to a level at which existence is impossible. But I must not drag down my fellow authors to that level also by accommodating the price of my books to it. I must refer the lady to the happily available communistic alternative: the public library.

I take the opportunity to say a word about the reception of the book in its first edition, already endeared to collectors by several errors, one of which was a mistake in the number of one of the Articles of the Church of England. It passed entirely unnoticed in this country, but was detected and very kindly pointed out to me by a well-known French atheist [Shaw's French translator, Augustin Hamon]. Of the general reception of the book I cannot speak, because I have no means of knowing what its readers felt; and I implore them not to write to me about it unless, like my French correspondent, they have a blunder to correct. The reviews mean little, because reviewers are not paid enough to read more than the chapter headings of a long book; that is why I made the chapter headings so complete, having been a reviewer myself once. A reviewer has to think of his wife and family as well as of the authors he reviews; and when I read

1. The original English edition of 16,000 copies in 1928 sold for fifteen shillings. The 'Popular Edition' a year later, consisting of 25,000 copies, sold at five shillings.

criticisms clumsily refuting fallacies which my book refutes with sound science and some elegance, or patronizingly calling my attention to considerations which I have insisted on in chapter after chapter, I bear no malice, but, as an old hand, estimate the price of the review and the burdens of the reviewer, and muttering "Two guineas: three children," or "Fifteen shillings: several children: husband an unappreciated artist" (for all these tragedies are wrapped up in our newspapers and oppress the conscience of an incorrigible economist like myself) I drop the press cutting into the wastepaper basket.

But the people who exasperate me most are those who have really read the book, or think they have. I took the utmost pains to make it intelligible, clear, lucid, unambiguous, simple and unmistakeable. The result appears to be that only one man in the civilized world has understood it; and that man is Albert Einstein. I begin to think that lucidity is self-defeating. I remember how, many years ago, when the mischief done by whisky was attributed to the fusel oil and other irrelevancies which it contained, the experiment was made of eliminating them all, and producing a pure spirit. It proved poisonous, maddening, and destructive beyond anything that the worst modern bootlegger has ever sold in the cheapest speakeasy. I have, at great cost of labor, eliminated from this book all the common adulterations of doctrine by mush, gush, nonsense, hypocrisy and humbug, only, it seems, to make it unfit for human consumption. People cannot take it in until they have reintroduced all the adulterations from their home supplies. Then they expatiate, at my expense, on their own adulterations.

Among the complaints of the price of the first edition of my book was one made in public by my friend Sir William Joynson Hicks,[2] who said, quite truly [in a speech in September 1928], that a Home Secretary could not, as such, afford to buy fifteen-shilling books. But, he added, a compassionate lady had made him a present of a copy. That well-intentioned lady did not know what I and all authors know: that people never read the books they get for nothing, or indeed any book at all unless they want it badly enough to buy it. But the lady did produce in Sir William's mind the illusion that he had read the book; for he proceeded to quote from it a string of propositions not one of which it contained, and most of which it

2. William Joynson Hicks, a Conservative MP, had been Home Secretary since 1924. He and Shaw frequently clashed over fiscal and political matters, and it is quite unlikely that 'Jix' (as he was commonly known), a vehement anti-Labourite who shortly afterwards declined to stand again for Parliament under the new Labour Government, would have looked upon Shaw as a friend.

disproved. And Sir William was presently quoted, without acknowledgment, but with vigorous intensifications, by the minor lights of his Party, and in particular by its lady election canvassers, the present prospect being a general election at which the country will be invited to vote for the Conservative Party to save it from the horrors of a Shavian Socialism which was bred in Sir William's fancy and not in my book.

But far be it from me to confute and contradict him. My aims and proposals go so much further than any of my hostile critics are yet capable of conceiving that I am only too thankful to be mistaken for a mere harmless Utopian instead of being hanged without benefit of clergy. When the spirit drives me to tell the truth, and the flesh reminds me of the police and of the fate of those who have yielded to that temptation in the past, I screw my courage up by reflecting on the extreme improbability of anybody seeing anything in my treatise but a paradoxical joke. For instance, when I point to groups of millions of people in all directions living on equalized incomes much more placidly and permanently than the handful of fevered speculators who never know from one day to another whether they are millionaires or bankrupts, I know that our statesmen will contemplate that overwhelming spectacle without seeing that it is there, and will assure me that people would never stand equality of income; that whenever two people get equal incomes one of them becomes a beggar and the other a plutocrat before the year is out; and that my notion that millions of citizens now have equal incomes without anything of the kind happening is the dream of an unobservant idealist, unversed in public affairs and ignorant of human nature.

Well, I take refuge with the intelligent women. As for the front-bench male politicians, I can point out the moon in the heavens to them; but I cannot persuade them that it is anything more than a piece of green cheese.

12th April 1929.   G. B. S.

Index to Volume 2

by David Bowron

═══════

Other than in the entry under his name, Shaw is referred to as S. Insignificant references to persons or works mentioned in Shaw's text and/or in the footnotes have not been indexed.